Glass in Early America

Glass in Early America

Selections from the
Henry Francis du Pont Winterthur Museum

Arlene Palmer

WINTERTHUR, DELAWARE

HENRY FRANCIS DU PONT WINTERTHUR MUSEUM

1993

DISTRIBUTED BY

W.W. NORTON

NEW YORK · LONDON

The publication of this book is supported in part by funds from
the National Endowment for the Arts.
Copyright © 1993 by The Henry Francis du Pont Winterthur Museum, Inc.

Printed in Italy

Library of Congress Cataloguing-in-Publication Data

Henry Francis du Pont Winterthur Museum.
Glass in Early America : selections from the Henry Francis du Pont
Winterthur Museum / by Arlene Palmer.
Includes bibliographical references and index.
ISBN 0-393-03660-X
1. Glassware—United States—History—18th century—Catalogs.
2. Glassware—United States—History—19th century—Catalogs.
3. Glassware—Europe—History—18th century—Catalogs.
4. Glassware—Europe—History—18th century—Catalogs.
5. Glassware—Delaware—Winterthur—Catalogs.
6. Henry Francis du Pont Winterthur Museum—Catalogs.
I. Palmer, Arlene M., 1950–
II. Title.
NK5112.A1H46 1993
748.2'074'7511—dc20   93-32489
                                                          CIP

ISBN 0-393-03660-X

First edition

The goblet with the cover in the frontispiece was probably made at the New
Bremen Glassmanufactory of John Frederick Amelung, 1791–93; see NO. 16.

All photographs in introductory essays Winterthur Museum except those
figures listed here.

Fig. 1, Charles B. Gardner Collection, Museum of American Glass, Wheaton
Village. Figs. 2, 4, 9, 10, 11, Arlene Palmer collection. Figs. 3, 5, 7, Winterthur
Library. Figs. 6, 13, 14, 16, 19, 20, Corning Museum of Glass. Fig. 8, Philadel-
phia Museum of Art, gift of J. W. Nixon. Fig. 12, Metropolitan Museum of
Art, gift of James Jackson Jarves, 1881. Fig. 15, Toledo Museum of Art; pur-
chased with funds from the Libbey Endowment, gift of Edward Drummond
Libbey. Fig. 17, Historical Society of Pennsylvania. Fig. 21, Maryland His-
torical Society, on loan from private collection. Figs. 23, 24, 28, 29, Winterthur
Archives. Fig. 25, Collection of W. B. Gest. Figs. 26, 27, SPNEA: photo,
David Bohl.

Contents

Preface

Winterthur, 1933.

The Henry Francis du Pont Winterthur Museum near Wilmington, Delaware, was founded in 1951 by Henry Francis du Pont (1880–1969). It houses the premier collection of decorative arts objects made or used in the United States between 1650 and 1850. The collection is comprehensive in scope and includes furniture, textiles, paintings, prints, ceramics, glass, and metalwares.

The Winterthur estate was part of the land owned by Eleuthère Irénée du Pont, whose gunpowder manufactory on the Brandywine River marked the beginning of the DuPont Company. In 1816 du Pont's daughter Evelina Gabrielle married his partner, Jacques Antoine Bidermann, and after Irénée's death the couple purchased a 450-acre tract of land from the estate. Their home was completed in 1839; they called it Winterthur in honor of the childhood years Bidermann spent in the Swiss town of that name. Winterthur passed to the Bidermanns' son, James Irénée Bidermann. Deciding to make his home abroad, Bidermann sold the property to his uncle, Henry du Pont, who served as president of the DuPont Company from 1850 until his death in 1889. Du Pont's son, Colonel Henry A. du Pont, made Winterthur his home from 1875 until his death in 1926. The last private owner of Winterthur was his son, Henry Francis du Pont.

By the time Henry Francis du Pont was born at Winterthur in 1880, the house had been considerably enlarged, but its greatest expansion occurred under his ownership. Bucking the fashion for interiors in European styles, H. F. du Pont decided in the 1910s and early 1920s that he wanted an "American house" and began to collect antique American furniture and accessories for Chestertown House, his retreat on Long Island. When he inherited Winterthur in 1926, du Pont made this familial property the focus of his collecting. During the late 1920s he added a huge wing that he filled with paneled rooms from eighteenth- and early nineteenth-century houses. He furnished the rooms with decorative art objects he believed were appropriate to them. By 1930 he had established Winterthur Corporation, initiating the steps of turning his house into a museum. In October 1951 the plans became reality, and Winterthur Museum welcomed its first guests.

Glass was one of du Pont's earliest collecting interests. The Winterthur collection is one of the very few glass collections formed between 1920 and 1950 that is still intact. Although he specialized in American-made glass, du Pont also acquired some European glass of the kind that was imported by early American merchants. Over the years museum staff has expanded this part of the collection to reflect archaeological and historical findings about the role of imported glass in America from 1650 to 1850.

Between 1955 and 1964 in his annual letters of instructions to the trustees of the museum, du Pont expressed his wish for a book on Winterthur's glass. It is my sincere hope that this book would have met his expectations.

Acknowledgments

I am most grateful to Olive Jones who read the manuscript in an early stage and offered many incisive comments and suggestions for its improvement.

I appreciate the assistance of the following friends and colleagues in responding to my queries or supporting my efforts in some other way: William Ambler, Mary Boydell, Geraldine Casper, Alice Cooney Frelinghuysen, JoAnne Fuerst, William B. Gest, Dorothy Hogan, Audrey Iacone, Greta B. Layton, Martin Mortimer, Christina H. Nelson, Kirk J. Nelson, Ada Polak, Jane Shadel Spillman, Laura Fecych Sprague, Kenneth M. Wilson, and Virginia Wright. In my footnotes I have acknowledged individuals who generously shared their research with me; I would like to thank here anyone I inadvertently might have overlooked. Ellen M. Rosenthal discovered the shop inventory of Leonard Keehmle, which has been a very useful source for me. Gary E. Baker kindly gave me a copy of the price list of Francis Plunkett which I cite throughout this catalogue.

Many current and former members of the Winterthur staff have been involved in this project. I am grateful for the help of Karol A. Schmiegel and the staff of the Registration Division. The Winterthur Conservation Division rose to the challenge of restoring numerous glass lighting devices. Janice H. Carlson, head of the Analytical Laboratory, has been extremely helpful over the years in providing and interpreting analytical data about the objects. The photography of Winterthur's glass was admirably accomplished by George J. Fistrovich. The groundwork for this catalogue was laid by Dwight P. Lanmon, now Winterthur's director, when he was glass curator. It was he who first looked into H. F. du Pont's purchase records for insights into the formation of the collection and undertook the important study of mold defects in mold-blown glass. Amanda E. Lange, assistant curator, kindly provided many bits of information that I was otherwise unable to obtain long distance. Wade Lawrence, formerly of the Curatorial Division, came to the rescue on several occasions. Lois F. McNeil Fellow Margaret H. Watson generously offered her time to solve some problems for me. Teresa A. Vivolo and Lisa L. Lock in the Publications Division have checked numerous details. Ian M. G. Quimby, former director of the Publications Division, gave initial guidance for the project. His successor, Catherine E. Hutchins, has been most patient, and her thoughtful editing of the manuscript has made it a far better book than it might have been.

FIG. 1
New England Glass
Company, 1822.

FIG. 2
Interior, New England
Glass Company. From
*Ballou's Pictorial Drawing-
Room Companion* (January
20, 1855): 41.

Glassmaking: A Brief Summary

FIG. 3
Denis Diderot, *Recueil de Planches . . .* (1765), 10: pl. 4.

FIG. 4
The World We Live On (February 1869): 79.

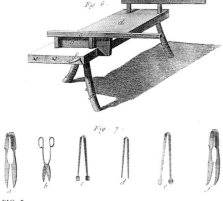

FIG. 5
Denis Diderot, *Recueil de Planches . . .* (1765), 10: pl. 18.

In physical terms, glass is a liquid that exists in a solid state. The secrets of making glass were discovered in ancient times and remained remarkably unchanged for centuries. The chief ingredient of glass, silica, was derived either from sand or flint. An alkaline flux such as potash from wood ashes, or soda in the form of ashes from marine plants, was added to lower the melting point of the silica. Lime or lead was necessary to stabilize the batch. Broken bits of fabricated glass (cullet) were often added to facilitate the melting process. Iron oxide occurring naturally as impurities in the raw materials would color the glass from green to black or yellow to dark brown. Other colors, such as blue, required the addition of metallic oxides. Achieving a truly colorless substance was a goal of manufacturers of table glass for centuries. To this end they would add manganese as a decolorizer to counter the tints caused by small amounts of iron.

The batch reached the desired molten state in special pots of fireclay placed in a furnace that was fired by wood or coal fuel (fig. 3). Glassblowers used a hollow iron blowpipe to take up a gather of glass from the pot. They formed the taffylike substance into a bubble by alternately blowing and rolling (marvering) it on an iron or marble table (fig. 4). The glass remained plastic for a length of time, which varied with the chemical composition. As they sat on their specially designed chairs with extended arms, glassblowers, or gaffers, used simple hand tools such as the pucellas and the battledore to refine the shape of the bubble (fig. 5). Constant reheating at the furnace kept the bubble pliable, and through blowing it could be expanded to the desired size. Once that was achieved a solid iron rod, the pontil, was attached opposite the blowpipe, and the blowpipe was cracked off. The gaffer could then finish the piece by adding and tooling glass for handles, feet, or ornamental devices, or by trailing threads of glass for decoration. Holding the vessel on the pontil, he could finish the top and fire polish the edge. The removal of the pontil left a characteristic mark or scar. A ring-shape mark indicates that the craftsman used a blowpipe for empontilling.

To ensure uniformity of shape and size the craftsmen sometimes blew glass into molds of wood or metal. Decorated metal molds, bearing ribbed, diamond, or other patterns, imparted an overall design to the body of the glass. Dip or part-size molds would pattern the glass; after removal from the mold the gather was blown and shaped as needed (figs. 6, 7). Glass blown into full-size molds received size and shape as well as decoration (fig. 8). By the second quarter of the nineteenth century, glassmakers used plungers to press molten glass into molds (fig. 9). With this tech-

FIG. 6
Cast iron dip mold, New
Geneva Glass Works, ca.
1797–1847.

FIG. 7
Denis Diderot, *Recueil de
Planches* . . . (1765), 10:
pl. 19–4.

FIG. 8
Cast iron bottle mold,
ca. 1850.

nological advance, the role of the glassblower became limited to the production of luxury or art ware.

Whether manually or mechanically shaped, hot glass objects had to be cooled gradually and uniformly in an annealing oven so as to relieve internal stresses that could cause breakage. Once annealed, glass could be enamel-painted or gilded, the colors affixed by firing in a furnace. Other decoration was possible through the "cold," wheel-driven processes of cutting and engraving (figs. 10, 11).

The manufacturer of glass required an extensive facility (fig. 1). At the core was the building with a glass furnace where glass was made (fig. 2). Other activities such as the preparation of raw materials, the production of pots, the decoration of glasswares, and the packing of finished products usually occurred in separate structures. Most factories had a blacksmith's shop where tools could be made or repaired. Larger glassworks had their own moldmaking shops. In the eighteenth and early nineteenth centuries, glass factories often included housing for the workers.

FOR ADDITIONAL READING
Charleston, Robert J. "Glass Furnaces through the Ages." *Journal of Glass Studies* 20 (1978): 9–33.
Charleston, Robert J. "Wheel-Engraving and Cutting: Some Early Equipment; 1, Engraving." *Journal of Glass Studies* 6 (1964): 83–100.
Charleston, Robert J. "Wheel-Engraving and Cutting: Some Early Equipment; 2, Water-Power and Cutting." *Journal of Glass Studies* 7 (1965): 41–54.
Frank, Susan. *Glass and Archaeology.* London: Academic Press, 1982.
Jones, Olive et al. *The Parks Canada Glass Glossary.* Studies in Archaeology, Architecture and History. Ottawa: National Historic Parks and Sites Branch, Parks Canada, Environment Canada, 1985.
Newman, Harold. *An Illustrated Dictionary of Glass.* London: Thames and Hudson, 1977.
Vose, Ruth Hurst. *Glass.* The Connoisseur Illustrated Guide. London: Connoisseur, 1975.

FIG. 9
*One Hundred Years'
Progress of the United States*
(1874), following p. 404.

FIGS. 10, 11
Charles A. Joy, "The
Manufacture of Glass,"
in *Frank Leslie's Popular
Monthly,* p. 251, figs. 13, 12.

European Glass

The Background of Table Glass Production in Europe

FIG. 12
Tazza, Venice, 16th century.

FIG. 13
Covered goblet, Venice, late
16th or 17th century.

From the fifteenth to the seventeenth century, Venice was the undisputed center of the fine table glass industry in Europe. Glassmakers on the island of Murano—some 3,000 in the late 1500s—developed many distinctive styles of luxury tablewares. From a transparent, colorless glass called *cristallo* because of its resemblance to rock crystal, they blew elegant vessels of great delicacy (fig. 12). They sought new formulas for richly colored transparent glasses and brought enamel-painting and gilding on glass to a high art. The soda-formula glass made in Murano set up quickly and enabled craftsmen to shape drinking vessels with tall, fanciful serpent or flower stems. By embedding canes of opaque glass into *cristallo*, they created wares of remarkable intricacy, a type of ware known as *vetro a filigrana* (fig. 13). Venetian artisans made opaque glass in imitation of agate, aventurine, and Chinese porcelain and revived the ancient Roman technique of *millefiore*. In the sixteenth century they developed a technique to make "ice glass" with a rough and crackled surface—the antithesis of *cristallo*.

These luxury wares supplied an international market. As one visitor to Venice remarked, "They utter here forth two hundred thousand crownes worth a yeare of this brickware; and they seem to have taken measure of every nations belly and humour, to fit them with drinking glasses accordingly; For the *High Dutch*, they have *high glasses*, called *flutes*, a full yard long. . . . For the *English* that love *toasts* with their drink, they have curious *tankards* of thick *crystal glasse*, just like our *silver tankards*. For the *Italians* that love to drink leasurely, they have glasses that are almost as large and flat *as sylver plat[e]s*, and almost as uneasy to drink out of."[1]

Archaeological excavations and early written records are gradually revealing the extent of the consumption of Venetian glass in England and her colonies. The 1547 household inventory of Henry VIII, for example, lists over 600 items of Venetian glass. During the later sixteenth century, the use of Venetian glass had spread to the lower strata of society. William Harrison observed in 1577, that

> wherein gold and silver most aboundeth, . . . our gentility, as loathing those metals (because of the plenty) do now generally choose rather the Venice glasses, both for our wine and beer, . . . and such is the estimation of this stuff that many became rich only with their new trade unto Murana. . . . And as this is seen in the gentility, so in the wealthy communalty the like desire of glass is not neglected. . . . The poorest also will have glass if they may; but . . . the Venetian is somewhat too dear for them.[2]

The Tudor interest in Venetian wares sparked several efforts to establish a Venetian-type industry in England. Although Venetian glassblowers had moved to London as early as 1549, the beginnings of refined tableware production date from 1567 when Jean Carré arrived from Antwerp and obtained a license to build a glass furnace. Venice-born Giacomo Verzelini assumed control of the works after Carré's death and in 1574 secured a royal patent to make "crystal drinking glasses." The earliest Venetian-style glasses associated with an English enterprise are attributed to Verzelini, who retired from glassmaking about 1592.[3]

A number of artisans managed to leave Murano and carry the secrets of glass manufacture to other parts of Europe, so that by the seventeenth century, table glass in the Venetian style (*façon de venise*) was blown in several centers besides London, notably in the Netherlands, France, and the Tyrol (fig. 14).

FIG. 14
Goblet, Netherlands, 1675–1700.

In spite of the endeavors of duke of Buckingham George Villiers, Sir Robert Mansell, and others who followed Verzelini's lead, Continental glasswares continued to dominate the English market in the seventeenth century, but their quality was uneven. Importer John Greene complained that the glass in a recent shipment was "indifferent good and cleer, but not so sound and strong as they should have bin made."[4]

Venetian glass and its imitations were intended for an urban clientele. For the less affluent and less sophisticated market, numerous forest glasshouses throughout Europe produced vessels of green glass, often highly ornamented with molded or applied decoration. From the Germanic *waldglas* tradition came many of the craftsmen who operated glass factories in eighteenth-century America. In England, a green glass industry, organized chiefly by French immigrants, flourished in the Weald area. After a ban on wood fuel was enacted in 1615, they carried their craft to the north and west. Glassblowers trained in those factories traveled to the North American colonies in the seventeenth century to blow glass.[5]

In the 1660s following the restoration of Charles II to the throne, English entrepreneurs renewed their efforts to break Venice's hold on the market and to create glass that could rival Venetian products. A leader in this endeavor was George Ravenscroft, a merchant familiar with the Venetian trade, who opened glasshouses in the Savoy and at Henley-on-Thames. Early in 1674 he secured a patent from the king, claiming that his glass was "of a finer sort and made of other ingredients than any other glasshouses in England have used, and that the invention may be of considerable public advantage as the glasses thereby made equalize, if not excel, those imported from Venice and France."[6] His claim was premature because only toward the end of 1676 was he able to produce a fairly stable glass (fig. 15). Using silica from calcined flints and pebbles, with lead oxide as a flux, Ravenscroft eventually produced a "crystalline" or "flint" glass that was softer and heavier than Venetian soda glass. The lead gave the glass a higher index of refraction; the new material exuded a brilliance

FIG. 15
George Ravenscroft, posset pot, London, 1677–78.

FIG. 16
Covered goblet, Bohemia,
1710–20.

FIG. 17
William Parker trade card
London, 1769.

unparalleled in Continental wares. The development of lead glass hastened the end of the Venetian export trade and ushered in the great age of English glassmaking.

At about the same period, glassmakers in Bohemia were also experimenting to refine a glass formula that offered improvements upon the Venetian. Their hard, colorless potash-lime glass was especially suitable for wheel engraving, a technique that central Europeans trained in lapidary traditions brought to new levels of accomplishment (fig. 16). Other Continental developments of the seventeenth century included Johann Kunckel's introduction of gold-ruby glass.

Ravenscroft's success had an immediate impact on the English industry, and factories making lead glass proliferated. Glass forms for drinking and dining multiplied: there were glass drinking vessels for every beverage from ratafia to chocolate, and serving pieces for everything from salt to sweetmeats. Glass assumed an important position on the dessert table, and by the end of the eighteenth century, complete services of glassware were made, often of richly cut styles. Lighting devices were manufactured of glass as were numerous objects of strictly ornamental purpose.

The extraordinary range of forms available in glass was matched by an equally extensive selection of decorative techniques. Delicate blown forms could be studded with air beads or have twisted stems of virtuoso effect reminiscent of *vetro a filigrana*. Glasses were engraved or enamel-painted in myriad patterns, and commemorative inscriptions were popular. Glasscutters from the Continent brought their skills to England and found the relatively soft lead oxide glass particularly suited to their art. The trade card of William Parker (fig. 17), a leading London glasscutter who sold to fashionable colonists, illustrates that any form of glass could be cut to capture and refract light with sparkling effects. English glasscutters developed a style that set the fashion for all of Europe in the neoclassical age. When John Adams visited a cut-glass manufactory in 1783 (possibly Parker's) he observed that cut glass "did as much honor to the English as the mirrors, the seve [Sèvres] China, or the gobeline [Gobelain] tapestry of France. It seemed to be the art of transmitting glass into diamonds."[7]

The nineteenth century saw an explosion of technical developments and stylistic changes in glass. Colorless cut glass continued to be popular for several decades, with British styles predominating. By 1820 French craftsmen had perfected an ornamentation known today as sulphides, in which white clay images attained the brilliance of silver by being embedded into colorless glass. French and English manufacturers produced molded and pressed glass as cheaper alternatives to cut glass. A taste for colored glass took hold during the 1840s; Bohemian glassmakers led the way with innovative colors and decorative techniques to enhance them, including casing or overlay glass. In the 1850s and 1860s fashionable blown tableware of fine colorless glass was embellished with delicate wheel engraving in patterns reflecting the aesthetic interests of the day.

European Glass in America before the Civil War

Our knowledge of European glass used in the seventeenth-century colonies is hampered by the lack of surviving examples with reliable histories, the generally vague descriptions found in probate inventories and other records, and the relatively few sites that have been archaeologically excavated. Available evidence indicates that the role of glass in the colonies before 1650 was minimal and probably limited to square, green bottles. By the 1650s globular bottles with long necks were used; small vials and other bottles are listed frequently in inventories from the second half of the century. Green tablewares, notably roemers and other drinking vessels of continental European production, have been unearthed from later seventeenth-century contexts at several sites.

Excavations at Fort Orange (now Albany), New York, St. Mary's City, Maryland, yielded fragments of sophisticated table glass made in either Venice or the Netherlands in the 1650–1700 period. These run the gamut from simple shapes of the type imported by John Greene to complex serpent-stem glasses. Beakers of a blue and white *vetro a fili* style usually dated to about 1600 have also been found. Venetian chalcedony glass, also imported by Greene, was known to the colonists, as were opaque red and opalescent wares. Some fragments of stemware of the type attributed to Robert Mansell's factory have been found in Virginia; his association is particularly interesting given his involvement in the Virginia Company that sponsored the Jamestown settlement and the glasshouses erected there. Any and all of these types of vessels could fit the description "venice glasses," which occasionally appears in period records.

The English industry's experimentations during the last quarter of the century are represented on American sites by a number of fragments bearing seals or factory marks. Most important among the fragments found at Jamestown is the spout of a posset pot bearing the logo of Ravenscroft's enterprise (see fig. 15).[8]

After 1700 until the Revolution, English glass dominated the colonial market, reflecting the success of the English industry and the concomitant legislation enacted to control the colonial trade. Although imports varied in quality, they apparently included the full range of forms available to the domestic English market (fig. 18). In spite of England's efforts to dominate the colonial market, some Continental table glass did find its way to America in the prerevolutionary period, probably the result of trade connections maintained by some of the thousands of emigrants who traveled to the colonies from areas of Germany throughout the eighteenth century.

After the Revolution, American shops were filled with German and Bohemian glasswares that were often cheaper than English or domestic products. Some idea of the scale of this trade can be gleaned from the records of Baltimore merchant Frederick

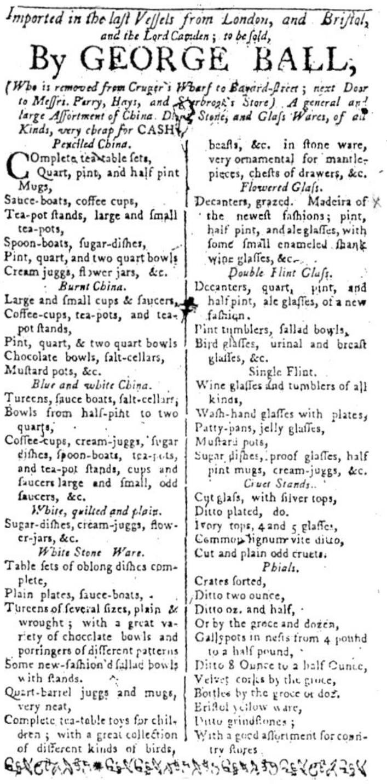

FIG. 18
New York Mercury,
February 23, 1767.

Hammer: an inventory of his warehouse taken in 1818 itemizes more than 140,000 pieces of German glass, including 85,000 tumblers, 12,000 decanters, and 10,000 wineglasses.[9] An illustrated trade catalogue in the Winterthur Library (see NOS. 17–19) provides clear evidence of the appearance of these imports. Although the Napoleonic Wars and the second war with Great Britain temporarily stemmed the flow of imported glass, by the 1820s United States manufacturers were complaining bitterly about the intense competition from foreign companies that accompanied the return of peace.

European manufacturers sent a variety of forms, but the quality often did not meet domestic standards, the claims of import merchants notwithstanding. On his travels through the States in the late 1810s, Axel Klinkowstrom remarked that English imports "are of such quality as not to allow close scrutiny. . . . In the English factories there is a slogan for inferior and less dependable merchandise: 'It is good enough for sale in America.'" A few years later, when English traveler Margaret Hall heard "some American ladies remarking . . . that they thought the American glass quite as prettily cut as the English," she thought it a "great stretch of national prejudice," until she remembered "how inferior a quality of goods of every description is sent to this country. You cannot really form an idea," she wrote, "of the trash that is to be found in the best shops."[10]

The role of imported glass in the United States after 1840, a time when America's own glass factories were flourishing, has not been well documented. Certainly glasswares from England, France, Bohemia, and Germany continued to be sold to American consumers. Bohemian cased or overlay glass was prominently featured in the 1853 New York Crystal Palace Exhibition, but the ware was already well known in this country. When Alexander Cummings, editor of the Philadelphia *Bulletin*, visited New England Glass Company in 1852 he was "especially struck with the fact . . . that most of the exquisite, richly colored and decorated glass-ware, which is so much admired under the name of 'Bohemian Glass,' is manufactured at these works"—in Cambridge, Massachusetts.[11]

Cummings's observation attests to what is the greatest problem facing collectors of American glass of eighteenth- and nineteenth-century origin, namely the difficulty of distinguishing the domestic product from its contemporary European import. American manufacturers looked to imports for fashions to copy. They employed immigrant glassblowers, cutters, and engravers who made and decorated glass in the styles they had made in the Old World. Undoubtedly much European glass has been, and still is, misidentified as American made and vice-versa. In the twentieth century, the enthusiasm of collectors and the misattributions of European wares as native products led to a new wave of imports to feed the demand for antique early American glass.

1. Richard Lassels, *The Voyage of Italy*, 2 vols. (Paris, 1670), 2:423–24, reference courtesy of Laura Sprague.

2. William Harrison, *Description of England,* as quoted in R. J. Charleston, "The Tudor Period: Pottery, Porcelain, and Glass," in *The Connoisseur's Complete Period Guide*, ed. Ralph Edwards and L. G. G. Ramsey (New York: Bonanza Books, 1968), pp. 122–23.

3. For a discussion of Verzelini glass see Charleston, *English Glass*, pp. 53–61, pls. 12–14.

4. Greene to Allesio Morelli, November 30, 1672, as quoted in Albert Hartshorne, *Antique Drinking Glasses* (New York: Brussel and Brussel, 1968), p. 448 (originally published as *Old English Glasses* [1897]).

5. Arlene Palmer, "Aspects of Glassmaking in Eighteenth-Century America," *Annales du 8e Congrès de l'Association Internationale pour l'Histoire du Verre* (Liège: Edition du Centre de Publications de l'A. I. H. V., 1981): 307–19.

6. Ravenscroft as quoted in Charleston, *English Glass*, pp. 110–11.

7. *Diary and Autobiography of John Adams*, ed. L. H. Butterfield, 4 vols. (Cambridge: Harvard University Press, Belknap Press, 1961), 3:151.

8. R. J. Charleston, "George Ravenscroft: New Light on the Development of His 'Christalline Glasses,'" *Journal of Glass Studies* 10 (1968): 156–67. Information on seventeenth-century excavated glass and its identification in Arlene Palmer, "English and Continental Glass in Colonial and Federal America" (paper read before the International Ceramics Fair and Seminar, London, 1989).

9. Hammer Account Books, 1796–1817, Maryland Historical Society, Baltimore.

10. *Klinkowstrom's America, 1818–1820*, trans. and ed. Franklin D. Scott (Evanston, Ill.: Northwestern University Press, 1952), p. 170. Margaret Hall, *The Aristocratic Journey: Letters of Mrs. Basil Hall . . . in America, 1827–28*, ed. Una Pope-Hennessy (New York: G. P. Putnam's, 1931), p. 289.

11. [Arlene Palmer], "Bohemian Glass at the New York Crystal Palace, 1853," *Glass Club Bulletin*, no. 152 (Spring 1987): 14–16. Cummings quoted in *Hunt's Merchants' Magazine and Commercial Review* 27, no. 1 (July 1852): 133.

FOR ADDITIONAL READING

Table Glass Production in Europe

Charleston, Robert J. *Masterpieces of Glass: A World History from the Corning Museum of Glass.* New York: Harry N. Abrams, 1980.

Charleston, R. J. *English Glass and the Glass Used in England, circa 400–1940.* London: George Allen and Unwin, 1984.

Drahotová, Olga. *European Glass.* New York: Excalibur Books, 1983.

Hajdamach, Charles R. *British Glass 1800–1914.* Woodbridge, Eng.: Antique Collectors' Club, 1991.

Klesse, Brigitte, and Hans Meyr. *European Glass from 1500–1800: The Ernesto Wolf Collection.* Vienna: Kremayr and Scheriau, 1987.

Polak, Ada. *Glass: Its Makers and Its Public.* London: Weidenfeld and Nicolson, 1975.

Tait, Hugh. *The Golden Age of Venetian Glass.* London: British Museum Publications, 1979.

Weiss, Gustav. *The Book of Glass.* Translated by Janet Seligman. New York: Praeger, 1971.

European Glass in America

Lanmon, Dwight P. "The Baltimore Glass Trade, 1780 to 1820." In *Winterthur Portfolio 5*, edited by Richard K. Doud, pp. 15–48. Charlottesville: University Press of Virginia, 1969.

Noël Hume, Ivor. *A Guide to Artifacts of Colonial America.* New York: Alfred A. Knopf, 1970.

Noël Hume, Ivor. *Glass in Colonial Williamsburg's Archaeological Collections.* Williamsburg, Va.: Colonial Williamsburg Foundation, 1969.

McKearin, Helen. "Eighteenth Century Advertisements of Glass Imports into the Colonies and the United States." *Glass Notes.* Compiled by Arthur Churchill. No. 14 (December 1954): 13–25.

Schwind, Arlene Palmer. "English Glass Imports in New York, 1770–1790." *Journal of Glass Studies* 25 (1983): 179–85.

Wilson, Kenneth M. "Heritage of New England Glass—Importations." In *New England Glass and Glassmaking*, pp. 5–36. New York: Thomas Y. Crowell, 1972.

An Overview of American Glass History

There were about a dozen glasshouses built in the American colonies. The Polish, Italian, Dutch, and German glassblowers who operated these ventures brought with them the manufacturing techniques and stylistic traditions of continental Europe. It was with English glass that domestic manufacturers primarily had to compete, but as far as is known, only one colonial glasshouse was entirely English in its operations.

Behind the first glasshouses at Jamestown, Virginia, was the idea that a colonial factory would export its product to the mother country. In 1608, when the Virginia Company built the Jamestown works, England was moving toward an industrial ban on wood fuel. How logical, then, for a glasshouse to be among the company plans for settlement in the thickly forested wilderness. The harsh winter of 1609–10, however, put an end to the dream and the factory. Between 1621 and 1624 a second glasshouse was tried at Jamestown, which may have been initiated by malcontent Venetians from Mansell's London works who saw an opportunity to set up a rival factory to meet English demands. It, too, failed.

By the eighteenth century, entrepreneurs were interested in building glasshouses in the colonies to meet the domestic need for glassware. Their efforts defied Parliament, which now viewed colonial manufactures as a threat to the home industry. The government's fears were needless, however, because few colonial glassmaking ventures were able to overcome technical difficulties, labor problems, and consumer resistance conditioned by high quality imports.

FIG. 19
Wistarburg Glassworks,
wine bottle, ca. 1739–77.

The major exception was Wistarburgh, a glasshouse founded by Caspar Wistar in 1739 and continued after his death in 1752 by his son, Richard. The factory operated until the Revolution. In 1717 Caspar Wistar traveled from Baden and arrived in Philadelphia where he learned the trade of brass-button making. Within a few years he had accumulated enough capital to acquire real estate and expand his interests. Business correspondents in Germany may have persuaded Wistar to construct a glassworks. The site he chose was near Alloway in Salem County, New Jersey. Four German glassblowers ran the factory. Bottles and window glass were their primary products (fig. 19), but records indicate that tablewares were also made as was scientific glass for Benjamin Franklin's electrical experiments.

Ironmaster Henry William Stiegel, a German immigrant like Wistar, established a glassworks in Manheim, Pennsylvania, in 1764, and for the first five years his German workmen blew bottles, window glass, and hollowwares of Germanic style. In response to the 1767 Townshend Acts levying import duties on manufactured goods, including glass, colonial merchants signed articles of nonimportation. By April 1769, British goods were in short supply. Stiegel seized the short-lived opportu-

nity to fill the void and manufacture refined table glass of English style and quality. He hired English artisans, introduced lead-formula glass, and employed an English glasscutter and engraver (fig. 20). Although he succeeded in making "FLINT GLASS, viz. decanters, wine glasses, tumblers, Etc." deemed "equal in beauty and quality to the generality of Flint Glass imported from England," and established an impressive network of agents, his plan failed.[1] In 1774 the factory closed and Stiegel went to debtor's prison.

The end of the revolutionary war brought a renewed call for domestic manu-factures and economic independence from Britain. At the urging of several promi-nent United States citizens, John Frederick Amelung (fig. 21) left his position as superintendent of a mirror glass factory in Germany to open a glassworks in the new nation. Having secured the financial backing of Bremen merchants, Amelung was ready to set sail with a large crew, but the English government got wind of the plan and tried to prevent Amelung from leaving. Eventually Amelung arrived in Balti-more in August 1784. He quickly acquired an existing glasshouse in western Mary-land, bought more land, and within a few years had four glasshouses in operation. The complex, known as New Bremen, produced a variety of tableware, bottles, and window glass, but Amelung was disappointed by the public's lack of support.

In 1787 he published his concerns, noting that in his experience many privileges were granted to manufacturers by "despotic Governments on the continent of Eu-rope" but none were extended to those who attempted to "bring the balance of trade in favour of the United States." From Maryland's legislature he hoped for loans or exemptions from taxes—significant considerations given the vast capital required for glass manufacture. Amelung urged the public to "be above the common prejudices that the foreign goods are better than the home manufactured, and . . . using them [home goods], through their good example, persuade others to follow them, even if the Manufactory had not arrived to the greatest perfection." His glass, he claimed, "is cheaper, and of a better quality, than a great deal of what is imported."[2] As further testimony of his workers' abilities, Amelung created a series of sophisticated presen-tation pieces, but still the support he required failed to materialize. On the brink of financial ruin, Amelung closed his enterprise in 1795.

In spite of such setbacks, early American glassmaking efforts continued. When-ever one factory closed, glassblowers traveled to another in search of work. Some-times they banded together to form their own business. For example when New Bremen failed, several workers stayed in the area and operated small-scale factories.

Between 1807 and 1814 the Embargo, Napoleonic Wars, and War of 1812 gave another boost to domestic industry: forty-four glasshouses were in production in the United States during that period alone. Following the War of 1812 few domestic glass manufacturers survived the peacetime competition from European glasshouses. Those that did complained bitterly to the census taker in 1820 and urged the government to increase the tariff on imported glass.[3] In 1824 a tariff was enacted, with the result that by 1829, the "*general price* of glass has been reduced not less than FORTY *per cent.*" The "domestic supply and competition . . . have mainly caused this benefit to the people; and . . . if our markets were thrown open to the gluts and swindlings of foreign manufacturers, . . . so that our own establishments should be paralized in their operations . . . the price of glass would return to its former high rate, *for the benefit of foreigners.*"[4] By 1840 the United States had eighty-one glasshouses; the number rose to ninety-four in 1850.

Window glass continued to be a staple of the American industry, and the production of containers for liquor, medicines, syrups, and inks became big business. Philadelphia and southern New Jersey were home to numerous bottle and window glass factories. New York had a prosperous industry, as did New Hampshire, Connecticut, and Ohio. Popular products in the 1815–70 period were mold-blown pocket-size flasks featuring personalities and politics of the era. Many bottle and window glass manufacturers also made tablewares blown of the same unrefined aqua or amber glass as their bottles and windowpanes.

In 1831 there were twenty-one furnaces in the nation dedicated to fine tableware or flint-glass production. The $1,300,000 worth of glass they yielded was almost equal to domestic consumption.[5] Most of these factories were located in coastal cities, such as Baltimore and Philadelphia, or in cities along major inland waterways, such as Wheeling. Boston and Pittsburgh gained renown for their cut and engraved table glass modeled after English and Bohemian imports. To expand the middle-class market, the industry developed lines of mold-blown wares of geometric patterns as less-expensive alternatives to cut glass. It was the refinement of pressed-glass technology, however, that made glass available to all strata of society and put the United States in the forefront of the industry.

1. *Pennsylvania Journal,* June 27, 1771.
2. John F. Amelung, "Remarks on Manufactures" (1787) reprinted in *Journal of Glass Studies* 18 (1976): 130, 133, 135.
3. Arlene Palmer Schwind, "Hard Times in 1820," *Glass Club Bulletin,* no. 147 (Fall 1985): 14–16.
4. [Hezekiah Niles], "Glass and Earthen Wares," *Niles' Weekly Register* 36, no. 933 (August 1, 1829): 361–62.
5. Timothy A. Pitkin, *A Statistical View of the Commerce of the United States of America* (1835; reprint, New York: Johnson Reprint Co., 1967), p. 500.

FOR ADDITIONAL READING

Harrington, J. C. *A Tryal of Glasse: The Story of Glassmaking at Jamestown.* Richmond: Dietz Press, [1957].

Innes, Lowell. *Pittsburgh Glass, 1797–1891: A History and Guide for Collectors.* Boston: Houghton Mifflin, 1976.

Lanmon, Dwight P., and Arlene M. Palmer, "The New Bremen Glassmanufactory of John Frederick Amelung." *Journal of Glass Studies* 18 (1976): 9–128.

McKearin, George S., and Helen McKearin. *American Glass.* New York: Crown Publishers, 1941.

McKearin, Helen, and George S. McKearin. *Two Hundred Years of American Blown Glass.* New York: Bonanza, 1950.

Palmer, Arlene. "Glass Production in Eighteenth-Century America: The Wistarburgh Enterprise." In *Winterthur Portfolio 11*, edited by Ian M. G. Quimby, pp. 75–101. Charlottesville: University Press of Virginia, 1976.

Palmer, Arlene. "'To the Good of the Province and Country': Henry William Stiegel and American Flint Glass." In *The American Craftsman and the European Tradition, 1620–1820*, edited by Francis J. Puig and Michael Conforti, pp. 202–39. Minneapolis: Minneapolis Institute of Arts, 1989.

Wilson, Kenneth M. *New England Glass and Glassmaking.* New York: Thomas Y. Crowell, 1972.

The Study of Early American Glass to 1950

During the nineteenth century collectors began to seek the tangible remains of their country's past, but little is known about those who were particularly interested in old glass. Some Americans collected glass objects because of family associations. Others apparently collected glass for purely aesthetic reasons.

If the publications about American glass history are reliable indicators, interest in glass collecting began to spread during the third quarter of the nineteenth century. In 1852 and 1853 Deming Jarves, founder of Boston and Sandwich Glass Company, wrote a series of essays for *Hunt's Merchants' Magazine and Commercial Review* concerning the history and technology of glass and the rise of the industry in the United States from the late eighteenth century; in 1854 these were bound for private circulation as *Reminiscences of Glass-Making*. In his comprehensive *History of American Manufactures from 1608 to 1860*, J. Leander Bishop publicized the fact that glassmaking was the nation's very first industry. Perhaps it was to Bishop and other historians of American manufactures that Jarves referred when he issued a revised edition of *Reminiscences* in 1865, "in order to meet the demand for information which has unexpectedly sprung up from those interested in the manufacture of glass in America."[1] Although it could not have been widely circulated, the next important contribution to the literature of United States glass history was Joseph D. Weeks's report on glass manufacture for the 1880 census. Weeks drew on the work of Jarves, Bishop, and several local historians and also conducted extensive research of his own.[2] He included a great deal of technical information and provided comparative statistics of European production. In spite of these contributions to the history of glassmaking, however, glass collecting remained the province of a few.

Among those interested in early American glass at the turn of the century was Edwin AtLee Barber, curator and then director of the Philadelphia Museum of Art and an indefatigable researcher best remembered for his work in the history of American ceramics. In 1900 Barber published the first book devoted to early American glass, *American Glassware Old and New*. Here he summarized the history of glassmaking in the United States and gave brief sketches of several factories. The only products he discussed were mold-blown pictorial flasks and bottles, which he divided into six types (by shape) and eighty-six designs. Because of Barber's book, collecting interest in these colorful containers grew rapidly. Dating from 1815 to 1870, pictorial flasks and bottles appealed to collectors not only because of their historical associations but also because many carried the name of the manufacturer and so were readily authenticated.

It was the lack of similar documentation that may have deterred collectors in the area of table glass. As Walter Dyer explained in his 1910 *Lure of the Antique*, "The whole matter of collecting should be approached with caution, glassware most of all. . . . A study of the subject reveals little more than a series of unrelated facts, and accuracy in collecting is to a large degree impossible. . . . There are no marks on old glassware, as on china and silver. To take an unknown piece and determine its age, maker, history, value, or even nationality is difficult and often impossible."[3]

Caution went to the winds in 1914 with Frederick William Hunter's *Stiegel Glass*. Even though publication was limited to 420 copies, news of the author's discoveries and attributions quickly spread, and a veritable glass-collecting mania ensued. Hunter's mission had been to learn all he could about Henry William Stiegel, a German-born ironmaster who operated a glassworks in Manheim, Pennsylvania, between 1764 and 1774. Several students of Pennsylvania history had already published articles about this flamboyant entrepreneur, but few had speculated about his products. Hunter, however, proposed a large corpus of "Stiegel" products based on fragments of glass he unearthed from Manheim gardens and on his interpretation of Stiegel's business records, which he discovered in the Historical Society of Pennsylvania. He credited Stiegel with glass of many styles: enamel-painted mugs, flasks, and tumblers; engraved drinking vessels; and pattern-molded pitchers, salts, and sugar bowls in blue, green, and amethyst. Because he wished to place Stiegel in context, Hunter included a chapter on Wistarburgh Glassworks founded by Caspar Wistar in 1739 in Salem County, New Jersey. Hunter presented previously unpublished primary material on this topic, but his analysis of Wistar production was as problematical as his Stiegel discussion. He described but did not illustrate the "bowls, dishes, and pitchers of various quaint shapes in crude brown, green or bluish green glass," which he felt were the work of Wistar's artisans. In particular, he attributed to Wistarburgh the techniques of lily pad decoration and embedded swirls of different colors.[4]

Thanks to Hunter, glass identification no longer seemed the impossible task outlined by Dyer. Collectors now had two names they could attach to their glass, although the dramatic tale of "Baron" Stiegel made him the favorite manufacturer. In analyzing the antiques market in 1916, Virginia Robie observed the growing interest "in early American [glass] specimens and in genuine Stiegel. Enameled Stiegel is valuable, but the present demand is for the flint glasswares made by . . . Stiegel. Some of the recent prices paid for Stiegel blue, green, and white flint have been almost sensational."[5] Maine collector and novelist Kenneth L. Roberts satirized the passion for Stiegel in his *Antiquamania* of 1928, in which the fictitious Professor

Milton Kilgallen concluded that Hunter's history was wrong: "'You can see for your-self,' said he, 'from the amount of genuine Stiegel in our best antique shops, that the Stiegel factory must have been about the size of a Ford assembly plant, and must have worked on twenty-four hour shifts for at least fifty years.'"[6]

Stiegel Glass inspired collectors and encouraged students to investigate other early American glasshouses. Throughout the 1920s, many articles and books opened new areas of American glass history for collectors to explore. Rhea Mansfield Knittle uncovered information about glasshouses in the Ohio River valley. Julia D. Sophronia Snow examined Franklin Glassworks of Warwick, Massachusetts. Based on his excavations of glass factory sites, Harry Hall White wrote about the glass in-dustry in Kentucky, New Hampshire, and New York. Charles Messer Stow, Walter Dyer, Frederick T. Irwin, and Lenore Wheeler Williams among others, studied Bos-ton and Sandwich Glass Company and pushed that enterprise into a triumvirate with Wistar and Stiegel.

Collector and dealer George S. McKearin and his daughter, Helen, began to establish themselves as the revisionist historians of early American glass with their articles questioning some of Hunter's theories concerning Stiegel and Wistar pro-duction. In 1926 George McKearin declared: "In the choicest collections, . . . many of the best specimens of early American glass, referred to as *Stiegel* or *Wistarberg*, were actually produced during [a] much later period." Not wishing to discourage collec-tors, he hastened to add that later dating does not "detract one jot or tittle from their interest or their beauty in form, color, and design; neither does it lessen their rarity."[7]

Bottle enthusiasts received new guidelines in 1920 from William S. Walbridge's *American Bottles, Old and New*, a project sponsored by Owens Bottle Company. Stephen van Rensselaer expanded Barber's classifications and in 1921 published an extensive *Check List of Early American Bottles*. He revised this in 1926, appending it to a larger, rather disjointed, general history based on his own research of glass fac-tories from city directories, period newspapers, trade catalogues, and local histories.

N. Hudson Moore took a different approach in 1924 by considering American glass styles in tandem with European production. In the section on the United States, Moore's *Old Glass, European and American* combined factory histories with well-illustrated discussions of various types of glass. Two years later Mary Harrod Northend wrote *American Glass*, a narrative intended for the general public that also highlighted the decorative value of antique glass. The best synthesis of American glass scholarship was Rhea Mansfield Knittle's *Early American Glass*, published in 1927. Cautioning that "the subject of early American glass is without doubt the most obscure and also the most uncertain, illusive, and deceptive in the entire field of

Americana," Knittle countered the Wistar–Stiegel–Sandwich obsession of previous authors and presented a careful, chronological survey of the industry that covered important developments in Ohio, western Pennsylvania, and West Virginia as well as the East. "Most of the glassware formerly sold and collected as 'Wistarberg,'" she wrote, "is now described as of 'South Jersey technique,' although much of it was made many miles removed from the State of New Jersey—in upper New York State and New England, and some of it in the middle West."[8] Without directly challenging most of Hunter's Stiegel attributions, Knittle observed that identifying the true Manheim product was often difficult.

In 1929 collectors had the first opportunity to see for themselves, in one place, the remarkable breadth of American glass production. The landmark "Loan Exhibition of Eighteenth and Early Nineteenth Century Furniture and Glass," held in New York as a benefit for the Girl Scouts of America, featured 500 examples of early American glass in the collection of George McKearin. The well-illustrated catalogue departed from previous publications in its focus on the objects and their attributions.

In spite of the Great Depression, interest in glass collecting grew. McKearin was forced to sell some of his 5,000-piece collection at auction in 1931 and 1932, and the sale catalogues with their detailed descriptions and commentary were useful reference tools for collectors. In 1933 glass enthusiasts founded the National Early American Glass Club in Boston and chapters soon spread across the country. The club's *Bulletin*, eventually issued as a quarterly, contained articles on many aspects of glass history and collecting. The more broadly based magazines *Antiques* and *American Collector* published more than sixty articles on glass in the 1930s: among them were pioneering studies of glasshouses in Cleveland, Albany, and Peterboro, New York; Portland, Maine; Coventry, Connecticut; and Lake Dunmore, Vermont. Knittle continued her work on midwestern factories. Lura Woodside Watkins meticulously researched several New England enterprises. She published the results of her study of New England Glass Company under the title *Cambridge Glass* (1930). Jarves's Boston and Sandwich glassworks continued to fascinate collectors and scholars, and with *Sandwich Glass*, issued in 1939, Ruth Webb Lee became the standard bearer. Lee also wrote extensively on other aspects of nineteenth-century production and was the first to publish information about glass reproductions and fakes.

Between 1900 and 1940, the literature concerning early American glass provided a great deal of historical information about glassmaking ventures but, in general, failed to offer much practical advice for the identification or authentication of any particular glass object. *American Glass*, published in 1941 by the McKearins, filled the void and gave collectors an authoritative analysis of the products of American glasshouses. With detailed descriptions and some 2,000 illustrations this monumental work presented the authors' opinions about hundreds of objects. Their attributions were based on glasswares they knew with histories in glassmaking regions. Through an exhaustive survey of city directories and newspapers, the McKearins outlined the stories of over 300 glasshouses and unraveled the often complicated ownership histories. Helen McKearin's early studies of the so-called blown three-mold glass culminated in *American Glass* with an analysis of the technique and a classification system for identifying patterns. She accomplished a similar task for mold-blown pictorial flasks, building on Barber's work and creating a classification system that is still used.[9] In *American Glass*, the McKearins took a cue from Weeks and explained in depth how glass was formed and decorated. They also placed the domestic industry within the larger context of world glassmaking. Their story is no dry compilation of facts but is woven against a background of American economic and political history.

Following the lead of the McKearins, Ruth Webb Lee and James H. Rose published a classification system for pressed-glass cup plates in 1948. During the 1940s some scholars researched glassmaking centers that were not well covered in *American Glass*: Josephine Jefferson issued a volume on Wheeling glass, Lura Woodside Watkins published her research of glassmaking in Providence, and Lowell Innes wrote his first articles on Pittsburgh production. In 1949 Pearce Davis wrote *The Development of the American Glass Industry*, the first survey of glassmaking in the United States from the academic viewpoint of business and labor history.

The McKearins continued to refine their views on American glass and in 1950 issued a second, sumptuously illustrated work, *Two Hundred Years of American Blown Glass*.[14] The year 1950 also saw the publication of Dorothy Daniel's *Cut and Engraved Glass, 1771–1905*, the first study devoted to this type of luxury ware.

Between 1920, when Henry du Pont bought his first examples of early American glass, and 1951, when he opened his extraordinary collection of decorative arts to the public as the Henry Francis du Pont Winterthur Museum, knowledge of the glass industry increased dramatically, thanks to the efforts of amateur historians, antiquarians, and committed collectors. Much of their work has been expanded or revised by recent scholars, but the importance of their pioneering contributions cannot be overestimated.

1. Jarves's *Reminiscences* were originally published in *Hunt's Merchants' Magazine and Commercial Review*, which was bound for private circulation by Eastburn Press of Boston in 1854. J. Leander Bishop, *History of American Manufactures from 1608 to 1860* (Philadelphia: Edward Young, 1866), vol. 1. Another example of manufacturing history published in the 1860s is L. Stebbins, *Eighty Years' Progress of the United States* (Hartford: L. Stebbins, 1868), vol 1. Deming Jarves, preface to *Reminiscences of Glass-Making* (2d ed., enl., 1865; reprint, Great Neck, N.Y.: Beatrice Weinstock, 1968), p. iv.

2. Joseph D. Weeks, "Report on the Manufacture of Glass," in *Report on the Manufactures of the United States at the Tenth Census (June 1, 1880)* (Washington, D.C.: Government Printing Office, 1883), pp. 1029–1152.

3. Walter A. Dyer, *The Lure of the Antique* (New York: Century Co., 1910), pp. 309–10, 313.

4 Hunter's Stiegel attributions continue to have a following among glass collectors in spite of revisionist theories that appeared in print over the years. The most recent reexamination of the Stiegel enterprise is Palmer, "To the Good." For Hunter's description of Wistar products, see Hunter, *Stiegel Glass*, pp. 163–65. He did not use the term *lily pad* but rather described the ware as having a "friezelike design suggestive of breaking waves."

5. Virginia Robie, *The Quest of the Quaint* (Boston: Little, Brown, 1916), pp. 238–39.

6. Kenneth L. Roberts, ed., *Antiquamania* (Garden City, N.Y.: Doubleday, Doran, 1928), p. 200.

7. Helen A. McKearin, "Three Mold Glass," *Antiques* 6, no. 2 (August 1924): 78–81, and "Fictions of 'Three-Mold,' Glass," *Antiques* 16, no. 6 (December 1929): 502–5; George S. McKearin, "Wistarberg and South Jersey Glass," *Antiques* 10, no. 4 (October 1926): 274–80.

8. Knittle, *Early American Glass*, pp. v, 95.

9. Although both *American Glass* and *Two Hundred Years* emphasized table glass, Helen McKearin had been assiduously researching the U.S. bottle industry and planned a comprehensive book on that subject. This project was only realized in 1978 when *American Bottles and Flasks and Their Ancestry* was released with the collaboration of Kenneth M. Wilson.

Henry Francis du Pont as a Collector of Glass

Henry Francis du Pont's collecting career virtually began with American glass (fig. 22). The first antique he acquired in November 1919, a maple table, was followed in January 1920 with nine lots of glass from the estate auction of Frederick William Hunter. Du Pont's purchases at the auction suggest he initially preferred table glass of the South Jersey type to the pattern-molded, engraved, or enamel-painted wares Hunter had assigned to Stiegel's Pennsylvania factory. Six of du Pont's lots were green glass objects described in the auction catalogue as products of Wistarburgh Glassworks: two vases (NO. 255), two bowls, and two pitchers (NO. 137), some with spherical or ball covers. The other three lots were chains of white and amber glass attributed to Millville, New Jersey.[1] In January 1922 du Pont successfully bid on a light green "Large Wistarburgh Glass Fruit Dish" in the collection of Jacob Paxson Temple of Chester County, Pennsylvania. At Temple's second sale fourteen months later du Pont again purchased New Jersey–type glass; among the five lots he secured were a pair of tall vases (64.888.1–.2) and a milk bowl attributed to Waterford Glass Works of Camden County.[2]

Between autumn 1923, when du Pont's collecting of Americana crescendoed, and the end of 1924, he had added more than seventy pieces of glass to his collection, including a "piece Wistarberg," a "large green glass milk bowl," a "Blue Stiegel Vase," two blown three-mold decanters, and four Boston and Sandwich candlesticks. His acquisitions went beyond cabinet pieces and included sets of sherry glasses, goblets, and tumblers, probably for table use: du Pont eventually had fifty-eight different antique luncheon and dinner services each of which required glassware of harmonious style and color. His purchase of several lamps, sixteen glass doorknobs, and seven green glass flower pots reflect other practical needs.

It is difficult to match the purchase records with specific objects at Winterthur today because neither the vendors' invoices nor du Pont's purchase lists are particularly descriptive. Moreover, some glass he bought, especially in the 1920s, he kept at Chestertown House, his Long Island estate.[3] Occasionally du Pont sold glass from his collection either because of a question of authenticity or because of a change in taste or direction.

A 1938 stereopticon view of the glass display at Winterthur (pl. 1) and a catalogue of the glass collection made by Neil Gest in August 1939 clarify some purchase records and confirm du Pont's preferences for three kinds of early American glass: blown glass of the so-called South Jersey style; colored and pattern-molded Stiegel-type wares; and table glass blown in full-size molds of geometric design commonly known as blown three-mold glass. Moreover, du Pont favored certain colors and from the outset wanted his glass collection to create a pleasing overall effect. His 1923 visit to Beauport, the retreat of Henry Davis Sleeper in Gloucester, Massachusetts, strengthened this resolve and drew his attention to specific hues. Nearly twenty years later he confessed to Gest, "I like the color of these two amethyst sugar bowls so much that I hate to take them out of the window." His interest in amber glass was only slightly less passionate, and as late as 1957 Gest offered an important Ohio bottle (NO. 343) because of du Pont's "fondness for amber." Blue was not a color du Pont admired in glass so an object in that color had to be extremely rare—and reasonably priced—for him to buy it.[4]

As his earliest glass purchases demonstrate, du Pont was drawn to the special production ware of bottle and window glass factories. Then known generically as Wistarburgh or South Jersey glass, these ranged from utilitarian objects such as milk pans or jugs (NO. 117) with clean, simple lines, to serving vessels such as bird-topped sugar bowls with intricate outlines (NO. 161). Among the forms he purchased were bowls, vases, mugs, pitchers, sugar bowls, lighting devices, and miniatures. Some were undecorated; others had swirl-rib gadrooning or the type of applied and tooled decoration known as lily pad. By 1940 he had acquired a number of important examples including two lily pad pitchers (NO. 140), a gadrooned bowl (NO. 219) and celery (NO. 244), two sugar bowls (NOS. 161, 166), an oil lamp (NO. 314), and a Jacob's Ladder (NO. 423). Because of their high cost ($425), the "3 South Jersey Glass Candle Sticks with Bobeches" that came from Renwick C. Hurry in November 1924 may be the ones with gadrooned sockets (NOS. 289, 290).

Du Pont acquired several sugar bowls from Gest in the 1940s. At the William Wood sale Gest had secured a dark amber one with heavy swagging that was considered a great rarity (NO. 178). Gest later found a more conventional lily pad example in aqua (NO. 177). In 1948 Gest provided a stunning sugar bowl with gadrooned ornamentation (NO. 176). Also in the late 1940s Gest sold du Pont two eighteenth-century bowls with swan finials (NOS. 152, 153). At the time, NO. 152 was attributed to New Jersey and NO. 153 to the New Geneva glasshouse of Albert Gallatin, but both may represent the work of German glassblowers employed by Henry William Stiegel.[5] NO. 152 is related to an aqua rib-molded vase with intricate handles that Gest sold him in 1940 (NO. 254).

Du Pont's collecting patterns prove he, too, succumbed to Stiegel mania. Of the enamel-painted and engraved wares that Hunter attributed to Manheim, however, du Pont acquired only a few token examples (for example, NOS. 39, 344, and 64.1031–.1033), either by aesthetic choice or because his exposure to similar glass on his European travels led him to doubt an American origin for such ware. What did attract du Pont's attention were colorful, pattern-molded objects, especially pocket bottles. By August 1939, du Pont owned twenty Stiegel pocket bottles: twelve in the diamond-daisy pattern (NO. 354) and two each of the ribbed, diamond, diamond-over-flute, and daisy-in-hexagon designs (NOS. 349, 352, 353, 357). Du Pont found these intellectually appealing as examples of the colonial industry as well as aesthetically satisfying in their rich amethyst hues. He also purchased the very rare blue and colorless diamond-daisy specimens (NOS. 355, 356) and a green ribbed one (see NOS. 369–71). Under the assumption they were also of Manheim manufacture, du Pont acquired two amethyst bowls of diamond-molded design (NO. 155), another of emerald green (NO. 156), and two blue, covered ones.[6] In 1928 he bought an amethyst rib-molded scent bottle attributed to Stiegel (NO. 329); later he found similar ones in blue and green glass.

Other Stiegel-attributed objects du Pont sought were colored, fluted vases with turned-over rims (NOS. 259–61), similar to the one published as the frontispiece in Hunter's book. His first, an amethyst example, came from McKearins' Antiques in August 1926 for $850; another followed in January 1927 from A. H. Rice for $1,080. By 1939 du Pont owned one in green and six in amethyst including a rare pair of diminutive size (NO. 261). Gest's classification of these as "Stiegel or Sandwich?" reflects a theory put forth by George McKearin in 1939 and still held today that such vases were of nineteenth-century origin and probably made in Massachusetts.[7]

The luxury cut glass made in the United States in the early 1800s held little attraction for du Pont, perhaps because of the difficulty of distinguishing American from European examples. Instead du Pont actively collected the imitations of cut glass blown in three-part molds of geometric design, which were, with few exceptions, peculiar to the American industry. Dealer Wilmer Moore of Hopewell, New Jersey, sold him his first example, a "Three-section mold Decanter," in August 1924. By November 1934 du Pont had accumulated enough to be able to set the table for a luncheon he gave for George McKearin.[8] The fifty-five specimens he owned by 1939 included sugar bowls, punch bowls, and celery vases; the majority were colorless, but four were amethyst and six were cobalt blue.

Du Pont's pursuit of mold-blown glass continued through the 1940s. He never set out to acquire an example of every pattern identified in the McKearins' *American Glass* but looked instead for the pleasing shape or unusual color. Among the striking forms the acquired in the 1940s were a butter tub and stand (NO. 213), a cruet or small decanter (NO. 100), and large round dishes (NO. 215). His purchases of colored specimens included an aqua sugar bowl (NO. 174) and vase (NO. 258), a blue tumbler (NO. 53) and salt (NO. 231), a pale pink pitcher (NO. 126), and a deep olive bottle (NO. 338). His attraction to rarity led him to buy eighteen objects that are now known to be fraudulent. Made in scarce and unrecorded shapes of amethyst, blue, and colorless glass (for example, NO. 133), they were designed to appeal to an advanced collector like du Pont. Indeed, the scheme may have been devised with du Pont as the intended ultimate customer.[9]

Du Pont focused on the colonial and federal periods in American decorative arts, so he naturally wanted to have representative examples of domestic glass from those eras. The Wistars and Henry William Stiegel were the well-known manufacturers of the eighteenth century, but in the late 1920s a third name came to the forefront: John Frederick Amelung. In 1928 the Metropolitan Museum of Art published a spectacular presentation goblet which, because of its inscription, was attributed to New Bremen Glassmanufactory established by Amelung in 1784.[10] The sophisticated form and accomplished engraving set it apart from all other American-made glass then known; indeed some collectors doubted it *was* American made. A large covered tumbler with engraved decoration lent to the Baltimore Museum of Art in 1934 corroborated the Maryland origin of the Metropolitan's goblet, and as *Antiques* editor Homer Eaton Keyes reported, this second Amelung glass—made for Charles Ghequiere in 1788—was withdrawn from public view after being "acquired rather mysteriously by an unnamed purchaser."[11] The purchaser was Henry du Pont and the Ghequiere tumbler took a place of honor in his glass cupboard (NO. 44).

Amelung's ambitious enterprise in Frederick County, Maryland, had captured du Pont's imagination, and he continued to seek New Bremen products. In 1939 he bought from Gest the amethyst presentation sugar bowl with swan finial (NO. 158). According to Gest, "It has been agreed among glass collectors that this bowl is the finest piece of American glass yet discovered. It is also the only existing piece of Amelung in any color. Nor has any other sugar bowl in Amelung been found. . . . undoubtedly the most important discovery in American Glass to date."[12] The following year Gest turned up an engraved amethyst cream jug attributed to New Bremen (NO. 110). Du Pont doubted it was made to go with the sugar bowl because it was "plainer in feeling," but he was "very much pleased to have it." "In fact," he wrote, "I think I should have it, inconvenient as it may be to have to purchase it at this time" (the price was $2,800). "I hope to God that too many pieces of the same family won't turn up, as now that I have started I suppose I had better corner the market in this particular line of glass."[13] No other engraved amethyst Amelung glass came to light in du Pont's lifetime, although he did acquire two amethyst checkered-diamond flasks believed to have been made at New Bremen (NO. 360).

In 1946 du Pont bought another Amelung presentation tumbler at auction (NO. 46). In October 1951 Gest offered du Pont an Amelung goblet engraved "A. Konig" but the pressures and expenses of opening the museum that month prompted du Pont to forego the purchase, a decision made less painful by Gest's assertion that the piece was "being peddled all around by the owner."[14] The very next year du Pont purchased another magnificent sugar bowl attributed to Amelung (NO. 157) that Gest had known about for many years and considered "the finest sugar bowl I have ever seen except your [Amelung] amethyst Geeting bowl."[15] Within a few weeks du Pont also bought a rare blue checkered-diamond flask (NO. 361) through Gest, who pointed out that "there are very few of these Amelung checkered diamond flasks in any color. You have the only blue Diamond Daisy, and this would give you the only blue Checkered Diamond. You would have a clear, an amethyst and a blue of both varieties, and that is absolutely unheard of in any collection."[16] More Amelung glass came on the market in the late 1950s. In 1958 du Pont acquired the JFCH tumbler (NO. 47) and the stunning Schley goblet (NO. 16) for Winterthur. Discovered in 1937 by George McKearin, the goblet was the third New Bremen object to come to light. "Because of his special feeling for you, and because there was no covered goblet among your Amelung pieces," Helen McKearin wrote du Pont, her father had "hoped its final home would be Winterthur." Du Pont had been keeping a close eye on this important object. In his annually up-dated "Letters and Notes" he authorized his executors and the museum trustees to pay up to $10,000 for the Schley goblet whenever it became available.[17] Du Pont did not live to see Winterthur curators discover another signed Amelung glass (NO. 45), but he doubtless would have approved of the tumbler, which relates to the Ghequiere.

Glass made in Ohio and western Pennsylvania factories was not among du Pont's initial interests, but he eventually assembled a choice collection of this ware. Between 1927 and 1931, guided by his love of amethyst glass, he purchased four amethyst sugar bowls of midwestern style: one with rib molding (NO. 165), one a blown three-mold (NO. 171), and two fakes (NO. 170, 59.3116). Of significant amber examples, he had ac-quired in the same period only a diamond-molded dish (NO. 199) and a plain but im-pressive globular bottle (NO. 341). In the 1940s, however, through Gest, du Pont purchased several important examples of midwestern production. To du Pont's delight, a mate to his amethyst blown three-mold sugar bowl became available in June 1940 (NO. 172). When a third came on the market later that year du Pont declared, "Two are enough for anyone to have and I do not wish to corner the market of any American commodity if I can help it."[18] Two other rarities in Ohio mold-blown glass surfaced in 1947: a pale pink pitcher (NO. 126) and a yellow vase (NO. 257). In pattern-molded midwestern glass du Pont found a blue diamond sugar bowl in 1946 (NO. 168), an amber sweetmeat stand in 1947 (NO. 200), and an amethyst ribbed tumbler in 1948 (NO. 59). Acquisitions of midwestern glass continued in the 1950s with an aqua sugar bowl (NO. 167) and an amber pitcher (NO. 120). Gest turned up the rare light olive green, diamond-molded jug in 1957 (NO. 119); two years later J. A. Lloyd Hyde offered du Pont a green glass mate to the blue diamond sugar bowl (NO. 169).

Henry Francis du Pont was also drawn to objects that bespoke the nationalistic pride of Americans after the revolutionary war. As a result, Winterthur abounds in artifacts that sport the American eagle and other symbolic motifs. Although the

American-market ceramics and textiles he bought were mass-produced, du Pont never responded to the mold-blown and mold-pressed commemorative glasswares manufactured during the first half of the nineteenth century. He preferred the hand craftsmanship of free-blown and engraved glass. As early as 1927 he found a blown goblet engraved with the Great Seal of the United States (NO. 21); twenty years later he bought three similar goblets from Gest (NOS. 23, 24). Once thought to be American made, they are now attributed to Europe (the decoration may have been added in the United States). Two eagle-engraved decanters at Winterthur are now believed to be period objects with later engraving (63.875a, b; 59.3064a, b).

Although du Pont purchased a copy of Edwin AtLee Barber's book on American glass in 1925, he never warmed to the pictorial flasks the author so enthusiastically described. The flasks he did buy from the McKearins in 1930 were of the scroll style, and these he soon sold. In 1940 Gest ventured, "I have been thinking a lot about your glass at Winterthur, and I wonder if you might be interested in making a small, very choice collection of historical flasks? It seems to me such a collection selected with great care might have a place with you and be a distinct asset to Winterthur, historically and in other ways."[19] Du Pont remained unpersuaded.

Similarly, pressed glass of historical design held no attraction for du Pont after a brief foray early in his collecting career. The Lafayette boat salt may have been purchased in 1925 (NO. 234). Cup plates featuring the ship *Cadmus* and Henry Clay's portrait he bought in 1927 he subsequently sold. What he did retain were several eagle-design cup plates of rare color (NOS. 78–80).

Du Pont had a greater interest in pressed wares of decorative impact. A stereopticon view of the South Room (now McIntyre Room) shows a color scheme carried out with amethyst glass accessories including pressed-glass oil lamps. These may have come from Flayderman and Kaufman in August 1924, although du Pont purchased several pressed lamps in this color (for example, NO. 323). In 1927 the McKearins sold du Pont a rare pair of lamps combining amethyst blown fonts with colorless pressed bases (NO. 319). He acquired numerous "Sandwich" lamps, presumably pressed, in the 1920s. Much of the pressed glasswares du Pont bought, such as various forms in the sawtooth pattern, must have been intended for table use, either at Winterthur or at Chestertown House. Two amethyst "Sandwich" vases came from Arthur J. Sussel in September 1926, but they have not been identified; of the rare pressed glass in the collection, only the canary yellow compotes (NO. 208) can be traced in the purchase records.

H. F. du Pont inadvertently added European pieces to his collection because so much foreign glass was misattributed to American factories. Some of the colored diamond-molded objects he thought were of Stiegel manufacture are of English make (for example, NO. 156). The three "blue urns" du Pont bought in December 1926 from the McKearins and the "Blue Stiegel Urn" purchased the following year from Sussel for $1,500 were of Norwegian origin but were the type Hunter had published as Stiegel.[20] In the 1940s du Pont acquired two Continental sugar bowls with animal finials because he thought they might have been blown at New Bremen (NOS. 159, 160).

Du Pont did actively collect several types of European glass, probably for their decorative appeal. He assembled a forty-piece collection of European eighteenth-century opaque white glass with enamel-painted decoration (for example, NO. 40). Although commonly identified in the purchase records as Bristol glass, these imitation porcelain wares are of Continental origin. Du Pont also formed a small collection of nineteenth-century Continental glasswares with bands of polychrome floral decoration (NO. 94). In 1945 he acquired several English wine bottles with personalized seals (for example, NO. 335) as appropriate accessories for his period rooms. He generally avoided English tableware but could not resist an impressive ceremonial goblet when it came up at auction in New York (NO. 3). During the 1930s and 1940s du Pont turned to English glass lighting devices to achieve the effects he desired for Winterthur's rooms. Lloyd Hyde scoured the globe for spectacular chandeliers, hanging lamps, and wall lights, often sending telegrams itemizing his finds. According to Hyde, the chandelier in Winterthur's Chinese Parlor came from "Li Bak Yee of Canton, who found it in Fat Shan" (fig. 23).[21] Hyde also sold du Pont several superb fixtures that had graced the Lisbon townhouse of the Count of Porto Covo (NOS. 301, 303).

Whether selecting lighting devices or Amelung sugar bowls, Henry Francis du Pont maintained rigorous standards in his collecting. He wanted only examples that were made of high quality glass and that were well crafted in their form and ornament. He gravitated to bold, well-proportioned shapes. Nearly every glass object he owned was in perfect condition; only for objects of extreme rarity, like a blue mold-blown pitcher (NO. 121) or an eighteenth-century sugar bowl (NO. 153) would he accept any damage.

Du Pont's areas of collecting interest were defined by his own taste and judgment, though he respected the opinions of trusted dealers like Gest. He paid little heed to popular trends, but he was sometimes torn between his desire for a well-rounded collection and his intuitive attraction to unusual if not unique specimens. When tempted by a pattern-molded sugar bowl of unusual color (NO. 162), he wrote: "The only thing about it is that it is not a typical Ohio bowl, and I feel I would be making a mistake getting it, as in my opinion I ought to have one typically Ohio representation in my collection. However, this piece is so unusual I think I ought to see it and possibly ought to keep it." To the vendor, Gest, it was quite evident that ordinary glassware had no place at Winterthur, and the rarity and beauty of the bowl in question made it "a typical Winterthur piece."[22]

FIG. 23
Chinese Parlor, 1935
stereopticon.

Although he was a very private collector, du Pont's interests became known to the trade and to other collectors, and he was offered many hundreds of glass objects. When he declined to buy something, du Pont never described its inadequacies to the owner but would merely write that he "could not use" the object in question, he "had no room for it," or he "could not afford it"—the last a response that many doubtless greeted with disbelief. In spite of du Pont's vast wealth, the extraordinary breadth of his collecting and the scope of his building project at Winterthur meant that he could not always buy what he wished at a given moment. He had set his priorities, and he deliberated over every purchase. In 1931 when Gest telegraphed him about an amethyst sugar bowl (NO. 171), claiming it was "undoubtedly the finest piece I have ever owned and [that it] would be the outstanding piece in your collection," du Pont cautiously replied, "in these times one does not feel like rushing a purchase by telegram, as every expense must be carefully considered."[23] McKearin offered an emerald green vase for sale for $2,250 in 1935, but du Pont demurred: "Those green paneled Stiegel vases always turn up when my resources are at their lowest, so I must turn this one down. This is the third one now that has escaped me."[24] He also regretted having to pass on an amethyst salt Gest had in 1938: "Unfortunately times are so bad now that I cannot buy any glass at all, much [as] I should like to own this rare piece of yours."[25]

In du Pont's opinion, President Roosevelt was to blame for much of the country's economic woes. "With this continuing administration," he wrote Gest in November 1940, "my glass buying of any importance is definitely over." Discussing the upcoming auction of William Howe's collection, du Pont said he found lot 275 "a beautiful piece; and had Willkie been elected I was going to ask you to try to get it for me." Instead, he commissioned Gest to get two lesser lots.[26] The taxes levied during the war years further frustrated du Pont. As he explained to Gest, "Now that the full import of the tax law has dawned upon me, I find to my chagrin that my buying of antiques must be very much curtailed, at least until 1943. It is very trying, but it has [to] be." By the end of 1942 du Pont had closed up much of Winterthur and was living in an area near the dining room. He thought the war would end by 1945, but he had the feeling "the taxes are with us forever."[27]

Henry Francis du Pont acquired much of his antique glass through dealers. He frequented antiques shops and shows and responded to dealers' advertisements in *Antiquarian* and *Antiques*. Dealers and private individuals bombarded du Pont with letters advising him of glass they had to sell. If the object was of interest, he would have it sent on approval because he never bought an antique without first seeing it. Du Pont never made offers nor did he bargain with vendors. If he thought an object was priced too high, he did not buy it. When glass collections were sold at auction, du Pont often previewed the sale but had an agent execute his bidding. Because much of his glass was

FIG. 24
McKearin invoice, 1924.

acquired "through the mail," there is considerable documentation of the general formation of the collection. Besides the correspondence to and from dealers, there is a daily list of antiques purchases, beginning November 1919 and continuing until Winterthur Museum opened in October 1951. This list provides the date (generally of payment), brief description of object, vendor name, and price.

The records indicate that many different dealers sold du Pont glass in the 1920s and early 1930s. Among them were Wilmer Moore, Dorothy O. Schubart, Katharine E. Willis, Katherine Wales and Ethel Staniar, D. N. Shanaman, A. M. Mason, M. Tilden, Arthur J. Sussel, and Schuyler Jackson. Most of these dealers were located on the East Coast, but some from farther afield got wind of du Pont's interest in glass. J. W. Young, who owned a fine arts and antiques gallery in Chicago, offered du Pont an amethyst diamond-daisy pocket bottle in 1929. Although he claimed that "patronage for these very rare items is as yet quite limited among Western collectors," he nonetheless revealed that Henry Ford had called about the bottle and was disappointed to learn it had gone out on approval to du Pont.[28]

Du Pont acquired a number of glass objects from George McKearin, the premier collector, dealer, and student of early American glass, who had begun collecting glass about 1916. An insurance agent from Hoosick Falls, New York, with an office in Manhattan, McKearin took advantage of the travel required by his business to indulge his passion for glass. By 1929 he had amassed a vast collection. McKearin opened an antiques shop in New York City in 1923 where he sold furniture, ceramics, pewter, and other accessories in addition to glass.[29] His daughters Helen and Katherine managed the shop, but Helen's true calling was in the field of glass research, and she left the business in 1930.

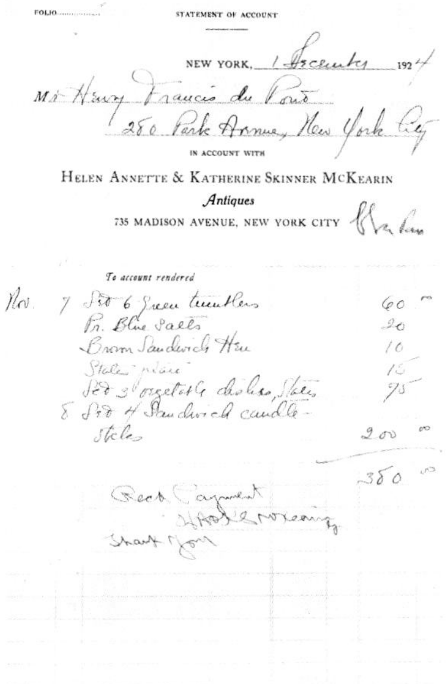

Du Pont first patronized the McKearins in December 1924 when he bought a "Set 6 green tumblers," a "Brown Sandwich Hen," some historical blue Staffordshire ceramics, and a set of four Sandwich candlesticks (fig. 24). His relationship with the McKearins had a difficult start, however. They sent several items on approval in an incorrectly addressed parcel. Du Pont fumed at the delay, and when the package did arrive at Winterthur, one of the glass candlesticks was broken. "I am not surprised," remarked du Pont caustically, "as they were in much too small a box for two glass candlesticks. Luckily the one broken is the one with the square base, as I want the one with the flared base, and you can send down the other three to match this one."[30] Nonetheless, du Pont continued to patronize the McKearins' New York shop and in August 1933 invited George and Helen to visit him in Southampton. The following year, George McKearin accepted du Pont's invitation to see Winterthur. "I saw so many rare and unique things," wrote an enraptured McKearin, "that it is difficult to even begin to visualize them all. . . . There is not any museum in this country whose collection of Americana can even begin to compare in comprehensiveness, rarity and beauty of arrangement with the collection in your homes at Winterthur and Southampton."[31]

McKearin closed his New York shop in 1935 but continued to exhibit in antiques shows and to deal from his Hoosick Falls address. Correspondence indicates that he often acted as a broker, and du Pont occasionally sought his expertise on items offered by other dealers.[32] Du Pont cooperated with the McKearins as they prepared their major publication, *American Glass*, supplying photographs and permitting Helen McKearin to examine his collection of blown three-mold glass in detail.

McKearin suffered a stroke in 1954; in 1957 his collection was dispersed. Although the bulk of it went to the new Corning Museum of Glass, du Pont acquired thirty-three pieces that McKearin had earmarked for Winterthur. When he learned of McKearin's death late in 1958, du Pont wrote Helen, "As he was so keen and interested, he was a real inspiration to me and every collector. He, undoubtedly, was the foremost American glass collector in his time, or of any time. I consider it was a privilege to have known him."[33]

George McKearin may have inspired du Pont, but it was Neil Chellis Gest (1893–1958) of Ohio who exerted the greater influence on du Pont (fig. 25). "The excellence of my collection is entirely due to you," du Pont wrote Gest in 1939, "and I appreciate very much the good advice you have been giving me through all these years."[34] Their thirty-year relationship began in July 1928 when du Pont responded to Gest's advertisement for an amethyst flask of rare daisy-in-hexagon pattern (NO. 357).

Gest was treasurer, and later president, of the Ohio Grain Company, but in between business transactions he gained considerable expertise in the field of early American glass. "I'm not an Antique Dealer," he explained, "I'm primarily in the grain business, and early American glass is my hobby. My interest lies greatly in the glass itself and the commercial end is only a means."[35] Gest can best be described as a private dealer, buying and selling glass as well as acting as a broker. He knew many private collections and worked hard to spring loose important pieces for du Pont. "I'm trying mightily hard to land this flask," he wrote in 1930, "and may have it any day."[36] Considered an authority on Ohio glass, Gest wrote the foreword to the auction catalogue of the important collection of William W. Wood III of Piqua, Ohio. With Parke G. Smith he published an article in *Antiques* about the Kramer family who blew glass in western Pennsylvania and Ohio.[37] Yet connoisseurship rather than scholarship was Gest's forte, and as his sales to du Pont prove, his expertise was by no means limited to Ohio production. A special concern was fake and misattributed glass in the marketplace. His research of a problematical group of pattern-molded vases or bowls of diamond-daisy pattern led du Pont to dispose of an example from his collection.[38] The work of "that chap at Vinelands" (presumably Emil Larson) made Gest "extremely suspicious of all glass," but a few problem pieces from that part of the world still managed to slip through his hands (for example, NO. 218).[39]

FIG. 25
Neil Chellis Gest.

When Gest finally met du Pont in June 1939 a personal rapport between the two men was forged. Gest, his wife, and children were frequent visitors to Winterthur, with Gest often joining du Pont on the golf course. Gest was awed by what du Pont had achieved. "One has to be [at Winterthur] several times," he wrote in 1940, "before grasping even a small conception of all you have done. I remember Mr. [Joseph] Downs remarking to you about having too many accessories and your reply 'nothing of the kind, I like accessories.' In this I heartily agree. Of course your major pieces are of the greatest importance, but after all the accessories bring out the same major pieces, and I believe are of equal importance. Winterthur is a wonderful place to me, and truly interests me more than anything I ever expect to know."[40]

Shortly after meeting Gest, du Pont asked him to inventory and appraise his glass collection and had him update the records over a period of at least seven years. It was Gest who acted as du Pont's agent at auctions, offering his opinion of the glass being sold and executing du Pont's bidding. When du Pont wanted to dispose quietly of a problem piece he turned to Gest. As the consummate collector, du Pont enjoyed hearing Gest's ideas about glass but did not always agree with him. In 1952 du Pont rejected a bowl Gest offered him because, as he explained, "it hasn't the quality of the different ones I have bought from you over a period of years." Du Pont added wryly, "you know you did set a very high standard for me."[41]

1. American Art Association, "Rare and Beautiful Oriental Art Treasures and . . . American Glass Formed by . . . the Late Frederick William Hunter" (January 7–14, 1920), lots 1346–48, 1398, 1475, 1477, 1479, 1480, 1499. Du Pont spent a total of $632.50.
2. Anderson Galleries, "The Jacob Paxson Temple Collection of Early American Furniture and Objects of Art," sale no. 1626 (January 23–28, 1922), lot 1221. It brought $130. Anderson Galleries, "Early American Glass . . . Collection of Jacob Paxson Temple," sale no. 1716 (March 1–3, 1923), lots 301, 306, 331, 334, 489, totaling $318.
3. In 1923 du Pont built Chestertown House. When he inherited Winterthur in 1926 he determined it should be an "American" house. He began extensive additions and moved some of his collections from Chestertown House to Winterthur. When George and Helen McKearin prepared to visit him in Southampton in 1933, he warned "that you are coming under false pretenses, as I have very little glass. I have some quite nice Pennsylvania pottery and fair furniture, but please do not expect too much of the glass" (du Pont to Helen McKearin Powers, July 31, 1933, Registration Division, Winterthur Museum, Winterthur, Del. [hereafter WM]). After du Pont's death in 1969 the museum sold items from Chestertown House, including some glass.
4. Du Pont to Gest, May 8, 1941; Gest to du Pont, December 3, 1957, WM. Du Pont reminded Gest of his dislike of blue glass in letters of June 19, 1944, and July 24, 1949.
5. Palmer, "To the Good," pp. 206, 207, 228.
6. The sources of the blue sugar bowls have not been identified. In 1925 du Pont bought "two blue glass sugar bowls" from H. H. Wetherstine, but their low price—$50 each—compared with that of other diamond-molded wares (for example, $1,000 for amethyst bowl 59.3148) suggest they were not the "Stiegel" ones.
7. George S. McKearin, "A Study of Paneled Vases," Antiques 36, no. 2 (August 1939): 60–63. More than 100 of these vases passed through the McKearins' hands.

8. George S. McKearin to du Pont, November 30, 1934; the luncheon was also mentioned in Gest to du Pont, January 25, 1935, WM.

9. Lanmon, Brill, and Reilly, "Suspicions."

10. R[uth] R[alston], "Accessions and Notes: A Recent Purchase of American Glass," *Bulletin of the Metropolitan Museum of Art* 23, no. 6 (June 1928): 166–68.

11. Homer Eaton Keyes, "Safe Clues in the Amelung Quest," *Antiques* 26, no. 3 (September 1934): 89.

12. Gest, Inventory of du Pont Glass Collection, August 21, 1939, no. 73, WM.

13. Du Pont to Gest, November 2, 1940, WM.

14. The Konig goblet went to Maryland Historical Society; see Lanmon and Palmer, "New Bremen," pp. 80–81, no. 16. Gest to du Pont, October 25, 1951; du Pont to Gest, October 30, 1951, WM.

15. Gest to du Pont, August 13, 20, 1952, WM.

16. Gest to du Pont, September 2, 1952, WM. The colorless checkered-diamond flask is a fake (NO. 362).

17. Helen McKearin Powers to du Pont, March 31, 1959, WM. H. F. du Pont, "Letters and Notes to the Executors and Winterthur Directors," February 16, 1955–February 29, 1964, p. 68, Archives, Winterthur Library (hereafter WL), Winterthur, Del.

18. Du Pont to Gest, October 24, 1940, WM. The amethyst blown three-mold sugar bowl from the Howe collection, sold in November 1940, was bought by Richard Loeb and was in turn offered in Loeb's auction sale in March 1947, lot 136.

19. Gest to du Pont, September 20, 1940, WM.

20. Hunter, *Stiegel Glass*, fig. 60.

21. Purchase from Lloyd Hyde recorded July 24, 1935, Purchase List, WM.

22. Du Pont to Gest, October 7, 1939; Gest to du Pont, October 5, 1939, WM.

23. Gest to du Pont, November 6, 1931; du Pont to Gest, November 17, 1931, WM.

24. Du Pont to McKearin, February 25, 1935, WM.

25. Du Pont to Gest, June 6, 1938, WM.

26. Du Pont to Gest, November 5, 1940. Parke-Bernet Galleries, "Early American Glass . . . Collection Formed by the Late William T. H. Howe," pt. 1, sale no. 227 (November 7–8, 1940), lots 71, 72, 133, 275.

27. Du Pont to Gest, October 1, 1941; December 9, 1942, WM.

28. Young to du Pont, April 19, 1929, WM. The purchase of this flask involved the exchange of seven letters between Young and du Pont between March 7 and April 19, 1929.

29. Among the nonglass objects McKearin sold du Pont were a Hadley chest, July 15, 1926, and a Queen Anne mirror, October 21, 1929.

30. Du Pont to McKearin, May 14, 1925, WM.

31. McKearin to du Pont, November 30, 1934, WM.

32. Vineland, New Jersey, dealer Arthur M. Mason offered du Pont a green bottle that he thought was made at Stiegel's factory. In du Pont to Mason, November 29, 1928, WM, du Pont reported, "I have taken the so-called Stiegel bottle to Mr. McKearin and he says that it is the same type as the bottles found in Ohio."

33. Du Pont to Mrs. Albert E. Powers, January 10, 1959, WM.

34. Du Pont to Gest, June 8, 1939, WM.

35. Gest to du Pont, May 12? 1939, WM.

36. Gest to du Pont, October 29, 1930, WM.

37. Parke-Bernet Galleries, "Early American Glass . . . Collection of William W. Wood, 3d," sale no. 338 (January 22–23, 1942). Neil C. Gest and Parke G. Smith, "The Glassmaking Kramers," *Antiques* 35, no. 3 (March 1939): 118–21.

38. Gest to du Pont, December 27, 1938, May 8, 1939; du Pont to Gest, May 17, 1939, WM. Examples of the group are shown in McKearin and McKearin, *American Glass*, pl. 32, nos. 1–3.

39. Gest to du Pont, September 15, 1941, WM.

40. Gest to du Pont, August 23, 1940, WM.

41. Du Pont to Gest, January 8, 1952, WM.

Glass Collecting by Winterthur Museum

Henry du Pont lived another eighteen years after transforming his Delaware estate into an unprecedented museum of American decorative arts. He continued to buy major pieces of glass for Winterthur, even though he felt his glass collection was largely complete. The guiding philosophy for the expansion of the glass collection between 1951 and 1969 was to build on its strengths, primarily those types of glass that had captured du Pont's attention.

Several significant tablewares made in bottle or window glass factories were sold to Winterthur by Helen McKearin in 1957, including an aqua candlestick (NO. 288), a pitcher of plain, olive green glass (NO. 112), and an olive green lily pad pitcher (NO. 141). From George McKearin's collection also came a colorless candlestick with a New Jersey provenance (NO. 284): today it is recognized as a product of Wistarburgh Glassworks because of its similarity to a taperstick donated to the museum in 1977 by a Wistar descendant (NO. 283). Another Wistar-attributed object, a rib-molded green sugar bowl (NO. 150), had been advertised for sale by Arthur J. Sussel Antiques in 1940, but it only joined the collection in 1959 when the museum bid successfully for it at Sussel's estate sale.

Winterthur did not venture into the problematical realm of Stiegel glass except to buy a tumbler enamel-painted with an English inscription (NO. 38) and to accept the gift of an engraved, "Stiegel-type" tumbler in 1955 (NO. 42). An important early sugar bowl purchased at auction in 1959 (NO. 151) was thought to be of South Jersey origin, but current scholarship suggests it could have been blown by German immigrant craftsmen at Stiegel's Manheim factory.

Du Pont acquired several notable examples of Amelung wares and Ohio glass for the museum during the 1950s and 1960s. To his extensive display of blown three-mold glass he added only a few important pieces, including an aqua sugar bowl attributed to Keene (NO. 163) and a rare cream jug in cobalt blue (NO. 128). The same year, William Van Winkle donated a decanter in a pattern unrepresented in the collection (NO. 95), and J. K. Danby bequeathed a pair of toy decanters (NO. 102). In 1958 James Rose and Earl Knittle offered Winterthur the rare flask NO. 381.

Building on the strengths of the existing American glass collection has continued to be the curatorial acquisition policy since du Pont's death in 1969. Du Pont had instructed his executors and the trustees of the museum that he had "no objection" to Winterthur's adding "a few outstanding pieces" of glass after his death, and indeed only a few were acquired in the special areas of his interest.[1]

Lewis Rumford II kindly donated the Wistar taperstick in 1977 (NO. 283), and the museum purchased two green glass objects that may represent Wistar production (NOS. 36, 225). A cream jug made in the MidAtlantic region after the Revolution was purchased at auction (NO. 111). In 1979 Enora Busler Berry donated an unusual pitcher from Lewis Glassworks, a factory of which hitherto little was known (NO. 116). In 1970 Winterthur bought three magnificent objects with lily pad decoration in 1970, objects that McKearin had sold to collector Mitchell Taradash (NOS. 142, 210, 217). The unrivaled group of Amelung glasswares at Winterthur was expanded in 1973 with an Amelung case bottle engraved for Baker Johnson (NO. 347). Ironically, the owner had tried to sell the case and bottles to du Pont in 1943, but du Pont had refused to make him an offer.[2] To supplement the presentation of common wares attributed to New Bremen, Winterthur bought a blue checkered-diamond salt in 1974 (NO. 227).

The museum acquired several objects made in molded patterns not found in du Pont's collection, including a pitcher donated by Mrs. Titus Geesey (NO. 122). A cream jug of unrecorded pattern was the gift of Emily Manheim in 1972 (NO. 131), and in the 1980s two tumblers of design interest were acquired by gift and purchase (NOS. 57, 58). To round out its presentation of rare forms in blown three-mold glass, Winterthur bought a complete caster set in its original frame (NO. 240).

After du Pont's death the museum determined to venture beyond its founder's preferences in order to create a more comprehensive presentation of glass made and used in early America. As a teaching institution Winterthur needed to exhibit the range of techniques practiced by early American glassmakers. To this end the museum sought and acquired examples of pillar molding (NO. 144), beehive tooling (NOS. 134, 175), and blowing over-the-mold (NO. 198). Du Pont had only a limited interest in pressed glass, and although Winterthur still focuses on hand craftsmanship rather than mechanical mass production, the museum staff believed that the collection of early pressed glass needed to be extended. Documented pieces, such as the marked Bakewell furniture knobs (NO. 414), were welcome gifts. In the 1970s the museum bought marked examples from New England Glass Company (NO. 236), Providence Flint Glass Company (75.101), and the Robinson firm of Pittsburgh (NO. 409). Winterthur also viewed pressed glass from the standpoint of design and sought objects reflecting broader stylistic movements and relating to other decorative arts in the museum. For this reason as early as 1959 Charles F. Montgomery had urged du Pont to approve the purchase of a Bakewell windowpane of Gothic motif (NO. 403) and in 1967 a compote of sophisticated empire design (NO. 207). Rare candlesticks of dolphin (NO. 293) and acanthus (NO. 292) motifs further enhanced the museum's interpretation of classical expression in American decorative arts. The most humble form in pressed glass, the cup plate, was manufactured in an astonishing range of patterns, many of which were commemorative or patriotic in nature. Few were in du Pont's Glass Room, however, so when the Ladies' Hermitage Association of Tennessee offered to donate a cup plate collection they could not use, Winterthur gratefully accepted.

Figured flasks, like cup plates, were inexpensive objects intended for mass consumption, but they, too, represent in their variety an extraordinary index to nineteenth-century popular taste. Again, Henry Francis du Pont disliked these pocket bottles and only a handful of rather ordinary ones were on view at Winterthur during his lifetime. Charles van Ravenswaay donated several appealing flasks during his tenure as Winterthur's director (NOS. 397, 399). In 1973 Mrs. Harry W. Lunger approached the museum about donating the figured flask collection of her father, Philip Francis du Pont (1878-1928), who was a cousin of Henry. Winterthur eagerly accepted the gift, and some 114 flasks joined the collection, besides other pattern-molded, blown three-mold, and pressed wares he had also collected. The Glass Room could not accommodate the flask collection so Mrs. Lunger generously donated funds to transform the windows in the Hall of Statues into suitable display cases (fig. 32). Known as the Oberod Collection, Mrs. Lunger's gift represents the production of many different glasshouses, and the flasks occur in a wide range of designs and colors. This gift gave Winterthur a new strength on which to build: even with the size and depth of the Oberod Collection there were gaps. Since 1973 Mrs. Lunger has continued to be a generous patron and has purchased several important flasks for Winterthur (for example, NO. 387) as well as other types of glass needed to enhance the American glass collection (for example, NO. 292). A strong subsection of the Oberod Collection is the group of 26 pocket bottles with pattern-molded ribbed decoration. Several were manufactured in New England, but the majority hail from glasshouses in western Pennsylvania and Ohio (NOS. 367–70, 372–79).

The production of fine tablewares in the United States during the first half of the nineteenth century was poorly represented at Winterthur before du Pont's death. McKearin felt the museum ought to have an example of the work of Thomas Cains and directed a chain-decorated pitcher to Winterthur (NO. 114). This was followed by a threaded dish in 1971 (NO. 201).

Several important documented objects with cut decoration have come to Winterthur over the years. In 1967 the museum bought a cut tumbler embellished with engraving in diamond point, made at Boston and Sandwich Glass Company (NO. 70). Mrs. E. I. du Pont Irving donated the beautifully cut and engraved tumbler made in 1821 at Bakewell's in Pittsburgh for Victorine du Pont Bauduy (NO. 60). From Louis Lyons in 1957 the museum acquired two cut and engraved Bakewell tumblers enclosing sulphide portraits of Washington and Franklin (NO. 63), although at the time of purchase they were thought to be French. Additional examples of Bakewell's venture into the sophisticated production of sulphide glasses came to Winterthur in 1978 and 1987 (NOS. 64, 65).

Du Pont's enthusiasm for European glass of American historical content (for example, NOS. 21, 415, 417) was shared by museum curatorial staff. Accepted for donation in the 1970s were an eagle-engraved goblet (NO. 22), the gift of Dr. and Mrs. James L. Price, and two tumblers engraved with Philadelphia buildings (NOS. 66, 67) from George R. Clark. The museum purchased an opaque white vase with a Philadelphia scene (NO. 268).

What the collection lacked was a good representation of the more ordinary foreign glass that dominated American importations. As the artifacts at Winterthur came to be interpreted as evidence of consumer habits and trading patterns, curators realized that European glass was underrepresented in the period rooms. By the late 1960s, decorative art historians and archaeologists had discovered that European tablewares of many forms were used in the colonies from 1607 onward; however, visitors to Winterthur saw little or no glass in the seventeenth- and eighteenth-century period rooms. This left the impression that glass was too expensive and fragile an item to have been owned by American colonists. Winterthur's first curatorial glass specialist, Dwight P. Lanmon, undertook to correct this situation when he joined the staff in 1968. He acquired numerous fine examples of eighteenth-century English table glass for the Winterthur rooms, including a variety of wineglasses, decanters, serving vessels, and dessert glassware. The effort continued in the mid and late 1970s during the author's tenure when it was greatly facilitated by the donation of funds from the Charles E. Merrill Trust, restricted to the purchase of English antiques. Several donors came forward with English or Irish objects that had histories in early America, notably an unusual sugar bowl owned in colonial Philadelphia (NO. 149) and a handsome cut fruit bowl from the Lothrop family of Boston (NO. 202). Major gifts include the marked Waterloo Glass Company jug from the Wunsch Americana Foundation (NO. 115) and several drinking glasses from Mrs. Hugh W. Kelly (NOS. 6, 7, 12, 14). From John C. Mayer, a generous patron of Winterthur's ceramics collection, came the gift of an opaque white glass vase enamel-painted in the manner of Chinese porcelain (NO. 253).

Continental European glass had a significant role in the seventeenth-century colonies and again in the federal period. To illustrate the dominance of Venetian products in the seventeenth century, Winterthur in 1975 acquired a rare Venetian goblet (NO. 1). From George McKearin's collection the museum acquired several examples of Bohemian export glass that exemplify the trade in Continental glass that followed the revolutionary war. These objects match the drawings of an important glass trade catalogue purchased in 1971 (see NOS. 17–19). Some European glasses have been acquired specifically to contrast with American-made glasses of related style or decoration, for example, a chain-decorated English cream jug (NO. 105) and an engraved French tumbler (NO. 61).

Winterthur is unique among museums in its active pursuit of decorative arts objects of didactic import. Gathered into the Study Collection are objects that are available to students enrolled in museum-sponsored graduate programs and museum visitors with specialized collecting interests. The Study Collection provides the opportunity to handle glass objects in order to understand techniques of manufacture and decoration. Other examples demonstrate the differences between European and American production. Yet another category of wares are fakes and legitimate reproductions, which allow students to compare and contrast the characteristics with genuine counterparts through hands-on experience.

1. Du Pont, "Letters and Notes to Executors and Winterthur Directors, February 16, 1955–February 29, 1964," p. 68, WL.
2. James C. Brand to du Pont, September 18, 1944; du Pont to Brand, September 22, 1944, WM.

Display of Glass at Winterthur

FIGS. 26, 27
Henry Sleeper's glass
display at Beauport, 1977,
1988.

For help with the interior decoration of Chestertown House, his Southampton residence, Henry du Pont turned to Henry Davis Sleeper (ca. 1878–1934). Du Pont had visited Sleeper's Gloucester, Massachusetts, home in 1923 and was struck by Sleeper's eye for color, texture, and shape. Sleeper had incorporated paneling from colonial houses into his rambling, picturesque retreat and arranged within the spaces his varied collections of Americana in imaginative and striking ways. To show his glass collection, Sleeper transformed door and window frames into display cases, cleverly using transmitted natural daylight. One large fan door from a Connecticut house carried twenty-four pressed-glass cup plates in its leading (fig. 26); shelves extending behind the muntins held more than 100 pieces of amber glass. Another window of Gothic outline contained a display of amethyst glass (fig. 27).[1]

In 1916 antiquarian Virginia Robie had reported a market enthusiasm for glass in "purple and amber tones" that may have been Sleeper's doing; surely no one better envisioned the decorative potential of one-color collecting.[2] Although du Pont pursued aqua and green table forms, the amber glass he acquired after 1923—snuff bottles, a handled flask, a fish flask, a celery vase, bowls, and figures of fish and turkeys (NO. 422)—suggest he intended to emulate Sleeper's appealing effects at Chestertown House. Later, at Winterthur, du Pont displayed his amethyst glass in a window display. The two collectors may have achieved similar visual results, but they differed in their approach to collecting glass. For Sleeper, color was everything; for du Pont, color was secondary to quality and rarity.

Because many of du Pont's amethyst glass purchases were pocket bottles and vases attributed to Stiegel, the space where he kept his glass was called the Stiegel Room (now Ulster County Room). In a 1938 view of the room (pl. 1), carefully hand-tinted at the time to record the accurate colors of the objects, these amethyst pieces are shown to dazzling advantage against natural light. Against the wall in the same room was a green country cupboard with orange-red interior that was the perfect setting for the aqua and green glasswares.

The stereopticon views of Winterthur taken in 1935 and 1938 reveal that virtually no glasswares except lighting devices were in any of the period rooms. One significant exception was du Pont's own bedroom (pl. 2) where nineteenth-century American glass bedecked the glorious eighteenth-century Newport furniture: on a slant-front desk were a pair of aqua lily pad pitchers (NO. 140) flanking a large aqua bowl with swirled decoration (NO. 219); on a card table opposite the bed, between two green plants, was the glassmaker's tour de force known as Jacob's Ladder

Aug. 21, 1939.

WINDOW DETAIL

Pitkin flask #29	Green fluted flask #1	Amethyst ribbed flask #2	Amethyst Small vase #3	Amethyst small vase #3	Amethyst diamond daisy #4	Amethyst small diamond #6
Amethyst diamond daisy #12	Green diamond bowl	Amethyst daisy-in-hexagon #7	Amethyst paneled vase #8	Amethyst diamond daisy #10	Amethyst 3-mold creamer #32	Amethyst 3-mold sweat-meat #33	Amethyst small diamond ribbing #22
Amethyst diamond daisy #13	Amethyst large diamond #20	Amethyst paneled vase #25	Amethyst diamond daisy #16	Blue diamond daisy #19	Amethyst daisy-in-hexagon #23	Amethyst paneled vase #24	Amethyst small ribbing
Amethyst diamond daisy #14	Amethyst 3-mold sugar #35	Amethyst ribbed salt #26	Amethyst baptismal bowl #27	Amethyst paneled #25	Amethyst salt #34	Amethyst sugar bowl #28
Amethyst Diamond daisy #11	Amethyst diamond daisy #18	Amethyst Pittsburgh sugar bowl #30	Amethyst Pittsburgh sugar bowl #31	Amethyst diamond daisy #17	Amethyst diamond daisy #9	Amethyst diamond daisy #15

Aug. 21, 1939.

SOUTH JERSEY GLASS IN GLASS ROOM

Candlestick #80	Goblet #75	Lamp #79	Goblet #76	Vase #74
	Wine #77		Goblet #78	
Miniature compote #82	Miniature Bowl #85	Chicken sugar bowl #87	Oil pot #83	Small bowl #84
	Miniature creamer #86		Pipe #81	
Vase #91	Compote #90	Vase #94	Bowl #89	Pitcher #88
	Miniature Bowl #93		Miniature Candlestick #92	
Bowl #97	Creamer #98	Bowl & cover #95	Sugar bowl #96

Pair of shoe hooks

FIGS. 28, 29
Neil Gest charts of glass
room displays, 1939.

(NO. 423), and another whimsy, a flip-flop.[3] As the primary accessories in the room these objects attest to du Pont's fondness for glass and indicate the pleasure he must have taken in seeing aqua glass in morning light. Another exception was the South Room (now McIntyre Room) where he displayed amethyst cornucopia vases, hurricane shades, and pressed lamps.

Du Pont's genius lay in choosing objects that were masterpieces of form or ornament in their own right but which worked visually with other things in the collection. "I have made it a rule," he said, "never to buy anything no matter how beautiful, how valuable, or how unusual, which does not go well with what I already have."[4] He also was unwilling to acquire something for which he had no space, although lack of room was sometimes a convenient excuse to decline a dealer's offer. In April 1939, du Pont told Gest "my room for showing glass is entirely filled" and lamented his "glass collecting is at an end."[5] It wasn't, of course. A few months later when Gest inventoried the collection, he drew up a chart of the exhibit in the Stiegel or Glass Room (figs. 28, 29). At that time, the cupboard held twenty-six pieces of "South Jersey" glass; thirty-seven examples of "Stiegel" and other wares, mostly amethyst, were arrayed in the window case. There were six aqua glass objects in du Pont's bedroom. Where the remaining fifty-five inventoried pieces—the colorless and blue blown three-mold glass and the two engraved Amelung objects—were displayed is unknown. An eighth floor alcove became a location for the display of glass only about 1942.

In the Stiegel Room, du Pont's display seems to have been guided by aesthetics alone, yet when he viewed McKearin's collection at the Girl Scouts exhibition in 1929, du Pont complained that the glass "would be much more interesting if it were displayed chronologically."[6] Discussing placement and arrangement of glass, du Pont wrote: the "clear daisy-in-hexagon I have placed to the left of the big paneled vase and between it and the blue flask comes the smaller amethyst daisy-in-hexagon, the three making a wonderful trio." Gest in turn offered suggestions, which du Pont usually tried and sometimes followed: "I have decided to make the exchange of the Pitkin flask for the big amethyst flask," du Pont reported, "as it does look very well on the bottom shelf as you suggested." On another occasion, du Pont profusely thanked Gest for his recommendation but insisted, "I can't possibly do what you would like as I do not wish to put my deep blue [Ohio sugar bowl] with the ambers and pale greens. In fact, I think it would look like the mischief and possibly like a 'thirty-center.' I have moved it to the other end of the case."[7]

The glass collection continued to grow and more acquisitions meant the rearrangement of displays. Updated charts of the window case in the Stiegel Room reveal

FIGS. 30, 31
Glass room, 1973.

FIG. 32
Hall of statues, post 1973.

that thirteen pieces were added to the shelves between August 1939 and July 1941. By 1947, even as he bought another three pieces of glass, du Pont pleaded with Gest, "for Heaven's sake don't send me anything else as I won't have room to put it."[8] Du Pont *was* running out of room, but he soon solved the problem by deciding to create a new, larger room just for the glass collection. "I have had temporary plans drawn for the glass room at the top of the house," he reported to Gest in 1948, "and I am arranging to have electric lights over the top and under the bottom of each set of shelves. One set of shelves has the North window behind it as in my present room, and all the other shelves have a skylight over them, so each shelf will have daylight as well as electricity."[9] The plan was implemented with the installation of cupboards and shelves in a ninth-floor space, and the Glass Room opened late in 1949 (figs. 30, 31). This room was an exception to du Pont's rule against having rooms devoted to only one type of artifact. "The Winterthur Museum is a house museum of the American decorative arts," he wrote, "and as soon as the Museum rooms begin to have collections of only one or two kinds of objects, it immediately puts it in a class with most museums which have a series of rooms and galleries to show their collections."[10] Winterthur was not to be like "most museums."

Since du Pont's death, a number of European glass objects and some American-made glasswares have been installed in the period rooms to illustrate the usage of glass in the early American home. By 1973 the Glass Room had to be expanded to accommodate American glass accessions, especially nineteenth-century objects manufactured at too late a date for display in the period rooms, the majority of which date from the eighteenth century. Three more display cabinets were added along one wall. The entire room was rearranged at that time by curators Lanmon and Palmer so as to convey a coherent and somewhat chronological story of the American industry. The window cases in the Glass Room, with their Stiegel pocket bottles and fluted vases, were left largely intact to reflect du Pont's original scheme. The Stiegel Room's country cupboard had been relocated to a hallway off the Courtyard, but the curators decided to incorporate its aqua and green glasswares into the newly expanded ninth-floor gallery. The Glass Alcove on the eighth floor became the repository for the museum's collection of midwestern blown glass, with the window case retaining a selection of pressed-glass whale-oil lamps. When the collection of mold-blown pictorial flasks formed by Philip Francis du Pont was donated later in 1973, it was installed in new window cases in the fourth floor's Hall of Statues (fig. 32).

As Winterthur moves toward the twenty-first century, other changes will affect the presentation of the glass collection. A climate control system, installed in the early 1990s, necessitated the dismantling of the Glass Room. Renovations accompanying the opening of the new gallery exhibition spaces in 1993, includes a display of the glass study collection. Glass is also part of the museum's long term "Perspectives on the Decorative Arts in Early America" exhibition and will be part of the changing exhibitions schedule. In a variety of formats, Winterthur will continue to make available to the public its superb collection of glass made and used in America before the Civil War.

1. Jay E. Cantor, *Winterthur* (New York: Harry N. Abrams, 1985), pp. 115–17. *Beauport: The Sleeper-McCann House* (Boston: SPNEA, 1990); Paul Hollister, "Beauport: Windows for the Eye," *Glass Club Bulletin*, no. 131 (Fall 1980): cover, 7-11.
2. Virginia Robie, *The Quest of the Quaint* (Boston: Little, Brown, 1916), p. 238.
3. The flip-flop, acquired from Karl Kaiser in 1929, was broken in 1983 (formerly 59.2633).
4. Quoted in Cantor, *Winterthur*, p. 142.
5. Du Pont to Gest, April 5, 1939, WM.
6. Quoted in Cantor, *Winterthur*, p. 141.
7. Du Pont to Gest, 1940; June 15, 1942; June 26, 1950, WM.
8. Du Pont to Gest, April 14, 1947, WM. The objects he purchased were 59.3104, 59.3112, 59.3170.
9. Du Pont to Gest, November 19, 1948, WM.
10. H. F. du Pont, "Letters and Notes to Executors and Winterthur Directors, February 16, 1955–February 29, 1964," p. 6, Archives, WL.

THE CATALOGUE

PL. 1
PL. 1
Stereopticon view of Stiegel Room in
1938.

PL. 2
Stereopticon view of Penn Room in 1935.

Nineteenth-century New York and New
Jersey glass with swagged and lily pad
decoration; NOS. 140, 210, 262, 138.

Nineteenth-century American glass with
gadrooned decoration; NOS. 219, 244, 176,
289, 136.

Pattern-molded pocket bottles from
eighteenth-century American
glasshouses; NOS. 360, 357, 353, 352.

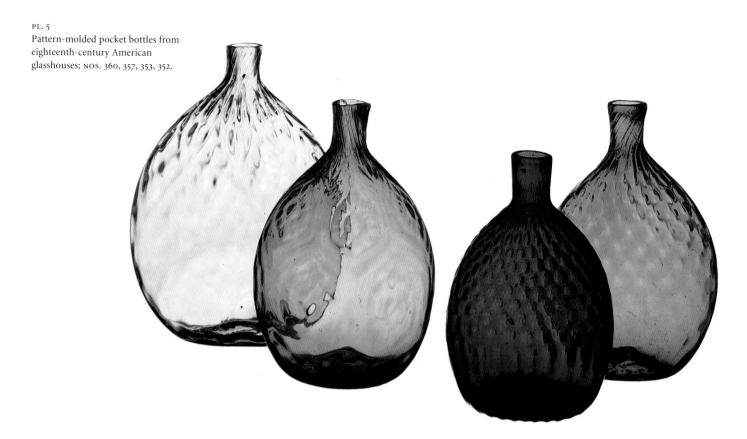

Eighteenth-century Steigel pocket bottles
and an English sugar bowl; NOS. 350, 155,
348, 349.

PL. 7
Glassware attributed to the Maryland glasshouse of John Frederick Amelung; NOS. 158, 110.

PL. 8
American pattern-molded glass of the early and mid nineteenth century; NOS. 165, 241, 228, 260.

American blown three-mold glass of
unusual color; NOS. 123, 257.

American blown three-mold glass of
unusual color; NOS. 126, 273.

PL. 11
Blown three-mold glass from New York
and New Hampshire; NOS. 174, 408, 163,
258.

PL. 12
Early nineteenth-century Ohio
blown three-mold glass and a
twentieth-century fake;
NOS. 171, 129, 216, 172.

PL. 13
American glassware of the colonial
period attributed to Wistarburgh
Glassworks; NOS. 36, 225, 150.

PL. 14
MidAtlantic glassware made about
1800; NOS. 153, 161, 111, 254.

PL. 15
Eighteenth-century Wistar and Stiegel glass and a later pitcher; NOS. 135, 283, 356.

PL. 16
Eighteenth-century European opaque white glass; NOS. 40, 253, 282, 251.

OCTOBER

PL. 17
Early pattern-molded glass from
England, Pennsylvania, Maryland, and
Ohio; NOS. 106, 351, 227, 168.

PL. 18
American blown three-mold glass of the
early nineteenth century; NOS. 53, 274,
121, 127, 124, 125.

PL. 19
Nineteenth-century mold-blown glass of
diamond design; NOS. 214, 162, 169.

PL. 20
Nineteenth-century American glass
made in bottle and window glass
factories; NOS. 255, 421, 314, 288.

PL. 21
American and English glassware in a
range of greens; NOS. 406, 238, 156, 259.

PL. 24
Free-blown Pennsylvania and Ohio glass
of the early nineteenth century; NOS. 116,
167, 166.

Notes to the Catalogue

Although primarily a catalogue of the American glass holdings at Winterthur, this catalogue also includes much of the significant European glass. It illustrates and describes with commentary, 423 of the approximately 1,500 objects in the collection. The decision was made to produce a partial rather than comprehensive catalogue so as to permit detailed descriptions and discussions of attribution and usage. Deciding which objects to include was not easy. Documented and historically significant objects, as well as the most aesthetically pleasing glasswares, were obvious choices. I included certain objects because they filled a gap in the general story of glass made and used in the United States or emphasized a point about du Pont's growth as a collector. Because many objects in the glass collection essentially duplicate others, I chose only one example and noted in the entry related glasses with their accession numbers. From the groups of such mass-produced glassware as cup plates, figured ("historical") flasks, and tablewares patterned in three-part molds of geometric design ("blown three-mold"), I have presented only a representative sampling. Appendixes, however, list all of Winterthur's holdings in these wares.

After considerable deliberation I decided to present the objects according to their function. The broad categories are vessels associated with drinking and the serving of liquids; table glass used to serve food; ornamental vases and desk accessories; lighting devices; bottles and flasks; and a miscellany category encompassing everything from windowpanes to bird fountains. Each section contains chapters devoted to single forms such as decanters, sugar bowls, and pocket bottles. Many chapters have a brief introduction discussing usage and development of the form. Within each chapter objects are arranged roughly in chronological order. Several forgeries from the Winterthur Study Collection have been included, not in a separate chapter, but following authentic objects to which they relate.

My arrangement by function may startle those who collect glass by manufacturing or decorative technique—say pressed glass or engraved ware—but too many objects combine techniques to make such an organization practical. By the same token, glasses from various geographic areas are mixed together in this format by function. Collectors of glass from England or New England may despair, but I believe there is value in seeing how factories from different regions or countries approached a single form. The arrangement by form also obviated the problem of those many objects for which no precise geographical location can be known. The more I learn about the marketing of early glass, and the backgrounds and migration patterns of American glass craftsmen, the less confidence I have in the structure of regional characteristics that has defined American glass connoisseurship for so long. I hope the extensive cross-references and index will alleviate any difficulties for the reader in trying to track specific interests.

For each object or group of objects I have proposed a date of manufacture in addition to a country of origin, region, state, or specific factory as I thought appropriate. In general, I have followed a conservative path. The descriptions in the entries are fairly detailed, a feature which, surprisingly, is rarely found in catalogues of glass collections published both here and abroad. Color terminology is always problematical and ultimately personal; color plates include what to my eye is standard "green" or "aqua," and I adjusted my descriptions of other objects accordingly. I have eschewed some of the picturesque terms found in books about glass, for example, peacock green and sapphire blue, but amethyst seems to be with us forever. When known, the composition of the glass has been noted with regard to the presence or absence of lead oxide; this knowledge can be helpful in determining the place of manufacture. For colorless glasses this was determined using an ultraviolet light. Many of the colored glasses were analyzed for lead content by the staff of Winterthur's Analytical Laboratory, using the Kevex spectrometer.

The verbal description of each object, intended to enhance the visual image, starts with the basic manufacturing technique and moves to a description of form and decoration. I have described the patterns of blown three-mold glass in some detail in addition to citing the classification system developed by George McKearin and Helen McKearin and published in their *American Glass*. Similarly, I have noted the designs of molded pictorial flasks with reference to the McKearins' system for flask patterns, which was updated in *American Bottles and Flasks and Their Ancestry* by Helen McKearin and Kenneth M. Wilson. For pressed-glass salts I have used the classifications developed by D. B. Neal; for cup plates I cite the pattern numbers assigned by Ruth Webb Lee and James H. Rose. Pontil marks are on the underside of objects unless another location is specified. Dimensions are given in inches and centimeters.

The history of each object before it came to the Winterthur collection has been provided where known, including the source of acquisition, whether donor or dealer. Unfortunately, it was not always possible to identify individual objects from the descriptions in du Pont's purchase records. Museum accession numbers are given not only for the entries but also for closely related objects not included in the catalogue. The exhibition and publication history of each object has been noted: the relatively small number of objects that have been previously published underscores the need for this catalogue. In my commentary for individual objects or groups of objects I have tried wherever possible to incorporate new research data regarding production or usage. Information is footnoted, with short titles used for frequently cited references.

Table Glass Associated with Beverages

Chapter 1
Stemmed
Drinking Vessels

Glass was a desirable material for drinking vessels because it did not alter the flavor of beverages. Its transparency allowed the imbiber to see the liquid—and see how little remained. Wine, in particular, was preferred from a glass. In 1657 Jeremias van Rensselaer reported from Albany that he had been unable to sell glassware he had imported from Holland because "there was no wine . . . so that people had no need of them."[1] Wineglasses traditionally had stems, but other beverages were drunk from stemware as well. Some beer glasses of the mid 1600s had conical bowls and short stems, and in eighteenth-century England, short- and long-stemmed vessels with deep, narrow bowls were designed for ale and cider.

Glassmakers exercised considerable imagination in their treatment of stems, from fanciful serpents to architectural balusters, from sturdy knops to airy twists. Although some stems seem designed to provide the drinker with a good grip, pictorial evidence reveals that people frequently held glasses by the foot while they drank.[2] Just as stems varied, so did the bowls of stemmed drinking glasses. They came in many sizes and shapes and were vehicles for molded, tooled, engraved, or enamel-painted decoration.

Many imported wines were available in the American colonies, but their cost restricted them to the upper echelons of society. According to one account of life in Charleston in 1770, "Madeira Wine and Punch are the common Drinks of the Inhabitants, yet few gentlemen are without Claret, Port, Lisbon, and other Wines, of the French, Spanish or Portugal Vintages."[3] Some idea of the quantities of wine kept in the best houses can be gleaned from the inventory of losses taken when fire destroyed the royal governor's residence in New York in 1773. Lost were two pipes and ten dozen bottles of Madeira, a barrel of peach brandy, a keg of French brandy, twenty-five dozen bottles of port, four dozen bottles of claret, three dozen bottles of Malmsey Madeira, two dozen bottles of Minorca wine, six dozen bottles of mountain (a variety of Malaga wine), two and one-half dozen bottles of hock (a German white wine), and two and one-half dozen bottles of the muscat wine made at Frontignan, commonly known as fronteniac.[4]

Advertisements of glass manufacturers and importers indicate that certain wines were meant to be drunk from glasses of particular shape or size, but today it is difficult to match wines with wineglasses. Illustrated trade catalogues from the later nineteenth century can provide some insights, but even in that period, when table customs were rigidly proscribed, individual preference and circumstance could prevail. Indeed, wineglasses could be as multipurpose as other table glass. "If you don't use egg cups and stands, you must put on wine glasses," advised Robert Roberts, butler to Massachusetts Governor Christopher Gore. This practice perhaps gave people the idea of cracking their soft-boiled eggs into a wineglass, where, "after being duly and disgustingly churned up with butter and condiment, the mixture, according to its degree of fluidity, is forthwith either spooned into the mouth, or drunk off like a liquid."[5]

1. Van Rensselaer to Jan Thomassen Van Wely, May 22, 1657, in *Correspondence of Jeremias van Rensselaer, 1651–1674*, trans. and ed. A. J. F. van Laer (Albany: University of the State of New York, 1932), p. 47.

2. See, for example, Jan Steen, *Margrite de Gojen* (engraving after the painting, collection of the author), and Sir Godfrey Kneller, *Duke of Newcastle*, ca. 1718, in Hughes, *Table Glass*, fig. 32.

3. Dr. George Milligin, *A Short Description of the Province of South Carolina*, quoted in Anna Wells Rutledge, "After the Cloth Was Removed," *Winterthur Portfolio 4*, ed. Richard K. Doud (Charlottesville: University Press of Virginia, 1968), p. 50.

4. B. D. Bargar, ed., "Documents: Governor Tryon's House in Fort George," *New York History* 35, no. 3 (July 1954): 306. A pipe was a large cask generally equal to 2 hogsheads or 4 barrels (about 126 gallons), but the capacity could vary according to the type of wine stored. A keg usually held less than 10 gallons. Malmsey was a strong, sweet wine that got its name from Monemvasia, Greece, where malmsey grapes were first pressed. In addition to wines, Governor Tryon lost large amounts of ale, porter, rum, and arrack—a fermented drink derived from coconut juice.

5. Robert Roberts, *The House Servant's Directory* (1827; facsimile ed., Waltham, Mass.: Gore Place Society, 1977), p. 43. Thomas Hamilton, *Men and Manners in America* (1833; reprint, New York: Augustus M. Kelley, 1968), p. 25.

1

DRINKING GLASS
PROBABLY VENICE (MURANO),
1660–80

Colorless nonlead glass of gray-green tint. Blown. Thin conical bowl set on hollow ball knop; conical foot with downward-folded edge; pontil mark. Paper label inscribed "15_/65/126."
H: 6¼ in (15.9 cm); Diam bowl: 3⁹⁄₁₆ in (9.1 cm)
Museum purchase, 1975: Alan Tillman Antiques, London.
Funds for purchase, gift of the Claneil Foundation
75.205

Published: Sotheby Parke Bernet, "Fine English and Continental Glass" (July 14, 1975), lot 316.
Smith and Hummel, "Winterthur Museum," p. 1282.

When a Dutchman visited Jamestown in 1633, the governor welcomed him "with a Venice glass of sack." In Boston, Samuel Sewall noted in his diary for July 18, 1687, "Mr. [Increase] Mather had two Venice Glasses broken at our Meeting."[1] The New York inventory of Colonel William Smith, taken in 1704/5, included "a case with Venis Glasses" valued at £3.[2] Fragments of simple drinking vessels comparable to Winterthur's glass have been excavated from Jamestown and other archaeological sites in Virginia. Venetian and *façon de venise* stemmed ware of more elaborate styles have been recovered from Virginia sites, St. Mary's City, Maryland, and Fort Orange in Albany.

In form, Winterthur's glass relates closely to Venetian wine and beer glasses ordered by the London Arm of Michael Measey and John Greene, members of the Company of Glass Sellers, between 1667 and 1672. Measey and Greene provided their Venetian supplier, Allesio Morelli, with more than 400 measured drawings of the glassware they wanted for their English clientele. In the accompanying letters, Greene insistently stated that the drinking glasses be made "exact according to the patterns both for size fashion and number and of noe other sorts or fashions."[3]

The scale drawings reveal that size rather than shape designated the beverage. Beer glasses had conical bowls, ball knops, and flaring feet and stood 6½ to 6¾ inches. In a letter of August 28, 1668, the merchants complained that the "beere glasses were something

smaller than the patterns," which may explain why Winterthur's glass falls slightly short.[4] Claret glasses were to be of similar shape but only 5¾ inches in height.

For the beer glasses, Greene had specified that "the Lower part . . . and the button must be sollid mettall and all the Rest of the glass I would have to be blowne thicker than usealy [usually] especially the feet must be strong." Yet in this and other examples only a tiny section of the base of the bowl is solid and the ball knop below is hollow.[5] The vessel is extremely thin-walled and light in weight. The foot, although folded at the edge, seems hardly "strong." Still, Venetian glasswares had distinct advantages over their English counterparts, as Greene reassured Morelli: "the exelencj of your Venice glasses [is] that they are generallij stronger than ours made heer, and soe not so soon broken."[6] English glassmakers, however, were struggling to achieve sound, crystallike glass that would compete successfully with Venetian imports. Early in 1673 Girolamo Alberti, the Venetian secretary in London, observed that the English could not yet match "the clearness and strength of venetian crystal," but a year later he warned, "They already made crystal glass here in perfection." By June 1674 Alberti reported that the English drinking glasses are "very white and thick in imitation of rock crystal, but very far from real perfection though they strike the eye and surpass those of Venice."[7]

1. David Peterson DeVries, *Voyages from Holland to America, A.D. 1632 to 1644*, trans. Henry C. Murphy (New York: Billin and Brothers, 1853), p. 50. *The Diary of Samuel Sewall, 1674–1729*, ed. M. Halsey Thomas, 2 vols. (New York: Farrar, Straus, and Giroux, 1973), 1:144. Sewall does not offer explanation; perhaps the gesture was to symbolize the fragility of life or to dramatize Mather's famous hatred of drunkenness. Among Mather's sermons was the 1673 "Wo to Drunkards."
2. St. Georges, Suffolk County, New York, Wills, liber 6, p. 123, Queens College, reference courtesy of Benno M. Forman.
3. Measey and Greene to Morelli, August 28, 1668, as quoted in Albert Hartshorne, *Antique Drinking Glasses* (New York: Brussel and Brussel, 1968), p. 441 (originally published as *Old English Glasses* [1897]).
4. Measey and Greene to Morelli, August 28, 1668, as quoted in Hartshorne, *Antique Drinking Glasses*, p. 441.

5. Drawing with instructions in Tait, *Golden Age*, p. 24, fig. 5. Examples similar to Winterthur's are in Victoria and Albert Museum, *Glass Table-Ware* (London, 1947), fig. 15; Rex Ebbott, *British Glass of the Seventeenth and Eighteenth Centuries*, National Gallery Booklets (Melbourne, Aus.: Oxford University Press, 1971), fig. 1a; *Glass at the Fitzwilliam Museum* (Cambridge, Eng.: Cambridge University Press, 1978), p. 83, fig. 187.
6. Greene to Morelli, November 30, 1672, as quoted in Hartshorne, *Antique Drinking Glasses*, p. 448.
7. Quoted in Charleston, *English Glass*, p. 108.

2

ALE GLASS

ENGLAND, 1690–1720

Colorless lead glass. Blown. Elongated bucket bowl; a
second gather pattern-molded with 24 ribs swirled to right
and pulled into points below rim; flattened knop; short,
flaring stem; disk foot; pontil mark.
H: 5⅛ in (13.0 cm); Diam bowl: 2⅜ in (6.0 cm)
Museum purchase, 1978: Christie, Manson & Woods,
London
78.196

Published: Christie, Manson & Woods, "Important English
and Continental Glass," sale no. 1125 (October 3, 1978),
lot 51.

Although the Greene and Measey drawings discussed in NO. 1 indicate that function varied
with size rather than shape, by the end of the
seventeenth century certain beverages were
equated with particular shapes. Chief among
these was ale, an alcoholic drink made from
malt, and, in this period, without hops.

    For this relatively potent liquor, a tall, nar-
row bowl with a three-to-four-ounce capacity
was set on a short stem. In the early eighteenth
century, the bowl, more commonly conical than
bucket- shape, was typically ornamented with
"wrythen" decoration, that is, mold-blown ribbing that spiralled from the top of the stem
two-thirds up the bowl.¹ On the Winterthur
example the ribbing is pincered into points
around the top, an embellishment indicative of
Venetian influence.

    Ale was a favorite beverage in the North
American colonies from the beginning of settlement, but the term *ale glass* has not been found
in colonial records prior to about 1750. Because
"Nippitate" described ale of particular strength
and quality, the "pair Nippto glasses" valued at
2*s*. 6*d*. in a Philadelphia inventory of 1708 were
probably ale glasses, perhaps of this style.²

1. See P. C. Trubridge, "The English Ale Glasses, 1685–
1830," *Glass Circle* 1 (1972): 46–57.
2. John Hunt inventory, 1708-108, Philadelphia County
Probate Records (microfilm), Joseph Downs Collection of
Manuscripts and Printed Ephemera, Winterthur Library,
Winterthur, Del. (hereafter, Downs, WL).

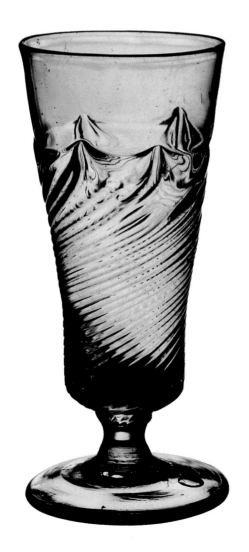

3

GOBLET

ENGLAND, 1690–1710

Colorless lead glass. Blown. Pointed round funnel bowl;
stem formed of inverted baluster and basal knop each
with a tear; conical foot with downward-folded edge;
pontil mark.
H: 14½ in (36.8 cm); Diam bowl: 8⅞ in (22.6 cm)
History: Lord Methuen; Joseph Bles; Frank Partridge &
Sons; Mrs. Howard Eric
H. F. du Pont purchase, 1949: Parke-Bernet Galleries,
New York City
63.685

Exhibited: Victoria and Albert Museum, 1923–34.
Published: Parke-Bernet Galleries, "Rare Chinese
Porcelains, Early English Silver, and English Furniture
from . . . Mrs. Howard Eric" (December 2, 1949), lot 38.

With its boldly knopped stem offset by an elongated, hollow air bead, this massive goblet
exemplifies the heavy baluster style that characterized English stemware between 1690 and
1720. Of unusually large size, this glass probably had a ceremonial purpose as a communal
toasting glass. Early eighteenth-century paintings depicting the host with a much larger
goblet than those of his guests support this inter-
pretation.¹

    Moralists in England and her colonies de-
cried the habit of toasting, which, when un-
checked, led to excessive consumption of intoxi-
cating beverages. In 1630, "upon consideration
of the inconveniences which had growne in England, by drinkinge one to another," John
Winthrop, Governor of the Massachusetts Bay
Colony, "restrayned it at his owne table and
wished others to doe the like, so as it grewe by
little and little to dysuse." Winthrop's model
must not have been emulated because in 1639
the General Court passed a law prohibiting the
"abominable practice of drinking healths" in
the colony. Transgressors were fined 12*d*.; in-
formers were given half the fine.²

1. Charleston, *English Glass*, pp. 137–40, pls. 35a, b. For
related glasses, see *Glass at the Fitzwilliam Museum*
(Cambridge, Eng.: Cambridge University Press, 1978),
p. 87, nos. 202a, b; Merseyside County Museums, *Historic
Glass from Collections in North West England* (Liverpool,
Eng., 1979), p. 63, no. E6; Museum of Fine Arts, Boston,
New England Begins: The Seventeenth Century, 3 vols.
(Boston, 1982), 2:283–84, no. 278.
2. *The Journal of John Winthrop*, in *The Winthrop Papers*,
5 vols. (Boston: Massachusetts Historical Society, 1931),
2:268–69.

4

DRAM GLASS

ENGLAND, 1700–1720

Colorless lead glass. Blown. Round funnel bowl; stem
formed of inverted baluster and basal knop; conical foot
with downward-folded edge; pontil mark.
H: 4⅛ in (10.6 cm); Diam bowl: 2⁵⁄₁₆ in (5.8 cm)
Museum purchase, 1976: A. U. Milford Antiques, London.
Funds for purchase, gift of the Charles E. Merrill Trust
76.311

Published: Smith and Hummel, "Winterthur Museum,"
p. 1282.

This diminutive drinking glass is known as a
dram glass. Although a dram is an apothecary's
measure of one-eighth fluid ounce, the term
was loosely used in the eighteenth century to
denote any small draught. Designed to serve
"strong-waters," cordials, or such "spirituous
liquors" as brandy, rum, and gin, the small bowl
enabled the drinker to swallow the contents in
one gulp and enjoy a quick succession of short
drinks—a practice called dramming. In recol-
lecting his Connecticut childhood around 1800,
S. G. Goodrich wrote of a cleric who decried
the dramming habit:

> I say nothing, my beloved brethren, against
> taking a little bitters before breakfast, and
> after breakfast, especially if you are used to
> it. What I contend against is this dramming,
> dramming, dramming, at all hours of the
> day. . . . I do not purpose to contend against
> old established customs, . . . rendered re-
> spectable by time and authority; but this
> dramming, dramming, is a crying sin in
> the land.[1]

Early references to dram glasses occur in
the probate records of Philadelphia County. The
"glass dram cup" and "dram glass" listed in inventories of 1698 and 1699 may well have been
of this heavy baluster style.[2]

1. Samuel Griswold Goodrich, *Recollections of a Lifetime;
or, Men and Things I Have Seen*, 2 vols. (New York: Miller,
Orton, and Mulligan, 1856), 1:69.
2. Hester Watts inventory, 1698-179, and John Burby
inventory, 1699-227, Philadelphia County Probate Records
(microfilm, Downs, WL).

5

WINEGLASS (ONE OF SIX)
ENGLAND, 1745–65

Colorless lead glass. Blown. Trumpet bowl; drawn,
straight stem containing multiple-spiral air twists; conical
foot; pontil mark.
H: 7½ in (19.2 cm); Diam bowl: 3 in (7.6 cm)
Museum purchase, 1970: Spink & Son, London
70.191.1 (mates are 70.191.2–.6)

English decorative art of the rococo period is
characterized by a lightness and fluidity of design. In stemmed glassware this taste was most
eloquently expressed by the air-twist stem,
which was probably introduced in the late
1730s, an outgrowth of the earlier practice of
inserting tears in the stems of glassware (NO. 3).
With a spiked tool, the glassmaker pricked a
gather of glass, trapping air bubbles in a decorative pattern. By drawing the bubbles out with
a twisting motion of the tool, he created the
spirals, which often have a silvery or mercurial
appearance. In the Winterthur examples the
bowls of the wineglasses seem to float atop a
hollow column defined by the twists—an almost disturbing illusion that recalls the per-
verse side of the rococo.

The period term for glasses with twisted
stems was "wormed," though occasionally
"twisted" was used. The earliest reference to
wormed glasses yet found in England or
America is William Randall's March 24, 1746,
advertisement, *Boston Evening Packet*.

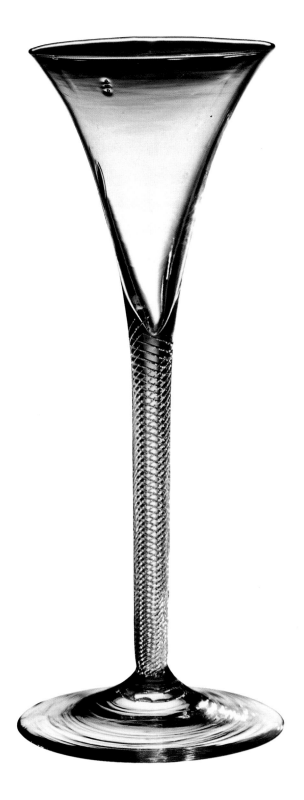

6

WINEGLASS
ENGLAND, 1765–75

Colorless lead glass. Blown. Ogee bowl, tooled horizontal ribbing; straight stem containing a double-series, white opaque twist consisting of a pair of corkscrew tapes outside a pair of heavy spiral threads; conical foot; pontil mark.
H: 4⅞ in (12.4 cm); Diam bowl: 1¹⁵⁄₁₆ in (4.9 cm)
History: Hugh W. Kelly, Lancaster, Pa.
Gift of Mrs. Hugh W. Kelly, 1987
87.123

7

WINEGLASS
ENGLAND, 1755–75

Colorless lead glass. Blown. Waisted ogee bowl, basal molding, tooled detail; straight stem containing a double-series, white opaque twist consisting of a multi-ply corkscrew twist outside a heavy single tape corkscrew; conical foot; pontil mark.
H: 6 in (15.4 cm); Diam bowl: 2⅛ in (5.4 cm)
History: Hugh W. Kelly, Lancaster, Pa.
Gift of Mrs. Hugh W. Kelly, 1987
87.126

8

WINEGLASS (ONE OF TWO)
ENGLAND, 1755–75

Colorless lead glass. Blown. Ogee bowl; straight stem containing a double-series, white opaque twist; conical foot; pontil mark. Wheel engraved with rosette and leaves; traces of gilding on the engraving.
H: 5½ in (14.0 cm); Diam bowl: 1¹³⁄₁₆ in (4.5 cm)
Museum purchase, 1968: Richard H. and Virginia A. Wood Antiques, Baltimore
68.311.2 (mate is 68.311.1)

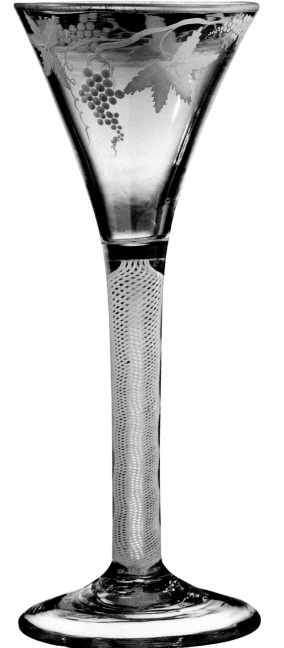

9

WINEGLASS (ONE OF TWO) ENGLAND, DECORATION ATTRIBUTED TO SHOP OF WILLIAM BEILBY, NEWCASTLE UPON TYNE, CIRCA 1765

Colorless lead glass. Blown. Trumpet bowl; straight stem containing multiple spiral, white opaque twist; conical foot; pontil mark. Painted in white enamel with a fruiting, leafy vine; gilded edge.
H: 6¾ in (17.3 cm); Diam bowl: 2¹¹⁄₁₆ in (6.9 cm)
History: George Horace Lorimer
Museum purchase through trade, 1975: Bernard and
S. Dean Levy, New York City
75.43.1 (mate is 75.43.2)

10

WINEGLASS (ONE OF TWO) ENGLAND, DECORATION ATTRIB- UTED TO SHOP OF WILLIAM BEILBY, NEWCASTLE UPON TYNE, CIRCA 1765

Colorless lead glass. Blown. Bell bowl; straight stem containing a double-series, white opaque twist, consisting of a multi-ply spiral band encircling a pair of spiral tapes; conical foot; pontil mark. Painted in white enamel with a fruiting, leafy vine; gilded edge.
H: 6⅜ in (16.3 cm); Diam bowl: 2¹¹⁄₁₆ in (6.9 cm)
History: George Horace Lorimer
Museum purchase through trade, 1975: Bernard and
S. Dean Levy, New York City
75.44.1 (mate is 75.44.2)

A second rococo style that came into fashion in mid eighteenth-century English tableware was the opaque-twist stem. To create this, the glass-maker placed the ends of enamel canes into a mold. He then picked up the canes with a gather of hot glass, embedded them within the glass by rolling the gather on a flat surface (marvering), and pulled and twisted out the gather.[1] Stems of varying lengths could be prepared in advance, cut as needed, and applied to bowls.

An extraordinary number of different complex spirals was produced for a wide range of effects, including an overall gauze, such as that of the sixteen spiralling tapes in NO. 9, and a zigzag design formed in NO. 10 by a twelve-ply band encircling a pair of spiral tapes. White was the common color, but some red, blue, green, and yellow canes were used.[2]

What spurred the manufacture of opaque-twist stems in England is not known. The technique is rooted in Venetian filigree styles of the sixteenth and seventeenth centuries, in which intricate patterns of opaque threads embellished many forms of tableware. Venetian craftsmen may have brought the technique to English glasshouses, but solid proof is lacking. Perhaps the idea came through Bohemian glassmakers who, by 1700, were twisting threads of ruby glass within the stems and finials of covered goblets(see p. 5, fig. 16).[3] In any case, English artisans developed a distinctive style and limited the technique almost exclusively to stemware; only a few other forms incorporating twisted decoration are recorded (NO. 149).

Introduced shortly before 1750, opaque-twist stems soon superseded air-twist stems and remained in vogue into the 1770s. The "new fashion twist stemed Wine Glasses" Henry Barnes advertised in Boston in 1751 may have had opaque twists.[4] Period notations of "enamel'd shank" and "enameled stem" wineglasses describe the style; "enameled" wineglasses probably refer more often to opaque-twist stems than to enamel-painted decoration. Both written and archaeological evidence attest to the widespread popularity of the style in colonial America.

Bowls of several different shapes surmounted opaque-twist stems. In modern parlance they include the round funnel, waisted ogee or tulip (NO. 7), ogee (NO. 8), trumpet or conical (NO. 9), and bell (NO. 10). Eighteenth-century names for bowl forms are rarely specified in period documents. An exception is a 1752 advertisement of Cooper and Curtin in Charleston, South Carolina, who advised the public that they carried "bell bowl" wines—probably similar in shape to NO. 10—as well as "Spanish," "Britannia," "olive and diamond," and "globe and olive egg bowl." In the 1770s a New York City merchant, Frederick Rhinelander, ordered dozens of drinking glasses from the Bristol glasshouse of Vigor and Stevens. Two shapes specified in his business papers are globe and lemon, the former probably denoting a hemispherical bowl and the latter probably an ogee (NO. 8).[5]

The bowls of wineglasses could be left plain or could be decorated in several ways. The "olive and diamond" wineglasses offered in Charleston, for example, probably had a pattern-molded diamond design. The bowls of some mid eighteenth-century wineglasses had tooled horizontal ribbing or corrugation, a style collectors call "Lynn-type," after the town of King's Lynn (NO. 6; see NO. 37). Others bore engraved designs. Fruiting vines had an obvious appeal, but the rose was also popular (NO. 8). Although some glasses of rose design may have symbolized Jacobite sentiments, it is likely that floral motifs were chosen for their own merits, particularly after the death of the Old Pretender in 1766. Indeed, naturalistic flowers were such a hallmark of English rococo glass that engraved glasses in the period were known as "flowered."[6]

The vine, a standard motif in the glass engraver's repertory, was also a favorite of enamelers. The enamel-painted and gilded bowls of NOS. 9 and 10 bear the same grapevine motif that is on a claret decanter (NO. 84). Enamel-painted glasses signed by William Beilby (1740–1819) of Newcastle upon Tyne have prompted Beilby attributions for most glasses of this type.[7]

In at least one instance, English enamel-painted glasswares were specifically ordered by colonists. In 1767 Brother Andrew Miller of a Masonic lodge in Halifax, North Carolina, was instructed to obtain from England six dozen wineglasses, twelve half-pint glasses, twenty-four pint glasses, three dozen punch glasses, and nine decanters, all "with the words Enameled upon them Halifax Lodge No Carolina."[8] The wines were to have "worm'd stalks," a term historians usually associate with air-twist stems, but in the 1760s it may have described opaque twists.

1. For an illustration of the technique see Wilson, *New England Glass*, p. 23.
2. L. M. Bickerton, *Eighteenth Century English Drinking Glasses: An Illustrated Guide* (London: Antique Collectors' Club, 1986), nos. 1,174–1,218.
3. Tait, *Golden Age*, pp. 49–50, 65–84.
4. Noël Hume, *Glass*, pp. 20–22. *Boston Evening Post*, May 27, 1751.
5. Cooper and Curtin advertisement, *South Carolina Gazette*, November 20, 1752, reference courtesy of Museum of Early Southern Decorative Arts (hereafter MESDA); Arlene Palmer Schwind, "English Glass Imports in New York, 1770–1790," *Journal of Glass Studies* 25 (1983): 182.
6. Flowered glass is first advertised in England in 1742; see Charleston, *English Glass*, p. 154.
7. James Rush, *The Ingenious Beilbys* (London: Barrie and Jenkins, 1973).
8. Bradford L. Rauschenberg, "Discovery: A Documented Bow Bowl Made for Hallifax Lodge/North-Carolina," *Journal of Early Southern Decorative Arts* 1, no. 1 (May 1975):4.

11

WINEGLASS (ONE OF TWELVE)
ENGLAND, 1750–70

Colorless lead glass. Blown. Trumpet bowl; straight stem containing a pair of air spirals encircling a multiple-spiral, white opaque twist; conical foot; pontil mark.
H: 7½ in (19.2 cm); Diam bowl: 2¼ in (5.7 cm)
Museum purchase, 1969: Spink & Son, London
69.76.1 (mates are 69.76.2–.12)

Published: Advertisement of Spink & Son, *Country Life* 145, no. 3750 (January 16, 1969): 102.

Occasionally, English glassmakers combined opaque twists with air twists for a virtuoso effect. Known to collectors as the mixed-twist stem, the result is a subtle interplay of white and silvery tones. It is possible that the "wormed and enameled wine-glasses" advertised by Walter Mansell in Charleston in 1763 refer not to two different styles of glasses but to this combination technique.[1]

1. *South Carolina Gazette*, October 15, 1763.

12

MASONS' OR FIRING GLASS
IRELAND OR ENGLAND, CIRCA
1795

Colorless lead glass. Blown. Ovoid bowl; short straight stem containing wide multiple-spiral, white opaque twist; thick disk foot; pontil mark. Wheel engraved with Masonic square and compasses on one side and "761" on the other.
H: 4 in (10.8 cm); Diam bowl: 2 in (5.1 cm)
History: Hugh W. Kelly, Lancaster, Pa.
Gift of Mrs. Hugh W. Kelly, 1987
87.125

Glasses with short stems and thick feet were specifically designed for ritualistic toasts that Freemasons offered at their meetings. When pounded upon the table in unison, the glasses generated a sound like cannon shot, hence the name "firing" glasses. Because they were so closely linked with Masonry, they were called Masons' or Freemasons' glasses even when undecorated.

The square and compasses symbolized reason and faith, and "761" denoted the particular lodge that owned this glass, the Young-Union Lodge No. 761, recorded in Ireland between 1792

and 1818.[1] The engraving may have been added to an earlier glass, but this is unlikely because twist-stemmed firing glasses remained fashionable until about 1800, long after the style had been superseded in other drinking vessels.

References to Masons' glasses in the American colonies occur as early as November 23, 1761, when merchant Mary Gallop advertised engraved examples in the *Boston Gazette*, and continue through the 1780s, reflecting the popularity of the Masonic movement. The first American glassmaker known to have manufactured Masons' glasses was Henry William Stiegel, who included them in a list of products made at his Manheim, Pennsylvania, factory in 1769. In that same year, at his Elizabeth Furnace ironworks, he also made stove plates bearing Masonic designs.[2]

1. I am grateful to Stephen E. Patrick, curator of the George Washington Masonic National Memorial Association, Alexandria, Va., for identifying lodge no. 761.
2. Scottish Rite Masonic Museum of Our National Heritage, *Masonic Symbols in American Decorative Arts* (Lexington, Mass., 1976), p. 30; Winterthur owns a stove plate of this design (60.145).

13

WINEGLASS
ENGLAND, 1770–90

Colorless lead glass. Blown. Round funnel bowl; straight stem; disk foot; pontil mark partially polished. Wheel engraved with rosettes, bud, leaves, and other flowers. Cut scales around base of bowl; facet-cut stem.
H: 6¾ in (17.3 cm); Diam bowl: 2⅛ in (5.4 cm)
History: Walter F. Smith, Jr., Trenton, N.J.
Museum purchase, 1968: Sam Laidacker, Bloomsburg, Pa.
68.167

14

WINEGLASS
ENGLAND OR POSSIBLY
PENNSYLVANIA, 1770–90

Colorless lead glass. Blown. Narrow, round funnel bowl; drawn straight stem; conical foot; pontil mark. Wheel engraved: at rim, a chain of alternating circles and stars; below, "R. Redman" within a heart shape of branches. Stem and base of bowl cut in irregular diamond facets.
H: 4⅜ in (11.2 cm); Diam bowl: 1⅞ in (4.7 cm)
History: Hugh W. Kelly, Lancaster, Pa.
Gift of Mrs. Hugh W. Kelly, 1987
87.127

Influenced by Bohemian and Silesian cut glass of the early eighteenth century, some English glassmakers practiced decorative cutting in the 1725–50 period. However, the technique only became widespread during the latter part of the century when the delicate geometry of the neo-classical style took hold. Stems were facet-cut with small diamonds or hexagons to reflect and refract the light in eye-catching ways. Known as "cut shanks" in the period, these stems appeared in the 1760s, and replaced the fanciful twisted styles during the following decade. In 1761 Benjamin Franklin purchased "Two large Glasses with cut Shanks & Feet" from London glasscutters Maydwell and Windle for shipment to Pennsylvania.[1] New York merchant Frederick Rhinelander's accounts document the growing popularity of cut styles and the decline in demand for twist stems. In August 1773 his Bristol suppliers sent fifty dozen "com[mo]n wines Diamond & plain stems," twenty dozen "Dwarf Wine Cut Stems Globe bowls," twenty dozen of the same with "lemon" bowls, and only twenty-five "enamild Stem Cyder Glasses." Subsequent invoices do not include any enameled or twist-stem glasses, although glasses with enameled shanks occur in his sales records until 1777.[2]

Glass could be cut and engraved on the glass manufactory premises or in an independent shop. Lazarus Isaac, the first glasscutter and engraver known to have worked in America, advertised in the May 17, 1773, issue of the *Pennsylvania Packet*, that he was capable of cutting the stems of wineglasses "in diamonds," for 2s. 6d. per dozen. In the summer of 1773 Isaac left Philadelphia to work as a cut-

ter and flowerer at Henry William Stiegel's glassworks in Manheim, Pennsylvania. Two decorated glasses have recently been attributed to Stiegel's factory during the 1773–74 period of Isaac's tenure: a twist-stem goblet engraved to commemorate the marriage of Stiegel's daughter Elizabeth to William Old (see p. 10, fig. 20); and a large covered goblet with facet-cut stem that was presented to Emmanuel Carpenter, representative of Lancaster County in the Pennsylvania legislature.[3]

The similarity of the engraving of NO. 14 to those two goblets suggests that Isaac may have been responsible for the decoration. The letters have the same heavy serifs and crudely rounded sections. The branches, with their almost abstract leaves and V-shape juncture, are rendered much the same way as those of the Old goblet. It is not clear if the glass was manufactured in England or in this country, because both Stiegel and the Philadelphia Glass Works were producing English-style, lead-formula glass. The irregularity of the stem diamonds in size and shape suggests that it may have been cut outside the factory.

The recipient, R. Redman, may be the Richard Redman of Philadelphia who sold John Cadwalader a hall lantern in 1770.[4]

1. Invoice, February 16, 1761, recorded in the Isaac Norris Account Book, p. 2, Library Company of Philadelphia (photostat, Downs, WL); the glasses in question, costing 7s. 6d. apiece, were apparently ordered for the use of Ephrata Cloister.
2. Invoice from Vigor and Stevens, August 30, 1773, and sale to the widow Montagnie, April 25, 1777, Daybook, Frederick Rhinelander Papers, New-York Historical Society (hereafter NYHS), New York.
3. For discussion of these glasses, see Palmer, "To the Good," pp. 234–39.
4. Nicholas B. Wainwright, *Colonial Grandeur in Philadelphia: The House and Furniture of General John Cadwalader* (Philadelphia: Historical Society of Pennsylvania, 1964), p. 42.

15

WINEGLASS
PROBABLY GERMANY, 1760–80

Opalescent white glass. Blown. Thistle bowl; stem formed of inverted baluster and basal knop; conical foot with downward-folded edge; pontil mark. Enamel-painted decoration in blue, green, orange, red, yellow, and rose: at rim, a band of oblique lines forming triangles; on one side an oval medallion containing half-length portrait of a man within scrolled cartouche; on the other, a floral spray. Stem has orange-red pointed ovals; foot, floral sprays.
H: 6⅝ in (16.9 cm); Diam bowl: 2⅞ in (7.3 cm)
H. F. du Pont purchase
58.1420

Beginning in the third quarter of the seventeenth century, glassmakers of central Europe created opaque white glass that simulated the appearance of ceramics. Johann Kunckel's 1679 book on glassmaking included a formula for such glass and spurred the production of this ware.[1] Although *milchglas* resembles porcelain and tin-glazed earthenwares (faience), it has an opalescent translucency absent from ceramic wares.

Because of their forms, opaque white glass teawares (NOS. 74–77) seem clearly based on porcelain prototypes, but this goblet, which probably had a cover, may have been inspired by faience examples.[2] Its shape contrasts sharply with stemware being made contemporaneously in England (NOS. 6–11) and demonstrates the persistence of baroque styles in Continental glass production.

The relationship of *milchglas* to ceramics is reinforced by decorative painting in enamel colors: a profile portrait of a gentleman is the focal point, and flowers embellish the opposite side of the bowl and encircle the foot. The narrow geometric border around the rim was derived from China trade porcelains of the early eighteenth century.

1. Johann Kunckel, *Ars Vitraria Experimentalis*, discussed in Olga Drahotová, *European Glass* (New York: Excalibur Books, 1983), p. 153.
2. Friedrich H. Hofmann, *Geschichte der Bayreuther Fayencefabrik* (Augsburg: Benno Filser, 1928), p. 31, pl. 19.

16

GOBLET WITH COVER
FREDERICK COUNTY, MARYLAND,
ATTRIBUTED TO NEW BREMEN
GLASSMANUFACTORY OF JOHN
FREDERICK AMELUNG, 1791–93

Colorless nonlead glass of gray tint. Blown. Goblet: round funnel bowl with collar below; inverted baluster stem with large tear; domed foot; pontil mark. Wheel engraved: foliate and scrolled sprays of flowers and fruit; "G. J. Schley." above an armorial asymmetrical cartouche suspended from a vine; in the cartouche a fish swimming in the sea beneath sunrays breaking from a bank of clouds. Cover: conical top and straight sides, inset with trailed ring that rests on edge of goblet; applied baluster finial with large tear; interior pontil mark. Cover shoulder wheel engraved with foliate spray.
OH: 11⅞ in (30.2 cm); H goblet: 8½ in (21.7 cm); Diam bowl: 4⅝ in (11.8 cm)
History: George Jacob Schley; probably Mary Schley Schroeder and descendants; George S. McKearin Museum purchase, 1959: estate of George S. McKearin, Hoosick Falls, N.Y.
59.47a, b

Published: McKearin and McKearin, *American Glass,* pl. 36, no. 3.
McKearin and McKearin, *Two Hundred Years,* frontis.
George S. McKearin, "This Is How It Happened," *Antiques* 58, no. 4 (October 1950): 290–93.
Florence M. Montgomery, "An Amelung Sugar Bowl," *Journal of Glass Studies* 1 (1959): 92, fig. 5.
Milo M. Naeve, "The Schley Goblet," *Winterthur Portfolio One* (Winterthur, Del: Winterthur Museum, 1964), p. 121.
Gustav Weiss, *The Book of Glass,* trans. Janet Seligman (New York: Praeger Publishers, 1971), p. 235.
Lanmon and Palmer, "New Bremen," pp. 84–85.

The glassmaking enterprise of John Frederick Amelung first came to the attention of glass historians in 1928 with the discovery of a signed goblet engraved on one side with the arms of the city of Bremen, Germany, and the inscription, "Old Bremen Success and the New Progress." Engraved on the reverse is the factory signature: "New Bremen Glassmanufactory. 1788 / North America, State of Maryland."[1] The goblet was probably sent to a Bremen investor to demonstrate the quality of his product. The Schley goblet was the second Amelung glass of this form to be found. In December 1937, it was

offered to George McKearin by the great-great-great-great-grandson of the original owner, a young man who needed funds to finance his undergraduate education at Princeton.[2] The glass remained a treasured prize in McKearin's personal collection until his death in 1959. Helen McKearin then offered the glass to H. F. du Pont.

Although there is no factory signature, the goblet is unquestionably of Amelung origin because of its similarity in form to the Bremen goblet and in engraving to other documented New Bremen products. The lettering here is most like that on glasses dating to 1791–93.[3] The Schley vessel is outstanding in the Amelung oeuvre in the near-colorless quality of its material. Achieving crystallike glass was a problem for Amelung as for so many glassmakers, and many of his New Bremen wares have a strong gray or green tint. Of the eleven extant decorated goblets, of which only three retain their original covers, the Schley example is the most successful in its line and proportion. The characteristic baluster finial effectively balances the base of the goblet with its inverted baluster stem.

Produced at a time when restraint, delicacy, and symmetry were the hallmarks of fashion, Amelung's presentation goblets, with domed feet, balusters, and asymmetrical rococo-style engraving, may have seemed out-of-date to Anglo-Americans (see NO. 3). In continental Europe, however, glasses of this style were made until about 1800: close contemporary parallels to the Schley and other New Bremen goblets are recorded among the products of the Kassel glasshouses as well as the Lauenstein factory in Hanover, not far from Grünenplan.[4]

The fish engraved within the cartouche is a pun on the owner's name because "schleie" is the German word for tench, a fish of the carp family. For George Jacob Schley it must have been a sort of heraldic bearing. The son of John Thomas and Margaret Winz von Winz Schley, George Jacob was probably born prior to the family's immigration to America in 1737. After eight years in Philadelphia, the Schleys moved to western Maryland and were among the founders of Frederick. During the revolutionary war, George Jacob Schley manufactured rifles for the American cause and

served in the militia. He also kept a tavern in Frederick and owned land in Georgetown.

Winterthur's vessel may well be the "1 Large Goblet" listed in the household inventory taken at Schley's death in 1811 and valued by appraisers for $1.25 ("1 smaller [goblet]" was appraised for 25¢). In accordance with his will, Schley's possessions were sold for the payment of debts and funeral charges. At the sale or vendue, his son Jacob purchased "a Goblet for his sister Shroeder, $1.25." The sister in question was Mary, familiarly known as Polly (b. 1775), who at the age of twenty married Henry Schroeder, a Baltimore merchant; so it must have been one of her descendants who sold the glass in the 1930s. Also sold at the 1811 vendue, but not listed in Schley's inventory, was "a Large tumbler, figured," for which son John Schley paid 31¢.[5] If this was also a New Bremen product, perhaps on the order of the Ghequiere or Guest tumblers in NOS. 44, 45, it remains to be discovered.

1. Collection of Metropolitan Museum of Art; see R[uth] R[alston], "Accessions and Notes: A Recent Purchase of American Glass," *Bulletin of the Metropolitan Museum of Art* 23, no. 6 (June 1928): 166–68; Lanmon and Palmer, "New Bremen," pp. 48–49.
2. McKearin and McKearin, *American Glass,* p. 107; George S. McKearin, "This Is How It Happened," *Antiques* 58, no. 4 (October 1950): 291–92.
3. Lanmon and Palmer, "New Bremen," pp. 45–46.
4. Franz Adrian Dreier, *Glaskunst in Hessen-Kassel* (Kassel: GmbH, 1969), fig. 79.
5. Genealogical data on the Schley family and transcripts of Schley probate and other records are in Downs, WL. Schroeder employed George Trisler, for whom Amelung made a similar pair of goblets in 1793; Lanmon and Palmer, "New Bremen," pp. 74–75.

17

WINEGLASS
PROBABLY BOHEMIA, 1790–1820

Colorless nonlead glass. Blown. Round funnel bowl, flat
ground and polished edge; drawn tapered stem; conical
foot; pontil mark. Wheel engraved: at rim, a row of
stylized sprigs above tall ovals and a horizontal line, the
line interspersed with tasseled stars and connected with
swags of ovals. Facet-cut stem and base of bowl.
H: 4¹¹⁄₁₆ in (11.9 cm); Diam bowl: 2³⁄₁₆ in (5.6 cm)
Museum purchase, 1957: McKearins' Antiques, Hoosick
Falls, N.Y.
57.18.38

18

LIQUEUR GLASS OR RUMMER
PROBABLY BOHEMIA, 1790–1820

Colorless nonlead glass. Blown; pressed. Narrow ovoid
bowl, flat ground and polished edge; double collar; solid,
pressed base comprised of 4-sided flaring stem and square
stepped foot with beveled edges; polished bottom. Wheel
engraved: at rim, a row of stylized sprigs above tall ovals
and a horizontal line, the line interspersed with tasseled
stars connected with swags of ovals. Seven cut ovals
around base of bowl; faceted collar.
H: 4 in (10.2 cm); Diam bowl: 1¾ in (4.4 cm)
Museum purchase, 1957: McKearins' Antiques, Hoosick
Falls, N.Y.
57.38.35

Published: McKearin and McKearin, *American Glass,*
pl. 41, no. 5.

19

FIRING GLASS
PROBABLY BOHEMIA, 1790–1820

Colorless nonlead glass. Blown. Truncated conical bowl,
flat ground and polished edge; drawn stem with large
tear; collar; thick, slightly domed foot; pontil mark.
Wheel engraved: at rim, a row of stylized sprigs above tall
ovals and a horizontal line.
H: 4¾ in (12.1 cm); Diam bowl: 2⅝ in (6.6 cm)
Museum purchase, 1957: McKearins' Antiques, Hoosick
Falls, N.Y.
57.18.46

Thousands upon thousands of drinking glasses,
decanters (NOS. 87, 88), and other tablewares
with delicate engraving and facet-cutting were
imported from continental Europe to the
United States in the postrevolutionary period.
Generally described in records only as "German" glass, such wares were made in the glasshouses of Bohemia as well as the German
states. Baltimore merchant Frederick Hammer
purchased a large portion of a cargo that John
Jacob Astor imported from the Swedish port of
Göteburg in 1814. According to Astor's advertisement, the "Bohemian Ware" included decanters, tumblers, and wineglasses, some of
them "cut and figured." "Westphalian" glass was
also in the shipment, indicating that factories
in that part of Prussia enjoyed an export trade.
More than 140,000 pieces of glass were in
Hammer's inventory in 1818. His "cut glass with
stars, guirlands [garlands], wreaths," probably
resembled NOS. 17 and 18.[1]

Glassmakers in Bohemia and the German
states used a lightweight, nonlead glass, and
their products were cheaper than English and
Irish wares of similar style. Although the transportation costs may have been higher than for
wares made in the British Isles, the overall price
still remained lower. In a Philadelphia glass and
china merchant's shop in 1813, for example, cut
and engraved "English" wines were valued at
$3.50 a dozen; cut and engraved "German"
wines were $2.00 a dozen.[2] The combination of
style and saving was most attractive to United
States merchants newly freed from their ties to
Britain and seeking other sources of manufactured goods. The quantities of this Continental
export glass that have survived indicate the
success of the makers' marketing strategy.

For many years, the role of imported glass
in America was imperfectly understood; it was
assumed that glasses like NOS. 17, 18, and 19
were manufactured in this country. The New
Bremen works of John F. Amelung was given
credit for glasses engraved in this style, even
though the documented and firmly attributed
Amelung products (for example, NOS. 16, 44,
45) are distinctly different. More recently,
scholars have found glasses identical to these in
the illustrated trade catalogues of a Bohemian
glass factor, Johannes Schiefner (see drawings).
Schiefner operated an "Export and Commission
Agency for export to Russia, America, Spain,
etc." It is not known which manufacturer's
goods are represented in his two-volume catalogue; nonetheless, the images provide strong
evidence of the Bohemian origin of these wares.[3]
The American owner of the catalogue and
price list was John Gardiner of Gardiner's Island, New York. In the catalogue a glass like
NO. 17 is described as a roemer with round
base, scaly stem, and engraved garlands." The
manufacturer's name for NO. 19 was a conical
tumbler, but to the American trade it was a
Mason's glass (see NO. 12). A 1763 Norwegian
pattern book showing undecorated glasses of
this form labeled them "Freemasons glasses."[4]

1. Kenneth Wiggins Porter, *John Jacob Astor: Business
Man,* 2 vols. (Cambridge: Harvard University Press, 1931),
1:306–7. Hammer Account Books, 1796–1817, Maryland
Historical Society, Baltimore (hereafter MdHS).
2. Leonard Keehmle inventory, 1813-131, Philadelphia
County Probate Records (microfilm, Downs, WL).
3. The Gardiner's Island Glass Catalogues, translated by
Maria R. Petri, are in Downs, WL. The glasses in this entry
match nos. 117, 101, and 77. See Dwight P. Lanmon, "The
Baltimore Glass Trade, 1780 to 1820," *Winterthur Portfolio 5,*
ed. Richard K. Doud (Charlottesville: University Press of
Virginia, 1969), pp. 15–48. For information about
Schiefner, see Francis N. Allen, "The Gardiner's Island
Glass Catalogs: A Question of Attribution," *Glass Club
Bulletin,* no. 123 (July 1978): 3–7.
4. Polak, "Illustrated Price-List," p. 104, fig. 49.

20

RUMMER (ONE OF TWO)
ENGLAND, 1800–1820

Colorless lead glass. Blown; pressed. Cup bowl with collar below; solid pressed base comprised of a 4-sided flaring stem and stepped foot; polished pontil mark. Wheel engraved: at rim with a horizontal band of alternating stars and polished ovals, enclosed within parallel lines and zigzag lines leading to oval medallion containing initials, "JAB"; stars on the body below. Fourteen flutes cut at base of bowl.
H: 5¹⁵⁄₁₆ in (13.5 cm); Diam bowl: 3½ in (8.9 cm)
History: possibly Jacques Antoine Bidermann
Bequest of H. F. du Pont, 1969
69.1371.2 (mate is 69.1371.1)

Drinking glasses with capacious, ovoid bowls, short stems, and sturdy square or round feet

were known from the late eighteenth century as rummers. These differed from the sixteenth- and seventeenth-century German and Dutch roemers, which had large, often hemispherical, bowls and cylindrical stems, typically ornamented with applied "raspberry" prunts. The new style of rummer dates from about 1770, the year it was included among the offerings of a Dublin glasshouse. When New Yorker Frederick Rhinelander first imported rummers from Bristol in 1778 he emphasized their half-pint capacity. He ordered four dozen plain rummers and two dozen each that were described as "cut shank," and "cut & beaded," and one dozen "Cut & Sprig'd very neat." The following year, while the revolutionary war still raged, Rhinelander ordered several dozen rummers to be "Cut very neat . . . to suit the best Decanters." Rummers continued in popularity for at least another three decades. Spencer Philpot of Albany imported some from Ireland in 1800. In Charleston, Thomas Scott sold "Plain and Elegant Cut" rummers from England in 1807. An English price list proves the form was still being produced in 1819.[1]

Rummer is confusing because people tend to link it with the liquor rum, of which considerable quantities were consumed in the 1780–1820 period. Yet there is no reason to believe the form was intended for that spirit exclusively. An English traveler stopping at a wayside inn requested the best bottle of port which he tossed off "in an ecstasy of two rummers—and died on the spot from sheer joy." One English print shows that hot drinks such as grogs and toddies were consumed from rummers, while another, "The Whim," proves rummers held cold drinks. The accompanying verse of "The Whim" reads, "If ever I marry a wife, I'll marry a landlord's daughter; Then I can sit in the bar, And drink cold brandy & water."[2] This further implies the rummer glass was suitable for liquors diluted with water; if so, the "wine and water" glasses of early advertisements and household inventories may be rummers.

Winterthur's rummer is one of several engraved with the initials "JAB" and reported to have belonged originally to Jacques Antoine Bidermann, builder of Winterthur. No documentation to support this association has been found.

1. Richard Williams & Co. advertisement, quoted in Westropp, *Irish Glass*, p. 57; orders to Vigor and Stevens, March 21, 1778, and September 21, 1779, Letter and Order Book, 1774–84, Rhinelander Papers, NYHS; Philpot advertisement, *Albany Centinel*, December 23, 1800, reference courtesy of Leigh Keno; Thomas Scott advertisement, *Charleston Courier*, January 16, 1807, reference courtesy of MESDA; "Prices of Glass Goods, arranged at a general meeting of the Flint Glass Manufacturers . . . Birmingham, . . . 1819," reference courtesy of Wendy Evans.
2. The traveler is quoted in G. Bernard Hughes, "English Rummers and Firing Glasses," *Antiques* 19, no. 2 (February 1931): 114, and a detail of a James Gillray print is illustrated on the same page; "The Whim" was published by Laurie and Whittle, London, 1808.

21–24

RUMMERS
BOHEMIA OR GERMANY,
ENGRAVING POSSIBLY ADDED
IN UNITED STATES, CIRCA 1795

NO. 21. Colorless nonlead glass of yellow tint. Blown; pressed. Cup bowl with flat ground and polished edge; faceted collar; solid pressed base comprised of 4-sided spreading stem on square stepped foot with beveled edges. Wheel engraved: at rim, a row of polished ovals on a matte-engraved, rope-bordered band; body bears Great Seal of the United States with 15 stars. Five long and 3 short ovals cut around base of bowl; faceted collar; underside of foot cut in 6-point star.
H: 5⅜ in (14.4 cm); Diam bowl: 3⁵⁄₁₆ in (8.5 cm)
History: tradition of ownership in family of Commodore John Barry, Philadelphia
H. F. du Pont purchase, 1927: Martha de Haas Reeves Antiques, Philadelphia
59.3063

Exhibited: Art Institute of Chicago, "Dinner with the Presidents," 1961.
Published: McKearin and McKearin, *American Glass*, pl. 48, no. 4.
McKearin and McKearin, *Two Hundred Years*, pl. 67, no. 2.
Art Institute of Chicago, *Dinner with the Presidents* (Chicago, 1961), inside front cover.

NO. 22. Colorless nonlead glass of gray tint. Blown; pressed. Cup bowl with flat ground and polished edge; collar; solid pressed base comprised of an 8-sided spreading stem on square foot. Wheel engraved: at rim, a row of polished ovals alternating with pairs of vertical lines on a matte-engraved band scalloped on lower edge; from band a swagged chain of ovals with pendant grapes and flowers extends around glass except above Great Seal of the United States with 15 stars. Engraved sprigs between the 9 cut flutes around the base of the bowl (one is shorter below Seal); faceted collar; panel-cut stem; underside of foot cut in a 6-point star.
H: 5⅜ in (13.7 cm); Diam bowl: 3¹¹⁄₁₆ in (9.4 cm)
History: tradition of ownership in the Lee family, Virginia
Gift of Dr. and Mrs. James L. Price, 1979
79.133

NO. 23. Colorless nonlead glass of blue-gray tint. Blown; pressed. Cup bowl with flat ground and polished edge; collar; solid pressed base comprised of 8-sided spreading stem on square foot with beveled edges; polished bottom. Wheel engraved: at rim, a row of polished beads on matte-engraved band scalloped on lower edge; from band hang a series of tassels, and a foliate garland with grape clusters extends around body except above Great Seal of the United States with 15 stars. Two horizontal lines encircle base of bowl, through 9 cut ovals containing triangles interspersed with an engraved sprig and topped by short rays; faceted collar; panel-cut stem.
H: 5⅜ in (13.7 cm); Diam bowl: 3⅝ in (9.2 cm)
H. F. du Pont purchase, 1947: Neil C. Gest, Mechanicsburg, Ohio (with NO. 24 and 59.3060)
59.3065

Published: McKearin and McKearin, *Two Hundred Years*, pl. 67, no. 3.

NO. 24 (one of two). Colorless nonlead glass of gray tint. Blown; pressed. Cup bowl with flat ground and polished rim; faceted collar; solid pressed base comprised of 8-sided spreading stem on square foot with beveled edges. Wheel engraved: at rim, a row of polished beads alternating with pairs of vertical lines on matte-engraved band scalloped on lower edge; from band a swagged chain of polished ovals with pendant grapes and flowers extends around body except above Great Seal of the United States with 15 stars. Nine cut flutes around base of bowl (one is shorter below Seal); faceted collar; panel-cut stem; underside of foot cut in a 6-point star.
H: 5⅜ in (13.7 cm); Diam bowl: 3⁹⁄₁₆ in (9.1 cm)
H. F. du Pont purchase, 1947: Neil C. Gest, Mechanicsburg, Ohio (with its mate 59.3060 and NO. 23)
59.3059

These rummers have received considerable attention over the years because of their decoration. Some historians have tried to associate them with presidential usage, but there is no evidence to support this.[1] The Great Seal would have appealed to any number of well-to-do, patriotic-minded citizens, including the Lees of Virginia, who reportedly owned NO. 22 and Commodore John Barry of Philadelphia, who may have owned NO. 21. It may have been one of the "4 Glass Goblets" of Barry's 1803 household inventory.[2] NOS. 23 and 24 belonged to an unidentified Boston family who moved to Columbus, Ohio, in 1831.[3]

In form, these glasses relate to the English rummers (NO. 20), and some Irish glass is decorated with the American eagle.[4] A central European origin is postulated for these rummers because of their nonlead composition.

The eagles of NOS. 22, 23, and 24 are similar in design, detail, and workmanship. The bird is thick-necked and somewhat chickenlike in the thrust of its head. Its open mouth seems to drop the motto rather than grasp it. The shield does not rest on the bird's breast as in the Great Seal but awkwardly conceals the lower body. Feathers are effected by short strokes within the outlines of the body and by a band of V-strokes edging the outer neck and knees. The tail feathers are rendered exactly as the laurel branch. It is tempting but risky to attribute the eagle engravings of NOS. 22, 23, and 24 to the same hand, but at the very least they emanated

from a similar vision of the Great Seal of the United States.

NO. 21 sports a bird of a different feather—literally. The body is composed of rows of feathered strokes. The shield is more nobly positioned, and the tail feathers are quite distinct from the laurel branch. The wings have a vertical thrust instead of a horizontal flutter. In short, a different hand was definitely at work. Like NOS. 22 and 24, two flutes were cut smaller to accommodate the eagle. The decoration may well have been executed in Bohemian or German glasshouses or decorating shops, either on special order or on the judgment of a factory manager who thought the design would be a commercial success. Bohemian glassmakers did have a long history of catering to the fashions of their markets; the Gardiner's Island trade catalogues include a listing, but no illustration of glasses with "Liberty Bird."[5] Another possibility is that the goblets were ornamented abroad with borders and flutes and a space left blank for a special decoration to be added later in this country.[6]

It is also possible that all of the decoration is the product of independent glass engravers in America. Several men and women are known to have practiced that art in America in the federal period, but no documented examples of their work are known. Of diverse national backgrounds, these glass engravers advertised their talents in newspapers and served both retailers and private customers. They offered to decorate the ware with initials, ciphers, coats of arms, borders, or any other design of the customer's fancy. For example, John Moss, a glass engraver who left the employ of Abbott and Turner in London to seek his fortune in America, promised Philadelphians in 1796 he had the skill to engrave on glass in a "superb elegant and masterly manner." Pertinent to Winterthur's rummers is his suggestion to merchants that they engage him to "have an engraving of something emblematical of their patriotic principles," because "elegance adds to the rapidity of the sale of goods."[7]

The only American eagle documented to a glass engraver working in the United States before 1800 is on an Amelung presentation tumbler. The craftsman responsible could have carried on his trade independently after New Bremen closed, but his eagle is too different from those on the Winterthur rummers to warrant an attribution.[8]

The Great Seal was designed by William Barton and Charles Thomson and adopted by Congress in 1782; the thirteen stars symbolized each of the colonies. Many seal-based designs on decorative art objects were made with a varying number of stars. It has been customary among curators and collectors to date such objects on the basis of the stars, assuming that the number corresponded to the number of states in the Union when the item was made.

While there may be some validity to this approach, the limitations of space and the ability and interest of the individual craftsman undoubtedly affected such details. On the basis of their fifteen stars, these rummers would date between 1792 and 1796; given their other stylistic characteristics they could well have been made in that period.

1. McKearin and McKearin, *American Glass*, p. 140. The McKearins thought NO. 21 might be part of the glass service made for President Monroe by Bakewell, Page, and Bakewell in 1818. According to the invoice and newspaper descriptions of the service, the forms were engraved with the coat of arms of the United States. Bakewell, however, produced lead glass. I am grateful to Milo Naeve for information about the exhibition of NO. 21 in 1961.

2. Inventory of Commo. John Barry, 1803, Downs, WL.

3. Neil C. Gest described the goblets inherited by the unnamed lady in Columbus as "five goblets with U.S. coat of arms, 15 stars, etc., almost identical to your goblet [NO. 21] with Eagle" (Gest to du Pont, April 2, 1947, WM). Another goblet virtually identical to NO. 23, provenance unknown, is shown in the advertisement of W. M. Schwind, Jr., Antiques, in *Antiques* 134, no. 3 (September 1988): 449. An apparent mate to NO. 24 is in Corning Museum of Glass (55.4.45).

4. Warren, *Irish Glass*, p. 134, fig. 105.

5. Arnost Klima, "Glassmaking Industry and Trade in Bohemia in the Seventeenth and Eighteenth Centuries," *Journal of European Economic History* 13 (Winter 1984): 499–520, reference courtesy of Olive Jones. Price List no. 163, Gardiner's Island Trade Catalogues, Downs, WL.

Given the position of this listing, it may refer to opaque white mugs with enamel-painted eagles, of which numerous examples are known.

6. Ada Polak, *Glass: Its Makers and Its Public* (London: Weidenfeld and Nicolson, 1975), pp. 107–8. American glass factories also decorated glass with stock patterns, leaving spaces blank for initials to order (see NO. 60).

7. Bevis Hillier, *Master Potters of the Industrial Revolution: The Turners of Lane End* (London: Cory, Adams and Mackay, 1965), p. 57. *Pennsylvania Packet*, December 1, 1796. Moss is listed in the Philadelphia directories as a glass engraver between 1799 and 1801.

8. Dated 1792, the Amelung tumbler features the Great Seal in reverse; Lanmon and Palmer, "New Bremen," cover illus. and pp. 66–67.

25

WINEGLASS
POSSIBLY MARYLAND, POSSIBLY BALTIMORE GLASS MANUFACTORY, 1814–15

Colorless nonlead glass. Blown. Round funnel bowl; straight stem; conical foot; pontil mark. Wheel engraved: rim inscribed, "Fair won, dearly belov'd" above a 12-star American flag flying from a serpent-entwined flagpole, planted in a bowknot connecting 2 laurel sprays.
H: 6³⁄₁₆ in (15.9 cm); Diam bowl: 2⅛ in (5.4 cm)
Gift of Mr. and Mrs. Norton Asner, 1971
71.137

Published: Lanmon and Palmer, "New Bremen," p. 42, fig. 16.

The patriotic decoration on this simple wineglass may have been designed to celebrate the successful defense of Fort McHenry against the British navy, which had previously laid waste to much of Washington and decided to inflict the same fate upon Baltimore. In September 1814 a dramatic engagement occurred at Fort McHenry, which guarded the entrance to Baltimore's harbor. It was during this "perilous fight" that Francis Scott Key observed the "broad stripes and bright stars" of the American flag flying over the fort and was moved to pen "The Star-Spangled Banner."

Because of its nonlead composition and eighteenth-century form, NO. 25 has at various times been attributed to John Frederick Amelung's New Bremen Glassmanufactory in Frederick County, Maryland. There are significant compositional differences between this glass and the documented Amelung products, however, and the engraving is dissimilar (see NOS. 44, 45). Moreover, the subject matter of the engraving postdates Amelung's 1785–95 venture. Although some workers continued to make glass on a small scale at New Bremen after Amelung closed the factory in 1795, there is no evidence that glassmaking continued on that site after 1808.[1]

The more likely source for the wineglass is the glasshouse that Amelung's son, Frederick Magnus Amelung, established in Baltimore in 1800. After his father-in-law, Alexander Furnival, withdrew his financial support, Amelung sold his leasehold in 1802 to Philip R. I. Friese but stayed on as manager until 1806.

Friese continued as proprietor during the War of 1812 and was joined by his brother, John F. Friese. The glasshouse operated into the 1880s. Although bottles and windowpanes were its chief products, from the beginning the Baltimore factory advertised its manufacture of "a general assortment of hollow white glass."[2] There is no record, however, of decorative cutting or engraving at the factory in the first part of the nineteenth century. Baltimore Glass Manufactory, as it was first called, was located at the foot of Federal Hill, on the south side of the harbor basin. Glass craftsmen were among those who defended the city against the British attack, so this glass may have been made to celebrate the victory.

It is possible that the glass was made at an earlier date and only engraved in 1814–15 by an independent glass engraver. As one glass engraver suggested, "Housekeepers may have their Plain Glass Engraved, to what pattern they choose."[3] Little is known about independent engravers in Baltimore in the early nineteenth century, but two are recorded in Baltimore before the War of 1812. In 1800 Robert Burford claimed his was "the first essay of the ingenious art in this city" and advertised "Devices, Cyphers, or coats of arms elegantly cut or engrav'd on Glass or Stone, in a superior style." By 1808 Joseph Myring had established a similar business, but he only stayed in Baltimore until 1810.[4]

1. NO. 25 has a potassium and calcium ratio equivalent to Amelung examples, but it lacks the traces of lead, arsenic, and antimony usually found in Amelung glass. It also contains more rubidium, strontium, and zirconium. Analytical Laboratory, Winterthur Conservation. Lanmon and Palmer, "New Bremen," pp. 45–46, 39–43.
2. Arlene Palmer, "The Baltimore Glassworks: A Report for the Maryland Archaeological Society" (April 1971), copy on deposit at Rakow Library, Corning Museum; McKearin and Wilson, *American Bottles*, pp. 71–74; Baltimore Glass Manufactory advertisement, *Federal Gazette and Baltimore Daily Advertiser*, August 15, 1800.
3. Joseph Myring advertisement, *Aurora and General Advertiser*, June 6, 1810.
4. Burford advertisement, *American and Daily Advertiser*, December 25, 1800. Myring advertised for an apprentice in *American and Commercial Daily Advertiser*, October 25, 1808, reference courtesy of MESDA. Myring was listed in the 1810 Baltimore city directory, but by June he had moved to Philadelphia.

26

FLUTE GLASS (ONE OF EIGHTEEN)

UNITED STATES, ENGLAND, OR IRELAND, 1815–35

Colorless lead glass. Blown. Conical bowl with collar below; spool stem with central bladed knop; disk foot; polished bottom. Bowl cut with strawberry-diamonds and fans above a horizontal band; panel-cut below.
H: 7 in (17.9 cm); Diam bowl: 2⅛ in (5.4 cm)
Museum purchase, 1968: estate of Helen DeLancey Watkins, Schenectady, N.Y.
68.128.1 (mates are 68.128.2–.18)

With its deep, tapered bowl, the flute glass was favored for effervescent beverages, especially champagne. Introduced into England during the reign of Charles II, champagne was "a fine liquor which all great beaux drink to make them witty," but it was not widely consumed in America until the early years of the nineteenth century.[1] A visitor to Washington in 1819 believed, "You will be much judged of by your Champagne & the Americans prefer the sweet & sparkling. I think a dinner or supper is prized and talked of exactly in proportion to the quantity of Champagne given and the noise it makes *in uncorking*!"[2]

The demand for champagne glasses was met by numerous American glasshouses in this period. Champagne glasses are included in the price lists of South Boston Flint Glass Works and Francis Plunkett and Company's Wheeling factory and in the advertisements of New England Glass Company. "Button stem champaigns," which could describe NO. 26, were manufactured by Boston and Sandwich Glass Company.[3]

The strawberry-diamond and fan pattern was probably the favorite Anglo-Irish design copied by American glasscutters. Collectors most often associate it with the Pittsburgh glassworks of Benjamin Bakewell (NO. 63), but the pattern is documented to several other factories and independent glasscutters.[4] Bakewell did sell flutes that are virtually identical to Winterthur's to Nicholas Biddle of Andalusia.[5] Without the original bill of sale for Winterthur's set of flutes and matching tum-blers, however, it is impossible to say whether the glass was produced in England, Ireland, or the United States, let alone at which factory.

1. Quoted in G. Bernard Hughes, "English Champagne and Strong Ale Glasses," *Antiques* 20, no. 2 (August 1931): 92.
2. "Charles Bagot's Notes on Housekeeping and Entertaining at Washington, 1819," *Transactions, 1924–1926*, Publications of the Colonial Society of Massachusetts, 26 (Boston, 1927), p. 442.
3. Prices Current, South Boston, 1819, Archives and Library, Edison Institute, Dearborn, Mich. (hereafter Edison Inst.); Wheeling Price Current. "Diamond Fluted and Fingered" champagnes from the New England Glass Co. were sold in Virginia by William Loyall, *American Beacon and Norfolk and Portsmouth Daily Advertiser*, May 8, 1820, reference courtesy of MESDA. Leinicke, "Production," p. 58.
4. For example, a compote from Jersey City Glass Company (Corning Museum 71.4.108), see "Recent Important Accessions," *Journal of Glass Studies* 14 (1972): 160–61, no. 54.
5. McKearin and McKearin, *American Glass*, pl. 50, nos. 2–3; p. 154.

27

WINEGLASS (ONE OF SEVEN)
UNITED STATES, ENGLAND, OR
IRELAND, 1815–35

Colorless lead glass. Blown. Truncated conical bowl; spool stem with central wafer knop; disk foot; pontil mark. Bowl: blown in 3-part mold of geometric design (McKearin G II-19): horizontal rings around rim above diagonal ribbing; band of diamond diapering between horizontal rings; vertical ribbing below. This wine and 3 others (59.3202, 59.3272, 59.3273) appear to have been made in the same mold, different from that used for the other 3 glasses in this pattern and bowl shape.
H: 4 in (10.2 cm); Diam bowl: 2³⁄₁₆ in (5.6 cm)
H. F. du Pont purchase, before 1941
59.3204 (mates are 59.3200–.3203; 59.3272–.3273)

28

WINEGLASS (ONE OF EIGHT)
UNITED STATES, ENGLAND, OR
IRELAND, 1815–35

Colorless lead glass. Blown. Incurved bucket bowl; spool stem with central bladed knop; disk foot; pontil mark. Bowl: blown in 3-part mold in same pattern as NO. 27. Seven of the 8 appear to have been made in the same mold; 59.3940 is of this bowl shape but was probably blown in the same mold as NO. 27.
H: 3⅞ in (9.8 cm); Diam bowl: 2 in (5.1 cm)
H. F. du Pont purchase, before 1940
59.3241 (mates are 59.3239–.3240; 59.3242–.3246)

Recognizing that customers of lesser means also wished to be fashionable, glass manufacturers developed a mold-blown technique that provided the look of "rich-cut" glass at an affordable price. Using a manufacturing technique known in ancient times, moldmakers copied the geometric patterns of cut glass in molds hinged in three or four parts.[1] Glassblowers would insert a gather into the mold, and by blowing, force the glass against the sides of the mold. When the glass was released from the mold, the blower could use hand tools to modify the shape as needed.

Such mold-blown glass was more popular in the United States than in England and Ireland, and may have been introduced by Thomas Cains, a Bristol-trained glassmaker who immigrated to Boston in 1813.[2] The glasshouses in the Boston area—South Boston Flint Glass Works, Boston and Sandwich Glass Company, New England Glass Company—were producing tremendous quantities of mold-blown tableware by the 1820s and shipping it to markets outside New England. In 1828 a Baltimore firm purchased "Tumblers and Wines diamond moulded sorts, new patterns" from the South Boston factory.[3] In 1825 a Philadelphia merchant advertised "Button Stem Tumbler Shape Wines," a phrase that seems to fit NO. 27.[4]

1. For an ancient prototype see R. J. Charleston, *Masterpieces of Glass: A World History from the Corning Museum of Glass* (New York: Harry N. Abrams, 1980), pp. 42–43.
2. For a discussion of molded Irish glass, see Warren, *Irish Glass*, pp. 199–212, 203, fig. 231b.
3. Wilson, *New England Glass*, chap. 7. Kenneth W. Lyon, "Blown Pattern Glass (Alias Blown Three Mold)," *Glass Club Bulletin*, no. 136 (Winter 1981/82): 12; Lovering & Penniman advertisement, *Baltimore American*, July 11, 1828.
4. Paul S. Brown advertisement, *Poulson's American Daily Advertiser*, May 6, 1825. "Tumbler bowl" goblets and wines also occur in an 1823 English sale catalogue, R. J. Charleston, "A Glassmaker's Bankruptcy Sale," *Glass Circle* 2 (1975): 7.

29, 30

TOY WINEGLASS
PROBABLY SANDWICH,
MASSACHUSETTS, PROBABLY
BOSTON AND SANDWICH GLASS
COMPANY, 1825–40

NO. 29 (one of two). Colorless lead glass. Blown. Conical bowl; drawn stem and foot; pontil mark. Blown in 3-part mold of geometric design (McKearin G III-12): faint vertical ribbing around rim; between horizontal rings are 3 repeat panels of sunburst and diamond diapering; vertical ribbing around stem; ringed bottom (type II).
H: 2¹⁵⁄₁₆ in (7.4 cm); Diam top: 1¹¹⁄₁₆ in (4.2 cm)
History: William T. H. Howe, Cincinnati
H. F. du Pont purchase, 1940: Parke-Bernet Galleries, New York City, through Neil C. Gest
59.3228 (mate is 59.3229)

Published: Parke-Bernet Galleries, "Early American Glass . . . Collection Formed by the Late William T. H. Howe," pt. 1, sale no. 227 (November 7–8, 1940), lot 68.

NO. 30 (one of two). Colorless lead glass. Blown. Conical bowl; drawn stem and foot; pontil mark. Blown in 3-part mold of geometric design (McKearin G II-16): horizontal rings above diamond diapering and vertical ribbing; ringed bottom (type II).
H: 2⁹⁄₁₆ in (6.5 cm); Diam top: 1⅝ in (4.1 cm)
H. F. du Pont purchase, probably 1941: Neil C. Gest, Mechanicsburg, Ohio
59.3231 (mate is 59.3230)

31

TOY WINEGLASS
UNITED STATES, 1815–35

Colorless lead glass. Blown. Truncated conical bowl, thick base; short stem comprised of flattened ball knop and small basal knop; disk foot; pontil mark.
H: 2¼ in (5.7 cm); Diam bowl: 1¼ in (3.2 cm)
History: found in New York
Gift of Mr. and Mrs. Edgar H. Sittig, 1959
59.94.1

These very small glasses were most likely made as children's toys. Toy wines, decanters, and tumblers are enumerated in the price lists and invoices of several American glasshouses in the 1815–40 period. "Toy molded wines," probably like NOS. 29 and 30, were sold by the Boston and Sandwich factory for about 50¢ a dozen in 1826–27.[1]

Full-size molds were used to pattern NOS. 29 and 30, and their stems and feet were drawn out by the glassblower, distorting the patterns. Considering their purpose and the price at which they sold, it is not surprising that little effort went into their production. NO. 31, on the other hand, is free blown and is remarkably well made for its size.

1. J. S. Cunningham Account Book, Boston, 1826–27, pp. 31, 37, Edison Inst.

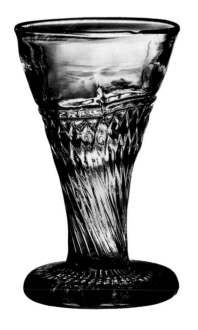

32

WINEGLASS

PROBABLY NEW JERSEY, 1810–35

Aqua nonlead glass. Blown. Ogee bowl; drawn stem with
ball knop and basal knop; disk foot; pontil mark.
H: 5⅜ in (13.7 cm); Diam bowl: 3³⁄₁₆ in (8.1 cm)
Museum purchase, 1957: McKearins' Antiques, Hoosick
Falls, N.Y.
57.90.5

The raw materials of glassmaking carried iron
impurities that colored the glass batch, frequently
in strong shades of green or aqua. In the flint
glass factories that specialized in fine tableware,
this effect was counteracted by adding manganese to the batch, but for glasshouses producing utilitarian bottle and window glass, refined
colorless glass was not required, so green or
aqua was the norm. Occasionally, these factories used unrefined glass to fabricate drinking
vessels and other table forms. A bottle or window glass establishment undoubtedly made
NO. 32. In the early 1800s there were many such
factories located in the southern counties of
New Jersey.

In the shape of its bowl the glass harks
back to the ogee of the eighteenth century
(NO. 8), but its stem style places it after 1800.

33

DRINKING GLASS (ONE OF TWO)
PENNSYLVANIA, 1865–85

Colorless lead glass. Blown. Cup bowl; 2 compressed
knops above cylindrical stem; disk foot; pontil mark.
Wheel engraved with the coat of arms of Pennsylvania.
H: 4¹³⁄₁₆ in (12.2 cm); Diam bowl: 3⁹⁄₁₆ in (9.1 cm)
H. F. du Pont purchase, 1929: Arthur J. Sussel,
Philadelphia
59.3061

Published: McKearin and McKearin, *American Glass*,
pl. 48, no. 6.
McKearin and McKearin, *Two Hundred Years*, pp. 254–55,
pl. 67.

This glass and its mate have been dated to the
early 1800s, but their bowl shape and stem
configuration point to the latter part of the
century. By 1843 Pennsylvania had twenty-eight
glass factories and fifteen glass-cutting establishments, more than any other state, so a
Pennsylvania attribution is plausible.[1] Given
the decoration, a Pennsylvania origin has been
assumed, but newspaper advertisements prove
that New York, New England, and Midwest
glassware was sold within Pennsylvania. It has
been suggested that Pittsburgh's Bakewell,
Page, and Bakewell manufactured the glasses,
but they do not sufficiently resemble any documented Pittsburgh glass to warrant that attribution (NOS. 60, 63–65).

The engraving is much stiffer than the
fluid rendition of the same coat of arms
achieved by Amelung's engraver (NO. 45).

1. *The American Laborer* (New York: Greeley and
McElrath, 1843), p. 79.

34

ALE GLASS (ONE OF ELEVEN)
FRANCE OR POSSIBLY BOHEMIA, 1855–85; ENGRAVING POSSIBLY LATER

Colorless nonlead glass. Blown. Narrow incurved bucket bowl with recessed rim; spool stem; thick octagonal foot. Bowl cut below rim and from base with 8 panels whose points meet near middle; underside of foot cut with 16-point star. Wheel engraved: on one panel, emblem of the Society of the Cincinnati.
H: 4¾ in (12.1 cm); Diam bowl: 2⅛ in (5.4 cm)
History: found in Bermuda
H. F. du Pont purchase: J. A. Lloyd Hyde, New York City
61.630.3 (mates are 61.630.4–.13)

35

WATER GOBLET (ONE OF FOURTEEN)
FRANCE, 1855–85; ENGRAVING POSSIBLY LATER

Colorless lead glass. Blown. Truncated conical bowl; recessed rim; hexagonal stem comprised of large knop with waisted sections above and below; flat hexagonal foot. Bowl cut in 8 panels below rim; underside of foot cut with 32-point star. Wheel engraved: on one panel, emblem of the Society of the Cincinnati.
H: 6¾ in (17.3 cm); Diam bowl: 3⅛ in (7.8 cm)
History: found in Bermuda
H. F. du Pont purchase: J. A. Lloyd Hyde, New York City
61.1592.1 (mates are 61.1592.2–.14)

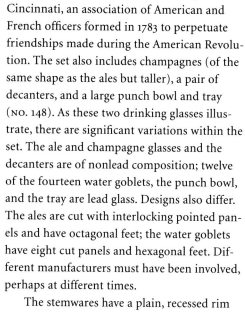

These glasses are part of a large service engraved with the emblem of the Society of the Cincinnati, an association of American and French officers formed in 1783 to perpetuate friendships made during the American Revolution. The set also includes champagnes (of the same shape as the ales but taller), a pair of decanters, and a large punch bowl and tray (NO. 148). As these two drinking glasses illustrate, there are significant variations within the set. The ale and champagne glasses and the decanters are of nonlead composition; twelve of the fourteen water goblets, the punch bowl, and the tray are lead glass. Designs also differ. The ales are cut with interlocking pointed panels and have octagonal feet; the water goblets have eight cut panels and hexagonal feet. Different manufacturers must have been involved, perhaps at different times.

The stemwares have a plain, recessed rim that seems to emerge from an outer layer or casing of cut glass, a feature typically seen on Continental glass and rarely found in American products. The shapes relate closely to glass made by the Saint-Louis factory in Lorraine in the 1860s, but the nonlead objects in the service could have been made in Bohemia.[1] As with all engraved glassware but especially with an assembled set like this, there is the possibility that the Cincinnati emblem was added outside the factory, possibly at a later date. Perhaps French members of the Society of the Cincinnati ordered this service for a 100th anniversary celebration.

It is curious that no glass of the federal period has been recorded with the Cincinnati emblem, because the society's founding members, including George Washington, were quick to order the Cincinnati badge as a decoration on Chinese export porcelain dinnerwares.[2]

1. Paul H. Dunlop, *The Jokelson Collection of Antique Cameo Incrustation* (Phoenix, Ariz.: Papier Press, 1991), pp. 80–81.
2. See Arlene M. Palmer, *A Winterthur Guide to Chinese Export Porcelain* (New York: Crown/Rutledge, 1976), pp. 53, 133–34. The author is grateful to John D. Kilbourne, director of the Library and Museum, Headquarters of the Society of the Cincinnati, Washington, D.C., for confirming that no other Cincinnati table glass is recorded.

Chapter 2
Tumblers and Mugs

Tumblers were probably the most common glass drinking vessel in early America. Basically cylindrical forms with flat bottoms, they suited a wide variety of beverages, especially the beer, cider, and ale that were consumed by most Americans. William Ellery's 1771 advertisement for "Tumblers (or beer glasses)" implies that beer in particular was associated with this form. Other colonial importers sold "punch tumblers" and "wine and water tumblers."[1] Pictorial and written sources of the nineteenth century reveal that tumblers were the standard containers used in taverns to serve distilled liquors such as rum, gin, and whiskey, as well as mixed drinks of the 1830s and 1840s with such picturesque names as *mint-sling, hail-stone, snowstorm, Tom and Jerry,* and *timber-doodle.*[2]

Collectors gave the name *flip glass* to large tumblers, implying they were for the beer and rum concoction known as flip. Period records, however, consistently use only "tumbler," regardless of contents, which are rarely noted, or capacity, which generally ranged from half-gill (one ounce) to quart, although tumblers of even gallon capacity are known. Larger tumblers frequently had covers.

A few household inventories list tumblers with handles, but mug or can more often denotes handled drinking vessels. These forms were more commonly fashioned of silver, pewter, or ceramic. *Mug* and *can* may have been interchangeable terms, but in one glass seller's advertisement they are listed separately, implying some difference between the two. Among the beverages associated with the forms in probate inventories are lemonade and sangaree, a punch composed of red wine and lemon juice.[3]

The expansive sides of tumblers and mugs provided a surface for decoration, whether applied, molded, cut, engraved, or enamel-painted. The shapes of these vessels changed little over time, so clues to dating often lie in the style of decoration.

1. Ellery advertisement, *Connecticut Courant*, October 15–22, 1771. Christopher Bancker advertised "Punch tumblers," *New York Gazette*, supplement, June 13, 1774; for "wine and water" tumblers see George Ball advertisement, *New York Gazette*, July 27, 1775.
2. These exotic drink names can be found in Charles Joseph Latrobe, *The Rambler in North America, 1832–1833*, 2 vols. (New York: Harper and Brothers, 1835), 2:51, and in Charles Dickens, *American Notes for General Circulation* (London: Chapman and Hall, 1892), p. 86.
3. Henry Barnes advertisement, *Boston Evening Post*, April 30, 1750. A large glass "Sangeree Mugg with Cover" worth 7s. 6d. was among the possessions of John Rogerson, inventory 1769-323, Philadelphia County Probate Records (microfilm, Downs, WL).

36, PL. 13

MUG

PROBABLY NEW JERSEY,

PROBABLY WISTARBURGH

GLASSWORKS OF CASPAR AND

RICHARD WISTAR, 1739–77

Yellow-green, bubbly nonlead glass. Blown. Barrel-shape body pattern-molded with 20 vertical ribs; applied threading at top and bottom; thin, rounded ear-shape handle applied with large pad at top and ending in short, tooled terminal; pontil mark.
H: 4½ in (11.4 cm); Diam top: 3¼ in (8.3 cm)
Museum purchase, 1976: Louis Lyons, New York City
76.172

It was a fashion among glassmakers, potters, and silversmiths of the eighteenth century to design mugs and dispensers for cider and ale in the form of common barrels. In Winterthur's version the glassblower achieved the effect of ribs and staves by molded ribbing and applied threads of glass wound around the vessel from either end. Although more frequently of Continental manufacture, "Barrel Canns" were among the English glasswares sold in colonial Boston.[1]

This mug is attributed to the South Jersey enterprise of Caspar and Richard Wistar. Patterned in a twenty-rib mold, it relates to several sugar bowls attributed to Wistarburgh (NO. 150). Two smaller mugs with thumbpieces and overall threading discovered in archaeological excavations are also attributed to the Wistar factory.[2]

Rim wear suggests the Winterthur mug may originally have had a cover.

1. Rebecca Abbot advertisement, *New England Journal*, January 24, 1731. For a German or Bohemian example, see Winterthur 87.122. For a French example excavated from a ca. 1745 context at Louisbourg, see E. Ann Smith, "Glassware from a Reputed 1745 Siege Debris Context at the Fortress of Louisbourg," *History and Archaeology*, no. 55 (Ottawa: National Historic Parks and Sites Branch, Parks Canada, 1981), p. 239, fig. 59. For an English rib-molded and threaded example, see Thorpe, *History*, 2: pl. 80, no. 1; a Bristol one dated 1760 is shown in Witt, Weeden, and Schwind, *Bristol Glass*, pl. 34. A cut and covered barrel mug is shown in the trade card of Maydwell and Windle, in Hughes, *Table Glass*, p. 60.
2. One was excavated in a 1740–60 context from a well at 314 Market St., Philadelphia; see Barbara Liggett, *Archaeology at Franklin's Court* (Harrisburg: McFarland Co., 1973), n.p.; Arlene Palmer, *The Wistars and Their Glass, 1739–1777* (Millville, N.J.: Museum of American Glass at Wheaton Village, 1989), p. 23, fig. 22. The other mug was found on Tindal's Island near Greenwich, N.J.; Andrew Stanzeski, Camden, N.J., to author, March 6, 1987.

37

TUMBLER (ONE OF TWO)
ENGLAND, 1760–80

Colorless lead glass. Blown. Cylindrical body, tooled
horizontal ribbing; thick base; pontil mark.
H: 4⅞ in (12.4 cm); Diam top: 4⅛ in (10.5 cm)
Museum purchase: W. M. Schwind, Jr., Antiques,
Yarmouth, Maine
80.89 (the other, 73.285, is smaller)

In 1897 glass historian Albert Hartshorne ar-
gued that glasses with this "horizontally corrugated" decoration emanated from Norfolk in
the east of England and suggested that the
factory responsible for this ware might be located in the town of King's Lynn.[1] Ever since,
tumblers, wineglasses (NO. 6), finger bowls,
and other forms tooled with such ribs have
been labeled as "Lynn" or "Lynn-type." None,
however, has a documented history or association with a Norfolk glasshouse. Indeed, research by scholars in recent years has yielded
no proof that a glasshouse was even operating
in King's Lynn after 1747.[2] Because Lynn-type
wineglasses have opaque-twist stems, most
Lynn-type glasses have been dated to the third
quarter of the eighteenth century. The context
of examples recovered from archaeological
sites in Canada suggests that the taste for horizontal ribbing endured into the nineteenth
century.[3] An exaggerated version of the same
tooling technique can be seen in the "beehive"
glass made at Boston and Sandwich Glass
Company in the 1830s (NOS. 134, 175).

1. Albert Hartshorne, *Antique Drinking Glasses* (New
York: Brussel and Brussel, 1968), p. 278 (originally
published as *Old English Glasses* [1897]).
2. L. M. Bickerton, "Glassmaking Traditions in King's
Lynn," *Country Life* 145, no. 3771 (June 12, 1969): 1514–15.
Elizabeth M. James, *King's Lynn and the Glassmaking
Industry* (Norfolk, Eng.: Norfolk Museums Service
Information Sheet, 1979).
3. Jones and Smith, *British Military*, p. 37, fig. 32.

38

TUMBLER

EUROPE, PROBABLY GERMANY,
1775–1825

39

MUG

EUROPE, PROBABLY GERMANY,
1775–1825

NO. 38. Colorless nonlead glass. Blown. Tapered body;
pontil mark. Polychrome enamel-painted decoration: a
bird perched on a heart, flanked by vertical floral sprays,
all on green band; opposite the bird the script inscription
"We two. will / be True"; scalloped line and painted bands
below rim.
H: 3¾ in (9.5 cm); Diam: 2¹⁵⁄₁₆ in (7.3 cm)
History: found in Lancaster Co., Pa.; Rhea Mansfield
Knittle
Museum purchase, 1956: Neil C. Gest, Mechanicsburg,
Ohio
56.71

Published: Schwind, "Pennsylvania German Glass," p. 206,
figs. 198–99.

NO. 39. Colorless, bubbly nonlead glass. Blown. Cylindrical
body flared out and rounded at base; applied, thin strap
handle; pontil mark. Polychrome enamel-painted decoration: opposite the handle, a white pelican plucking her
breast, flanked by diagonal sprays of fruit and flowers, the
decoration contained within horizontal painted bands;
below the rim, a white scalloped line.
H: 4¾ in (12.05 cm); Diam top: 3⁷⁄₁₆ in (8.7 cm)
H. F. du Pont purchase
64.1034

Europe had a long tradition of enamel-painted
glassware. Throughout the eighteenth and well
into the nineteenth century, a tremendous number of glasswares were crudely but colorfully
painted in a limited range of designs including
birds, flowers, landscapes, and figures. Many of
these glasses were made for export, and some,
like NO. 38, bear inscriptions in the language of
the market country.[1]

Fragments of enamel-painted glassware have
been recovered from early eighteenth-century
contexts in the Spanish settlements of Florida,
but similar archaeological evidence from the
English colonies is slim. Among the few written
references is the listing of "3 painted Dutch tumblers" in the 1753 inventory of Daniel Dulany of
Maryland. The expansion of trade with continental Europe after the Revolution brought
increased quantities of the ware to the United
States. The "three painted glass muggs" Elizabeth Drinker purchased in Philadelphia in 1795
were probably like NO. 39.[2]

Over the years, enamel-painted tumblers, mugs, and bottles (NO. 344), especially ones with English inscriptions, have been attributed to Henry William Stiegel's glassworks in Lancaster County, Pennsylvania, for two reasons. First, because Stiegel had both workers and local customers who were German-born, it has been assumed that glasses in this style would have had strong appeal. Stiegel's production records do mention "German" cans, but their decoration is not specified. After 1770 Stiegel employed both German and English glassblowers, and his record books and advertisements prove that his market extended beyond the Pennsylvania German community.

The second basis for the attribution of enamel-painted glassware to Stiegel is the "enamelled" glass he lists in his newspaper advertisements after 1772: "blue and plain enamelled" salts, "common and enamelled" servers [salvers], "enamelled and plain" cream jugs, "enamelled common, and twisted" smelling bottles, and "plain, enamelled and twisted" wineglasses. Stiegel published these advertisements at a time when his avowed aim was to create quality table glass in the English manner, and in records of the English glass industry, "enameled" could refer not only to enamel-painted but also to opaque white glass and opaque-twist stems. The enameled forms Stiegel offered are known in English opaque white glass but are rarely seen with painted decoration like that of NOS. 38 and 39. "Enameled and twisted" accurately describes the characteristic treatment of English stemware that Stiegel is known to have emulated. Enamel-painted glasswares like NOS. 38 and 39 are of nonlead composition; by 1771 Stiegel was successfully manufacturing English-type lead glass.[3]

In Europe, enamel-painted decoration was frequently applied and fired onto the glass in small workshops independent of the glasshouses. No such shop in colonial America has been identified.

1. Axel von Saldern, "Baron Stiegel and Eighteenth-Century Enameled Glass," *Antiques* 80, no. 3 (September 1961): 232–35.

2. Kathleen Deagan, *Artifacts of the Spanish Colonies of Florida and the Caribbean, 1500–1800, 1: Ceramics, Glassware, and Beads* (Washington, D.C.: Smithsonian Institution Press, 1987), p. 141, fig. 6.19. Fragments of enamel-painted glass have been found in excavations at Pemaquid, Maine. Daniel Dulany inventory, 1753, box 55, no. 42, Maryland Hall of Records, Annapolis. Diary of Elizabeth Drinker, October 19, 1795, Historical Society of Pennsylvania, Philadelphia (hereafter HSP).

3. Stiegel Records, HSP. *Pennsylvania Packet*, July 6, 1772; see also Schwind, "Pennsylvania German Glass," pp. 205–7. An English price list includes "Wine Glasses, plain Shanks, Ditto enamelled or twisted," Whitefriars Glassworks Collection, Museum of London, reference courtesy of Wendy Evans. Williams, Dunbar and Co. of Chepstow advertised their "flint and enamel glass manufactory" in 1764, see Delomosne and Son, *Gilding the Lily*, p. 4. Palmer, "To the Good," pp. 212–18.

40, 41, PL. 16

MUGS

PROBABLY BOHEMIA OR SOUTH GERMANY, 1770–90

NO. 40. Opaque white glass. Blown. Barrel form, flat ground and polished edge; applied rounded loop handle with tooled terminal; ground pontil mark. Polychrome enamel-painted scene representing October: a fruit seller holds aloft a huge berry from his basket while a woman with a basket on her back walks away; in the treetop, above a moon face, is a scorpion; gilded rim band.
H: 5¾ in (14.6 cm); Diam top: 3½ in (8.9 cm)
H. F. du Pont purchase
69.1428

NO. 41. Opaque white glass. Blown. Body: cylindrical form flaring sharply at base; applied flat loop handle with tooled terminal; pontil mark. Polychrome enamel-painted land-scape setting in which a man grasping a tree trunk tickles a sleeping woman with a long stalk, while another man on the right fires a gun at him; a horse and grazing sheep stand to the far left and a birdcage hangs from the tree; dog and basket in foreground; gilded rim.
OH: 5¾ in (14.6 cm); Diam top of mug: 4 in (10.1 cm)
H. F. du Pont purchase
69.1426a, b

The enamel-painted decoration of these drink-ing vessels, more finely executed than that of NOS. 38 and 39, relates stylistically to painted porcelains of the period. The subject matter was derived from print sources. The same genre scene painted on NO. 41 is recorded on a barrel-shape mug of opaque white glass. The

"October" mug was doubtless part of a set; besides the months and seasons of the year, the
four continents were also celebrated on painted
glass. Perhaps it was such a "sett glass china
mugs" that Leonard Keehmle had in his Philadelphia shop in 1813. *Glass china* was an early
nineteenth-century term for glass that imitated
white porcelain or china.[1]

1. Sotheby Parke Bernet, "The Krug Collection of Glass,"
pt. 1 (July 7, 1981), lot 16; the same mug was sold again at
Christie, Manson & Woods, "Fine English and Continental
Glass and Paperweights" (June 19, 1984), lot 262. For other
versions of this decoration see Walter Spiegl, *Glas*
(Munich: Battenberg Verlag, 1979), pp. 96–97, nos. 149, 151.
Leonard Keehmle inventory, 1813-131, Philadelphia County
Probate Records (microfilm, Downs, WL). Keehmle's set
was valued at $5.

42

TUMBLER

GERMANY OR BOHEMIA,

1780–1820

43

MUG WITH COVER

GERMANY OR BOHEMIA,

1780–1820

NO. 42. Colorless nonlead glass of yellow tint. Blown. Tapered form; ground pontil mark. Wheel engraved: on one side, a basket containing large tulip and 2 leafy sprays; squiggled lines spring from basket and flank blossom; on the reverse, stylized flower on stem with 4 broadly scrolled leaves, central squiggled lines. (Originally it may have had a cover.)
H: 7½ in (19.0 cm); Diam top: 5⅞ in (15.0 cm)
Gift of Charles K. Davis, 1955
55.65.3

NO. 43. Colorless nonlead glass. Blown. Body: cylindrical, flared sharply at base; applied strap handle; pontil mark. Wheel engraved: opposite the handle a sunburst motif containing in the center roundel 2 birds perched on a heart set on the ground; a dotted border above. Cover: low, domed top and straight sides inset below rounded flange;

applied finial of angle-knop form on short waisted stem; interior pontil mark. Wheel engraved: 2 wavy bands around the upper rim.
OH: 9 in (23.0 cm); Diam top of mug: 3½ in (8.9 cm)
History: Hugh W. Kelly, Lancaster, Pa.
Gift of Mrs. Hugh W. Kelly, 1987
87.129a, b

Ever since the publication of Frederick William Hunter's 1914 *Stiegel Glass*, curators and collectors have attributed engraved tumblers and mugs of this type to Henry William Stiegel's glassworks. Hunter found examples in Pennsylvania homes and collections and assumed they had been locally manufactured. Knowing that Stiegel was a German who employed glassblowers of Continental background, and that Pennsylvania was heavily populated with German emigrants, Hunter then concluded that much of Stiegel's production was in this style.[1]

What Hunter did not comprehend was the vast extent to which seventeenth- and eighteenth-century America relied on imported glass. Prior to the Revolution, English manufacturers supplied most of the bottles, windowpanes, and table glass used in the colonies. After independence was won, however, other nations established trade with America. Many German and Bohemian glass factories quickly found a market in the new nation. Their products were generically referred to as "German" by importers and auctioneers.

Although the naive or "peasant" quality of the engraving seen in NOS. 42 and 43 has been cited as evidence of colonial manufacture, an illustrated trade catalogue (see NOS. 17–19) of a Bohemian glass factory proves that crudely engraved drinking vessels were commercially produced for export: a tumbler decorated with a similar basket of flowers (see drawing) is described in the catalogue as "common."

Among the United States consumers who lamented the influx of these cheap, coarse glasswares was one Charlestonian songster:

A long farewell to sparkling old Madeira,
No longer sipped from English glass in this unhappy era.
Our democratic grog must now be drank from German tumblers,
Thick as the heads, coarse as the minds of Democratick Bunglers.[2]

This lament also indicates that the European glasshouses enjoyed a market well beyond the German settlements of America, a surmise borne out by fragments of such glasses found in archaeological sites from Maine to Virginia. That they tend to surface in post-1780 contexts further supports the theory that Stiegel, whose factory closed in 1774, was not responsible.

This is not to say that Stiegel did not produce glass of a Continental character. Given the training of his workers and his local clientele, glass of Germanic-style was inevitable, especially in the 1764–69 period. Pint- and quart-size mugs were made by Stiegel's workmen as early as 1765, probably in green glass. "German cans with covers" are listed among the products in 1774; perhaps they were similar in form to NO. 43.[3]

To achieve his new aims as a manufacturer of glass in the English mode, Stiegel hired English artisans and introduced an expanded line of table glass. To advertise this new phase he submitted specimens of his flint glassware— "decanters, wineglasses, tumblers, etc."—to the American Philosophical Society in 1771. The judges assessed them "Equal in beauty and quality to the generality of Flint Glass, imported from England," an opinion published in English newspapers.[4] A key feature of English glass was its lead composition, and Stiegel succeeded in making lead glass tablewares at his manufactory by 1771.

There is no record of engraved glass from Manheim before Lazarus Isaac was hired as "cutter and flowerer" in 1773. Isaac came from England where engraving in the design and manner of NOS. 42 and 43 (a mixture of light engraving and variable matting known as *mattschnitt*) was not practiced. Two engraved glasses that reflect Isaac's English training in both subject and style are currently the only engraved glasses that can be firmly attributed to the Stiegel enterprise.[5]

Tumblers of this large size have traditionally been known as flip glasses among collectors, but there is no evidence that glasses of a particular shape or size were associated with that eighteenth-century beverage. Contemporary records such as merchants' advertisements, factory ledgers, and household inventories consistently use "tumbler" in conjunction with a designation of capacity, not contents.

1. Hunter, *Stiegel Glass*, pp. 219–20, figs. 114–34.
2. Published in 1788 in the *Charleston Courier*, quoted in Mrs. H. M. Milford, "Amelung's Glass Manufactory," *Glass Club Bulletin*, no. 34 (December 1953): 5.
3. Daybook, July 30, 1774, Stiegel Records, HSP.
4. *South Carolina Gazette*, July 8, 1771; *Felix Farley's Bristol Journal*, August 31, 1771.
5. See Palmer, "To the Good," pp. 234–39, nos. 93, 96.

44

TUMBLER WITH COVER
FREDERICK COUNTY, MARYLAND,
NEW BREMEN GLASSMANUFAC-
TORY OF JOHN FREDERICK
AMELUNG, DATED 1788

Colorless nonlead glass of gray tint. Blown. Tumbler: tapered form with thick base; pontil mark. Wheel engraved: on one side, "Charles Ghequiere" within 2 branches of flowers and leaves joined with a flower at the bottom, surmounted by a dove holding a leafy spray in its beak; above the wreath, "Floreat Commercium" in an arc above a crown; inscribed, "New Bremen Glasmanufactory / the 20the of June 1788" on the reverse. Cover: domed top and high, tapered sides, inset with trailed ring that rests on edge of tumbler; applied baluster finial with large tear; interior pontil mark. Wheel engraved: on one side along the shoulder a scrolled, foliate spray.
OH: 12¼ in (31.1 cm); H tumbler: 8⅛ in (20.4 cm); Diam top of tumbler: 5¹³/₁₆ in (14.8 cm)
History: Charles Ghequiere; his great-grandson, Charles G. Fenwick
H. F. du Pont purchase, ca. 1934: Charles G. Fenwick
59.3009a, b

Exhibited: Baltimore Museum of Art, 1934.
Published: Homer Eaton Keyes, "Safe Clues in the Amelung Quest," *Antiques* 26, no. 3 (September 1934): 89, figs. 3–4.
McKearin and McKearin, *American Glass*, p. 105, pl. 38, nos. 1, 3.
Lanmon and Palmer, "New Bremen," pp. 52–53.

This tumbler, made for Charles Ghequiere (d. 1819) of Baltimore, helped unravel the story of John Frederick Amelung's glassworks because it was the second signed example of Amelung's work to come to light and the first of this form (see NO. 16). Like the Bremen goblet at Metropolitan Museum of Art, Ghequiere's tumbler is dated 1788 and carries the factory name. Of the ten large tumblers now identified as New Bremen products, three are at Winterthur (NOS. 44–46) and six retain their original covers. Amelung's newspaper advertisement for quart-size tumblers does not mention covers.[1]

Many eighteenth-century tumblers and stemmed drinking glasses were probably intended to have covers. In 1769, Richard Eagles of North Carolina owned "3 large Tumblers with Tops to suit" and three covered glass mugs. William Vanderspiegel, a Philadelphia merchant, had a half-gallon tumbler and cover. Two tumblers in John Fulford's 1780 inventory were itemized as having "Covers broke"—undoubtedly the fate of many such glass parts. These eighteenth-century covered glasses were probably of English manufacture, though relatively few English ones survive in contrast to Continental examples.[2]

Whether such large covered tumblers were meant to be used for specific beverages or on particular occasions is unknown. The engraved date, June 20, 1788, suggests that NO. 44 was of a commemorative nature, and family tradition maintains that it was presented to Ghequiere by admiring friends. The tumbler is inscribed "Floreat Commercium" (may commerce flourish), a slogan that is found on Silesian goblets of earlier date.[3] Perhaps the glass was commissioned to celebrate some new venture of the enterprising Ghequiere. The 1788 date predates his powder mill on Gwinn's Falls (1791) and his role as president of Baltimore Fire Insurance Company. Amelung must have hoped his own commerce would benefit from his association with Ghequiere, who imported quantities of window glass from Bohemia; however, the merchant's post-1788 advertisements do not indicate that he added Amelung's products to his inventory.[4] Some business connection did exist between the two men because in 1795 Ghequiere and two other merchants forced Amelung and James Labes to mortgage land holdings to cover their debts.

It is a curious coincidence that the son of George Jacob Schley, recipient of the goblet shown in NO. 16, was the appraiser of Ghequiere's estate in 1819. Winterthur's tumbler cannot be identified in the document because Schley did not itemize the household furnishings.[5]

1. Keyes, "Safe Clues," pp. 88–91. For other examples see Lanmon and Palmer, "New Bremen," pp. 50–51, 66–67, 94–97, 100–103. These are all over 7⅛ in. in height and range from 11⁵/₁₆ in. to 13 in. with covers. Two somewhat smaller coverless tumblers are known of 6 in. and 6⅜ in. in height. Amelung's glass is described in James Labes advertisement, *Maryland Journal*, March 18, 1790.
2. J. Bryan Grimes, *North Carolina Wills and Inventories* (Raleigh: Edwards and Broughton, 1912), p. 487; William Vanderspiegel inventory, 1768-206, Philadelphia County Probate Records (microfilm, Downs, WL); John Fulford inventory, 1780, liber 12, fol. 260, Baltimore County Probate

Records (microfilm, Downs, WL). One example dated 1774 is in Percy Bate, *English Table Glass* (London: B. T. Batsford, 1913), fig. 242.
3. Keyes, "Safe Clues," p. 88. For a Silesian goblet of 1740 engraved with the same slogan, see Sotheby Parke Bernet, "English and Continental Glass," (June 13, 1977), lot 215. Also, Museum für Kunsthandwerk, *Europäisches und Aussereuropäisches Glas* (Frankfurt am Main, 1980), pp. 184–86, no. 395.
4. *Maryland Gazette*, July 18, 1788, and *Maryland Journal*, February 12, 1790; in 1795 Ghequiere notified the public that he had received a "supply of the real Bohemia Glass, in boxes. . . . Which I will sell at as moderate prices as I can afford" (*Maryland Journal*, September 18, 1795).
5. Baltimore City Will Book, liber 31, fol. 524–25 (microfilm, Downs, WL).

New Bremen Glassmanufactory.
1791

45

Colorless nonlead glass of slight gray (body) and green (cover) tints. Blown. Tumbler: tapering form; thick base; pontil mark. Wheel engraved: on one side, the coat of arms of Pennsylvania; the reverse, inscribed "New Bremen Glassmanufactory-/1791-." Cover: low, conical top and curved sides, inset with trailed ring that rests on edge of tumbler; applied baluster finial with large tear; interior pontil mark. Wheel engraved along shoulder with foliate spray. Cover broken in 2 parts and repaired.
OH: 11¼ in (28.7 cm); H tumbler: 8½ in (21.7 cm); Diam top of tumbler: 6 in (15.3 cm)
History: John Guest; his nephew, George Guest Williams (1793–1879); his daughter, Sarah Williams Emlen (1830–1913); her granddaughter, Mary Emlen Metz
Museum purchase, 1969: Robert A. and Mary E. Metz 69.139a, b

Published: "Museum Accessions," *Antiques* 99, no. 2 (February 1971): 208.
Lanmon and Palmer, "New Bremen," pp. 64–65.

One of seven glasses that bears the signature of Amelung's glassworks, this covered tumbler is splendidly decorated with the arms of the state of Pennsylvania as depicted from 1790 to 1805. The same arms occur on another New Bremen–made glass dated 1791, a goblet presented to Thomas Mifflin who was elected governor of the state that year.[1] The owner of the Winterthur tumbler, John Guest (1768–1817), held no political office in Pennsylvania and had been born in New Jersey. Philadelphia, however, was the center of his extensive mercantile business and the home of his ancestors, including George Guest who had settled there in 1681.

The lid of this tumbler is considerably flatter than the very swelled one of the Ghequiere example (NO. 44), and were it in perfect condition it would still fit the body poorly. The distinctive finial and engraving identify it as Amelung's product, but it may have originally been made for a different tumbler, perhaps a mate to the one that has survived.

1. The Mifflin goblet (Metropolitan Museum of Art, New York) is in Lanmon and Palmer, "New Bremen," p. 61.

46

TUMBLER

FREDERICK COUNTY, MARYLAND, ATTRIBUTED TO NEW BREMEN GLASSMANUFACTORY OF JOHN FREDERICK AMELUNG, 1785–95

Colorless nonlead glass of greenish tint. Blown. Tapered form, thick base; pontil mark. Wheel engraved: on one side, an oval wreath composed of stylized branches and flowers surrounding the initials, "A.G." (Originally it may have had a cover.)
H: 8⅛ in (20.8 cm); Diam top: 5⅞ in (15.0 cm)
History: Grosz family; Charles Woolsey Lyon; Richard Loeb
H. F. du Pont purchase, 1946: Parke-Bernet Galleries, New York City, through Neil C. Gest
59.3004

Published: Parke-Bernet Galleries, "Fine English and American Furniture and Decorations," sale no. 805 (November 9, 1946), lot 82.
McKearin and McKearin, *Two Hundred Years*, pl. 78, no. 3.
Lanmon and Palmer, "New Bremen," p. 92.

Each signed or otherwise documented example from Amelung's Maryland glassworks provides evidence of form and ornament that can be used to identify unsigned glass objects. Attributed glasses in turn can offer new details or design concepts that further extend the picture of this important factory of the federal era.

This unsigned tumbler has engraved decoration that incorporates elements found on documented objects, for example the Guest tumbler (NO. 45), yet the arrangement of stylized leaves and flowers is different. The rather stiff "A" is also unusual; however, the chevron crossbar is recorded on the set of tumblers made for Abigail and William Goddard.[1] The "G" is typical of the New Bremen engraver's work.

Noted antiques dealer Charles Woolsey Lyon reportedly obtained this glass from the Grosz family of Frederick, Maryland. The initials were later identified as those of Anthony Grosz (1735–95), about whom nothing is known. There were at least six other men with initials "AG" living in Frederick during the period of the New Bremen operation. Moreover, many of the owners of Amelung's "Flint-Glass" cut with "Devices, cyphers, Coats of arms, or any other Fancy Figures" were prominent people living outside the local community and often beyond the state lines.[2]

1. Lanmon and Palmer, "New Bremen," pp. 94–95.
2. Amelung advertisement, *Maryland Journal*, May 22, 1789.

47

TUMBLER

FREDERICK COUNTY, MARYLAND,
ATTRIBUTED TO NEW BREMEN
GLASSMANUFACTORY OF
JOHN FREDERICK AMELUNG,
DATED 1788

Colorless nonlead glass. Blown. Tapered form; thick base;
pontil mark. Wheel engraved: on one side, laurel branches
joined with a flower at the bottom frame "J.F.C.H./1788."
H: 3⅝ in (9.2 cm); Diam top: 2¹⁵⁄₁₆ in (7.5 cm)
History: Ira Hostetter, Lancaster Co., Pa.; Katharine
Woodward, Middleburg, Va.
Museum purchase, 1958: James H. Rose, Canton, Ohio, and
Richard H. Wood, Baltimore
58.9

Published: Lanmon and Palmer, "New Bremen," pp. 54–55.

This small tumbler parallels the larger, covered
ones (NOS. 44, 45) in its gently tapered form and
thick bottom, and its simple, engraved decoration
relates to that on other Amelung ware. The date is
virtually identical in its execution to that on the
Johnson case bottle (NO. 347). The "J," "F," and
"C" are similar to those on documented glasses,
but the less successful "H" is not.

Amelung apparently employed only one engraver, and examination of the dated New Bremen
objects indicates his skill improved somewhat
over time. As yet anonymous, this engraver practiced the round-hand lettering that was common
in English-language areas, even though he was
certainly of German origin and training.[1]

The placement of initials or a name within
a wreath was a device employed by many glass
decorators over a long period of time. An Irish
example dated 1810 is shown in NO. 113 while an
American example of the 1850s is seen in NO. 71.

Several other decorated Amelung glasses also
bear the date of 1788, most notably the Bremen
goblet, and the "Tobias and the Angel" tumbler.[2]

1. For the Amelung "alphabet" created from letters found on
documented glasses and a glass with German inscription in
round-hand lettering, see Lanmon and Palmer, "New
Bremen," pp. 45, 76–77.
2. Lanmon and Palmer, "New Bremen," pp. 54–55.

48

TUMBLER

UNITED STATES OR ENGLAND, ENGRAVED IN PHILADELPHIA, DATED 1806

Colorless lead glass. Blown. Cylindrical form of uneven height with thick base; polished bottom. Row of narrow flutes cut around lower body. Engraved in diamond-point cursive: around rim, the Lord's Prayer (in 3 lines), followed by "JW. 1806"; on one side of body, "James McAlpin/Philadelphia/July 24th", and on the opposite side, "Ann S. Mc.Alpin."
H: 3¾ in (9.5 cm); Diam top: 3¼ in (8.2 cm)
History: James Burke, Decatur, Ind.
Museum purchase, 1976: The Stradlings, New York City
76.321

Exhibited: Henry Ford Museum, 1960.
Published: Sotheby Parke Bernet, "The American Heritage Society Auction of Americana," sale no. 3923 (November 18–20, 1976), lot 492.
Arlene M. Palmer, "Religion in Clay and Glass," *American Art and Antiques* 2, no. 4 (July–August 1979): 84.

Glasses have been decoratively engraved with a diamond point since ancient times. Because no equipment beyond the diamond was needed, the technique attracted amateur as well as professional practitioners. There were several professional engravers working in Philadelphia around 1806, but none is recorded with the initials "JW." Perhaps the decorator was an amateur, a friend of the McAlpins who originally owned the glass.

The obviously local origin of the decoration does not prove the tumbler itself was blown and cut in Philadelphia. Indeed, cut-glass tumblers were among the many English and Irish glasswares imported into that city, so it is possible this tumbler was made abroad. In 1806 the only flint glass factory in the city was the old Philadelphia Glass Works, which James Butland and two partners had purchased in 1800. Cut glass had been manufactured there from 1775, but there is no record showing the new owners continued to offer this luxury ware. No glasscutters are listed in the directories from 1802 to 1807.

According to city directories, James McAlpin was a merchant tailor from 1803 to 1817; after 1818, he is described as a gentleman. He died in 1848.

49, 50

MUGS

PROBABLY BOHEMIA, 1790–1820

NO. 49. Violet-blue, nonlead glass. Blown. Barrel form;
applied ear-shape handle; pontil mark. Gilded band
around rim; 7 rows of gilded stars on body.
H: 4⅜ in (11.1 cm); Diam top: 2¹³⁄₁₆ in (7.1 cm)
Museum purchase, 1974: Brianwood Antiques and
Interiors, Ithaca, N.Y.
74.69

NO. 50. Colorless nonlead glass, slight green tint. Blown.
Barrel form; flat ground and polished edge; applied solid
handle; flat polished bottom. A band of flutes cut around
the base; small, 8-point stars engraved around body;
at rim a row of triangles above a twisted rope from which
hang fringed swags, each containing a flower; between
each swag, a flower from which hang crossed lines each
with a flower at the bottom.
H: 2¹³⁄₁₆ in (7.1 cm); Diam top: 2⅜ in (6.1 cm)
Museum purchase, 1957: McKearins' Antiques, Hoosick
Falls, N.Y.
57.18.42

Barrel-shape mugs like NOS. 49 and 50 were
made in the glasshouses of Bohemia for export
to foreign markets. Proof of this can be seen in
an illustration from a Bohemian trade catalogue
of the 1790–1810 period (see NOS. 17–19). In that

catalogue, number 165 is described as a "Mug,
of dark blue glass, with gilt rim and small stars,"
available in three sizes. On Winterthur's gilded
mug, the stars, which are remarkably intact,
parallel the engraved ones that are often featured on Continental as well as English and Irish
glass (NO. 20). Winterthur's smaller colorless
mug (NO. 50) is similar to item 123—with "scalloped base and delicate festoons"—in that same
trade catalogue.[1]

Although the catalogue descended in the
Gardiner family of Gardiner's Island, New York,
it documents the type of central European glasswares that merchants throughout postrevolutionary America were importing. In Baltimore,
such wares competed with Amelung's products—and in the twentieth century were erroneously attributed to the New Bremen factory.[2]

In the trade catalogue, handled drinking
vessels are called "mugs" regardless of their capacity, but collectors and curators have traditionally identified small ones like NO. 50 as
punch glasses. The evidence suggests that punch
cannot be associated with a vessel of specific size
and shape. New York merchant George Ball sold
punch glasses "of several sizes" in 1775. A few

years later Frederick Rhinelander was importing English punch glasses "with handles," implying that handles were an option. Several references exist to punch glasses "covered" or "with tops." In a 1767 drawing of a convivial drinking party, a punch bowl dominated the table, yet the only drinking glasses shown are stemmed "wine-glasses."[3]

1. Gardiner's Island Glass Catalogues, Downs, WL.
2. Dwight P. Lanmon, "The Baltimore Glass Trade, 1780 to 1820," *Winterthur Portfolio 5*, ed. Richard K. Doud (Charlottesville: University Press of Virginia, 1969), pp. 35–36. Among the foreign glasses advertised were blue glass mugs.
3. Rhinelander advertisement, *Rivington's New York Gazetteer*, July 27, 1775; Arlene Palmer Schwind, "English Glass Imports in New York, 1770–1790," *Journal of Glass Studies* 25 (1983): 182; See George Roupell's ink and wash drawing *Mr. Peter Manigault and His Friends* (Winterthur 63.73a) in Anna Wells Rutledge, "After the Cloth Was Removed," *Winterthur Portfolio 4*, ed. Richard K. Doud (Charlottesville: University Press of Virginia, 1968), p. 49. Tall, stemmed glasses are also shown in Joseph Highmore, *A Punch Party*, ca. 1740, in Hughes, *Table Glass*, p. 78, fig. 31.

51

TUMBLER

PROBABLY BOHEMIA, 1790–1820

Colorless nonlead glass of blue-gray tint. Blown. Tapered form; polished pontil mark. Cut band of tall flutes around lower body. Wheel engraved: border design of pointed frosted ovals containing zigzag line; between each oval is a rosette; from the middle of each oval hangs a double tassel; a beaded chain connects the pairs of tassels.
H: 5 1/16 in (12.9 cm); Diam top: 3 5/8 in (9.2 cm)
Museum purchase, 1957: McKearins' Antiques, Hoosick Falls, N.Y.
57.18.44

Published: McKearin and McKearin, *American Glass*, pl. 41, fig. 6.

Continental glasswares were widely used in federal America. In the Gardiner's Island trade catalogues a glass like NO. 51 is described as a beer glass with cut base and "delicate festoons." Although the label and drawing in the trade catalogue would seem to settle the question of what glass form was designed for beer in the 1790–1820 era, other references indicate that "beer glass" was by no means a standardized concept. William Ellery of Hartford advertised

"Tumblers (or beer glasses) from half a gill to a pint," which confirms that tumblers functioned as beer glasses but also implies that beer glasses might be of various sizes. The advertisement of Salem merchant Stephen Higginson for beer glasses "of all Sizes and Shapes" could be taken to mean that vessels besides tumblers were appropriate for that beverage. Indeed, in Boston Joseph Barrel sold "Beer Glasses with cut Shanks," that is, with cut stems. His advertisement harks back to the seventeenth century

when short-stemmed conical glasses (NO. 1) were described as beer glasses. Adding to the confusion are a 1764 reference to beer mugs and a 1768 listing of "2 large Beer glasses with Covers" in merchant William Vanderspiegel's inventory.[1]

1. Ellery advertisement, *Connecticut Courant*, October 15–23, 1771; Higginson advertisement, *Essex Gazette*, September 14–21, 1773; Barrel advertisement, *Boston Evening Post*, October 26, 1772; Martin Ashburn inventory, 1764-59, and Vanderspiegel inventory, 1768-206, Philadelphia County Probate Records (microfilm, Downs, WL).

52

MUG

PROBABLY KEENE, NEW
HAMPSHIRE, PROBABLY KEENE
GLASS WORKS, 1815–17

Colorless lead glass. Blown. Cylindrical body; applied,
rounded hollow-blown handle. Body blown in 3-part
mold of geometric design (McKearin G III-20): faint
vertical ribbing around rim with horizontal ring and
diagonal ribbing below; between horizontal rings are 3
repeat panels of diamond diapering and waffle sunburst;
vertical ribbing around base; rayed bottom (type VI-A);
pontil mark.
H: 3⁵⁄₁₆ in (10.0 cm); Diam top: 2¹⁵⁄₁₆ in (7.5 cm)
History: William T. H. Howe, Cincinnati
H. F. du Pont purchase, 1941: Parke-Bernet Galleries,
New York City
67.837

Published: McKearin and McKearin, *American Glass*, pl. 106,
no. 9.
Parke-Bernet Galleries, "Early American Glass . . .
Collection Formed by the Late William T. H. Howe,"
pt. 2, sale no. 273 (April 3–4, 1941), lot 446.

53, PL. 18

TUMBLER
KEENE, NEW HAMPSHIRE,
ATTRIBUTED TO KEENE GLASS
WORKS, 1815–41

Blue nonlead glass. Blown. Barrel shape; blown in 3-part mold of geometric design (McKearin G III-16): faint vertical ribbing around rim with horizontal ring and diagonal ribbing below; between horizontal rings are 3 repeat panels of diamond diapering and bull's-eye sunburst; vertical ribbing around base; rayed bottom (probably type VI-A); pontil mark.
H: 4⅝ in (11.8 cm); Diam top: 3⅜ in (8.6 cm)
H. F. du Pont purchase, 1946: McKearins' Antiques, Hoosick Falls, N.Y.
59.3282

Published: Wilson, *New England Glass*, p. 167, fig. 126b.

The glassworks erected in 1815 on Marlboro Street in Keene, New Hampshire, is best known for its mold-blown flasks (NO. 384), but tablewares are also attributed to the factory. In 1816 the proprietors advertised for sale an "assortment of Flint Glass Ware, consisting of Tumblers, Wines, Decanters, Pitchers, &c &c." A contemporary description of the factory notes it even had facilities for "cutting and polishing all sorts of glass."[1] Although no cut glass from Keene is known, mold-blown tablewares imitative of cut designs have been attributed to the works. That the Keene factory's "flint" glass was of lead composition is proved by documented lead-glass flasks (73.423.6, 73.420.6, 73.411.2), but newspapers indicate that the manufacture of flint glass ceased by August 1817. In 1820 new factory owner Justus Perry reported to the federal government that "bottles and common glass" were his only products.[2]

The small mug (NO. 52) may have been made in Keene during the two-year period of lead-glass production. NO. 53 is unusual in its blue color; most of the blown three-mold tablewares attributed to Keene are of common bottle glass in olive and aqua (NOS. 163, 258). The waffle sunburst pattern of NO. 52 also occurs in olive green decanters.[3]

Any defects in the design of a metal mold will be imparted to every piece of glass blown in that mold, hence the mapping of imperfections can aid in making attributions. Mold-defect evidence reveals that two dishes in the

Winterthur collection were blown in the same mold as NO. 52 (59.3156, 59.3157). Two tumblers of G III-20 pattern were blown in a different mold, presumably at a different factory.

1. Keene advertisement quoted in Wilson, *New England Glass*, pp. 160–61.
2. Wilson, *New England Glass*, p. 161; 1820 Census of Manufactures, s.v. "New Hampshire." For a discussion of lead-glass production see Wilson, *New England Glass*.
3. Wilson, *New England Glass*, p. 166, fig. 125.

54, 55

TUMBLERS

UNITED STATES, 1815–40

NO. 54 (one of two). Colorless lead glass. Blown. Cylindrical form blown in 3-part mold of geometric design (McKearin G III-6): faint vertical ribbing around rim; horizontal rings with diagonal ribbing below; between horizontal rings are 3 repeat panels of sunburst and diamond diapering; vertical ribbing; rayed bottom (type VI-A); pontil mark.
H: 3½ in (9.0 cm); Diam top: 2⅞ in (7.3 cm)
H. F. du Pont purchase, between 1939 and 1941
59.3252 (mate is 59.3253)

NO. 55 (one of two). Colorless lead glass. Blown. Large cylindrical form blown in 3-part mold of geometric design (McKearin G II-34): faint vertical ribs around rim; diagonal ribbing between horizontal rings; band of vertical flutes above a horizontal ring and diamond diapering; horizontal ring above vertical flutes around base and onto bottom; bottom patterned with diamonds (type X); pontil mark.
H: 7½ in (19.2 cm); Diam: 5⅞ in (15.0 cm)
H. F. du Pont purchase, 1946: Neil C. Gest, Mechanicsburg, Ohio
59.3330 (mate is 59.3293)

56

TUMBLER

PROBABLY WESTERN
PENNSYLVANIA OR OHIO, 1815–45

Colorless lead glass of slight green tint. Blown. Barrel form
swelled in the middle. Blown in 3-part mold of geometric
design (McKearin G III-10): vertical ribbing swirled to right
at rim above horizontal ring; 6 large diamonds filled with
small diamonds, fans in the spaces between; horizontal ring
above vertical ribbing; bottom patterned with petals (type
II); pontil mark.
H: 3½ in (8.9 cm); Diam top: 2¾ in (6.9 cm)
H. F. du Pont purchase, 1947: Neil C. Gest, Mechanicsburg,
Ohio
59.3170

Written records shed little light on the introduction and development of the technique of patterning glass in full-size, three- or four-part
molds of geometric designs. References to "moulded" tablewares in price lists and advertising
notices date to the late 1810s, but that term was
also used to refer to pattern-molded styles (for
example, NO. 59).

It is widely thought that Thomas Cains
(NO. 114) brought the so-called blown three-mold
technique from England to Boston in 1812, but
hard evidence is lacking. Certainly glasswares of
this kind were made at his South Boston Flint
Glass Works between 1813 and 1830. On Cape
Cod, numerous fragments of mold-blown glass
have been plucked from the site of Boston and
Sandwich Glass Company, resulting in the attribution of many patterns to that undertaking.
Numerous designs have also been attributed to
New England Glass Company in Cambridge.
Attributions are difficult to make because glasshouses freely pirated one another's patterns,
which were derived from the intricate geometric
designs of luxury cut glass, domestic and imported. Production of mold-blown tumblers
extended beyond New England, but records are
vague. Baltimore Glassworks, for example, offered "Moulded S[hip]" tumblers (half-pint size)
in 1831 and "moulded" tumblers of gill capacity.
The molded diamond and molded flute tumblers
made by Philadelphia's Union Flint Glass Works
in the late 1820s cannot be absolutely identified
but may have been of the blown three-mold
variety.[1]

The price lists of South Boston Flint Glass
Works supply important evidence of the price
levels of mold-blown tumblers. In the 1818 list,
"mo[lded]" tumblers were available in the following sizes with the cost given per dozen: gill,
$1.00; half-pint, $1.50; pint, $2.00; quart, $3.00;
and two-quart, $6.00. Prices were lower on the
1819 list, perhaps in response to the panic of 1819
and the general economic depression. On that
list, "best moulded" tumblers were priced as
follows: gill, $.90; half-pint, $1.34; pint, $2.00;
quart, $3.00; and two-quart, $5.00. "Best plain"
tumblers were considerably more expensive,
running from $1.34 per dozen for the gill size to
$9.00 per dozen for the two-quart tumbler. Cut
tumblers, described as "fingered" cost $2.40 per
dozen for the gill size and $4.50 for the
half-pint.[2]

The pattern of NO. 54 was made at several
factories. Fraudulent glasswares were made in
this same design in the twentieth century (see
NO. 133). NO. 55, remarkable for its very large
size, has a small diamond design that clearly
evokes Anglo-Irish cut glass.

The Winterthur collection includes two
cylindrical tumblers that seem to have been
blown in the same mold as NO. 56. The G III-10
design is rare and has been associated with
midwestern production. When Neil Gest offered
NO. 56 to du Pont, he wrote that it had been
found "right out here in the sticks," but this is
no guarantee of origin, because glass manufacturers were remarkably efficient in distributing
their goods to the most remote areas.[3]

1. Gilpin Invoice Book, pp. 15, 17, HSP; December 23, 1831,
entry, Chapman-Baker Day Book, p. 19, MdHS.
2. Prices Current, South Boston, 1819, Edison Inst.
3. McKearin and McKearin, *American Glass*, p. 283, pl. 123,
no. 2; Gest to du Pont, March 31, 1947, WM.

57, 58

TUMBLERS

PROBABLY MASSACHUSETTS,
1825–40

NO. 57. Colorless lead glass. Blown. Cylindrical form blown in 3-part mold of geometric design (McKearin G IV-3): a band of pointed arches with 2 branches extending up between each arch; the bottom patterned with diamonds (type II); pontil mark.
H: 3¼ in (8.2 cm); Diam top: 3 in (7.6 cm)
Museum purchase, 1983: The Stradlings, New York City
83.2

NO. 58. Colorless lead glass. Blown. Cylindrical form blown in 3-part mold of geometric design (McKearin G IV-2): a band of rounded arches with fan motif extending up between each arch; the bottom patterned with diamonds (type XIII); pontil mark.
H: 3⅝ in (9.2 cm); Diam top: 3⅛ in (8.0 cm)
History: Hugh W. Kelly, Lancaster, Pa.
Gift of Mrs. Hugh W. Kelly, 1987
87.121

In 1826 Boston and Sandwich Glass Company sold fifteen dozen "flute and pinetree" tumblers for $3 a dozen—a price that indicates they were cut.[1] Fragments of glass unearthed from the factory site demonstrate that the company also manufactured cheaper mold-blown versions of that pattern, such as NO. 58. The Sandwich "arch and pinetree" molded wares included decanters and tumblers, perhaps like NO. 57.

Glasshouses outside of New England produced similar tumblers: in 1830 in Philadelphia, Union Flint Glass Works sold "flute & tree" tumblers for 50¢ a dozen, a price that indicates they were mold-blown and not cut.[2] Perhaps not coincidentally the blowers at this factory included several who had worked in the Boston area.

Although mold-blown glass was inexpensive, the metal molds were costly and carefully executed. In these examples heavy outlines on the recessed arches enhance the three-dimensional, pseudo-cut effect.

NO. 57 reflects a taste for the Gothic style that was fashionable in the second quarter of the nineteenth century. In this pattern the forked branches, sprouting from the spandrels of the arches, almost meet to create a double-arch effect. Although a cut-glass design may have provided inspiration, no exact prototype has been located. In NO. 58 the decoration between the flutes or Roman arches is a fan-shape motif that relates more closely to cut-glass designs such as on NOS. 26 and 63.

1. Boston and Sandwich Glass Company to J. Waldren, September 1, 1826, Rakow Library, Corning Museum. In the accounts of James Cunningham there is an entry for Sandwich-made "flint cut Pine Tree Tumblers," some 7 dozen for $21.25, or $3.00/dozen, confirming the price for cut tumblers of this style; Cunningham Account Book, p. 36, Edison Inst.
2. Invoice, December 29, 1830, Gilpin Invoice Book, p. 29, HSP. A dozen "cut" tumblers, by contrast, cost the Gilpins $1.75 on December 2, 1828.

59

TUMBLER

OHIO OR WESTERN
PENNSYLVANIA, 1820–50

Pale amethyst lead glass. Blown. Tapered form, pattern
molded with 24 vertical ribs; pontil mark.
H: 3¾ in (9.6 cm); Diam top: 3 in (7.6 cm)
H. F. du Pont purchase, 1948: Neil C. Gest, Mechanicsburg,
Ohio
59.3007

Students of American glass have tried to pinpoint the origins of rib-molded wares based on
the slim evidence of fragments found at factory
sites or surviving objects with histories. Harry
Hall White dug sites in Ohio and drew up a classification based on the number of ribs or diamonds, while Rhea Mansfield Knittle focused on
above-ground archaeology in tracking down
glass in local families and tracing the histories of
the Ohio factories in early newspapers and other
documentary sources. Glass molded with 16 or
32 ribs was attributed to Mantua; 20-rib specimens were thought to be from Kent, and those
with 24 ribs, from Zanesville. An 1816 advertisement for Zanesville Glass Works (one of the few

for an Ohio glasshouse but typically unin-
structive) notified the public that a "large and
general assortment of White Hollow-ware" was
on hand. The following year the factory was
offered for sale, and prospective buyers were
assured that among the assets were "all the
moulds of the best and newest fashions."[1]

"White" was a period term used to describe
clear, colorless glass, yet much surviving
rib-molded midwestern glass occurs in aqua,
green, or amber, colors that reveal the bottle-
glass orientation of most of the factories. The
rare amethyst color of NO. 59 and its lead formula, indicate this tumbler came from a table
glass factory, possibly in Pittsburgh where
there was a strong emphasis on pattern-
molded, flint tablewares.

1. Harry Hall White, "The Story of the Mantua Glass
Works," *Antiques* 28, no. 5 (November 1935): 199–203;
Rhea Mansfield Knittle, "Zanesville Glass," *Antiques* 22,
no. 6 (December 1932): 224–28; *Western Courier*
(Louisville, Ky.), January 24, 1816, reference courtesy of
Mr. and Mrs. J. G. Stradling; *New Hampshire Gazette*,
May 20, 1817, quoted in "The Editor's Attic: Regarding
Zanesville Glass," *Antiques* 40, no. 3 (September 1941):
163.

60

TUMBLER

PITTSBURGH, BAKEWELL, PAGE,
AND BAKEWELL, CIRCA 1821

Colorless lead glass. Blown. Tapered form; thick base; cut
8-point star on bottom. Cut decoration: diamonds over
flutes. Wheel engraved: on one side, a cipher "VB" beneath
floral swags; on the other, a reclining greyhound chained
to an urn surmounted by a pair of birds; rosebushes and
leafy sprays between.
H: 3⅜ in (8.6 cm); Diam top: 3⅛ in (8.0 cm)
History: Victorine du Pont Bauduy; descended in the
du Pont family
Gift of Mrs. E. du Pont Irving, 1955
55.4

Exhibited: National Gallery of Art, "In Praise of America,"
1980.
Published: Innes, *Pittsburgh Glass*, pp. 120–21, figs. 69–71.
Karol A. Schmiegel, "Tokens of Friendship," *Antiques* 115,
no. 2 (February 1979): 369, figs. 2, 3.
Wendy A. Cooper, *In Praise of America* (New York: Alfred
A. Knopf, 1980), p. 155, no. 176.

This tumbler is important because of its documentation to the Pittsburgh factory of Bakewell,
Page, and Bakewell and because of the information known about its giver and recipient. The
initials are those of Victorine du Pont Bauduy
(1791–1860), daughter of Eleuthère Irénée
du Pont, founder of what was to become E. I.
du Pont de Nemours & Co. She was the great-
aunt of Henry Francis du Pont. The glass was a
gift to Victorine from her teacher and friend
Antoinette Brevost (1790–1823) whom Victorine
had met at Madame Rivardi's seminary in
Philadelphia. In 1814 Antoinette moved to Pittsburgh and taught at a girls school established
there by her parents. She continued to correspond with Victorine, and the two women ex-
changed numerous gifts.[1]

In Pittsburgh the Brevost family knew the
Bakewells socially, and, as Antoinette wrote in
1820, "Our back windows overlook Mr.
Bakewell's glass house." Antoinette selected this
tumbler "of Mr. Bakewell's manufacture" in the
spring of 1821 and sent it as a gift to Victorine,
in Wilmington, who on at least one occasion
used it to hold some birthday flowers.

Victorine was curious about the design of
the tumbler, and Antoinette hastened to assure
her: "The engravings on your tumbler was not
designed by me . . . I could not have had time to
do anything of the kind if even I had had the

capacity." She went on to say, "I saw a great many other or[n]amented glasses at Mr. Bakewells, most of which had like this one a place for a cypher. I found this very convenient and Mr. Bakewells' engraver is so expeditious that in the course of the same afternoon your cypher was put on."

The main element of the design is the recumbent greyhound chained to an urn on a pedestal upon which two doves are perched. A symbol of fidelity in love, this motif is also seen in European glass of the period (NO. 61).[2] That the Bakewell engraver did turn to European prototypes for this pattern is suggested by Anne Royall's observations of the Bakewell operation in 1829:

> The patterns are mostly obtained from Europe, and the pattern executed when I was in, for beauty and taste, was exquisite, particularly a greyhound with its head erect as though looking at something and though not an inch in length it was perfect and entire, the eyes, ears, nose being life itself.[3]

The comment also indicates that the greyhound design was in the repertory for a number of years. According to Royall, such engraved glassware was expensive, sometimes $5 per tumbler.

In its arrangement of cut diamonds over flutes, the Bauduy tumbler relates to another Bakewell greyhound tumbler.[4] Other examples have only flutes below the scene (NO. 64).

NO. 60 was made at a time when Bakewell, like other glass manufacturers, was struggling to compete with European imports. As he reported in 1820, the value of his firm's product slipped from $100,000 in 1815 to $20,000 in 1820 because of the "incessant importations of foreign glass and the sales of it at auction much below its intrinsic value." Bakewell's plight and push for a protective tariff was championed in the press by others. In a communique to the editor of *American Farmer*, a concerned American patriotically averred that Bakewell's manufactory "furnishes glass superior to any that I have ever seen imported from England, and assuredly at less price. The fine cutting, polishing, and engraving surpass in execution, all I have ever seen. My good sir, . . . do we purchase imported cloth and glass, and a hundred other things imported which we could have better made at home?"[5]

Even allowing for cultural chauvinism, a favorable comparison can be drawn between Bakewell's fine glass and that of Europe because most of the Bakewell cutters and engravers had been trained abroad. Some had come from England, and at least one, Alexander Jardelle, was of French origin. When Thomas Bakewell traveled abroad in 1816 to seek workmen for the Pittsburgh glasshouses, he reported the willingness of Parisian glass decorators to emigrate, noting that if Mr. [Benjamin] Bakewell were here, "he might by giving them some rich work as well as common to do, have all the glasscutters in Paris."[6]

1. Karol A. Schmiegel, "Tokens of Friendship," *Antiques* 115, no. 2 (February 1979): 367–69. Quotes in this entry from the Brevost-Bauduy correspondence are taken from this article.
2. For a Portuguese example, see Vasco Valente, *O Vidro em Portugal* (Pôrto: Portucalense Editora, 1950), figs. 69, 70.
3. Quoted in Innes, *Pittsburgh Glass*, p. 118.
4. The Reynolds tumbler, presented to William Reynolds of Meadville, Pa., by Benjamin Bakewell (collection of the Historical Society of Western Pennsylvania) is in Innes, *Pittsburgh Glass*, pp. 116–17, figs. 65–66.
5. 1820 Census of Manufactures, s.v. "Pennsylvania"; see also Arlene Palmer Schwind, "Hard Times in 1820," *Glass Club Bulletin*, no. 147 (Fall 1985): 14–16. Letter to Mr. [John] Skinner, ed., "Occasional Extracts," *American Farmer* (Baltimore) 1, no. 34 (November 19, 1819): 273.
6. Thomas C. Pears III, "Sidelights on the History of the Bakewell, Pears and Company from the letters of Thomas and Sarah Pears," *Western Pennsylvania Historical Magazine* 31, nos. 3–4 (September–December 1948): 63.

61

TUMBLER
FRANCE, 1815–35

Colorless lead glass. Blown. Waisted beaker form; polished base. Cut flutes around lower body. Wheel engraved: on one side, greyhound seated near altar surmounted by 2 hearts; on opposite side, "LA / FIDELITE" flanked by flowers.
H: 3¹³⁄₁₆ in (9.7 cm); Diam top: 3⅜ in (8.6 cm)
Museum purchase, 1978: Christie, Manson & Woods, London
78.197

Published: Christie, Manson & Woods, "Important English and Continental Glass," sale no. 1125 (October 3, 1978), lot 125.

The waisted shape of NO. 61 is typical of Continental production; the language of the inscription and the lead glass composition point to a French origin. The engraved design of this tumbler relates to that of the preceding American example (NO. 60), but the greyhound is less competently rendered and the marital symbol-ism is reinforced with an inscription. A similar scene is recorded on a marriage tumbler made in 1811 by the Saint-Louis factory in Lorraine.[1]

Some glass of French manufacture was exported to America after the period of the Napoleonic wars. In Pittsburgh, for example, merchant Nathaniel Richardson notified the public that he had "french cut glass" for sale.[2]

1. James Barrelet, *La verrerie en France: De l'époque Gallo-Romaine à nos jours*, Arts, Styles, et Techniques series, ed. Norbert Dufourcq (Paris: Librairie Larousse, 1953), pl. 65.
2. Richardson advertisement, *Pittsburgh Mercury*, May 17, 1817, reference courtesy of Mr. and Mrs. J. G. Stradling.

62

TUMBLER
UNITED STATES OR ENGLAND,
DATED 1824

Colorless lead glass. Blown. Short cylindrical form, thick base; polished bottom with central concavity. Wheel engraved: script initials "RWV" above "June 25.th / 1824."
H: 3³⁄₁₆ in (8.2 cm); Diam top: 3 in (7.5 cm)
Museum purchase, 1978
78.84

Because tumblers were among the chief products of every fine glass factory in England and the United States, it is impossible to pinpoint the origin of this particular example. Some factories had decorating shops where custom engraving would be executed, but in many cities and towns, glass engravers worked independently. The engraving here is obviously of commemorative significance, perhaps marking a birth, wedding, or death.

63–65

TUMBLERS

PITTSBURGH, BAKEWELL, PAGE, AND BAKEWELL, CIRCA 1825

NO. 63 (one of two). Colorless lead glass; white clay (sulphide). Blown. Cylindrical form with thick base; polished bottom. Cut decoration: strawberry-diamonds with tall fans between; above two horizontal rings and paneled base. Wheel engraved: "MAS" within a vine of leafy-stemmed roses; the same vine encircles the rim. Embedded in the base, a sulphide profile portrait: (.1) Benjamin Franklin facing right; (.2) George Washington facing left.
H: 3⅜ in (8.6 cm); Diam top: 2⅞ in (7.3 cm)
Museum purchase, 1957: Louis Lyons, New York City
57.76.1 (mate is 57.76.2)

Exhibited: National Gallery of Art, "In Praise of America," 1980.
Published: Advertisement of Louis Lyons, *Antiques* 72, no. 4 (October 1957): 300.
Palmer, "American Heroes," p. 15, fig. 15.
Wendy A. Cooper, *In Praise of America* (New York: Alfred A. Knopf, 1980), p. 155, no. 177.

NO. 64. Colorless lead glass; white clay (sulphide). Blown. Cylindrical form, slightly curved in at base; polished bottom. Cut decoration: narrow flutes around the base. Wheel engraved: around the body, a seated dog, basket of flowers, altar surmounted by 2 birds and blank shield; around the rim, leafy-stemmed roses. Embedded in the base, a sulphide portrait of Benjamin Franklin facing right.
H: 3¼ in (8.3 cm); Diam top: 3 in (7.6 cm)
Museum purchase, 1978: Philip H. Bradley Company, Downingtown, Pa. Funds for purchase, gift of Mrs. Alfred P. Harrison
78.30

Published: Palmer, "American Heroes," pp. 14, 15, figs. 14, 16.

NO. 65. Colorless lead glass, crizzled; white clay (sulphide). Blown. Cylindrical form; thick base; polished bottom. Cut decoration: strawberry-diamonds set off with horizontal rings from short blaze cuts above and wide panels below. Embedded in the base, a sulphide profile portrait of George Washington facing left.
H: 3¼ in (8.3 cm); Diam top: 3 in (7.7 cm)
History: Hugh W. Kelly, Lancaster, Pa.
Gift of Mrs. Hugh W. Kelly, 1987
87.128

In his March 19, 1825, issue of *Weekly Register*, Hezekiah Niles reported on a display in a Baltimore shop of a

> novel, curious, and elegant specimen of American industry and talent, from the glass making establishment of Messrs. Bakewell, Page and Bakewell, of Pittsburg. It consists of cut-glass tumblers, in the bottom of each of which, by a very ingenious process is embedded an excellent likeness of some distinguished American citizen, as Adams, Jackson, Lafayette, &c. The likeness is formed of a composition having the appearance of silver, and although presented in bold relief, every part of it is enclosed in solid glass, and is, consequently, indelible.[1]

The process that Niles so admired was known in the period as cameo incrustation, and it was inspired by interest in the gemstone cameos and medals of ancient Rome. Cameo incrustation was perfected in England and France between 1812 and 1818 and enjoyed its greatest vogue from that time into the 1830s. Scholars of the late nineteenth century believed that the silvery-looking substance of the images or cameos was silver sulphide, hence the name sulphide became attached to the technique. In fact, the cameos were of white clay paste cast in molds and baked to hardness.

Probably the first method developed to encase the cameo was that described by Pierre Honoré Boudon de Saint-Amans in 1818:

> Prepare a copper mold, whose size and depth depends upon the size and thickness of the cameo. . . . The first workman pours in molten crystal from his dipper; a second levels the surface with his copper palette knife and puts in the cameo, face downwards; a third workman pours more molten crystal on the back of the cameo, which is thus between two layers of crystal; the second man with his palette knife gently presses the mass in the mold. An apprentice carries the hot mold in a pair of tongs to the oven. Two minutes' baking generally is sufficient to set the crystal.[2]

Another process is illustrated in Apsley Pellatt's *Curiosities of Glass Making* (London, 1849). The gather of glass was opened with pucellas, creating an air pocket into which the cameo was inserted. The glassblower then collapsed the air bubble over the image by inhaling on the blowpipe. Great skill was required at this step to ensure that no bubbles remained around the cameo.

That cameo incrustation was practiced in Pittsburgh attests to the determination of United States glass manufacturers to compete with European goods. Compared to the French and English examples (NO. 417), however, Bakewell's versions look gray, and air bubbles detract from the clarity of the portraits. Bakewell's used the Saint-Amans technique in making a sulphide mantel ornament.[3] The basal cutting of the tumblers obscures any seams that would indicate whether that technique was also followed in the production of sulphide tumblers.

Although likenesses of Franklin and Washington were not specified by Niles, the Winterthur tumblers are unquestionably of Bakewell production: there is no evidence that any other American glasshouse made sulphide glasses prior to 1850. The Bakewell firm is not named, but it was certainly the source of the "extensive assortment of plain and cut flint glassware," including "double flint cut tumblers containing medalions of Washington, LaFayette, &c.," offered at auction in Philadelphia by J. and W. Lippincott, March 22, 1825.[4] This auction notice and Niles's description are also important because they prove that the Pittsburgh manufacturers marketed their glass on the East Coast.

In their cut and engraved decoration, NOS. 63–65 relate closely to tumblers containing sulphides of Lafayette and Jackson and other tumblers that are documented to the Pittsburgh concern. The leaves engraved around the rims of NOS. 63 and 64, for example, are of the same style and execution as those on NO. 60 to the right of the greyhound. NO. 65 has no engraved decoration, but it documents to the Bakewell endeavor another cut pattern, one that features diagonal or blaze cutting above a wide band of strawberry-diamonds.

The Franklin portraits here were taken either from a Sèvres porcelain plaque first produced in 1778 or its jasperware counterpart by Josiah Wedgwood. Bakewell also produced a different sulphide portrait of Franklin from the Franklin Institute medal awarded to the glassworks in 1825 (NO. 416). One tumbler has the image placed on the side rather than in the bottom of the vessel.[5]

The Washington portraits were derived from a medal recorded in Snowden's catalogue of the collection of the United States Mint, probably from the design of Christian Gobrecht, a Phila-

delphia engraver and die-sinker. Identical portraits are in a decorative plaque (NO. 415), two mantel ornaments, and another three tumblers.[6]

Glasswares of patriotic intent, whether expensive tumblers like these or cheap, mold-blown pocket bottles (NOS. 386–90), very much reflected the self-conscious pride of a nation approaching the fiftieth anniversary of its independence. Washington and Franklin were the favorite icons of the age: in the words of a toast offered to their memory on New Year's Day, 1825, "Nature cast them in a gigantic mould, to be founders of a mighty Republic."[7]

1. *Niles' Weekly Register* 28, no. 705 (March 19, 1825), p. 34.
2. Saint-Amans quoted in Paul Hollister, Jr., *The Encyclopedia of Glass Paperweights* (New York: Bramhall House, 1969), p. 256.
3. Dean M. Zimmerman, "On the Cover," *Glass Club Bulletin*, no. 158 (Spring 1989): cover, 2, 16.
4. *Poulson's American Daily Advertiser*, March 9, 1825, reference courtesy of Susan H. Myers. A Lafayette sulphide tumbler (National Museum of American History) is in Palmer, "American Heroes," p. 4, fig. 1; p. 10, fig. 8.
5. Palmer, "American Heroes," p. 6, figs. 2–3; Corning Museum, gift of Jerome Strauss.
6. James Ross Snowden, *A Description of the Medals of Washington . . . in the Museum of the Mint* (Philadelphia: Lippincott, 1861), pl. 6, no. 14; Palmer, "American Heroes," p. 23, fig. 23.
7. Yardleyville, Pa., *Bucks County Patriot* (Doylestown), January 31, 1825.

66–68

TUMBLERS

PROBABLY BOHEMIA, POSSIBLY
ENGRAVED IN PHILADELPHIA,
1830–40

Colorless nonlead glass. Blown. Thick cylindrical form,
recessed plain rim; bottom cut with 24 shaped rays. Cut
decoration: one side, pillar cuts below 3 double swags
supporting field of small diamonds; on the other, a
crosshatched frame; base cut with quartered diamonds.
Wheel engraved within frame: Philadelphia buildings, each
identified with inscription beneath: NO. 66, "GIRARDS BANK
/ in Philadelphia"; NO. 67, "SWEDISH LUTHERAN CHURCH /
in Philadelphia"; NO. 68, "UNIVERSITY / in Philadelphia."
H: (NOS. 66, 67) 4⅜ in (11.1 cm); Diam top: 3⅛ in (7.9 cm)
H: (NO. 68) 4⁷⁄₁₆ in (11.2 cm); Diam top: 3³⁄₁₆ in (8.1 cm)
NOS. 66, 67: Gift of George R. Clark, 1977
77.165.1, .2

NO. 68: Museum purchase, 1976: The Stradlings, New York
City. Funds for purchase, gift of the Claneil Foundation
76.7
Published: (NO. 67) Smith and Hummel, "Winterthur
Museum," p. 1282.
(NO. 68) Jane Shadel Spillman, "Glasses with American
Views," *Journal of Glass Studies* 19 (1977): 135, fig. 5.

These tumblers are among eight known with
different views of Philadelphia.[1] The scenes were
copied from C. G. Childs's 1829 *Views in Philadelphia and Its Environs from Original Drawings
Taken in 1827–30.* The drawings were first printed
separately and then published in book form in
1830. George Strickland executed the original
drawings for the university and the bank, while
the view of the church was rendered by Thomas
Sully. The glass engraver closely copied the
buildings but excluded human figures.

The tumblers fall into a larger group of Continental glasses with United States views that are
generally believed to have been produced abroad
on American order.[2] The recessed rim and pillar
and swag cutting (which forms a backdrop for
the scene) are characteristic of Bohemian glasses
of the early nineteenth century, as is the nonlead
composition. Although the Philadelphia subject
matter has given rise to suggestions that the
tumblers were manufactured at Union Flint
Glass Works, that factory, like the other "flint
glass" factories of America in the 1830s, probably
made lead glass.[3]

Another possibility is that the tumblers were
cut as blanks in Europe and were engraved in
Philadelphia by one or more of the twenty-five
glasscutters who lived in that city during the
1830s. "Glasscutter" applied to decorative cutters, engravers, and those who cut windowpanes. In the 1833 directory Joseph Myring is
listed as a glasscutter, but in earlier directory
entries, he is variously described as a glass and
seal cutter, a lapidary, and a lapidary and engraver on glass. Myring detailed his services in
an 1810 newspaper advertisement:

> He also Engraves on Glass, any inscription
> that may be wanted; and all kinds of Fancy
> Borders, Flowers, Birds, Cyphers, &c. &c. on
> Large Passage Lamps, Decanters, Goblets,
> Wine Glass, &c. Storekeepers may have their
> Glass Engraved. . . . Housekeepers may have
> their Plain Glass Engraved, to what pattern
> they choose, at his manufactory, No. 45,
> North Third street.[4]

Whoever was responsible for the engraving
on the tumblers was fairly proficient in his art.
Philadelphia's landmarks are rendered with a
good sense of perspective and a remarkable
amount of architectural detail. The windows are
polished for a glistening effect that is charming.
Some of the details may originally have been
highlighted with gilding.

The Bank of the United States was built
1795–97 and was immediately hailed as an architectural triumph in America's premier city, "An
elegant exhibition of simple grandeur and chaste
magnificence." Congress failed to renew its char-
ter in 1811, and the building was purchased by

Stephen Girard for a private banking establishment. It was known as "Girard's Bank" until
1862. Erected between 1698 and 1700, Gloria Dei
(Old Swedes') Church stands as testament to the
early Swedish settlement of the Delaware River
valley. The University of Pennsylvania acquired
the impressive mansion engraved on NO. 68
in 1800. The building had been intended as a
residence for the nation's presidents, but John
Adams declined to live in it, and the capital
soon moved to Washington. Benjamin H.
Latrobe altered the interior for the university's
use and added the wing to the left to house the
medical department. Known as the "President's
House," it was demolished in 1829.[5]

1. The other Philadelphia views are the Widow and
Orphan's Asylum, Sedgeley Park (Corning Museum);
Bank of Pennsylvania (Metropolitan Museum of Art);
Pennsylvania Academy of Fine Arts and Bank of the
United States (private collections); see Jane Shadel
Spillman, "Glasses with American Views," *Journal of Glass
Studies* 19 (1977): 134–35.
2. Spillman, "Glasses with American Views," pp. 134–46.
3. Kenneth M. Wilson, "Union Flint Glass Works
(1826–44)," in Philadelphia Museum of Art, *Philadelphia:
Three Centuries of American Art* (Philadelphia, 1976),
nos. 252a–b, pp. 296–97. Several cut-glass objects from this
period have been attributed to the Union Works on the
basis of descent in the family of a glasscutter known to
have been employed there. They are all of lead-formula
glass. Kenneth M. Wilson, "Cut Glass Lamps Attributed to
the Union Flint Glass Works, Kensington, Philadelphia,"
Journal of Glass Studies 25 (1983): 221–24. The composition
of the tumblers is similar to that of an opaque white vase
with painted Philadelphia view, see NO. 268.
4. Myring advertisement, *Aurora General Advertiser,*
June 6, 1810.
5. Philadelphia Museum of Art, *Philadelphia: Three
Centuries,* pp. 172–73, 11–12; Martin Meyerson and Dilys
Pegler Winegrad, *Gladly Learn and Gladly Teach* (Philadelphia: University of Pennsylvania, 1978), pp. 202–3,
reference courtesy of Amanda Lange.

66

67

68

68 (side)

69

TUMBLER
FRANCE, 1825–55

Colorless lead glass with blue-white tint. Blown pressure-molded. Cylindrical form; recessed rim; rounded pillars separate 6 panels of relief decoration containing circular motifs at the top and 3 drapes or scales falling beneath, the lowest forming a foot; rayed bottom.
H: 3⁹⁄₁₆ in (9.0 cm); Diam top: 2¹⁵⁄₁₆ in (7.5 cm)
Museum purchase, 1981: W. M. Schwind, Jr., Antiques, Yarmouth, Maine
81.74

This tumbler was fashioned by a pressure-blown technique by which the glass was mechanically blown into a full-size mold. The technique was introduced in the early 1820s by Ismael Robinet of the Baccarat glassworks in France. He invented a pump or piston that attached to the mouthpiece of the blowpipe and created a pressure to inflate the gather of glass at the other end and force it evenly against the walls of a mold. Because this invention spared the lungs of the glassblowers, Robinet was hailed for his contribution to the health of the workers.

Blown pressure-molded tableware, known as *moulé en plein*, is differentiated in several ways from mechanically pressed glass and from glass blown into a mold by a gaffer. It is much heavier in weight. On the exterior of the vessel, the design is deep and sharply defined, having almost a carved appearance. The interior surface ware has a tactile, corresponding design on the interior surface, unlike pressed glass, but this design is less pronounced than that on gaffer blown-molded glassware. Pressure-molded glasses generally received additional handwork, such as the grounding and polished rims, and on occasion, decorative cutting.[1]

The trade catalogue of Parisian glass merchants Launay, Hautin, et Cie. illustrates this pattern as "Service Moulé à draperies." Although the catalogue dates from about 1840, the drapery pattern was made as early as 1834.[2]

Drapery pattern tumblers may have been made even in the preceding decade, because such a tumbler was supposedly Deming Jarves's first essay in pressed glass at Boston and Sandwich Glass Company in 1827. According to the *Crockery and Glass Journal*, "So great was the indignation of the glass blowers at the time against Mr. Jarvis' 'new invention,' that his life was threatened, and he was obliged to seclude himself for more than two months, and it was nearly one year before he dare venture out after nightfall."[3]

Through the efforts of F. C. Sieman and John A. Dobson & Co., that first pressed tumbler was shown at the Centennial Exposition in Philadelphia as part of the display of J. H. Hobbs, Brockunier, and Company of Wheeling, along with a letter in which Jarves described the reaction to this invention. Hobbs may have fared little better than Jarves; he had the misfortune to drop and smash the historic tumbler during centennial ceremonies. The design of the famed tumbler survives in a drawing by Thomas Gaffield, a merchant and window glass manufacturer who had a keen interest in the history of New England's glass industry.[4]

All of the tumblers currently recorded in this pattern are of the French pressure-molded type and are not pressed.

1. Miriam E. Mucha, "Mechanization, French Style Cristaux, Moulés en Plein," *Glass Club Bulletin*, no. 126 (September 1979): 3–8.
2. Spillman, *Pressed Glass*, p. 30, fig. 3; Mucha, "Mechanization," p. 7.
3. *Crockery and Glass Journal* (April 3, 1875): 6.
4. Ruth Webb Lee, *Sandwich Glass* (3d ed., Framingham Centre, Mass.: By the author, 1939), p. 83. Lura Woodside Watkins, "Deming Jarves and the Pressing of Glass," *Antiques* 20, no. 4 (October 1931): 220.

70

TUMBLER

SANDWICH, MASSACHUSETTS, BOSTON AND SANDWICH GLASS COMPANY, ENGRAVED AND POSSIBLY CUT BY JOHN M. L. BADGER, DATED 1844

Colorless lead glass. Blown. Cylindrical form; thick base; flat bottom cut with 16-point star; beveled edge. Cut decoration: between 2 horizontal, triangular bands is a field of miter-diamonds with cross-cut points, surrounding a large shield cut on one side. Engraved in diamond-point within shield, memorial urn and inscription, "Mary Masters / Aged 101 Years / And 3 Month / Died July / 4th 1844." Below, on the foot rim, in similar, smaller script is engraved, "John M. L. Badger / Glass Cutter / Sandwich Mass."
H: 4⅞ in (12.4 cm); Diam top: 3½ in (8.9 cm)
Museum purchase, 1967: Robert Carlen, Philadelphia
67.233

Published: Edith Gaines, ed., "Collectors' Notes: Signed Sandwich," *Antiques* 102, no. 2 (August 1972): 270.

Handsomely cut, this tumbler was doubtless made for stock with a blank shield to be wheel engraved to the order of the purchaser. John M. L. Badger's responsibility for the amateurish diamond-point memorial decoration is inferred from his signature. He called himself a glasscutter, so he may also have executed the considerably more successful diamond pattern and shield; however, the records of the Sandwich factory contain no mention of an employee of this name, even though a John Badger is called a glassblower in the Sandwich census of 1850.

Genealogical records reveal that the remarkably long-lived Mary Masters, who died on her nation's birthday, was the grandmother of Badger (d. 1872). Her daughter, Mary, married Nathaniel Badger. They had two children, Elmira and John M. L. In 1836 Elmira married Francis Kern, a scion of a well-known family of artisans associated with Boston and Sandwich. Their daughter, also named Elmira, wed her first cousin, Gustavus Adolphus Badger, the son of John M. L. Badger and his wife, Mary A. Collins.[1]

Memorial glassware is rather rare in American production, although glass had a role in the rituals of mourning. Those grieving the loss of a loved one often drowned their sorrows with alcoholic beverages served in glass vessels. At the funeral of Peter Jacob Marinus in seventeenth-century New York, mourners consumed twenty-nine gallons of wine—and broke 3s. 7d. worth of glassware in the process.[2]

1. I am grateful to Russell A. Lovell, Jr., and Martha Hassell of Sandwich Glass Museum for providing information about the Badger and Masters families. Christina Nelson kindly checked for Badger in the Boston and Sandwich factory records at Edison Inst.
2. Hewson L. Peeke, *Americana Ebrietatis: The Favorite Tipple of Our Forefathers and the Laws and Customs Relating Thereto* (1917; reprint, New York: Hacker Books, 1970), p. 124.

71

TUMBLER

NEW ENGLAND OR POSSIBLY PITTSBURGH, 1850–55

Colorless lead glass; white clay (sulphide). Blown. Cylindrical form; thick base; polished bottom. Wheel engraved leafy border and heart-shape wreath enclosing the script inscription "Jeny Lind." Embedded in the base, a sulphide profile portrait of Madame Sévigné.
H: 3⁹/₁₆ in (9.0 cm); Diam top: 3⅛ in (7.9 cm)
Museum purchase, 1978: The Stradlings, New York City 78.43

Published: Palmer, "American Heroes," pp. 24–25, figs. 24–25.

This tumbler has a sulphide portrait embedded in its base in the same manner as the Bakewell examples of the 1820s (NOS. 63–65); however, its commemoration of Jenny Lind, the Swedish singer, suggests it was made and engraved around 1851 when Lind made a grand tour through America.

What is of particular interest is that the portrait is not of Jenny Lind but of Marie de Rabutin-Chantal Sévigné (1626–96), a French aristocrat whose published correspondence with her daughter was widely read in the nineteenth century.

Cast from a medal designed by Raymond Gayrard in 1816, Sévigné's sulphide is recorded in French glass plaques and tumblers of the 1820s and 1830s.[1] The portrait here has gouge marks on the underside, suggesting that the sulphide maker's name may have been impressed there (see NO. 417) and removed. The word Sévigné was partially obliterated from the shoulder, further indicating that the glassmaker planned to use the sulphide to represent someone else—like Jenny Lind. Hence the tumbler would seem to be contemporary with the Swedish star's tour. Manufacturers hastened to profit from the popularity of Lind as she sang her way across the country. Glassmakers offered thirteen different commemorative designs in mold-blown bottles (NO. 394). (Four spell Jenny with only one *n* as on Winterthur's tumbler.) A Portsmouth merchant purchased from Boston and Sandwich Glass Factory some "J. Lind dishes" and "Jane Lind dec[an]t[er]s," the exact appearance of which is unknown. As late as the 1870s glass manufacturers continued to list "Lind" patterns in their trade catalogues. In Pittsburgh, for example, M'Kee and Brothers offered a "Lind" tumbler pressed in a geometric pattern of pointed arches below flutes.[2]

It is curious that the maker of NO. 71 turned to a decorative technique that had been in fashion for drinking vessels more than twenty years before. By the 1850s sulphides were commonly limited to paperweights (NOS. 275–78) and marbles. A notable exception was the Scottish firm of John Ford, which continued to produce expensive tablewares embellished in this manner. Although the Bakewell factory is the only documented maker of sulphide tumblers in the United States, other American factories may have been making sulphide paperweights in the third quarter of the nineteenth century (see NO. 277). New England Glass Company had a strong interest in glass portraiture in this period, using an intaglio technique to commemorate Queen Victoria and Prince Albert and the Lawrence brothers, yet no sulphides have been documented to that factory. Similar wreaths appear on New England Glass Company products, but it was a conventional device of the glass engraver.[3]

Whoever made the tumbler experienced the same technical difficulties as the earlier Bakewell craftsmen in removing the air around the cameo. The quality of the glass is rather poor, but not surprising given the souvenir nature of the product.

1. Paul Jokelson, *Sulphides: The Art of Cameo Incrustation* (New York: Galahad Books, 1968), p. 93, fig. 95; Museum der Stadt Regensburg, *Gläser: Antike, Mittelalter Neuere Zeit* (Karlsruhe: Corona-Verlag Karl Heine, Sammlung Brauser, 1977), p. 152, no. 316.
2. John Sise invoice as quoted in Wilson, *New England Glass*, p. 294; *M'Kee Glass*, pp. 16, 24, 49, 85, 150, 184.
3. Watkins, *Cambridge Glass*, pl. 30.

72

MUG

UNITED STATES, PROBABLY NEW JERSEY, 1865–1910

Aqua glass. Blown. Narrow, cylindrical body; applied double-ribbed handle; pontil mark. Body blown in 2-part mold: 4 sets of horizontal ribs divide the body; opposite the handle the inscription in relief letters, "W. E. BONNEY." Crack next to top of handle.
H: 5¼ in (13.1 cm); Diam top: 3½ in (9.0 cm)
H. F. du Pont purchase
64.907

Published: William E. Covill, Jr., *Ink Bottles and Inkwells* (Taunton, Mass.: William S. Sullwold, 1971), p. 150, fig. 662.

For the ink he manufactured in South Hanover, Massachusetts, William E. Bonney engaged a bottle glass factory, probably in New Jersey, to make barrel-shape glass containers. The bottle not only simulated the shape of a barrel, but it also had rings in imitation of barrel hoops. The Bonney ink barrel is recorded in four sizes from two ounces to one quart.[1] To create this unusual drinking vessel a glassblower used the ink-bottle mold and added a handle.

1. McKearin and Wilson, *American Bottles*, pp. 268, 278–79, ill. 76, no. 13. William E. Covill, Jr., *Ink Bottles and Inkwells* (Taunton, Mass.: William S. Sullwold, 1971), pp. 147–48.

Chapter 3
Teawares

Although sugar bowls and cream jugs are the glass forms most readily associated with the consumption of tea, the primary vessels required for this hot beverage—teapots, tea canisters, and cups and saucers—were occasionally fabricated of glass in the eighteenth century. Most extant examples are blown of opaque white glass and painted in the manner of porcelain. Continental European glasshouses apparently produced more glass teawares than did their English counterparts. Glass teawares other than sugar bowls, creamers, and cup plates are virtually unknown in American production.

Brought from China along with porcelains and silks, tea became a popular beverage in England during the second half of the seventeenth century and by the 1690s was available, at considerable expense, in New England. When he visited the United States in 1781, the Abbé Claude Robin observed that Americans "use much tea," and that "the greatest mark of civility and welcome they can show you is to invite you to drink it with them."[1]

1. Quoted in Rodris Roth, "Tea Drinking in Eighteenth-Century America: Its Etiquette and Equipage," *United States National Museum Bulletin*, No. 225 (Washington, D.C.: Smithsonian Institution, 1961): 63.

73

TEAPOT

ENGLAND, 1730–45

Colorless lead glass. Blown. Body: globular form with short cylindrical neck, applied hollow curved spout and solid rounded loop handle with tooled terminal; 3 applied curved legs with relief-molded masks at top, paw feet; pontil mark. Cover: low, hemispherical top and straight sides, inset with wide flange pulled out to rest on edge of body; air hole; applied acorn finial containing 6 tears; interior pontil mark.
OH: 6³⁄₁₆ in (15.7 cm); L: 8¹⁄₁₆ in (20.5 cm)
Museum purchase, 1981
81.67a, b

Published: Alan Tillman Antiques, *Glass through the Ages* (Privately published, 1974), p. 21, no. 28.

Although glass hardly seems a practical substance for holding and serving hot liquids, manufacturers of the eighteenth century produced glass pots as well as cups and saucers for tea, coffee, and chocolate. Because porcelain was the favored material for such vessels, most glass teapots were imitatively fashioned of opaque white glass (NO. 75). Colorless glass examples are extremely rare.[1]

Winterthur's teapot features the cabriole legs, masks, and paw feet found in English ceramic teapots of the period. Glass cream jugs and salts (NO. 224) of similar decoration are known.[2] The acorn element is found in candle-

stick stems and other wares of the early eighteenth century.

Glass tea sets were advertised in Boston in 1732 by Rebecca Abbot.[3] The "white" glass teawares she stocked may have included teapots like this because *white* was a term for colorless glass.

1. An English cut-glass teapot, ca. 1760, is in W. A. Thorpe, "The Development of Cut-Glass in England and Ireland," pt. 1, *Antiques* 18, no. 4 (October 1930): 300, fig. 3. An engraved teapot of the 1760s was sold at Sotheby's, "English and Continental Glass from 1500–1960" (March 25, 1991), lot 65.
2. A related cream jug is shown in Buckley, *Old English Glass,* pl. 54.
3. Abbot advertisement, *New England Journal,* July 31, 1732, quoted in Wilson, *New England Glass,* p. 14.

74

TEACUP AND SAUCER

GERMANY OR BOHEMIA, 1740–75

Opalescent white glass. Blown. Teacup: circular form with curved sides, everted rim, applied foot ring; pontil mark. Saucer: circular form, with deeply curved sides, applied foot ring; pontil mark. Both with polychrome enamel-painted decoration that matches NO. 74. Traces of gilding on both.
H cup: 1⅝ in (4.1 cm); Diam saucer: 4³⁄₁₆ in (10.7 cm)
H. F. du Pont purchase, possibly 1937: possibly J. A. Lloyd Hyde, New York City
58.1431–.1432

75

TEAPOT

GERMANY OR BOHEMIA, 1740–75

Opalescent white glass. Blown. Body: globular shape with short, waisted neck, applied, hollow curved spout and solid rounded loop handle with tooled terminal; applied foot ring; pontil mark. Cover: hemispherical top and short, straight sides, inset with wide flange pulled out to rest on edge of body; drawn, pointed finial; interior pontil mark. Polychrome enamel-painted decoration: on each side of body a bird on a grassy nest with large floral sprays alongside; a bird painted below spout; decorative borders painted in red. On cover, floral sprays, with red dashes and rings.
OH: 5¾ in (14.7 cm); L: 7¼ in (18.6 cm)
H. F. du Pont purchase
58.1449a, b

76

TEACUP AND SAUCER

GERMANY OR BOHEMIA, 1740–75

Opalescent white glass. Blown. Teacup: circular form with sides curved in at base to applied foot ring; pontil mark. Saucer: circular form with curved sides, applied foot ring; pontil mark. Polychrome enamel-painted decoration: bold, floral design with red geometric border designs.
H cup: 1¾ in (4.4 cm); Diam saucer: 4¾ in (12.1 cm)
H. F. du Pont purchase
58.1433a, b

77

TEA BOTTLE

GERMANY OR BOHEMIA, 1740–75

Opalescent white glass. Blown. Rectangular body curved in at shoulder to short cylindrical neck; flat base with pontil mark. Polychrome enamel-painted decoration consisting of a bird and floral sprays.
H: 4⅛ in (10.55 cm); W: 2⅜ in (5.7 cm)
H. F. du Pont purchase, 1952: J. A. Lloyd Hyde, New York City
58.1448

The eighteenth century was the age of porcelain, with millions of Chinese porcelains exported to Europe, many shaped and decorated to Western order. European potters and princes alike became fascinated with unraveling the oriental secrets of porcelain production and porcelain factories were established all over Europe with varying degrees of success. Glassmakers were also influenced by "china mania" and offered "glass china" as a substitute for the real thing.

Continental glassmakers were more interested than their English counterparts in creating glass copies of the highly fashionable and rather expensive porcelain tewares. In reflected light these wares have the whiteness of porcelain, but under transmitted light they exhibit a fiery, red and blue opalescence that is characteristic of Continental "milk" glass. Although the ultimate

inspiration for such glass vessels must have been oriental porcelains, glassmakers may have actually copied their painted designs from German-made chinaware.

Glass teawares of this kind were apparently enjoyed in colonial America. At his death in 1734, Capt. James Pecker of Boston owned "3 painted Glass tea Cupps and Saucers and 1 Server," all valued at 7s.[1] Given the date, it is interesting to speculate that he had purchased them from Rebecca Abbot (see NO. 73) whose "Japanned Glass" tea sets must have been painted in an oriental style.

Glass tea bottles and canisters are recorded in colonial American household inventories and other records. In 1713 Mary Dickinson of Pennsylvania received as a gift from an English friend, "a German Cutt Glass kinester for Tea on the Tea table." Sometime later in the eighteenth century a family descendant, referring to this canister, wrote: "It is a singular fact, that Glass Vessels, so good to keep other substances will not keep Tea, but quite alters its taste; This was first observed to me by Charles Thomson Esqr and I have proved it to be so."[2] Elizabeth Davey may have come to the same conclusion; when appraisers inventoried her Maryland estate in 1782 they found "a little starch" in one of her glass tea bottles.[3] Certainly colorless glass was unsuitable because exposure to sunlight can alter the strength and taste of tea leaves. This may have been another reason that glassmakers made tea bottles of opaque glass.

1. No. 6589, Suffolk County Probate Records (microfilm, Downs, WL), reference courtesy of Patricia Chapin O'Donnell.
2. John Askew to Jonathan Dickinson, March 28, 1713, with a later note signed "D.L." (Deborah Logan), Maria Dickinson Logan Papers, HSP.
3. Elizabeth Davey inventory, 1782, Baltimore County Probate Records, liber 13, fol. 73 (microfilm, Downs, WL).

78

CUP PLATE
POSSIBLY PHILADELPHIA,
POSSIBLY UNION FLINT GLASS
WORKS, 1827–35

Light green lead glass. Pressed. Circular form of irregular circumference; narrow flaring rim, deep well. Relief pattern on the exterior well (Lee-Rose 651-A): an American eagle with wings spread and head raised to right, clutching arrows, within a beaded circle, surrounded with concentric rings; on the interior rim, relief design of flowering vine.
Diam: 3¼ in (8.3 cm)
H. F. du Pont purchase, before 1944
59.3073

79

CUP PLATE
PROBABLY PITTSBURGH, 1835–50

Deep violet-blue lead glass. Pressed. Circular form with scalloped edge; narrow curved rim, flat circular well. Smooth upper side; relief pattern on underside (Lee-Rose 677-A): in the rope-bordered well, a large American eagle with shield on breast, wings crookedly raised and head facing right, clutching arrows and laurel branch; the upper edge of the well outlined with 13 stars. Around rim, a design of 4 large daisies, with interspersed palmettes in circles and dotted circles.
Diam: 3³⁄₁₆ in (8.2 cm)
H. F. du Pont purchase
59.3076

80

CUP PLATE
NEW ENGLAND, 1830–45

Deep blue lead glass. Pressed. Circular form with edge of alternating scallops and points, rim curved in to flat circular well; recessed bottom. Smooth upper surface; relief pattern on underside (Lee-Rose 807): in the well, an American eagle with shield on breast, wings spread and head facing right, clutching arrows and laurel branch, within beaded ring and grapevine wreath. Around rim, against a stippled ground, are 4 motifs of stylized leaves and scrolls flanking a trapezoidal shape, small stars between; stippled ground on edge.
Diam: 4⁵⁄₁₆ in (11.0 cm)
H. F. du Pont purchase
59.3045

Cup plates were made in United States glass factories by the thousands in response to a table custom that was widely practiced in the second quarter of the nineteenth century. From the 1770s the English had been pouring their tea and coffee out of the cup into the saucer, allowing the hot liquid to cool, then drinking it from the saucer. This custom did not apparently take hold in North America until the very end of the eighteenth century. Only about 1820 did someone—probably frustrated by the rings left on fine furniture and linens by dripping cups—conceive of the idea of a special plate on which to set the empty cup. Household etiquette books indicate that the practice was still strong in the 1840s, but after the Civil War cup plates disappear from the trade catalogues and price lists published by United States glasshouses.[1]

These plates vary somewhat in diameter. Those over 4 inches like NO. 80 have been called "toddy" plates but most likely these were used with breakfast cups, which were larger than the standard tea or coffee cups.

The first cup plates were made of English pottery, but American glassmakers quickly outdistanced their ceramic rivals both in quantity and variety. While cup plates are known in blown glass it was the development of mechanical pressing that enabled glass manufacturers to take over this market. The shallow, 3- to 5-inch plates were naturally suited to the pressing technology and were among the first forms to be made in pressed glass.

Like the pictorial, mold-blown liquor flasks (see chap. 23), cup plates provide an interesting index to popular taste in the 1825–65 period.

There were intricate geometric and floral patterns as well as historical motifs of national and local concern. Particularly appealing to collectors have been cup plates of patriotic inspiration, such as the eagle examples. Few cup plates bear a factory mark, and attributions to individual glasshouses have been hampered by a lack of primary source material. It is clear, however, that factories pirated one another's designs almost as soon as they were issued. Henry Whitney, agent of the New England Glass Company, complained in 1828, "So. Boston Co. has already copied our patterns and Mr. Jarves [of Boston and Sandwich Glass Co.] will do the same probably."[2]

Attributions have also been based on the region where cup plates have surfaced, but this is problematical because glasshouses enjoyed

markets far beyond their factory walls. Agent Whitney, for example, was writing to a Baltimore firm that had purchased a large quantity of the Cambridge-made cup plates. By 1831 a Baltimore glasshouse was making cup plates.[3]

The manufacture of cup plates was apparently limited to urban factories, basically in the three areas represented by the examples seen here: New England, western Pennsylvania, and the MidAtlantic region.

The cup plate shown in NO. 78, with decoration on both sides and produced without use of a cap ring, has been attributed to Philadelphia because several have come to light in that vicinity. Union Flint Glass Works is known to have made cup plates, though period documents have not yielded any specifics as to design. For example, cup plates that the Gilpins purchased from that firm in March 1831, are merely described as "new pattern" cup plates. The design of NO. 78 relates to cup plates ascribed to New

England with the eagle facing the other direction. Workers from Boston-area factories were among the founders of the Union factory, and perhaps they adapted the concentric ring eagle motif from flasks they had made in Cambridge.[4]

The majority of cup plates were fashioned of colorless glass, but collectors have always sought the rarer colored examples.

1. Jane S. Shadel, "Documented Use of Cup Plates in the Nineteenth Century," *Journal of Glass Studies* 13 (1971): 128–33.
2. July 26, 1828, Whitney to William E. Mayhew & Co., quoted in Shadel, "Documented Use of Cup Plates," p. 128.
3. Chapman-Baker Day Book, December 23, 1831, MdHS, lists 172 dozen "2nd" cup plates at 25¢ per dozen; first-quality cup plates cost 33¢ per dozen (August 8, 1832); white and blue cup plates are listed in the 1832 inventory. No patterns are described.
4. Gilpin Invoice Book, p. 31, HSP; Lee-Rose 650; Spillman, *Pressed Glass*, p. 139, no. 442; see McKearin and Wilson, *American Bottles*, p. 675.

Chapter 4
Decanters

Wine was stored in large wooden barrels or binned in green glass bottles and had to be drawn off or decanted without disturbing the sediment. Although green glass bottles could function as serving vessels on the dining table, during the last quarter of the seventeenth century, colorless, refined glass objects were introduced in England specifically for pouring wine at table. Kersey's *Dictionary* of 1715 defines a decanter as "a Bottle made of clear Flint-glass, for the holding of Wine, etc. to be pour'd off into a Drinking-Glass." An early reference to a decanter in the American colonies dates from 1714.[1] Although wine was the common liquid contained in decanters, "labeled" examples prove that beer, various distilled liquors, and punch were poured from them as well.

Throughout the eighteenth century, decanters were among the most important products of flint-glass manufacturers. Plain blown-glass decanters filled the shelves of taverns, but in homes decanters were meant to be ornamental as well as functional. Like wineglasses, decanters were an integral part of entertaining and so were often expensively decorated.

Decanters sold in the United States ranged in capacity from a half-pint to a gallon. Shapes changed over time. Collectors have given them such names as *globe-and-shaft, mallet*, and *taper*, but the period names are far more evocative: *sugar loaf, champagne, barrel, spiral, globe*. The "French and Prussian decanters" sold in Charleston in 1772 refer to shapes, not places of origin. The records of a New York importer prove that many decanters were not fitted with stoppers.[2]

1. Quoted in Hughes, *Table Glass*, p. 253. The household inventory of Edward Shippen included "An od decanter and ½ doz. broken glasses on mantle," 1714-24, Philadelphia County Probate Records (microfilm, Downs, WL).
2. Joshua Lockwood advertisement, *South Carolina Gazette*, supplement, December 3, 1772. Arlene Palmer Schwind, "English Glass Imports in New York, 1770–1790," *Journal of Glass Studies* 25 (1983): 183.

81

DECANTER-JUG

ENGLAND, 1725–50

Colorless lead glass. Blown. Squat body with rounded
shoulders; tall, cylindrical neck pulled out to form pouring
lip; trailed neck ring below; applied rounded handle curled
back at lower terminal; pontil mark.
H: 7⅝ in (19.4 cm); Diam: 5 in (12.7 cm)
Museum purchase, 1978: Maureen Thompson Antiques,
London. Funds for purchase, gift of the William Penn
Foundation in memory of Mrs. Leola J. Willaman
78.202

Green glass serving bottles had been used on
English dining tables as early as the 1660s for
wine and other beverages. By 1677 George
Ravenscroft was offering "Cristalline or Flint"
glass bottles, including ones with handles.

The shapes of refined glass decanters and
handled decanter-jugs frequently imitated green
bottles. Here, a spout and handle were added
to the standard bottle form. A related example
even has a high push-up in the bottom in the
manner of common green bottles.[1]

The six dozen quart "bottle decanters, with
handles" ordered by Governor Dunmore of
Virginia in 1773 must have been later versions
of NO. 81.[2]

1. W. A. Thorpe, "The Evolution of the Decanter,"
Connoisseur 83, no. 332 (April 1929): 201, no. 6.
2. Frances Norton Mason, ed., *John Norton and Sons:
Merchants of London and Virginia* (Richmond: Dietz,
1937), p. 329.

82

DECANTER

ENGLAND, 1730–50

Colorless lead glass of gray tint. Blown. Molded cruciform body with round shoulders; tall, cylindrical neck with triple-ring collar; pontil mark.
H: 8⅞ in (22.6 cm); W: 3⅞ in (9.8 cm)
Museum purchase, 1970: A. U. Milford Antiques, London 70.265

Published: Palmer, "Beer to Birdcages," p. 83, fig. 1.

The distinctive cross-shape body of this decanter was achieved by blowing the glass into a metal mold. The difference in temperature between the mold and the molten gather gave the glass a blemished, wavy appearance, but the cruciform design enabled the wine to be thoroughly chilled when the decanter was placed in ice or iced water. These decanters were not intended to have glass stoppers and were primarily used to serve wine at the table.

Introduced by 1730, true cruciform decanters are believed to date before 1750, but the related square examples with chamfered corners were made into the third quarter of the century. A decanter of the later type survives in the Jonathan Sayward House, York Harbor, Maine, and apparently belonged to Jonathan Sayward (1713–97).[1]

1. Ivor Noël Hume, *A Guide to Artifacts of Colonial America* (New York: Alfred A. Knopf, Borzoi Book, 1970), pp. 199, 201, fig. 66; Jones and Smith, *British Military*, p. 28, fig. 17; Laura Fecych Sprague, "Glass in Maine, 1630–1820," *Glass Club Bulletin*, no. 135 (Fall 1981): 5, fig. 3.

83

DECANTER

ENGLAND, 1765–75

Colorless lead glass. Blown. Body: flared mallet form; tapered cylindrical neck with tooled lip, ground inside; flat polished bottom. Wheel engraved: "MADEIRA" inscribed within cartouche suspended from engraved chain around neck; grapevine motif below cartouche. Stopper: disk with edge cut in triangular facets, on tapered ground plug.
OH: 11½ in (29.3 cm); Diam: 4¼ in (10.9 cm)
Museum purchase, 1976: Alan Tillman Antiques, London. Funds for purchase, gift of the Charles E. Merrill Trust 76.165a, b

Published: Sotheby Parke Bernet, "English and Continental Glass and Glass Paperweights" (July 12, 1976), lot 91.

In 1755 an English merchant advertised "New-fashion'd Decanters with Inscriptions engraved on them viz. Port, Claret, Mountain, White Wine, Lisbon, Madeira, Florence, Rhenish, Burgundy, Hock, Beer and Cyder, decorated with Vine Leaves, Grapes, etc." Decanters bearing the name of the liquor they were intended to contain quickly became known as "labeled." The decoration echoes a more expensive practice of the period where silver or enamel bottle tickets were hung on chains around the necks of bottles and decanters as a means of identifying the contents.[1] Glass engravers mimicked these labels even to the conceit of a chain motif. The taste for labeled decanters continued well into the nineteenth century (NOS. 95–97), but the shouldered, mallet body and the style of engraving indicate this example was made around 1770.

Colonists in America apparently enjoyed these decanters as much as English consumers. In 1763 James Gilliland of New York offered the following for sale: "gallon, three quarts, and quart Champaign decanters, cut and ground Madeira, Port, Claret and Mountain ditto." Ten years later importer Frederick Rhinelander sold a pair of quart-size labeled decanters for 13*s*. Among the glassware offered by Joseph Stansbury in Philadelphia in 1776 were "Two quart decanters, labeled Madeira." Fragments of labeled decanters similar to the Winterthur example have been excavated from archaeological sites in Virginia and Maine.[2]

At least two American glass manufacturers were producing engraved English-style decanters in the 1770s. Both Henry William Stiegel at his Manheim, Pennsylvania, factory and John Elliott at Philadelphia Glass Works advertised decanters, and both claimed to make lead-formula glasswares in the English taste. Stiegel was able to offer engraved glass only after July 1773 when he secured the services of an engraver, Lazarus Isaac. Earlier that year while self-employed in Philadelphia, Isaac advertised that "he cuts upon decanters a name of the wine, &c. for 1s." Curiously, it was the same day Isaac's advertisement was published that William Logan wrote Cornelius Fry in Bristol about "some Glass Cutters" who had "lately Come over" to Philadelphia and could cut "Words—Grapes Coats of Arms or any Device that may be desired," and charged 3½*d*. for engraving a decanter with grapevines.[3]

Wine from the Madeira Islands was consumed by American colonists from at least the 1670s and became one of the most popular eighteenth-century beverages. Visiting America after the Revolution, the Comte de Ségur reported to his wife, "My health continued excellent, despite the quantity of tea one must drink with the ladies out of gallantry, and of madeira all day long with the men out of politeness."[4]

1. Jonas Phillips advertisement, *Norwich Mercury,* December 27, 1755, quoted in Sheenah Smith, "Glass in Eighteenth Century Norwich," *Glass Circle* 2 (1975): 54; G. Bernard Hughes, "Old English Decanters and Their Labels," *Antiques* 15, no. 6 (June 1929): 479–80.
2. Gilliland advertisement, *New York Mercury,* April 4, 1763. Rhinelander sold his decanters to Silas Howell; see Order Book, 1772–74, p. 320, Rhinelander Papers, NYHS. Stansbury advertisement, *Pennsylvania Evening Post,* April 30, 1776. Noël Hume, *Glass,* p. 26, fig. 15, illustrates a fragment from a madeira decanter found in Virginia; Sondy Sanford, "Monticello—Archaeological Glass," *Glass Club Bulletin,* no. 139 (Winter 1983): 9–10, shows another. A "white wine" decanter has been excavated at Tate House, Portland, Maine, information courtesy of Laura Fecych Sprague. Winterthur owns a slightly later example labeled "Port" (69.47).
3. Lazarus Isaac advertisement, *Pennsylvania Packet,* May 17, 1773; Logan to Fry, May 17, 1773, Smith Papers, Library Company of Philadelphia.
4. Comte de Ségur quoted in Charles H. Sherrill, *French Memories of Eighteenth-Century America* (1915; reprint, New York: Benjamin Blom, 1971), p. 78.

84

DECANTER

ENGLAND, DECORATION

ATTRIBUTED TO SHOP OF

WILLIAM BEILBY, NEWCASTLE

UPON TYNE, CIRCA 1765

Colorless lead glass. Blown. Body: mallet form with
rounded shoulders; tall cylindrical neck ground inside;
polished bottom. White enamel-painted: "CLARET"
inscribed within a scrolled cartouche on dotted chain,
fruiting grapevine below; on the reverse a sunflower; a
leafy-scroll band around the neck. Stopper: facet-cut
spire shape on tapered plug.
OH: 11 1/16 in (28.1 cm); Diam: 4 3/8 in (11.0 cm)
History: George Horace Lorimer
Museum purchase by trade, 1975: Bernard and S. Dean
Levy, New York City
75.42a, b

Published: Smith and Hummel, "Winterthur Museum,"
p. 1282.

The advertisement of Boston's Elizabeth Perkins
for "Cut, label'd, enamel'd, engrav'd and plain"
decanters reveals the range of decorative options
available in decanters in 1773.[1] As discussed in
NO. 83, it became fashionable to inscribe or "label" decanters with the name of the liquor they
were intended to contain. This could be done
not only by means of wheel engraving but also
with enamel colors and gilding affixed in a low-
temperature furnace.

The white enamel painting of this claret decanter is typical of the decorative work executed
by members of the Beilby family in Newcastle
upon Tyne in the 1760s. Among the objects that
bear William Beilby's signature is a smaller decanter of the same shape, painted with the same
cartouche, fruiting vine, and inscription.[2] The
Winterthur collection includes several wineglasses with related decoration that are also attributed to the Beilby workshop (NOS. 9, 10).

Few gentlemen in colonial America were
without a stock of claret. The wine cellar of Lord
Botetourt, Royal Governor of Virginia, included
twenty-seven dozen and five bottles of claret,
and another eighty-six bottles were stored in the
vault.[3] Acquiring a suitable supply was not always easy, however, as Landon Carter learned in
1772: "Opened Mr. Lee's claret, and had 5 bottles
broke in it out of the 6 dozen, intirely by the
loose careless way of Packing it up and this from
the most [experienced?] dealers of claret in all
Britain, as the Merchant says at the bottoms of
their shop note."[4]

1. Perkins advertisement, *Boston Evening Post*, September
13, 1773.
2. Delomosne and Son, *Gilding the Lily*, p. 42, figs. 67a, b.
Related decanters are in the Lorimer Collection,
Philadelphia Museum of Art.
3. "An Inventory of the Personal Estate of His Excellency
Lord Botetourt . . . 1770," *Inventories of Four Eighteenth-
Century Houses in the Historic Area of Williamsburg*
(Williamsburg, Va.: Colonial Williamsburg Foundation,
n.d.), p. 12.
4. Entry of April 21, 1772, *The Diary of Colonel Landon
Carter of Sabine Hall, 1752–1778*, ed. Jack P. Greene
(Charlottesville: University Press of Virginia, 1965), 2:671.

85

DECANTER

PROBABLY ENGLAND, 1775–1800

Colorless lead glass. Blown. Body: barrel form tapered to short neck flared at lip, ground inside; polished bottom. Stopper: flat, tear shape with facet-cut edges on ground cylindrical plug. Stopper not original to decanter.
OH: 15⅛ in (38.6 cm); Diam: 5¾ in (14.7 cm)
Museum purchase, 1958: McKearins' Antiques, Hoosick Falls, N.Y.
58.4.2a, b

Published: McKearin and McKearin, *American Glass*, pl. 29, fig. 1.
Papert, *Illustrated Guide*, p. 46.

It was probably decanters of this elegant shape that were described as "barrel" in the eighteenth century. In 1782 New York importer Frederick Rhinelander placed an order with the Bristol manufactory of Vigor and Stevens for thirty dozen decanters to be "chiefly of the New Sugar loaf pattern, the remainder of the barrel shape." Such decanters could be left plain or carry cut decoration. In 1775 English glasscutter Christopher Haedy offered barrel decanters "cut on an entire new pattern." One cut pattern reinforced the barrel theme with vertical lines and rings cut in imitation of staves and hoops. American glasscutters embellished barrel decanters with a variety of patterns, at least through the 1830s.[1]

The Winterthur decanter is very large, having a half-gallon capacity. Most of the decanters recorded in early American sources were of quart and pint sizes. Only as part of small, special-order sets did Rhinelander ever import half-gallon and gallon decanters. Interestingly, it was a Philadelphia glass manufacturer, not an importer, who first advertised the sale of larger decanters. In 1775 "Decanters from one gallon to half a pint" were available from the Philadelphia factory. That such large decanters may have had a particular purpose is suggested by a Charleston advertisement offering "large Decanters for Punch."[2]

When this decanter was published in *American Glass* and later sold to Winterthur, it was described as being of soda lime composition and possibly of Stiegel manufacture. Spectrographic analysis, however, has shown that it is fashioned of lead glass.[3] Both the Manheim and Philadelphia glasshouses made lead-glass tablewares, but the American origin of this decanter cannot yet be proved.

1. Order of January 25, 1782, Letter and Order Book, 1774–83, Rhinelander Papers, NYHS; Haedy advertisement, *Bath Chronicle*, December 21, 1775, quoted in Buckley, *Old English Glass*, p. 124. A barrel-decorated example in Corning Museum is in Hughes, *Table Glass*, p. 281, pl. 220. Arlene Palmer Schwind, "Joseph Baggott, New York Glasscutter," *Glass Club Bulletin*, no. 142 (Winter 1983): 10–11.
2. Philadelphia Glass Works advertisement, *Pennsylvania Packet*, February 27, 1775; Brian Cape advertisement, *South Carolina Gazette*, August 23, 1773.
3. McKearin and McKearin, *American Glass*, p. 87, pl. 29, fig. 1. Invoice, object files, Registration Division, WM. Analytical Laboratory, Winterthur Conservation.

86

WINE FOUNTAIN
IRELAND OR ENGLAND,
1790–1810

Colorless lead glass. Blown. Body: deep, round funnel bowl; applied near base is a hollow cylinder with folded lip and ground interior into which fits a curved spigot; tall stem with central bladed knop, flaring out to circular base; flat foot of scalloped outline; polished bottom. Bowl is cut with narrow flutes extending down from rim, panels around base of bowl and a band of stylized leaves around the middle; cut stem of 6 sides; edge of foot scallop-cut and faceted. "N 8" is scratched with a diamond point on the bowl above the cylindrical opening. Cover: high, domed top and short, straight sides inset below thick flange; applied knob finial on waisted stem. Cut with a row of circles around flange; cut panels extending around base and below finial; 6-sided finial spiral-cut at top. Spigot: hollow form swelled and blocked at middle, curved tip; end ground to fit into body; ground vertical cylindrical opening in center to hold valve; "6" scratched on one side of center section. Valve: facet-cut rectangular form with tapered cylindrical ground plug; horizontal cylindrical opening through plug; "6" scratched on base of plug.
OH: 16³⁄₁₆ in (41.0 cm); OW: 8¹³⁄₁₆ in (22.3 cm)
Museum purchase, 1975: Rare Art, New York City
75.17a–d

Published: "Recent Important Acquisitions," *Journal of Glass Studies* 18 (1976): 245, no. 30.
Smith and Hummel, "Winterthur Museum," p. 1282.

NO. 86 is a glass version of silver hot water urns that graced tea tables in the neoclassical era. Glass urns presumably dispensed cool water, wine, or punch, but few examples of this form are recorded. A much larger one in Corning Museum has a bowl and cover of the same shape as Winterthur's. Others are of different design with an ovoid body, narrow neck, and galleried rim.[1] Remarkably, Winterthur's urn retains its original glass spigot.

The cut decoration of NO. 86 is traditionally associated with Cork, Ireland, but current scholarship indicates that factories within England were responsible for much of the luxury cut glass made, especially after 1800. A virtual mate to Winterthur's wine fountain, produced in Bohemia of nonlead glass, indicates the pervasive influence of Anglo-Irish cut glass in this period.[2]

1. John D. Davis, *English Silver at Williamsburg* (Williamsburg, Va.: Colonial Williamsburg Foundation, 1976), pp. 95–96, no. 92. Corning's example, with a replacement metal spigot, is in Warren, *Irish Glass*, p. 108, fig. 63. Cover and spigot are missing from one in Christie, Manson & Woods, "Fine English and Continental Glass and Glass Paperweights" (November 25, 1986), lot 52. Another (St. Louis Art Museum) is in "Recent Important Acquisitions," *Journal of Glass Studies* 30 (1988): 107, no. 14.
2. Catherine Ross, "The Excise Tax and Cut Glass in England and Ireland, 1800–1830," *Journal of Glass Studies* 24 (1982): 57–64. The nonlead example is in Carnegie Museum of Art.

87, 88

DECANTERS

PROBABLY BOHEMIA, 1790–1820

NO. 87. Colorless nonlead glass. Blown. Body: flared mallet form with sloping shoulders; tapering neck with tooled lip, ground inside; flat polished bottom. Cut flutes extend down from neck to shoulders with 2 horizontal bands cut around neck; flutes around base. Encircling the body is a wheel-engraved garland of flowers tied with bowknots and hanging tassels. Stopper: flat, pear-shape with bevel-cut edge, short cylindrical plug.
OH: 10¾ in (27.4 cm); Diam: 4 in (10.2 cm)
H. F. du Pont purchase
66.1012a, b

NO. 88 (one of two). Colorless, nonlead glass of yellow-green tint. Blown. Body: tall, conical form with tooled and facet-cut lip; neck ground inside; flat polished bottom. Cut flutes extend down from neck to shoulders; below, a horizontal row of tiny ovals; flutes around base. On one side, wheel-engraved Masonic symbols within an oval medallion framed with floral sprays that hang from a bowknot. Stopper: flat, flame-shape with bevel-cut edge, short cylindrical ground plug.
OH: 9¹⁄₁₆ in (23.2 cm); Diam: 4⅜ in (10.7 cm)
Bequest of Waldron Phoenix Belknap, 1959
60.296.2 (mate is 60.296.1)

Decanters of this style, commonly found all along the East Coast, were once attributed to the Maryland glassworks of John Frederick Amelung. Although blown of nonlead glass, these decanters vary significantly from the characteristic composition of documented Amelung glasses.[1] Moreover, the style of their engraving bears no resemblance to that of the known products of the New Bremen works (for example, NOS. 16, 44–47).

A Bohemian glass agent's trade catalogue in the Winterthur Library, known to have been used in New York State, depicts decanters of similar shape and decoration, even examples embellished with Masonic symbols. Perhaps inspired by English and Irish glass but manufactured in Bohemia for export abroad, these decanters were shipped to America in tremendous quantities in the years following the Treaty of Paris (see NOS. 17–19, 49–51). Many were shipped through Hamburg and hence were described as "German." The 1813 inventory of a Philadelphia shopkeeper, for example, lists cut and engraved German decanters of pint and quart sizes.[2]

The delicate festoons, garlands, wreaths, and swags that adorn these wares clearly bespeak the neoclassical age. NO. 88, designed to appeal to the many Freemasons of federal America, exhibits a restrained style of Masonic engraving characteristic of the early nineteenth century. English-made decanters "curiously engrav'd with the Mason's Arms" had been available in the colonies as early as 1763.[3]

With its conical form NO. 88 would have been described in the period as a "sugar loaf" decanter, a term derived from the resemblance of the decanter to the cones in which sugar was molded.[4] The earliest record of the style in America occurs in the 1769–70 production list from Henry William Stiegel's Manheim, Pennsylvania, manufactory, where glassblowers produced some 735 decanters of "sugar loaf," "champain," and unspecified shapes. Importer Frederick Rhinelander, who purchased Bristol-made sugar loaf decanters in 1770, by 1781 was offering decanters of a "new sugar loaf" style.[5]

There are five other related Bohemian export decanters in the Winterthur collection (57.18.32–.34, 58.101.1–.2).

1. McKearin and McKearin, *American Glass*, pl. 42, figs. 1–9. See Robert H. Brill and Victor F. Hanson, "Chemical Analyses of Amelung Glasses," *Journal of Glass Studies* 18 (1976): 216–23.
2. Leonard Keehmle inventory, 1813-131, Philadelphia County Probate Records (microfilm, Downs, WL).
3. Joseph Barrel advertisement, *Boston Gazette*, July 11, 1763.
4. Belden, *Festive Tradition*, pp. 103–5, figs. 3:6, 3:7.
5. Ledger B, Stiegel Records, HSP; Arlene Palmer Schwind, "English Glass Imports in New York, 1770–1790," *Journal of Glass Studies* 25 (1983): 183.

89

DECANTER (ONE OF TWO)
ENGLAND, PROBABLY BRISTOL,
1800–1810

Blue lead glass. Blown. Body: mallet form with rounded shoulders and short neck with wide, tooled lip; pontil mark. Gilded decoration: "Hollands" inscribed in script letters within a label of rectangular outline with canted corners, hanging by a double chain from a bowknot at neck ring. Stopper: flat tear shape with bevel-cut edge; cylindrical plug. A gilded line outlines the shape and surrounds an "H" in gilded script.
OH: 9¼ in (23.6 cm); Diam: 2¾ in (7.0 cm)
History: Philip Francis du Pont
Gift of Mrs. Harry W. Lunger, 1973
73.459.1a, b (mate is 73.459.2)

In this version of the labeled decanter (see NOS. 83, 84), the decoration is gilded. After the glass was annealed, gold powder was applied and affixed in a low-temperature firing.

There are a few references to blue glass in colonial American sources of the late seventeenth and early eighteenth centuries, but colored glass did not come into general use until the 1770s. "Blue quart decanters for port or claret, cut bottoms and tops," were advertised in 1775 by New York importer George Ball (see p. 6, fig. 18). Another merchant carried "blue and white soy crewets and stands, with gilt labels."[1]

Condiment bottles in this period had the same shapes as decanters. Both forms were frequently sold in sets, with the bottles placed in frames that ranged from leather-covered tin to sterling silver. In 1807 the *Charleston Courier* carried a notice for "Liquor frames with gilt blue decanters."[2]

Hollands, brandy, and rum are the spirits most commonly named on decanters of this type. The mate to this example is labeled "Brandy." Hollands geneva, the contemporary term for gin from the Netherlands, was distilled from grain and flavored with juniper berries. "Gin" is a corruption of "genièvre," the French word for juniper berry.

A closely related Hollands decanter that is signed by Isaac Jacobs, a Bristol decorator, is in Bristol City Art Gallery. One of a set of three, it has a somewhat wider body, but its gilded script and label device are virtually identical to the Winterthur example.[3] Colored glass is traditionally associated with Bristol, even though it was manufactured throughout England.

1. Ball advertisement, *Rivington's New York Gazetteer*, July 27, 1775; James and Arthur Jarvis advertisement, *New York Gazette*, December 9, 1771.
2. Importer's advertisement, *Charleston Courier*, January 16, 1807, reference courtesy of MESDA.
3. Witt, Weeden, and Schwind, *Bristol Glass*, p. 47, pl. 21.

90

DECANTER

PROBABLY IRELAND, POSSIBLY UNITED STATES, 1790–1820

Colorless lead glass. Blown. Body: cylindrical form with sloping shoulders; cylindrical neck with tooled lip, ground inside; concave bottom, pontil mark. Wheel engraved with floral and leafy sprays, featuring a daisylike flower with cross-hatched center, surrounding the word "RUM." Stopper: hand-pressed disk with vertical ribs on one side and horizontal ribs on the other; tapered plug.
OH: 10⅝ in (27.1 cm); Diam: 3⅝ in (9.2 cm)
Museum purchase, 1965: Leon S. Stark Antiques, Philadelphia
65.29a, b

Although this rum decanter recalls the English styles represented by NOS. 83 and 84, significant differences in form and decoration suggest the decanter is not of English origin and is of a later date. The transition from neck to shoulder is abrupt, and the bottom has a sizable push-up with a pontil mark left unpolished, characteristics that do not reflect the sophisticated state of English table glass production. The lack of a defined label shape and neck chain in its engraved design points to a date after 1790.

NO. 90 could be a product of one of America's early table glass factories, but it is more likely an example of the Irish ware that was exported to the United States after the Revolution, even though it does not have the molded fluting so typical of Irish production. The engraving is poorly executed, but similarly careless engraving can be seen on some Irish glasswares.

The glass exported to North America varied in quality. George Ball was just one of the importers who kept on hand "an assortment of cheap glass fit for the country" as well as better "flower'd and cut pint and quart decanters" for more particular—presumably urban—customers.[1]

1. Ball advertisement, *New-York Gazette and the Weekly Mercury*, April 15, 1771, in Rita Susswein Gottesman, *The Arts and Crafts in New York, 1726–1776: Advertisements and News Items from New York City Newspapers*, Collections of New-York Historical Society 69 (New York, 1938), p. 98.

91

TOY DECANTER (ONE OF TWO)
BOSTON, ATTRIBUTED TO THOMAS
CAINS, SOUTH BOSTON FLINT
GLASS WORKS OR PHOENIX GLASS
WORKS, 1815–35

Colorless lead glass. Blown. Body: tapered form with
mercurial ring at shoulder; sharply angled to cylindrical neck
with applied ring and irregular horizontal lip; pontil mark
with iron oxide deposit. Stopper: disk on cylindrical plug.
OH: 3⅜ in (8.6 cm)
H. F. du Pont purchase
58.2925a, b (mate is 58.2926)

This toy decanter is attributed to the Boston area
glasshouses operated by Thomas Cains on the
basis of its so-called mercurial ring. This feature is
found in English glass, including objects made in
Bristol where Cains had apprenticed. Indeed,
Cains is credited with having introduced the mercurial ring as well as other English techniques to
the American industry.[1]

Although the ring that encircles the shoulder
appears to be filled with mercury or quicksilver, it
contains only air. To achieve this effect the gaffer
made an indentation in the body and then
paddled and tooled the glass together from both
sides of the groove, thereby trapping air inside.
This distinctive ring occurs on the stoppers of
large chain-decorated decanters as well as on
lamp fonts and cream jugs attributed to Cains.[2]
Here the ring creates a particularly interesting
visual effect because of its placement at the
widest point of the shoulder where it echoes the
applied neck ring and the wide lip. The toy does
not follow exactly the shape of decanters Cains
made for adults' use but is more sharply angled
and straight-sided.

The popularity of glass toys for children is
indicated by an 1816 order of Boston merchant
Horace Collamore, who requested from his
English agents "few Doz. Toy Decanters, pitchers, Tumblers, Wines for Children. They must
be quite small and come low charged." How
"low charged" these could be is suggested in the
record book of a Baltimore glasshouse where in
the 1830s toy decanters cost 50¢ per dozen.[3]

1. Witt, Weeden, and Schwind, *Bristol Glass*, p. 66, pl. 36,
pp. 88–89. The Phoenix Goblet, made ca. 1814 at Phoenix
Glasshouse of Ricketts, Evans, & Co., in Bristol has this
feature.
2. Wilson, *New England Glass*, pp. 221, 223, 225, figs. 174,
180, 182, 183.
3. Order to Jackson-Alderson of Warrington, Collamore
Papers, Baker Business Library, Harvard University,
reference courtesy of Barbara Gorely Teller; "Invoice of
Glass on Hand 6 May 1834," Chapman-Baker Day Book,
p. 14, MdHS.

92

DECANTER (ONE OF TWO)
PROBABLY NEW YORK CITY OR
BROOKLYN, 1825–45

Colorless lead glass. Blown. Body: compressed mallet
shape; cylindrical neck with 3 applied rings and wide
scalloped lip. Overall cut pattern of strawberry-diamonds
on body; paneled neck and rings; bottom cut in rays with
smooth polished center. Stopper: mushroom form with
knop below; cylindrical plug; upper surface cut in rays.
OH: 9⅛ in (23.2 cm); Diam: 4¹⁄₁₆ in (10.4 cm)
Gift of Mr. and Mrs. Robert Trump, 1977
77.181.1a, b (mate is 77.181.2)

Decanters blown of heavy lead glass and deeply
cut in an overall geometric pattern were described in the first half of the nineteenth century as "rich cut" and commanded high prices.
This decanter is cut in strawberry-diamonds,
a favored motif of a glasscutter's repertory
(NOS. 26, 63). Its ray-cut bottom repeats the
pattern of the stopper, while the rounded knop
of the stopper stem is complemented by the
unusual scalloped lip.

Although NO. 92 may be based on English
models, its rather squat body and scalloped lip
suggest an American origin. Related decanters
have been traditionally associated with the
Brooklyn Flint Glass Works of John Loftus
Gilliland. Advertisements of this factory, which
opened in 1823, state that plain, molded, and
pressed wares were made; no mention of cut
glass occurs until the 1840s, and only one glasscutter is recorded in the Brooklyn city directories before 1850. Gilliland's factory, however, is
known to have supplied independent decorators
with blanks for cutting. Among the entries for
cut glass in the first Franklin Institute exhibition
(1825) were wares from the Brooklyn factory that
had been cut in Philadelphia.[1]

Some Brooklyn glass was almost certainly
cut in New York, which became an important
center of the glasscutting business in the second
quarter of the nineteenth century. In Philadelphia Gilliland employed the same agent as independent New York glasscutter Joseph Baggott,
suggesting there was a link between the two
establishments. In Baltimore Alexander Mitchell
had the agency "for the sale of PLAIN GLASS
from the extensive Glassworks of Messrs. Jno. R.
Gilliland & Co. Brooklyn, New York, and of CUT

GLASS from the celebrated establishment of Edward Yates, N. York; the character of both of which, being so well known, nothing here is deemed necessary to be said in recommendation."[2] Again, it may be inferred that Gilliland supplied some blanks to Yates.

Between 1825 and 1835 New York city directories list sixty-nine glasscutters. Decorating shops like Baggott's employed a large number of cutters. According to Hezekiah Niles, editor and advocate of protectionism: "One gentleman at New York [probably Baggott] employs *forty* hands in the cutting of glass." He went on to inform his readers:

> There are many other highly respectable establishments for this purpose in the United States. . . . In fact, the finest and most beautiful glass-wares, lately imported, are now excelled by the work of our own artizans, and at one-half less price than such articles, very lately commanded in the market. Protection has accomplished much for *consumers*—but, perhaps, reduced the apparent profits of *manufacturers*. The business, however, is a more steady one, and the domestic competition must regulate itself.[3]

Glass made or cut in the New York area enjoyed a widespread market, beyond the eastern seaboard. In 1830 a New Orleans shop offered "80 packages from the Brooklyn Glass Company; all new and taste[ful] articles."[4]

1. A related decanter (New-York Historical Society) is in Dorothy Daniel, *Cut and Engraved Glass, 1771–1905* (New York: M. Barrows, 1950), pl. 57. Franklin Flander is listed as a glasscutter in the 1834 city directory for Brooklyn. A facsimile of the report of the committee on Manufacturers of Cut Glass, Franklin Institute, is reproduced in Innes, *Pittsburgh Glass*, p. 30; no glasscutter is named.
2. John Southan advertisements, *Poulson's American Daily Advertiser*, January 1 and 8, 1830; Alexander Mitchell advertisement, *Baltimore American Mercury*, September 1, 1828; Arlene Palmer Schwind, "Joseph Baggott, New York Glasscutter," *Glass Club Bulletin*, no. 142 (Winter 1983): 9–13.
3. *Niles' Weekly Register* 38, no. 975 (May 22, 1830): 232.
4. Thomson and Grant advertisement, *New Orleans Argus*, January 18, 1830, reference courtesy of Deborah Dependahl Waters.

93

DECANTER (ONE OF TWO)
UNITED STATES, 1825–40

Colorless lead glass. Blown. Body: globular shape, sloping shoulders, tall neck with 3 applied rings and wide lip; applied disk foot, polished bottom. Cut decoration: short panels around shoulder; peacock eye or comet pattern around lower body, consisting of curved panels of alternating diamonds and feathers below rondels; horizontal rings above and below. Stopper: blown sphere on waisted stem and cylindrical plug; cut star on top and rondels around middle.
OH: 9 9/16 in (24.2 cm); Diam: 4 1/4 in (10.8 cm)
Gift of William A. Henry in memory of Bessie Maynard Henry
84.96.1a, b (mate is 84.96.2)

In the second quarter of the nineteenth century, decanters of this shape were described as "globe or pear shaped" in a Wheeling price list and as "globe decanters on foot" in the records of a Baltimore factory. These two references indicate the widespread popularity of the shape: too often, all decanters of this form are automatically attributed to Bakewell's of Pittsburgh because of several that have been documented to that firm.[1]

NO. 93 is cut in a variation of the peacock eye or comet pattern, one that is also recorded in pressed glass (NOS. 221, 223). While some collectors have suggested this design dates from the appearance of Halley's comet in 1835, "comet" cut-glass wares are recorded as early as 1828, when a New Orleans merchant advertised the pattern. In 1829 Philadelphia's Union Flint Glass Works offered "flute and comet" decanters for $2.50 a pair.[2]

1. Wheeling Price Current. Oglebay Inst.; Chapman-Baker Day Book, p. 14, MdHS; Innes, *Pittsburgh Glass*, p. 138, fig. 92, and a similar pair, p. 148, fig. 108.
2. Thomson and Grant advertisement, *New Orleans Argus*, March 24, 1828, reference courtesy of Deborah Dependahl Waters; Gilpin Invoice Book, p. 29, HSP.

94

DECANTER

CONTINENTAL EUROPE, 1825–65

Colorless glass, nonlead body and lead stopper. Blown.
Body: bulbous form with molded flutes around base;
shoulders taper sharply to slim, cylindrical neck flaring at
rim with 3 applied rings and wide lip, ground inside;
molded star on bottom; pontil mark. Wide band of painted
flowers in polychrome colors on the exterior with white
enamel on the interior. Stopper: pressed in mushroom
form with 14-petal flower above knop, cylindrical plug.
Stopper not original to decanter.
OH: 11⅛ in (28.4 cm); Diam: 4⅛ in (10.6 cm)
H. F. du Pont purchase
64.2067a, b

Decanters of this form came into fashion at the
end of the eighteenth century and continued to
be made into the middle of the nineteenth century. Frequently seen in Irish glass (NO. 115), the
molded flutes around the base imitate more
costly cut fluting. The molded basal star in imitation of cut rays, however, is not found in the
Irish decanter tradition.

The nonlead composition of the glass, as
well as the style of decoration, points to a continental European source, but it is difficult to
pinpoint a place of origin. Early nineteenth-
century glasses enamel-painted in this manner
have been attributed to Spain, but some scholars
believe they were made in Bohemia for export to
the Spanish market. Similar examples are also
believed to have been manufactured at
Mylenberg Glassworks in Denmark between
1852 and 1863.[1]

The decanter is one of eight examples of
table glass at Winterthur that feature this distinctive floral decoration (others are 64.2061,
.2062, .2063, .2065, .2066, .2068).

1. Alice Wilson Frothingham, "Enameled Glass from the
Spanish Royal Factory," *Journal of Glass Studies* 3 (1961):
118–29; Alice Wilson Frothingham, *Spanish Glass* (New
York: Thomas Yoseloff, 1963), fig. 83; Victoria and Albert
Museum, *Danish Glass, 1814–1914: The Peter F. Heering
Collection* (London, 1974), pp. 56–57.

95

DECANTER

UNITED STATES, 1820–45

Colorless lead glass. Blown. Body: barrel form tapered to cylindrical neck; thick tooled lip with inward-folded edge. Blown in 3-part mold of geometric design (McKearin G I-8): broad vertical ribs, swirled slightly on neck and extending to mid body; on one side a rectangular panel with "WINE" in large letters; a band of short ribs behind on the other side; tall ribs around the base; pontil mark. Stopper: sphere on hollow plug, partly ground. Mold-blown with top boss of 14-petal flower, ribbing below (type 12).
OH: 10½ in (26.8 cm); Diam: 3¾ in (9.5 cm)
Gift of William M. Van Winkle, 1956
56.36a, b

96

DECANTER (ONE OF FOUR)

UNITED STATES, 1820–45

Colorless lead glass. Blown. Body: squat cylindrical form, rounded shoulders and tapered neck with tooled lip, ground inside. Blown in 3-part mold of geometric design (McKearin G III-2, type 2): faint vertical ribbing around neck above horizontal ring; wide vertical ribs around shoulder swirled to right into neck; between horizontal rings a wide band containing a row of sunbursts in diamonds flanking panel containing word "RUM" within wreath design; vertical ribbing around base; pontil mark. Stopper: sphere on hollow plug partly ground. Mold-blown with shaped, diagonal ribbing; rayed top (type 16).
OH: 10⅞ in (27.8 cm); Diam: 3¾ in (9.5 cm)
H. F. du Pont purchase, before 1932
59.3303a, b (mates are 59.3306a, b, bearing the word "GIN"; 59.3305, "BRANDY"; and 59.3304a, b, "WINE")

97

DECANTER (ONE OF TWO)
SANDWICH, MASSACHUSETTS,
ATTRIBUTED TO BOSTON AND
SANDWICH GLASS COMPANY,
1825–45

Colorless lead glass. Blown. Body: squat cylindrical form
curved in to wide, molded collar; tall angled neck with
tooled lip, ground inside. Blown in 3-part mold of geometric design (McKearin G IV-7): row of wide arches
separated by vertical branches, each arch containing leafy
branch; double horizontal rings with the word "CHERRY" on
one side within a narrow oval formed by 2 snakes, their tails
entwined below and extending to bottom; around the base a
row of arches, each containing leafy branch ringed and
rayed base (type II); pontil mark. Stopper: compressed
globular form on hollow plug. Mold-blown with diagonal
ribbing around flat, rayed top (type 16).
OH: 10⅝ in (27.1 cm); Diam: 4 in (10.2 cm)
H. F. du Pont purchase, 1931: McKearins' Antiques,
New York City
59.3260a, b (mate is 59.3258, bearing the word "WHISKEY")

These three decanters represent a continuation of
the labeled decanter tradition that began in the
mid eighteenth century (see NOS. 83, 84, 89, 90).
Here the liquor names are part of the molded
design rather than engraved or gilded, and they
are more limited in the range of liquors named
than their eighteenth-century counterparts, with
only wine, rum, brandy, gin, h[olland] gin, whiskey, and cherry recorded. The whiskey decanters
attest to the increasing importance of American-
made corn whiskey. *Cherry* could refer to either a
cherry wine or liqueur. George McKearin told du
Pont that the cherry decanter was "the rarest of
all the threemold decanters" and added that he
had seen only one other.[1]

The 8⅓ dozen "Mo[lded] letter.d qt." decanters valued at 18*s*. in the 1829 inventory of Troy
merchant Horace Jones must refer to decanters
like NOS. 95–97, but the manufacturer of the glass
Jones sold is not known. That John Gilliland's
Brooklyn Flint Glass Works produced labeled
decanters is indicated by an advertisement of
Alexander Mitchell, the firm's Baltimore agent,

for "Labeled qt Decanters" among other
molded wares. At about the same time, Boston
and Sandwich Glass Company was manufacturing "Mo[lded] Reeded" decanters with and
without neck rings that may have resembled
NO. 95. Fragments of the "arch and fern" pattern have been found at the Sandwich factory
site, so decanters like NO. 97 are attributed to
that company.[2]

1. McKearin to du Pont, December 10, 1931, WM. The
other cherry decanter McKearin referred to is in Corning
Museum.
2. Horace Jones inventory, Albany Institute of History
and Art, reference courtesy of Nancy Dickinson; Mitchell
advertisement, *Baltimore American*, March 16, 1829;
William M. Muzzey orders, January 30, 1828, in Bishop
and Hassel, *Your Obdt. Servt.*, p. 74; Wilson, *New England
Glass*, pp. 270–71.

98

DECANTER

PROBABLY MASSACHUSETTS, 1815–40

Colorless lead glass. Blown. Body: barrel form with sloping shoulders; cylindrical neck with 3 applied double, milled rings, wide tooled lip. Blown in 3-part mold of geometric design (McKearin G II-18): vertical ribbing above and below a band of diamond diapering within horizontal rings; bottom patterned with diamonds (type XII); pontil mark. Stopper: compressed globular shape with pointed top, hollow cylindrical plug. Mold-blown with diamond diapering and vertical ribbing below, the top with radial ribbing (type 3).
OH: 10⅜ in (26.5 cm); Diam: 3¾ in (9.5 cm)
H. F. du Pont purchase
59.3206a, b

Published: Arlene M. Palmer, "Through the Glass Case: The Curator and the Object," *in Material Culture and the Study of American Life,* ed. Ian M. G. Quimby (New York: W. W. Norton, 1978), p. 238, fig. 6.

99

DECANTER

PORTUGAL, ATTRIBUTED TO VISTA ALEGRE GLASSWORKS, 1825–40

Sea green, bubbly nonlead glass. Blown. Body: elongated barrel form with sloping shoulders; tapering neck around which is applied a spiraling thread with large flat terminal; wide horizontal lip; flat smooth bottom. Blown in 3-part mold of geometric design (McKearin G II-27 variant): around shoulders, vertical ribbing slightly twisted; between wide horizontal rings are 3 sections of diamond diapering separated by 5 vertical ribs; vertical ribbing below.
H: 9¼ in (23.6 cm); Diam: 3⅝ in (9.2 cm)
History: George Horace Lorimer
H. F. du Pont purchase, 1945: Neil C. Gest, Mechanicsburg, Ohio
59.3320

The simple diamond patterning of these decanters well illustrate the use of molds to simulate costlier cut glass. New England Glass Company advertised "Diamond Moulded" decanters in 1820; in 1827 diamond-molded, quart-size decanters made in Sandwich sold for 12¢ apiece. Other glasshouses doubtless used diamond-design molds as well.[1]

In period price lists and advertisements the collar arrangement of NO. 98 was described as "triple ring neck" or "3 ring'd neck," and the term "pulley" ring may have denoted the serrated or milled tooling seen here.

In the late 1820s the Boston retail firm of J. S. Cunningham offered New England-made "Snake ring" decanters, a term that aptly describes the neck treatment of NO. 99.[2] That this example was not made in the United States, however, is proposed for several reasons. The decanter is of a green nonlead glass which is extremely bubbly. Although mold-blown tablewares were made in nonlead compositions by American glasshouses (for example, NO. 53), they are not of this hue and rarely bubbly. The molded pattern is similar to that recorded by the McKearins as G II-27, but it lacks the beverage label included in that design. Irish decanters and other table forms are known in a similar pattern, but they are invariably of lead-formula glass. The decanter most nearly matches a design shown in an 1829 trade catalogue of Vista Alegre Glassworks in Portugal.[3] A flask in the Winterthur collection, unlike anything made in America and identified as Portuguese through the Vista Alegre catalogue, is also fashioned of bubbly green glass (NO. 383).

The Vista Alegre catalogue illustrates other examples of molded glass, including another three-ring decanter resembling NO. 98. That firm also made wares of colorless lead glass, however, as shown by a decanter in Corning Museum.[4]

1. New England Glass Company advertisement, *American Beacon and Norfolk and Portsmouth Daily Advertiser*, May 8, 1820, reference courtesy of MESDA.
2. Cunningham Account Book, p. 47, Edison Inst. The Boston and Sandwich Sloar Book includes references to snake ring decanters at 20¢ each; Leinicke, "Production," p. 64; Bishop and Hassell, *Your Obdt. Servt.*, p. 31, fig. 9.
3. McKearin and McKearin, *American Glass*, p. 251, pl. 104, no. 3; an example without label with snake ring and of aquamarine glass is shown on pl. 127, no. 2, which may be the other one Gest knew of when he wrote December 1, 1945, offering NO. 99 to du Pont. For Irish decanters see McKearin and McKearin, *American Glass*, pl. 104, fig. 3; Warren, *Irish Glass*, p. 202, fig. 229, p. 204, fig. 232. Vasco Valente, *O Vidro em Portugal* (Pôrto: Portucalense Editora, 1950), p. 84.
4. Valente, *O Vidro,* p. 83. The Corning decanter is published in Palmer, "Through the Glass Case," p. 239, fig. 7.

100

DECANTER OR CRUET
UNITED STATES, 1815–40

Colorless lead glass. Blown. Body: spherical upper section on tapered base with flat bottom; short cylindrical neck with tooled lip, ground inside. Blown in 3-part mold of geometric design (McKearin G III-6): vertical ribbing from neck to shoulder; horizontal ring and diagonal ribbing below; between horizontal rings are 3 repeat panels of sunburst and diamond diapering; vertical ribbing around base; rayed bottom (type VI-A); pontil mark. Stopper: sphere on ground cylindrical plug. Mold-blown with vertical ribbing above and below diamond diapering (type 2); ground plug.
OH: 7¼ in (18.5 cm); Diam: 3⅛ in (8.0 cm)
H. F. du Pont purchase, 1947: McKearins' Antiques, Hoosick Falls, N.Y.
59.3249a, b

101

DECANTER (ONE OF TWO)
UNITED STATES, 1820–40

Colorless lead glass of yellow tint. Blown. Body: tall, narrow cylindrical form with rounded shoulders; cylindrical neck with tooled lip, ground inside. Blown in 4-part mold of geometric design (McKearin G III-33): vertical ribs around the neck above collar; diagonal ribbing around shoulder above horizontal ring; diamond diapering; between horizontal rings a band of bull's-eye diamonds with diagonal ribs in between; vertical ribbing; diamond diapering between horizontal rings; vertical ribbing around base; plain bottom; pontil mark. Stopper: pressed mushroom shape with knop below on cylindrical plug; ribbed upper surface (type 19).
OH: 10¹⁵⁄₁₆ in (27.9 cm); Diam: 3¹³⁄₁₆ in (9.7 cm)
History: Philip Francis du Pont
Gift of Mrs. Harry W. Lunger, 1973
73.489.1a, b (mate is 73.489.2)

102

TOY DECANTER (ONE OF THREE)
PROBABLY SANDWICH,
MASSACHUSETTS, PROBABLY
BOSTON AND SANDWICH GLASS
COMPANY, 1825–40

Colorless lead glass. Blown. Body: squat globular shape; cylindrical neck with irregularly tooled lip with inward-folded edge. Blown in 3-part mold of geometric design (McKearin G III-12): horizontal ring around neck with vertical ribbing below; between horizontal rings are 3 repeat panels of sunburst and diamond diapering; vertical ribbing around base; ringed bottom (type II); pontil mark. Stopper: pressed disk on cylindrical plug; plain circular center and rayed outer band (type 24).
OH: 3½ in (9.0 cm)
Gift of J. K. Danby estate, 1956
56.38.36a, b (mates are 59.3174, 59.3175)

These three decanters illustrate the range of shapes and sizes made in mold-blown glass by United States glass manufacturers between 1820 and 1850. The very large decanter (NO. 101) with an intricate pattern was blown in a four-part, rather than three-part, mold. Its pressed mushroom-style stopper is the inexpensive counterpart to cut examples (see NO. 92). The stopper of NO. 102, pressed with a hand tool, may be the kind of "prest star" stopper advertised by New England Glass Company in 1820.[1]

The unusual shape of NO. 100 suggests it was intended to fit into a frame, but what it was intended to contain is difficult to know. Sets of decanters for liquors as well as cruet bottles for oils and condiments were sold in metal frames.[2]

Miniature or "toy" glasswares were made by many glasshouses. Molded toy decanters appear in the records of Boston and Sandwich Glass Company for 1828; Union Flint Glass Works in Philadelphia sold toy decanters, probably molded, for 50¢ a dozen in 1831.[3]

The G III-6 pattern of NO. 102 was copied in the 1920s.[4]

1. *Boston Commercial Gazette*, March 27, 1820, facsimile in Watkins, *Cambridge Glass*, p. 65.
2. For a similar example see McKearin and McKearin, *American Glass*, pl. 127, no. 5.
3. Wilson, *New England Glass*, p. 270. For Union products see Gilpin Invoice Book, p. 31, HSP.
4. Lanmon, Brill, and Reilly, "Suspicions." NO. 133 is an example of these fakes.

103

DECANTER

SANDWICH, MASSACHUSETTS,
ATTRIBUTED TO BOSTON AND
SANDWICH GLASS COMPANY,
1825–45

Colorless, bubbly lead glass. Blown. Body: squat
cylindrical shape curved in to wide molded collar; tall
neck with wide tooled lip. Blown in 3-part mold of
geometric design (McKearin G V-8): extending below
collar are ribs of varied length; 3 pairs of large, scrolled
forms around middle; wide ribs of varied height around
base; plain bottom; pontil mark. Stopper: tapered ground
plug. Mold-blown in 12-rib pattern (type 28).
OH: 11½ in (29.3 cm); Diam: 4¹³⁄₁₆ in (12.3 cm)
History: Philip Francis du Pont
Gift of Mrs. Harry W. Lunger, 1973
73.460.1a, b

104

DECANTER

CAMBRIDGE, MASSACHUSETTS,
ATTRIBUTED TO NEW ENGLAND
GLASS COMPANY, 1825–45

Colorless lead glass. Blown. Body: narrow cylindrical
form curved in to wide molded collar; waisted neck with
tooled lip. Blown in 3-part mold of geometric design
(McKearin G IV-6): wide ribs on neck; tall, pointed
arches ending in short wide ribs; plain bottom; pontil
mark. Stopper: sphere on ground cylindrical plug.
Mold-blown in 12-rib pattern (type 29).
OH: 6⁷⁄₁₆ in (16.4 cm); Diam: 4¹¹⁄₁₆ in (12.0 cm)
History: Philip Francis du Pont
Gift of Mrs. Harry W. Lunger, 1973
73.461a, b

Long known to collectors as the baroque scroll
pattern, NO. 103 in fact reflects the classical
scroll and pillar elements of empire design.
Similar wide or melon ribbing was fashionable
in silverware of the period, and the scroll element suggests the stylized shell seen in the
ornamentation of furniture and silver.[1]

NO. 104 received its design impetus from
the Gothic revival movement, when architects
and designers looked to the Middle Ages for
decorative motifs such as the pointed arch. In
1829 W. E. Mayhew and Company ordered two
dozen "Qt. Mo[lded] Arch flute" decanters
from New England Glass Company at a price
of $3.50 per dozen. Because this description
seems to match NO. 104, the G IV-6 pattern has
been attributed to that Cambridge factory.
Decanters of similar style were also made in
Baltimore, however, because a manufacturer
there was offering quart-size "double arch &
flute" decanters at $2.50 a dozen.[2]

1. Berry B. Tracey and William H. Gerdts, *Classical
America, 1815–45* (Newark, N.J.: Newark Museum, 1963).
2. Invoice of Mayhew and Co., April 18, 1829, in Helen
McKearin, "New England Glass Company Invoices," pt. 1,
Antiques 52, no. 3 (September 1947): 175, fig. 3; also
Wilson, *New England Glass*, pp. 242–43. Chapman-Baker
Day Book, August 16, 1832, MdHS.

Chapter 5
Pitchers, Jugs, and Creamers

Handled vessels used at table to pour liquids were called jugs or pitchers in eighteenth-century records. The terms were often interchangeable, but "pitcher" may have always denoted a vessel with a pouring lip, and some "jugs" had narrow mouths without a spout so they could also function as drinking vessels if necessary. As early as 1699, a glass jug was recorded in the estate of a Philadelphia weaver. Glass pitchers are first mentioned in a merchant's advertisement of 1750. The 1818 South Boston price list includes both pitchers and jugs, indicating differences between the two forms. Their prices were comparable, but pitchers ranged in capacity from one-third pint to four quarts; jugs were not available beyond the one-quart size. The 1819 price list of the firm had pitchers only.[1]

American colonists were not noted for their consumption of water, but by the federal era, water was an acceptable alternative to alcoholic beverages and was generally offered at meals, preferably in elegant cut-glass pitchers that enhanced its status. When setting out the dessert course, Robert Roberts states in his *House Servant's Directory*, that the "sugar basin and cut-glass water pitcher [go] between the top and bottom dishes, in a right line down the centre of the table." For suppers, Roberts recommended "four or six water decanters or cut glass pitchers, on your supper table, as the company generally help themselves at supper without the formality of more attendance than is necessary for comfort." Decanters for water, also known as carafes, traditionally lacked stoppers and frequently had globular bodies.[2] Besides water, pitchers and jugs also served other beverages such as ale, beer, and milk.

Small jugs were necessary accessories for the tea table because tea was commonly served with cream. Glass cream vessels are most often cited as jugs or pots; glass cream pots "pearl'd and plain" were among the items sold in Boston in 1737.[3] Cream jugs were often modeled after silver or ceramic prototypes, with cabriole legs, pedestal bases, or flat bottoms. Glass cream basins, cream buckets, and cream cups are also mentioned in colonial source material, but these may have referred to nonpouring shapes used for clotted or whipped cream.

1. John Burby inventory, 1699-227, Philadelphia County Probate Records (microfilm, Downs, WL). Henry Barnes advertisement, *Boston Evening Post*, April 30, 1750. Prices Current, South Boston, 1818, 1819, Edison Inst.
2. Robert Roberts, *The House Servant's Directory* (1827; facsimile ed., Waltham, Mass.: Gore Place Society, 1977), pp. 60, 65. See the water bottles in Apsley Pellatt's abridged price list of 1838, in Hugh Wakefield, *Nineteenth-Century British Glass* (2d ed., rev.; London: Faber and Faber, 1982), p. 36.
3. Mehetabel Kneeland advertisement, *Boston Gazette*, April 25, 1737.

105

CREAM JUG

ENGLAND, 1770–1800

Colorless lead glass. Blown. Baluster-shape body; gadrooning around base made of added gather molded with 16 flutes; tall cylindrical neck flared at rim and pulled out to form spout; trailed threading around rim and chain motif below; applied rounded handle with thumbpiece at top, curled back at lower terminal; applied pedestal foot; pontil mark. In bottom of body, a 3d. coin of the reign of George III.
H: 4 in (10.2 cm)
Museum purchase, 1978: Alan Tillman Antiques, London. Funds for purchase, gift of the Charles E. Merrill Trust
78.19

Published: Sotheby Parke Bernet, "Fine English and Continental Glass" (October 3, 1977), lot 108.

Glasses containing coins were made by English glassmakers from the late seventeenth century. The coin provides only a date after which the glass was made; late nineteenth- and twentieth-century glasses are known incorporating coins of a much earlier date.

This cream jug is one of a group of English mugs and jugs manufactured toward the end of the eighteenth century that displays decorative devices more commonly associated with the very beginning of the century. Glassmakers of the late 1600s—George Ravenscroft and his successors—embellished their wares with gadrooning, presumably in imitation of silver fashions, and with twisted chains of glass.[1] Derived from Venetian glass of the Renaissance, and ultimately from ancient Roman glass, chains continued to be adapted by English glassworkers through the 1730s. The technique was revived about 1770 chiefly for mugs and jugs.[2] Bristol-trained Thomas Cains brought this decorative tradition to South Boston, where he established a glassworks in 1813 (NO. 114).

1. *Glass at the Fitzwilliam Museum* (Cambridge, Eng.: Cambridge University Press, [1978]), pp. 76, 79, 80, 81, 84, figs. 174, 176, 179, 181, 197. Ashmolean Museum, *Glass Exhibition*, l'Association Internationale pour l'Histoire du Verre (Oxford, 1979), p. 11, fig. 20.
2. Wilson, *New England Glass*, p. 220, figs. 171–2; Ward Lloyd, *Investing in Georgian Glass* (London: Barrie and Jenkins with Corgi Books, 1971), p. 157.

106, PL. 17

CREAM JUG

ENGLAND, 1760–90

Blue lead glass. Blown. Sharply angled ovoid body with
short neck and flared rim pulled out to form spout;
pattern-molded with 14 lateral rows of 20 diamonds;
thick, applied rounded handle crimped and curled back
at lower terminal; applied pedestal foot; pontil mark.
H: 4⅜ in (11.2 cm)
History: Philip Francis du Pont
Gift of Mrs. Harry W. Lunger, 1973
73.474.1

107

CREAM JUG

ENGLAND, 1770–1820

Blue lead glass. Pear-shape body with sharply flared rim
pulled out to form spout; pattern-molded with 6 lateral
rows of 11 diamonds, above a row of 11 pointed flutes;
applied rounded handle crimped and curled at lower
terminal; applied pedestal foot; pontil mark.
H: 5 in (12.8 cm)
History: Philip Francis du Pont
Gift of Mrs. Harry W. Lunger, 1973
73.474.4

108

CREAM JUG

PROBABLY ENGLAND, 1790–1825

Blue lead glass. Blown. Pear-shape body with sharply
flared rim pulled out to form spout; pattern-molded with
16 vertical ribs; applied rounded handle with long terminal, crimped and curled back at lower terminal;
applied pedestal foot; pontil mark.
H: 5 in (12.7 cm)
History: Philip Francis du Pont
Gift of Mrs. Harry W. Lunger, 1973
73.473.3

109

CREAM JUG (ONE OF TWO)

PROBABLY UNITED STATES,
1900–1920

Blue lead glass. Blown. Elongated pear-shape body with
flared rim pulled out to form short spout; pattern-
molded with 14 vertical ribs; applied rounded handle
of tightly looped form, crimped and curled at lower
terminal; applied pedestal foot; pontil mark with bits
of colorless glass.
H: 5 in (12.7 cm)
History: Philip Francis du Pont
Gift of Mrs. Harry W. Lunger, 1973
73.473.1 (mate is 73.473.2)

There are numerous pattern-molded cream
jugs in American collections. Although many
are of deep blue glass, colorless, purple, and
green examples are also known. Their appeal
to American collectors dates from 1914 when
Frederick William Hunter attributed such
creamers to the legendary glassworks of Henry
William Stiegel.[1] Hunter understood the English derivation of the style and attempted to
differentiate between American and English
products, but his theory was not based on any
documented examples.

The production of colored, pattern-molded
English glass has been poorly researched, and
doubtless many of the wares were exported to
America at the time they were made, further
hampering identification. During the Revolution, Loyalist Frederick Rhinelander bought
blue and purple milk jugs from Bristol manufacturers Vigor and Stevens. In Hartford in
1788, Thomas Tisdale advertised blue cream
jugs among his "plain and moulded" imported
glass.[2] The study of mold defects in specific
patterns, and in objects that have never crossed

the Atlantic Ocean, allows certain patterns like the 11-diamond-over-flute design of NO. 107 to be attributed to England with some authority (see NO. 156).

Stiegel produced lead-formula glass at his Manheim works as early as 1769 using melted cullet and by 1771 using raw ingredients. Moreover, he was determined to emulate the styles and quality of English imports and employed English workers to that end. His glasshouse made cream pots from at least 1765 (during the German period of the factory) when Martin Greiner was supplementing the standard bottle and window glass production with a limited range of table forms. Those creamers were fashioned of bottle-green and possibly nonlead colorless glass, but no description of their specific shapes or ornamentation exists in Manheim records. In 1772 Stiegel and his agents sold three-footed cream jugs, a style of somewhat earlier English glass.[3] Both flint and common cream jugs were offered, suggesting that nonlead glass continued to be used even after the secret of lead or flint glass technology was introduced.

Creamers were among the enamelled forms sold by Stiegel in 1772. As discussed in the entry for NOS. 38, 39, this term probably denoted opaque white glass rather than enamel-painted decoration. Blue glass was manufactured at Manheim, but no evidence exists for the production of emerald green glass. Such cream jugs as NO. 106, therefore, that have mold mates in green, were probably made abroad. Stiegel certainly used part-size molds, but details of the patterns have not been documented. That he offered some variety in design and quality is implied by the range of prices for cream jugs, from 8*d.* to 1*s.* 3*d.* apiece.

Mold-blown, colored glass of this kind is difficult to date precisely. The taste for richly colored tableware in England emerged in the last quarter of the eighteenth century and continued well into the nineteenth. The shape of NO. 106 may be an attempt to replicate the ogee body found in English rococo silver. The pear shapes of NOS. 107 and 108 roughly approximate English ceramic forms of the late eighteenth and early nineteenth centuries.

The unusual high-waisted proportion of NO. 109 and its tightly looped handle suggest it is not of the period but a later reproduction. Examples are recorded in colorless as well as blue glass. Although many are made with lead oxide, these fourteen-rib creamers are of bubbly, poor quality glass. Their origin is not known. The handles relate to those on documented objects by Clevenger Brothers of Clayton, New Jersey, and several cream jugs have the conical push-up so often seen in Clevenger production. The Clevengers did not open their factory until 1930, however, and Hunter had published one of these jugs in his 1914 book.[4]

1. Hunter, *Stiegel Glass*, pp. 214–15, figs. 71–74, 88, 95, 101–2.
2. Orders to Vigor and Stevens, September 15, 1780, January 20, 1781, Letter and Order Book, Frederick Rhinelander Papers, NYHS. Tisdale advertisement, *Connecticut Courant*, June 30, 1788.
3. Buckley, *Old English Glass*, pl. 54.
4. Gay LeCleire Taylor, *Clevenger Brothers Glass Works: The Persistence of Tradition* (Millville, N.J.: Museum of American Glass at Wheaton Village, 1987), p. 8, nos. 16, 17.

110, PL. 7

CREAM JUG

FREDERICK COUNTY, MARYLAND,
ATTRIBUTED TO NEW BREMEN
GLASSMANUFACTORY OF JOHN
FREDERICK AMELUNG, 1785–95

Dark amethyst (striated) nonlead glass. Blown. Globular
body, cylindrical neck with flared rim pulled out to form
spout; applied rounded handle crimped and curled at
lower terminal; applied irregular pedestal foot; pontil
mark. Wheel engraved: on body below spout, 8-point star
within wreath studded at 4 points with flower and sprays.
H: 4¾ in (12.0 cm)
H. F. du Pont purchase, 1940: Neil C. Gest,
Mechanicsburg, Ohio
59.3010

Published: McKearin and McKearin, *Two Hundred Years,*
p. 177, pl. 28.
Lanmon and Palmer, "New Bremen," pp. 112–13.

This is the only cream jug presently attributed
to the Amelung enterprise. Its wheel-engraved
wreath relates to those found on other New
Bremen objects, but the only other star yet recorded in the New Bremen oeuvre has six points
and lacks the accomplished three-dimensional
effect of this one. The wreath is similar to that
on a sugar bowl (NO. 158), but there is no evidence that the two objects were originally
paired. George and Helen McKearin speculated
that the creamer and bowl may have been blown
from the same batch, but spectrographic analysis of the objects has shown sufficient variation
in formula to dispute that point.[1]

Archaeological excavation of Amelung's
factory site yielded fragments of feet of similar
size, perhaps from similar vessels, in green,
blue, and purple glass.[2] The color of the creamer
is irregular because of pronounced striae in
the glass.

According to Neil Gest, who secured it for
du Pont in 1940, the jug was "found near
Hagerstown," after a year of scouting. Subsequent correspondence claimed a history in a
Chambersburg, Pennsylvania, family.[3]

1. The "L.S." tumbler, which includes a star in its engraved
Masonic decoration, is in Connecticut Historical Society;
see Lanmon and Palmer, "New Bremen," pp. 102–3.
McKearin and McKearin, *Two Hundred Years,* p. 176.
Analytical Laboratory, Winterthur Conservation.
2. Ivor Noël Hume, "Archaeological Excavations on the
Site of John Frederick Amelung's New Bremen Glassmanufactory, 1962–1963," *Journal of Glass Studies* 18 (1976):
189, fig. 38.
3. Gest to du Pont, October 28, 1940, Isabel Laurence to
Winterthur Museum, November 11, 1968, WM.

111, PL. 14

CREAM JUG

PENNSYLVANIA OR NEW JERSEY,
1785–1820

Pale yellow-green nonlead glass. Blown. Wide pear-
shape body, with flared rim pulled out to form small
spout; pattern-molded with 20 vertical ribs; trailed
threading around rim; applied triple-rib handle curled
back at lower terminal; push-up; pontil mark with traces
of iron oxide.
H: 3¾ in (9.5 cm)
History: Eleanor M. Dowd; James Burke, Decatur, Ind.
Museum purchase, 1976: Sotheby Parke Bernet, New
York City
76.320

Published: Sotheby Parke Bernet, "The American
Heritage Society Auction of Americana," sale no. 3923
(November 18–20, 1976), lot 459.

This cream jug came with an old paper label,
handwritten by Eleanor M. Dowd, stating that
the jug was "Blown in Glass Factory in Philadelphia, Pennsylvania in 1813." The identity of
Dowd has not been ascertained nor has this
documentation been verified.

Specific attributions are difficult to make
in the federal period, when more than sixty
glasshouses were in operation. Factories operated for short periods of time and then reopened under new management and with different craftsmen. The products of these
glasshouses were marketed nationally: an object can have a history in Philadelphia without
having been manufactured there.

The history of the glass industry in Philadelphia in this period is complex, and it is not
clear whether or not a glass factory was in
business during the War of 1812 when this
creamer was supposedly made. There were two
areas of Philadelphia where glasshouses were
erected: on the Delaware River and on the
Schuylkill River.

At Kensington on the Delaware, fine table
glass, some of lead-formula composition, was
produced in the 1770s. At one point the works
was leased by former Stiegel workers, and it
operated sporadically during the 1780s under
the ownership of snuff manufacturer Thomas
Leiper, presumably for the production of snuff
bottles. Utilitarian ware was the focus of the
factory in 1798 when Christopher Trippel
[Triepel], a former employee of John Frederick
Amelung and of John Nicholson, leased the

"Old Glass Manufactory at Kensington" from Leiper, renamed it the Philadelphia Glass Manufactory, and blew green bottles and chemical glass.[1] In 1800 Leiper sold the property to James Butland and Co., which operated it as a bottle glass factory. An auction there in February 1812, suggests the works was going out of business. In 1815 James Rowland bought out Butland and converted the plant for steel production, but a new Kensington glassworks for bottles was built on an adjacent lot in 1816 by Hewson, Connell, and Co. Christopher Lee, described in the city directories between 1817 and 1821 as a glass manufacturer in Kensington, may have been involved in that undertaking. By 1820 "Doctor" Thomas Dyott (NO. 389), an agent for several New Jersey glasshouses, acquired an interest in Hewson, Connell, and Co. In 1833 he purchased the old glasshouse from Rowland's son.[2] The tradition of fine tableware in Kensington was revived in 1826, when several glass craftsmen from New England founded Union Flint Glass Works.

The other location that attracted potential glass manufacturers was along the Schuylkill River. John Nicholson erected an extensive bottle works at the Falls of the Schuylkill in 1794, but that site does not seem to have been continued as a glasshouse after Nicholson's failure in 1797.[3]

In December 1806 Thomas Harrison, William McIlheney, Philip Jones, and John Encell rented a lot along the Schuylkill at South and Water streets, and, according to the 1811 census directory, built a glass factory that was capable of producing fine tableware in 1808. English-born Encell, the only practical glassmaker among the four, must have misrepresented his experience with "white flint glass," because "the proprietors found their manager inadequate to the undertaking; they therefore resorted to making green glass hollow ware, of various kinds, including bottles."[4] Encell left, McIlheney sold his interests, and in June, 1809, Harrison withdrew from the partnership. Success eluded the enterprise, renamed Philip Jones and Co., and the proprietors put the glassworks on the market. There were apparently no buyers; advertisements for the property were still being issued in 1813.[5] Exactly

when glass ceased to be made is not known.

This may be the same site where John Lawrence by 1820 was making "plain glass" and window glass.[6] That other entrepreneurs may have been manufacturing glass there in the interim is suggested by city directory listings for George Rees, Jr., and Peter Wikoff as glass manufacturers in the 1813–19 period. (Although glassblowers were sometimes designated as "manufacturers," Rees's designation as a "furrier and glass manufacturer" implies he was an investor and not a skilled craftsman.) The 1813 city directory does list a handful of glassblowers, mostly with addresses in Kensington, so perhaps Butland and Co. was still in operation. Among them was Philip Stenger of a New Jersey family of glassmakers. Stenger may have also been working in New Jersey at this time, but he is listed in the Philadelphia directories for both 1813 and 1814.[7]

This New Jersey connection is intriguing because NO. 111 has pattern-molded ribs and threading that are more reminiscent of eighteenth-century Wistarburgh glass (NOS. 36, 150) than of anything else documented in the MidAtlantic region—and the Stenger family

was brought over by Wistar to blow glass at his Salem County factory. A very similar pitcher, "acquired in the neighborhood of the glassworks section of New Jersey," was used to illustrate an early study of South Jersey glassmaking.[8]

1. Pennsylvania Packet, April 13, 1798, quoted in Alfred Coxe Prime, comp., The Arts and Crafts in Philadelphia, Maryland, and South Carolina, 1786–1800: Series Two, Gleanings from Newspapers (Topsfield, Mass.: Walpole Society, 1932), p. 157.
2. Helen McKearin, Bottles, Flasks, and Dr. Dyott (New York: Crown Publishers, 1970), pp. 135–36.
3. Arlene M. Palmer, "A Philadelphia Glasshouse, 1794–1797," Journal of Glass Studies 21 (1979): 102–14.
4. Philadelphia Land Deeds, book EF 32, pp. 248–49 (microfilm, Downs, WL); Encell is named as a glass manufacturer "of Great Britain" in the deed. A John Encell is listed in the Bristol Burgess Rolls for 1803, Bristol Record Office; Philadelphia census directory (1811), p. 476. According to this same census directory, p. 472, $8,000 worth of glass was made in Philadelphia city per annum and "Glassworks" in Philadelphia County were valued at $18,800.
5. Aurora General Advertiser, July 24, 1810; Poulson's American Daily Advertiser, August 28, 1813.
6. 1820 Census of Manufactures, s.v. "Pennsylvania."
7. Pepper, Glass Gaffers, pp. 47, 114.
8. Palmer, "Glass Production," p. 78; Rhea Mansfield Knittle, "Various South Jersey Operations," Antiques 14, no. 1 (July 1928): 52, fig. 1.

112

PITCHER

NEW ENGLAND, POSSIBLY

CONNECTICUT, 1790–1825

Olive green, bubbly nonlead glass. Blown. Globular body; tapered neck with flared rim pulled out sharply to form spout; applied, rounded handle, crimped and curled at lower terminal; pontil mark.
H: 6⅝ in (16.9 cm)
History: Mrs. George W. Mitton, Boston; George S. McKearin
Museum purchase, 1957: McKearins' Antiques, Hoosick Falls, N.Y.
57.90.6

This pitcher is a pleasing example of the tableware that was made on a limited scale by many early bottle factories in New England. It is blown of the same unrefined dark green glass as common bottles, replete with striae, bubbles, and unvitrified matter.

George McKearin had attributed this pitcher to Pitkin Glassworks in East Hartford, Connecticut, which operated from the 1780s until about 1830. Bottles were certainly the focus of production although some window glass was manufactured there. A 1791 petition of the factory owners, which mentions cups and pitchers, indicates other hollowware forms were also made there.[1] Without a specific history, however, it is impossible to identify this pitcher as a Pitkin product.

1. Petition to have a lottery to benefit the glassworks, submitted to the Connecticut General Assembly, quoted in Wilson, *New England Glass*, pp. 63–64.

113

PITCHER

ENGLAND OR IRELAND,

DATED 1810

Colorless lead glass. Blown. Tapered body sharply angled in at shoulder; short neck with flared rim pulled out to form squared spout; applied rounded handle curled back at lower terminal; polished pontil mark. Wheel engraved: on one side a 3-masted ship, framed on right with branch; on the opposite side a large anchor with branch placed on left; below the spout is "W / J*E / 1810" within branches; around the rim, scattered stars and sprigs.
H: 6⅝ in (16.9 cm)
Museum purchase, 1961: Richard H. and Virginia A. Wood, Baltimore. Funds for purchase, gift of H. F. du Pont
61.18

Acquired as an example of Pittsburgh engraved glass, this pitcher is now thought to be of English or Irish manufacture. The Pittsburgh attribution was based on a decanter engraved by Charles Ihmsen in 1813 that features the naval battle of the *Hornet* and the *Peacock* during the War of 1812.[1] The ship of the Winterthur jug, however, does not seem to have been rendered by the same hand. Although this jug and Ihmsen's engraved decanter share certain characteristics, such as the feathered initials and stylized branches, these reflect the universal fashion of the day rather than a uniquely national or regional statement.

Winterthur's pitcher does not relate closely to any documented Pittsburgh glass. Cut glass was apparently made in Pittsburgh as early as 1804–6 at the pioneer establishment of Craig and O'Hara, but none has been identified. The sustained production of fine flint glass only began in 1808 with the founding of Bakewell and Ensell. Benjamin Bakewell bought Edward Ensell's interests early in 1809 and operated the firm as Bakewell and Co., but an early advertisement of the firm mentions no large pitchers or jugs, nor does it specify decoration of any kind. By 1812, however, Bakewell was making luxury cut glass, as evidenced by his gift of cut vases to the Pennsylvania Academy of the Fine Arts. Ensell in the meantime had taken Charles Ihmsen as a partner and in 1810 formed Ensell, Wendt, and Co. Their intention was to manufacture bottles and window glass; the *Hornet and Peacock* decanter is the only indication that Ensell's company may have been making

fine table glass, although Ihmsen could have engraved a decanter blown elsewhere. It is not known how many glass engravers were working in Pittsburgh in 1810, but there were at least two in the city by 1813.[2]

The ship engraved here presumably represents an American vessel, although the flag displays only stars and no stripes. This does not mean the decoration had to have been executed in this country: English, Irish, and Continental glass was custom decorated for American consumers (for example, NOS. 21–24, 66–68). Further, ships and anchors were stock devices of the period. A 1799 invoice of London glass merchant Elizabeth North and Son for example specifies "6 ro[un]d foot Goblets engravd ship & anchor."[3]

Large ship-decorated pitchers are far more common in cream-colored earthenware than in glass. Many American sea captains returned from abroad with a pitcher bearing their name or initials, a patriotic scene, and a view of a ship. Ship views were standardized; the engraver of this pitcher probably used the same design sources as did the decorator of creamware. Perhaps this jug was produced or engraved in Liverpool, where so many creamware pitchers were decorated for American customers on special order. Several glasshouses were operating in Liverpool in this period, but little is known of their products.[4]

The style of the engraving appears to be contemporary with the pitcher, and 1810 is a plausible date for its manufacture.

1. Now in Corning Museum. McKearin and McKearin, *Two Hundred Years*, pp. 286–87.
2. Innes, *Pittsburgh Glass*, p. 18; Bakewell advertisement, *Western World* (Frankfort, Ky.), June 8, 1809, reference courtesy of Mr. and Mrs. J. G. Stradling; Benjamin Bakewell to Talbot Hamilton, May 16, 1812, records of Pennsylvania Academy of the Fine Arts (microfilm, Downs, WL). Early in 1813, Philadelphia glass engraver Joseph Myring was in Pittsburgh; see Trevor and Ensell to Charles Wilson Peale, March 2, 1813, Rakow Library, Corning Museum. Richard James, lapidary and glass engraver, advertisement, *Pittsburgh Mercury*, April 1, 1813.
3. For examples of custom-decorated glass, see Warren, *Irish Glass*, p. 134, fig. 105; Witt, Weeden, and Schwind, *Bristol Glass*, p. 86. Invoice, Elizabeth North and Sons to S. Williams, p. 15b, Downs, WL.
4. Robert H. McCauley, *Liverpool Transfer Designs on Anglo-American Pottery* (Portland, Maine: Southworth-Anthoensen Press, 1942), pl. 12, bottom left. Francis Buckley, "Old Lancashire Glasshouses," *Journal of the Society of Glass Technology: Transactions* 13 (1929): 231–42. For related English examples see Ward Lloyd, *Investing in Georgian Glass* (London: Barrie and Jenkins with Corgi Books, 1971), p. 156.

114

PITCHER

BOSTON, ATTRIBUTED TO

THOMAS CAINS, SOUTH BOSTON

FLINT GLASS WORKS OR PHOENIX

GLASS WORKS, 1812–27

Colorless lead glass of gray tint. Blown. Modified barrel-shape body with 2 trailed chains; short neck flared at rim and pulled out to form spout; applied rounded handle crimped and curled at lower terminal; pontil mark.
H: 6⅜ in (16.3 cm)
Museum purchase, 1957: McKearins' Antiques, Hoosick Falls, N.Y.
58.4.1

Published: McKearin and McKearin, *American Glass*, pl. 55, fig. 1.

Because its chain decoration parallels that of the "Bishop's Mug" that descended in the family of Thomas Cains, this pitcher is attributed to the Boston area glasshouses Cains operated in the second and third decades of the nineteenth century. To achieve the chain effect, the glassmaker applied two thick threads of glass and nipped them together at intervals to form linklike motifs. Similar chains can be found on Roman, Venetian, and late seventeenth-century English glass.[1] As discussed in NO. 105, the technique reappeared in English glass of the second half of the eighteenth century and must have been popular in the Bristol factories where Cains served his apprenticeship.

The period designation for chain decoration is not known, but perhaps the "hooped" pitchers listed in the South Boston Flint Glass Works price list of 1819 were of this style. "Hooped or threaded" pitchers were the most expensive offered: those with a three-pint capacity sold for $18 a dozen, plain pitchers were $14 a dozen, and molded versions cost only $10 a dozen.[2] In addition to pitchers, Cains applied chains to decanters, plates, oil lamps, shallow bowls, and sugar bowls.

1. Wilson, *New England Glass*, p. 214, fig. 163, p. 220; Donald Ferland, "Chain Decoration: Thomas Cains, His Predecessors, and His Contemporaries," *Glass Club Bulletin*, no. 159 (Fall 1989): 7–14.
2. Prices Current, South Boston, 1819, Edison Inst.

115

PITCHER

CORK, IRELAND, WATERLOO
GLASS HOUSE COMPANY, 1815–25

Colorless lead glass. Blown. Wide barrel-shape body with
rounded shoulders; tall neck with flaring tooled rim
pulled out to form spout; applied rounded handle with
long crimped terminal curled back at end. Body
pattern-molded around base with band of 60 narrow
vertical flutes; below, a band of 30 shorter flutes that
extend onto bottom; molded legend in a ring on the
bottom, "WATERLOO CO. CORK"; pontil mark in center.
Wheel engraved: bowknots connected with swagged lines,
and stylized flower in between; a leafy frond on either
side of neck.
H: 6⅜ in (16.2 cm)
History: George Horace Lorimer
Gift of Wunsch Americana Foundation, 1975
75.47

Waterloo Glass House Company was founded
in Cork in 1815 by Daniel Foley and apparently
commenced production the following year.
According to a newspaper notice, "His workmen are well selected, from whose superior
skill the most beautiful glass will shortly make
its appearance to dazzle the eyes of the public,
and to outshine that of any other competitor."
The simple engraved pattern on Winterthur's
pitcher is also found on other signed Waterloo
glass, including jugs of the same form.[1]

That products of the Irish glasshouses were
widely exported to America is seen in the customs records cited by M. S. Dudley Westropp,
noted historian of Irish glass. The advertisements of glass importers document the great
diversity of forms and styles that were available. Spencer Philpot of Albany, for example,
offered "a quantity of plain flint and double
flint cut and engraved glass, consisting of Decanters, Wine Glasses, Rummers, Tumblers,
Goblets, Pickle Glasses, Butter Keelers [cool-
ers], wine glass coolers, Wash-hand glasses,
nob salts, sugar dishes, Salad Bowls, Cider
Flutes, Enamelled Egg cups &c. &c." In Alexandria, Triplett and Neale notified the public of
the arrival of glass from Dublin in 1817. The
cut and plain wares included celery glasses,
jellies, flower root glasses, lemonades, hock
glasses, inks, mustards, urinals, and pitchers.
Between 1818 and 1824 Boston merchant
Horace Collamore placed several orders for

glassware with the proprietors of the Waterloo
factory; perhaps the quart jugs he ordered
were of this kind.[2]

1. *Cork Overseer*, December 24, 1816, quoted in Westropp,
Irish Glass, p. 121. Examples at Victoria and Albert Museum
and Toledo Museum of Art are in Warren, *Irish Glass*,
pl. 17a, b.
2. Westropp, *Irish Glass*, pp. 145–57; Philpot advertisement,
Albany Centinel, December 23, 1800, reference courtesy of
Leigh Keno; Triplett and Neale advertisement, *Alexandria
Herald*, April 18, 1817, reference courtesy of MESDA;
Barbara Gorely Teller, "Table Glass Importations in
Boston, 1812–24: Evidence from the Horace Collamore
Papers," copy in author's files.

116, PL. 24

PITCHER

EAGLES MERE, PENNSYLVANIA,
LEWIS GLASSWORKS (ALSO
KNOWN AS EAGLES MERE
GLASSWORKS), CIRCA 1819

Light olive green body and aqua handle, nonlead glass.
Blown. Tall cylindrical body; tapered neck; flared rim
pulled out to form spout; applied rounded handle curled
back at lower terminal; ring-shape pontil mark.
H: 5¾ in (14.6 cm)
History: Elizabeth Wisner Morris; Ermina Morris Busler;
William Sherwood Busler; Enora Busler Berry
Gift of Enora Busler Berry in memory of William Sherwood
Busler, 1979
79.56

Published: W. S. Busler, "A Perfect Lewis' Glass Works
Pitcher," *Now and Then* (Muncy Hist. Soc.) 7, no. 1
(January 1942): 6–9, fig. 7.
"Recent Important Acquisitions," *Journal of Glass Studies*
22 (1980): 94, fig. 26.

The interruption of foreign trade during the
Napoleonic Wars and America's second war with
Britain spurred many entrepreneurs to build
glasshouses to meet domestic demand for glass.
Some products of the large table glass factories
of this era have been identified, but those of the
smaller glassworks have generally eluded documentation. Especially difficult to trace are table
forms made of unrefined window and bottle
glass. Objects that can be attributed to specific
factories are, therefore, of particular importance.

The history of this unusual, two-color
pitcher was recorded by William Sherwood
Busler (1858–1947): "This pitcher was blown at
the Lewis Glass Works, Lewis' Lake Sullivan
County Pa about the year 1819 and presented to
Elizabeth Wisner as a souvenir by one of the
workmen there." Elizabeth Wisner, Busler's
grandmother, was born in 1801 in Penn Township, Lycoming County. She married David
Morris, and from the mid 1850s she lived with
her daughter Ermina Morris Busler (1835–1913)
and her family. She died in 1881. William Busler
recalled his grandmother's pitcher at their daily
table, filled with cream or milk. Sometime after
Elizabeth Wisner Morris died, probably in the
1890s, Ermina Busler gave the pitcher to her son,
who was then living in Philadelphia.[1]

The attribution of the glass to the little-
known Lewis Glass Works is supported by a now
fragmentary pitcher that descended in the family
of a Mr. Huckle, who worked for George Lewis,
founder of the glassworks. That example has
the same distinctive short-necked form as the
Wisner one, and its handle is similarly applied at
the rim. The Huckle pitcher was also fashioned
of two colors, having a green body and an
amber handle.[2]

The glasshouse at Eagles Mere remained
under the control of George Lewis until about
1829. In 1831 it was sold to John J. Adams of
Washington, D.C. Three years later, Thomas
Wells and E. G. Lyon acquired the business. The
factory continued to operate into the 1840s.[3]

1. Undated note from William S. Busler, object folder,
Registration Division, WM; W. S. Busler, "A Perfect Lewis'
Glass Works Pitcher," *Now and Then* 7, no. 1 (January
1942): 6–9.
2. Katherine Ecroyd Kirk, "The Lewis Glass Works: A
History of George Lewis, Lewis' Lake, and the
Development of Eagles Mere as a Summer Resort," *Now
and Then* 6, no. 9 (January 1940): 220.
3. Kirk, "Lewis Glass Works," pp. 217–43.

117

JUG

UNITED STATES, 1820–40

Aqua glass. Blown. Spherical body; short, narrow
cylindrical neck and everted lip; applied triple-rib
handle curled back at lower terminal; conical push-up;
pontil mark.
H: 8 in (20.4 cm)
H. F. du Pont purchase
64.901

Exhibited: Hagley Museum, "Technological Innovation
and the Decorative Arts," 1973.

Blown of a brilliant aqua glass, this jug is a fine
example of utilitarian hollowwares produced at
America's bottle and window glass factories.
Wonderfully bold in its body shape and handle
formation, the jug parallels a container form
more commonly known in earthenware dating
from the early nineteenth century.[1]

1. See for example, the earthenware jug by Daniel Clark,
Concord, N.H., in Susan H. Myers, "The Business of
Potting, 1780–1840," in Ian M. G. Quimby, ed., *The
Craftsman in Early America* (New York: W. W. Norton,
1984), p. 193, fig. 1.

118

CREAM JUG
OHIO, 1820–40

Light green glass. Blown. Cylindrical body swelled in
middle and pulled out at rim to form tiny spout; pattern-
molded from base to rim with 18 ribs swirled to right;
applied, double-rib handle with long terminal curled up
at bottom; pontil mark.
H: 3⅞ in (9.9 cm)
History: Philip Francis du Pont
Gift of Mrs. Harry W. Lunger, 1973
73.466

Numerous glasshouses were built in Ohio during
the first half of the nineteenth century, with the
best known located in Zanesville, Cincinnati,
Kent, and Mantua. Although there has been considerable research into their complex histories
of ownership and operation, there is little
documentation concerning the glassblowers or
the products they made. Few objects survive
with firm histories; newspaper advertisements
are rarely specific about forms or ornamentation. The site of only one Ohio factory,
Franklin Glass Works, has been professionally
excavated.[1] In spite of this spotty picture, collectors and scholars have identified a large
group of hollowwares as Ohio products. Often
of striking forms and colors, many of these
wares have mold-blown decoration.

This cream jug was one of the generic
green hollowwares made by Ohio glass manufacturers. Typically midwestern in its swelled
shape and rudimentary, slightly upturned
spout, the jug is smaller than related examples
in other collections.[2]

1. Franklin Glass Works was excavated by David S. Brose
from 1968 to 1970 under the sponsorship of Case Western
Reserve University and Western Reserve Historical
Society. The artifacts recovered from the excavation are
in Western Reserve Historical Society, Cleveland. For a
history of the site, see George L. Miller, "History of the
Franklin Glass Works, Portage County, Ohio," *Glass Club
Bulletin*, no. 152 (Spring 1987): 3–9.
2. A 24-rib pitcher in Corning Museum stands 7¼ in.,
see McKearin and McKearin, *Two Hundred Years*,
pp. 200–201. Another, 6½ in. high, is in Rhea Mansfield
Knittle, "Zanesville Glass," *Antiques* 22, no. 6 (December
1932): 225, fig. 6.

119, PL. 23

JUG

OHIO, PROBABLY ZANESVILLE,
1820–45

Yellow-green nonlead glass. Blown. Ovoid body; short
cylindrical neck; lip with outward-folded edge; pattern-
molded with rows of 10 diamonds above a basal row of
flutes; applied ribbed handle with tooled lower terminal
(lower part missing); pontil mark.
H: 4¹⁵⁄₁₆ in (12.6 cm)
Museum purchase, 1957: Neil C. Gest, Mechanicsburg,
Ohio
57.132.1

This jug exemplifies the characteristics that
have made Ohio glass so avidly sought by collectors. It is a rare form of good proportions,
blown of a brilliant glass of unusual "citron"
color, and clearly decorated with an expanded
diamond pattern. When Gest offered it to du
Pont he described it simply as "the most beautiful Ohio piece I have ever had." There is a
similar one in red-amber glass at Corning
Museum and a flask of the same yellow-green
color at Minneapolis Institute of Arts.[1] Two
covered bowls at Winterthur were blown in
the same mold (NOS. 168, 169).

1. The Corning jug is in McKearin and McKearin,
American Glass, pl. 237, no. 1, and *Two Hundred Years*,
pp. 336–37, pl. 108, no. 3.

120, PL. 22

PITCHER

OHIO, POSSIBLY ZANESVILLE,
1820–50

Red-amber nonlead glass. Blown. Spherical body; tall
neck with flaring tooled rim pulled out for spout; applied
rounded handle with lightly ribbed, crimped and curled
lower terminal; applied pedestal foot with scalloped edge;
pontil mark.
H: 6 in (15.4 cm)
History: Tracy Clark, Richmond, Ind.; William W. Wood
III, Piqua, Ohio; Richard Loeb
Museum purchase, 1951: Neil C. Gest, Mechanicsburg,
Ohio. Funds for purchase, gift of H. F. du Pont
51.59

Published: Parke-Bernet Galleries, "Early American
Glass . . . Collection of William W. Wood, 3d," sale no. 338
(January 22–23, 1942), lot 375.

Parke-Bernet Galleries, "Rare Early American Glass . . .
Property of Richard Loeb," sale no. 853 (March 27, 1947),
lot 82.

This handsome pitcher with its nearly spherical
body, flaring lip, and tall foot has all the boldness of form and richness of color that glass
enthusiasts associate with the "Midwest," which
in glass parlance means the manufactories of
western Pennsylvania, West Virginia, and Ohio.
The scalloped foot of this pitcher is related to
those of the 10-diamond sugar bowls and creamers (NOS. 168, 169) attributed to Zanesville.[1]
Lower, flatter petal versions of this foot appear
on eighteenth-century ware (NO. 153). Often
found in English pattern-molded dessert glassware and salts of the late eighteenth century, the
petal foot was perhaps a crude attempt to imitate the cut scallops found on the bases of
luxury cut glass (NO. 86).

Du Pont viewed the pitcher at the William
Wood sale in 1942, but Richard Loeb was the
buyer at $200. This was a "cheap" price in Gest's
opinion because the pitcher and its companion
sugar bowl were "great rarities in Zanesville's
output, much rarer, in fact, than the ribbed and
patterned pieces." Du Pont apparently had the
opportunity to buy it again from Gest in 1948
but did not act until 1951, after Winterthur
opened as a museum. Gest said this was the
same pitcher sold at the Wood auction in 1942,
and the illustration in the sale catalogue seems
to confirm this, even though the pitcher's height
is there recorded as 6½ inches. Gest had acquired the pitcher when Loeb consigned it to
Parke-Bernet in 1947. In the catalogue for that
sale, the "brilliant honey amber" pitcher was not
illustrated, the description makes no mention of
the scalloped foot, and the height is specified as
6¼ inches. In 1946 Loeb had sold from his collection another Zanesville-type "dark amber
glass blown pitcher with scalloped foot" that
stood 5¾ inches.[2]

1. Helen McKearin, "Early Nineteenth-Century Glassmaking in Ohio," *Antiques* 49, no. 1 (January 1946): 52,
fig. 1.
2. Notes of Gest in sale catalogue, Parke-Bernet Galleries,
"Early American Glass . . . Collection of William W. Wood,
3d," sale no. 338 (January 22–23, 1942), lot 375, WL; Gest to
du Pont, September 14, 1948, WM. Parke-Bernet Galleries,
"Fine English and American Furniture and Decorations,"
sale no. 805 (November 9, 1946), lot 73.

121, PL. 18

PITCHER (ONE OF TWO)
KEENE, NEW HAMPSHIRE,
ATTRIBUTED TO KEENE GLASS
WORKS, 1815–41

Blue nonlead glass. (Handle darker shade than body.) Blown. Barrel-shape body; tall cylindrical neck flared slightly at rim and pulled out for small spout; applied rounded handle crimped at lower terminal. Blown in 3-part mold of geometric design (McKearin G III-16): faint vertical ribbing around rim with horizontal rings and diagonal ribbing below; between horizontal rings are 3 repeat panels of diamond diapering and bull's-eye sunburst; vertical ribbing around base; rayed bottom (type VI-A); ring-shape pontil mark. Rim repaired.
H: 5¾ in (14.7 cm)
History: Louis G. Myers; William T. H. Howe, Cincinnati H. F. du Pont purchase, 1946: Neil C. Gest, Mechanicsburg, Ohio
59.3280 (mate, 59.3318, is of light green glass)

Published: Parke-Bernet Galleries, "Early American Glass . . . Collection Formed by the Late William T. H. Howe," pt. 1, sale no. 227 (November 7–8, 1940), lot 265. Wilson, *New England Glass,* p. 167.

From mold defects in the pattern it is evident that this pitcher, its light green mate, four decanters (59.3172, 59.3173, 59.3213, 59.3316), a sugar bowl (NO. 163), a vase (NO. 258), and a tumbler (NO. 53) were blown in the identical mold, which was probably designed for pint-size decanters. The craftsmen used the mold for the pattern only and freely worked the pieces into various forms.

The glasshouse on Marlboro Street in Keene was the ambitious undertaking of Henry Rowe Schoolcraft in 1815. For two years he and his partners manufactured lead-formula glass (NO. 52) and also had facilities for cutting table glass.[1] The enterprise failed and was taken over by Justus Perry. Although fine cut glass was no longer made, this pitcher attests to the continued production of quality tablewares mold-blown in the styles of cut glass. Most examples recorded from this glasshouse are blown of dark green bottle glass.

1. See Harry Hall White, "Henry Rowe Schoolcraft, Glassmaker," 3 pts., *Antiques* 34, no. 6 (December 1938): 301–3; 35, nos. 2, 4 (February, April 1939): 81–83, 186–88. Schoolcraft's description of the works was published in the *Literary and Philosophical Repertory* (Middlebury, Vt.) 2 (February 1816) and is partially quoted in Wilson, *New England Glass,* p. 161.

122

PITCHER

UNITED STATES, 1820–40

Colorless lead glass. Blown. Broad baluster-shape body; tall neck flared at rim and pulled sharply out to form spout; high, hollow handle applied at rim and crimped and curled up at lower terminal; short cylindrical foot. Blown in 4-part mold of geometric design (McKearin G V-7): around the neck a row of fanlike leaves; narrow band of diagonal ribbing within horizontal rings; wide vertical ribs around base; plain bottom; pontil mark.
H: 6⁷⁄₁₆ in (16.3 cm)
History: Titus Geesey
Gift of Mrs. Titus Geesey, 1976
76.32

Published: Smith and Hummel, "Winterthur Museum," p. 1282.

One carafe and a number of pitchers in this pattern are known, including one in blue glass.[1] The Winterthur pitcher is noteworthy because of its particularly bold proportions, broad spout, and elegant handle.

Several examples surfaced in the western Maryland area, so the distinctive pattern has been ascribed to Maryland or Pennsylvania glasshouses. Records indicate that both Baltimore Flint Glass Works and Union Flint Glass Works (Philadelphia) produced mold-blown pitchers in this period, but the patterns they made are not described nor have any examples been positively identified.

The style of the pitcher as well as its hollow, blown handle sets it apart from the mold-blown glass associated with New England and Ohio (for example, NOS. 123, 124, 126). Nonetheless, attributions cannot be based on location-where-found, because the flint glass factories of this period enjoyed far-flung markets. Baltimore glasswares were sold as far north as Portland; South Boston products were advertised in Baltimore, in competition with glass from Philadelphia and Brooklyn. Boston and Sandwich glass was retailed in Philadelphia, and the rival New England Glass Company reached markets in Virginia and Missouri. New Orleans merchants advertised glass made in Brooklyn, Philadelphia, and Sandwich, as well as Cambridge. Benjamin Bakewell, noted Pittsburgh glass manufacturer, advertised his wares in Baltimore, Philadelphia, and Portland, even though he testified in Congress that his glass was distributed "to the Southwest and West, principally; [and] some to the northeast part of Ohio."[2]

What is most interesting about this object is its design, which in both concept and detail is an expression of the empire or classical style. As with several mold-blown tumblers (see NOS. 57, 58), the fan motif seen here was derived from cut glass. Shape, reeding, and ribbed detail, however, owe more to contemporary silver than to glass. A pair of Boston-made silver pitchers, for example, exhibit these characteristics.[3] Other molded patterns (McKearin G V-3 and G V-6) can be interpreted as exaggerated variations on the same theme.

1. McKearin and McKearin, *American Glass*, pp. 271–72.
2. "Testimony in Relation to Window and Other Glass," January 17, 1828, *Minutes of Evidence Taken before the Committee on Manufactures*, 20th Cong., 1st sess., p. 148.
3. The pitchers made by John B. Jones and presented to Capt. Nathaniel Garland of Salem in 1823 are in David B. Warren et al., *Marks of Achievement: Four Centuries of American Presentation Silver* (Houston: Museum of Fine Arts, 1987), p. 89, fig. 95.

123, 124, PLS. 9, 18

CREAM JUGS

UNITED STATES, 1820–40

NO. 123. Light yellow-green lead glass. Blown. Barrel-shape body; tall neck with flared rim, pulled to form spout; applied handle with medial rib, crimped and curled at lower terminal. Blown in 3-part mold of geometric design (McKearin G III-24): faint vertical ribbing around neck above horizontal ring and diagonal ribbing; a band of diamond diapering within horizontal rings; below are 9 large diamonds each containing a sunburst, with diagonal ribs in between; vertical ribbing around base below horizontal ring; rayed bottom (probably type VI-A); pontil mark; ".5310" scratched into base.
H: 4⅜ in (11.2 cm)
H. F. du Pont purchase, 1947: Neil C. Gest, Mechanicsburg, Ohio
59.3322

NO. 124. Deep blue body, colorless handle; lead glass. Blown. Cylindrical body; tall neck with flaring tooled rim, pulled out to form spout; applied triple-rib handle with tooled terminal (lower part missing). Blown in same 3-part mold as NO. 123 (McKearin G III-24); rayed bottom (type III); pontil mark of colorless glass.
H: 4⅜ in (11.2 cm)
H. F. du Pont purchase
59.3286

Examination of the mold defects in the G III-24 pattern indicates these two small pitchers were blown in the same mold, and the differences in color, rim treatment, and handle illustrate the visual variety that was possible even when the same mold was used. The majority of American mold-blown wares of geometric design were made of colorless glass. The yellow-green color of NO. 123 is extremely rare: Gest knew of only one other in what he called "absinthe" color.[1] The color contrast of NO. 124 makes a more striking statement; similar blue jugs with colorless handles in the Garvan collection at Yale University Art Gallery and the Metropolitan Museum of Art were apparently blown in the identical mold. Another means of achieving color contrast was to ornament a colorless object with a thread of colored glass around the rim. More commonly seen in English production, this technique is recorded on at least one American blown three-mold pitcher.[2]

1. Gest to du Pont, September 8, 1947, WM.
2. A pitcher similar to NO. 132 but with blue rim (Bennington Museum) is in Richard Carter Barret, *Handbook of Blown and Pressed American Glass* (Manchester, Vt.: Forward's Color Productions, 1971), pl. 9.

125, PL. 18

CREAM JUG

SANDWICH, MASSACHUSETTS,
ATTRIBUTED TO BOSTON AND
SANDWICH GLASS COMPANY,
1825–40

Blue lead glass. Blown. Barrel-shape body with sloping
shoulders; wide neck with flared rim pulled out to form
broad spout; inward-folded edge; applied rounded handle
crimped and curled at lower terminal. Blown in 3-part
mold of geometric design (McKearin G I-29): faint fluting
around shoulders with 2 horizontal rings below, 21 broad
vertical ribs encircle body with 2 horizontal rings below;
concentric-ring bottom (type III); pontil mark.
H: 4½ in (11.5 cm)
History: Philip Francis du Pont
Gift of Mrs. Harry W. Lunger, 1973
73.463

Fragments of the G I-29 pattern have been dug
up at the site of the Sandwich factory, so both
the blue and colorless examples recorded in this
design are attributed to that famous enterprise
founded by Deming Jarves.[1] Objects molded with
a similar design but blown of aqua nonlead glass
are believed to have been made in Mount Vernon, New York (NO. 174 and a creamer [58.4.4]).

The pattern is modeled on cut glass, having
the type of broad ribs or flutes known in the
cutting trade as pillars (NOS. 66–68).

1. Helen McKearin, "Blown Three-Mold Fragments
Excavated at Sandwich," *Antiques* 35, no. 5 (May 1939): 240,
fig. 12b, 242.

126, PL. 10

PITCHER

OHIO, POSSIBLY KENT, 1825–45

Pale lavender-pink lead glass. Blown. Wide, squat body
angled sharply at shoulders; cylindrical neck pulled out
at rim to form tiny, squared spout; applied rounded
handle patterned with 16 ribs crimped and curled at
lower terminal. Blown in 3-part mold of geometric design
(McKearin G II-6): vertical ribbing around neck; between
horizontal rings a band of diamond diapering; broad
vertical ribs above a horizontal ring; diamond diapering
below; pontil mark.
H: 5¾ in (14.7 cm)
H. F. du Pont purchase, 1947: Neil C. Gest,
Mechanicsburg, Ohio
59.3006

In the difficult period following the War of
1812, some glassmakers turned to the West as a
way of literally putting distance—and the cost
of overland transportation—between themselves and the European competition.[1] Encouraged by a stronger protective tariff passed in
1824, some sixty-four new glasshouses were
built between 1824 and 1837, of which nearly
half were built in Ohio and the western sections of Pennsylvania and Virginia. Ironically,
English emigrant glassblowers were among
those who found employment in the Ohio
factories.

   Harry Hall White's finds at the site of the
Kent glasshouse are the basis for the attribution of this G II-6 pattern.[2] Decanters, bowls
(NO. 214), vases (NO. 257), and pitchers are
known in this pattern, both in lead and
nonlead glass, but the pink color of NO. 126 is
unique. The handle proves that a sixteen-rib
mold was also used at this factory.

1. George L. Miller, "History of the Franklin Glass Works,
Portage County," *Glass Club Bulletin*, no. 152 (Spring
1987): 3–4.
2. McKearin and McKearin, *American Glass*, pp. 229–30,
274–75.

127, PL. 18

CREAM JUG

UNITED STATES, 1820–40

Blue glass. Blown. Squat cylindrical body with shoulders
angled to short neck; flared rim pulled out to form spout;
applied narrow rounded handle with long lower terminal
with multiple crimps and curled at end. Blown in 3-part
mold of geometric design (McKearin G III-23): diagonal
ribbing around the neck within horizontal rings; wide
band of diamond diapering; between horizontal rings are
9 large diamonds each containing a sunburst with
diagonal ribs in between, vertical ribbing around base;
rayed bottom (type IV); pontil mark.
H: 3 in (7.6 cm)
H. F. du Pont purchase, before August 1933
59.3276

128

CREAM JUG

UNITED STATES, 1820–40

Blue lead glass. Blown. Barrel-shape body; short neck,
flared rim pulled out to form spout; applied rounded
handle crimped at lower terminal. Blown in 3-part mold
of geometric design (McKearin G III-21): diagonal ribbing
around neck; between horizontal rings are 3 repeat panels
of diamond diapering and diamond-center sunburst;
diagonal ribbing to the left separated by a horizontal ring
from diagonal ribbing to the right; rayed bottom (type
VII-A); pontil mark.
H: 3⅟₁₆ in (7.8 cm)
History: possibly Louis G. Myers
Museum purchase, 1956: Neil C. Gest, Mechanicsburg,
Ohio
57.10.3

129, PL. 12

CREAM JUG

OHIO OR WESTERN

PENNSYLVANIA, 1815–45

Deep amethyst glass. Blown. Ovoid body with short neck;
flared rim pulled out to form spout; applied rounded
handle curled at lower terminal. Blown in 3-part mold
of geometric design (McKearin G II-17): vertical fluting
around neck above diamond diapering; 2 horizontal
rings above tall vertical ribs at base; pontil mark.
H: 3¾ in (9.6 cm)
History: a Mrs. Norton
H. F. du Pont purchase, before 1940
59.3109

NOS. 127–29 illustrate ways in which moldmakers
working for early American glasshouses would
combine motifs from cut glass: complex designs
cover the surface of these very small objects. In
fine cut glass, however, strong colors were rarely
used. Intricate cut patterns refracted the light
and were intended to enhance the brilliance of
colorless lead glass, and strong colors tended to
diminish the dazzling effect considerably. Although there is little documentation of mold-
blown patterns to specific factories, variations in
shape, color, and pattern may indicate regional
preference. The creamer NO. 129 differs markedly in shape from the other two, which probably emanated from New England. Amethyst is
recorded in other mold-blown midwestern
wares (see NOS. 171, 172).

130

TOY JUG
PROBABLY SANDWICH,
MASSACHUSETTS, PROBABLY
BOSTON AND SANDWICH GLASS
COMPANY, 1825–40

Colorless lead glass. Blown. Squat barrel-shape body; tall neck; flaring, tooled rim pulled out to form spout; applied rounded handle, crimped and curled at lower terminal. Blown in 3-part mold of geometric design (G III-12): vertical ribbing around the neck, swirled somewhat to right; between horizontal rings are 3 repeat panels of diamond diapering and sunburst; vertical ribbing around base; ringed bottom (type II); pontil mark.
H: 2¼ in (5.7 cm)
H. F. du Pont purchase, 1950: Neil C. Gest, Mechanicsburg, Ohio
59.3310

Miniature or toy glasswares for children appear in the price lists and records of several glasshouses, although primary information about their use in children's play remains undiscovered. NO. 130 and a matching toy decanter (NO. 102) were blown in the same mold. This was probably one of the toy molded jugs listed at 50¢ a dozen in J. S. Cunningham's accounts with Jarves. In 1827 alone more than 2,000 toy jugs, many molded, were made at Sandwich.[1]

1. Cunningham Account Book, p. 31, Edison Inst.; Leinicke, "Production," p. 497.

131

CREAM JUG
UNITED STATES, ENGLAND,
OR IRELAND, 1820–45

Deep violet-blue lead glass. Blown. Cylindrical body with curved shoulder; tall neck with flared rim pulled out to form spout; applied rounded handle curled at lower terminal. Blown in 3-part mold of geometric design (McKearin G II-45 variant): paneled rim; around the neck between pronounced horizontal rings is swagged drapery against vertical ribbing; below are 3 panels of diamond diapering separated by triple reeds; horizontal ring above vertical ribbing around base; pontil mark.
H: 3⅞ in (9.9 cm)
Gift of Emily Manheim, D. M. & P. Manheim Antiques, 1972
72.117

This unrecorded creamer has a drapery pattern that is reminiscent of cut patterns in Irish glass.[1] In their study of blown three-mold glass, the McKearins note condiment bottles in the closely related G II-45 pattern. The overall shape and highly positioned handle of this cream jug differ from most American examples, so a European origin cannot be ruled out.

1. Warren, *Irish Glass*, p. 147, fig. 128.

132

PITCHER (ONE OF TWO)

PROBABLY MASSACHUSETTS,
1815–40

Colorless lead glass. Blown. Broad barrel-shape body; tall neck; widely flared rim pulled out to form spout; applied, 5-rib handle, crimped and curled at lower terminal. Blown in 3-part mold of geometric design (McKearin G III-5): around the neck a band of vertical ribbing separated by a horizontal ring from diagonal ribbing below; between horizontal rings are 3 repeat panels of diamond diapering and sunburst; vertical ribbing around base; rayed bottom (type VI-A); pontil mark.
H: 6½ in (16.6 cm)
H. F. du Pont purchase, one before 1939; one acquired 1941 from Neil C. Gest, Mechanicsburg, Ohio
59.3221 (mate is 59.3222)

Published: Lanmon, Brill, and Reilly, "Suspicions," p. 146, figs. 4a, b.

133

PITCHER

UNITED STATES, PROBABLY

PHILADELPHIA AREA, 1920–30

Colorless lead glass. Blown. Globular body with sloping shoulders; curved neck with flaring, tooled rim pulled out to form spout; thin, applied rounded handle, flat and rounded at lower terminal; drawn disk foot. Blown in 3-part mold of geometric design, same pattern as NO. 132; pontil mark.
H: 6½ in (16.6 cm)
H. F. du Pont purchase, 1940: Neil C. Gest, Mechanicsburg, Ohio
59.3180

Published: Lanmon, Brill, and Reilly, "Suspicions," pp. 162–63, fig. 22.

NOS. 132 and 133 were selected to contrast the characteristics of genuine mold-blown products of the early nineteenth century with those of fake specimens fabricated a hundred years later. Although both are colorless, NO. 132 has a gray cast and an occasional stone or air bubble; NO. 133, on the other hand, is blown of a truly colorless material that exhibits a purity indicative of technological advancements postdating the early 1800s. NO. 132 has a shape well known in mold-blown pitchers, but NO. 133 has a globular body and drawn foot that are extremely unusual.[1] This shape is believable for the period, but its rarity in mold-blown glass was calculated to attract the advanced collector. However appealing in form, NO. 133 lacks in its details the boldness and assurance of early products that were designed to bear up under daily use on the tables of American homes. For example, the handle of NO. 133 seems barely attached at the rim, while the flat terminal differs markedly from the typical handle of the period. In short, the object seems to be designed for a collector's cabinet rather than practical use, an observation corroborated by the lack of wear marks.

The bogus pitcher is one of a group of about fifty mold-blown objects that were apparently made as deliberate fakes and placed with leading dealers and collectors in the 1920–40 period (see NO. 216). The group was identified and their properties analyzed in detail in 1973 in the *Journal of Glass Studies*. Eighteen of them are at Winterthur; du Pont had acquired four examples by 1933.

NO. 133 did not come to Winterthur with any history, but related examples in the G III-5, G III-6, and G II-18 patterns were identified in 1940 as the handiwork of one Frederick Mutzer, a nineteenth-century German immigrant glassblower.[2] Dealer George McKearin obtained a number of the glasses from Mutzer's descendant along with an affidavit that explained the history in a somewhat contradictory fashion. The descendant claimed that Medford, New Jersey, was the place of manufacture. Subsequent research has failed to yield any factory located there or anyone named Mutzer working at an American glassworks.

The exact origin of the spurious moldblown glass remains to be discovered, but the Philadelphia region seems likely. The problem is confused—perhaps deliberately so—by the legitimate reproductions in similar patterns made by Clevenger Brothers in Clayton, New Jersey, from about 1930.[3] The so-called Mutzer wares exhibit greater technical skill and occur in more believable colors than the Clevenger ones. The Mutzer glasses were obviously produced under the direction of people familiar with early American glass, but the identities of the instigators of this fraud remain unknown.

1. What appears to be a genuine example of this shape is in Helen A. McKearin, "Fictions of 'Three-Mold' Glass," *Antiques* 16, no. 6 (December 1929): 505, fig. 8b.
2. George S. McKearin, "From Family Glass Cupboards," *Antiques* 59, no. 2 (February 1951): 131–33, frontis.
3. Lanmon, Brill, and Reilly, "Suspicions," pp. 144–45.

134

CREAM JUG

SANDWICH, MASSACHUSETTS,

ATTRIBUTED TO BOSTON AND

SANDWICH GLASS COMPANY,

1830–40

Colorless lead glass of slightly yellow tint. Blown.
Compressed spherical body, cylindrical neck pulled up and
out to form spout; tall pedestal foot; body and foot tooled
with wide, rounded horizontal rings; applied rounded
handle crimped and curled at lower terminal; pontil mark.
H: 5⅞ in (14.9 cm)
Museum purchase, 1975: Ruth Troiani Fine Antiques,
Pound Ridge, N.Y. Funds for purchase, gift of the Claneil
Foundation
75.70.2

Cream jugs, sugar bowls, lamps, and candlesticks featuring this distinctive, bold tooling are
attributed to Boston and Sandwich Glass Company because of several examples that can be
traced to workers of that factory.[1] More exaggerated than the English "Lynn" rings (NO. 37), the
tooling of this creamer and its matching sugar
bowl (NO. 175) is known today as "beehive" ware.
From the 1780s until the 1820s English silversmiths made honey pots that looked like beehives; other forms, like teapots, had a modified
beehive shape with the same pronounced horizontal rings.[2] Such silver may have inspired the
Sandwich glassblowers, some of whom had emigrated from England.

It was probably a creamer with a similarly
high spout that South Boston Glass Works
described in their 1819 price list as having a
"ewer mouth."[3]

1. See Frederick T. Irwin, *The Story of Sandwich Glass and Glass Workers* (Manchester, N.H.: Privately printed, 1926), p. 98. Dwight P. Lanmon, comp., *Glass from Six Centuries* (Hartford, Conn.: Wadsworth Atheneum, 1978), p. 101, fig. 113. Wilson, *New England Glass*, pp. 267–68, fig. 219a, b, fig. 220a, b.
2. G. Bernard Hughes, *Small Antique Silverware* (New York: Bramhall House, 1957), pp. 197–98, fig. 238.
3. Prices Current, South Boston, 1819, Edison Inst.

135, PL. 15

PITCHER (ONE OF TWO)
UNITED STATES, POSSIBLY NEW
JERSEY, 1830–50

Deep gray-blue nonlead glass. Blown. Compressed
globular body; tall cylindrical neck with flaring, tooled
rim pulled out to form tiny pouring spout; applied
double-rib handle, curled back at lower terminal; thick
disk foot with pincered detail; ring-shape pontil mark.
H: 5⅛ in (13.1 cm)
History: Frederick K. Gaston, Greenwich, Conn.
H. F. du Pont purchase, 1940: Neil C. Gest,
Mechanicsburg, Ohio
59.3074 (mate is 59.3075)

Published: Parke-Bernet Galleries, "Early American
Glass . . . Collection of the Late Frederick K. Gaston,"
sale no. 187 (March 29–30, 1940), lot 171.

These pitchers and related examples are distinguished by low-slung bodies and tall necks. A
larger pitcher of this form, but embellished
with threading around the neck, has a history
of being blown by Joel Duffield at Whitney
Glass Works in Glassboro, New Jersey, in the
late 1830s.[1] A blue mug in the Winterthur collection also relates to the group because of its
color and double-rib handle (64.644).

1. Others are in Pepper, *Glass Gaffers*, pl. 7; another is
shown in McKearin and McKearin, *American Glass*, pl. 13,
no. 7; Parke-Bernet Galleries, "Early American Glass and
Ceramics, Collection of Alfred B. Maclay," sale no. 100
(March 23–25, 1939), lot 466. The Duffield pitcher
(Corning Museum) is in McKearin and McKearin, *Two
Hundred Years*, pp. 200–201, pl. 40, no. 1.

136, PL. 4

PITCHER

UNITED STATES, 1835–55

Aqua glass. Blown. Compressed spherical body below a
heavy ring; gadrooning made of added gather molded with
11 swirled ribs; widely flared threaded neck pulled out to
form spout; outward-folded edge; broad applied handle
with pronounced medial rib, crimped and curled at lower
terminal; applied disk foot; ring-shape pontil mark.
OH: 5¾ in (14.7 cm)
H. F. du Pont purchase, before 1939
59.3055

This pitcher is a superb example of the tableware produced in bottle or window glass factories in the middle part of the nineteenth century.
The pitcher and a related sugar bowl and vase
(NOS. 176, 244) are based on high-style, colorless

prototypes made in the Boston area.[1] Although
the flint glass versions are more refined in execution, the vigor and character of the aquamarine
wares give them a special appeal.

Objects of this type have traditionally been
associated with southern New Jersey, where numerous bottle and window factories were located
in the nineteenth century. The attribution is not
based on any documentation, however. The concept of the "South Jersey tradition" grew out of
the early years of glass collecting when all glass
was attributed to the triumvirate of Wistar,
Stiegel, and Sandwich. Most aqua glass was as-

signed to Wistarburgh. When it was realized that
certain shapes dictated a date of manufacture
long after Wistarburgh had shut down (1777),
the attribution was regionalized and pushed
ahead in time. The problem with this line of
thinking was recognized as early as 1927 when
Rhea Mansfield Knittle wrote: "Most of the
glassware formerly sold and collected as
'Wistarberg' is now described as of 'South Jersey
technique,' although much of it was made many
miles removed from the State of New Jersey—in
upper New York State and New England, and
some of it in the then middle West." Glassblower
migration was seen as the basis of this phenom-
enon, even though little hard data about the
craftsmen and their movements were gathered
after the initial theory was set forth by Harry
Hall White.[2]

Because the flint glass models for this
pitcher and its associated wares can be documented to the Boston area, it is possible that
these renditions in aqua glass were also made in
New England. This notion is not without prece-
dent because a related pitcher is recorded with a
history in Stoddard, New Hampshire. That object posed a dilemma for the McKearins, who
felt its features were "so definitely South Jersey,"
but, in the end, its history outweighed stylistic
considerations.[3] The New Hampshire attribution
was bolstered by the dark red-amber color commonly found in the bottle factories of New
Hampshire but rarely linked to New Jersey.

There were bottle and window factories in
New England—Chelmsford, Suncook, and
Keene, to name but a few—that definitely produced tableware of aqua glass.[4] That Massachusetts glasshouses influenced the production of
glass in New York State as well is suggested by
the occurrence of certain mold-blown patterns
at both Sandwich and Mount Vernon. The products of the former are rendered in nonlead aqua
glass (NO. 174), while the Sandwich tablewares
are fashioned of fine flint glass (NO. 125).

Although a definite attribution cannot be
proposed at this time, the group composed of
this pitcher, its mates in other collections, and
related objects of other forms is large enough to
indicate a deliberate strategy on the part of some
clever entrepreneur to provide the market with
inexpensive copies of the fine table glass made

by New England Glass Company and the South Boston glasshouses.

There is another, smaller cream jug with gadrooning at Winterthur (59.3050) and a footed bowl that was cut down from a jug originally similar to NO. 136 (68.725).

1. A cream pitcher and matching sugar bowl were made in 1838 for Thyrza Barnes at the time of her marriage to George Leighton, son of Thomas Leighton of New England Glass Company. Watkins, *Cambridge Glass*, pp. 73, 75, pl. 29; also shown in Wilson, *New England Glass*, p. 247, fig. 207a.
2. Knittle, *Early American Glass*, p. 95; Harry Hall White, "Migrations of Early Glassworkers," *Antiques* 32, no. 2 (August 1937): 64–67; Arlene Palmer Schwind, "The Glassmakers of Early America," in *The Craftsman in Early America*, ed. Ian M. G. Quimby (New York: W. W. Norton, 1984), pp. 158–89.
3. McKearin and McKearin, *American Glass*, p. 216, pl. 72a, no. 6.
4. Examples from the Chelmsford factory are on loan to Chelmsford Historical Society, Chelmsford, Mass.; for Suncook objects, see Wilson, *New England Glass*, p. 90.

PITCHER
UNITED STATES, 1835–65

Aqua body; pale yellow-green handle. Blown. Elongated barrel-shape body; tall neck; flaring, tooled rim pulled out to form spout; applied rounded handle with crimped and curled lower terminal; pontil mark.
H: 5½ in (14.0 cm)
History: Frederick W. Hunter
H. F. du Pont purchase, 1920: American Art Association, New York City
64.886

Published: American Art Association, "Rare and Beautiful Oriental Art Treasures and . . . American Glass Formed by the . . . Late Frederick William Hunter" (January 7–14, 1920), lot 1477.

This well-proportioned pitcher was one of du Pont's early acquisitions in American glass. It is hardly surprising that as a budding collector of Americana he patronized the sale of the estate of the famous Frederick W. Hunter, whose 1914 *Stiegel Glass* had revolutionized the collecting of American glass. Although Hunter's focal point was the Lancaster County enterprise of Henry William Stiegel, he included a well-researched history of the glassworks of Caspar Wistar, Stiegel's predecessor and rival. Hunter's understanding of Wistar production, however, was not accurate (see NO. 150). He attributed this pitcher and numerous other objects of nineteenth-century date to Wistarburgh, thereby spawning a misunderstanding of Wistar and South Jersey glass production that endured for decades.

138, PL. 3

PITCHER

PROBABLY NEW YORK OR NEW JERSEY, 1835–65

Blue-green nonlead glass. Blown. Globular body with added gather tooled into 7 short peaks of equal height; tall cylindrical neck with trailed threading; flared rim pulled out to form small spout; applied handle with pronounced medial rib, crimped and curled back at lower terminal; applied disk foot; ring-shape pontil mark. Crack in body at lower handle terminal.
H: 8¼ in (21.1 cm)
History: George Hamersley, Germantown, Pa.
Museum purchase, 1956: Margaretta Hamersley, Philadelphia
56.102

Published: Pepper, *Glass Gaffers,* p. 106, fig. 83.

139

CREAM JUG

PROBABLY NEW YORK OR NEW JERSEY, 1835–65

Aqua glass. Blown. Narrow pear-shape body with added gather tooled into 4 peaks of equal height; threaded neck; flared rim pulled out to form spout; rounded handle with large upper terminal and protruding thumbpiece, and with curled at lower terminal; pincered pedestal foot of irregular circumference; ring-shape pontil mark.
H: 2¹⁵⁄₁₆ in (7.5 cm)
H. F. du Pont purchase, before 1939
59.3021

140, PL. 3

PITCHER

PROBABLY NEW YORK, 1835–65

Green-blue nonlead glass. Blown. Tapered body with rounded shoulders; added gather tooled into 4 tall peaks with 4 shorter peaks in between; threaded neck; flared rim pulled out to form spout; applied rounded handle crimped and curled at lower terminal; push-up; pontil mark.
H: 7⅝ in (19.5 cm)
H. F. du Pont purchase, before 1935
59.3024

141

PITCHER

PROBABLY STODDARD, NEW HAMPSHIRE, 1842–73

Olive-amber nonlead glass. Blown. Globular body with sloping shoulders; added gather tooled into 4 scrolls with 4 short, straight peaks in between, each ending in a pad; tall threaded neck; flared rim pulled into small spout; applied rounded handle crimped and curled at lower terminal; applied pedestal foot; pontil mark. Crack in body near handle terminal.
H: 7¼ in (18.5 cm)
Museum purchase, 1957: McKearins' Antiques, Hoosick Falls, N.Y.
58.4.7

Published: "Recent Important Acquisitions," *Journal of Glass Studies* 1 (1959): 115, no. 47.
Papert, *Illustrated Guide,* p. 31.

138

139

142

PITCHER

NEW YORK, 1835–65

Aqua nonlead glass. Blown. Large globular body with sloping shoulders; thin, added gather tooled into 6 tall, curved peaks each ending in an oval pad; threaded neck; flared rim pulled out to form spout; applied rounded handle crimped and curled at lower terminal; applied disk foot; pontil mark. Cracked at lower handle terminal.
H: 10⅝ in (27.0 cm)
History: found near Watertown, N.Y.; George S. McKearin; Mitchell Taradash, Ardsley-on-Hudson, N.Y. Museum purchase, 1970: Robert Burkhardt, Kutztown, Pa. 70.84

Published: "A Glimpse of Early Glass," *Antiques* 17, no. 2 (February 1930): 140.
Glass Club Bulletin, no. 42 (March 1957): cover.
"Important Recent Acquisitions," *Journal of Glass Studies* 13 (1971): 146, no. 65.

These pitchers feature a type of decoration known to collectors since about 1930 as "lily pad." The term is imperfect because, as the group illustrates, the added gather of glass could be pulled into vertical or scrolled shapes of varying heights, few of which resemble the botanical specimen. The water lily *was* a source of inspiration to designers of silver and porcelain in the mid nineteenth century, particularly after the spectacular *Victoria regia* variety from South America was successfully cultivated in England in 1849. It is highly unlikely, however, that the glassblowers responsible for these objects were actually inspired by nature, nor do their products copy the naturalistic water lily designs found in metalwares and ceramics.[1]

Prototypes are known in eighteenth-century glass from Spain, Portugal, and Norway, but how the style became part of nineteenth-century American glassmaking vocabulary is not clear. No nineteenth-century descriptions of lily pad ware have been uncovered. There are related techniques seen on contemporary, high-style glass, but lily pad wares are typically blown from unrefined aqua or amber glass.[2]

From the several hundred examples that survive, it is certain that lily pad wares were popular products of America's bottle and window glass factories and not merely "offhand" or "end of day" wares made for the personal use of the craftsmen. Utilitarian containers and windowpanes were the principal products of glassworks throughout New Jersey, New York, and New England. C. B. Barrett's factory in

140

141

142

Stoddard, New Hampshire, was typical of these glasshouses in offering "all kinds of BLACK, GREEN, and AMBERWARE" in addition to demijohns, flasks, and other bottles.[3]

NO. 141 was probably made at one of the Stoddard glasshouses; pitchers of this type with the double lily pad have been attributed to the hand of Matt Johnson. NO. 142 surfaced near Watertown, New York, and was probably produced at either the Redford or the Redwood works, where lily pad wares are known to have been made. Other lily pad glasswares have been traced to glasshouses in New London, Connecticut; Lancaster, New York; and Mallorytown, Ontario.[4]

The Winterthur pitchers not only illustrate the variety that was possible within the style, but they also show the range of size and shape within the pitcher form, ranging from the giant NO. 142, the largest example recorded, to the tiny creamer NO. 139, one of the smallest. The lily pad technique was used to embellish other vessel forms (see NOS. 177, 210, 219, 262), but none were perhaps as suited to the style as the pitcher. The Winterthur collection has another pitcher (67.834) and cream jug (59.3022).

1. The story of the discovery of enormous lilies, with leaves some 5 feet in diameter, was the subject of a book by John Fisk Allen entitled *Victoria Regia; or, The Great Water Lily of America* (1854), which was reviewed in *The Horticulturalist and Journal of Rural Art and Rural Taste*, n.s., 5 (January 1855): 52. For a silver pitcher of lily pad design, made in 1857, see Metropolitan Museum of Art, *Nineteenth-Century America: Furniture and Other Decorative Arts* (New York, 1970), no. 143. Between 1850 and 1858 parian porcelain pitchers with lily pad decoration were made in Bennington, Vt. See Richard Carter Barret, *Bennington Pottery and Porcelain* (New York: Bonanza Books, 1958), p. 49, pl. 64. These were apparently based on English examples.
2. See for example, *Spanish Glass in the Hermitage* (Leningrad: Aurora Art Publishers, 1974), pl. 26, cat. 51. A colorless, lead-glass sugar bowl and pitcher in a private collection on loan to Metropolitan Museum of Art have a type of lily pad as part of an overall drapery design; they are attributed to the Boston area.
3. Reproduced in McKearin and Wilson, *American Bottles*, p. 177.
4. Lura Woodside Watkins, "Stoddard Glass," *Antiques* 24, no. 2 (August 1933): 54–55. Clinton County Historical Museum, *Reflections: The Story of Redford Glass* (Plattsburgh, N.Y.: Clinton Co. Historical Association, 1979); Wilson, *New England Glass*, pp. 151–52; Ernest W. Young, "Authenticated Lancaster Glass," *Antiques* 24, no. 2 (August 1933): 51; Gerald Stevens, *Canadian Glass, 1825–1925* (Toronto: Coles, 1979), pp. 4–8.

143

TOY CREAM JUG
UNITED STATES, 1840–65

Gray-blue glass. Pressed; tooled. Cylindrical body with curved shoulders; tooled neck with flared rim pulled out to form spout; body molded with 16 pointed flutes; applied handle crimped and curled at lower terminal; concentric rings on bottom, pontil mark within center depression.
H: 2⅜ in (6.0 cm)
Museum purchase, 1955: Henrietta Bonsal. Funds for purchase gift of H. F. du Pont
55.136.84

Using a mold that was probably designed for a gill-size tumbler, the glassmaker freely shaped the rim and added a handle to create this charming miniature. As discussed above (NO. 130) the production of toy glassware for children was enormous. The arch pattern illustrates the continued popularity of the Gothic taste in American decorative arts (see NO. 104).

144

PITCHER

UNITED STATES OR POSSIBLY
ENGLAND, 1845–70

Colorless lead glass. Blown. Pear-shape body; widely
flared rim pulled out to form broad spout; mold-blown
with 8 pronounced vertical ribs (pillar molding),
extending from the center of the bottom to the rim; ribs
are flattened around the base and cut around central
polished circle; applied rounded handle crimped and
curled at terminal; pontil mark.
H: 8½ in (21.6 cm)
Museum purchase, 1976: Tontine Emporium, Ridgefield,
Conn.
76.162

This pitcher is an example of pillar molding, a
decorative process which exploits the properties
of glass to glorious effect. Developed in Roman
times, pillar molding was revived about 1840
in England and soon became popular in American glass.

London glass manufacturer Apsley Pellatt
described the production process, noting that a
metal mold about a third the size of the object
to be made was required:

> The metal [glass] is first gathered upon a
> rod in the ordinary manner, except that the
> first gathering should be allowed to cool to a
> greater degree of hardness than usual; the
> second coating should be pressed into the
> mould . . . as hot as possible, that the exte-
> rior coating only shall be acted upon by the
> pressure of the moulding, and that the inte-
> rior shall preserve its smooth circular area.
> When about half formed, the projecting
> parts [ribs] have a centrifugal enlargement
> given to them by a sharp trundling of the
> iron at, or immediately after, the moment
> the workman is blowing; during the
> re-heating process.[1]

Characteristics that might distinguish
American from English pillar-molded glass have
not been satisfactorily delineated, nor has the
extent of pillar-molded production in the
United States been documented. American collectors have categorically attributed all pillar-
molded ware to Pittsburgh. The trade catalogues
of M'Kee and Brothers prove that pillar-molded
glass was made in that city, but the technique
was certainly practiced in other glassmaking
centers.[2] Pillar-molded glass has also been long
associated with usage on river steamboats, but
no documentation of this has been located.

1. Apsley Pellatt, *Curiosities of Glass Making* (1849; reprint,
Newport, Eng.: Ceramic Book Co., 1968), pp. 104–5. The
popularity of the ware in Britain is suggested by unusual
parian porcelain pitchers made in imitation of pillar-
molded glass by Samuel Alcock and Co. of Burslem,
Staffordshire, in the 1850s (collection of the author).
2. Innes, *Pittsburgh Glass*, pp. 193–201; *M'Kee Glass*
(1859/60) p. 19; (1864) p. 50; (1868) p. 138. Pitchers only are
shown in this style and are described as "quart ribbed
pitcher."

Chapter 6
Punch Bowls

Introduced to western Europe from the East in the late 1600s, punch became a very popular beverage in the 1700s. Recipes varied, but most punches contained an alcoholic base such as brandy or rum, hot or cold water, sugar, lemon or lime, and spices.

Punch was especially refreshing when served cold. When he arrived at his Philadelphia hotel, British traveler Henry Wansey ordered "a glass of cool punch." He noted that it contained pineapple juice "to heighten its flavor," but he seemed surprised by the lump of ice in the glass.[1]

Punch was prepared in bowls that were most frequently made of porcelain or earthenware. Because the beverage was particularly associated with celebrations or special occasions, punch bowls were often inscribed or custom decorated. A rare glass example was engraved to celebrate the wedding of Elizabeth Hannaford and John Davey in London in 1769. A Captain Blaiklock, stationed at Quebec City, owned a small glass punch bowl engraved "September 14, 1766," presumably commemorating a special event.[2]

English glass punch bowls are known from the late seventeenth century, but the first colonial references to them date from the 1720s.[3] Glass punch bowls were uncommon in the United States until the end of the nineteenth century, when brilliant cut-glass and pressed-glass punch bowl sets became a mark of middle-class propriety.

Punch was typically ladled from the bowl, and even ladles were fashioned from glass at an early date. Glass was the preferred material from which to drink punch, whether stemmed wineglasses, tumblers, cups, or mugs. The small size of the Blaiklock bowl indicates that it also served as a drinking vessel. That people even drank directly from rather large punch bowls can be seen in eighteenth-century illustrations of drinking parties. To the Comte de Ségur, traveling in the United States in the late 1700s, one of the most shocking customs he encountered was "when the time came for toasts, to pass around the table a great bowl of punch from which each guest was obliged in turn to drink."[4]

1. Henry Wansey, *An Excursion to the United States of North America in the Summer of 1794* (2d ed.; Salisbury, Eng.: J. Easton, 1798), p. 118.
2. W. M. Schwind, Jr., Antiques advertisement, Antiques 137, no. 3 (March 1990): 633. The Blaiklock bowl, in National Museum of Man, Ottawa, is pictured in Jones and Smith, *British Military*, p. 55, fig. 63.
3. For an early English punch bowl and ladle, see London Museum, *The Garton Collection of English Table Glass* (London: Her Majesty's Stationery Office, 1965), p. 15, no. 4. Two glass punch bowls are listed in the 1728 probate inventory of Arthur Allen, Surry County, Va., in Surry County Deed Book, 1715–30, pt. 3, pp. 807–10, reference courtesy of John C. Austin.
4. Merchant Mehetabel Kneeland listed glass ladles in her advertisement in *Boston Gazette*, April 25, 1737. An Annapolis drawing from the 1740s entitled "The Royalist Club," showing a man drinking from a punch bowl, is in Carl Bridenbaugh, ed., *Dr. Alexander Hamilton's Itinerarium* (Chapel Hill: University of North Carolina Press, 1948). Ségur quoted in Charles H. Sherrill, *French Memories of Eighteenth-Century America* (1915; reprint, New York: Benjamin Blom, 1971), p. 86.

145

PUNCH BOWL

GERMANY OR BOHEMIA, 1740–75

Opalescent white, bubbly glass. Circular form with curving sides; applied foot ring; concave bottom; pontil mark. Polychrome enamel-painted decoration: 3 large floral sprays on the exterior, 4 on the interior.
H: 3½ in (8.9 cm); Diam: 8 in (20.3 cm)
H. F. du Pont purchase
59.59.1

Like the related tewares (NOS. 74–77) at Winterthur, this glass punch bowl imitates the form, substance, and decoration of ceramics.

In the seventeenth century, glassmakers in France and Germany experimented with the manufacture of opaque white glass, thus continuing a tradition of Venetian glassmaking. In Munich in 1669 Joachim Becher produced a

porcelainlike glass using lead, tin, and bone ash. Johann Kunckel's recipe for opal glass, published in his 1679 *Ars Vitraria Experimentalis*, utilized bone and horn ash and created an opalescent, rather than truly opaque, white glass. Formulas varied, but German production of opalescent milk glass in the eighteenth century was based on Kunckel's work.[1]

1. Olga Drahotová, *European Glass* (New York: Excalibur Books, 1983), pp. 153–56.

146

PUNCH BOWL WITH COVER
HURDALEN, NORWAY,
ATTRIBUTED TO HURDALS VERK
GLASSHOUSE, CIRCA 1800

Blue lead glass. Blown. Bowl: wide hemispherical form with
outward-folded edge, drawn cylindrical foot; pontil mark.
Cover: high, domed form flared at base to vertical edge
made to fit over rim of bowl; drawn flattened ball finial
with pontil mark on top.
OH: 8⅛ in (20.6 cm); Diam top of bowl: 9¹¹⁄₁₆ in (24.6 cm)
H. F. du Pont purchase, probably from Israel Sack
69.1476a, b

Published: Knittle, *Early American Glass,* pl. 12, after p. 76.

Products from Norwegian glasshouses have long
been erroneously attributed to the United States,
starting with the large blue covered urns published by Hunter as examples of Stiegel glass.[1]
In 1927 Knittle labeled this bowl a rare Stiegel

specimen. Although neither the urns nor this
punch bowl bears any relationship to known
American products, there are interesting parallels between the glass industries of Norway and
the United States. In both countries, workers
of German and Bohemian origin formed the
nucleus of the labor pool. Members of the
Wentzel family of glassblowers, for example,
are recorded both at Nøstetangen in Norway
and at Wistarburgh in New Jersey. In both coun-

tries English artisans introduced the technology
of lead glass in the third quarter of the eighteenth century.[2]

English punch bowls, whether of metal,
glass, or ceramics, generally lacked covers, but
price lists of Norwegian glasshouses in 1763 and
1787 prove that punch bowls there were commonly covered, as were their ceramic counterparts. No parallels are known in American glass,
but a similar form in American pewter is in the
Winterthur collection.[3]

1. Hunter, *Stiegel Glass,* fig. 60.
2. Polak, "Illustrated Price-List," pp. 87–88; Ada Buch
Polak, *Gammelt Norsk Glass* (Oslo: Gyldendal Norsk
Forlag, 1953), pp. 221–25; Ada Polak, *Glass: Its Makers and
Its Public* (London: Weidenfeld and Nicolson, 1975), p. 26;
Palmer, "Glass Production," p. 78.
3. For similar bowls attributed to Hurdals Verk, see Polak,
Gammelt, pp. 232–34, pl. 83, no. 197; pl. 88, no. 209; pl. 87,
no. 200. Documentation on the use of covers is based on
Ada Polak to the author, May 22, 1990. Charles F.
Montgomery, *A History of American Pewter* (New York:
Praeger Publishers, 1973), p. 144, figs. 8–11.

147

PUNCH BOWL (ONE OF TWO)
UNITED STATES, 1815–40

Colorless lead glass. Blown. Deep circular form with curved sides and outward-folded edge; blown in 3-part mold of geometric design (McKearin G II-21): faint vertical ribbing around rim; narrow band of diagonal ribbing within horizontal rings; wide band of diamond diapering; diagonal ribbing within horizontal rings above vertical ribbing; applied disk foot of irregular circumference; pontil mark.
H: 6⅜ in (16.3 cm); Diam: 9⁵⁄₁₆ in (23.5 cm)
H. F. du Pont purchase, before 1939
59.3274 (mate is 67.849)

Winterthur's two large punch bowls are among the rare survivals of mold-blown American glass. Close inspection of defects in the ribbed areas of the G II-21 design indicates that the two were blown in the same mold.

It is unclear from du Pont's records where and when he acquired NO. 147. Neil Gest included it as no. 65 in his 1939 inventory of the glass at Winterthur but gave no hint of its provenance. A smaller bowl of this pattern had been sold in 1938 from the William Van Winkle collection and was considered "probably unique." It had a history of having been purchased in Rustburg, Campbell County, Virginia, from a family "who had lived there all their lives."[1]

The mate to NO. 147 came to Winterthur in November 1946. Its owner, collector Richard Loeb, sold it at auction in New York where Gest acquired it for du Pont.[2] Both bowls have plain feet, but an example with a rayed foot was published by the McKearins in 1941.[3]

These bowls presumably functioned as punch bowls because in size and shape they follow the standard ceramic ones, yet no mention of the form in mold-blown glass has been found in glasshouse price lists or advertisements of this period. Instead, glass punch bowls were generally described as cut or engraved, suggesting the luxury status of the form. In 1819 South Boston Flint Glass Works offered punch bowls among their "Rich Cut Glass." The rival New England Glass Company made "Husked, Fingered & Beaded Punch Bowls" as well as engraved ones in quart and half-gallon sizes. These could be purchased in Norfolk, Virginia, in 1820 from "a complete assortment of plain and Rich Cut Glass" manufactured by that Cambridge firm.[4] Thus the Virginia history of the Van Winkle bowl by no means precludes a New England origin.

In Baltimore in 1832, Baltimore Flint Glass Works manufactured punch bowls in 8-, 9-, and 10-inch diameters of different styles. Eight-inch

148

ones came in $1.50, $2.00, and $2.50 varieties, and the 10-inch size cost $4.00 each.[5] Documentary evidence proves that the Baltimore factory was producing plain, molded, cut, and pressed glass, but no mold-blown wares from the works have been identified.

1. Parke-Bernet Galleries, "Important Early American Glass . . . Collected by William Mitchell Van Winkle," sale no. 34 (April 28–29, 1938), lot 426.
2. Parke-Bernet Galleries, "Fine English and American Furniture and Decorations," sale no. 805 (November 9, 1946), lot 83.
3. McKearin and McKearin, *American Glass*, pl. 109, no. 5.
4. Prices Current, South Boston, 1819, Edison Inst. Hugh and William Pannell, auctioneers, advertisement, *American Beacon and Norfolk and Portsmouth Daily Advertiser*, May 8, 1820, reference courtesy of MESDA.
5. Invoice to William and James Neal, August 8, 1832, Chapman-Baker Day Book, MdHS.

PUNCH BOWL
FRANCE, 1855–85; ENGRAVING
POSSIBLY LATER

Colorless lead glass of gray tint. Blown. Heavy, hemispherical form with panel-cut sides below a recessed rim. Wheel engraved: on opposite sides, an oval medallion containing the emblem of the Society of the Cincinnati. Star-cut bottom.
H: 8 in (20.4 cm); Diam: 14½ in (36.3 cm)
History: found in Bermuda
H. F. du Pont purchase: J. A. Lloyd Hyde, New York City
61.630.2

This punch bowl and its matching tray (61.630.1) are part of a large service of colorless cut glass engraved with the emblem of the Order of the Cincinnati (NOS. 34, 35). The idea of a punch bowl and tray with matching drinking glasses is documented as early as 1788 when Philadelphian Thomas Hutchins bought such a service "ornamented with crest."[1] Apparently this Cincinnati set was assembled and engraved to special order, perhaps for French members of the society. Found by dealer Lloyd Hyde in Bermuda, the specific history of the service is as yet unknown.

1. Invoice from Jacob Schrinier, Downs, WL.

Table Glass for the Serving of Food

Chapter 7
Sugar Bowls

When West Indian sugar became more widely available in Europe during the seventeenth century, it was liberally added to all manner of fish, meat, egg, and salad dishes. By 1700, sugar was used chiefly to cure meat, preserve fruits, and sweeten dessert foods. It was also frequently mixed with beverages.

Putting sugar in wine to "temper the roughness" was a common custom of the eighteenth century. In 1709 William Byrd of Westover, Virginia, recorded in his diary that he "drank a glass of Rhenish wine and sugar."[1] Sugar was a necessary ingredient of most punches. Many colonists found that sugar greatly enhanced the flavor of tea, coffee, and chocolate. Peter Kalm visited Albany in the mid eighteenth century and observed that the Dutch settlers there "never put sugar into the cup, but take a small bit of it into their mouths while they drink." Traveling through New Sweden, Israel Acrelius was surprised to find "tea, coffee, and chocolate are so general as to be found in the most remote cabins, if not for daily use, yet for visitors"; he notes that these drinks were "mixed with Muscovado or raw sugar."[2]

Although North American maple sugar could meet some sweetening needs, most housewives endeavored to buy the best quality imported sugar they could afford. There were as many as nine grades of sugar, and prices varied accordingly. Coarse muscovado sugar was brown; ordinary refined sugar was yellow, and increased refining whitened the color. Carolus Linnaeus described the process at a Swedish refinery in 1741:

> The coarse and unrefined raw sugar was pulverized and boiled in water, diluted with limewater, mixed with ox blood or egg white, skimmed and poured into inverted cone-shaped moulds, perforated at the tip; from these a syrup trickled down into a bottle; this was repeated, and then the mould was covered with a white, dough-like French clay like a lid.[3]

The clay filtered water through the sugar carrying impurities with it. When removed from the clay cones, sugar was wrapped in paper and marketed as a loaf. The loaf could be cut into lumps or grated to a powder.

Just as "the kind of sugar they use marks generally poverty or richness," the sugar container, whether of silver or pewter, porcelain or earthenware, cut glass or common green glass, made a statement about the household.[4] In spite of their frequent service on the tea table, silver and ceramic sugar bowls did not always match the teapot and other vessels in shape or pattern, perhaps because of their role in other dining and drinking situations. Some consumers may have preferred glass sugar bowls because they harmonized more readily with vessels of other materials.

An early record of glass sugar containers in colonial America occurs in the 1731 advertisement of Boston importer Rebecca Abbot.[5] Eighteenth-century documents refer to glass sugar containers as boxes, pots, dishes, bowls, and basins, suggesting considerable variation in shape and style. Sugar bowls in the eighteenth and nineteenth centuries often had covers, but there was also a tradition of open sugars, particularly in English provincial production. Early covers usually fit inside the bowl with a pulled-out flange that rested on the rim of the bowl. After about 1800, the fashion changed to high, domed covers resembling bells that rested inside the galleried rims of bowls. The finials on English sugar bowl lids were generally of simple geometric shape, such as balls or spires. Craftsmen at Wistarburgh, New Bremen, and other American factories followed Continental practice in making finials whimsically tooled into birds and swans. Many nineteenth-century sugar bowls had simple finials. Some sugar bowls came with stands as well as covers, as seen in an 1819 advertisement for "rich cut Globe sugars with tops and stands."[6]

1. G. Bernard Hughes, *Small Antique Silverware* (New York: Bramhall, 1957), p. 32. Louis B. Wright and Marion Tinling, eds., *The Secret Diary of William Byrd of Westover, 1709–12* (Richmond: Dietz Press, 1941), pp. 28, 69.
2. Adolph B. Benson, ed., *Peter Kalm's Travels in North America* (New York: Wilson-Erickson, 1937), p. 347. Acrelius is quoted in Rodris Roth, "Tea Drinking in Eighteenth-Century America: Its Etiquette and Equipage," *United States National Museum Bulletin*, no. 225 (Washington, D.C.: Smithsonian Institution, 1961): 66.
3. Quoted in glossary to Hannah Glasse, *The Art of Cookery* (facsimile ed.; London: Prospect Books, 1983), p. 201.
4. Louis L. B. J. S. Robertnier's 1780 comment quoted in Belden, *Festive Tradition*, p. 104.
5. *New England Journal*, January 24, 1731.
6. T. Twitchell advertisment, *Petersburg Intelligencer* (Virginia), January 18, 1819, reference courtesy of MESDA.

149

SUGAR BOWL WITH COVER
ENGLAND, 1725–45

Colorless and opaque white lead glass. Blown. Bowl: tall
and U-shape, flaring out at rim and curved in at base;
applied pedestal foot; pontil mark. Cover: conical top and
straight sides, inset with flange pulled out to rest on edge
of bowl; applied spire finial containing 2 rows of air beads
around a central bead; interior pontil mark. Marvered into
the glass and radiating from the base of bowl and the finial
of cover are filigree canes of twisted white enamel threads;
intertwined canes encircle the rims of both pieces. Paper
label inscribed with history adhered to the bottom.
OH: 8⅛ in (20.6 cm); Diam top of bowl: 5 in (12.7 cm)
History: Mary Lefevre Deshler; Catherine Deshler Roberts;
Esther M. Roberts; Samuel Canby; Elizabeth Morris Canby
Rumford; Lewis Rumford; Lewis Rumford II
Gift of Mr. and Mrs. Lewis Rumford II, 1979
79.62a, b

Exhibited: Wilmington Society of Fine Arts, January 10–28,
1940.
Published: "From Kiln and Glory Hole," *Antiques* 37, no. 3
(March 1940): 133.
Arlene Palmer Schwind, "Tale of a Twist," *Glass Club
Bulletin*, no. 133 (Spring 1981): 9–11.

This covered bowl is one of the few English glass
objects that survives above ground with a firm
history in colonial America. The original owner
was Mary Lefevre (1715–74), a Philadelphian of
French Huguenot heritage. In 1739 she married
David Deshler, nephew of America's pioneer
glass manufacturer, Caspar Wistar (NO. 150).
This unusual English bowl was inherited by
their daughter, Catherine Roberts; upon her
death in 1837 it passed to her daughter Esther
Morton Roberts, who in turn left it to her
nephew, Samuel Canby of Wilmington. It was
Samuel's wife, Elizabeth Clifford Morris Canby
(1813–92), who carefully preserved the history of
the bowl as well as that of other important glass
and ceramic items (NO. 283).[1]

The rather tall and narrow bowl is a baroque
form better known with gadroon-molding
around the base and guilloche bands of colorless
glass applied around the middle.[2] That plan of
ornament is repeated here, but the glassblower
substituted white twists for the gadrooning and
created a chain of ribbons of white glass. This

unusual filigree work seems to presage the
twist-stemmed vessels that were a hallmark of
English glass of the third quarter of the eighteenth century (NOS. 6–12). At the same time,
the decoration evokes the *vetro a filigrana* made
in Venice some two hundred years before.[3]

Although Thorpe has described bowls of
this shape as posset pots, this bowl was probably intended to hold sugar, which in the eighteenth century was in the form of fairly large
lumps cut from the loaf.[4]

1. The bowl was no. 78 in Mrs. Canby's catalogue,
described as "Bowl with lid-glass with white figurings
through it," the manuscript of which is in the collection
of Mr. and Mrs. Lewis Rumford II.
2. For covered bowls of the same form but with gadroon-
molded and applied decoration, see Hughes, *Table Glass*,
p. 57, fig. 24.
3. Tait, *Golden Age*, p. 69, fig. 92.
4. Thorpe, *History*, 2: pl. 75, no. 3.

150, PL. 13

SUGAR BOWL WITH COVER
ALLOWAY, NEW JERSEY,
ATTRIBUTED TO WISTARBURGH
GLASSWORKS OF CASPAR AND
RICHARD WISTAR, 1739–77

Yellow-green nonlead glass. Blown. Bowl: wide and U-shape, faintly pattern-molded with 20 vertical ribs, probably dipped twice in the mold; 2 applied rounded handles, curled back at lower terminal; applied pedestal foot of irregular circumference; pontil mark. Cover: free blown; low, domed top and straight sides, inset with flange pulled out to rest on edge of bowl; applied finial of 2 balls on a wafer, surmounted by a disk faintly pincered with a chevron pattern on one side and cross-hatching on the other; around the lower ball is an applied band of glass pulled out into 6 protruding disks and pincered at the top disk; interior pontil mark.
OH: 7¼ in (18.5 cm); Diam top of bowl: 4¹³⁄₁₆ in (12.2 cm)
History: Arthur J. Sussel, Philadelphia
Museum purchase, 1959: Parke-Bernet Galleries, New York City
59.30.2

Exhibited: Museum of American Glass, Wheaton Village, "The Wistars and Their Glass, 1739–1777," 1989.
Published: Advertisement of Arthur J. Sussel, *Antiques* 38, no. 6 (December 1940): 264.
Agnes Marshall, "Shopping Around," *American Collector* 16, no. 12 (January 1948): 25.
Advertisement of Arthur J. Sussel, *Antiques* 69, no. 5 (May 1956): 380.

Parke-Bernet Galleries, "American and Other Decorative Arts . . . Part Three: Collection of the Late Arthur J. Sussel," sale no. 1888 (March 19–21, 1959), lot 79.
Palmer, "Glass Production," p. 92, fig. 17.
Arlene Palmer, *The Wistarburgh Glassworks: The Beginning of Jersey Glassmaking* (Alloway, N.J.: Alloway Bicentennial Committee, 1976), p. 22, fig. 15.
Schwind, "Pennsylvania German Glass," p. 202, fig. 192.
Arlene Palmer, *The Wistars and Their Glass, 1739–1777* (Millville, N.J.: Museum of American Glass at Wheaton Village, 1989), p. 22, fig. 20.

Although bottles and window glass were the major products of the Wistar enterprise, factory records indicate that tablewares of green and even refined "white" (colorless) and colored glass were also made. Objects that have descended in the Wistar family have provided a key to Wistar production (NO. 283).

No sugar bowl has retained a Wistar family history, but there are several that can be attributed to Wistarburgh. Winterthur's bowl relates closely to two with histories in southern New Jersey: one in the Salem County Historical Society and one in the Newark Museum.[1] Both the lid and bowl of the Newark example were patterned in a twenty-rib mold; those of the Salem County example were molded with sixteen ribs. All three covers have the distinctive tripartite finial with applied band of pincered wafers, a decorative device that harks back to *façon de venise* stemware and is seen again in some English glass of the early 1700s.[2] The handles of the three sugar bowls are formed in the same manner, although the one at Newark is embellished with tooled finger rests. The generous size of the bowls, the form of the covers, and the decorative details are indicative of eighteenth-century origin and a strong Germanic influence. Although a wine bottle made at Wistarburgh for the personal use of Richard Wistar emulates the English imported bottles that dominated the colonial market, these sugar bowls bear no relation to the contemporary English models that would have graced the finest tables in Philadelphia.

1. See Arlene Palmer, *The Wistarburgh Glassworks: The Beginning of Jersey Glassmaking* (Alloway, N.J.: Alloway Bicentennial Committee, 1976), pp. 21, 23.
2. A related finial is recorded on an English covered bowl of the late seventeenth century, in L. M. Bickerton, *Eighteenth-Century English Drinking Glasses, An Illustrated Guide* (London: Antique Collectors' Club, 1986), no. 44. See also Grant R. Francis, *Old English Drinking Glasses* (London: Herbert Jenkins, 1926), pl. 2, no. 18.

151, 152

SUGAR BOWLS WITH COVERS
PENNSYLVANIA OR NEW JERSEY,
POSSIBLY MANHEIM GLASSWORKS
OF HENRY WILLIAM STIEGEL,
1765–90

NO. 151. Colorless low-lead glass of greenish-gray tint.
Blown. Bowl: bulbous body, pattern-molded with 16
vertical ribs over 16 swirled ribs; 2 applied rounded handles
curled back at lower terminal; thick, applied foot of irregular square form curved down and pincered with a V at
corners; pontil mark. Cover: free blown; conical top and
straight sides, inset with flange pulled out to rest on edge
of bowl; applied finial of tooled swan on wafer; interior
pontil mark.
OH: 7 in (17.9 cm); Diam top of bowl: 3³⁄₁₆ in (8.2 cm)
History: Mrs. J. Amory Haskell; Arthur J. Sussel,
Philadelphia
Museum purchase, 1959: Parke-Bernet Galleries, New
York City
59.30.1a, b

Published: Parke-Bernet Galleries, "The Americana
Collection of the Late Mrs. J. Amory Haskell," pt. 3, sale
no. 587 (October 11–14, 1944), p. 50, lot 223.
Advertisement of Arthur J. Sussel, *American Collector* 15
(December 1946): inside cover.
Advertisement of Arthur J. Sussel, *Antiques* 55, no. 5
(May 1949): 327.
Parke-Bernet Galleries, "American and Other Decorative
Arts . . . Part Three: Collection of the Late Arthur J.
Sussel," sale no. 1888 (March 19, 1959), lot 78.
Pepper, *Glass Gaffers*, p. 18, fig. 16.

NO. 152. Colorless nonlead glass of bluish tint. Blown.
Bowl: bulbous body, tapered sharply at base; 2 applied
handles of thin, intertwined loops, curled back at lower
terminal; thick, applied foot of irregular square form
curved down and pincered with a V at corners; pontil
mark. Cover: flat top and straight sides, inset with flange
pulled out to rest on edge of bowl; applied finial of tooled
swan on flattened ball and wafer; interior pontil mark.
OH: 6¾ in (17.3 cm); Diam top of bowl: 3½ in (8.9 cm)
History: W. G. Russell Allen (1926); Mrs. Frederick S. Fish;
W. Griffin Gribbel
H. F. du Pont purchase, 1948: Neil C. Gest, Mechanicburg,
Ohio
59.3028a, b

Published: Parke-Bernet Galleries, "Early American
Glass . . . Collection Formed by Mrs. Frederick S. Fish,"
sale no. 159 (January 5–6, 1940), lot 367.
McKearin and McKearin, *American Glass*, pl. 15, no. 3.
McKearin and McKearin, *Two Hundred Years*, p. 181, pl. 30.
Thomas S. Buechner, "Origins of American Glass,"
Antiques 68, no. 6 (December 1955): 560, fig. 2.
Margaret E. White, *Decorative Arts of Early New Jersey*
(Princeton: Van Nostrand, 1964), p. 13.
Pepper, *Glass Gaffers*, p. 18, fig. 14.

These are two of a group of five related bowls.[1]
Although their exact origin is unknown, they
appear to have been made at the same glassworks. All are of a similar shape and proportion
and are blown of colorless glass. The four bowls
that retain their covers are capped with swan
finials (or remains thereof), each fashioned in
the same distinctive manner with a tall, erect tail
tooled into narrow feathers. Another bowl at
Winterthur (NO. 153) has a closely related finial
but shares none of the other characteristics. The
bowl at the Metropolitan Museum is pattern
molded with 16 ribs like NO. 151, the gather having been dipped in the mold and swirled and
then dipped again for a broken swirl or basket-
weave effect. NO. 152 features unusual intertwined
handles that look heart-shaped from above. This
detail is paralleled on the Ford Museum example,
but that bowl is set on a round rather than square
foot. The thick square feet of NOS. 151 and 152 link
the group to a green vase in the Winterthur collection (NO. 254).

With their whimsical animal finials, the
bowls clearly reflect a continental European
glassmaking tradition (see NOS. 159, 160). No
parallels for this style are recorded in English
production, but the handles of NO. 152 are reminiscent of English ceramic sugar bowls made of
creamware and pearlware in the last quarter of
the eighteenth century.[2]

The majority of glass craftsmen who worked
in eighteenth-century America emigrated from
areas of Germany, so it is difficult to pinpoint
which American factory was responsible for the
important group of sugar bowls. None has survived with a history of ownership. The refined
material as well as the form of the bowls suggest a
glasshouse where tableware was an integral facet
of production.

As discussed in NOS. 283 and 284, workers at
Wistarburgh did manufacture some colorless and
blue glass objects. Sixteen- and twenty-rib molds
were also used for patterning there (see NO. 150),
and a bowl in the Newark Museum is decorated
in the broken-swirl style. Bird finials are recorded
on two cream buckets and a green glass covered
bowl attributed to Wistarburgh, but they are not
of the same feather as the swans seen here.[3]

Henry William Stiegel's glass manufactory is
a more likely source than Wistarburgh because
Stiegel was more concerned with the production
of refined tableware than any other glassmaker
before the Revolution. Bottles and window glass
dominated production from 1764 to 1769, but it
is now known that Martin Greiner, a craftsman
from Saxe-Weimar, also fashioned numerous
table forms, including sugar bowls, in that period. Although most of these would have been
blown of the same unrefined glass as the bottles
and windows, the factory records do mention
"white" or colorless glass.[4] Greiner and the other
Germanic blowers continued at the Manheim,
Pennsylvania, glasshouse even after Stiegel
turned his attention toward the production of
glass in the English taste. Lead glass was blown,
at first from cullet and then, by 1771, from raw
materials. The low lead content of NO. 151 suggests it could have been made at Manheim in
the 1769–71 period of experimentation with
lead cullet.[5]

Another contender for the source of these
bowls is the Stenger (also spelled Stanger) glasshouse in Gloucester County, New Jersey. Members of this glassmaking family emigrated from
Germany in 1768 and blew glass for Richard
Wistar. When Wistarburgh closed, Solomon
Stenger bought land in what later became Glassboro and during the winter of 1779/80 erected a
glassworks of his own.[6] By 1786 Thomas Heston
and Thomas Carpenter had acquired the business, but they retained the Stengers as managers
and workers. A newspaper notice of 1788 must
refer to the Glassboro works: "A White Glass
Manufactory has lately been set on foot in New
Jersey, and the glass pronounced equal to the
English White Glass and is sold here [Philadel-
phia] considerably cheaper."[7] The British consul
in Philadelphia was quick to allay any fears in the
home industry by noting in his report to the
British Foreign Office that the local "white glass
is of a very mean quality and they rely upon
what broken flint glass they can procure to make
their white glass."[8] As at Manheim, then, this
firm was reworking melted flint cullet. Currently,
only one glass object, a green bottle, has any firm
association with the Glassboro undertaking.

The Stengers' connections with several glasshouses over a period of time illustrate the complexity of the early American glass trade and suggest the dangers of attempts at rigid attribution. Of the immigrants, Adam, Christian, and Daniel Stenger are mentioned in the records of the Friesburg Emmanuel Lutheran Church near Wistarburgh, so it can be assumed they were employed by the Wistars. Jacob Stenger absconded from Richard Wistar, who placed a notice for his arrest in the Philadelphia newspapers. Solomon Stenger is named in passing in Stiegel's records; it was he who subsequently purchased the land in Gloucester County for the new factory. Presumably he worked there until his death in 1794.[9] Francis Stenger, probably a son of one of the immigrants, was the owner of a famous flask made at Amelung's New Bremen glassworks in 1792.[10]

1. The others are in Corning Museum, Metropolitan Museum of Art, and Henry Ford Museum, Edison Inst.
2. Peter Walton, *Creamware and Other English Pottery at Temple Newsam House, Leeds* (London: Lund Humphries, 1976), pp. 158, 183, nos. 658, 742.
3. For an illustration of the Newark bowl, see Palmer, "Glass Production," p. 91, fig. 16. The colorless cream bucket is in the Melvin Billups Collection, New Orleans

Museum of Art; the blue one is in Corning Museum. The green bowl (private collection) is in Arlene Palmer, *The Wistars and Their Glass, 1739–1777* (Millville, N.J.: Museum of American Glass at Wheaton Village, 1989), p. 22, fig. 21.

4. Palmer, "To the Good," p. 205.

5. A 2–3 percent lead content was detected. Analytical Laboratory, Winterthur Conservation; Palmer, "To the Good," pp. 211–12, 229.

6. Johan Adam Stenger or Stanger, Sr., traveled with Adam, Christian, Jacob, Daniel, Solomon, and Jacob Stenger on the *Betsey* as listed in I. Daniel Rupp, *A Collection of Thirty Thousand Names of German, Swiss, Dutch, French, and Other Immigrants in Pennsylvania from 1727 to 1776* (Philadelphia: Kohler, 1876), pp. 386–87. Deed, Jacob Gosling to Solomon Stenger, in Robert D. Bole and Edward H. Walton, Jr., *The Glassboro Story, 1779–1964* (York, Pa.: Maple Press, 1964), app. An advertisement for a tract of land notes "A Glass-house . . . lately erected within a mile of it," *Pennsylvania Packet*, March 11, 1780.

7. *Maryland Journal*, July 1, 1788; *Gazette of Georgia*, July 1, 1788, the latter reference courtesy of MESDA.

8. Phineas Bond to the Duke of Leeds, November 10, 1789, American Historical Association, *Annual Report for the Year 1896* (Washington, D.C.: Government Printing Office, 1897), 1:652. Bond erroneously located the glass-house in Woodbury.

9. Advertisement for runaway Stenger in *Pennsylvania Chronicle*, April 18, 1770. Solomon Stenger is named as a glassblower at Manheim in September 1774, but it is not clear how long he may have been there; Ledger C, no. 3, 1774, p. 98, Stiegel Records, HSP.

10. Lanmon and Palmer, "New Bremen," pp. 72–73, no. 12.

153, PL. 14

SUGAR BOWL WITH COVER
PENNSYLVANIA OR MARYLAND, 1770–1810

Green nonlead glass. Blown. Bowl: deep and U-shape;
2 applied rounded handles curled back at lower terminal;
applied pedestal foot with irregularly scalloped edge;
ring-shape pontil mark. Cover: conical top and straight
sides, inset with thick flange pulled out to rest on edge of
bowl; applied, tooled swan finial on wafer; interior pontil
mark. Bowl is cracked and repaired.
OH: 7¾ in (19.7 cm); Diam top of bowl: 3¾ in (9.5 cm)
H. F. du Pont purchase, 1949: Neil C. Gest, Mechanicsburg, Ohio
59.3032a, b

Published: Schwind, "Pennsylvania German Glass," p. 210,
fig. 202.

A sugar bowl virtually identical to Winterthur's
in color, shape, and bird finial was said to have
been found in a farmhouse some thirty miles
from New Geneva in western Pennsylvania.[1] On
this basis, both bowls have long been attributed
to the glasshouse that was built in that town
about 1797. A third bowl, closely related but
blown of light blue glass, can also be considered
part of this "New Geneva" group. Although its
finial was broken, enough remains to indicate it
had been tooled in the same manner as the
finials of the other bowls.[2] Although New
Geneva is certainly a possible source for these
bowls, the migratory history of the glassblowers
there suggests additional prospects.

The New Geneva Glass Works was established by James Nicholson and Albert Gallatin,
member of the House of Representatives and
later Secretary of the Treasury. The most plausi-
bly documented object attributed to the early
period of the glassworks is a large blown goblet
in the Strauss Collection of Corning Museum.
Made of green glass, the goblet encloses in its
stem a silver "Prix de Diligence" that was apparently awarded Albert Gallatin while a student at
University of Geneva.[3] This goblet does not bear
any particular relationship to the sugar bowls.

Gallatin hired glassmakers from John
Frederick Amelung's defunct factory, New
Bremen, in western Maryland. Chief among
them was Baltzer (Baltasar, Balthaser) Kramer,
who had once worked for Henry William
Stiegel. A Kramer descendant researching his
family genealogy had long ago unearthed this
Stiegel-Amelung connection, but what has
more recently been discovered is that Kramer
built and operated another glassworks in the
interim. Located in Frederick County, Maryland, this factory was founded as a partnership
between Baltzer, his brother, George, and his
brothers-in-law Martin Everhart (Eberhardt)
and Conrad Foltz (Voltz). Glass was made there
between 1780 and 1784.[4]

The peripatetic record of Baltzer Kramer
clearly demonstrates the difficulties of positively identifying the products of America's
glasshouses in the 1770–1810 period. Workers
carried their knowledge, skills, tools, and molds
from factory to factory. The only extant molds
associated with early American glassmaking are
three part-size molds used at New Geneva,
which descended in the family of a Christian
Kramer (the relationship to Baltzer, if any, is
not known)(see p. 2, fig. 6).[5] Given the history
of the workmen, it is conceivable they were
used at several glasshouses: New Geneva, New
Bremen, the Kramer-Everhart-Foltz factory,
and Manheim.

None of the three "New Geneva" bowls
share any obvious characteristics with the bowls
attributed to Wistarburgh (NO. 150) or New
Bremen (NOS. 157, 158). In the shape and proportion of its body, handles, and petal foot,
NO. 153 relates to a colorless lead glass bowl in
Cincinnati Museum of Art that bears a Wistar-
type finial and is now thought to be of Stiegel
manufacture.[6] The finial of NO. 153 is similar to
those on NOS. 151 and 152: the swan was con-
ceived in the same way, although on NO. 153 it
was tooled with too much glass and was less
well executed. The cover of NO. 153 has the same
conical form as NO. 151. Although a Manheim
origin is also possible for NO. 153, the weight
and color of the glass support an attribution to
one of Stiegel's successors in the region.

1. Owned by Neil C. Gest when published by him and
Parke G. Smith, "The Glassmaking Kramers," *Antiques* 35,
no. 3 (March 1939): 182, fig. 9. Owned by Smith when
shown in McKearin and McKearin, *American Glass*, pl. 45,
no. 3, and since 1955 this bowl, pattern molded with 24
ribs, has been in the collection of Cincinnati Art Museum
(1955.810); it is in Palmer, "To the Good," p. 207, fig. 2.
2. This was apparently also owned by Gest and
subsequently by James Burke. Peter Tillou, antiques
dealer of Litchfield, Conn., acquired it and sold it to
Crawford Wettlaufer.
3. Jerome Strauss, "Another Gallatin Glass," *Antiques* 36,
no. 2 (August 1939): 79; also in McKearin and McKearin,
Two Hundred Years, pl. 69.
4. LeRoy Kramer, comp., *Johann Baltasar Kramer . . .
Pioneer American Glass Blower: A Record of His Known
Descendants and Relatives* (Chicago: Privately printed,
1939). Lanmon and Palmer, "New Bremen," pp. 18–19. The
four men had emigrated together from Europe, traveling
on the *Britannia*, which landed in Philadelphia in
September 1773; I. Daniel Rupp, *A Collection of Thirty
Thousand Names of German, Swiss, Dutch, French and
Other Immigrants in Pennsylvania from 1727 to 1776*
(Philadelphia: Kohler, 1876), p. 408.
5. One with 16 ribs, one with 20 ribs, and one with a 16-
diamond pattern are in McKearin and McKearin, *American Glass*, pl. 46, nos. 8, 10, 11; see also Kramer, *Johann
Baltasar Kramer*, p. 13. Collection of Corning Museum.
6. American Art Association/Anderson Galleries, "Early
American Glass, Collection of Alfred B. Maclay," sale
no. 4211 (December 5–7, 1935), lot 325, ex collection
Minnie I. Meacham. Later owned by W. T. H. Howe. The
petal foot became popular in western Pennsylvania and
Ohio glass in the early nineteenth century (NOS. 120, 168,
169) although there are English wares of the eighteenth
century with the same foot.

154

SUGAR BOWL WITH COVER
PROBABLY ENGLAND, 1760–1800

Blue lead glass. Blown. Bowl: hemispherical body, pattern-molded with rows of 20 diamonds; applied pedestal foot of irregular circumference; pontil mark. Cover: conical top and straight sides, inset with flange pulled out to rest on edge of bowl; pattern-molded with rows of 20 diamonds; swirl-ribbed spire finial on wafer; interior pontil mark.
OH: 5½ in (14.05 cm); Diam top of bowl: 4⅜ in (11.2 cm)
H. F. du Pont purchase
59.3299a, b

Published: Schwind, "Pennsylvania German Glass," p. 204, fig. 196.

155, PL. 6

SUGAR BOWL

PROBABLY ENGLAND, 1760–1800

Purple lead glass. Blown. Hemispherical bowl pattern-molded with rows of 18 diamonds; applied tall pedestal foot with downward-folded edge; pontil mark.
H: 3¾ in (9.6 cm); Diam: 4 in (10.2 cm)
H. F. du Pont purchase, before 1940
59.3146

156, PL. 21

SUGAR BOWL
ENGLAND, 1770–1820

Emerald green lead glass. Blown. Shallow hemispherical bowl pattern-molded with 3 lateral rows of 11 diamonds above a row of 11 pointed flutes; applied, cylindrical foot flared at base; pontil mark.
H: 2½ in (6.3 cm); Diam: 4¼ in (10.4 cm)
H. F. du Pont purchase, 1928: D. N. Shanaman, Richmond, Pa.
59.3137

Published: Schwind, "Pennsylvania German Glass," p. 205, fig. 197.

The appeal of expanded diamond or honeycomb designs has ancient Roman roots. Diamond molding appeared in English glass from the late seventeenth century onward, but the fashion for brightly colored wares in this style did not take hold until later in the eighteenth century. Importers' records reveal the popularity of such wares in America in the latter part of the eighteenth century. In 1774, for example, New York merchant Frederick Rhinelander offered "Moulded Sugar basons & Covers" from a Liverpool factory; blue and purple are colors specified for sugar basins in his invoices.[1]

Dozens of colored mold-blown sugar bowls of this type have been attributed to the Manheim glasshouse of Henry William Stiegel, but none has been documented to that factory. Stiegel did produce colored glass, and sugar bowls are among the numerous tablewares listed in the factory's records. By 1771 Stiegel achieved full lead glass, and isolating his products from English imports is problematical.[2] Careful examination of molded patterns has revealed defects in some molds that were transmitted to every piece patterned in them. The 11-diamond-over-flute design of NO. 156, for example, has a defect in the form of a horizontal ridge across the top of one flute; this defect has been found in objects of this pattern that have apparently never left England.[3] The English attribution of this object is also strengthened by the brilliant green color, which cannot yet be associated with American production.

Period documents indicate that sugar bowls did not always have covers; NO. 156 may originally have had one, but NO. 155 with its tall foot probably did not. There is a tradition of sugar bowls of that form in the north of England, which refutes the popular notion that they were baptismal bowls.[4]

1. Josiah Perrin to Keeling and Davis, June 2, 1774, Rhinelander order to Vigor and Stevens, September 15, 1780, Letter and Order Book 1774–84, Rhinelander Papers, NYHS.
2. Palmer, "To the Good," pp. 210–12. When asked about colored glass bowls of this type, J. Bernard Perret of Delomosne and Son, a prominent London firm specializing in antique glass, replied: "I am quite sure that when I used to sell these English pieces before the war they were frequently reattributed to Stiegel when they arrived in the States" (Perret to author, September 9, 1974).
3. A salt with this defect is in the collection of Sheffield City Art Gallery; a bowl in Corning Museum, acquired in England, also carries this defect.
4. Blue glass footed bowls of later date, not molded but of similar proportion, are inscribed "A Present from Newcastle"; collection of Laing Art Gallery, Newcastle upon Tyne. Another has the gilded inscription, "Be canny with the sugar"; Richard W. Oliver Auction Gallery, "Important Sale of Glass from the Lowell Innes Collection" (May 3, 1986), lot 137a.

157

SUGAR BOWL WITH COVER
FREDERICK COUNTY, MARYLAND,
ATTRIBUTED TO NEW BREMEN
GLASSMANUFACTORY OF JOHN
FREDERICK AMELUNG, 1785–95

Colorless nonlead glass of green tint. Blown. Bowl: bulbous
body, curved in at rim and base; a ring of glass trailed
below rim to support cover; 2 applied rounded handles
each with tooled trailing and curled back at lower terminal;
applied pedestal foot; pontil mark. Cover: hemispherical
form, flattened at top, that fits over rim of bowl; applied,
hollow baluster finial to which glass was applied and tooled
to create swan above 4 curved leaves; interior pontil mark.
OH: 8½ in (21.2 cm); Diam top of bowl: 4⅜ in (11.2 cm)
History: member of Stevens family; Nancy Boyington;
Mary Edgerton; Mrs. James Bryant; Ralph N. Hamilton;
James R. Gabell

Museum purchase, 1952: Neil C. Gest, Mechanicsburg,
Ohio. Funds for purchase, gift of Henry Francis du Pont
52.279a, b

Published: Florence M. Montgomery, "An Amelung Sugar
Bowl," *Journal of Glass Studies* 1 (1959): 89–93.
Gustav Weiss, *The Book of Glass,* trans. Janet Seligman
(New York: Praeger Publishers, 1971), p. 233.
Papert, *Illustrated Guide,* p. 68.
Lanmon and Palmer, "New Bremen," pp. 108–9, no. 32.

Sugar bowls attributed to Amelung's glassworks
are distinct from other early American sugars
because instead of an inset cover they have a lid
that rests on a trailed ring applied below the rim
of the bowl. Close European parallels for this are
known, including eighteenth-century bowls of
similar construction preserved in the collections
of Nationalmuseum in Nuremburg and Museum
für Glaskunst in Lauscha. Described as a butter
dish, this same form is also illustrated in a 1763
pattern book of Norwegian glass, and German
glassmakers who emigrated to Norway were
probably responsible.[1]

The fanciful swan finial, which also has parallels in eighteenth-century Continental glass,

began as a hollow baluster knop, now considered
an Amelung "trademark" (nos. 16, 44, 45). By
adding and tooling blobs of glass for a neck,
wings, and tail the blower cleverly transformed
it into a swan. Then he applied four leaves to the
broad part of the baluster, creating a graceful
setting for the bird.

Balancing this ornate finial are bold, nearly
hemispherical handles embellished with pincered bands curled outward at the top. Fragments of similar trailing were excavated from
Amelung's factory site.[2] Known as rigaree, this
was a time-honored technique used by glassmakers around the world.

Although the bowl exhibits a great deal of
artistry in its form and ornamentation, the glass
itself is not of good quality, having a strong
green tint. In his advertisements, of course,
Amelung admitted no technical difficulties with
his flint glass (a confusing period term used to
denote a fine quality, colorless tableware irre-
spective of chemical composition). Such critics
as the British consul in Philadelphia, however,
were quick to point out the flaws in New Bremen
products: "Their white glass if it may be so
called, is of a very mean quality, vastly thick and
heavy and full of specks."[3] Just how formidable a
process it was to achieve a satisfactory colorless
glass can be understood by Amelung's comments
of the following year, 1790:

> The quality of Glass is coming to Perfec-
> tion from degree to degree almost every
> Month, owing to the Experience I have ac-
> quired since these 6 Years past which enabled
> me to be better acquainted with the Mater-
> ials here.[4]

The bowl is said to have been a wedding gift
to a member of the Stevens family who carried
it from Maryland to New York State. A great-
granddaughter of the original owner gave it
to Nancy Boyington of Marshall, Michigan,
about 1909.

1. Polak, "Illustrated Price-List," p. 98, fig. 30.
2. Ivor Noël Hume, "Archaeological Excavations on the Site
of John Frederick Amelung's New Bremen Glassmanufactory, 1962–1963," *Journal of Glass Studies* 18 (1976): 191,
fig. 39, nos. 28, 30.
3. Phineas Bond to the Duke of Leeds, November 10, 1789,
American Historical Association, *Annual Report for the
Year 1896* (Washington, D.C.: Government Printing Office,
1897), 1:654.
4. John F. Amelung, appended notes of 1790 in *Remarks on
Manufactures,* 1787, reprinted in *Journal of Glass Studies* 18
(1976): 136.

158, PL. 7

SUGAR BOWL WITH COVER
FREDERICK COUNTY, MARYLAND, ATTRIBUTED TO NEW BREMEN GLASSMANUFACTORY OF JOHN FREDERICK AMELUNG, 1785–95

Dark amethyst nonlead glass. Blown. Bowl: bulbous body, tapered sharply at base; a ring of glass trailed below rim to support cover; 2 applied rounded handles, each with tooled trailing and curled under at both terminals, curled back again at lower; applied pedestal foot of irregular circumference; pontil mark. On one side, the wheel-engraved inscription: "To Mis. C.G. / In Washington C.ty" within wreath. Cover: low, domed top and high straight sides that fit over rim of bowl; applied finial composed of a ball on cylindrical stem to which glass was applied and tooled to create a swan above 4 winglike leaves; interior pontil mark. Wheel engraved on one side with floral spray.
OH: 8 in (20.4 cm); Diam top of bowl: 3¾ in (9.5 cm)
History: probably Christina Geeding Bovey; Elizabeth Bovey Jones; Sophia Rosanna Jones Beck; Naomi Elizabeth Beck Young; Dolly Young Harper
H. F. du Pont purchase, 1939: Neil C. Gest, Mechanicsburg, Ohio
59.3011a, b

Exhibited: National Gallery of Art, "In Praise of America," 1980.
Published: Antiques 36, no. 2 (August 1939): frontispiece. McKearin and McKearin, *American Glass*, pl. 39, no. 2. McKearin and McKearin, *Two Hundred Years*, pp. 176–77, pl. 28, no. 1.
Papert, *Illustrated Guide*, p. 67.
Lanmon and Palmer, "New Bremen," pp. 104–5, no. 30.
Wendy A. Cooper, *In Praise of America* (New York: Alfred A. Knopf, 1980), p. 105, pl. 18.

Although this bowl is less successful than NO. 157 in its proportions and tooled ornament, it is generally considered a masterpiece of New Bremen production because of its rich color and deep engraving. Related amethyst glass fragments were unearthed from the factory site, but this is, to date, the only known Amelung presentation piece of colored glass.[1] The lettering, wreath, and floral spray are closely paralleled on other Amelung objects (for example, NOS. 44, 47, 110).

That at least one other decorated purple sugar bowl of this type was made by Amelung workmen is evidenced by the survival of a lid engraved by the Amelung "hand" in a similar floral motif.[2] A scar on the convex side is all that remains of the finial; on the interior surface there is the usual pontil mark. Wear marks indicate that once shorn of its finial, the lid was turned over and used as a small bowl.

H. F. du Pont acquired the CG bowl after it was published as the frontispiece in the August 1939 issue of *Antiques* and hailed as "one of the most significant pieces of American glass thus far discovered." Neil Gest had purchased the piece in June 1939 from a Mr. Kohler who owned a jewelry store in Hagerstown, Maryland. It was said to have belonged to Catherine Geeting (or Geeding) of Washington County, Maryland, but this history was not substantiated. In 1961 Winterthur learned that Kohler had acquired the bowl from descendants of Naomi Beck Young (b. 1860). Recent information from a descendant has revealed that the original owner must have been Christina Geeding (1779–1814), a direct ancestor of Young.[3]

1. Ivor Noël Hume, "Archaeological Excavations on the Site of John Frederick Amelung's New Bremen Glassmanufactory, 1962–1963," *Journal of Glass Studies* 18 (1976): 189, fig. 38, no. 2.
2. Bayou Bend Collection, Museum of Fine Arts, Houston, ex coll. John T. Gotjen, who acquired it at the sale of the collection of Col. M. Robert Guggenheim (Richard A. Bourne Co., "Rare American Glass" [May 7, 1977], lot 594).
3. First mentioned in Neil C. Gest to du Pont, May 24, 1939, the purchase was agreed upon in August; Mrs. Robert Beck to Charles F. Montgomery, May 16, 1961; Irvin F. Muritz to Winterthur, September 19, 1987, Registration Division, WM. Christina Geeding became the wife of Jacob Bovey.

159

SUGAR BOWL WITH COVER
CONTINENTAL EUROPE, POSSIBLY
FRANCE, 1750–1800

Colorless nonlead glass. Blown. Bowl: shallow bulbous
body, pattern-molded with 16 vertical ribs; a ring of glass
trailed below rim to support cover. On either side an
applied flower with pincered petals; 2 applied rounded
handles each with 2 pulled finger rests and curled back at
lower terminal; drawn knopped stem; applied disk foot;
pontil mark. Cover: tall, domed, hemispherical form that
fits over rim of bowl; pattern-molded with 16 vertical ribs
and ornamented with 4 applied flowers with pincered
petals; applied knob finial to which glass was applied and
tooled in a stag shape; pontil mark on top of stag's body.
OH: 8¼ in (20.8 cm); Diam top of bowl: 3½ in (9.0 cm)
H. F. du Pont purchase, 1940: Neil C. Gest, Mechanicsburg, Ohio
59.3014a, b

Published: McKearin and McKearin, *Two Hundred Years,*
pp. 178–79, pl. 29, no. 2.

160

SUGAR BOWL WITH COVER
CONTINENTAL EUROPE,
1800–1840

Colorless nonlead glass of strong yellow-gray tint. Blown.
Bowl: heavy, hemispherical body bearing tooled decoration
of double chainlike effect; 2 applied handles each with 2
tooled finger rests and flat lower terminals; applied disk
foot crimped with long V's; pontil mark. Cover: flat top
and straight sides that fit over rim of bowl; a gather of glass
tooled into double chainlike effect as on the bowl; applied
finial composed of a large tooled chicken on a mushroom
shape; interior pontil mark.
OH: 9 in (23.0 cm); Diam top of bowl: 4⁵⁄₁₆ in (11.0 cm)
H. F. du Pont purchase, 1946: Neil C. Gest, Mechanicsburg,
Ohio
59.3012a, b

Published: McKearin and McKearin, *Two Hundred Years,*
p. 179, pl. 29.

H. F. du Pont acquired both these bowls because
he believed them to be products of Amelung's
New Bremen glassworks, operating in western Maryland between 1785 and 1795. As Gest
wrote, "The Amelung bowl with the chicken top
[NO. 160] is the finest thing yet since your amethyst Geeting bowl turned up." Gest admitted
that "the 'swag' decoration is unique to me,"
but his attribution was later supported by the
McKearins who published both bowls in their
1950 book on American blown glass.[1]

The association with New Bremen was based on the way the lids fit over the rims of the bowls and rest on applied rings. The amethyst bowl (NO. 158) by Amelung, already in du Pont's collection by 1946, is constructed in this manner, as are NO. 157 and all other attributed Amelung sugars.[2] The style, however, was firmly rooted in European practice (see NO. 157).

Other than this point of construction these bowls bear no relationship to documented and well-attributed Amelung glasses now known. NO. 159 has a lid that is remarkably elongated, leading Gest to describe it as "a sort of honey dish with cover"; later, he referred to it as "more like a cheese dish."[3] Its stemmed base is also unparalleled in the Amelung oeuvre. Although the stag was a motif often found on Continental glass, none surmounts known Amelung glass. Applied floral ornament of the kind seen here, rooted in Venetian traditions, is also unrecorded in American glass. Fragments of rib-molded glass have been excavated from the New Bremen factory site, but no extant tablewares with rib molding have yet been identified.

NO. 160 also differs from known Amelung sugars in several respects. No New Bremen objects are recorded with the gogglelike swagging seen on this bowl, nor do any have crimped feet. The chicken finial lacks the grace of the Amelung swans. Moreover, this example seems much later in date than the New Bremen period, particularly when viewed in conjunction with a closely related footed bowl illustrated in *American Glass.*[4]

Spectrographic analysis has shown that the chemical compositions of NOS. 159 and 160 vary significantly from those of documented Amelung products.[5]

1. Gest to du Pont, January 13, 1946, WM; McKearin and McKearin, *Two Hundred Years*, pp. 178–79, pl. 29.
2. Lanmon and Palmer, "New Bremen," pp. 104–11.
3. Gest to du Pont, September 20, 1940, and December 13, 1946, WM.
4. McKearin and McKearin, *American Glass*, pl. 41, fig. 8.
5. Analytical Laboratory, Winterthur Conservation; Robert H. Brill and Victor F. Hanson, "Chemical Analyses of Amelung Glasses," *Journal of Glass Studies* 18 (1976): 215–37.

161, PL. 14

SUGAR BOWL WITH COVER
NEW JERSEY, MARYLAND, OR
PENNSYLVANIA, 1790–1820

Light green nonlead glass. Blown. Bowl: deep, U-shape body,
faintly pattern-molded with 24 vertical ribs, and threaded
around the rim; 2 applied rounded handles with pulled
thumb rest and curled back at lower terminal; applied disk
foot with scalloped edge, each scallop pincered in diamond
design; ring-shape pontil mark. Cover: low, hemispherical
top and straight sides, inset with flange pulled out to rest on
edge of bowl; finial composed of roosterlike bird perched on
cylindrical stem; interior pontil mark.
OH: 8⅞ in (22.6 cm); Diam top of bowl: 4³⁄₁₆ in (10.7 cm)
H. F. du Pont purchase, 1930: Mrs. Ridgeway, Mickleton,
N.J., through Arthur Mason, Vineland, N.J.
59.3018a, b

Published: Pepper, *Glass Gaffers*, p. 18, fig. 14.

NO. 161 offers a distinctive interpretation of
the characteristics associated with sugar bowls
of the MidAtlantic region. It combines a rib-
molded bowl with a scalloped foot that has unusually delicate pincering. The handles are reminiscent of the Wistar sugar bowl at Newark Museum, but the thumbpieces have an almost
comical effect. Another Wistar bowl is rib molded
and threaded like NO. 161, but no other bowl has
this large capacity.[1] Birdlife abounds on a number
of early American sugar bowls, but the creature
here is a unique specimen.

   Sugar bowls with handles and inset covers
are normally associated with eighteenth-century
production. The proportions of NO. 161, with a
foot that seems too small to support the body and
a lid that lacks the usual overhang suggest, however, that the object dates from the early 1800s.

1. See Arlene Palmer, *The Wistarburgh Glassworks: The
Beginning of Jersey Glassmaking* (Alloway, N.J.: Alloway
Bicentennial Committee, 1976), p. 23, fig. 16.

162, PL. 19

SUGAR BOWL WITH COVER
PROBABLY UNITED STATES,
POSSIBLY ENGLAND, 1800–1825

Green lead glass. Blown. Bowl: elongated hemispherical
body pattern-molded with rows of 20 small diamonds;
applied disk foot; pontil mark. Cover: conical top and
straight sides, inset with flange pulled out to rest on edge
of bowl; pattern-molded with rows of 20 diamonds; short
spire finial on wafer; interior pontil mark.
OH: 6¼ in (16.0 cm); Diam top of bowl: 4⅛ in (10.5 cm)
H. F. du Pont purchase, 1940: Neil C. Gest, Mechanicsburg,
Ohio
59.3339a, b

After pursuing it for some time, Ohio glass
dealer Neil Gest finally secured this unusual pattern-molded sugar bowl and offered it to H. F.
du Pont in the fall of 1939. He felt it was "another
typical 'Winterthur' piece"—an object of great
beauty and rarity. Gest attributed the bowl to
the Mantua, Ohio, glassworks because of a sugar
bowl of similar color and shape that was included
in the landmark Girl Scouts exhibition of 1929.
That bowl, however, was blown of nonlead glass
and was patterned in a mold of fifteen, not twenty, diamonds. Its inset lid was patterned with
sixteen ribs and capped with a flattened knop.[1]

Winterthur's bowl is unlike most Ohio
sugar bowls in its proportion, style, and color
(NOS. 167–69, 171, 172).[2] Indeed, it seems to pre-
date Ohio production. Realizing this was "not a
typical Ohio bowl," du Pont hesitated but then
accepted Gest's judgment, writing: "As you say it
is the last word in Ohio glass, I have decided to
keep it."[3]

With its pointed knop finial and small diamond design this sugar bowl seems closer to English styles of the eighteenth century (NO. 154)
than to American midwestern glass. Given that it
is blown of lead glass, the possibility of English
manufacture should probably not be dismissed.
Although rarely published and little studied, light
green tablewares in the shapes and styles of more
expensive colorless glass were made by numerous
provincial English glasshouses.

Prior to the revolutionary war, lead glass
was made in Pennsylvania at Manheim and in
Philadelphia. Sugar bowls were among the forms
produced at both factories but none have been
positively identified. Benjamin Bakewell was

apparently making lead glass soon after he
opened his Pittsburgh plant in 1808, but no
wares have been documented to his early period.
Few other American glassworks are known to
have made lead glass before 1815.

Although it is a poor fit, the cover of NO. 162
does match its bowl both in color and pattern.

1. George S. McKearin, "Early American Glass," in
American Art Galleries, *Loan Exhibition of Eighteenth and
Early Nineteenth Century Furniture and Glass . . . for the*
Benefit of the National Council of Girl Scouts, Inc. (New
York, 1929), no. 192. McKearin included the bowl as a
"Stiegel-type" object, explaining that "it must necessarily
be very difficult to distinguish . . . between different pieces
which may have been produced in Stiegel's factory and
taken into Ohio and similar pieces blown afterward by
Stiegel workmen and their descendants in other factories."
Harry Hall White found fragments of 15-diamond molded
glass at the Mantua site, so when the McKearins published
this bowl in *American Glass*, pl. 79, no. 1, they attributed it
to Mantua. The bowl is now in Corning Museum.
2. See also Rhea Mansfield Knittle, "American Glass Sugar
Bowls," *Antiques* 20, no. 6 (December 1931): 344–48.
3. Gest to du Pont, September 12 and 19, October 5 and 9,
1939; du Pont to Gest, October 7 and 14, 1939, Registration
Division, WM.

163, PL. 11

SUGAR BOWL WITH COVER
KEENE, NEW HAMPSHIRE,
ATTRIBUTED TO KEENE GLASS
WORKS, 1815–41

Aqua (bowl) and light green (cover) nonlead glass.
Blown. Bowl: heavy globular body curved in below
galleried rim; blown in 3-part mold of geometric design
(McKearin G III-16): diagonal ribbing below rim;
between horizontal rings are 3 repeat panels of diamond
diapering and bull's-eye sunburst; vertical ribbing
around base; slightly concave bottom, rayed (type VI-A);
pontil mark. Cover: free blown; high, domed form flared
at base to fit inside rim of bowl; drawn wafer finial with
pontil mark on top.
OH: 5¾ in (14.6 cm); Diam: 4⅜ in (11.2 cm)
History: Charlotte and Edgar Sittig; probably William W.
Wood III
Museum purchase, 1956: Neil C. Gest, Mechanicsburg,
Ohio
57.10.2a, b

Published: Wilson, *New England Glass*, p. 167.

The body of this sugar bowl was blown in a
mold of geometric design that was intended
for the production of pint decanters. One of a
remarkable series of objects (NOS. 53, 121, 258)
from the Marlboro Street glassworks in Keene,
the bowl illustrates just how versatile a single
full-size mold could be. By skillful manipula-
tion of the glass after removing it from a mold,
the glassblower could shape it into a decanter,
pitcher, vase, tumbler, or a sugar bowl.
Whether this was an isolated experiment or
special order is not clear, for although numerous decanters are known, only one other bowl
like this is recorded.[1]

1. McKearin and McKearin, *American Glass*, pl. 119; this
was exhibited in the Girl Scouts show as no. 354.

164

SUGAR BOWL WITH COVER
UNITED STATES, 1815–35

Colorless lead glass of grayish tint. Blown. Bowl: heavy, globular body curved in below tall, galleried rim; short, solid cylindrical foot; pontil mark. Wheel engraved with design of fringed swags containing stylized flowers and leaves, the swags connected with bowknots and tassels; above one swag are the initials "LB"; above the others is a star; around the rim a feathered line connecting flowers. Cover: high, domed form flared at base to fit inside rim of bowl; applied flattened ball finial on wafer, polished top. Wheel engraved with swag and tassel design to match bowl.
OH: 6¹⁵⁄₁₆ in (17.7 cm); Diam top of bowl: 5¹⁄₁₆ in (13.0 cm)
H. F. du Pont purchase
59.3120a, b

The swags and tassels of this sugar bowl represent the international vocabulary of the neoclassical era. The delicacy of the design and the details of the motifs and lettering echo the ornamentation found on silverware of the period.[1]

Swags and tassels were engraved by Bohemian glass decorators on glass intended for export to western Europe and North America (NOS. 17, 18, 87); more abstract versions can be seen on Irish glass (NO. 115). Of the various objects bearing this design and believed to be of American origin, no example executed in exactly the same manner as this bowl has been found. The engraver feathered the ropes from which the tassels hang to create the illusion of fiber, but the ball tops of the tassels are cross-hatched. The skill of the craftsman is evident from the execution of the design and in its placement upon the glass. The pendant tassels fall perfectly on the curve of the bowl so as to compliment the shape; the swags are carefully balanced in between. The tassels of the lid hang in judicious proportion to the rather tall form.

American engraved glasswares of the early nineteenth century have been primarily documented to glasshouses in Boston and Pittsburgh, although there is written evidence that manufacturers in other cities also produced engraved glass. The 1837 price list of Francis Plunkett and Company of Wheeling mentions engraved sugars and covers at $6.00 per dozen, and an inventory of stock at the Baltimore Flint Glass Works includes cut "Festoon" sugars at $3.50 a pair.[2] Besides those engravers working for glasshouses, there were many who operated independent decorating shops throughout the republic.

The Winterthur bowl is extremely heavy and has an unusual foot. Unpolished pontils occur more frequently on American than on English or French table glass.

1. For example, an English silver tea caddy by J. Hampston and J. Prince of York in 1784/85 has the same border as on the rim of the sugar bowl; see Victoria and Albert Museum, *Adam Silver* (London: Her Majesty's Stationery Office, 1953), no. 24.
2. Wheeling Price Current, Oglebay Inst.; inventory of stock ca. 1832, Chapman-Baker Day Book, p. 10, MdHS.

SUGAR BOWL WITH COVER
PROBABLY PITTSBURGH, 1825–50

Amethyst lead glass. Blown. Bowl: elongated, pear-shape body tapered in at top below short, curved galleried rim; pattern-molded with 12 vertical ribs; applied pedestal foot; pontil mark. Cover: domed form flared at base with wide, downward-folded edge that fits inside rim of bowl; pattern-molded with 12 vertical ribs; drawn, wafer finial with pontil mark on top.
OH: 6½ in (16.6 cm); Diam top of bowl: 3¹³⁄₁₆ in (9.7 cm)
H. F. du Pont purchase, 1927: McKearins' Antiques, Hoosick Falls, N.Y.
59.3114a, b

Similar boldly ribbed sugar bowls are recorded in blue, green, and colorless glass. George McKearin referred to NO. 165 as one of the "Ohio type," indicating an uncertainty of attribution that remains today. None has a history, but the twelve-rib bowls have been linked with the enterprise of Benjamin Bakewell which opened in Pittsburgh in 1808. Most of the documented or well-attributed Bakewell objects are of colorless glass (NOS. 60, 63–65), but by 1809 Bakewell was advertising tablewares, including sugar basins and cream jugs, of "assorted colours."[1] In his report for the 1820 Census of Manufactures, he described his products as "white & coloured flint Glass of all kinds whether Chemical. Philosophical or ornamental."

The overall pear shape created by body and lid is complemented by the widely spaced ribs. In this design glassmakers may have been influenced by the work of silversmiths.

1. B. Bakewell and Co. advertisement, *Western World* (Frankfort, Ky.), June 8, 1809, reference courtesy of Mr. and Mrs. J. G. Stradling; 1820 Census of Manufactures, s.v. "Pennsylvania."

166, PL. 24

SUGAR BOWL WITH COVER
PENNSYLVANIA OR NEW JERSEY,
1815–40

Green glass. Blown. Bowl: hemispherical body with horizontal rim and inward-folded edge; applied disk foot; pontil mark. Cover: conical top and short straight sides, inset with thick flange pulled out to rest on edge of bowl, downward-folded edge; applied mushroom finial with pontil mark on top.
OH: 7 in (17.9 cm); Diam top of bowl: 5¾ in (14.7 cm)
H. F. du Pont purchase, before 1939
68.745a, b

This boldly shaped bowl of clear green glass is a fine example of the tableware made on a limited scale by domestic window glass factories in the first half of the nineteenth century. One related bowl has the same distinctive shape and proportion as Winterthur's and is crowned with a similar mushroom finial. It is associated with Bethany Glass Manufactory because it was "found about 15 miles from the Bethany plant at Lake Ariel, Pennsylvania," and "family tradition placed its early purchase at Honesdale (about 4 miles from the Bethany plant)."[1] Unfortunately the popular location-where-found argument is a tenuous basis for attribution, and documentary evidence proves that American glassmakers reached markets far beyond their immediate neighborhood.

What little information there is about the Bethany glasshouse is incomplete and somewhat contradictory. According to a legal opinion prepared in 1829, "a family of Germans named Greiner" purchased 641 acres of land in Wayne County in May 1816, on which they "built a Glass House . . . and carried on the business of Glass making for some years, but became Insolvent." According to the research of L. G. Van Nostrand, Adam Greiner and Nicholas Greiner were but two of a partnership of five—Christopher Faatz was the main force behind the establishment of the factory. As early as 1810 Faatz was operating a window glass factory and advertising his products in the New York City papers to all "Lovers of American manufactures."[2]

When the 1820 Census of Manufactures was taken, Jacob S. Davis answered for Bethany Glass Manufactory. Thirty men and six boys produced $20,000 worth of window glass annually at a single furnace with six pots. Davis added:

Manufactory has been established about 5 years, is esteemed of great importance to the vicinity, and notwithstanding that the natural impediments to transportation are not yet totally removed, is in a prosperous condition. The measure of success which this establishment has obtained is to be ascribed to the quality of the manufacture, which has always been in good demand.[3] The picture was perhaps not as rosy as this implies; in 1824 the property was taken over by two principal creditors of the partners. They, in turn, sold the land in 1828, but glassmaking continued. In 1829 the factory was "owned and occupied by Messrs. Greele and Taatz [Faatz]" who employed forty men and eight boys at making "chiefly window glass"—450,000 feet or 9,000 boxes valued at $3 per box.[4] The plant continued to operate until 1848.

1. Collection of Mrs. U. A. Noble; L. G. Van Nostrand, "The Bethany, Pennsylvania, Glass Works . . . ," in "The Glass and China Cupboard," *Antiques* 43, no. 5 (May 1943): 226–28.
2. Thomas Stewardson to Horace Binney, January 10, 1829, Henry S. Drinker Papers, HSP; Van Nostrand, "Bethany Glass Works," p. 226. *New York Evening Post*, November 3, 1810, reference courtesy of Neil Larson; the location of Faatz's factory is not given in the advertisement. Van Nostrand's assertion that Faatz's factory was in Philadelphia has not been proved.
3. 1820 Census of Manufactures, s.v. "Pennsylvania."
4. Hazard, *Register of Pennsylvania* 3 (February 1829): 137.

167, PL. 24

SUGAR BOWL WITH COVER
OHIO, 1815–45

Green-blue, slightly bubbly nonlead glass. Blown. Bowl:
tapered body with round shoulders curved sharply in
below galleried rim; pontil mark. Cover: tall, double-
domed form flared at base with downward-folded edge
that fits inside rim of bowl; drawn ball finial with pontil
mark on top. Small crack on body of bowl.
OH: 7⁷⁄₁₆ in (18.1 cm); Diam top of bowl: 4¹³⁄₁₆ in (12.3 cm)
History: Neil C. Gest; William W. Wood III
H. F. du Pont purchase, 1950: Neil C. Gest,
Mechanicsburg, Ohio
68.713a, b

Published: Parke-Bernet Galleries, "Early American
Glass . . . Collection of William W. Wood, 3d," sale
no. 338 (January 22–23, 1942), lot 281.

In 1931 Rhea Mansfield Knittle published a
very similar sugar bowl with a history in the
glassmaking town of Zanesville, Ohio.[1] Certainly in its bold lines and brilliant glass this
bowl exhibits the characteristics associated
with Ohio glassmaking, but it is difficult to
make attributions to individual factories without specific documentation.

1. Rhea Mansfield Knittle, "American Glass Sugar Bowls,"
Antiques 20, no. 6 (December 1931): 346, fig. 9.

168, 169, PLS. 17, 19

SUGAR BOWLS WITH COVERS
OHIO, PROBABLY ZANESVILLE,
1820–45

NO. 168. Blue lead glass. Blown. Bowl: globular, curved in
below wide, galleried rim; pattern-molded in rows of 10
large diamonds with 10 pointed flutes around the base;
applied pedestal foot with irregularly scalloped edge; pontil
mark. Cover: double-domed form flared at base with
downward-folded edge that fits inside rim of bowl; pattern-
molded with row of 10 pointed flutes at top and rows of 10
large diamonds below; drawn ball finial with pontil mark
on top.
OH: 6⁷⁄₈ in (17.6 cm); Diam top of bowl: 5 in (12.7 cm)
H. F. du Pont purchase, 1946: Neil C. Gest, Mechanicsburg,
Ohio
59.3070a, b

NO. 169. Green nonlead glass. Blown. Bowl: globular, curved in below wide, galleried rim; pattern-molded in rows of
10 large diamonds with 10 pointed flutes around the base;
applied pedestal foot with irregularly scalloped edge (one
scallop broken off); pontil mark. Cover: double-domed
form flared out at base with downward-folded edge that fits
inside rim of bowl; pattern-molded with row of 10 pointed
flutes at top and rows of 10 large diamonds below; drawn
flattened ball with pontil mark on top.
OH: 7 in (17.9 cm); Diam top of bowl: 4⁷⁄₈ in (12.4 cm)
History: William T. H. Howe, Cincinnati
Museum purchase, 1959: J. A. Lloyd Hyde, New York City
59.7.13a, b

Published: Parke-Bernet Galleries, "Early American
Glass . . . Collection Formed by the Late William T. H.
Howe," pt. 1, sale no. 227 (November 7–8, 1940), lot 317.
"The Almanac," *Antiques* 38, no. 5 (November 1940): 238.

Perched on their petaled feet these richly colored
bowls must have made quite a statement on the
tea or dining table of their day. The distinctive
double-domed cover—it looks like a salt dish
upside-down (for example, NO. 228)—is peculiar
to glass production in the Ohio River valley. The
arrangement of the lid resting inside a galleried
rim, however, is merely indicative of a nineteenth-century date. American silversmiths had
adopted the style for their hollowware in the
later years of the eighteenth century.

Close examination of the molded design and its defects reveals that the two bowls and their lids were patterned in the same mold as a yellow-green jug (NO. 119) and an amber dish (NO. 199) at Winterthur. If only one factory was responsible, it must have been set up to manufacture both flint tableware and the more utilitarian bottle products. The attribution of this group of 10-diamond molded wares to

Zanesville is tenuous, based only on flasks in this pattern that surfaced in the Zanesville area.[1] Rhea Mansfield Knittle, a pioneer historian of Ohio glassmaking, published a 10-diamond sugar bowl that had a history in Pittsburgh which led her to attribute it to Benjamin Bakewell's factory in that city.[2]

The 10-diamond sugar bowls have long been among the most sought-after forms of early American glass. When Neil Gest offered the blue one to H. F. du Pont he cited the similar one published by the McKearins and remarked that George McKearin "used to say he wanted it buried with him."[3]

1. McKearin and McKearin, *Two Hundred Years*, p. 116; Helen McKearin, "Early Nineteenth-Century Glassmaking in Ohio," *Antiques* 49, no. 1 (January 1946): 52.
2. Rhea Mansfield Knittle, "American Glass Sugar Bowls," *Antiques* 20, no. 6 (December 1931): 345, fig. 5. Another light green one was in the Maclay collection, published in *Antiques* 35, no. 3 (March 1939): 144, and sold by Parke-Bernet Galleries, "Early American Glass and Ceramics, Collection of Alfred B. Maclay," sale no. 100 (March 23–25, 1939), lot 503. According to Gest, that one did not have the original cover.
3. Gest to du Pont, December 13, 1946, WM.

170

SUGAR BOWL WITH COVER PROBABLY VINELAND, NEW JERSEY, PROBABLY EMIL J. LARSON, 1925–30

Gray-amethyst glass. Blown. Bowl: globular body, curved in below tall galleried rim; pattern-molded in rows of 15 diamonds; applied pedestal foot; pontil mark. Cover: high, domed form flared at base to fit inside rim of bowl; pattern-molded in rows of 15 diamonds; applied finial of compressed ball shape with pontil mark on top.
OH: 6¾ in (17.3 cm); Diam top of bowl: 4⅜ in (11.2 cm)
H. F. du Pont purchase, 1930: McKearins' Antiques, New York City
59.3107a, b

Although this bowl appears to relate to some early Pittsburgh and Ohio sugar bowls in the Winterthur collection, there is reason to believe it was made as a twentieth-century reproduction. The most damning evidence is the faked wear on the bottom of the foot: instead of the haphazard arrangement of lines, heavier in some places than others, that is typical of genuine wearmarks, this bowl has a tidy, even ring of wear that was achieved by grinding. The color is a dull grayish amethyst, not the rich, vibrant hue that is seen in early glass. The proportions are also unusual, with a lid that is far too tall for the size of the body.

As with the so-called Mutzer fakes (NOS. 133, 216), the provenance of this object seems curious. On his invoice to du Pont George McKearin described the object simply as "amethyst diamond sugar bowl and cover" and recorded no attribution to justify the substantial price of $3,000. Later that year, while inventorying the Winterthur collection, Neil Gest described this as the "only specimen I have ever seen in what appears to be an American bowl. Not Stiegel in my estimation, but a wonderful specimen of some 40 or 50 years after Stiegel. Fine quality and color. . . . Origin, Philadelphia." He added: "Found in Germantown, Pa." Gest would have known its provenance because

it was he who had sold it to McKearin. Gest later sold an almost identical example to Richard Loeb that Brooklyn Museum bought at the Loeb auction in 1947.[1]

It seemed very important to Gest and presumably to McKearin that the bowl had surfaced in the Philadelphia area. According to the tenets of the day, the piece must have been made there, and indeed, it was probably made in nearby New Jersey.

Emil Larson was born in 1879 in Sweden, the son of a glassblower.[2] After the family came to America, his father worked at the Dorflinger factory in White Mills, Pennsylvania. Emil Larson learned the craft there and was employed by Dorflinger's until it closed in 1921. He then blew glass for the Pairpoint Company, Quezal, and Durand. When Durand closed in 1931 he turned full time to his own one-pot furnace at his home in Vineland. At the urging of Philip Glick, a local glass collector and dealer, Larson tried his hand at making such "Stiegel" reproductions as diamond-daisy and ribbed pocket bottles. Among his wares were "Footed sugar bowls with domed, knopped covers which Larson made with a diamond pattern." These were blown of cobalt blue and a "rich wine-colored" glass. Larson's antique copies were marketed through a handful of dealers and George McKearin is said to have collected samples of all his reproductions. There may not have been any intention of deception on Larson's part, but the opportunity for misrepresentation of these very competent, unmarked reproductions was too tempting for the unscrupulous to ignore. Wending its way from Vineland to Germantown to Mechanicsburg to Hoosick Falls to Winterthur all before February, 1930, this bowl must have been one of the first such "Stiegel" reproductions Larson made.

1. Invoice, McKearin to du Pont, February 18, 1930, WM; Neil C. Gest, Inventory of Winterthur Glass Collection, August 1939, no. 28, Archives, WM; Gest to du Pont, November 9, 1931, WM; Parke-Bernet Galleries, "Rare Early American Glass . . . Property of Richard Loeb," sale no. 853 (March 27, 1947), lot 85.
2. All the information about Larson that follows is taken from Pepper, *Glass Gaffers*, pp. 278–80, 286–89.

171, 172, PL. 12

SUGAR BOWLS WITH COVERS
OHIO, 1820–45

Amethyst lead glass. Blown. Bowl: deep, U-shape body with wide galleried rim. Blown in 3-part mold of geometric design (McKearin G II-32): short vertical flutes above a wide band of quartered-diamond diapering within horizontal rings; vertical ribbing around base above a smooth area; applied pedestal foot; pontil mark. Cover: conical (NO. 171), and domed (NO. 172) form with downward-folded edge that fits inside rim of bowl; pattern-molded with 16 ribs, swirled to left; drawn ball finial with pontil mark on top.
NO. 171: OH: 6⅝ in (16.9 cm); Diam top of bowl: 4⁹⁄₁₆ in (11.6 cm)
NO. 172: OH: 6½ in (16.6 cm); Diam top of bowl: 4¾ in (12.1 cm)
H. F. du Pont purchases, 1931 (NO. 171), 1940 (NO. 172): Neil C. Gest, Mechanicsburg, Ohio
59.3152a, b (NO. 171); 59.3153a, b (NO. 172)

Published: (NO. 171) McKearin and McKearin, *American Glass,* pl. 123, no. 3.

These sugar bowls and covers, combining the techniques of full-size and part-size molding, are among the rarest of Ohio glass; fewer than a dozen examples are recorded.[1] NO. 171 was found near Richmond, Indiana. According to family tradition, it had been a wedding present in 1806 to an ancestor in Pennsylvania who later moved to Richmond. Gest told du Pont the other was a wedding gift to a couple "named something like Boerger," who migrated from Lancaster County to Pittsburgh and then to Warren County, Ohio. A Mrs. Smith, daughter of the original owners, sold the bowl to a Mr. Browne, who died early in 1940. According to Gest, the six or seven bowls known in 1940 had surfaced in the vicinity of Richmond or in nearby Ohio.[2]

Glass students of the 1920s and 1930s formulated the theory that Ohio glass was rooted firmly in Stiegel traditions. As George McKearin wrote:

> Many fine pieces of glass, characteristic of Stiegel in color, form, and decorative technique, have been found in Ohio, especially in that portion of the State near the Pennsylvania line and in the territory settled by Mennonites from the Stiegel section of Pennsylvania. . . . after the failure of Stiegel's enterprise, workmen from his factory and their descendants found employ-ment in the early factories of the Pittsburgh and Ohio River Districts. . . . it is entirely possible that many fine pieces actually made in Stiegel's factories were taken into Ohio by the early settlers from Pennsylvania.[3]

Indeed, it was once widely believed that blown three-mold glass was made at Stiegel's colonial venture. These bowls bear no relationship to Stiegel production, however, and reflect instead the Anglo-Irish origins of many of the glass workers in the Ohio River valley.

1. Others are in Metropolitan Museum of Art, Corning Museum, Yale University Art Gallery (without cover); one was published in *American Collector* 3, no. 8 (April 4, 1935): 11; another was in the Norman Rose collection sold at Christie's East, "American Paintings, Furniture, and Decorative Arts," (April 26, 1988), lot 111.
2. Gest to du Pont: November 6, 1931, May 29, 1940, July 2, 1945; Gest, Inventory of Winterthur Glass Collection, August 1939, no. 35, Archives, WM.
3. George H. McKearin, "Early American Glass," in American Art Galleries, *Loan Exhibition of Eighteenth and Early Nineteenth Century Furniture and Glass . . . for the Benefit of the National Council of Girl Scouts, Inc.* (New York, 1929), after no. 191.

173

SUGAR BOWL WITH COVER PROBABLY SANDWICH, MASSACHUSETTS, PROBABLY BOSTON AND SANDWICH GLASS COMPANY, 1825–40

Colorless lead glass. Blown. Bowl: hemispherical body with short galleried rim. Blown in 3-part mold of geometric design (McKearin G II-18): vertical ribbing above and below a band of diamond diapering within horizontal rings; bottom patterned with diamonds; applied pedestal foot; pontil mark. Cover: domed form flared at base with downward-folded edge that fits inside rim of bowl; blown in 3-part mold of similar pattern as bowl; drawn mushroom finial with pontil mark on top. OH: 5³⁄₁₆ in (13.3 cm); Diam top of bowl: 4⁹⁄₁₆ in (11.6 cm) H. F. du Pont purchase, 1946: Neil C. Gest, Mechanicsburg, Ohio
59.3271a, b

Although NO. 173 shares the design concept of the previous two bowls (NOS. 171, 172), its shape and proportion vary dramatically and demonstrate the differences between glass products from the western Pennsylvania/Ohio area and those from the East Coast. Mold-blown sugars on feet were among the wares manufactured at Boston and Sandwich and fragments of the G II-18 pattern have been found at the factory site on Cape Cod. The New England Glass Company probably made the pattern as well. NO. 173 appears to have been blown in the identical mold as NO 213.

Contrary to popular belief, some mold-blown sugar bowls were no more expensive than pressed ones. An 1829 invoice from New England Glass Company to a Baltimore merchant shows that "2d quality" molded sugar bowls sold for $6 a dozen—the same price as second quality pressed ones. A glassblower at Boston and Sandwich was credited with 16²⁄₃¢ for each mold-blown footed sugar bowl he made and twice that amount for free-blown ones that would later be cut.[1]

1. New England Glass Company to William E. Mayhew, in Helen McKearin, "New England Glass Company Invoices," pt. 1, *Antiques* 52, no. 3 (September 1947): 175–76; Leinicke, "Production," pp. 60–61.

174, PL. 11

SUGAR BOWL WITH COVER
POSSIBLY NEW YORK, POSSIBLY
MOUNT VERNON GLASS WORKS,
1825–45

Aqua bubbly lead glass. Blown. Bowl: bulbous body with
rounded shoulders curved in below galleried rim. Blown in
3-part mold of geometric design (McKearin G I-30): faint
fluting at neck with 3 horizontal rings around shoulder; 21
broad vertical ribs encircle body with 2 faint horizontal
rings below; slightly concave base patterned with diamonds (probably type I); pontil mark. Cover: free blown;
domed form flared at base with downward-folded edge
that fits inside rim of bowl; drawn ball finial with pontil
mark on top, retaining iron oxide matter.
OH: 5½ in (14.0 cm); Diam top of bowl: 3⅞ in (9.8 cm)
H. F. du Pont purchase, 1945: Neil C. Gest, Mechanicsburg,
Ohio
59.3047a, b

The mold-blown design of this sugar bowl
approximates the effect of pillar cutting, one
of the most difficult types of cuts to achieve
(NOS. 66–68). Because it is blown of a brilliant
aqua glass, however, even the casual viewer
would never mistake this bowl for its costlier
counterpart.

The attribution of this pattern (see also
NO. 408) to Mount Vernon is based on amateur
excavations conducted by Harry Hall White in
the 1920s. This G I-30 design is believed to be
unique to Mount Vernon Glass Works, yet glasswares in the very similar G I-29 pattern have
been assigned both to Mount Vernon and to
Boston and Sandwich.[1] Unfortunately there is
little documentary evidence concerning the
tableware production at Mount Vernon. The
factory's bottle output is described in some
detail in advertisements, and marked bottle
seals were discovered at the site.

1. Harry Hall White, "New York State Glasshouses," pts. 2,
3, *Antiques* 16, nos. 3, 5 (September, November 1929):
193–96, 394–96; McKearin and McKearin, *American Glass*,
pls. 121–22, pp. 186, 275–76, 279.

175

SUGAR BOWL WITH COVER
SANDWICH, MASSACHUSETTS,
ATTRIBUTED TO BOSTON AND
SANDWICH GLASS COMPANY,
1830–40

Colorless lead glass, slight yellow tint. Blown. Bowl:
compressed spherical body with applied pedestal foot;
body and foot tooled with horizontal rings; pontil mark.
Cover: conical top and short straight sides, inset below
flange; tooled with horizontal rings; drawn, flattened ball
finial containing large tear, polished top.
OH: 7¹³⁄₁₆ in (19.8 cm); Diam top of bowl: 3¾ in (9.6 cm)
Museum purchase, 1975: Ruth Troiani Fine Antiques,
Pound Ridge, N.Y. Funds for purchase, gift of the Claneil
Foundation
75.70.1a, b

The horizontal tooling seen here is much bolder
than the rings of the eighteenth-century Lynn-
type glasses (NOS. 6, 37). With its rounded shape
and corrugated surface the bowl seems to simulate a beehive. The Boston and Sandwich glassmakers may have been inspired by English silversmiths, who from about 1780 indulged in the
conceit of honey pots shaped and ridged like
beehives; they also made teapots in this style.
Anglo-Irish glassmakers imitated this fashion in
costly cut glass.[1]

The beehive was a Masonic symbol of in-
dustriousness, an image which doubtless suited
the glassworkers. Moreover, because glass furnaces often resembled beehives in their conical
shape, the style could have had a special appeal
for the blowers, who, when working their glass,
moved quickly to and from the furnace—
much like busy bees.

This sugar bowl and its matching creamer
(NO. 134) can be attributed to Boston and
Sandwich Glass Company because similar examples of this distinctive decoration are
known to have descended in the families of
workers from that factory. About the time
these blown wares were made, the Sandwich
factory and its rival in Cambridge were also
making pressed glass with beehive motifs.[2]

The stock of a Philadelphia glass importer,
inventoried in 1813, included a "diamond cut
beehive," and "beehives & covers" appear in the
1829 price list of an English glassworks.[3] Although these descriptions presumably referred
to honey pots, sugar bowls, or other serving
vessels of beehive shape, there is evidence that
a beehive made of glass was used by an American apiarist in the 1820s. Exhibited at a fair in
Brighton, Massachusetts, was "a glass beehive
filled with honey, as the bees had left it. . . . It
was sent by Gen. Dearborn, of Roxbury, and
added much to the interest of the exhibition.
The hive is of a globular form—was filled by
the bees in 22 days and is estimated to weigh
nearly an hundred pounds. The experiments as
made by Gen. Dearborn subserves the cause of
humanity, as four only of those useful insects
the bee were found in the hive when removed
from its stand."[4]

1. G. Bernard Hughes, *Small Antique Silverware* (New
York: Bramhall House, 1957), p. 191, fig. 238, pp. 197–98;
Cincinnati Art Museum, *Folger Coffee Company Collection of Antique English Silver Coffee Pots* (Cincinnati,
1961), p. 44; Warren, *Irish Glass*, p. 161, fig. 153.
2. A similar sugar bowl (Sandwich Glass Museum) was
made in 1829 by William Kern for the wedding of his
sister Catherine to Frederick Eaton; Frederick T. Irwin,
The Story of Sandwich Glass and Glass Workers
(Manchester, N.H.: Privately printed, 1926), p. 98.
Another sugar bowl in the family of Leonard Rogers,
who worked at Sandwich in the 1830s (probably as a
blacksmith), is in Dwight P. Lanmon, comp., *Glass from
Six Centuries* (Hartford, Conn.: Wadsworth Atheneum,
1978), p. 101, fig. 113; Dorothy Hogan, Sandwich Glass
Museum, to author, July 7, 1987. Spillman, *Pressed Glass*,
p. 50, nos. 100–102, p. 172, no. 640.
3. Leonard Keehmle inventory, 1813-131, Philadelphia
County Probate Records (microfilm, Downs, WL);
Beatson, Clark and Co., *The Glass Works Rotherham,
1751–1951* (Rotherham, Eng., 1952), p. 10.
4. *Bucks County [Pennsylvania] Patriot*, November 15,
1824.

176, PL. 4

SUGAR BOWL WITH COVER
UNITED STATES, 1835–55

Deep aqua glass. Blown. Bowl: urn-shape body with galleried rim and wide medial ring; gadrooning around
the base made of added gather molded with 10 swirled ribs;
baluster stem; thick, disk foot; ring-shape pontil mark.
Cover: high, flattened hemispherical top, flared below to
rest on edge of bowl; gadrooning around top made of
added gather molded with 10 swirled ribs; applied flattened
knop finial on wafer, pontil mark on top.
OH: 9¼ in (23.6 cm); Diam top of bowl: 4⅜ in (11.2 cm)
History: (probably) Louis G. Myers; George S. McKearin;
Mrs. Frederick S. Fish; W. Griffin Gribbel
H. F. du Pont purchase, 1948: Neil C. Gest, Mechanicsburg,
Ohio
59.3056a, b

Exhibited: American Art Galleries, "Loan Exhibition of
Eighteenth and Early Nineteenth Century Furniture and
Glass for the Benefit of the National Council of Girl Scouts,
Inc.," 1929.
Published: George S. McKearin, "Early American Glass," in
American Art Galleries, *Loan Exhibition of Eighteenth and
Early Nineteenth Century Furniture and Glass . . . for the
Benefit of the National Council of Girl Scouts, Inc.* (New
York, 1929), no. 134.
American Art Association/Anderson Galleries, "Early
American Glass, the Private Collection of George S.
McKearin," sale no. 3938 (January 6–7, 1932), lot 338.
Parke-Bernet Galleries, "Early American Glass . . .
Collection Formed by Mrs. Frederick S. Fish," sale no. 159
(January 5–6, 1940), lot 365.
McKearin and McKearin, *American Glass,* pl. 16, no. 5.
Pepper, *Glass Gaffers,* p. 17, fig. 11.

This sugar bowl is a stunning example of how a
glassblower at a bottle or window glass factory
used unrefined glass to imitate high-style design.
Aqua colored glass was the standard material for
liquor bottles, pharmaceutical vials, food storage
containers, and other such utilitarian objects.
Much of the American window glass at this time
was of strong aqua tint (NO. 402). Tablewares
blown of unrefined aqua glass were sometimes
described as "common" in period records. At
many factories these wares were an integral part
of commercial production and not just keep-
sakes made by the workmen for themselves and
their families.

A clever and skillful craftsman who was familiar with the ornamental techniques of fine,
colorless glassware and who knew the work of
the Boston area glasshouses must have been responsible for this object. Numerous vessels made
by the South Boston factories and New England
Glass Company in the 1830s display characteristics that were imitated here: the waisted body,

the medial ring, the swirled gadrooning on the
lower body and upper lid. The most accomplished statement of the style is a sugar bowl
in Toledo Museum of Art that is attributed to
New England Glass Company.[1] The contours of
NO. 176 are less bold, but its concept is identical. In both cases, when the cover is inverted its
shape echoes that of the bowl. Even closer to
the aqua version in profile and finial is a bowl
with a history of ownership in Cambridge.[2]

In spite of their stylistic relationship to
sophisticated New England bowls, NO. 176 and
others like it, including two in dark amber,
have been attributed in the past to New Jersey
and New York, particularly to Mount Vernon
Glass Works.[3] Other vessel forms with similar
characteristics include pitchers (NO. 136), vases
(NO. 244), and candlesticks (NOS. 289, 290). The
tremendous movement of glass craftsmen
within the industry in the nineteenth century
could explain how the style spread to the Mid-
Atlantic, but bottle and window glass factories
in New England should not be ruled out as the
source for this group.

1. Toledo Museum of Art, *The New England Glass
Company, 1818–1888* (Toledo, 1963), p. 40, no. 13; for other
Boston examples see Wilson, *New England Glass,* p. 247.
2. Watkins, *American Glass,* p. 45, pl. 11b; McKearin and
McKearin, *American Glass,* pl. 55, no. 2, and p. 159, where
a history in Cambridge is mentioned.
3. The McKearins discuss the Mount Vernon attribution
in *American Glass,* pl. 67, nos. 2, 3, p. 176. A dark amber
sugar bowl in the Henry Ford Museum, Edison Inst., is
attributed to Ellenville, N.Y. Another (private collection)
is attributed because of family history to the Batsto Glass
Works, a window factory operating in New Jersey
between 1846 and 1867; information courtesy of Kenneth
M. Wilson. An aqua sugar bowl (Corning Museum)
similar to NO. 176 is in McKearin and McKearin , *Two
Hundred Years,* pl. 7. The Winterthur collection includes
another sugar bowl that has been cut down (59.3051a, b).

177

SUGAR BOWL WITH COVER
PROBABLY NEW JERSEY OR NEW
YORK, 1835–65

Aqua nonlead glass. Blown. Bowl: globular body flared
out at top to wide horizontal rim; added gather tooled
into 4 tall, thin peaks of equal height; thick disk foot;
ring-shape pontil mark. Cover: low, domed form flared
widely at base to rest on rim of bowl; added gather tooled
into 5 short peaks ending in oval pads; drawn ball finial
with pontil mark on top.
OH: 6¾ in (17.3 cm); Diam top of bowl: 6⅞ in (17.6 cm)
H. F. du Pont purchase, 1945: Neil C. Gest, Mechanicsburg, Ohio
59.3038a, b

Sugar bowls are among the rarer forms bearing
lily pad decoration (see NOS. 138–42, 210, 217,
262), and several varieties are recorded. One
bowl that is documented to Clinton County,
New York, has a tall centrally knopped stem
and circular foot. Others have low disk feet like
NO. 177, but an olive green example has a tall
pedestal foot. Lily pad sugar bowls occur with
and without handles. Several have galleried
rims and plain, domed covers.[1] Winterthur's is
unusual because the cover also has lily pad
decoration. Although it is ill-fitting, it probably is original to the bowl.

   Just as the shapes of lily pad sugar bowls
vary, so do the styles of the lily pads. NO. 177 is
distinguished by its spare, tentacle-like fronds.
Because many craftsmen at different glasshouses were apparently responsible for lily pad
glasswares, additional research is needed to
substantiate specific regional or factory attributions.

1. See Jane Shadel Spillman, *Glass Tableware, Bowls, and
Vases*, Knopf Collectors' Guides to American Antiques
(New York: Alfred A. Knopf, 1982), no. 122.

178

SUGAR BOWL WITH COVER
NEW ENGLAND OR NEW YORK,
1850–75

Deep amber bubbly glass. Blown. Bowl: heavy U-shape
body flared out at top to a thick, rounded edge; applied
and tooled band of thick, irregular swagging around base;
applied thick disk foot; pontil mark. Cover: domed form
flared at base to rest on rim of bowl; applied finial of flattened ball on cylinder, pontil mark on top.
OH: 8¼ in (21.1 cm); Diam top of bowl: 6 in (15.4 cm)
History: Alfred B. Maclay; William T. H. Howe; Neil C. Gest
H. F. du Pont purchase, 1941: Neil C. Gest, Mechanicsburg,
Ohio
59.3042a, b

Published: Parke-Bernet Galleries, "Early American Glass
and Ceramics, Collection of Alfred B. Maclay," sale no. 100
(March 23–25, 1939), lot 469.
Parke-Bernet Galleries, "Early American Glass . . .
Collection Formed by the Late William T. H. Howe," pt. 2,
sale no. 273 (April 3–4, 1941), lot 127.

This large sugar bowl stands in marked contrast
to other American glass sugar bowls of the nineteenth century. Normally these icons of the tea
and dining table were made of a clear glass and
embellished with a light touch. The glass here,
however, is so thick it appears to be opaque
black. In the Maclay collection sale of 1939 it is
pictured and described as a "unique 'black' glass
sugar bowl and cover—one of the Greatest Rarities in American Hand-blown Glass." When held
to the light the true color of the piece is apparent,
namely a deep red-amber for the bowl and a
more yellowish amber for the lid.

The color and weight of the glass indicate the
bowl was manufactured at a bottle glass factory.
As such, it is indeed a great rarity because few
sugar bowls are known that were blown of dark
bottle glass. Tablewares blown of similar glass
have been attributed to bottle glasshouses in New
York, Connecticut, and New Hampshire.[1]

Here the glassblower was obviously aware of
the fashion for gadrooned and swagged decoration in glass tableware, seen on colorless glass
and aquamarine glass made in bottle and window factories in New Jersey and New York (for
example, NO. 138). The swagging on NO. 178 is so
thick and low that it has the effect of being a
decorative holder for the bowl rather than a band
of ornament. Instead of making a vertical gallery
for the rim to rest upon, the glassblower merely
rolled the lip of the bowl.

1. McKearin and McKearin, *American Glass*, pls. 69–72a.

Chapter 8
Dessert Wares

While the Continental Congress was in session in Philadelphia in 1774, Samuel Powel gave a dinner party that concluded with "Curds and Creams, Jellies; Sweet meats of various sorts, 20 sorts of Tarts, fools, Trifles, floating Islands, whippd Sillabubs &c. &c." In short, there was "Every Thing which could delight the Eye, or allure the Taste."[1] This dessert course accompanied an evening meal, but dessert foods, known generally as sweetmeats, were frequently offered as light refreshment at other times of the day. Wet varieties of sweetmeats, such as the jellies, creams, and floating islands served at the Powel home, were consumed with a spoon. Dry sweetmeats, eaten with the fingers, included nuts, chocolates, small cakes, and dried, preserved, or fresh fruits.

Specialized forms of silver, ceramics, and glass were devised to prepare and serve these foods. On many fashionable tables, the presentation of dessert was enhanced by fanciful decorations. New York's royal governor, William Tryon, for example, had "1 Sett Desert frames with Italian temples, Vases, China Images, Basket & flowers, etc."[2]

Among the most spectacular centerpieces designed for sweetmeats were glass pyramids and dessert stands. These required a dazzling array of such glass forms as salvers, jelly glasses, flower holders, orange glasses, and baskets. Glasses for syllabubs, possets, custards, comfits, and trifles are also mentioned in period records. The exact identification of many of these glasses is clouded by a lack of illustrated price lists and by conflicting evidence in early cookbooks and household manuals. Moreover, house-wives were not limited in their imaginative use of objects: then, as now, "the setting out a table is guided by Fancy and varied by Fashion."[3]

Serving dishes and plates for dessert were generally made of porcelain or earthen-ware, but during the second half of the eighteenth century, serving bowls, dessert dishes, and matching plates made of glass came into vogue. One of the earliest records of such a service is the "handsome service of glass for a dessert, four middlesized and six lesser dishes, and three dozen plates of hard metal" ordered from London in 1768 by George Wythe of Virginia.[4] Dessert wares like these were often of costly cut glass. By the 1820s America's glasshouses and independent glasscutters were manufacturing cut-glass dessert sets to rival imports. Technological developments soon led to the production of cheaper mold-blown and pressed glasswares for the dessert table.

1. *Diary and Autobiography of John Adams*, ed. L. H. Butterfield, 4 vols. (Cambridge: Harvard University Press, Belknap Press, 1961), 2:127. A room from Powel's house is installed at Winterthur.
2. B. D. Bargar, ed., "Governor Tryon's House in Fort George," *New York History* 35, no. 3 (July 1954): 305.
3. Helen McKearin, "Possets, Syllabubs, and Their Vessels," *Glass Circle* 5 (1986): 57–67. A 1795 quotation from an unidentified source cited in Helen McKearin, "Sweetmeats in Splendor: Eighteenth-Century Desserts and Their Dressing Out," *Antiques* 67, no. 3 (March 1955): 224.
4. George Wythe to John Norton, August 18, 1768, in Frances Norton Mason, ed., *John Norton and Sons: Merchants of London and Virginia* (Richmond: Dietz Press, 1937), p. 58.

179

PYRAMID SALVERS

CONTINENTAL EUROPE, 1720–70

Colorless nonlead glass; tin (probably added to conceal and strengthen a repair). Blown. Pyramid composed of 3 separate salvers held in place by a solid glass rod with stamped tin sleeve; the salvers have nearly flat circular tops with upturned and tooled rims; the center of each opens into a hollow stem of inverted baluster form, the stems apparently drawn from the tops; conical foot with downward-folded edge. On the largest salver the base of stem is closed; pontil mark on underside; on the 2 smaller salvers the stems are open through the feet with pontil scars around the holes.
OH: 19 in (48.2 cm)
Museum purchase, 1968: estate of Helen DeLancey Watkins, Schenectady, N.Y.
68.153a–d

Published: Palmer, "Beer to Birdcages," p. 85, fig. 3.
Belden, *Festive Tradition*, pl. 2:20.
Tim Udall, "Glasses for the Dessert 2—Eighteenth-Century English Jelly and Syllabub Glasses," *Glass Circle* 5 (1986): 43, fig. 6.

180

PYRAMID SALVERS

ENGLAND, 1740–80

Colorless lead glass. Blown. Flat circular top with upturned and tooled rim; hollow molded pedestal stem ringed at base; domed foot with downward-folded edge; pontil mark.
H (.1): 5¼ in (13.4 cm); Diam top: 11¾ in (29.9 cm)
H (.2): 5 in (12.7 cm); Diam top: 9 in (22.9 cm)
History: Taylor family, Monmouth Co., N.J.
Museum purchase, 1965: Ginsburg and Levy, New York City
65.111.1–.2

The glass salver, or server as it was sometimes called, was modeled after silver. In the 1661 edition of his *Glossographia*, Thomas Blount defined the form as a "new fashioned piece of wrought plate; broad and flat, with a foot underneath, and is used in giving Beer, or other liquid thing, to save or preserve the Carpit and Cloathes from drops." "Savers," or salvers, made of glass are mentioned in English records as early as 1620, and like their silver counterparts they functioned as serving trays.[1] In period paintings they are often shown supporting one or more wineglasses.

English examples from the late seventeenth and early eighteenth centuries have the wide pedestal foot seen on silver ones (NO. 181), but this generally gave way to a baluster stem on a domed foot. Stems composed of multiple knops are sometimes seen on glass salvers (NO. 183), but the most popular style was the molded pedestal stem seen in NO. 180. This stem lingered well into the nineteenth century; after 1800 the edge of the foot is usually folded upwards. Open-stemmed salvers like NO. 179 were made in England, but most had solid tops like those of NO. 180. Colonial American advertisements for glass included salvers "of all kinds"—varying sizes, singly or in sets, double or single flint (indicating weight and quality), and at least one merchant assured his customers that the salvers he offered were "genteel."[2]

Glass salvers became closely associated with the serving of desserts, as depicted in a Joseph Highmore painting of 1741–45 where a single glass salver supports a set of jelly glasses arranged around an orange glass. Besides functioning as a stand for individual jelly glasses, salvers could handsomely hold single, large gelatinous creations and baked goods. At an early nineteenth-century wedding celebration the bride's cake "was simply decorated with the white jassamine sprigs and lemon blossoms laid round it on the glass salver on which it stood."[3]

The most spectacular role of the salver was in a dessert pyramid comprised of two to five salvers of graduated diameter set one upon the other to create a pyramidal effect. Each layer bore an arrangement of glassware filled with jellies, creams, whipped syllabubs, and dry sweetmeats. The smallest salver at the top was usually crowned with a "top glass" for preserved fruit such as oranges. Winterthur's three-tier pyramid of salvers is presented according to Hannah Glasse's description in her 1762 *Complete Confectioner*:

In the middle a high pyramid of one salver above another, the bottom one large, the next smaller, the top one less; these salvers are to be fill'd with all kinds of wet and dry sweetmeats in glass, baskets or little plates, colour'd jellies, creams, &c. biscuits, crisp'd almonds and little knicknacks, and bottles of flowers prettily intermix'd. The little top salver must have a large preserv'd Fruit in it.[4]

Although the term *pyramid* was not used by the estate appraisers, the 154 jelly glasses and five salvers listed in the 1734 inventory of Charles Calvert of Maryland's proprietary family must have been displayed in some form of a pyramid. Most American written references to glass pyramids as such date to the third quarter of the eighteenth century, and descriptions range from the very detailed to the succinct. Mansell, Corbett, and Co. of Charleston offered "cut salvers and pyramids containing 9 cut jellys, 4 sullibubs, 4 cut bottles with flowers, 8 cut sweet-meat cups with flower handles, and a cut and scallop'd top glass"; a household inventory of 1757 included "1 p[y]ramed glass some crackt." That pyramids were not restricted to private dining is indicated by the record of "412 Pieces of Glass ware for Pyramids," valued at £15, in the 1771 inventory of the Raleigh Tavern in Williamsburg.[5]

Salvers were first made in America in the early 1770s in Philadelphia. South Boston Flint Glass Works listed the form among its products in 1818; their salvers ranged from 8 to 15 inches in diameter and cost from $1.67 to $6.00 each. The following year the firm extended the range down to 6 and up to 17 inches.[6]

1. For Blount quotation and discussion of English salver form in silver, see John D. Davis, *English Silver at Williamsburg* (Williamsburg, Va.: Colonial Williamsburg Foundation, 1976), pp. 123–25. Hughes, *Table Glass*, 289.

2. For English open-stem salvers see Thorpe, *History*, 1:331. Double and single flint glass salvers were advertised by Samuel Gray, *Boston Evening Post*, May 3, 1773; "genteel" ones were offered by James and Arthur Jarvis, *New York Gazette*, December 9, 1771.
3. Joseph Highmore, *Pamela and Lady Danvers*, National Gallery of Victoria, Melbourne; cake description as quoted in Belden, *Festive Tradition*, p. 83.
4. Hannah Glasse, *The Complete Confectioner* (London, 1762), p. 263.
5. Calvert inventory, Probate Inventories, liber 20, fols. 153–67, Maryland Hall of Records, Annapolis; John Moore inventory, New York, Downs, WL; Mansell, Corbett, and Co. advertisement quoted in Belden, *Festive Tradition*, p. 56; *Inventories of Four Eighteenth-Century Houses in the Historic Area of Williamsburg* (Williamsburg, Va.: Colonial Williamsburg Foundation, n.d.), p. 21.
6. Prices Current, South Boston, 1818, 1819, Edison Inst.

181

SALVER
ENGLAND, 1720–60

Colorless lead glass. Blown. Shallow circular top curved up at edge; applied pedestal foot with downward-folded edge; pontil mark on bottom of top.
H: 1⅝ in (4.1 cm); Diam top: 4⅝ in (11.8 cm)
Museum purchase, 1968: Lois W. Spring, Sheffield, Mass. 68.174

This small salver has a tall pedestal foot copied from seventeenth-century English silver, and the shallow, curved bowl is reminiscent of early Venetian glass tazzas. The miniature size of this glass suggests it functioned on the dessert table as a container for such sweetmeats as preserved fruits, nuts, or small cakes.

182

SWEETMEAT OR ORANGE GLASS

ENGLAND, 1720–50

Colorless lead glass. Blown. Ogee bowl with horizontal
rim; pattern-molded with 20 vertical ribs; flattened ball
knop containing multiple air beads; molded pedestal
stem with diamond-topped shoulders and ringed base;
domed foot pattern-molded with 20 ribs,
downward-folded edge; pontil mark.
H: 6 in (15.4 cm); Diam top: 4⅛ in (10.5 cm)
Museum purchase: Sotheby & Co., London
69.122

Published: Sotheby & Co., "Catalogue of Fine English and
Continental Glass" (June 23, 1969), lot 45.

This glass held a preserved orange or other
large fruit and served as the top of the dessert
pyramid. Its form is echoed in the uppermost
section of the sweetmeat pole (NO. 191). Many
sweetmeat glasses are mentioned in early
American records, but their exact shapes cannot always be determined because sweetmeats
ran the gamut from custards to candied violets. When importers used the terms *orange* or
top glasses, however, they were describing vessels like NO. 182.

Sweetmeat glasses can be difficult to date
because their decorative features remained in
fashion over a long period of time. Introduced
in English glasswares about 1715, the molded
pedestal stem is found on wineglasses into the
1740s, but the style lingered in sweetmeat
glasses and salvers. Domed feet similarly stayed
on sweetmeat glasses long after they disap-
peared from wineglasses. Pattern molding also
continued to be popular for the form throughout the century as is evident from the "Ribb'd
Top Glasses" William Lambert advertised.[1]

1. Lambert advertisement, *Boston News Letter,* October
10, 1771.

183

SWEETMEAT STAND

ENGLAND, 1710–40

Colorless lead glass. Blown. Shallow circular bowl with
curved, vertical sides; applied stem composed of 4 solid
ball knops; slightly domed foot with downward-folded
edge; pontil mark.
H: 2½ in (6.3 cm); Diam top: 3 in (7.6 cm)
History: George S. McKearin
Museum purchase, 1968: Sam Laidacker, Bloomsburg, Pa.
68.166

184

SWEETMEAT GLASS

ENGLAND, 1740–70

Colorless lead glass. Blown. Ogee bowl with horizontal
rim; inverted baluster stem containing white enamel
threads; applied, conical foot of irregular circumference
pincered with long V's; pontil mark.
H: 3¼ in (8.3 cm); Diam: 3½ in (8.9 cm)
Museum purchase, 1973: estate of Edna H. Greenwood,
Marlborough, Mass.
73.296

With its boldly knopped stem and domed and
folded foot, NO. 183 stylistically dates from the
early part of the eighteenth century. The form
is often described in the literature as a patch
stand, a container for the fashionable cosmetic
patches of the eighteenth century, but no period references to such glass items are recorded
in American sources. NO. 184, made between
1740 and 1770, features a "pear" bowl. The
opaque enamel threads are not twisted but have
a striped effect harking back to Venetian glass.

The advertisement of "the Federal Confectioner" in New York identifies the toothsome
delights that filled sweetmeat glasses: coriander,
caraway, almond, and cinnamon comfits; burnt
almonds; barley sugar, peppermint, orange,
lemon, cinnamon, and hartshorn drops.[1]

1. Adam Pryor advertisement, quoted in Thomas E. V.
Smith, *The City of New York in . . . 1789* (1889; reprint,
Riverside, Conn.: Chatham Press, 1972), p. 118.

185

COMFIT GLASS (ONE OF TWO)

ENGLAND, 1730–70

Colorless lead glass. Blown. Shallow circular form with flared sides; pattern-molded with 15 ribs; applied disk foot; pontil mark.
H:⅞ in (2.2 cm); Diam top: 2⅝ in (6.7 cm)
History: Milton H. Biow
Museum purchase, 1969: Parke-Bernet Galleries, New York City
69.37.1 (mate is 69.37.2)

Published: Parke-Bernet Galleries, "Fine French Paperweights," sale no. 2804 (February 14, 1969), lot 16. Belden, *Festive Tradition,* p. 56, fig. 2:17.

Small glass pans or dishes containing comfits—"crisp'd almonds," sugared nuts, and seeds—were often placed upon pyramid salvers. Comfit glasses were advertised in England in the eighteenth century, but as yet no reference to this form has been found in American source material.[1]

   Displayed on Winterthur's pyramid, these glasses have strongly rib-molded sides that echo the ribs of the jelly glasses and flower vases and add to the vertical effect of the centerpiece.

1. *Liverpool Chronicle,* March 24, 1758, quoted in Buckley, *Old English Glass,* p. 149, no. 133.

186

PYRAMID VASE (ONE OF SIX)

ENGLAND, 1725–50

Colorless lead glass. Blown. Slim tapered form with hollow rounded interior; mold-blown into an octagonal shape, rounded at base with diamonds at end of ribs; applied pedestal foot of irregular shape; pontil mark.
H: 3¾ in (9.6 cm)
Museum purchase, 1969
69.142.1 (mates are 69.142.2–.6)

Published: Belden, *Festive Tradition,* p. 56, fig. 2:18.

187

MINIATURE VASE (ONE OF TWO)

ENGLAND, 1775–1825

Colorless lead glass. Blown. Cylindrical shape with waisted neck and everted rim; thick base, flat bottom; pontil mark.
H: 3 in (7.6 cm)
Museum purchase, 1969
69.138.2 (mate is 69.138.1)

"Prettily intermix'd" among the jelly glasses on Winterthur's pyramid (NO. 179) are rare and elegant little flower vases. NO. 187 resembles a miniature decanter or carafe. The six of octagonal form are merely inverted versions of the molded pedestal stems found in English table glass and must have been made in the same molds (NOS. 182, 281).[1] The earliest molded pedestal stems had four sides; octagonal ones such as these came into fashion in the late 1720s.

1. For additional examples of molded pedestal stems, see L. M. Bickerton, *Eighteenth Century English Drinking Glasses: An Illustrated Guide* (London: Antique Collectors' Club, 1986), chap. 5.

188

JELLY GLASS (ONE OF FOURTEEN)
ENGLAND, 1750–90

Colorless lead glass. Blown. Funnel bowl, pattern-molded with 16 ribs swirled slightly at rim; applied conical foot, pattern-molded with 24 ribs; pontil mark. (One of set has downward-folded foot.)
H: 4 in (10.2 cm); Diam top: 2¼ in (5.7 cm)
Museum purchase, 1968: estate of Helen DeLancey Watkins, Schenectady, N.Y.
68.154.5 (rest of set is 68.154.1–.4, .6–.14)
Published: Palmer, "Beer to Birdcages," p. 85, fig. 3.

189

JELLY GLASS (ONE OF EIGHT)
ENGLAND, 1765–85

Colorless lead glass. Blown. Funnel bowl with cut, scalloped rim and flattened basal knop; applied conical foot; pontil mark.
H: 4 in (10.2 cm); Diam top: 2⅜ in (7.3 cm)
History: Taylor family, Monmouth Co., N.J.
Museum purchase, 1965: Ginsburg and Levy, New York City
65.111.3 (rest of set is 65.111.4–.10)

190

SYLLABUB GLASS WITH HANDLES
ENGLAND, 1720–60

Colorless lead glass. Blown. Waisted bell bowl, pattern-molded with 8 vertical ribs; applied rounded handles curled back at lower terminals; applied domed foot, pattern-molded with 8 ribs; pontil mark.
H: 4¼ in (10.8 cm); Diam rim: 2¹³⁄₁₆ in (7.1 cm)
Museum purchase, 1969: Tontine Emporium, Ridgefield, Conn.
69.8

In the mid eighteenth century a Philadelphia woman used the following recipe to make jelly from deer antler:

> take a large Gallipot & fill it full, of hartshorn, & then fill it full with spring water & tie a double Cloth over Ye Gallipot, & Let it in ye bakers oven, wth household bread in ye morning take it out & run it through a Jelly bag and Season wth juice of Lemons & double refined Sugar, & ye whites of eight eggs well beaten, let it have a boil & run it through ye Jelly bag again into your Jelly Glasses put a bit of Lemon peel in ye bag.[1]

Jellies could be colored by adding such things as saffron or cowslip's juice for yellow, beetroot juice or cohineal for red, spinach juice for green, and powdered violets for purple.[2] Both clear and colored jellies would be served in glasses like NOS. 188 and 189.

Syllabub was essentially made by adding cream or milk to a spiced liquor. In the first American cookbook, Amelia Simmons reveals the preference for fresh ingredients:

> Sweeten a quart of cyder with double refined sugar, grate nutmeg into it, then milk your cow into your liquor, when you have thus added what quantity of milk you think proper, pour half a pint or more, . . . of the sweetest cream you can get all over it.

Her "whipt" syllabub called for two porringers of cream, one of white wine, grated lemon peel, and two or three sweetened egg whites, all whipped with a whisk into a froth.[3]

Hannah Glasse recommended placing glasses with colored jellies on the pyramid salvers and positioning those with clear jellies

on the table surface next to ice creams, whipped syllabubs, nonpareils, blancmange "stuck with almonds," postalia nuts, lemon cream, golden pippins, and almonds and raisins. The advertisement of merchant Joshua Lockwood of Charleston suggests a seasonal serving pattern because in addition to his "very large Assortment of Glass Ware of all Sorts," he stipulated "as Christmas is near," he "must particularize Patty-pans and whip Syllabub and Jelly Glasses."[4]

English jelly glasses of the eighteenth century typically have deep but fairly narrow funnel bowls set on round feet. Syllabub glasses, of similar size and shape, have bell or funnel bowls generally with one or two handles. Glasses with "pan" tops are believed to have been used for whipped syllabub whether they have handles or not. Both jelly and syllabub glasses were available in plain, pattern-molded, and cut styles. Rib-molded decoration, seen in NOS. 188 and 190, was popular into the nineteenth century. "Scallop'd" jellies might have looked like NO. 189 with its scallop-cut rim.[5]

Jelly glasses occur in American records from at least 1716 when appraisers valued at 11s. the five and one-half dozen jelly glasses left among the shop goods of Anne Cheetam in Philadelphia. The earliest colonial reference to syllabub glasses occurs in a 1731 advertisement of Boston merchant Rebecca Abbot. English examples dominated the American trade, but in Pennsylvania in the 1770s, the factories in Manheim and Philadelphia advertised jelly and syllabub glasses of their own manufacture. Stiegel offered jellies in acorn and bell-bowl styles. Some objects, known to collectors as salts, are of acorn shape and so may have originally functioned as jelly glasses (NOS. 225–28). Stiegel also advertised jellies of "bubble button" style, referring to an air-beaded knop often found below the bowl.[6] American glasshouses continued to produce jelly and syllabub glasses throughout the first half of the nineteenth century.

1. Elizabeth Coultas Receipt Book, 1749–50, p. 18a, Downs, WL.
2. Tim Udall, "Glasses for the Dessert 2—Eighteenth-Century English Jelly and Syllabub Glasses," *Glass Circle* 5 (1986): 35.
3. Amelia Simmons, *The First American Cookbook*, intro. Mary Tolford Wilson (facsimile ed.; New York: Dover Publications, 1984) (originally published as *American Cookery*, 1796), pp. 31–32.
4. Lockwood advertisement, *South Carolina Gazette*, December 19, 1774. Lockwood went on to explain that "Had his good Friends enabled him to make a better Remittance last Year, his Stock would have been better; it is imprudent to cry for shed Milk."
5. For a pan-top syllabub, see Udall, "Glasses for the Dessert 2," p. 51, fig. 22b. McKenzie and McNeill advertised London "Jelly Glasses ribb'd hoop'd & scallop'd plain," *Charleston Courier*, October 5, 1803, reference courtesy of MESDA.
6. Anne Cheetam inventory, 1716-89, Philadelphia County Probate Records (microfilm, Downs, WL); Abbot advertisement, *New England Journal*, January 24, 1731; Stiegel advertisements, *Pennsylvania Packet*, July 6, 1772, and *New-York Gazette and Weekly Mercury*, February 8, 1773; Philadelphia Glass Work advertisement, *Pennsylvania Packet*, February 27, 1775; Palmer, "To the Good," p. 217, fig. 9.

191

SWEETMEAT POLE WITH BASKETS
ENGLAND, 1765–75

Colorless lead glass; silver. Pole: solid, tapered shaft
facet-cut with diamonds, ball knop at base; silver collars
with rings to hold glass arms; domed foot cut with diamonds and panels and having a cut, shaped edge; pontil
mark. Top glass: blown ogee cup with everted rim and
scalloped and pointed edge, the cup cut with diamonds
and ovals; cylindrical stem facet-cut with elongated
diamonds. Lower arms: 4 double-curved arms with
pointed ends, facet-cut with ovals. Upper arms: 4 angled
glass arms with pointed ends, facet-cut with ovals.
Baskets: 8 blown baskets of oval shape with straight sides
and flat base, shallow cut with large diamonds and a star
motif on bottom; applied curved handle facet-cut with
diamonds and attached with raspberry prunt. Two
baskets are modern replacements.
OH: 17⅛ in (43.5 cm); Diam base: 7⅛ in (18.1 cm)
Museum purchase, 1979: China Shop, Montreal, Quebec
79.63a–r

Published: "Recent Important Acquisitions," *Journal of
Glass Studies* 22 (1980): 92, no. 20.
Belden, *Festive Tradition*, p. 58, fig. 2:21.
R. J. Charleston, "Glasses for the Dessert I—Introduc-
tory," *Glass Circle* 5 (1986): 44, fig. 10.

This dessert centerpiece offered a dramatic
alternative to the pyramid (NOS. 179, 180). The
large top glass was designed to hold a preserved
orange or other fruit, and the small baskets,
swinging somewhat precariously from glass
arms, were for sweetmeats.

A product of the glasscutter's art, the pole
came into fashion in the third quarter of the
eighteenth century. The "Sweetmeat poles with
spires and glasses" advertised in New York in
1762 may have been of this type. The only glass
sweetmeat pole known with a history in early
America is at Monticello; Thomas Jefferson
gave it to John Wayles Eppes and Martha Burke
Jones when they married in 1809. It is similar
to Winterthur's but has eight glass arms in its
lower range.[1]

A third type of glass dessert centerpiece
combines features of both the sweetmeat pole
and the pyramid. As depicted on the trade card
of a London glasscutter (see p. 5, fig. 17), it has
a pole, top glass, arms, and baskets. In addition, below the baskets is a large, revolving
plate encircling the base of the pole on which
jelly and syllabub glasses can stand.[2] This was
probably the type of centerpiece George Washington acquired in 1761 that was described as a
"glass Pyramid in 8 arms." A more elaborate
stand of this kind with matching sets of glasses
was in another Virginia estate. If the appraiser's
description is accurate, it must have made quite a
statement: "one Epergne—Cut-glass containing
twelve Branches, twelve Baskets, twelve Ornaments, six Cream Glasses, six Syllabub Glasses,
six Jelly ditto, large Salver to turn round, one
glass Branch and a large Cut-glass for the top."[3]

Winterthur's sweetmeat pole illustrates the
taste for luxury cut glass that steadily grew in the
eighteenth century. In 1760 cut-glass salts, tumblers, and covered sugar dishes were sold in
Charleston; by the next decade, the newspapers
of many cities carried advertisements offering
English cut glass. Also by the 1770s American
manufacturers made cut glass in competition
with the imports.[4]

1. James Gilliland advertisement, *New York Mercury,*
October 4, 1762; Edwin Morris Betts and James Adam Bear,
Jr., eds., *The Family Letters of Thomas Jefferson* (Columbia:
University of Missouri Press, 1966), p. 285 n. 1. The pole is
pictured in James A. Bear, Jr., "The Furniture and Furnishings of Monticello," *Antiques* 102, no. 1 (July 1972): 116.
Additional information courtesy of Mary Forbes Nicoll.
2. Shreve, Crump, & Low advertised one for sale in *Antiques*
59, no. 4 (April 1951): back cover. The glass forms may have
inspired Wedgwood, who made dessert stands of similar
concept in cream-colored earthenware and showed them in
his 1774 trade catalogue; Wolf Mankowitz, *Wedgwood*
(London: B. T. Batsford, 1953), pl. 10.
3. Richard Farrer supplied Washington with the pyramid;
Susan Gray Detweiler, *George Washington's Chinaware* (New
York: Harry N. Abrams, 1982), p. 43. John Randolph, Deed
of Trust, August 25, 1775, James City County Records, Va.,
reference courtesy of Mary Forbes Nicoll.
4. Richard Baker advertisement, *South Carolina Gazette,*
May 10–17, 1760. In 1771 Stiegel advertised that a "Glass
cutter and flowerer, on application will meet with good
encouragement," but it was not until 1773 that he was able
to hire one (*New York Gazette*, July 9, 1771). The Kensington
glassworks in Philadelphia advertised cut glass in 1775
(*Pennsylvania Packet*, February 27, 1775).

192

BASKET

ENGLAND, 1730–60

Colorless lead glass, slight grayish tint. Blown. Cylindrical
form with outward-folded edge; 3 loops of solid glass
applied to rim as handles, with molded berrylike prunts
applied at points of contact with the rim; pontil mark.
H: 3¾ in (9.6 cm); Diam: 5⅛ in (13.1 cm)
History: Milton H. Biow
Museum purchase: Parke-Bernet Galleries, New York City
69.36

Published: Parke-Bernet Galleries, "Fine French
Paperweights," sale no. 2804 (February 14, 1969), lot 17.
Palmer, "Beer to Birdcages," p. 87, fig. 4.

Glass baskets are mentioned in the records of
colonial households as early as 1717 when estate
appraisers noted a "glass baskitt and tray"
among the effects of Sarah Quary of Philadelphia. References to the form continue throughout the eighteenth century. Some baskets were
intended to hang from the branches of a sweetmeat tree or pole as seen in NO. 191, and others
served as additional containers for sweetmeats
on the dessert table. "Baskets with handles and
feet for desserts" were among the products of
the Round Glass House in Dublin advertised in
1729. Philadelphians John and Elizabeth
Cadwalader owned a "glass basket for sweet
meats" in 1771.[1] Glass baskets sometimes came
with stands or trays.

The handle arrangement here is rather
simple compared to some English examples
where a second row of loops extend from the
middle of one lower loop to the next. The berrylike prunts that ornament the juncture of the
handles recall those on the stems of Continental roemers of the sixteenth and seventeenth
centuries, although English glassmakers continued the tradition on roemers and other
wares made in lead glass in the 1680–1720 period and tripodal salts (NO. 224) and cream
jugs of the mid eighteenth century. Such loops
and prunts are also recorded on tall sweetmeat
glasses with molded pedestal stems. A related
handle treatment occurs on one example of
eighteenth-century American-made glass: a
cream bucket attributed to Wistarburgh Glassworks of Salem County, New Jersey. The workman responsible for that object may have been
inspired by earlier English cream buckets or
sweetmeat baskets like NO. 192.[2]

1. Sarah Quary inventory, 1717-113, Philadelphia County
Probate Records (microfilm, Downs, WL); Thorpe,
History, 1: pl. 76.
2. *Faulkner's Dublin Journal,* November 1729, quoted in
Westropp, *Irish Glass,* p. 41; Nicholas B. Wainwright,
*Colonial Grandeur in Philadelphia: The House and
Furniture of General John Cadwalader* (Philadelphia:
Historical Society of Pennsylvania, 1964), p. 55. For the
cream bucket in Billups Collection, New Orleans
Museum of Art, see Palmer, "Glass Production," p. 96,
fig. 24.

193

BASKET

UNITED STATES, 1815–40

Colorless lead glass. Blown. Circular bowl with inward-folded edge, curved below rim then extending straight to base; blown in 3-part mold of geometric design (probably McKearin G II-18): band of diamond diapering above vertical ribbing. Applied handle, terminals impressed with waffle motif; bottom patterned with diamonds (type VII or XI); pontil mark.
H: 2¾ in (6.9 cm); Diam: 3 in (7.6 cm)
H. F. du Pont purchase
59.3248

The fashion for expensive, diamond-cut dessert glassware spawned imitative examples in cheaper mold-blown ware. The extreme rarity of the basket form in American molded glass, as well as the size and shape of this example, sug-gest that NO. 193 may have been made to replace a lost basket from an earlier cut-glass sweetmeat pole. Sweetmeat baskets were advertised among the products of Boston Glass Manufactory in 1816, but no hint of style or decoration is given.[1]

1. Another taller mold-blown basket is described in McKearin and McKearin, *American Glass*, pp. 270, 286. Boston Glass Manufactory advertisement, *Columbian Centinel*, January 17, 1816, reproduced in Wilson, *New England Glass*, p. 202, fig. 156.

194

SAUCEPAN

ENGLAND, 1770–1800

Colorless lead glass, grayish tint. Blown. Squat, pear-shape body with flared rim pulled out to form spout; pontil mark. Applied cylindrical handle with ball knop, pontil mark on end.
H: 2⅛ in (5.4 cm); L: 5⅛ in (13.1 cm)
History: Milton H. Biow
Museum purchase: Parke-Bernet Galleries, New York City
69.35

Published: Parke-Bernet Galleries, "Fine French Paperweights," sale no. 2804 (February 14, 1969), lot 16.

This unusual glass form is derived from silver prototypes. Made from the reign of James I until the time of Victoria, silver saucepans or chafers were found on the dining tables of the wealthy. Saucepans of this size were used to melt butter and prepare the piquant sauces so important in the serving of food.[1]

This glass version probably served sauces for the dessert course. Period recipe books indi-cate that whether hot or cold, various pud-dings—Sunderland, Indian rice, marlborough, cream almond—were to be covered with a sweet sauce of melted butter, wine, and sugar.[2]

The shape of this glass saucepan closely follows the silver style that came into fashion in the latter part of the eighteenth century. In silver examples, the handle is set at a 45 degree angle to facilitate the removal of the pan from the brazier or chafing dish. Although the handle of this example is shorter than those of its metal counterparts, it is similar in length to those of two other glass saucepans in private collections.[3]

1. G. Bernard Hughes, *Small Antique Silverware* (New York: Bramhall House, 1957), p. 78, figs. 108, 112; pp. 80–84.
2. Belden, *Festive Tradition*, p. 208.
3. Michael Parkinton collection, exhibited at Broadfield House Glass Museum, Kingswinford, Eng., 1989; Christopher Sheppard and John Smith, *A Collection of Fine Glass from the Restoration to the Regency* (London: Mallett and Sheppard and Cooper, 1990), p. 44, no. 59.

195

NEST OF DISHES

ENGLAND OR IRELAND,
1785–1810

Colorless lead glass. Blown. Oval forms with cut, shaped
edges, sides cut with large ovals each containing a lozenge
design having a central faceted square, narrow cut lines
near base; flat bottom cut with rays.
H: from (.1) 1⁵⁄₁₆ in (3.5 cm) to (.7) 3 in (7.7 cm)
L: from (.1) 5½ in (14.0 cm) to (.7) 12¾ in (32.4 cm)
History: Dabney family
H. F. du Pont purchase
62.153.1, .3, .5, .6 (62.153.2 and .4 duplicate .1 and .3;
the largest, .7, is not pictured)

Published: Phelps Warren, *Irish Glass* (New York: Charles
Scribner's Sons, 1970), pl. 63a.

196

PLATE (ONE OF TWO)

ENGLAND OR IRELAND,

1785–1810

Colorless lead glass. Blown. Circular form with curved
rim and cut, shaped edge; cut on exterior with short
panels, a band of diamonds, and swirl cuts around a
central star on the flat bottom.
H: 1⅜₆ in (3.5 cm); Diam: 8⅜ in (21.4 cm)
History: Dabney family
H. F. du Pont purchase
62.154.1 (mate is 62.154.2)

Cut, "Scollop'd" plates are itemized in colonial
records as early as 1758, but it was in the final
quarter of the century that the production and
use of luxury cut glass expanded. During that
period, sets of cut-glass serving dishes became
fashionable for serving cold desserts. At a private dinner party in Boston in 1795, the "third

course was served in a most elegant service of
brilliant cut glass, with everything proportion-
ally splendid." Even proponents of domestic
economy were drawn to the fashion and justi-
fied the expense by pronouncing cut glass to
have "the advantage of being stronger and
thicker; and therefore, it may be considered
more serviceable" than cheaper plain glass.[1]

Although the glasshouses of Ireland are
traditionally credited with much cut glass of
this period, there is reason to believe that more
high-quality cut glass, particularly after 1800,

was produced in English rather than Irish factories.[2] Throughout the federal period, however, American importers advertised "elegant"
cut glass from both English and Irish sources.

1. Inventory of merchant Francis Thurman, 1758, New
York City, p. 59, Downs, WL; R. J. Jeyes, *The Russells
of Birmingham in the French Revolution and in America,
1791–1814* (London: George Allen, 1911), p. 202; Mrs. Wm.
Parkes, *Domestic Duties* (1st American ed.; New York,
1828), p. 187, reference courtesy of Wendy Kaplan.
2. Catherine Ross, "The Excise Tax and Cut Glass in
England and Ireland, 1800–1830," *Journal of Glass Studies*
24 (1982): 57–64.

197

DISH

ENGLAND, PROBABLY LONDON, 1800–1810

Colorless lead glass. Blown. Oval, boat-shape form with curved sides and flat bottom. Overall cut decoration with horizontal bands separating motifs: scalloped rim, a band of large diamonds around the sides interrupted by 4 oval medallions, 3 of which have stars, the other contains engraved script initials "APP." Below, a ring of tiny cut ovals; on the bottom, graduated rays extend from a central polished circle.
H: 2⅜ in (6 cm); L: 10⅜ in (26.5 cm)
History: Ann Pierce Parker Cowper; Thomas Frederick P. P. Cowper; Christine Reddick Cowper Jordan; Esther Ann Jordan to her cousin Marylyn Reeve Downes
Museum purchase, 1970: Marylyn Reeve Downes
70.252

This dish was part of a service made for Ann Pierce Parker (1774–1849) of Isle of Wight County, Virginia, who in 1802 married William Cowper (1770–1819). Upon the death of her father, Josiah Parker (1751–1810), who had served in Congress from 1789 to 1801, Ann inherited an entire "elegant set of cut glass imported from London with the initials of her name on them."[1]

Pieces of the service were distributed to various descendants upon Ann's death.

Possibly one of a nest similar to NO. 195, the dish was most likely used on the dessert table. Such glass was often termed *rich cut* in the period, in reference to its weight, the fullness and complexity of the design, and the quality of the cutting. The geometric patterns of imported glass like NO. 197 inspired not only American glass-cutters but also moldmakers whose products enabled glass manufacturers to offer cheaper imitations of cut glass.

1. Josiah Parker will, Macclesfield, Va., 1810, Downs, WL. It is not clear why the set was in Parker's possession at the time of his death since it was obviously made for Ann who had already married and left home. (Ann's mother's name was Mary, so it had not been hers.) Ann also inherited "a small platte [plate? platter?] of pompadore coloured save [Sèvres] china."

198

DISH

PROBABLY MASSACHUSETTS, POSSIBLY ENGLAND, 1815–30

Colorless lead glass, bluish tint. Blown. Thick oval form with curved sides, tapered in at base below ridge to oval foot; flat ground and polished edge; molded pattern of diamond diapering around sides with a horizontal ring beneath and a band of short vertical ribs around the base; on the flat bottom, a rayed sunburst.
H: 1⅞ in (5.0 cm); L: 9¾ in (24.5 cm)
Museum purchase, 1977: Allan J. Hodges Antiques, Beachwood, Ohio
77.206

NO. 198 was formed by a technique known in the nineteenth century as "blown-over" or "blown-off" glass. According to London manufacturer Apsley Pellatt,

> Nearly all dessert dishes, especially those of an oval or square form, are made upon this principle. An oblong dish, of ten inches long, weighs about six pounds, and requires two or three gatherings of metal. When it has been well rolled and flatted into a crude

square or other form upon the marver, the workman ascends the chair, and presses it into a brass mould previously placed upon the floor; urging the pressure by blowing, lifting it up repeatedly, and again, as it were, stamping it into the mould; and at last, increasing the inflation from the lungs, and greatly expanding the upper part of the dish called the blow-over, till it becomes so thin at parts as sometimes to explode. A piece of wood is used to knock off the lower part of the overplus, leaving the dish, of considerable substance, which is then turned out of the mould for annealing.

The above mode of blowing-*off* . . . [is] distinguished from blown-*over*, . . . [which] is similar . . . but less expanded upwards; the surplusage is, therefore, thicker, and must be flown off by the glass-cutter when cold, which incurs great risk.[1]

The walls of vessels made in this manner are very thick and have a smooth interior surface. After annealing, their rough rims were ground and polished, if not cut in decorative scallops. Although blown-over dishes and even sugar bowls are known, salts are the most numerous extant examples of the technique.

The time-saving blown-over process enabled glass manufacturers to offer their customers the look of cut glass at considerably lower cost. In her *American Domestic Cookery*, "formed on principles of economy," Maria Eliza Rundell suggested: "Those who wish for trifle-dishes, butter-stands, &c. at a lower charge than cut glass, may buy them, made in moulds, of which there is a great variety that look extremely well, if not placed near the more beautiful articles."[2] Distance was key: the diamond and sunburst designs of molded glass faithfully followed cut models, but up close the soft edges and blurriness characteristic of mold-blown glasses were readily visible.

Distinguishing between blown-over dishes made in England and those made in the United States is problematical. No documented American examples are recorded, but it is believed that the molded "fan end" and "octagon" salts listed in New England invoices refer to a particular blown-over type. The blown-over process may have been brought to New England by the Bristol-trained Thomas Cains (NO. 114), whose South Boston Flint Glass Works was making "Moulded" round and oval dishes in 1819. By 1820 rival New England Glass Company was selling "Diamond Moulded" oval dishes. Between 1825 and 1828 Boston and Sandwich Glass Company manufactured 5- to 11-inch "Blowover dishes" priced from 20¢ to 90¢.[3]

1. Apsley Pellatt, *Curiosities of Glass Making* (1849; reprint, Newport, Eng.: Ceramic Book Co., 1968), p. 96.
2. Maria Eliza Ketelby Rundell, *American Domestic Cookery* (New York: Evert Duyckinck, 1823), p. 16, reference courtesy of Susan B. Swan.
3. Wilson, *New England Glass*, p. 210. Prices Current, South Boston, 1819, Edison Inst.; the 1818 list does not include molded dishes. New England Glass Company wares were advertised by William Loyall, *American Beacon and Norfolk and Portsmouth Daily Advertiser*, May 8, 1820, reference courtesy of MESDA. Account Book of Glass Made 1825–28, Boston and Sandwich Factory Records, Edison Inst.

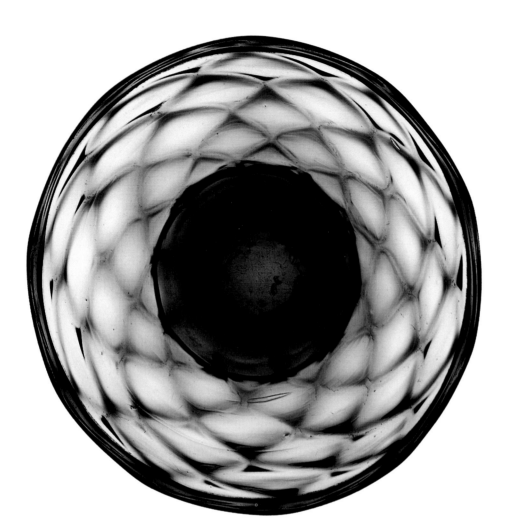

199

DISH

OHIO, PROBABLY ZANESVILLE, 1815–35

Amber glass. Blown. Shallow circular form with curved sides, inward-folded rim and drawn circular foot; pattern-molded with rows of 10 diamonds above a row of flutes; concave bottom; pontil mark.
H: 1¹¹⁄₁₆ in (4.3 cm); Diam: 6³⁄₁₆ in (15.9 cm)
H. F. du Pont purchase, 1929: McKearins' Antiques, New York City
59.3039

200, PL. 22

SWEETMEAT STAND

OHIO, PROBABLY ZANESVILLE, 1815–35

Amber glass. Blown. Shallow circular bowl with nearly flat bottom and slightly curved vertical sides; pattern-molded with rows of 10 diamonds; drawn knopped stem molded with 10 ribs; applied conical foot; pontil mark.
H: 3⁹⁄₁₆ in (9.1 cm); Diam: 5⅝ in (14.4 cm)
H. F. du Pont purchase, before 1947: possibly acquired at the Maclay sale, 1945
59.3035

Both of these objects reflect earlier English glassmaking traditions. NO. 199 is patterned the same way as English colored bowls of the late eighteenth century (NOS. 154–56), and in size and configuration NO. 200 recalls English sweetmeat glasses or stands (NO. 183), many of which were decorated with diamond molding on both the bowl and the foot. Their particular shapes and rich amber color, however, point to a nineteenth-century Ohio origin.

In 1822 the proprietors of the Mantua, Ohio, glasshouse presented the editor of *Western Reserve Chronicle* with an "elegant sweetmeat," perhaps like NO. 200.[1] The attribution of Ohio glass is problematical, but Winterthur's sweetmeat and dish relate to other mold-blown forms currently believed to have been made in Zanesville.[2]

In 1823 J. Shepard & Co. acquired a glassworks in Zanesville that had been founded in 1815 and operated it until 1838. Among Shepard's documented products are amber pictorial flasks that bear the company name (73.420.1). When Stephen C. Smith advertised for a buyer of Zanesville Glass Manufacturing Company in 1817, he described the factory as a producer of "white hollow ware," and his sale price included "all the moulds of the best and newest fashions."[3]

NO. 200 was possibly sold from the Alfred B. Maclay collection in 1945. A similar example was published in *American Glass* and may be the one that is now in Henry Ford Museum. A third amber diamond-molded stand is in Corning Museum. Similar stands are also known in plain blown amber glass and rib-molded amber glass.[4]

1. W. B. Honey, *Glass: A Handbook; . . . A Guide to the [Victoria and Albert] Museum Collection* (London, 1946), p. 105, pl. 54a. Quoted in Harry Hall White, "The Story of the Mantua Glass Works, Part 1," *Antiques* 26, no. 6 (December 1934): 215.

2. For example, a similar bowl was published by Knittle in 1932 that had been "found in the vicinity of Zanesville in 1930." She also illustrates a 10-diamond pitcher that descended in the family of a Zanesville glassworker until 1929; Rhea Mansfield Knittle, "Zanesville Glass," *Antiques* 22, no. 6 (December 1932): 224.

3. *New Hampshire Gazette* (Portsmouth), May 20, 1817, quoted in "The Editor's Attic: Regarding Zanesville Glass," *Antiques* 40, no. 3 (September 1941): 163.

4. Parke-Bernet Galleries, "Early American Bottles and Flasks and Other Rare American Glass Collected by the Late Alfred B. Maclay," sale no. 644 (March 7–8, 1945), lot 488; du Pont acquired at least two objects from this sale (lots 460, 461, 463; NO. 335). For the Henry Ford Museum example see McKearin and McKearin, *American Glass*, pl. 79, fig. 7 (it stands 3⅝ in. and has a diameter of 6¼ in.), and Helen McKearin, "American Glass from the McKearin Collection at the Henry Ford Museum," *Antiques* 77, no. 6 (June 1960): 584–85, no. 11. Corning Museum (58.4.24); it was acquired from James Rose.

201

DISH

BOSTON, ATTRIBUTED TO SOUTH BOSTON FLINT GLASS WORKS, 1812–23

Colorless lead glass. Blown. Shallow, circular form with straight sides, outward-folded edge; pontil mark. A thread of glass trailed on exterior surface and wound around from top to bottom in a spiral.
H: 2 in (5.1 cm); Diam: 8½ in (21.6 cm)
Museum purchase, 1971: Richard H. and Virginia A. Wood Antiques, Baltimore
71.279

In American production, threading is most commonly found around the rims of pitchers. It was a decorative technique favored for the aqua and green tablewares made in window glass and bottle factories, but in the Boston area, chains and threads of glass were applied to fine flint glass in a wide variety of forms from sugar bowls to oil lamps. "Threaded" dessert plates, perhaps like NO. 201, were available in 1818 from South Boston Flint Glass Works in 5- to 7-inch diameters. The following year the firm offered them in 4- to 8-inch sizes, costing from $3 to $7 a dozen. By contrast "moulded" dessert plates of the same sizes ranged from $2 to $5 a dozen.[1]

The bold horizontal design created by overall threading that is seen in NO. 201 is similar to the effect of the tooled "beehive" objects made at Sandwich in the 1830s (NOS. 134, 175).

1. An unusual pair of threaded lamps in Henry Ford Museum, Edison Inst. is in Wilson, *New England Glass,* p. 226, fig. 185, as are similar dishes with chain decoration (pp. 221, 223, figs. 174, 179). Prices Current, South Boston, 1818, 1819, Edison Inst.

Chapter 9
Footed Bowls
and Compotes

Fresh fruits were consumed with gusto in the eighteenth and nineteenth centuries, usually as the finale of the dessert course. Special ceramic and glass forms were developed to present this bounty. One traditional shape was the oval or round basket on stand, and ceramic versions often had openwork sides. A glass basket with tray is listed in a colonial inventory of 1717; by the 1790s elegant cut-glass ones were offered by many merchants. Cut-glass fruit bowls were also designed to be placed in silver or silver-plated epergnes or *surtouts de table* for stunning decorative effect.[1]

A tall, footed shape known as a compote (comport) also became a favored vessel for serving fruit. According to a late seventeenth-century definition cited in the *Oxford English Dictionary*, compote was fruit stewed in sugar in the French manner. It was served in a "compote dish," which eventually became just "compote." These tall bowls made dramatic centerpieces for the table as had fruit pyramids in the seventeenth century. Compotes may have also held salads and other foods besides fruits.

1. Belden, *Festive Tradition*, pp. 219–28, 65–69. A "glass baskitt & tray" worth 12*s.* was in the household effects of Sarah Quary, 1717-113, Philadelphia County Probate Records (microfilm, Downs, WL).

202

FOOTED BOWL
ENGLAND OR IRELAND,
1790–1810

Colorless lead glass. Blown; pressed. Deep oval blown bowl with curving sides; cut decoration composed of a faceted rim with alternating notched and serrated edges, a wide central band of diamond diapering within horizontal rings, fluting around the base. Tiered stem and square, double-step pressed foot with impressed rosette on underside.
H: 7½ in (18.2 cm); L: 10¹¹⁄₁₆ in (27.1 cm)
History: Lothrop family, Boston
Gift of Mr. and Mrs. Francis B. Lothrop, 1977
77.68

Anglo-Irish glass of the 1780–1830 period is best known for cut designs that, as in this example, exploit to the fullest the brilliance of lead-formula glass. Decorative cutting added considerably to the cost of an object because of the additional time and skill required, yet glassmakers often combined cut bowls with feet made by the labor-saving process of pressing.

Some blown goblets, candlesticks, and other wares had solid feet formed in plain, square, stepped molds; often the edges were sharpened by cutting (for example, NOS. 21–24). Deming Jarves, founder of Boston and Sandwich Glass Company, recalled importing such glass in the early 1800s, including English glass "table centre-bowls, plain, with pressed square feet, rudely made." The practice was also followed in Continental glass factories and, by the 1810s, in the glasshouses of the United States. The South Boston Glass Works price list of 1819, for example, includes "cast foot" wineglasses. For a lighter and more decorative foot as in NO. 202, glassmakers used a hand press with a star or rosette design that was imprinted into the underside of the foot. The period name for it may have been rose foot: in 1790 importer Thomas Tisdale of Hartford sold "scallop'd and diamon'd Salts with rose feet," and "Rose Feet Lamps" were made at Sandwich from 1825.[1]

Shallow oval bowls on tall stems are more common than ones with deep bowls and short stems, like NO. 202.[2] Although its rim is reminiscent of monteith bowls, where wineglasses were hung by the stem from the notches in the rim, this bowl was probably used to serve salad or fruit, or function, in Jarves's words, as a "table centre-bowl."

With its history in a Boston family, this elegant bowl well represents the quality glasswares that were available to the American consumer in the period following the Revolution. Cut glass of this kind was once automatically attributed to Irish factories, but recent scholarship has refocused attention on the production of cut glass in England. Certainly, the records of American importers indicate that both countries shipped cut glass to the United States, and, indeed, vied for the transatlantic market. Writing to American correspondents, a merchant in Cork reported, "there has been lately a Glass Manufactory established at Waterford about 60 Miles from hence, which for goodness of Metal and Cheapness of prices is allowed to equal if not excel those in England. I am constantly supplied with that article for the convenience of American Vessels to my address."[3]

1. Deming Jarves, *Reminiscences of Glass-Making* (2d ed., enl., 1865; reprint, Great Neck, N.Y.: Beatrice C. Weinstock, 1968), pp. 93–94; Prices Current, South Boston, 1819, Edison Inst.; Wilson, "American Contributions," pp. 168–72; Tisdale advertisement, *Connecticut Courant*, June 21, 1790; Bishop and Hassell, *Your Obdt. Servt.*, pp. 23, 25. Collectors describe such feet as "lemon squeezer" feet.
2. A related bowl is shown in Hughes, *Table Glass*, p. 352, fig. 282; he illustrates the more typical forms in pls. 281, 283. See also Warren, *Irish Glass*, p. 120, fig. 80.
3. Catherine Ross, "The Excise Tax and Cut Glass in England and Ireland, 1800–1830," *Journal of Glass Studies* 24 (1982): 57–64; Reuben Harvey to Christopher Champlin et al., April 15, 1784, in *Commerce of Rhode Island*, vol. 2, *1775–1800*, Collections of Massachusetts Historical Society, 7th ser., 10 (1915): 201.

203

FOOTED BOWL WITH COVER
UNITED STATES, POSSIBLY NEW
ENGLAND, 1815–30

Colorless lead glass; bowl of slight yellow tint. Blown.
Bowl: wide hemispherical form with outward-folded edge;
applied pedestal foot with downward-folded edge; pontil
mark. Cover: hemispherical form inset with flange pulled
out to rest on edge of bowl; drawn ball finial with flat,
polished top.
OH: 7¼ in (18.5 cm); Diam top of bowl: 7 in (17.9 cm)
Museum purchase, 1957: McKearins' Antiques, Hoosick
Falls, N.Y.
57.18.22a, b

The original function of this object is not known.
Similar but coverless English and Irish examples
are described as fruit or salad bowls.[1] Although
there is written evidence of glass salad bowls and
dishes in America from the 1760s, no mention
of ones with covers has been found.

A related bowl with applied ring decoration
is attributed to Thomas Cains. The 1818 price
list of the cut, plain, and molded ware made at
his South Boston Flint Glass Works included
"Sallad Stands," which may be interpreted to
mean a high-based form. These were priced at
$1.00 apiece; an 8-inch salver cost $1.67. Ap-
pearing on the 1819 list for the first time were
"Bowls, plain, on feet." These ranged in capacity from one to four quarts and cost between
$1.00 and $3.34 a dozen. "Sallad Bowls" were
only listed at the end of the price list among
the forms available in "Rich Cut" styles.[2]

Elegant in its simplicity, NO. 203 harks back
to the "standing bowls" of Venetian *cristallo* produced in the fifteenth century. Its tall pedestal
base, folded foot, and inset cover are characteristic of eighteenth-century glass; its ball finial
is seen on American nineteenth-century sugar
bowls. Several related bowls bear engraved
decoration associated with Bakewell's in Pittsburgh in the 1820s, signalling caution in the
attribution of plain versions to any specific

factory or region. The form continued to be
popular in pressed glass well into the century
as the 1871 catalogue of M'Kee and Brothers
of Pittsburgh illustrates.[3]

1. Hughes, *Table Glass*, fig. 282b, pp. 339, 344.
2. Larger and deeper than NO. 203, the bowl lacks a cover
and may never have had one; see Wilson, *New England
Glass*, p. 219, fig. 170. Prices Current, South Boston, 1818,
1819, Edison Inst.
3. Tait, *Golden Age*, p. 29, no. 4; p. 31, no. 10. For a
similar, larger bowl with a mushroom finial, see Eileen
O. Birk, "Current and Coming: Glass Products—
Pairpoint and Others," *Antiques* 90, no. 1 (July 1966): 26;
then in the collection of Lowell Innes, it was attributed
to New England Glass Company. Innes, *Pittsburgh Glass*,
p. 158, fig. 122; *M'Kee Glass*, pp. 163, 166.

204–206

FOOTED BOWLS

UNITED STATES, 1815–40

NO. 204. Colorless lead glass. Blown. Hemispherical bowl with wide outward-folded edge; blown in 3-part mold of geometric design (McKearin G II-18): vertical ribbing above and below a band of diamond diapering within horizontal rings; bottom patterned with diamonds (type XII). Applied pedestal foot with wide, downward-folded edge; blown in 3-part mold of the same pattern as the bowl except top is rayed (type VI-A); pontil mark.
H: 6¼ in (16.0 cm); Diam top: 7⅝ in (19.5 cm);
Diam foot: 5¹⁵⁄₁₆ in (15.2 cm)
H. F. du Pont purchase, before 1939: possibly 1934, McKearins' Antiques, Hoosick Falls, N.Y.
59.3190

NO. 205 (one of two). Colorless lead glass. Blown. Circular bowl with sides curved sharply in at base, wide outward-folded edge; blown in 3-part mold of geometric design (McKearin G III-5): narrow bands of vertical and diagonal ribbing separated by horizontal ring; between horizontal rings are 3 repeat panels of sunburst and diamond diapering; vertical ribbing below; rayed bottom (type VI-A). Applied pedestal foot with downward-folded edge; blown in 3-part mold of same pattern as bowl; pontil mark.
H: 5½ in (14.0 cm); Diam top: 8¼ in (21.1 cm);
Diam foot: 5⅞ in (15.0 cm)
H. F. du Pont purchase, 1947: Neil C. Gest, Mechanicsburg, Ohio
59.3232 (mate is 59.3247)

NO. 206. Colorless lead glass. Blown. Hemispherical bowl with outward-folded edge; blown in 3-part mold of geometric design (McKearin G II-18): vertical ribbing above and below a band of diamond diapering within horizontal rings; rayed bottom. Applied pedestal foot with downward-folded edge; blown in 3-part mold of geometric design (probably G III-6): vertical ribbing around stem; between horizontal rings are 3 repeat panels of sunburst and diamond diapering; faint diagonal ribbing; pontil mark.
H: 6 in (15.3 cm); Diam top: 9⅜ in (23.9 cm); Diam foot: 6⅜ in (16.4 cm)
H. F. du Pont purchase, before 1939: probably 1934, McKearins' Antiques, Hoosick Falls, N.Y.
59.3183

Published: (possibly NO. 206) McKearin and McKearin, *American Glass*, pl. 126.
McKearin and McKearin, *Two Hundred Years*, pp. 160–61, pl. 20.
Helen McKearin, "Early American Glass," *Antiques* 40, no. 2 (August 1941): 84.

Of imposing size and bold geometric design, these bowls well demonstrate the intentions of manufacturers to create the illusion of cut glass at a cheaper cost. Diamond and sunburst patterns were especially popular designs in cut glass and were made by English, Irish, and continental European, as well as American glasshouses.[1]

Unlike their cut-glass prototypes, the mold-blown footed bowls tend to be uneven in height and diameter, and their feet are sometimes off-center. Glassmakers encountered difficulties in controlling the patterns in wares of this size, as clearly seen in NO. 205—the bowl that Gest considered du Pont's best. The feet were apparently patterned in large tumbler molds then shaped into the desired form, which explains the variations. As evidence of handcraftsmanship, however, such irregularities subsequently enhanced the appeal of mold-blown wares for collectors. The tremendous rarity of bowls of this kind also outweighed any aesthetic inadequacies.

Large, footed bowls of this kind are often classified as punch bowls, but punch bowls, best known in pottery and porcelain, almost never stand on tall feet in this period. These glass bowls probably functioned instead as salad or fruit bowls, or perhaps as compotes for the dessert table. Irish "Centre Bowls & Stands," although of two parts, have a similar visual effect so perhaps these American footed bowls also served as table centerpieces.[2]

1. For example, large diamond-cut bowls were among the inventory of imported glasswares sold by Philadelphia merchant Leonard Keehmle, 1813-131, Philadelphia County Probate Records (microfilm, Downs, WL).
2. Westropp, *Irish Glass*, p. 232.

207

COMPOTE

PROBABLY SANDWICH,

MASSACHUSETTS, PROBABLY

BOSTON AND SANDWICH GLASS

COMPANY, 1830–45

Colorless lead glass. Pressed. Circular bowl with flaring
sides and flat base; scalloped edge; smooth interior
surface; in relief on exterior surface, a design of leaves
and flowers in the center, around the rim scrolling vine
with leaves and flowers, all against a stippled ground
(nectarine pattern); joining wafer below; central, 4-sided
shaft supported by 3 large C scrolls; shaped base with
hairy paw feet.
H: 5⅝ in (14.4 cm); Diam top: 7⅜ in (18.8 cm)
Museum purchase, 1967: Robert Carlen, Philadelphia
67.97

Published: "Recent Important Acquisitions," *Journal of
Glass Studies* 10 (1968): 189, fig. 55.

This compote is a handsome example of the
classical taste as expressed in glass. In such
designs the glassmakers were not slavishly
copying silver or ceramic models; instead, they
seem to have dipped into the rich vocabulary
of empire furniture. Vigorous C-scroll supports on the stem of the compote repeat the
pillar-and-scroll bases of center tables. The
finely beaded and ribbed detail of the base
simulates carving, and the contrasting surface
textures convey the effect of the figured ve-
neers characteristic of empire furniture. Paw
feet were a trademark of the classical style and
occur in objects of all media.

in this compote were possible only with the
new technology of pressed glass. The compote
was pressed in two separate sections and
joined by a wafer. This so-called nectarine
pattern, fragments of which were found at the
site of Boston and Sandwich Glass Company, is
also known in smaller flat-bottomed serving
pieces. Both bowl and base designs are recorded in other combinations. In one instance
the base was paired with a free-blown and
tooled candlestick holder of beehive style, a
decoration associated with Boston and Sandwich Glass Company production of the 1830s
(NOS. 134, 175).[1]

1. McKearin and McKearin, *American Glass,* pl. 157, no. 3;
Spillman, *Pressed Glass,* p. 60, no. 137; Wilson, *New
England Glass,* p. 268, fig. 220b.

208

COMPOTE (ONE OF TWO)
MASSACHUSETTS, 1830–45

Yellow lead glass. Pressed. Shallow rectangular bowl with curved sides and horizontal rim with wavy edge, against a stippled ground is a center panel bordered with a wave design surrounding a shaped medallion; on each long side is a cartouche with scroll outline containing diamond diapering and flanked by leafy branches; on each short end is a small stylized heart within larger scrolls (princess feather pattern); joining wafer below; tall, ribbed column sloping at base to scalloped edge, each lobe patterned with a large fern.
H: 6¼ in (16.0 cm); L: 10⁹⁄₁₆ in (27.0 cm)
H. F. du Pont purchase, probably 1931: McKearins' Antiques, New York City (mate was in collection by 1940) 59.3068 (mate is 59.3069)

This compote, basically a vegetable dish placed upon a tall foot, again illustrates the versatility that the technology of pressing permitted.[1] The princess feather pattern of the bowl is a typically intricate arrangement of scroll and leaves upon a stippled ground, and it contrasts sharply with the simple, clean lines of the stem and base.

The pattern also occurs in porcelain made by the Royal Saxon Porcelain Factory at Meissen, Germany. For years scholars thought that such porcelains inspired American glassmakers, but recent research into the Meissen archives has proved that the reverse was the case.[2] In the early 1830s the Meissen factory formed a collection of glass models including dessert plates, fruit baskets, bowls, vases, decanters, and candlesticks of both cut and pressed glass. The appeal of the pressed glass for Meissen designers seemed to be in the fine detail of the relief designs "in imitating raised decoration of flowers, fruits, and other products of nature." Crisply molded of thin, white porcelain, these Meissen versions could be embellished with enamel painting but more often were highlighted with a lustre gilding that had just been developed.

In 1835 Gotthelf Emil Frenkel, manager of the Leipzig warehouse of the royal factory, referred to "a substantial quantity of pressed glass ware from North America with the most appealing designs on hollowwares and flatwares of a distinctive appearance." The identity of the American manufacturers is not known. According to a government report published in 1832, New England Glass Company exported

$20,000 worth of glass annually to Europe, the West Indies, and the American South. Boston and Sandwich Glass Company reported overseas sales of about $55,000, but the markets named were South America, the West Indies, and the East Indies, not Europe.[3] Very likely the Germans had their own agents in this country who acquired the glass.

Meissen was the sole manufacturer of porcelains "in the crystal manner" that were so tremendously popular in the 1830–55 period. (These have been shunned completely by modern students of porcelain history.) Merchants from London to Budapest to Tiflis, Persia, eagerly purchased porcelains made in the styles of glass. The very success of this line of goods kept the factory on a firm financial footing at that time. Meissen records indicate that porcelains patterned after glass enjoyed a stronger market than the glass itself. The irony did not

escape Carl Friedrich Scheuchler of the Saxony ministry of finance who reported to the Meissen administration in 1840: "It is exceptional that the sale of exactly those cut and pressed crystal glass vessels, with their variety of facets and magnificent and impressed ornamentation, which had served the Meissen factory as models for those type of dinnerwares, on which the new lustre gilding could be applied with perfection, should be surpassed by the sale of those porcelain articles by the factory. The profits from the porcelain surpassed those gained by the sales of similar articles, which had been made from glass."

1. Spillman, *Pressed Glass*, p. 94, no. 266.
2. The information and quotes from the Meissen archives in this entry are taken from Joachim Kunze, "Meissen Porcelain Designed from Glass Patterns (1831 to 1855)," trans. Henry Pachter, *Glass Club Bulletin*, no. 153 (Fall 1987): 3–7; no. 154 (Winter 1987/88): 3–10. Kunze's original article, in German, was published in *Keramos* 105 (July 1984): 17–34.
3. Lura Woodside Watkins, "The Distribution of Early American Glass," *Antiques* 32, no. 1 (July 1937): 10–11.

209

COMPOTE

SANDWICH, MASSACHUSETTS,
ATTRIBUTED TO BOSTON AND
SANDWICH GLASS COMPANY,
1850–70

Deep amethyst lead glass. Pressed. Circular bowl with
flaring sides and irregular, rectangular openwork slits;
sawtooth edge; conical base of bowl has alternating long
and short rays from a circular ring above a hexagonal
knop; hexagonal pedestal foot.
H: 8¹⁄₁₆ in (20.5 cm); Diam: 8⅝ in (21.8 cm)
Bequest of H. F. du Pont, 1969
69.1032

The eighteenth-century fashion for openwork
or pierced porcelain compotes only increased
in the nineteenth century. The type of piercing
on Winterthur's basket was associated with
gold-trimmed Parisian porcelains, many of
which were exported to America. William Ellis
Tucker copied the style at his Philadelphia porcelain factory.[1]

Creating this form in glass was a considerable
technical achievement requiring a complex mold.
That the glassmakers had difficulty is evident
from the warping in the rim and the minute surface cracks.

1. Winterthur 91.1172. Philadelphia Museum of Art,
Tucker China, 1825–1838 (Philadelphia, 1957), p. 23, pl. 9.

210, PL. 3

COMPOTE

PROBABLY NEW YORK, 1835–65

Aqua nonlead glass. Blown. Hemispherical bowl with wide everted rim and outward-folded edge; added gather tooled into 4 scrolls ending in circular pads; applied stem with central compressed ball knop; thick disk foot; pontil mark.
H: 4¼ in (10.8 cm); Diam top: 8⅝ in (22.0 cm)
History: George S. McKearin; Mitchell Taradash, Ardsley-on-Hudson, N.Y.
Museum purchase, 1970: Robert Burkhardt, Kutztown, Pa.
70.85

Exhibited: Hagley Museum, "Technological Innovation and the Decorative Arts," 1973.

Hailing from the same collection as Winterthur's impressive lily pad pitcher (NO. 142) and bowl (NO. 217), the compote is a striking achievement of this style of decoration. Curving scrolls with nearly round ends cleverly echo the curves of the bowl and knop, and the extreme width of the rim balances the strength of the decoration. Spectrographic analysis revealed significant compositional similarities between the compote and the pitcher, suggesting that one manufacturer was responsible.[1] As discussed in NOS. 138–42, lily pad wares have been traced to several glasshouses.

There is considerable evidence of wear on the interior surface, so perhaps the compote was used more frequently for serving puddings and the like rather than as a fruit bowl.

1. Wade Lawrence, "Grouping Lilypad Glassware by Chemical Analysis," Winterthur Program in Early American Culture paper, May 1986 (author's collection). Related examples are in Corning Museum and Henry Sleeper's Beauport in Gloucester, Mass.

Chapter 10
Miscellaneous Bowls

211

FINGER BOWL (ONE OF TWO)
ENGLAND, 1755–75

Colorless lead glass. Blown. Circular form with curved sides flaring out at rim; pattern-molded with 16 vertical ribs swirled at rim; pontil mark.
H: 3³/₁₆ in (8.1 cm); Diam: 4 in (10.2 cm)
Museum purchase, 1972: Bardith, New York City
72.405.1 (mate is 72.405.2)

Published: Palmer, "Beer to Birdcages," p. 87, fig. 6.

Described as "wash-hand" glasses or basins for much of the eighteenth century, these refinements of the dining table were known as "finger cups" in the 1790s and "finger bowls" by the 1810s. The earliest colonial reference to the form occurs in 1750.[1] Fanny Kemble's report of a meal in New York implies, however, that finger bowls lacked widespread use even by the 1830s:

> The dinner was plenteous and tolerably well-dressed, but ill served: there were not half servants enough, and we had neither water-glasses nor finger-glasses. Now, though I don't eat with my fingers, (except peaches, whereat I think the aborigines, who were paring theirs like so many potatoes, seemed rather amazed,) yet do I hold a finger-glass at the conclusion of my dinner a requisite to comfort.[2]

Another function of finger bowls is recorded by French traveler François de la Rochefoucauld who observed in the 1780s, "after the sweets you are given water in small bowls of very clear glass in order to rinse out your mouth—a custom that strikes me as extremely unfortunate. The more fashionable folk do not rinse out their mouths, but that seems to me even worse; for, if you use the water to wash your hands, it becomes dirty and quite disgusting."[3]

The practice had not become common in the United States—or at least had gone out of favor by 1840—as a relieved Miss Leslie reported: "The disgusting European custom of taking a mouthful or two of the water, and, after washing the mouth, spitting it back again into the finger-glass, has not become fashionable in America." As la Rochefoucauld's account suggests, the ablutionary functions of the finger bowl could make it an unattractive feature of

212

the dining table, particularly if the glass were plain and "very clear," so decoration and color were practical means of obscuring the sullied contents from view. Some, like NO. 211, carried bold, pattern-molded designs. Others were cut and engraved or blown of dark colored glass. In New York, Frederick Rhinelander sold Bristol wash-hand glasses of blue, purple, and opaque white glass, some of which were scalloped and beaded. In 1781 he imported ones "Cut with a star and hanging border." South Boston Flint Glass Works, the first American glasshouse known to have made this form, offered only "plain" ones, for $4 a dozen in 1818 and 1819.[4]

According to merchants' advertisements and household inventories, such glasses often had accompanying stands or plates, generally of glass, but one Philadelphia household had "12 wash hand Glasses with China Saucers." That the form was available in various sizes is suggested by a 1765 reference to "large and small" wash-hand glasses fashioned of cut glass. Examination of other examples indicates that Winterthur's bowls are of a "large" size.[5]

1. Richard Capes advertisement for glass "finger cups," *New-York Daily Advertiser*, January 5, 1797, in Rita Susswein Gottesman, *The Arts and Crafts in New York, 1777–1799: Advertisements and News Items from New York City Newspapers*, Collections of New-York Historical Society 81 (New York, 1954), pp. 99–100, no. 303; Henry Barnes advertisement for glass "washing cups and saucers," *Boston Evening Post*, April 30, 1750.
2. Frances Anne Butler, *Journal*, 2 vols. (London: John Murray, 1835), 1:106, describing a dinner at the Philip Hone home, New York; see also *The Diary of Philip Hone, 1828–1851*, ed. Allan Nevins, 2 vols. (New York: Dodd, Mead, 1927), 1:146–47.
3. François de la Rochefoucauld as quoted in Jones and Smith, *British Military*, p. 55.
4. *Miss Leslie's House Book* (Philadelphia, 1840), quoted in Charleston, *English Glass*, p. 174; Arlene Palmer Schwind, "English Glass Imports in New York, 1770–1790," *Journal of Glass Studies* 25 (1983): 184; Prices Current, South Boston, 1818, 1819, Edison Inst. (on the 1818 list they were called finger basins; on the 1819 list, finger bowls).
5. Thomas Lawrence inventory, 1775-86, Philadelphia County Probate Records (microfilm, Downs, WL); Arthur Dobbs inventory, in J. Bryan Grimes, *North Carolina Wills and Inventories* (Raleigh: Edwards and Broughton, 1912), p. 484. A finger bowl with a 3¼ in. diameter is in Delomosne and Son, *Gilding the Lily*, p. 13, fig. 5.

COVERED BOWL AND STAND (ONE OF TWO)

ENGLAND, 1730–50

Colorless lead glass. Blown. Stand: shallow circular form with everted rim; polished bottom. Bowl: cylindrical form with concave bottom; polished pontil mark (mate has rough pontil mark). Cover: flat top and straight sides, inset with wide flange pulled out to rest on edge of bowl; applied ball finial containing multiple tears and capped with bead; interior pontil mark.
OH: 5¼ in (12.7 cm); Diam stand: 6¾ in (17.3 cm)
Museum purchase, 1969: W. G. T. Burne Antique Glass, London
69.141.1a–c (mate is 69.141.2)

The exact function of NO. 212 and its mate is not known. A similar object appears on a table in the aftermath of a drinking party of an Annapolis social club of the 1740s, where it had perhaps served as a container for sweetmeats or for the

sugar that sweetened the punch the men were imbibing. There are cut-glass covered bowls of the same size and shape, with or without stands, that are usually identified as butter coolers. Butter containers are not mentioned in written records until about 1770, however, and the bold, beaded finial of NO. 212 indicates an earlier date of manufacture.[1]

1. Westropp, *Irish Glass*, pls. 28, 30; Jones and Smith, *British Military*, p. 82, fig. 101; "*The Grand Clubical Battle of the Great Seal*, Minutes of the Tuesday Club with Illustrations by the Secretary, Dr. Alexander Hamilton," in Carl Bridenbaugh, ed., *Gentleman's Progress: The Itinerarium of Dr. Alexander Hamilton, 1744* (Chapel Hill: University of North Carolina Press, 1948), after p. 48.

213

BUTTER COOLER, COVER, AND
STAND
PROBABLY SANDWICH,
MASSACHUSETTS, PROBABLY
BOSTON AND SANDWICH GLASS
COMPANY, 1825–40

Colorless lead glass. Blown. Bowl: cylindrical form with
galleried rim; pontil mark. Cover: domed form flared at
base with downward-folded edge that fits inside rim of
bowl; drawn, flattened mushroom finial with pontil mark
on top surface. Stand: circular form with deep well and
everted rim with inward-folded edge; flat bottom with
pontil mark. All pieces blown in 3-part mold of
geometric design (McKearin G II-18): vertical ribbing
above and below a band of diamond diapering within
horizontal rings. Cover not original.
OH: 4⅞ in (12.4 cm); Diam (c): 6⁷⁄₁₆ in (16.5 cm)
History: Alfred B. Maclay; Richard Loeb
H. F. du Pont purchase, 1946: Neil C. Gest,
Mechanicsburg, Ohio
59.3275

Published: Parke-Bernet Galleries, "Early American Glass
and Ceramics, Collection of Alfred B. Maclay," sale no.
100 (March 23–25, 1939), lot 490.

Parke-Bernet Galleries, "Fine English and American
Furniture and Decorations," sale no. 805 (November 9,
1946), lot 75.

The history of this glass clearly demonstrates the
difficulty in discerning the original purpose of
objects made in the past. At the Maclay sale in
1939, NO. 213, without a cover, was catalogued
as a jam dish. Seven years later, when collector
Richard Loeb sold this item, then with a cover,
it was catalogued as "Covered Jam Dish and
Plate." After the Loeb sale Neil Gest called it a
cheese dish. A nearly identical example from
the McKearin collection and now at Corning
Museum was used for honey, according to
family tradition. Old Sturbridge Village has
one that has been labeled as a "covered preserve
dish." Although these names offer plausible
uses for the form, jam, cheese, honey, and preserve dishes of glass do not appear as such in
early advertisements and factory price lists.
The only period descriptions that fit this form

are "Butter coolers with covers and stands" and
"sweet meat tubs with stands." Butter coolers
were among the mold-blown products of South
Boston Flint Glass Works from at least 1819,
according to a price list printed that year. They
sold for $8 per dozen with stands and $6 without. The Winterthur cooler may well be one of
these South Boston products, although fragments of the G II-18 pattern found at the site
of Boston and Sandwich Glass Company have
led glass historians to attribute this pattern to
that factory. The reference to sweetmeat tubs
occurs in an 1830 auction advertisement for
glass from the Sandwich factory.[1]

   Prototypes for the form occur in English
and Irish cut glass of the late eighteenth century; they have traditionally been associated
with butter and known variously as butter
coolers, butter tubs, or butter basins. Those
depicted in an 1838 illustrated price list of London manufacturer Apsley Pellatt resemble NO.
213, but covers and stands were optional.[2]

   Butter tubs seem to have been introduced
in the American colonies during the 1760s. At
his death in 1770, Governor Botetourt of Virginia owned five with covers. The following
year "Elegant" cut-glass butter coolers were
available at the New York shop of James and
Arthur Jarvis. For the Loyalist trade in British-
occupied New York, Frederick Rhinelander
ordered Bristol butter coolers of "low flat
shape." Some Americans were apparently slow
to buy this form, and in 1788, merchant Thomas
Tisdale attempted to boost sales by explaining
that, "if once experienced in hot weather, every
family would use that is able to buy a pound of
butter in a week." Tisdale's imported examples
were of blue and white (colorless) glass.[3]

   The molded decoration of Winterthur's
American-made butter cooler obviously imitates
the diamond-cut patterns of English and Irish
ones and may have been directly inspired by
cheaper molded tubs made by some Irish glasshouses. In spite of the mass production that
molds made possible, only a handful of glass
butter coolers like this are known. Although he
recognized it as a rarity, du Pont told Gest he
did not want to pay an "exorbitant" price.[4]

1. Gest to du Pont, November 11, 1946, WM; McKearin
and McKearin, *Two Hundred Years*, pp. 186–87, pl. 33;
Wilson, *New England Glass*, p. 270, fig. 224; Prices

214, PL. 19

Current, South Boston, 1819, Edison Inst.; auction notice of Thomas Anderson and Co., *Louisville Public Advertiser*, December 14, 1830, reference courtesy of Mr. and Mrs. J. G. Stradling.

2. An Anglo-Irish cut-glass one (Corning Museum) is in Hughes, *Table Glass*, p. 152. Other Irish ones are shown in Westropp, *Irish Glass*, pl. 30. In the Waterford company patterns of about 1830 a different form—a rounded bowl with two short vertical handles—is described as a butter cooler; see Westropp, *Irish Glass*, endpapers. Phelps Warren, "Apsley Pellatt's Table Glass, 1840–1864," *Journal of Glass Studies* 26 (1984): 122, fig. 5. Hugh Wakefield dated the list to 1838 in *Nineteenth-Century British Glass* (2d rev. ed.; London: Faber and Faber, 1982), p. 36.

3. *Inventories of Four Eighteenth-Century Houses in the Historic Area of Williamsburg* (Williamsburg, Va.: Colonial Williamsburg Foundation, n.d.); Jarvis advertisement, *New York Gazette*, December 9, 1771; September 21, 1779; order to Vigor and Stevens, Letter and Order Book, Rhinelander Papers, NYHS; Tisdale advertisement, *Connecticut Courant*, June 30, 1788.

4. Westropp, *Irish Glass*, pl. 30; du Pont to Gest, November 6, 1946, WM.

BOWL

OHIO, POSSIBLY KENT, 1825–45

Light green nonlead glass. Blown. Circular form with straight, flaring sides and wide, outward-folded rim; blown in 3-part mold of geometric design (McKearin G II-6): vertical ribbing around top; between horizontal rings a band of diamond diapering; broad vertical ribs above a horizontal ring and basal ring of diamonds; pontil mark.
H: 3 in (7.6 cm); Diam rim: 7¼ in (18.5 cm)
Museum purchase, 1954: Neil C. Gest, Mechanicsburg, Ohio
54.36.2

The G II-6 pattern seen here (also NOS. 126, 257) traditionally is attributed to Franklin Glass Works near Kent, Ohio, and relates closely to Irish molded glass made in the early nineteenth century. Richard and George Parks, the presumed partners of James H. Edmunds in the Franklin undertaking, had emigrated from Great Britain and perhaps were responsible for introducing the pattern.[1] The green color of the glass is unparalleled in European examples, however, and the form is typically American. The specific purpose of the bowl is unknown.

1. Warren, *Irish Glass*, p. 205, pl. 233; George L. Miller, "History of the Franklin Glass Works, Portage County," *Glass Club Bulletin*, no. 152 (Spring 1987): 6.

215

BOWL (ONE OF TWO)
PROBABLY MASSACHUSETTS, 1815–40

Colorless lead glass. Blown. Shallow circular form with curved sides and wide outward-folded edge; flat bottom. Blown in 3-part mold of geometric design (McKearin G III-5): narrow bands of vertical and diagonal ribbing below rim separated by horizontal rings; between horizontal rings are 3 repeat panels of diamond diapering and sunburst; vertical ribbing; rayed bottom (type VI-A); pontil mark.
H: 2⅜ in (6.0 cm); Diam top: 10⅛ in (25.8 cm)
H. F. du Pont purchase, 1944 or 1946: Neil C. Gest, Mechanicsburg, Ohio
59.3160 (mate is 59.3161)

What foods these large dishes were meant to contain remains undetermined. The 1819 price list of South Boston Flint Glass Works lists "moulded round" dishes at a cost of 8¢ per inch. Union Flint Glass Works in Philadelphia sold 10-inch "plates" in 1832 for $4.50 per dozen.[1] The geometric pattern seen here is more often recorded in decanters, pitchers (NO. 132), and other forms. Indeed, that these dishes were blown in a mold designed for quart-size decanters is revealed by the pattern of mold defects that matches exactly those of a decanter in the Winterthur collection (59.3171). The G III-5 pattern is traditionally associated with Boston and Sandwich Glass Company; it was also one of the patterns chosen for insidious reproduction (NO. 133) in the twentieth century.

1. Prices Current, South Boston, 1819, Edison Inst.; Gilpin Invoice Book, p. 41, HSP.

216, PL. 12

BOWL
UNITED STATES, PROBABLY PHILADELPHIA AREA, 1920–30

Amethyst lead glass. Blown. Cylindrical form with sides sharply swelled below curving neck and everted rim. Blown in 3-part mold of geometric design (McKearin G III-6): narrow band of vertical ribbing above horizontal ring and diagonal ribbing; between horizontal rings are 3 repeat panels of diamond diapering and sunburst; narrow vertical ribbing below; pontil mark.
H: 2⅝ in (6.6 cm); Diam top: 3½ in (9.0 cm)
H. F. du Pont purchase, 1931: Neil C. Gest, Mechanicsburg, Ohio
59.3111

Published: Lanmon, Brill, and Reilly, "Suspicions," p. 169, fig. 36.

As the Winterthur collection demonstrates, America's early glasshouses produced a wide range of bowl styles. The bowl seen in NO. 216, however, is not of nineteenth-century shape. An example of the spurious Mutzer group of blown three-mold glass (NO. 133), it illustrates the manufacturer's predilection for unrecorded forms. This was a shrewd philosophy because a bowl like this was so rare that it was bound to appeal to collectors. When Gest wrote du Pont about the bowl he said it was "Unique in every way." Never had he seen "a piece so shaped in any glass." The Mutzer group was probably made near Philadelphia; Gest wrote that NO. 216 had been "found in Pennsylvania by a dealer who sold it directly to me."[1]

1. Gest to du Pont, May 19, 1931, WM.

217

BOWL

NEW YORK, 1835–65

Aqua nonlead glass. Blown. Deep circular form with widely flaring sides and outward-folded rim; added gather tooled into 5 tall peaks with 5 shorter in between; applied disk foot with pincered edge; pontil mark.
H: 4⅝ in (11.8 cm); Diam top: 14⅜ in (36.5 cm)
Museum purchase, 1970: Robert Burkhardt, Kutztown, Pa.
History: George S. McKearin; Mitchell Taradash, Ardsley-on-Hudson, N.Y.
70.83

Exhibited: American Art Galleries, "Loan Exhibition of Eighteenth and Early Nineteenth Century Furniture and Glass for the Benefit of the National Council of the Girl Scouts, Inc.," 1929.
Published: George S. McKearin, "Early American Glass," in American Art Galleries, *Loan Exhibition of Eighteenth and Early Nineteenth Century Furniture and Glass . . . for the Benefit of the National Council of the Girl Scouts, Inc.* (New York, 1929), no. 298.
"A Glimpse of Early Glass," *Antiques* 17, no. 2 (February 1930): 140.
McKearin and McKearin, *American Glass*, pl. 64, no. 2.
McKearin and McKearin, *Two Hundred Years*, pp. 150–51, pl. 15.
Cover, *Glass Club Bulletin*, no. 42 (March 1957).
"Recent Important Acquisitions," *Journal of Glass Studies* 13 (1971): 146, no. 64.

218

BOWL

CLAYTON, NEW JERSEY,
ATTRIBUTED TO CLEVENGER
BROTHERS, 1927–49

Aqua nonlead glass. Blown. Circular form with curved
sides that flare sharply at rim; outward-folded rim; added
gather tooled into 4 short wavelike peaks; applied disk
foot with pincered edge; pontil mark.
H: 3¹¹⁄₁₆ in (10.0 cm); Diam top: 10 in (25.5 cm)
H. F. du Pont purchase, 1949: Neil C. Gest, Mechanicsburg,
Ohio
59.3259

NO. 217 is arguably the finest bowl known that
bears the distinctive lily pad decoration (see
NOS. 138–42). Blown of a brilliant aqua glass,
its attenuated spikes have a masterful boldness
and spontaneity. When viewed from the side
the lily pads seem to lift and support the form.

A similar effect is seen on an early Spanish
tazza. On that piece, bright blue glass applied
to the underside of the colorless bowl was tooled

into eleven pad-capped fronds radiating from
the center. Around the rim is a blue glass chain,
indicating the maker's debt to Venice. Indeed,
the ultimate inspiration for lily pad wares may
be pillar-molded Venetian glass of the fifteenth
and sixteenth centuries, which in turn was
derived from ancient Roman prototypes.[1]

In marked contrast to the vitality of NO. 217
is the lily pad bowl NO. 218, in which there is
nothing spontaneous or bold about the four
clumsy, wavelike stalks. The color of the glass
is believable for the nineteenth century but
lacks the brilliance of NO. 217. Such details as
the folded rim and pincered foot are accurately
rendered, but the deep conical pontil mark so
characteristic of Clevenger products is unknown in genuine specimens.

The glasswares blown by the Clevenger
brothers—Tom, Reno, and Allie—were originally marketed as "hand blown replicas." The
1939 Ritter-Carlton Company catalogue, *Authentic Reproductions of Early American Glass*,
illustrates a similar lily pad bowl, noting that
its "graceful spread will form a base for a

flower arrangement." It was available in colonial blue, light green, and light blue and was
priced at $3.00.[2] Besides bowls, the Clevengers
made pitchers and two-handled vases with lily
pad decoration, always with the same regular
and uninspired treatment. Du Pont's acquisition of this bowl in 1949 indicates that whatever
the Clevengers' intentions, their reproductions
fooled collectors from the time of manufacture.

1. Attributed to Catalonia, 17th–18th century, in *Spanish
Glass in the Hermitage* (1970), pl. 8, cat. 28. For Venetian
glass see Tait, *Golden Age*, p. 37, no. 27.
2. Ritter-Carlton Co., *Authentic Reproductions of Early
American Glass* (New York, 1939); copy courtesy of
Thomas C. Haunton. Gay LeCleire Taylor, *Clevenger
Brothers Glass Works—The Persistence of Tradition*
(Millville, N.J.: Museum of American Glass at Wheaton
Village, 1987).

219, PL. 4

BOWL

UNITED STATES, 1835–55

Aqua glass. Blown. Hemispherical body with gadrooning made of added gather molded with 12 swirled
ribs; applied disk foot; pontil mark.
H: 5½ in (14.1 cm); Diam top: 5⅞ in (15.0 cm)
H. F. du Pont purchase, before 1935
59.3049

With its gadrooned decoration this bowl relates to several other tablewares at Winterthur
(NOS. 136, 176, 244). Although the concept is
rather sophisticated, the bowl is the product
of a bottle or window glass factory, as yet unidentified. It must have been one of du Pont's
favorite objects because he displayed it in his
bedroom (pl. 2).

220

BOWL

UNITED STATES, 1827–30

Colorless lead glass. Pressed. Shallow circular form with
curved sides and everted rim. On top of rim are diagonal
ribs in relief; remainder of upper surface is smooth. Relief
design on the underside consists of spirally radiating rows
of strawberry diamonds around a central circle with rays.
H: 1¼ in (3.2 cm); Diam top: 6⅛ in (15.7 cm)
Museum purchase, 1968: Richard H. and Virginia A.
Wood Antiques, Baltimore
68.348

This bowl is a hitherto unrecorded object from
the early years of American machine pressing.
It is dated to the late 1820s because it was pressed
without the use of a cap-ring, a device that
permitted the glassmaker to control the uniformity of rim thickness and that was probably
in general use by 1830.[1] The strawberry-
diamond pattern of this bowl also points to an
early date because it is derived directly from
cut-glass motifs.

1. See Kirk J. Nelson, "Early Glass Pressing Technology in
Sandwich," *Acorn* 1 (1990): 38–50.

221, 222

DISHES

SANDWICH, MASSACHUSETTS,
ATTRIBUTED TO BOSTON AND
SANDWICH GLASS COMPANY,
1830–50

NO. 221. Colorless lead glass. Pressed. Large, shallow circular bowl with ogee sides and edge of alternating scallops and double points; short foot ring, flat base. Smooth upper surface; pressed design in relief on underside against a stippled ground: around the rim a row of beads; 4 scrolled medallions in leafy frame enclosing diamond diapering around an oval; in between are 4 comets, 2 with diapering and 2 with strawberry-diamond diapering; around the well is a row of beads and a band of strawberry diamonds; in the base is a star within a frame of bellflowers and 6 thick S scrolls, 3 with diamond diapering and 3 with strawberry-diamond diapering.
H: 2¼ in (5.7 cm); Diam top: 11¹⁵⁄₁₆ in (30.4 cm)
H. F. du Pont purchase
59.3119

NO. 222. Colorless lead glass. Pressed. Large deep circular form with curved sides and scalloped edge; flat base. Smooth upper surface; pressed design in relief on underside: around the sides against a stippled ground are beaded oval medallions containing diamond diapering alternating with crossed comets framing a diamond, all with diamond diapering; a beaded ring around the well; 18 rays of triple ribs each on the base.
H: 3 in (7.6 cm); Diam top: 14 in (35.6 cm)
H. F. du Pont purchase
59.3015

Exhibited: Corning Museum, "Pressed Glass, 1825–1925," 1983.
Published: James H. Rose, "Unrecorded Rarities in American Glass," *Antiques* 71, no. 2 (February 1957): 160.

The patterns of these objects are pressed in very sharp, crisp relief, exemplifying the best of the early pressing accomplished in America's glasshouses. The design of NO. 222 demonstrates the manufacturer's reliance on cut-glass styles, but unlike the earlier strawberry-diamond dish (NO. 220), the pattern is set off against a stippled ground. Although traditionally associated with the first phase of pressed glass technology, the design of NO. 222 was still being made in 1860 as the "Ray" pattern by M'Kee Brothers, Pittsburgh.[1]

NO. 222 is also distinguished by its tremendous size: it and its virtual mate at Los Angeles County Museum of Art are the largest pieces of stippled-ground American pressed glass known.[2] Although Winterthur's dish is uniform in thickness, its rough inner surface indicates that technical problems were encountered in pressing such a large object.

1. *M'Kee Glass*, p. 21.
2. "Recent Important Acquisitions," *Journal of Glass Studies* 28 (1986): 111, no. 45.

223

COVERED BOWL

PROBABLY PITTSBURGH,

POSSIBLY BAKEWELL, PEARS,

AND CO., 1840–80

Colorless lead glass. Pressed. Bowl: circular form with
tapered sides and nearly flat bottom, everted rim; shaped
edge of alternating arches and points; in between wide
swirled ribs are rondels above diamond diapering
(peacock-eye or comet pattern). Short stem and circular
stepped and domed foot with vertical ribbing. Cover:
domed form flared at base to rest on rim of bowl;
cylindrical finial flared at top, 11-petal pattern; pressed
in same pattern as bowl.
OH: 5 in (12.5 cm); Diam top (a): 6¼ in (16.0 cm)
Museum purchase, 1974: The Stradlings, New York City
74.78a, b

The pattern of this covered bowl, derived from
cut glass (NO. 93), was made in pressed glass from
about 1830. In shape and foot Winterthur's bowl
relates closely to a "Comport & Cover" illustrated
in a trade catalogue of Bakewell, Pears, and Co.
that can be dated about 1875. That bowl is also
patterned in a "lacy" design (Rochelle pattern)
thus proving that intricate, stippled-ground
designs continued to be made long after 1850.[1]

The exact intended function of NO. 223 is
not clear. Nineteenth-century trade catalogues
describe similar forms as nappies, and ones of
6- to 8-inch diameter are named as "comports"
or compotes in the Bakewell catalogue.[2]

1. Thomas C. Pears III and Lowell Innes, *Bakewell, Pears,
and Co. Glass Catalogue* (Pittsburgh: Thomas C. Pears
III, 1977), p. 16; Wilson, "American Contributions," pp.
189–90, fig. 12. Spillman has attributed a similar example
in Corning Museum to the Midwest and dated it 1840–
50; *Pressed Glass*, p. 89, no. 246.
2. *M'Kee Glass* (1864), p. 45.

Chapter 11
Salts and Condiment Containers

In the days before refrigeration, salt was needed to preserve many foods, especially meats, as well as to prepare numerous recipes. It was an important seasoning added to dishes at the table to suit individual taste.

For table use, low, open salt containers, generally arranged in pairs, were made of silver, pewter, ceramics, or glass. In many period records they are merely called "salts," but other descriptions of salt dishes, cellars, and stands suggest a variety of shapes. Glass liners inside silver salts protected the metal from corrosion, but glass itself could be clouded by the salt. Some glass salts can be dated by the silver styles they imitated, but certain glass shapes were made over long periods of time. The technology of pressing led to the production of novelty salts, a fashion that continued through the nineteenth century.

An 1829 domestic economy book offered the following directions on the preparation of salt for salt cellars like these:

> Take a lump of Salt of the size you think proper and if not quite dry, place it in a plate before the fire to make it so, then pound it in a Mortar till it is perfectly fine; this done, fill your Salt-cellars with it higher than the brim, and with the flat side of a knife that has a smooth edge, take it off and press it down even with the top. If the salt-cellars are not smooth on the top, but cut in notches, a Table-spoon is the tool to press and smooth the salt in them—or it makes them look very neat, if bottom of the salt-cellar is ornamented, to place the bottom of one on the top of the other for the same purpose.
>
> The Salt should be in a lump that it may be free from dirt, and the knife must have a smooth edge—if it has the *least ruggedness*, it will leave the marks on the salt.[1]

In the kitchen, bottles and jugs of green glass or salt-glazed stoneware held the various liquids required in food preparation. On the dining table, more refined vessels were preferred. From the seventeenth century on, household inventories list glass cruets for oil and vinegar, most frequently combined for salad dressings. These often followed the styles of decanters, even to being "labelled," that is, engraved, enameled, or gilded with the name of the intended contents. At Stiegel's glasshouse in Pennsylvania, workers made oil and vinegar cruets in the joined "crossbill" style common in central Europe.[2] Sets of matching bottles for condiments were grouped in frames for convenient use during dining and by the mid nineteenth century became the centerpiece of the family dining table.

1. William Kitchiner, *The Housekeeper's Oracle* (London: J. Moyes, 1829), as quoted in Leinicke, "Production," pp. 470–71.
2. Palmer, "To the Good," p. 216.

224

SALT

ENGLAND, POSSIBLY NORWAY,
1740–70

Colorless lead glass. Blown. Hemispherical bowl with
tooled horizontal rings; three applied legs, each with a
molded raspberry prunt at top; pontil mark.
H: 2¹⁄₁₆ in (5.2 cm)
Museum purchase, 1973: estate of Edna H. Greenwood,
Marlborough, Mass.
73.295

Published: Palmer, "Beer to Birdcages," p. 85, fig. 2.
Smith and Hummel, "Winterthur Museum," p. 1282.
Laura F. Sprague, "Glass in Maine, 1630–1820," *Glass
Club Bulletin,* no. 135 (Fall 1981): 5, fig. 4.
Palmer, "To the Good," p. 218, fig. 11.

Salt cellars fashioned of glass had a place on
many colonial American dining tables, especially in the second half of the eighteenth
century. An early reference to the form is the
"blew [blue] glass Saltcellar" found in the 1677
household inventory of Mary Norton of Boston.
In 1701 three "salts of glass" in the stock of a
Philadelphia shopkeeper were valued at 6*d.*
each. Fifteen years later, glass salts remaining
in the estate of another merchant, Anne
Cheetam, were appraised for 3*d.* per dozen.[1]
Written references to glass salts become more
numerous after about 1730.

Many eighteenth-century glass salts were
made in a trencher form modeled after silver
and pewter. Others were blown into hemispherical bowls on circular feet. Rococo silver
salts inspired NO. 224 with its three cabriole

legs, but instead of the lion mask the glass salt
carries a traditional glassmaker's device, the
raspberry prunt, to conceal the juncture of leg
and bowl.[2] The horizontally tooled rings of the
bowl here are reminiscent of the English Lynn-
type glasses (NOS. 6, 37).

Boston merchant Henry Barnes imported
English "3 Feet Salts" in 1751. In Portsmouth,
New Hampshire, a salt like NO. 224 has been
found in archaeological excavations. Related
examples with pattern-molded bowls have been
excavated in Canada from mid eighteenth-century contexts at Fort Beauséjour/Cumberland
and the Fortress of Louisbourg.[3]

Three-legged, prunted salts were also made
in Norway, as a 1763 illustrated price list demonstrates. Between 1769 and 1774 English-trained
glassblowers produced three-legged salts for
Stiegel's American Flint Glassworks in Manheim.[4]

1. Norton inventory, 1677, Suffolk County Probate
Records, 12:197, reference courtesy of Benno M. Forman;
James Fox inventory, 1701-41, Anne Cheetam inventory,
1716-89, Philadelphia County Probate Records (microfilm,
Downs, WL).
2. Half of a glass trencher salt was excavated at Marlborough
Plantation, Va., see C. Malcolm Watkins, "The Cultural
History of Marlborough, Virginia," *United States National
Museum Bulletin,* no. 253 (Washington, D.C.: Smithsonian
Institution Press, 1968): 153, illus. 47, fig. 82a. John D. Davis,
English Silver at Williamsburg (Williamsburg, Va.: Colonial
Williamsburg Foundation, 1976)," pp. 144–45.
3. Barnes advertisement, *Boston Evening Post,* March 11, 1751;
Jones and Smith, *British Military,* p. 71, fig. 81.
4. Polak, "Illustrated Price-List," p. 97, fig. 25; Stiegel
advertisement, *New York Journal,* January 14, 1773; Palmer,
"To the Good," p. 218.

225, PL. 13

SALT

PROBABLY NEW JERSEY, PROBABLY
WISTARBURGH GLASSWORKS OF
CASPAR AND RICHARD WISTAR,
1739–77

Yellow-green low-lead glass. Blown. Bowl of angular
acorn form having shallow top and bulbous lower section,
faintly pattern-molded with 20 ribs; applied domed foot
with thick, downward-folded edge; ring-shape pontil mark.
H: 2¼ in (5.7 cm); Diam top: 2³⁄₁₆ in (5.6 cm)
History: Caleb Ewing
Museum purchase, 1982: The Stradlings, New York City
82.319

Exhibited: Museum of American Glass at Wheaton
Village, "The Wistars and Their Glass, 1739–1777," 1989.
Published: Arlene Palmer, *The Wistars and Their Glass,
1739–1777* (Millville, N.J.: Museum of American Glass at
Wheaton Village, 1989), p. 23, fig. 23.

The overall form of this salt, and such details
as the domed and folded foot, point to a mid
eighteenth-century date. It relates to contemporary pewter salts made in the MidAtlantic
region.[1] The color, quality, and chemical composition of the glass parallel known Wistarburgh
products. Although tablewares were never a
significant part of production at that pioneer
South Jersey glassworks, salts, like sugar bowls
(NO. 150), would have been among the forms
Wistar workers made of green bottle glass. Green
glass salts were also blown by Martin Greiner
at Stiegel's glassworks in the 1764–69 period,
when bottles and windowpanes were the principal products.[2]

1. See a pewter salt attributed to William Will, Donald L.
Fennimore, *Silver and Pewter,* Knopf Collectors' Guides
to American Antiques (New York: Alfred A. Knopf, 1984),
no. 252.
2. Palmer, "To the Good," p. 205.

226

SALT

PROBABLY ENGLAND, POSSIBLY UNITED STATES, 1770–1800

Amethyst lead glass. Circular bowl swelled below rim and curved in to drawn, knopped stem; pattern-molded with rows of 14 diamonds; applied pedestal foot; pontil mark.
H: 3⅛ in (8.0 cm)
H. F. du Pont purchase, probably 1940: Neil C. Gest, Mechanicsburg, Ohio
59.3141

227, PL. 17

SALT

POSSIBLY MARYLAND, POSSIBLY NEW BREMEN GLASSMANU-FACTORY OF JOHN FREDERICK AMELUNG, 1785–95

Blue nonlead glass. Blown. Deep circular bowl with sides curving in to shallow lower section with flat bottom and drawn knopped stem; pattern-molded with rows of 7 large diamonds, each containing 4 ogival diamonds; applied disk foot; pontil mark.
H: 2⅞ in (7.2 cm)
Museum purchase, 1974: William P. Williams, Holly Hill Antiques, Reading, Pa.
74.149

228, PL. 8

SALT

OHIO, 1815–35

Amethyst glass. Blown. Wide circular bowl of acorn shape with drawn knopped stem; pattern-molded with 22 vertical ribs over 22 swirled ribs; applied disk foot; pontil mark.
H: 2¾ in (7.0 cm)
H. F. du Pont purchase, 1951: Neil C. Gest, Mechanicsburg, Ohio
59.3100

Although there are silver salts like these, there is some question as to whether the glass versions were intended to be salt containers. E. Barrington Haynes has pointed out that they rarely exhibit any of the cloudiness that would result from salt. English collectors have traditionally called these items "monteith" and "bonnet" glasses without defining their function; at least one period reference mentions "bonnet" salts. There is also the possibility, as Robert Charleston has suggested, that these objects were designed to hold dry or wet sweetmeats on the dining table. Jelly glasses made by Stiegel workers are described as acorn-shaped, so perhaps NOS. 226–28—which do resemble acorns—functioned in that way.[1] Whatever their usage, such objects must have been extremely common because a great number have survived in museum and private collections.

The styles of some glass objects changed radically over time, but salt glasses like these were remarkably static in size, shape, and decoration. Pattern molding was the common decorative treatment for the form. Diamond molding (NO. 226) was popular in English and American ware for decades; an 1821 billhead of the agents for Boston Glass Manufactory shows a diamond-patterned salt. The checkered-diamond design of Amelung manufacture has parallels in earlier as well as later Continental glass.[2] NO. 228 illustrates the same broken-swirl type of molding that was used in colonial sugar bowls but which became a hallmark of midwestern glass production in the nineteenth century.

1. See one of 1768 by William Bond in Douglas Bennett, *Irish Georgian Silver* (London: Cassell, 1972), pp. 120–21. E. B. Haynes, "Monteiths," *Apollo* 33, no. 194 (February 1941): 47–49. Among English glass imports advertised in colonial Boston were "round and oval Pillar Cut Salts, and bonnet ditto" (*Boston News-Letter*, November 28, 1771, in George Francis Dow, *The Arts and Crafts in New England, 1704–1775: Gleanings from Boston Newspapers* [Topsfield, Mass.: Wayside Press, 1927], p. 94); Charleston, *English Glass*, p. 171; Palmer, "To the Good," p. 218.
2. Billhead of Wing and Sumner in Wilson, *New England Glass*, p. 203, fig. 157; a Bohemian example is pictured in *Antiques* 57, no. 1 (January 1950): 35; a Scandinavian checkered-diamond flask is shown in Arnstein Berntsen, *En samling norsk glass* (Oslo: Gyldendal Norsk Forlag, 1962), pl. 4, no. 336a. For a discussion of the Amelung attribution see Lanmon and Palmer, "New Bremen," pp. 118–19.

229

SALT

UNITED STATES, 1820–40

Colorless lead glass of slight green tint. Blown. Hemispherical bowl with inward-folded rim; drawn stem and thick disk foot. Blown in 3-part mold of geometric design (probably McKearin G II-18): vertical ribbing above and below a band of diamond diapering within horizontal rings; pontil mark.
H: 1½ in (3.8 cm)
H. F. du Pont purchase, before 1933
59.3331

230

SALT

UNITED STATES, 1820–40

Colorless lead glass. Blown. Wide bowl of acorn shape with drawn disk foot. Blown in 3-part mold of geometric design (McKearin G III-4 variant): vertical ribbing; between horizontal rings are 3 repeat panels of diamond diapering and sunburst; vertical ribbing below; rayed bottom (type I); pontil mark.
H: 2⅝ in (6.6 cm)
H. F. du Pont purchase, probably 1926: Dorothy O. Schubart Antiques, New Rochelle, N.Y.
59.3185

231

SALT (ONE OF TWO)

UNITED STATES, 1820–40

Blue bubbly lead glass. Blown. Globular bowl with tall galleried rim; drawn stem and disk foot. Blown in 3-part mold of geometric design (McKearin G III-13): around the rim faint diagonal ribbing to the right; between horizontal rings are 3 repeat panels of diamond diapering and bull's-eye sunburst; diagonal ribbing to the left separated by a horizontal ring from diagonal ribbing to the right; pontil mark.
H: 2¹¹⁄₁₆ in (6.8 cm); Diam top: 3⅛ in (8.0 cm)
H. F. du Pont purchase, 1944: Neil C. Gest, Mechanicsburg, Ohio
59.3278 (mate is 59.3279)

Published: McKearin and McKearin, *American Glass,* pl. 110, fig. 10.

232

SALT

UNITED STATES, 1820–40

Colorless lead glass. Blown. Compressed globular bowl curved in below everted rim; drawn stem and thick disk foot. Blown in 3-part mold of geometric design (McKearin G III-21): diagonal ribbing; between horizontal rings are 3 repeat panels of diamond diapering and diamond-center sunburst; diagonal ribbing around stem with vertically ribbed foot; rayed and ringed base (type III); pontil mark.
H: 2¼ in (5.7 cm)
H. F. du Pont purchase, 1941: Neil C. Gest, Mechanicsburg, Ohio
59.3238

233

SALT

MASSACHUSETTS, 1820–40

Colorless bubbly lead glass. Blown. Inverted hat-shape form with tapered sides and flaring rim; flat bottom. Blown in 3-part mold of geometric design (McKearin G III-18): faint diagonal ribbing around top; between horizontal rings are 3 repeat panels of diamond diapering and sunburst; vertical ribbing around the base; rayed bottom (type VI-A); pontil mark.
H: 3⁵⁄₁₆ in (8.7 cm)
H. F. du Pont purchase
59.3267

These examples of mold-blown salt dishes reveal how much variation was possible within the form. NO. 229 was blown in a castor bottle mold and shaped into a low, footed salt with shallow bowl reminiscent of metalwork examples. Gest described NO. 232 as "urn-shaped" because of its rim. NO. 231 is perhaps the most unusual because of its galleried rim, as if it were to have a cover.

The rare shape of NO. 231 was reproduced in the 1920–40 period, but the pattern used was not G III-13 but G III-6. Two of these forgeries in amethyst are at Winterthur. H. F. du Pont also purchased amethyst salts in the G II-18 pattern that were clever fakes, part of the Mutzer group that remained undetected until the early 1970s.[1]

Collectors have long been drawn to whimsical blown glass hats. That these were novelty salt dishes is indicated by an 1825 advertisement in Philadelphia for "oval and hat salts." James Cunningham, who sold glass from both New England Glass Company and Boston and Sandwich Glass Company, had "molded" hats in stock in 1826–27. Invoices from New England Glass Company in 1829 list molded hats in both white (colorless) and blue glass. Both colors were priced wholesale at 42¢ a dozen.[2]

1. Lanmon, Brill, and Reilly, "Suspicions," pp. 167–68, 170–71; Winterthur 59.3094, 59.3097, 59.3101, 59.3104.
2. J. and W. Lippincott advertisement, *Poulson's American Daily Advertiser*, August 31, 1825; Cunningham Account Book, p. 32, Edison Inst.; Helen McKearin, "New England Glass Company Invoices," pt. 1, *Antiques* 52, no. 3 (September 1947): 179, notes the sale to William E. Mayhew and Co.

234

SALT (ONE OF TWO)

SANDWICH, MASSACHUSETTS,

BOSTON AND SANDWICH GLASS

COMPANY, 1827–35

Blue lead glass. Pressed. Boat-shape form with relief
details in imitation of a paddlewheel steamboat (Neal BT
5): on the flat sternboard the inscription "B. & S./GLASS./
CO"; on the paddlewheel, "Lafayet"; on both surfaces of
the oval bottom the word "SANDWICH."
H: 1⁹⁄₁₆ in (4.0 cm); L: 3⁹⁄₁₆ in (9.1 cm)
H. F. du Pont purchase, possibly 1925
59.3072 (mate in colorless glass [59.3079] was published in
"Collector's Notes," *Antiques* 72, no. 2 [August 1957]: 155.)

235

SALT (ONE OF TWO)

PITTSBURGH, STOURBRIDGE

FLINT GLASS WORKS, JOHN

ROBINSON & SON, 1829–31

Blue lead glass. Pressed. Boat-shape form with relief
details in imitation of a paddlewheel steamboat (Neal BT
1): on the sternboard the inscription "ROBINSON & SON/
PITTSBURGH."; on each paddlewheel is a large star against
a stippled ground; an anchor on the bottom.
H: 1½ in (3.9 cm); L: 3⅝ in (9.0 cm)
H. F. du Pont purchase
59.3067 (mate is amethyst; 59.3078)

Boat salts are among the few examples of
American pressed glass that bear makers'
marks. Although produced several years after
the Marquis's famous tour of the United States,
the Lafayette salt has a souvenir character that
is heightened by the multiple factory signa-
tures. Of the eleven versions known to have
been made, two are unmarked. Numerous
colors have been recorded in this pattern.

According to Boston and Sandwich factory
records, "Lafayette salts" were made as early as
March 1827 by Benjamin Haines and John
Snowden. A New Jersey–built steamboat named
the *Lafayette* may have inspired the pattern.[1]

That a Pittsburgh glasshouse hastened to
copy the Sandwich product proves the popularity of the item as well as the market competition that prevailed in the period. There are
differences in design between the boat salts of
the two firms. The color of the Sandwich salt is
more blue gray than the Pittsburgh one, and
the relief detail of Robinson's boat is crisper.

John Robinson founded the Stourbridge
Flint Glass Works in Pittsburgh in 1823; his son
and namesake joined him between 1829 and
1831. Although the senior Robinson lived until
1836, he was not an active partner in the business
after 1831. About that time Thomas Robinson
joined his brother John, Jr., and the factory
operated under their names (NO. 409). An immigrant who presumably had some connection
with the glass industry in Stourbridge, England,
John, Sr., first worked for Benjamin Bakewell
when he came to Pittsburgh sometime before
1819. When he left Bakewell's to open his own
factory, he was applauded by the press for
"daring to compete with the old and reputable
white flint glass establishment." Although Robinson also concentrated on flint glass from the
beginning, his was a smaller operation. According to the 1826 city directory, he employed only
eighteen workers and produced $22,000 worth
of glass annually. Bakewell, on the other hand,
had sixty-one employees and manufactured an
average of $45,000 worth of glass. The editor of
the directory observed that some "very beautiful,
and highly finished articles have been produced"
at Robinson's Stourbridge works, "and we take
great pride in noting it."[2]

1. Leinicke, "Production," pp. 82, 83, 470; "Model for the
Lafayet Salt?" *Antiques* 72, no. 2 (August 1957): 155.
2. S. Jones, *Pittsburgh in the Year 1826* (Pittsburgh:
Johnston and Stockton, 1826), p. 71; Robinson advertised
a general assortment of candlesticks, lamps, and cut oval
fruit dishes in the *Pittsburgh Gazette*, April 25, 1823.

236

SALT

CAMBRIDGE, MASSACHUSETTS, NEW ENGLAND GLASS COMPANY, 1826–30

Opaque white lead glass. Pressed. Rectangular form with shaped edge and columns and ball feet at the corners; pressed design in relief on exterior surface (Neal NE 1A): paneled sides outlined with rope molding enclosing a rose on the ends and basket of fruit and flowers on the long sides; on the bottom, "NE/GLASS/COMPANY/BOSTON."
H: 1⁵⁄₁₆ in (3.7 cm); L: 3 in (7.6 cm)
Museum purchase, 1973: Philip H. Bradley Company, Downingtown, Pa. Funds for purchase, gift of Mrs. E. du Pont Irving
73.116

237

SALT

PROBABLY PROVIDENCE, PROBABLY PROVIDENCE FLINT GLASS COMPANY, 1831–33

Light yellow-green glass. Pressed. Deep 8-sided form with flaring sides and scalloped edge; pressed design in relief on exterior surface (Neal EE 5): stippled side panels with leaf and lyre motifs, stippled corner panels with small flowers in circles, and stippled end panels with fleurs-de-lis; on the bottom an American eagle within a beaded border.
H: 1¼ in (3.1 cm); L: 4 in (10.1 cm)
Museum purchase, 1974: The Stradlings, New York City
74.79

Every household required salt cellars of some kind; pressed glass ones were cheap enough for even the humblest of tables. Like cup plates (NOS. 78–80), pressed salts provided tremendous scope for glass manufacturers who competed for the market with an array of appealing and novel designs.

NO. 236 with its rose-embellished ends may represent the "rose salts" of the Mayhew invoices, which sold for $1.25 a dozen in 1829. What seems remarkable is that a company would go to the trouble and expense of having different molds made in essentially the same pattern: Neal records five variations. The style attracted the attention of the competition because a very similar version was made by Jersey City Glass Company.[1]

From the few advertisements of Providence Flint Glass Company it is clear that a full range of glasswares was manufactured at this short-lived venture. Cut glass in a variety of forms was produced, yet the only objects that can be firmly attributed to this factory are pressed.[2] A large salt bears the word "PROVIDENCE" in the base; Winterthur has a damaged example of that pattern in colorless glass (75.101). The salt shown here is closely related but carries an eagle motif in lieu of the factory name.

1. Helen McKearin, "New England Glass Company Invoices," pt. 2, *Antiques* 52, no. 4 (October 1947): 276–77; L. W. Neal and D. B. Neal, *Pressed Glass Salt Dishes of the Lacy Period, 1825–1850* (Philadelphia: Privately printed, 1962), pp. 124–25.
2. Lura Woodside Watkins, "The Providence Flint Glass Company," *Antiques* 55, no. 3 (March 1949): 190–91.

238, PL. 21

MUFFINEER
ENGLAND, 1760–1800

Emerald green lead glass. Blown. Pear-shape form tapered at top to point and small hole; pattern-molded with rows of 21 diamonds; applied pedestal foot with central hole; polished pontil mark.
H: 3¾ in (9.5 cm)
History: Mrs. Warden Lynch; William T. H. Howe; Richard Loeb
H. F. du Pont purchase, 1947: Neil C. Gest, Mechanicsburg, Ohio
59.3092

Published: Antiques 38, no. 5 (November 1940): 238. McKearin and McKearin, *American Glass*, pl. 32, fig. 11. Parke-Bernet Galleries, "Collection of Early American Glass," pt. 2 (April 3–4, 1941), lot 376. Parke-Bernet Galleries, "Rare Early American Glass . . . Property of Richard Loeb," sale no. 853 (March 27, 1947), lot 102.
Palmer, "Beer to Birdcages," p. 87, fig. 5.

Blown of emerald green glass and strongly patterned with diamonds, this unusual object was considered a rare example of Stiegel-type glass. As its provenance suggests, it caught the eye of numerous collectors of early American glass. Until related documentary objects are found, however, it must be assumed that no eighteenth-century American glasshouses made glass of this rich color (see NO. 156). When Gest saw the muffineer or shaker at the Howe sale he felt it was "definitely English"; nonetheless, he bought it for du Pont when it came up for sale again in 1947. Another green diamond example, patterned in the identical mold as NO. 238, is in a private collection in England.

NO. 238 has been variously described in the literature as pepper shaker, salt shaker, and sander, but it closely resembles silver muffineers made for sprinkling cinnamon, pepper, or other spices. Glass "muffins" were among the goods auctioned by Hoffman, Bend and Company in Baltimore in 1829.[1]

1. G. Bernard Hughes, *Small Antique Silverware* (New York: Bramhall House, 1957), pp. 51–58, 63; *Baltimore American*, April 9, 1829.

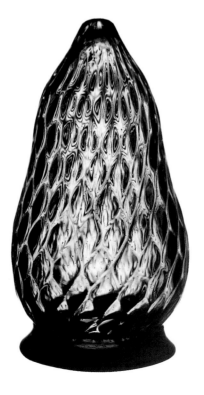

239

CRUET SET
ENGLAND, 1750–70

Colorless lead glass; wood; silver. Blown. Three bottles of mallet shape with flat bottoms; 2 casters of baluster shape with disk feet. Cut diamonds overall on each. Each cruet fitted with sterling silver cap; mounted in lignum vitae frame with ivory supports and silver handle marked with EL in rectangle (possibly London silversmith Edward Low).
H tallest bottle: 5⅝ in (14.2 cm); OH frame: 9¼ in (23.5 cm)
Museum purchase, 1975: Bardith, New York City. Funds for purchase, gift of the Claneil Foundation
75.269a–f

240

CRUET SET
UNITED STATES, 1815–35

Colorless lead glass; silver-plated copper, tin, lead. Blown. Six cylindrical containers with varying shoulder and neck treatments. Blown in 3-part mold of geometric design (McKearin G I-24): vertical ribbing around neck above a horizontal ring and short vertical ribbing; horizontal rings above a wide band of diagonal ribbing; 5 wide horizontal rings around base; pontil marks. Handled silver-plated frame with ringed supports for the bottles and stoppers; 2 bottles have silver-plated caps.
OH: 7 in (17.9 cm)
Museum purchase, 1983: W. M. Schwind, Jr., Antiques, Yarmouth, Maine
83.10a–m

Many condiments enhanced the preparation and presentation of food in the past as they do today. These included pepper, cayenne pepper and sauce, India soy sauce, ketchup in such flavors as mushroom and walnut, essence of anchovy, mustard, vinegar, and oil. Caster bottles of opaque white or blue glass often had the names of their intended contents painted upon them.[1]

Glass vinegar cruets are recorded in colonial inventories as early as 1694, when two valued at 3s. were in the Philadelphia home of William Salway. English cut-glass cruets, datable by their hallmarked silver mounts, are known from the 1620s. The bottles in NO. 239 represent mid eighteenth-century style both in shape and cutting. A later style of cutting with large, faceted diamonds can be seen on the glass in a London silver frame made in 1771–72 for Charles Carroll of Carrollton, Maryland.[2]

Cruet frames or stands were made of a variety of materials, ranging from sterling silver to paper. Cut glass was placed in the most expensive frames, but molded glass cruets were typically set into frames of lesser value. Early eighteenth-century frames held only two bottles for vinegar and oil. By the 1740s they were expanded to hold three bottles and two casters or sifters. A wooden frame similar to that of NO. 239 was owned by Gov. Thomas Mifflin of Philadelphia.[3] The frame of NO. 240, which may have been made in Birmingham, is enriched with classical ornament in the manner of sterling silver. The molded patterns of the bottles closely follow cut-glass fashions, and the designs were carefully planned so as to be shown to best advantage when placed in the ring supports.

Cruet bottles were made at Stiegel's glasshouse in Lancaster County from 1766, but there is no evidence that cut-glass cruets were manufactured in America before the nineteenth century. "Moulded bottles for castor frames," such as NO. 240, were among the glasswares offered by Pittsburgh's Bakewell firm in 1824. For "4, 5, and 6 Hole Plated and Japan Castors," New England Glass Company in 1820 provided "Prest Glasses," but this term is thought to mean mold-blown glass of the kind seen in NO. 240. In 1829 the company's "old stock" castor bottles wholesaled for 75¢ a dozen.[4]

1. See Jones and Smith, *British Military*, pp. 60–62, 69–70; Delomosne and Son, *Gilding the Lily*, pp. 11, 17.
2. William Salway inventory, 1694-121, Philadelphia County Probate Records (microfilm, Downs, WL). A cut cruet similar to those in NO. 239 has silver mounts of 1743, shown in W. A. Thorpe, "The Development of Cut-Glass in England and Ireland, 1: The Period from 1715 to 1780," *Antiques* 18, no. 4 (October 1930): 301, fig. 4. See also Charleston, *English Glass*, pp. 176–78, pl. 48a–c. The silver frame of Carroll's cruet set was made by Charles Aldrich and H. Green; it is in Baltimore Museum of Art.
3. Mifflin's frame has a mixture of glass styles, indicating some of the cruets and casters are later replacements. They carry silver mounts made by Edmund Milne, working in Philadelphia between 1757 and 1773. The set is at Historical Society of Pennsylvania.
4. For a discussion of Stiegel's cruets, see Palmer, "To the Good," p. 216. *Pittsburgh Mercury*, March 9, 1824. William Loyall advertisement, *American Beacon and Norfolk and Portsmouth Daily Advertiser*, May 8, 1820, reference courtesy of MESDA. Mayhew invoice, May 2, 1829, in Helen McKearin, "New England Glass Company Invoices," pt. 1, *Antiques* 52, no. 3 (September 1947): 179.

241, PL. 8

CRUET (ONE OF TWO)
OHIO OR WESTERN
PENNSYLVANIA, 1815–35

Light amethyst lead glass. Blown. Mallet form with
sloping shoulders and tall cylindrical neck flared out at
edge; pattern-molded with 16 ribs swirled; pontil mark.
H: 5¾ in (14.6 cm)
History: Philip Francis du Pont
Gift of Mrs. Harry W. Lunger, 1973
73.454.1 (mate is 73.454.2 [aqua])

242

CRUET (ONE OF TWO)
SANDWICH, MASSACHUSETTS,
ATTRIBUTED TO BOSTON AND
SANDWICH GLASS COMPANY,
1825–45

Blue lead glass. Blown. Barrel-shape body with sloping
shoulders and short cylindrical neck flared out at
edge. Blown in 3-part mold (McKearin G I-3, type 2):
overall pattern of 19 swirled ribs; ringed base (type III);
pontil mark. Stopper: ball finial on wafer with tapered
ground plug.
OH: 6⅜ in (16.3 cm)
Gift of Mrs. E. du Pont Irving, 1970
70.382.1a, b (mate is 70.382.2a, b)

Although small vessels like NOS. 241 and 242
have been published as toilet or cologne bottles,
their size and shapes echo contemporary
decanters, suggesting that they were designed
as cruets to serve vinegar, oil, or other sauces
at the dining table.

   NO. 241 is an elegant example of the colored
and patterned glass made in Ohio and western
Pennsylvania glasshouses. NO. 242, attributed
to the Sandwich factory on the basis of fragments found at the site, provides an interesting
contrast because here the manufacturer used a
full-size mold to achieve the same swirled effect
as the part-size pattern mold used for NO. 241.
With the full-size mold, however, the mold
seams are completely visible and detract from
the diagonal thrust of the design. Half-pint
"mo[lded] Blue Cruits" were among the glasswares recorded in the Boston and Sandwich
Sloar Book.[1]

1. Leinicke, "Production," p. 52.

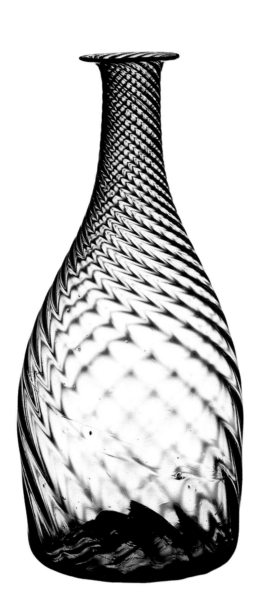

Chapter 12
Celery Glasses

Celery was considered a luxury food for much of the nineteenth century. A vegetable of the carrot family, celery was costly to cultivate because the process was labor-intensive: to preserve their whiteness and sweetness, celery stalks were grown in deep trenches or were individually wrapped with paper collars.

According to household adviser Isabella Beeton, celery was best eaten raw with cheese. It was washed, quartered lengthwise, and placed root down in a vase half-filled with water.[1] Silver vases were suitably lavish for presenting celery on the table, but glass ones allowed the quality of the stalks to be seen and admired.

No eighteenth-century American references to glass containers for celery have been discovered. By the 1820s, however, household inventories and shopkeepers' advertisements typically include "glasses," "stands," or "vases" for celery. These were wide-mouth vessels about 6 inches deep, usually raised upon stems to give them prominence on the dining table. Cut glass dramatically emphasized the status of celery and of those who served it, so expensively decorated celery glasses became popular presentation gifts. Those who did not wish to spend $3 to $10 for a pair of cut-glass celeries made do with plain blown, mold-blown, or pressed ones.[2]

By 1890 tall celery glasses had been relegated to "a dark corner of the china closet" and replaced with low shallow dishes. "Who," asked the author of *American Domestic Cyclopedia*, "has not mentally anathematized the old fashioned tall celery glass, from which it is almost impossible to remove one stalk without dragging two or three more out upon the spotless damask?"[3]

1. Isabella Beeton, *The Book of Household Management* (1861; reprint, London: Jonathan Cape, 1968), p. 566. This reference and information about the celery plant comes from Mary Ellen Hern, "The Celery Glass," Winterthur Program in Early American Culture paper, WL.
2. A number of presentation celeries made in the U.S. have been published. See, for example, frontispiece of *Antiques* 60, no. 4 (October 1951): 290–91. The price range is for "Cut, fluted, &c. celery vases" made by Francis Plunkett in Wheeling in 1837, Wheeling Price Current, Oglebay Inst.
3. *The American Domestic Cyclopedia* (New York: F. M. Lupton, 1890), p. 540, reference courtesy of Mary Ellen Hern.

243

CELERY GLASS

PROBABLY PENNSYLVANIA, 1815–40

Colorless lead glass of yellowish tint. Blown. Cylindrical body flaring sharply out at rim; gadrooning around the base made of added gather molded with 20 swirled flutes; cylindrical stem with button knop; applied conical foot; pontil mark.
H: 8⅝ in (22.0 cm); Diam top: 4¹⁵⁄₁₆ in (12.6 cm)
H. F. du Pont purchase
58.2843

Some silver vessels of the seventeenth and eighteenth centuries were ornamented around the base with a type of fluted chasing known as gadrooning. Glassmakers imitated the effect by applying a second gather of glass to the bowl of a piece and dipping it in a mold with deep concave flutes. Sometimes, as in this celery glass, the vessel was twisted slightly as it was removed from the mold or tooled with the pucellas for more pronounced swirling. The effect is dramatic, creating the illusion of a holder or cup in which the body rests.

Although gadrooning declined in fashion as a means of decorating silver, glass versions continued to be popular well into the nineteenth century, both in the U.S. and abroad. In his illustrated price list of 1838 London glassmaker Apsley Pellatt shows a custard that appears to be gadrooned and describes it as "medicean shape, purled," in reference to the second gather of glass known as the "pearl." A "medicean, fluted" jelly glass shown by Pellatt has a similar appearance but may lack the extra gather. The "ribbed and pearled" celeries sold by Lippincott & Co., a Philadelphia auction house, in 1825 were probably molded as NO. 243.[1]

In United States glass production of the second quarter of the nineteenth century, the gadrooned technique seems to have been frequently applied to celery glasses, judging from the number that have survived. Pittsburgh, Baltimore, and Philadelphia are often cited as the sources for these celeries, but no firmly documented examples have been published. Indeed, virtually no fine tablewares have been attributed with any assurance to either Baltimore or Philadelphia. A celery of the same shape as NO. 243 is engraved with the three-leaf-and-daisy motif that can be associated with some

assurance to Pittsburgh, and specifically to the Bakewell enterprise. Perhaps the "fluted celeries" sold by Bakewell, Page and Bakewell for $6 a dozen in 1830 were gadrooned ones like NO. 243.[2] Bakewell glass was marketed in Philadelphia, and it is possible that the glassware auctioned by Lippincott & Co. was made in Pittsburgh.

1. Published in Phelps Warren, "Apsley Pellatt's Table Glass, 1840–1864," *Journal of Glass Studies* 26 (1984): 122. Hugh Wakefield pinpointed the 1838 date of an abridged version of the price list in his *Nineteenth-Century British Glass* (2d rev. ed.; London: Faber and Faber, 1982), p. 36. J. and W. Lippincott & Co. advertisement, *Poulson's American Daily Advertiser*, August 31, 1825, reference courtesy of Susan H. Myers. The source of the Lippincott consignment is not given.
2. McKearin and McKearin, *American Glass*, pls. 7, 22, 44. That celery (Brooklyn Museum) was published in Lura Woodside Watkins, *American Glass and Glassmaking* (New York: Chanticleer Press, 1950), pl. 8, p. 36. For a discussion of the engraved three-leaf-and-daisy design, see Innes, *Pittsburgh Glass*, pp. 154–62. Bakewell invoice to Horman, Taylor & Co., October 4, 1830, Rakow Library, Corning Museum; the price indicates they were not cut with flutes.

244, PL. 4

CELERY GLASS
UNITED STATES, 1835–55

Green-blue nonlead glass. Blown; thistle-shape with tooled
rings around the rim; gadrooning around the base made
of added gather molded with 10 swirled ribs; flattened
knop and spreading stem; applied disk foot of irregular
circumference; remains of ring-shape pontil mark.
H: 8⅝ in (22.0 cm); Diam top: 4⅛ in (10.6 cm)
H. F. du Pont purchase, before 1939
59.3017

Blown of a strong green-blue glass, this vase
seems to represent a bottle or window glass
manufacturer's version of gadrooned celery
glasses discussed in NO. 243. In high-style examples the body is not usually of a thistle shape
but rises straight from the gadrooned casing.
Here the ribbing extends higher and is looser
and less distinct than in the flint glass models.

The vase relates to a group of objects including a sugar bowl and cream jug at Winterthur (NOS. 136, 176) in which the influence of
molded Boston-area high-style glass is very
apparent. There are no documented gadrooned

celery glasses from Boston or Cambridge glasshouses, but the large two-handled cups made
there do offer certain parallels.[1] The bodies of
the cups have the same shape as NO. 244 but
are more exaggerated. The celery glass lacks
the horizontal ring seen on the Massachusetts
objects, but the tooled rings around the top
simulate the applied threading of the cups.

1. Wilson, *New England Glass*, pp. 215, 217, figs. 166, 167.

245

VASE OR CELERY GLASS
UNITED STATES, POSSIBLY
PENNSYLVANIA, 1815–35

Colorless lead glass of gray tint. Blown; pressed. Blown
bowl of tall cylindrical shape flaring sharply out at rim;
gadrooning around the base made of added gather
molded with 20 flutes; above, on one side, an engraved
script "E" within a leafy oval; double collar below bowl;
applied, pressed base composed of short cylindrical stem
and hollow high-domed foot having 12 flutes on the
interior, thick square base with bevel-cut edges.
H: 11 in (28.1 cm); Diam top: 6 3/16 in (15.9 cm)
H. F. du Pont purchase
59.3118

Although this vase relates to celery glasses like
NO. 243, its large size suggests a purely ornamental function. The history of the vase is lost, but
the engraved "E" doubtless identified the original owner. A vase of the same shape, also with
gadrooning and a pressed foot, is engraved "BB"
for Bartholomew Berthold, who immigrated to
America in 1798. He lived in Philadelphia, moved
to St. Louis in 1809, and died there in 1831. Another, shorter vase bears the engraved initials
of an unidentified member of the Biddle family.[1]

Glass vases of this classical urn form with
flared rim and gadroon molding more often
have knopped stems and plain feet than pressed
feet, although the price list of a Wheeling manufacturer proves that both options continued
into the 1830s. In NO. 245 the ribbing of the high-
domed, pressed foot visually balances the
gadrooning of the bowl, but the square base
seems uncomfortably small. Hand-pressed bases
of this kind are first recorded in the European
table glass industry about 1780 (see NO. 287),

although the basic technique had been known to ancient craftsmen and the medieval glass-workers of the Islamic world. In the United States, pressed feet can be documented to the glassworks of Thomas Cains (NO. 114), where the feet of oil lamps were pressed into molds of several different patterns.[2] These may have been called rose feet in the period because of the floral appearance of the underside (see NO. 202).

The vogue for pressing feet in simple stars and rosettes declined by the 1830s as the development of fully mechanical pressing enabled more ambitious designs to be realized. Cup plates, for example, became popular as bases for blown lamp fonts and were denoted in factory records as "plate feet." The combination of blown and pressed techniques in the making of one object continued to be practiced into the 1840s (NOS. 319–21) and beyond.

Gadrooned and engraved vases have been attributed to Philadelphia glasshouses because several such vases have histories in that city. Attributions based on location-where-found are problematical, particularly with regard to fine tableware, because the leading glass factories had sophisticated and widespread marketing systems. As discussed in NO. 243, Bakewell's of Pittsburgh may be the source of some gadrooned ware, and Bakewell glass was sold in Philadelphia. Indeed, Nicholas Biddle owned the set of cut glassware made by Bakewell that was exhibited at the Franklin Institute Fair of 1825.[3]

The engraved decoration of NO. 245 is not the usual swags and festoons found on gadroon-base celeries and other vases but may have been executed by one of the many independent engravers who operated small shops in cities throughout the country. The workmanship is crude: the medallion is not perfectly oval, and the "E" was created with laborious curves.

1. The Berthold glass is in Missouri Historical Society and was published as the frontispiece in *Antiques* 60, no. 4 (October 1951): 290–91. The Biddle vase is in the Quattlebaum collection, Los Angeles County Museum of Art.
2. In 1837 the Wheeling firm of Francis Plunkett produced celery vases "heavy plain or figured knob stem, round or pressed foot" that sold from $4.50 to $7.50 per dozen, Wheeling Price Current, Oglebay Inst. Wilson, "American Contributions," pp. 169–71; Wilson, *New England Glass*, pp. 224–26; Spillman, *Pressed Glass*, pp. 27–29.
3. McKearin and McKearin, *American Glass*, pls. 50, 51, p. 155.

246–249

CELERY GLASSES

UNITED STATES, 1815–45

NO. 246. Colorless lead glass. Blown. Deep, waisted cylindrical body curved in at base and flaring at rim with outward-folded edge; blown in 3-part mold of geometric design (McKearin G II-18): vertical ribbing above and below a band of diamond diapering within horizontal rings; bottom patterned with diamonds (type XII). Applied conical foot with downward-folded edge; blown in 3-part mold of geometric design (probably G II-21): patterned with diamonds at top (type XII); bands of vertical and diagonal ribbing, above diamond diapering, separated by horizontal rings.
H: 8¾ in (22.3 cm)
H. F. du Pont purchase, before 1939
59.3197

NO. 247. Colorless bubbly lead glass with green tint. Blown. Deep bucket-shape bowl, flared at rim; blown in 4-part mold of geometric design (McKearin G III-32): diagonal ribbing around the rim above horizontal ring; diamond diapering; within horizontal rings are 8 bull's-eye diamonds with diagonal ribs in between; below is vertical ribbing, horizontal ring, and diamond diapering; plain bottom; applied stem composed of collar above, 2 ball knops; conical foot; pontil mark.
H: 8⅜ in (21.4 cm)
H. F. du Pont purchase, before 1946
59.3178 (a pair of celeries on low feet patterned in the same mold are 59.3223–.3224)

NO. 248. Colorless lead glass. Blown. Deep waisted cylindrical body curved in at base and flaring at rim; blown in 4-part mold of geometric design (McKearin G III-34): around the rim, diagonal ribbing above horizontal rings and diamond diapering; within horizontal rings are 8 large diamonds alternately containing bull's-eye sunbursts and circles; vertical ribbing above a horizontal ring and diamond diapering; plain base; applied disk foot; pontil mark with iron oxide deposit.
H: 7¼ in (18.6 cm)
H. F. du Pont purchase
59.3225

NO. 249. As NO. 246, but of straight-sided beaker form without foot; patterned in the identical mold.
H: 5⅞ in (15.0 cm)
H. F. du Pont purchase
59.3184

Given the market for cut-glass celeries in the first half of the nineteenth century, it is hardly surprising that astute glass manufacturers would offer the public mold-blown examples with the look but not the cost of cut glass. These four examples demonstrate the success of both the moldmakers and the glassblowers in simulating the geometry of cut glass.

There is so little primary information concerning the production of mold-blown glass and so few objects or patterns can be docu-mented to specific factories that it is impossible to make attributions with any assurance. The 1818 price list of South Boston Flint Glass Works includes celery stands with "low feet" and "high feet," which may denote the varied stem treatment seen here. The ones with high feet cost 50 percent more than the low. In 1820 New England Glass Company advertised celery stands among their "Diamond moulded" forms. The "flint and tale hollow glassware, cut, plain, moulded and pressed" glass manufactured by Union Flint Glass Works in Philadelphia in 1828 included celeries.[1] That firm had been founded by workers from the Boston factories who may well have copied patterns created in New England.

1. Prices Current, South Boston, 1818, Edison Inst.; William Loyall advertisement, *American Beacon and Norfolk and Portsmouth Daily Advertiser*, May 8, 1820, reference courtesy of MESDA; Union Flint Glass Works advertisement, *Baltimore American and Commercial Daily Advertiser*, October 27, 1828.

250

CELERY GLASS (ONE OF TWO)
NEW ENGLAND, 1845–65

Amethyst lead glass. Pressed. Eight-panel, bell-shape
body with scalloped rim, on short cylinder; joining wafer
below; octagonal pedestal foot.
H: 9¾ in (24.8 cm)
Gift of Mrs. G. Brooks Thayer, 1961
61.390.1 (mate is 61.390.2)

The pattern of this celery reflects the midcentury taste for broad flute or panel patterns.[1]
Although glasscutters throughout the country
conformed to that style, glass scholars have
traditionally attributed pressed versions to
New England. Slight variations in the panels as
they taper to the bottom of the bowl and other
differences in the profile of the bowl certainly
indicate that more than one factory was responsible. Examples are recorded in blue, green,
yellow, colorless, and amethyst glass.

The fashion for broad flutes extended to
pottery: vases of the same design as NO. 250 were
made of flint enamelware and graniteware at
Bennington Pottery in Vermont between 1849
and 1858.[2]

1. The ultimate expression of this style is a 4 ft. 10 in.
cut-glass covered urn made by the Sweeneys in Wheeling
(Oglebay Institute-Mansion Museum).
2. Richard Carter Barret, *Bennington Pottery and
Porcelain* (New York: Bonanza Books, 1958), pp. 146–47.

Accessories

Chapter 13
Ornamental Vases

Glass has always had a decorative as well as functional value. From the early eighteenth century, colonial probate inventories list glasswares on mantelpieces. Forms are rarely specified. Drinking vessels or decanters may have been placed high for safe-keeping, but they could also have been deliberately displayed for their ornamental impact. Some of the "mantlepiece truck," particularly the sets of glasses upon the mantels, must have been glass vases.[1] Pairs or sets of ceramic vases called *garniture* were displayed in the best homes on mantelpieces, wall brackets, or furniture, and this concept was imitated in glass. Indeed, the shapes and decoration of glass vases were generally derived from silver or ceramic forms and can be dated accordingly. In the nineteenth century, urn-shape vessels became popular, and many were manufactured in glass of all styles.

Garniture vases often held cut flowers.[2] Housewives did not need such specialized containers for their garden treasures: pictorial sources show flowers in simple glass tumblers or pitchers. Although large vases of flowers adorned the centers of fashionable European dining tables from the seventeenth century, this practice did not come to the United States until the second quarter of the nineteenth century. Small flower vases were preferred, and they often formed part of the table decoration for the dessert course. Glass vases designed to hold bulbs were available in the colonies from the mid eighteenth century. English-made "hyacinth" glasses were sold in Charleston in 1752. "Tulip and flower glasses" of the "neatest" patterns were offered in New York in 1762; the following year the same merchant had what he called "flower root glasses."[3]

1. "Glasses and other mantlepiece truck" were in a Philadelphia estate, 1757-29, Philadelphia County Probate Records (microfilm, Downs, WL). Jacob Amsden, Cambridge, Massachusetts, had a "Mantle tree Sett glasses," at his death, Middlesex County Probate Records, Middlesex County Court House, Cambridge, p. 455, reference courtesy of Robert F. Trent.
2. Belden, *Festive Tradition*, p. 81, fig. 2:45.
3. James Laurens advertisement, *South Carolina Gazette*, May 20, 1752; James Gilliland advertisements, *New York Mercury*, October 11, 1762, April 4, 1763.

251, PL. 16

GARNITURE

GERMANY OR POSSIBLY

BOHEMIA, 1740–65

Opalescent white glass. Blown. Two vases (58.1417, 58.1418): compressed globular body on flattened knop with tall neck flaring at rim; applied domed foot with downward-folded edge; pontil mark. The other (58.1416): globular body on flattened knop, thick collar and short flaring neck; applied domed foot with downward-folded edge; pontil mark. Polychrome enamel-painted decoration: on one side a scene of 2 seated Chinese figures at a table, one smoking a pipe and the other holding aloft a shallow bowl; on the reverse, a profusion of flowers; red dashes embellish the collar and knop; floral sprays painted around the foot; stylized florets around the neck.
H (58.1417): 9 in (22.9 cm); H (58.1416): 8⅛ in (20.6 cm)
H. F. du Pont purchase
58.1416–.1418

252

VASE WITH COVER

GERMANY OR POSSIBLY

BOHEMIA, 1745–70

Opalescent white glass. Blown. Vase: inverted pear-shape body extending from narrow neck with everted lip; applied domed foot with downward-folded edge; pontil mark. Polychrome enamel-painted decoration: on one side, within a cartouche stand a European man and woman in a landscape setting; diaper bands and panels above, with scrolls and sprays extending from the bottom of the cartouche; around lower body are floral elements; floral sprays surround the foot above a lozenge border with rosettes in reserves. Cover: elongated crown shape with 4 applied loops each capped with a colorless rigaree band; drawn double-knop finial. Enamel-painted diapered shield and other details.
OH: 15⅞ in (40.3 cm)
H. F. du Pont purchase
58.1415a, b

NO. 252 was also originally part of a garniture like NO. 251 intended to ornament a chimney mantelpiece or piece of furniture. Generally composed of three or five objects of two different shapes, such sets were more commonly made in delftware or porcelain than in glass. The vases in NO. 251 feature chinoiserie designs of the kind seen in ceramics of the 1720–40 period. NO. 252 depicts a European couple, but the lozenge border around the foot was ultimately derived from Chinese export porcelains. Enamel-painted opaque white glass has been attributed to both German and Bohemian glasshouses.[1]

1. For a vase similar to NO. 251 attributed to Thuringia, see *Europäisches und Aussereuropäisches Glas* (Frankfurt am Main: Museum für Kunsthandwerk, 1980), p. 215, no. 462.

251

253, PL. 16

VASE

SOUTH STAFFORDSHIRE,
ENGLAND, 1755–65

Opaque white glass. Blown. Globular body with tall
cylindrical neck; applied pedestal foot; pontil mark.
Polychrome enamel-painted decoration on one side
consisting of a floral spray.
H: 3⅞ in (9.9 cm)
Gift of John C. Mayer, 1983
83.37

English manufacturers made opaque white glass in imitation of porcelain by 1700, but production of this "mock china" greatly increased at midcentury as a result of improved technology and in response to the ceramics industry's success with porcelain. In 1743 the Countess of Hertford reported: "They have made a great improvement in Southwark upon the manufacture of glass, and brought it so nearly to resemble old white china, that when it is placed upon a cabinet at a convenient distance it would not easily be distinguished by an indifferent judge."[1] The art of what was often called "enamel glass" soon spread from the London area to the Midlands, where NO. 253 is believed to have been made. Its decoration, like that of its porcelain counterparts, was inspired by the floral painting on Chinese export porcelain.

1. Charleston, *English Glass*, pp. 187, 185. Examples of early English opaque white glass are shown in Charleston, *English Glass*, pl. 31b, c. The first English porcelain was made at Chelsea by 1745.

252

253

254, PL. 14

VASE

PENNSYLVANIA OR NEW JERSEY, 1790–1820

Light green nonlead glass. Blown. Elongated ovoid body with tooled, everted rim, pattern-molded with 32 vertical ribs; 2 thin, applied handles of double-loop form with long flat terminals curled back at end; applied, thick, square foot pincered with V's at the corners; pontil mark.
H: 7⅝ in (19.5 cm)
History: Mrs. Frederick S. Fish
H. F. du Pont purchase, 1940: Neil C. Gest, Mechanicsburg, Ohio
58.3058

Published: McKearin and McKearin, *American Glass*, pl. 21, no. 12.
Parke-Bernet Galleries, "Early American Glass . . . Collection Formed by Mrs. Frederick S. Fish," sale no. 159 (January 5–6, 1940), lot 366.

This distinctive vase is an ambitious product of an unidentified bottle or window glass factory. Its attribution to Pennsylvania or New Jersey is based on its relationship to sugar bowls (NOS. 151, 152, 161), cream jugs (NO. 111), and other pattern-molded wares manufactured by glasshouses in that region. The glass made there developed from the traditions brought by continental European craftsmen in the eighteenth century.

The handles of NO. 254 are somewhat reminiscent of Spanish glass. Two different vases with related double-loop handles are attributed to Ohio glasshouses of the early nineteenth century.[1]

1. The one at Corning Museum is in McKearin and McKearin, *Two Hundred Years,* pl. 3; that at New Orleans Museum of Art is in Corning Museum, *A Decade of Glass Collecting* (Corning, N.Y., 1962), p. 53, no. 85.

255, PL. 20

VASE

PROBABLY NEW JERSEY, 1825–50

Aqua glass. Blown. Baluster-shape body flared at rim
with threading trailed in a spiral around the neck; applied
stem composed of 2 ball knops and a flattened knop;
applied disk foot; ring-shape pontil mark.
H: 6½ in (16.6 cm)
History: Frederick William Hunter
H. F. du Pont purchase, 1920: American Art Association,
New York City
68.724

Published: American Art Association, "Rare and Beautiful
Oriental Treasures and . . . American Glass Formed by . . .
the Late Frederick William Hunter" (January 14, 1920),
lot 1398.

This vase and a related one that lacks threading
(64.909) were among du Pont's earliest purchases
of American glass. Frederick William Hunter
had gained fame in collecting circles for his study
of America's eighteenth-century glasshouses,
particularly that of Henry William Stiegel, so
it was natural for du Pont to participate in the
auction of his renowned collection.

In the sale catalogue, both vases were attributed to the Wistarburgh glasshouse. Although
southern New Jersey is a very likely source for
them, their shapes obviously belong to the
nineteenth century, and Wistarburgh had closed
by 1777.

256

VASE

PROBABLY NEW JERSEY, 1830–50

Blue-green glass. Blown. Compressed globular body with
tall cylindrical neck flared and tooled at rim; applied and
crimped disk foot; pontil mark.
H: 6½ in (16.6 cm)
H. F. du Pont purchase, before 1939
59.3046

In its graceful body this vase relates to a pair of
blue glass pitchers in the Winterthur collection
(NO. 135). The sophistication of the body, however, is countered by the heavy foot with web-
like crimping. Blown of unrefined aqua glass,
NO. 256 was probably made in one of New
Jersey's many bottle and window glass factories.

257, PL. 9

VASE

OHIO, POSSIBLY KENT, 1825–45

Light yellow nonlead glass. Blown. Wide bulbous body
tapered at shoulder to everted lip; conical push-up in
bottom. Blown in 3-part mold of geometric design
(McKearin G II-6): vertical ribbing around upper neck;
between horizontal rings a band of diamond diapering;
broad vertical ribs above a horizontal ring; diamond
diapering below; pontil mark.
H: 6 1/16 in (15.5 cm)
History: W. Griffin Gribbel; Mrs. Frederick S. Fish
H. F. du Pont purchase, 1947: Neil C. Gest,
Mechanicsburg, Ohio
59.3003

Published: McKearin and McKearin, *American Glass,*
pl. 117, no. 1.
Parke-Bernet Galleries, "Early American Glass . . .
Collection Formed by Mrs. Frederick S. Fish," sale no. 159
(January 5–6, 1940), lot 340.

Some of the most distinctive midwestern
mold-blown glasswares occur in this G II-6
pattern. Fashioned of unusual colors such as
the lavender pink of NO. 126 and the yellow
seen here, they also demonstrate a flair for
form within the idiom peculiar to Ohio production. Although three-part molds imparted
size and shape as well as pattern, the glassblowers responsible for objects in the G II-6
pattern used the mold merely as a starting
point toward a more creative expression. Defects
in the G II-6 pattern indicate that the identical
mold was used to make this bold vase, a wide-
bodied pitcher (NO. 126), and a shallow bowl
(NO. 214).

258, PL. 11

VASE

KEENE, NEW HAMPSHIRE,
ATTRIBUTED TO KEENE GLASS
WORKS, 1815–41

Aqua nonlead glass. Blown. Globular body curved in at
shoulder below tall, tapered neck; blown in 3-part mold
of geometric design (McKearin G III-16): faint vertical
ribbing around neck with horizontal ring and diagonal
ribbing below; between horizontal rings are 3 repeat
panels of diamond diapering and bull's-eye sunburst;
vertical ribbing around below; rayed bottom (type VI-A);
pontil mark.
H: 5¼16 in (13.3 cm)
History: Webster(?) sale (per Gest)
H. F. du Pont purchase, 1947: Neil C. Gest,
Mechanicsburg, Ohio
59.3315

Blown in the same mold as a tumbler (NO. 53),
sugar bowl (NO. 163), and pitcher (NO. 121), the
vase demonstrates how a skillful glassblower
was able to create a variety of shapes using a
single mold. Given the expense of molds, such
versatility may have been economically moti-
vated, especially at a small business such as
Keene Glass Works.

259–261, <small>PLS. 8, 21</small>

VASES

PROBABLY NEW ENGLAND,
1840–60

NO. 259 (one of two). Teal blue lead glass. Blown.
Cylindrical body with rounded shoulders, short neck,
and wide turned-over rim; the body and bottom
unevenly molded with 12 flutes; push-up; pontil mark.
H: 7¹¹⁄₁₆ in (19.9 cm); Diam top: 5¼ in (13.4 cm)
History: Israel Sack, New York City
H. F. du Pont purchase, 1940: Neil C. Gest,
Mechanicsburg, Ohio
59.3140 (mate is 59.3098)

NO. 260 (one of four). Amethyst lead glass; colorless glass
pontil mark. Blown. Bulbous body curved in at shoulder;
tall neck flaring at top with turned-over rim; the body
and bottom molded with 12 flutes; conical push-up;
pontil mark.
H: 8½ in (21.7 cm)
H. F. du Pont purchase, before 1940, probably before 1931
59.3103 (mates are 59.3093, 59.3128, 59.3150)

NO. 261 (one of two). Amethyst lead glass; colorless glass
pontil mark. Blown. Ovoid body curved in at shoulder;
cylindrical neck with turned-over rim; the body and
bottom molded with 9 flutes; push-up; pontil mark.
H: 6½ in (16.6 cm)
H. F. du Pont purchase, 1931: McKearins' Antiques,
Hoosick Falls, N.Y.
59.3154 (mate is 59.3115)

These three vases were selected from eight in the
collection to show variety within the form. The
nine-flute vase (NO. 261) is rarer than the others
because of the small size. Other fluted vases are
recorded in blue and colorless glass. NO. 260 is
the most gracefully proportioned one in the
Winterthur collection and is blown of a high-
quality glass. In contrast, NO. 259 is wavy and
seed-filled, and its flutes are poorly molded.

Because Frederick William Hunter published
a blue fluted vase as the frontispiece to his 1914
Stiegel Glass, du Pont and his contemporaries
scrambled to acquire similar vases as choice
examples of an important eighteenth-century
glasshouse. By 1939 George McKearin had
pushed the dating of these vases into the nineteenth century and their place of origin considerably north of Stiegel's Lancaster County
operation. Their discovery of a related vase with
a scalloped rim characteristic of Victorian glass
helped to support their arguments for revised
dating. Certainly the broad, molded flutes echo

the cut-flute style that came into fashion in the
1830s and that in turn inspired pressed glass
designs (NO. 250). The turned-over rims reflect
the influence of Irish imports and occur on
several vases documented to New England
Glass Company.[1] The variety in execution and
in quality of glass suggests that more than one
glasshouse was responsible.

1. George S. McKearin, "A Study of Paneled Vases,"
Antiques 36, no. 2 (August 1939): 60–63; McKearin and
McKearin, *American Glass*, pp. 90–93, pl. 34, no. 3;
Warren, *Irish Glass*, pp. 117, 187, 204, pls. 77, 210, 232;
Alice Cooney Frelinghuysen, "A Masterpiece of the New
England Glass Company at the Metropolitan Museum
of Art," *Journal of Glass Studies* 25 (1983): 226, fig. 1, 229,
fig. 4.

262, PL. 3

VASE

PROBABLY NEW YORK, 1835–65

Aqua glass. Blown. Globular body flared out at rim; added thick gather tooled into 4 wide peaks curved out at top with slight scallops in between; applied disk foot; ring-shape pontil mark.
H: 3 5/16 in (8.5 cm)
H. F. du Pont purchase
59.3025

This vase is one of the smaller objects at Winterthur bearing the lily pad type of decoration. The fronds are symmetrically disposed but boldly executed for an almost liquid effect. Similar execution of the lily pad can be seen on a small jug published in *American Glass*. The McKearins also recorded a vase of similar size and proportion that they attributed to New London Glass Company on the basis of location-where-found, but it does not relate to the one documented New London lily pad pitcher.[1]

1. McKearin and McKearin, *American Glass*, pl. 17, no. 1; pl. 73, no. 1. The documented New London pitcher is in McKearin and McKearin, *American Glass*, pl. 72a, no. 3, and discussed in Wilson, *New England Glass*, pp. 151–52.

263

VASE

UNITED STATES, 1845–70

Aqua, opaque white glass. Blown. Deep trumpet bowl
flaring widely at rim; collar above compressed globular
base; loops of opaque white glass embedded in the aqua
bowl; aqua baluster stem and disk foot; pontil mark.
H: 9⅞ in (25.2 cm)
H. F. du Pont purchase
67.857

Glassmakers of ancient times incorporated
loops or threads of opaque glass into glass of
contrasting color. Venetians elevated the technique to a high art in the seventeenth and
eighteenth centuries. Looping remained a
decorative option in European glasshouses into
the nineteenth century and was frequently used
for bottles and flasks. England's colorful looped
glasses of the nineteenth century, commonly
known as Nailsea ware, were characterized by
bright red, pink, and blue swirls in a colorless
base. Influenced by English examples, glasshouses in Massachusetts and western Pennsylvania made vases, pitchers, and whimsical
forms using colorless lead glass with colored
loopings. The peculiarly American statement
seen here, where the base glass is aqua window
glass, is traditionally associated with New Jersey,
but the shape reflects high-style versions attributed to Pittsburgh.[1]

Other objects at Winterthur with looped
decoration are a pair of vases (64.658, 64.659),
a bowl (67.850), three pitchers (67.852, 67.854,
67.858), and four balls (67.851, 67.7853.1–.2,
67.856).

1. Tait, *Golden Age*, pp. 50, 83, 84; Keith Vincent, *Nailsea
Glass* (London: David and Charles, 1975); Innes,
Pittsburgh Glass, pp. 98, 103, 104.

264

VASE

UNITED STATES, POSSIBLY
MASSACHUSETTS, 1840–60

Deep blue glass. Pressed. Bowl of trumpet shape with
scalloped edge; 6 elongated convex ovals above 6 shorter
ones (Bigler pattern); joining wafer above annulated
knop; hollow hexagonal baluster on square foot.
H: 11¼ in (28.7 cm)
History: Philip Francis du Pont
Gift of Mrs. Harry W. Lunger, 1973
73.481

265–267

VASES

MASSACHUSETTS, 1840–60

NO. 265 (one of two). Red-amethyst glass. Pressed. Bowl
of flaring, hexagonal form with scalloped edge; 6 long
vertical ovals each below a small horizontal oval; joining
wafer; spreading stem on hollow, square plinth with
recessed plain sides, stepped foot.
H: 10⅞ in (27.8 cm)
H. F. du Pont purchase
59.2999 (mate is 59.2998)

NO. 266 (one of two). Deep amethyst lead glass. Pressed.
Bowl of trumpet shape flared at top with scalloped edge;
6 rounded panels above 6 pointed flutes; joining wafer
above annulated knop; hexagonal, 4-tier base; 6 circular
relief marks on bottom.
H: 11½ in (29.3 cm)
H. F. du Pont purchase
64.653.1 (mate is 64.653.2)

NO. 267 (one of two). Pale gray-purple lead glass. Pressed.
Bowl of trumpet shape with scalloped edge; 6 long
convex ovals (loop pattern); joining wafer above
annulated knop; hollow, octagonal baluster on square
foot with chamfered corners.
H: 8⅞ in (22.6 cm)
H. F. du Pont purchase
64.648 (mate is 64.649)

These vases illustrate some variants of loop-
pattern pressed glass from the middle of the
nineteenth century. Each vase was pressed in
two parts and joined with a wafer of glass. The
technology of pressed glass allowed for interchangeable parts so that vases with the same
bowls seen here might have bases of different
design. The scalloped edges were not made
freely by hand but were created with the aid
of a special tool.

H. F. du Pont acquired a small group of
purple pressed glass vases to balance visually
his extensive collection of mold-blown pocket
bottles of the eighteenth century (see chap. 23).
Besides amethyst, pressed vases like these were
produced in blue (NO. 264), green, and yellow.

Boston and Sandwich Glass Company is
most often credited with vases in these patterns,
but other factories may have manufactured them.

268

VASE

BOHEMIA, 1835–60

Opalescent white nonlead glass. Blown. One-piece, hollow, mold-blown form, with trumpet bowl rising from compressed sphere; knopped stem and tall cylindrical foot with smooth, flat bottom. Gilded rectangular panel on one side contains river view with bridge painted in sepia enamel, the scene identified below the panel in gilt script: "Upper Ferry Bridge. Philadelphia." Gilded bands around rim and knops, gilded leafy band around compressed sphere and base of stem.
H: 8⅛ in (20.5 cm); Diam top: 4¼ in (10.6 cm)
History: Titus Geesey
Museum purchase, 1975: Charlotte & Edgar Sittig Antiques, Shawnee-on-Delaware, Pa.
75.222

With its opaque white body and painted and gilded decoration, this vase represents one of the four recorded types of Bohemian glass designed for sale in the United States in the mid nineteenth century. A second type is seen in NOS. 66–68—colorless, cut tumblers engraved with Philadelphia scenes. The third type is also engraved with American views, but the colorless glass is usually flashed with red, a style that Bohemian manufacturers had made famous by the 1840s. Finally, there are a few objects blown of brilliant yellow ("vaseline") glass and engraved after prints of American interest.[1]

A number of Bohemian glasshouses made glass like NO. 268, and specific factory attributions are impossible. In his landmark study of nineteenth-century glass, Gustav Pazaurek published a page from the pattern book of F. F. Palme of Steinschoenau showing similar vases.[2]

The majority of vases that have survived bear generalized, often floral, designs, and their use as flower containers has been documented in contemporary paintings and photographs.[3] In design, the form was particularly suited for this purpose because the hollow foot would fill with water and weight the vase. The contours of NO. 268 are so perfectly formed that a mold must have been used. The thinly blown glass has a milky texture and appears opalescent by transmitted light.

For years, opaque white glasswares of this period and style were believed to have originated in the factories of Bristol, but none have been documented to that glassmaking center or any other English source. Even though one vase of this kind is known to have an English view, the colored and opaque white glass produced in England was lead glass—even those opalescent wares of lesser quality from the northern provincial factories. Spectrographic analysis has shown that NO. 268 was blown of nonlead glass typical of Continental production.[4]

The source of the painted scene was a view by Charles Burton that was published as a print in the fall of 1830. Titled "Upper Ferry Bridge and Fair Mount Water Works, Philadelphia," the print was engraved and published in London by Jennings and I. T. Hinton. Early in his career Burton was a painter on glass for magic lanterns and transparencies. An English artist who worked in America between about 1819 and 1842, Burton is best known for his miniature views of New York and Philadelphia. Upper Ferry Bridge was designed by Robert Mills and opened about 1813. Other American scenes recorded on vases of this style include New York City Hall, United States Capitol in Washington, and Race Street Bridge, Philadelphia.[5]

1. Jane Shadel Spillman, "Glasses with American Views," *Journal of Glass Studies* 19 (1977): 134–46.
2. Gustav Pazaurek, *Gläser der Empire- und Biedermeierzeit* (Leipzig: Klinkharat u. Biermann, 1923), p. 361, fig. 306.
3. Henry F. Darby, *The Reverend John Atwood and His Family* (1845, oil on canvas; Museum of Fine Arts, Boston) and a daguerreotype of a young girl (private collection) both published in C. Peter Kaellgren, "The Bohemian Urn Vase: A Forgotten Form in American Decorative Art," *Glass Club Bulletin*, no. 133 (Spring 1981): 3–8.
4. E. Barrington Haynes, "White Glass," *Antiques* 48, no. 6 (December 1945): 346, fig. 10; Analytical Laboratory, Winterthur Conservation; Witt, Weeden, and Schwind, *Bristol Glass*. See Haynes, "White Glass," p. 347 for illustrations of Tyneside opaque white glass.
5. George C. Groce and David H. Wallace, *The New-York Historical Society's Dictionary of Artists in America, 1564–1860* (New Haven, Conn.: Yale University Press, 1957), s.v. "Burton." A vase with New York City Hall is in the collection of the Museum of the City of New York; Richard T. French advertised a pair with New York City Hall and the Capitol in *Connoisseur* 172, no. 693 (November 1969): cxlvi. A pair with the Upper Ferry and Race Street bridges were pictured in Helen Comstock, "Living with Antiques: The Ardmore, Pennsylvania Home of Mr. and Mrs. David B. Robb," *Antiques* 74, no. 2 (August 1958): 147.

269

VASE

PROBABLY CONNECTICUT, 1850–75

Very dark, amber-olive bubbly glass. Blown. Body of baluster shape with everted rim, tapered in sharply to small round base; 2 applied angular handles curled back at lower terminals; applied, thick cylindrical foot; pontil mark.
H: 7¼ in (18.5 cm)
Museum purchase, 1961: Richard H. and Virginia A. Wood Antiques, Baltimore. Funds for purchase, gift of H. F. du Pont
61.17

This vase probably emanated from a Connecticut bottle factory such as Westford, which operated into the 1870s. Stylistically, the vase suggests something of the neo-grec taste that emerged in the third quarter of the century.[1]

1. The Woods had sold the mate to this vase to George S. McKearin; it is now in Newark Museum; see Papert, *Illustrated Guide*, p. 32.

Chapter 14
Desk Accessories

270

POUNCE POT OR SANDER

PROBABLY SPAIN, 1750–1800

Olive green nonlead glass. Blown. Body of barrel form; central circular area pierced with small holes; applied and crimped horizontal rim with inward-folded edge; wide applied and crimped disk foot; pontil mark.
H: 3 in (7.6 cm)
H. F. du Pont purchase
58.134

Pounce, a fine powder such as pulverized gum sandarac, was shaken onto paper to prevent ink from spreading. Pounce pots or sanders were thus essential writing desk items up until the late nineteenth century. Most were made of wood or pewter. With its emphatic crimped detail, Winterthur's sander has the exuberant ornamentation characteristic of Spanish glass. A closely related one with applied ribbons of glass on the body is attributed to Almerían province.[1]

Nineteenth-century pounce pots made in the United States were fitted with metal perforated tops and were often made to match the square ink bottles for drawer or lap desk compartments. Somewhat reminiscent of NO. 270 are the columnar pressed-glass sanders with cable-edged feet made by Boston and Sandwich Glass Company in the second quarter of the nineteenth century.[2]

1. Hispanic Society of America, T-361, New York City.
2. William E. Covill, Jr., *Ink Bottles and Inkwells* (Taunton, N.J.: William S. Sullwold, 1971), pp. 402–9, esp. figs. 1725–27.

271

INKSTAND

UNITED STATES, 1815–40

Olive green, bubbly nonlead glass. Blown. Tapered form having a flat top with central hole within a folded rim; pattern-molded with 36 ribs swirled to right on the sides and continuing onto the bottom; push-up; pontil mark.
H: 1¾ in (4.4 cm); Diam base: 2¼ in (5.7 cm)
Gift of Mrs. E. du Pont Irving, 1970
70.377

Attributed for many years to Pitkin Glassworks in East Hartford, Connecticut, green swirl-ribbed inkstands, both round and square, are now known to have been manufactured at bottle factories throughout New England. Archaeological excavations at Glastenbury Glass Factory Company in Glastenbury, Connecticut, have yielded fragments of identical swirl-ribbed inkstands. An entry in the daybook of a Baltimore glass factory offering "green rib Inkstands" at 50¢ a dozen indicates that the style extended well beyond New England.[1]

1. See William E. Covill, Jr., *Ink Bottles and Inkwells* (Taunton, Mass.: William S. Sullwold, 1971), pp. 267–75, for illustrations of the variety within the form. Wilson, *New England Glass*, pp. 69, 140–41, figs. 54, 101 (an 1818 order included "inkstands"); Chapman-Baker Day Book, February 14, 1832, MdHS.

272, 273, PL. 10

INKSTANDS
UNITED STATES, 1820–45

NO. 272. Light blue lead glass. Blown. Body of slight barrel form curving in at top to rounded collar around central, depressed, circular hole; blown in 3-part mold of geometric design (McKearin G III-25): between horizontal rings are 3 repeat panels of diamond diapering and bull's-eye sunburst in diamond; herringbone ribbing below; ringed bottom (type II); pontil mark.
H: 1⅞ in (4.7 cm); Diam base: 2 in (5.1 cm)
History: Richard Loeb
H. F. du Pont purchase, 1947: Neil C. Gest, Mechanicsburg, Ohio
59.3319

NO. 273. Pale amethyst glass. Blown. Cylindrical form rounded at top and sloping down to central raised circular neck and opening; blown in 3-part mold of geometric design (McKearin G III-13): diagonal ribbing on the top; between horizontal rings are 3 repeat panels of diamond diapering and bull's-eye sunburst; diagonal ribbing to the left, separated by a horizontal ring from diagonal ribbing to the right; rayed bottom (type IV); pontil mark.
H: 2 in (5.1 cm)
History: Charles Woolsey Lyon; Richard Loeb
H. F. du Pont purchase, 1947: Neil C. Gest, Mechanicsburg, Ohio
59.3323

These inkwells are rarer than the Pitkin type (NO. 271), having been fashioned by means of three-part molds and occurring in colored glass. Often the mold used for inks was intended for other forms, such as tumblers. An example of this is NO. 272, which carries the identical mold defects as on some mugs, salts, and dishes.

A person of means in the early 1800s would have owned an inkstand of silver with cut-glass bottles. The designs seen here suggest cut patterns, but the lively colors belie any reliance on cut prototypes.

274, PL. 18

INKSTAND (ONE OF THREE)
UNITED STATES, 1820–45

Gray-blue glass. Blown. Cylindrical form with rounded shoulder and rounded collar around central circular hole; blown in 3-part mold of geometric design (McKearin G II-15): around the body between horizontal rings is a band with rows of alternating dots and diamonds; short vertical ribbing around base; plain bottom; pontil mark.
H: 1¾ in (4.4 cm)
H. F. du Pont purchase
59.3317 (others are 59.3321 in green and 73.492 in amber)

275

PAPERWEIGHT

CLICHY-LA-GARENNE, FRANCE,

CLICHY GLASSWORKS, 1845–55

Colorless and green glass; white clay (sulphide). Solid
rounded form of colorless glass; flat bottom with slight
indentation around center; contains white sulphide
profile portrait of Benjamin Franklin facing left, placed
on thin wafer of green glass. "Franklin" inscribed in black
at base of bust.
H: 2⅛ in (5.4 cm); Diam: 2¾ in (7.0 cm)
H. F. du Pont purchase
58.2580

Published: John A. Sweeney, *Treasure House of Early
American Rooms* (New York: Viking Press, 1963), pp. 96–
97.

276

PAPERWEIGHT

FRANCE, POSSIBLY CLICHY

GLASSWORKS, 1845–55

Pale lavender glass; white clay (sulphide). Solid rounded
form with flat bottom; contains white sulphide profile
portrait of Lafayette facing right. "Lafayette" inscribed in
blue at base of bust.
H: 2 in (5.1 cm); Diam: 2⅞ in (7.3 cm)
H. F. du Pont purchase
64.1116

Published: Palmer, "American Heroes," p. 10, fig. 9.

277

PAPERWEIGHT

BACCARAT, FRANCE, ATTRIBUTED

TO BACCARAT GLASS FACTORY,

1848–50

Colorless lead glass; white clay (sulphide). Solid rounded
form with flat bottom; contains white sulphide profile
portrait of John Quincy Adams facing left.
H: 1⅞ in (4.9 cm); Diam: 2¹¹⁄₁₆ in (7.5 cm)
Museum purchase, 1989: W. M. Schwind, Jr., Antiques,
Yarmouth, Maine. Funds for purchase, gift of Mrs. Harry
W. Lunger
89.83

278

PAPERWEIGHT

PROBABLY FRANCE, PROBABLY

CLICHY GLASSWORKS; POSSIBLY

UNITED STATES, 1848–50

Colorless glass; white clay (sulphide). Solid rounded
form with smooth, flat bottom; contains white sulphide
three-quarter portrait of Zachary Taylor.
H: 2⅛ in (5.5 cm); Diam: 3⅜ in (8.3 cm)
Gift of Mrs. Alan Renshaw, 1982
82.109

Although the heyday of sulphides or cameo incrustations occurred between 1815 and 1830 (see NOS. 63–65), the paperweight form introduced at midcentury presented a new opportunity for this type of decoration. Illustrious men of the eighteenth century as well as current celebrities were featured by the great French paperweight makers at the factories of Baccarat, Clichy, and Saint-Louis.

Heroes of the revolutionary war were popular subjects for nineteenth-century United States manufacturers, whether bottlemakers or creators of fine tableware. Lafayette's visit to America in 1824–25 apparently prompted the Bakewell factory to introduce commemorative sulphide tumblers and ornaments in the French style (see NOS. 63–65), but there is no evidence that Bakewell's made any sulphide paperweights. The Lafayette portrait of NO. 276 is from a different and more intricate medallic source than

that used for the Pittsburgh tumblers; however, the Augustin Dupré medal of Franklin, the source for the image in NO. 275, seems to have inspired one Bakewell sulphide tumbler.[1]

Bakewell's apparently made sulphide tumblers with likenesses of Adams, but none have come to light. Those would have been made at the time of his presidency; the later paperweight (NO. 277) was perhaps made at the time of Adams's death in 1848 and produced to honor in particular his strong antislavery stance.

Factory identification is based on shape and color, but attributions are not always clear-cut.[2] These examples demonstrate that little care was taken in manufacture, perhaps because such weights were considered no more than trifling souvenirs. The portraits of Lafayette and Franklin are off-center, and the glass of NO. 275 is of poor quality, being irregularly colored and filled with seeds.

Because Zachary Taylor did not have the international appeal of Franklin or Lafayette, sulphide paperweights featuring his portrait have been attributed to the United States, even

though some have a millefiori ring typical of Clichy production. Glass factories in all parts of the United States did issue pictorial flasks with the portrait of this hero of the Mexican-American War who became the twelfth president of the nation (NO. 393). Although Boston-area glasshouses have been suggested as the source of weights like NO. 278, there is no proof that sulphide weights were among their products.[4]

1. The Lafayette portrait is from a medal by François Augustin Caunois. See Palmer, "American Heroes," p. 4, fig. 1; p. 13, fig. 13; J. F. Loubat, *The Medallic History of the United States of America, 1776–1876* (1878; reprint, New Milford, Conn.: N. Flayderman, 1967), pl. 15.
2. Paul Hollister and Dwight P. Lanmon do not attribute a similar Lafayette weight to any factory, *Paperweights: "Flowers which Clothe the Meadows"* (Corning, N.Y.: Corning Museum of Glass, 1978), pp. 116, 165, no. 306.
3. Paul Jokelson, *Sulphides: The Art of Cameo Incrustation* (New York: Galahad Books, 1968), unnumbered pl., fig. 26.
4. New England Glass Company made paperweights with intaglio portraits of Queen Victoria and Prince Albert; see Paul Hollister, Jr., *The Encyclopedia of Glass Paperweights* (New York: Bramhall House, 1969), pp. 196–97, fig. 192a.

279

PAPERWEIGHT

CAMBRIDGE, MASSACHUSETTS,
ATTRIBUTED TO NEW ENGLAND
GLASS COMPANY, 1850–75

Lampwork. Pear-shape ornament shaded from peach to
deep rose with tip and colorless stem; partially embedded
in flat, circular base of colorless glass; smooth bottom.
H: 2 3/16 in (5.6 cm); Diam base: 2 15/16 in (7.5 cm)
H. F. du Pont purchase, 1924: Charles Woolsey Lyon,
New York City
64.642

A fashion for artificial fruit and flowers dates
from at least the seventeenth century, when
creations of sugar and gum arabic or painted
alabaster adorned the dessert table and con-
founded the unwary guest. Glass soon became
recognized as a suitable medium for such arti-
fice because its colors would not fade nor its
form disintegrate, and by the early 1700s Venetian glassblowers were making a variety of
fruits in glass.

In the mid nineteenth century, fruit forms
were adapted to the new concept of paperweights. The glass factory at Saint-Louis, France,
was noted for its hollow glass fruits set on
square cushions of colorless glass. It may have
been someone from the Baccarat works, however, who brought the fashion to America.
François Pierre (1834–72) left Baccarat at the
age of fifteen and came to work for New England
Glass Company as a fancy glassblower. He is
believed to have been responsible for many of
the millefiori and fruit paperweights manufactured there in the 1850s.[1]

NO. 279 and an apple weight also at Winterthur (64.643) are examples of lampwork composed of several layers of glass. In this process
the workman manipulated pre-formed glass
rods and tubes at a "lamp" or small flame. He
created realistic effects of bloom and mottling
by skillfully working tubes of thin casings of
colored glass over a core of colorless glass
cased with opaque white glass. In their shaded
effects the fruit weights anticipate by thirty
years the peachblow, amberina, Burmese, and
other heat-sensitive art glass.

In 1853 New England Glass Company displayed apple and pear paperweights at the New
York Crystal Palace Exhibition. The following
year a Portsmouth merchant bought a "Fruit
Paper Weight" from the Company for 62¢. For
"Common" weights he paid $4.50 a dozen, or
37½¢ apiece, while one described on the bill as
"fancy" cost him 75¢. An apple paperweight
similar to the Winterthur example is recorded
with a history of ownership in the family of a
New England Glass Company worker.[2]

1. Paul Hollister and Dwight P. Lanmon, *Paperweights:
"Flowers which Clothe the Meadows"* (Corning, N.Y.:
Corning Museum of Glass, 1978), p. 153, fig. 232;
Paul Hollister, Jr., *The Encyclopedia of Paperweights*
(New York: Bramhall House, 1969), pp. 196–97.
2. List of C. Goodrich as quoted in Wilson, *New England
Glass,* p. 325; invoice, New England Glass Company to
John Sise, May 5, 1854, Downs, WL; McKearin and
McKearin, *Two Hundred Years,* pl. 98, no. 4.

Lighting Devices

In the eyes of one critical foreign visitor, "one thing that the Americans manage very well is the lighting of their rooms." Indeed, she claimed that in the course of her travels she had "not yet been in a dark room."[1]

Most lighting fixtures had some glass parts, usually shades, chimneys, or oil fonts. The material was also used for the primary component in lighting devices of every kind, from candle holders to oil lamps, whether freestanding for table tops or mantelpieces or affixed to walls and ceilings. With its transparency and a refractory index enhanced by cutting, glass became the preferred material for chandeliers in the most luxurious homes and public rooms.

Unlike brass or silver, glass devices did not need to be polished, although they required careful cleaning for the best effect. As butler Robert Roberts recommended, "You should wash your lamp glasses every morning. . . . You should always have a clean towel when you are lighting your lamps, in order to dust your lamp glasses before you put them on, as they will show much better light."[2]

Winterthur's collection of lighting fixtures is quite large because of H. F. du Pont's desire to reproduce the effect of soft candlelight and oil light in the period rooms.

1. Una Pope-Hennessy, ed., *The Aristocratic Journey: Letters of Mrs. Basil Hall . . . 1827–28* (New York: Putnam's, 1931), p. 87.
2. Robert Roberts, *The House Servant's Directory* (1827; facsimile ed., Waltham, Mass.: Gore Place Society, 1977), p. 22.

Chapter 15
Candlesticks and
Candle Shades

280

TAPERSTICK

ENGLAND, 1720–40

Colorless lead glass. Blown. Deep, narrow cylindrical
socket; solid cylindrical stem with 3 annulated knops at
top and bottom, above short inverted baluster; domed
foot with central depression on top; pontil mark.
H: 6 in (15.4 cm); Diam foot: 2¾ in (7.0 cm)
H. F. du Pont purchase, 1948: Steuben Glass, New York
City
68.715

Small taper candlesticks may have had several
functions in the eighteenth century. Following
silver and brass prototypes, they could have
been placed on writing tables and desks for the
purpose of melting sealing wax.[1] G. Bernard
Hughes contends they were tobacco candlesticks, used by smokers to light their pipes.
Christopher Haedy's 1766 advertisement for
"Tea and other Candlesticks" supports a third
theory: that small candlesticks provided decorative illumination on the tea table.[2]

    Glass tapersticks have deep and narrow
sockets, as do their metal counterparts. The
knops on the long plain stem serve as a convenient gripping point, however the stick was used.

1. John D. Davis, *English Silver at Williamsburg*
(Williamsburg, Va.: Colonial Williamsburg Foundation,
1976), pp. 36–37, records a writing candlestick in an early
inventory and taper candlesticks among the silver in
Governor Botetourt's inventory of 1770.
2. Hughes, *Table Glass*, p. 315; G. Bernard Hughes, *Small
Antique Silverware* (New York: Bramhall House, 1957),
pp. 163–65; *Bath Chronicle*, November 20, 1766, as quoted
in E. M. Elville, *Paperweights and Other Glass Curiosities*
(London: Spring Books, 1954), p. 67.

281

CANDLESTICK

ENGLAND, 1725–45

Colorless lead glass. Blown. Rib-molded cylindrical socket with wide, upturned rim; angular knop with tears and flattened knop above octagonal molded pedestal stem with quartered diamonds at shoulder, annulated knop at bottom above angular knop with tears and flattened basal knop; applied domed foot molded with 8 ribs, each with a diamond protruding at top of dome; pontil mark.
H: 8⅞ in (22.6 cm); Diam base: 5¼ in (13.4 cm)
Museum purchase, 1986: W. M. Schwind, Jr., Antiques, Yarmouth, Maine. Funds for purchase, Collector's Circle 86.129

The English molded pedestal stem may have had its origins in Thuringia and Hesse, where from the early 1700s glassblowers used four-, six-, or eight-sided molds to imitate costlier facet-cut stems of Bohemian and Silesian glassware. The introduction of the style in English production seems to coincide with the Hanoverian succession in 1714.[1] Readily adaptable to wineglasses and dessert wares (NO. 182), the molded pedestal style was especially suited to candlestick shafts because it closely approximated the shouldered and faceted stems found in contemporary silver lighting devices.[2]

Fragments of a similar candlestick were excavated at the Fortress of Louisbourg, Nova Scotia, Canada.[3]

1. Charleston, *English Glass*, pp. 145–46. For examples of cut Silesian stems and molded Thuringian ones, see Brigitte Klesse and Hans Mayr, *European Glass from 1500–1800: The Ernesto Wolf Collection* (Vienna: Kremayr and Scheriau, 1987), nos. 107, 153.
2. John D. Davis, *English Silver at Williamsburg* (Williamsburg, Va.: Colonial Williamsburg Foundation, 1976), nos. 10, 11, 13, 14.
3. Jones and Smith, *British Military*, p. 104, fig. 124.

282, PL. 16

CANDLESTICK

CONTINENTAL EUROPE,
PROBABLY GERMANY, 1740–70

Opalescent white glass. Blown. Cylindrical socket with
everted rim, drawn flattened knop below; inverted baluster
stem; applied triple-domed foot with everted rim; pontil
mark. Polychrome enamel-painted decoration of floral
sprays and bands, bird on branches around foot, red
dash detail.
H: 6⅛ in (15.7 cm); Diam foot: 4⅛ in (10.6 cm)
History: found in Dartmouth, Mass.
H. F. du Pont purchase, 1950: Winsor White,
Mamaroneck, N.Y.
58.1427

The shape of this candlestick with its exaggerated foot was derived from European metalwork.
Pewter and brass candlesticks with similar
bases were made in the Netherlands and elsewhere from the early seventeenth century.[1]
These sometimes had pierced floral designs,
but the painted bird and flowers of Winterthur's candlestick are drawn from Chinese
export porcelain, perhaps through the medium
of German porcelain painting.

1. Kurt Jarmuth, *Lichter Leuchten im Abendland*
(Brunswick, Ger.: Klinkhardt and Biermann, 1967), p. 236,
fig. 227; Ronald F. Michaelis, *Old Domestic Base-Metal
Candlesticks from the Thirteenth to the Nineteenth
Century* (Woodbridge, Eng.: Antique Collectors' Club,
1978), pp. 63, 72, 105, references courtesy of Donald L.
Fennimore, Jr.

283, PL. 15

TAPERSTICK

ALLOWAY, NEW JERSEY,
ATTRIBUTED TO WISTARBURGH
GLASSWORKS OF CASPAR AND
RICHARD WISTAR, 1765–75

Light blue lead glass of uneven tint. Blown. Narrow
cylindrical socket slightly swelled at lip, thick rounded
drip pan and ball knop all from a single gather; stem
formed of angular and basal knops; applied conical foot
with wide, downward-folded edge; pontil mark. Remains
of paper label on bottom with inscription: "[blown] at
C[aspar] [Wistar]s glassh[ouse] ab[ou]t [17]30."
H: 4⅜ in (11.0 cm); Diam foot: 2⅝ in (6.5 cm)
History: Rebecca Wistar Morris; Caspar Wistar Morris;
Elizabeth Clifford Morris Canby; Elizabeth Canby
Rumford; Lewis Rumford; Lewis Rumford II
Gift of Mr. and Mrs. Lewis Rumford II, 1977
77.17

Exhibited: Wilmington Society of Fine Arts, Delaware Art
Center, 1940.
Corning Museum, "Glassmaking: America's First
Industry," 1976.
Museum of American Glass at Wheaton Village,
"The Wistars and Their Glass, 1739–1777," 1989.
Published: "From Kiln and Glory Hole," *Antiques* 37,
no. 3 (March 1940): 133.
Palmer, "Glass Production," p. 93, fig. 18.
Lanmon and Palmer, "New Bremen," p. 16, fig. 3.
Eleanor H. Gustafson, "Museum Accessions," *Antiques*
112, no. 6 (December 1977): 1088.
Smith and Hummel, "Winterthur Museum," p. 1282.
Wendy A. Cooper, *In Praise of America* (New York:
Alfred A. Knopf, 1980), p. 44, pl. 7.
Arlene Palmer, *The Wistars and Their Glass, 1739–1777*
(Millville, N.J.: Museum of American Glass at Wheaton
Village, 1989), p. 24, fig. 24.

284

CANDLESTICK

ALLOWAY, NEW JERSEY,
ATTRIBUTED TO WISTARBURGH
GLASSWORKS OF CASPAR AND
RICHARD WISTAR, 1765–75

Colorless lead glass. Blown. Tall cylindrical socket with
tooled, everted rim, rounded drip pan, and drop knop all
from a single gather; flattened ball knop above stem
formed of angular and basal knops; applied conical foot
with downward-folded edge; pontil mark.
H: 6¾ in (17.3 cm); Diam foot: 4⅟₁₆ in (10.4 cm)
Museum purchase, 1957: McKearins' Antiques, Hoosick
Falls, N.Y.
57.90.3

Published: Palmer, "Glass Production," p. 94, fig. 21.
Arlene Palmer, *The Wistarburgh Glassworks: The
Beginning of Jersey Glassmaking* (Alloway, N.J.: Alloway
Bicentennial Committee, 1976), p. 26, fig. 18.

The attribution of the blue taperstick (NO. 283)
to America's first successful glassworks is based
on its history in the Wistar family. Originally
owned by Rebecca Wistar (1735/36–91), a daughter of Caspar Wistar, who married Samuel
Morris in 1755, the taperstick was passed down
through the family to the donors. A matching
taperstick that originally belonged to either
Rebecca or her sister, Catherine Wistar Greenleafe (1731–71), descended in a different branch
of the family.[1]

Elizabeth Clifford Morris (1813–92), who in
1832 married Samuel Canby of Wilmington,
Delaware, inherited or collected from her rela-

tives some two hundred glass and ceramic objects with family associations (see NO. 149). The taperstick retains part of her label identifying it as number 21 in her collection. The history of this example led to the attribution of NO. 284 to Wistarburgh. That colorless candlestick repeats the form of the taperstick and was made in the same distinctive manner with a one-piece upper section. George McKearin had found NO. 284 in southern New Jersey and believed it had been made there.

A heavy baluster style remained fashionable in German glass throughout the eighteenth century (NOS. 15, 282) but enjoyed a much briefer period of favor in England (see NO. 3). Although more German than English in style—as would be expected considering the German origins of the workers—the Wistar candlesticks were blown of English-type composition. Spectrographic analysis revealed that the taperstick contains about 18 percent lead oxide; related blue and colorless glass cream buckets attributed to Wistarburgh are even higher in lead content.[2] Although white (colorless) glass was mentioned in the factory record book as early as 1744, lead glass was probably not attempted much before the late 1760s, when nonimportation agreements following the Townshend Acts encouraged manufacturers to seek new directions. There is no written evidence that Wistar used raw lead; presumably he had lead-glass cullet remelted and blown.[3] In these respects the Wistar taperstick illustrates the opposing influences on eighteenth-century American glassmaking: immigrant craftsmen skilled in the technical and stylistic traditions of continental Europe tried to accommodate a colonial market accustomed to English glass fashions.

The first advertisements for American-made glass candlesticks occur in the 1770s: Stiegel was making "ornamented" candlesticks in 1772, and Philadelphia Glass Works offered glass candlesticks and sockets in 1775.[4]

1. Now in Corning Museum. See Palmer, "Glass Production," p. 94, fig. 19.
2. The blue glass bucket that descended in the Wistar family is in the Corning Museum; a colorless one is in the Billups collection at New Orleans Museum of Art. See Palmer, "Glass Production," pp. 95–96, figs. 22–24. The blue color was achieved with copper, not cobalt oxide; Analytical Laboratory, Winterthur Conservation.
3. United Glass Company account book, p. 10, Wistar Papers, HSP. Stiegel's first "American flint glass" was also made solely of remelted cullet; by 1771 lead glass was being made from raw materials at the Manheim factory; see Palmer, "To the Good," pp. 210–12.
4. *Pennsylvania Packet*, July 6, 1772; *Pennsylvania Packet*, February 27, 1775.

285

CANDLESTICK (ONE OF FOUR)
ENGLAND, 1760–80

Colorless lead glass. Blown. Waisted cylindrical socket cut in large diamonds; facet-cut stem with central, angular knop; applied domed foot with 8 facet-cut panels, the bottom edge cut into 8 scalloped points; pontil mark.
H: 8¾ in (22.3 cm); Diam foot: 4¹³⁄₁₆ in (12.2 cm)
H. F. du Pont purchase, 1940: Arthur Ackerman, New York City
69.593.1 (mates are 69.593.2, 60.1188.1–.2)

Given the high refractive index of English lead glass, lighting devices are obvious forms to be embellished with facet cutting. Cut-glass candlesticks may have been somewhat inspired by silver prototypes that had diamond faceting on the candle cups and octagonal bases with faceted triangles. The technique of facet cutting was introduced into England from Germany in the early eighteenth century, and at least one example of German cut glass was in the colonies by 1713. "Diamond-cut and scalloped Candlesticks" were advertised by Jerome Johnson in London in 1742.[1]

"Rich cut," a term frequently used by American glass importers, could be applied to these candlesticks where no surface was left untouched by the cutter's wheel. Joseph Barrel of Boston offered "Very rich cut glass candlesticks" from London in 1772, while Philadelphia merchant Joseph Stansbury sold cut glass candlesticks in three sizes in 1776.[2]

Winterthur's examples may have had removable bobeches.

1. John D. Davis, *English Silver at Williamsburg* (Williamsburg, Va.: Colonial Williamsburg Foundation, 1976), pp. 23–24, nos. 8–9. A "German Cutt Glass kinester for Tea" was sent to Mary Dickinson of Philadelphia as a gift in 1713 (John Askew to J. Dickinson, March 28, 1713, Maria Dickinson Logan Papers, HSP; see NO. 77). Johnson as quoted in Charleston, *English Glass*, p. 181.
2. Barrel advertisement, *Boston Evening Post*, October 26, 1772; Stansbury advertisement, *Pennsylvania Evening Packet*, April 30, 1776.

286

CANDLESTICK (ONE OF TWO)
LONDON, 1775–95

Colorless and blue lead glass; ormolu. Blown; drops are pressed and cut. Urn-shape socket cut in a band of diamonds between panel cutting, upturned rim shaped with vandyke cuts from each of which hang a spangle and teardrop; below, metal mount and star-shape cut drip pan hung with double teardrops; cut pineapple form on metal mount above square plinth of dark blue glass gilded on 2 sides with a classical female figure and with floral bouquets on the other 2 sides, each panel outlined with circular scrolling; plinth mounted on a square, stepped ormolu base with concave sides and ball feet.
H: 11⅞ in (30.2 cm)
H. F. du Pont purchase, probably 1930: Arthur J. Sussel, Philadelphia
61.1067.1 (mate is 61.1067.2)

This candlestick embodies the neoclassical style of the late eighteenth century with its contrasts of blue and colorless glass and cut and gilded decoration. The gilded, blue glass plinth may be the glassmakers' response to candlestick bases of blue jasperware made by Josiah Wedgwood in this period (58.1176, .1177). James Giles was among the first decorators of glass to offer gilded designs of classical inspiration in the very early 1770s. These candlesticks and related candelabra in the collection (NO. 301) may be the work of his followers in the last decades of the eighteenth century.

In addition to exhibiting the costly techniques of cutting and gilding, the candlesticks were enhanced by ormolu mounts. They may represent the kind of work William Parker of London patented in 1781 as "a Method of making pedestals or supporters for Candlesticks Girandoles Chandeliers Candelabrums Lamps."[1]

1. Parker as quoted in Delomosne and Son, *Gilding the Lily*, p. 34.

287

CANDLESTICK (ONE OF FOUR)
ENGLAND, 1790–1815

Colorless lead glass. Blown; pressed; drops are pressed
and cut. Urn-shape socket cut in diamonds over panels,
everted scallop-cut rim hung with double teardrops;
brass fitting above cut star-shape drip pan hung with
double teardrops; panel-cut stem with central knop,
above hollow ovoid element panel cut, and with
horizontal rings above and below a band of diamonds;
faceted collar and short stem spreading to rounded
bottom; square, pressed base with fluted design on
interior.
H: 10¾ in (27.4 cm)
H. F. du Pont purchase
61.550.1 (mates are 61.550.2–.4)

A new feature seen in glass candlesticks of the
late eighteenth century is the pressed base with
decorative underside in a fluted or rosette design. Deming Jarves, founder of Boston and
Sandwich Glass Company, which gained renown
for its pressed glass, recalled that around 1800
"glass candlesticks and table centre-bowls, plain,
with pressed square feet, rudely made" were
imported from England.[1] NO. 287 proves that
expensive and decorative cut-glass wares received this mechanically produced foot as well
as plain candlesticks. The practice continued
to be followed in England, Ireland, and the
United States into the 1830s (see NO. 245).

1. Deming Jarves, *Reminiscences of Glass-Making* (2d ed.,
enl., 1865; reprint, Great Neck, N.Y.: Beatrice C.
Weinstock, 1968), pp. 93–94.

288, PL. 20

CANDLESTICK
UNITED STATES, 1815–40

Green-blue nonlead glass. Blown. Elongated cylindrical
socket with everted rim and bulbous bottom on
spreading collar; large, hollow, pear-shape element on
wide collar; central knop on short cylindrical stem,
spreading at base; thick conical foot; pontil mark.
H: 7⅞ in (20.0 cm); Diam foot: 3⅜ in (8.6 cm)
Museum purchase, 1958: McKearins' Antiques, Hoosick
Falls, N.Y.
58.4.3

Although the long socket and bloated central
knop of this candlestick recall English hollow-
knopped candlesticks of the late seventeenth
century, cut examples with bulbous shafts made
in the late eighteenth century (NO. 287) were
probably the immediate inspiration for this
lighting device. Still, the effect is jarring, almost as if a candle holder were placed as an
afterthought on top of an oil font. A related
candlestick at Metropolitan Museum of Art
makes this connection even more closely because its tall knopped stem and saucer base is
so typical of the early New England oil lamps
(NOS. 315, 316).[1]

 Although George McKearin had attributed
NO. 288 to southern New Jersey, the glass has a
shiny brilliance more often found in New York
products. The form is so singular, however,
that a specific attribution cannot be proposed.

 Even though the use of whale oil lamps
grew rapidly in the nineteenth century, candles
remained an important source of light. The
properties—and prices—of candles varied with
their composition and method of manufacture.
According to an 1829 London publication, six
best wax candles of 9-inch length cost 3s. 10d.,
and each would burn eight hours. At the other
end of the scale, ten dipped candles of 8¼-inch
length cost 7½d., but each candle would burn
only five hours.[2]

1. Thorpe, *History*, 2: pl. 54; Metropolitan Museum of Art
example published in McKearin and McKearin, *Two
Hundred Years*, pp. 304–5, pl. 92, no. 2.
2. William Kitchiner, *The Housekeeper's Oracle*, as quoted
in Leinicke, "Production," pp. 276–77.

289, 290, PL. 4

CANDLESTICKS

UNITED STATES, 1835–55

NO. 289 (one of two). Aqua nonlead glass. Blown.
Cylindrical socket with wide horizontal lip and globular
base with gadrooning made of added gather molded with
10 swirled ribs; cylindrical stem with knops above and
below a central annulated knop; applied disk foot; pontil
mark.
H: 9 ⅛ in (23.2 cm); Diam foot: 3⅝ in (9.2 cm)
H. F. du Pont purchase, possibly 1924: possibly Renwick
C. Hurry, New York City
59.3026 (mate, which is broken and repaired at rim, is
59.3027)

NO. 290. Blue-green nonlead glass. Blown. Cylindrical
socket with wide horizontal lip and globular base with
gadrooning made of added gather molded with 14 swirled
ribs; stem formed of 2 balusters separated in the center
with an annulated knop; applied irregular disk foot;
pontil mark.
H: 8⅞ in (22.6 cm); Diam foot: 4⅛ in (10.5 cm)
H. F. du Pont purchase, possibly 1924: possibly Renwick
C. Hurry, New York City
59.3053

Published: Pepper, *Glass Gaffers*, p. 78, fig. 51.

A small group of these striking candlesticks
were made by an as-yet-unidentified American
glasshouse. Metropolitan Museum of Art owns
a pair similar to NO. 289, and examples like
NO. 290 are in the Billups collection at New
Orleans Museum of Art and in a private collection.[1] In their distinctive gadrooning they relate to a sugar bowl, cream jug, and vase in the
Winterthur collection (NOS. 136, 176, 244). As
discussed in other entries (see NO. 176), the group
has traditionally been associated with New York
and New Jersey, but because of their relationship to certain high-style colorless glass objects, a
New England origin should be considered.

1. For the Metropolitan Museum example, see McKearin
and McKearin, *American Glass*, pl. 14, no. 3; Corning
Museum, *A Decade of Collecting* (Corning, N.Y., 1962),
no. 75; Arman Absentee Auctions, "Early American
Glass" (February 4, 1987), lot 33.

291

CANDLESTICK

CONNECTICUT OR NEW

HAMPSHIRE, 1840–60

Deep red-amber nonlead glass. Blown. Short, waisted
cylindrical socket on solid stem formed of 3 graduated
ball knops; drawn conical foot; ring-shape pontil mark.
H: 5⅝ in (14.4 cm); Diam foot: 3¹¹⁄₁₆ in (9.4 cm)
H. F. du Pont purchase, 1947: McKearins' Antiques,
Hoosick Falls, N.Y.
59.3023

According to McKearin, NO. 291 surfaced in the
vicinity of the Westford and West Willington
glasshouses in northeastern Connecticut. In a
letter to du Pont he cited a similar pair he had
acquired in 1919 (now in Corning Museum),
but they are heavy and clumsy by comparison.
McKearin attributed a more closely related
candlestick to Stoddard, New Hampshire,
which Kenneth Wilson has since identified as a
Connecticut product.[1]

Regardless of where it was made, Winterthur's candlestick proves that nineteenth-
century bottle glasshouses continued the
long-standing tradition of making refined forms
from common glass batch. The style of its
simple knopped stem owes nothing to artistic
movements of the day but represents instead
a timeless and universal solution to a design
problem.

1. McKearin to du Pont, February 24, 1947, WM;
McKearin and McKearin, *Two Hundred Years*, pp. 298–99,
pl. 89, nos. 1, 3; Wilson, *New England Glass*, p. 157, fig. 115
(now in Corning Museum).

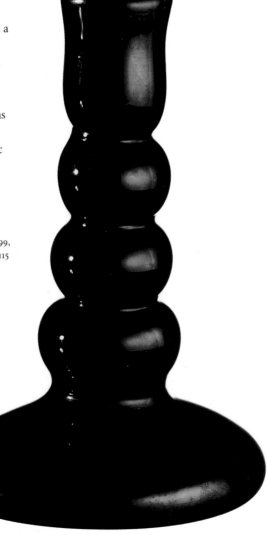

292

CANDLESTICK (ONE OF TWO)
PROBABLY SANDWICH,
MASSACHUSETTS, PROBABLY
BOSTON AND SANDWICH GLASS
COMPANY, 1840–60

Opaque blue glass. Pressed. Hexagonal urn-shape socket
with wide stepped lip and pedestal base, the center bearing
leafy scrolls in relief; irregular joining wafer below;
hexagonal baluster stem with acanthus leaves and bellflowers in relief, extending from top and bottom; plain
stepped section above spreading hexagonal foot with
leafy scrolls in relief; stepped hollow base.
H: 9⅜ in (23.9 cm); Diam base: 4½ in (11.5 cm)
History: Henry Iasello; William J. Elsholz; The Stradlings,
New York City
Gift of Mrs. Harry W. Lunger, 1988
88.32.2 (mate is 88.32.1)

Published: Richard A. Bourne Co., "The Elsholz
Collection of Early American Glass," 3 vols. (May 5–6,
1987), 2: lot 939.

These candlesticks reveal how generalized classical themes of the empire period were expressed
in American glass. The crisply press-molded
acanthus leaves and scrolls echo those of contemporary furniture and metalwork.

Attributed to Boston and Sandwich Glass
Company, the acanthus pattern candlestick is
known in three sizes. It is found in a two-color
combination of white stem and blue socket
more often than in the overall brilliant opaque
blue seen here.[1]

1. Raymond E. Barlow and Joan E. Kaiser, *The Glass
Industry in Sandwich* (Windham, N.H.: Barlow-Kaiser
Publishing Co., 1983), 4:58, no. 4041.

293

CANDLESTICK (ONE OF TWO)
PROBABLY SANDWICH,
MASSACHUSETTS, PROBABLY
BOSTON AND SANDWICH GLASS
COMPANY, 1845–65

Turquoise glass. Pressed. Tulip-shape hexagonal socket
with thick petaled rim on short hexagonal inverted
baluster stem, petaled at base; joining wafer below; figure
of a dolphin with tail upright and curved in S form; high,
square, hollow base.
H: 10⅜ in (26.4 cm); Base: 3¾ in square (9.6 cm)
History: Philip Francis du Pont
Gift of Mrs. Harry W. Lunger, 1973
73.495.2 (mate is 73.495.1)

The dolphin as a stem design in the decorative
arts has its roots in ancient art, but designers
of this popular glass candlestick were probably
more inspired by objects made closer to their
own time, such as earthenware candlesticks
produced at the Leeds Pottery in Yorkshire.[1]

Recorded in several colors, glass dolphin
candlesticks were made with scalloped bases
and stepped square bases as well as the plain
square foot seen here. There were also variations
in the style of the candle holder, and on some
examples the details of the dolphin's body were
highlighted with gilding. In 1857 Boston and
Sandwich Glass Company sold "Dolphin
candlesticks" wholesale for $3.50 a dozen, but
production was not limited to New England.
The 1859–60 trade catalogue of M'Kee and
Brothers illustrates a circular footed dolphin
candlestick made by that Pittsburgh firm.[2]

There was such demand for dolphin candlesticks among early collectors of pressed glass
that reproductions were made in Czechoslovakia
in the 1920s and 1930s.[3]

1. Trade catalogue of Leeds Pottery in Donald Towner,
The Leeds Pottery (New York: Taplinger Publishing Co.,
1965), no. 108.
2. Spillman, *Pressed Glass*, pp. 224–25, nos. 874–78; Metropolitan Museum of Art, *Nineteenth-Century America:
Furniture and Other Decorative Arts* (New York, 1970),
no. 94; invoice, Boston and Sandwich Glass Co. to John
Sise, February 14, 1857, Downs, WL; *M'Kee Glass*, p. 24.
3. Ruth Webb Lee, *Antique Fakes and Reproductions*,
supplementary pamphlet no. 1 (Framingham Centre,
Mass.: By the author, 1940), pp. 4–6.

294

CANDLE SHADE (ONE OF TWO)
ENGLAND OR POSSIBLY UNITED
STATES, 1780–1820

Colorless glass. Blown. Tall, truncated conical form with
outward-folded lip and downward-folded bottom edge.
H: 23½ in (59.9 cm)
H. F. du Pont purchase, before 1935
58.2841.1 (mate is 58.2841.2)

295

CANDLE SHADE
ENGLAND OR IRELAND,
1770–1800

Colorless lead glass. Blown. Hollow cylinder swelled at
center; 2 rows of rondels cut around the top; body facet-cut
with diamond shapes; row of rondels around base.
H: 20¼ in (51.7 cm)
Gift of H. F. du Pont, 1958
53.70

296

CANDLE SHADE (ONE OF TWO)
ENGLAND, 1800–1820

Colorless glass. Blown. Hollow cylinder swelled at center
and flared at bottom with downward-folded edge; cut
design of large sunbursts around the middle with linear
leafy sprays diagonally arranged above and below.
H: 22¼ in (56.8 cm)
H. F. du Pont purchase
58.3105.1 (mate is 58.3105.2)

Known today as hurricane shades, these forms
were called candle shades or India shades in the
eighteenth and nineteenth centuries. Designed
to fit over a candlestick to protect the flame
from the effects of wind and drafts, the hollow
form took several shapes. The 1760s trade card
of London's fashionable glasscutter, William
Parker, shows a waisted form with folded foot
and flaring scalloped rim (see p. 5, fig. 17). The
swelled cylinder shape, pictured as a lantern in

the 1763 illustrated price list of Norwegian
glass, remained a popular candle shade form
into the nineteenth century.[1] It is unclear where
the unusual and severely elegant shape of
NO. 294 fits into the development of the form.

As the name India implies, many of these
shades were destined for the Asian and West
Indian markets that had climates subject to
hurricanes and monsoons. A humorous drawing of 1802, "Segar Smoking Society in Jamaica,"
shows barrellike shades on the dining table
while numerous wall-mounted candles are
protected with shades of conical form.[2] English
glass manufacturers enjoyed a tremendous
export business in India shades as well as other
glass lighting fixtures throughout the nineteenth century.

The earliest record of domestically manufactured candle shades occurs in the 1775 advertisement of Philadelphia Glass Works. "India Shades, for Candles" were among the
products of Boston Glass Manufactory in 1816;
Boston and Sandwich Glass Company, in the
late 1820s, offered them from 20 to 27½ inches
in height. Candle shades were in demand until
the 1840s when oil lamps superseded candles.
Glassmakers then devised chimney or lamp
glasses to protect the flame of those lamps.[3]

Candle shades were blown of colored as well
as colorless glass. Some were plain, like NO. 294;
others had a roughed or frosted surface achieved
by means of wheel engraving or, by the mid
nineteenth century, by acid etching. The costli-
est ones were engraved or cut. In 1818, for example, South Boston Flint Glass Works offered
plain candle shades for $2.67 each, engraved
ones for $6.00, and "etched" ones of uncertain
decoration for $8.00.[4] The overall faceting of
NO. 295 would refract the candlelight for sumptu-
ous effect, and the sunbursts of NO. 296 were
strategically placed so as to enhance the glow
of the flame.

1. Polak, "Illustrated Price-List," p. 94, fig. 16.
2. The drawing by Ens. Abraham James (Barbados
Museum and Historical Society) is published in Jones
and Smith, *British Military*, p. 106.
3. *Columbian Centinel*, January 17, 1816, as quoted in
Wilson, *New England Glass*, p. 202; *Pennsylvania Packet*,
February 27, 1775; Leinicke, "Production," p. 278. The
1839 inventory of New York glasscutter Joseph Baggott
included 134 "lamp glasses" for oil lamps, 104 9- and
10-inch shades, and 720 chimneys, but only 1 pair of
candle shades (Baggott inventory, Downs, WL).
4. Prices Current, South Boston, 1818, Edison Inst.

Chapter 16
Candelabras

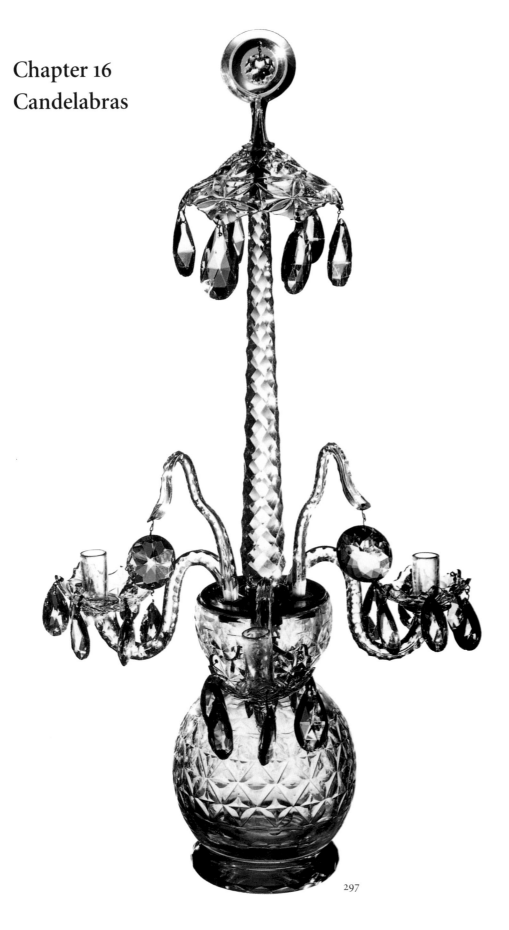

297

297

CANDELABRA (ONE OF TWO)
CONTINENTAL EUROPE, POSSIBLY
FRANCE OR BELGIUM, 1760–80

Colorless nonlead glass; metal. Blown; drops are pressed and cut. Hemispherical glass receiver cut in diamonds and fitted with a metal cover; spherical base cut in large diamonds; thick disk foot with facet-cut edge. Rising from the receiver is a solid, tapered spire cut in small diamonds; at the top, a conical canopy cut in petal design with 6 large teardrops, surmounted by a cut ring finial on stem with a pendant spangle drop. Around the shaft are 3 notch-cut arms of S shape with cylindrical sockets and upturned cut drip pans hung with teardrops; between are 2 crook-shape, notch-cut rods hung with large spangle drops. (Some drops replaced.)
H: 29 in (74.0 cm)
H. F. du Pont purchase, possibly 1940: possibly J. A. Lloyd Hyde, New York City
61.874.1 (mate is 61.874.2)

298

CANDELABRA (ONE OF TWO)
ENGLAND, PROBABLY LONDON,
1765–85

Colorless lead glass; silver plate. Blown; drops are pressed and cut. Small hemispherical glass receiver cut in diamonds, fitted with a metal cover; hollow stem cut in diamonds with central knop, enclosing a metal rod; domed foot cut in diamonds above plain rim and scalloped edge. From the socket rises a solid, tapered, notch-cut spire; at the top a domed canopy cut in diamonds and hung with chains of teardrops, surmounted by a cut crescent in metal mount. Flanking the spire are 2 notch-cut arms of S shape terminating in cylindrical sockets cut with vertical ovals, above a cut, star-shape drip pan hung with teardrops; between the arms is a notch-cut rod curved forward, from which hang a small and large teardrop.
H: 19⅜ in (49.3 cm)
History: Lord Durham
H. F. du Pont purchase, probably 1931: probably W. F. Cooper, New York City
63.934.3 (mate is 63.934.2)

299

CANDELABRA (ONE OF TWO)

ENGLAND, 1785–1800

Colorless lead glass; brass. Blown; drops are pressed and
cut. Hemispherical glass receiver cut in diamonds, fitted
with metal cover; solid, square pedestal stepped at top,
base with concave underside. From the receiver rises a
solid, triangular spire; at the top, a domed, cut canopy
surmounted by a cut star and hung with teardrops and a
central chain of teardrops connected with a rosette. Flanking
the spire are 2 S shape, notch-cut arms terminating in cut
cylindrical sockets above cut star-shape drip pans hung
with teardrops. (Some drops are replaced.)
H: 24 in (61.0 cm)
H. F. du Pont purchase
61.553.1 (mate is 61.553.2)

300

CANDELABRA (ONE OF TWO)

LONDON, 1796–1810

Colorless lead glass; ormolu. Blown; drops are pressed
and cut. Hollow ovoid element cut in band of diamonds
with panels above and below; faceted collar, 4-sided solid
spreading stem, stepped base. Rising above is a knopped
baluster shaft, panel cut, and enclosing a metal rod;
ormolu fitting, detailed with guilloche, supporting a
socket for a tall, notch-cut rod curved down at top, and
also supporting 2 large notch-cut, C scroll arms
terminating in bulbous sockets with upturned rims shaped
with vandyke cuts; below a metal joint are star-cut drip
pans each hung with tear, spangle, and rosette drops; the
central rod and C scrolls are connected with chains of
drops. The metal fitting stamped "LAFOUNT/ PATENT."
H: 24½ in (62.3 cm)
H. F. du Pont purchase
61.902.1 (mate is 61.902.2)

298

299

In the eighteenth century, multiple-armed candlesticks were called branches or girandoles, "and when made of glass, lustres."[1] A New York merchant, however, seemed quite certain they should be called girandoles when in 1762 he advertised "some curious four arm'd Cut Glass Candlesticks, ornamented with Stars and Drops, properly called Girandoles."[2] By the nineteenth century such forms were also known as candelabras.

Stars, drops, and other ornaments were used with more reserve in the 1750s and 1760s than in the final decades of the century when multiple chains of drops virtually obscured the central spire and branches. Because the cut surfaces refracted the candlelight, candelabras were often placed on pier tables or on mantelpieces in front of mirrors to enhance the lighting and make a room sparkle.

Ornamental drops were made in many shapes, but as the Winterthur lighting collection demonstrates, the tear-shape ones, round spangles, and long icicles were among the most common.[3] They were pressed into the desired shapes by hand-operated molds in a process known as drop pinching. As explained by glass manufacturer Apsley Pellatt, "Lumps of Glass made expressly for drop pinching, when softened sufficiently by a blast-furnace, . . . are shaped in twin brass dies, affixed to tongues, . . . [they] receive only the crude form; they afterwards require cutting, and polishing on a lead lap, to produce the required brilliancy." Pellatt added, "A considerable number of the Glass drops used for chandeliers, girandoles, and candlesticks, in England, are pinched from thick tumbler bottoms, or waste glass, causing a variety of tint, and inferior refraction."[4]

Aside from a few illustrations on glass manufacturers' trade cards, the styles of candelabras from the 1750–75 period are not well documented. Even though its nonlead composition indicates it was made on the Continent, NO. 297 reveals the influence of English styles. Its cut spherical base relates to early English glass chandeliers (NO. 308), and its diamond cut shaft parallels that on sweetmeat poles (NO. 191). The umbrella-shape canopy, which the drip pans echo in reverse, gives the object a Chinese air in keeping with the prevailing rococo taste.

William Parker's trade card shows a candelabra similar to NO. 298, in which the ball base of NO. 297 has been replaced by a knopped stem. Parker's light is capped with a crescent, perhaps a remnant of the "Turkish fashion" offered by glasscutter Jerome Johnson in 1752.[5] The square bases of NOS. 299 and 300 create a lighter effect than NOS. 297 and 298, indicative of the later neoclassical taste. Although the canopy was still an important feature of the form, the chains of drops diminished its exotic flavor. The dating of NO. 300 is aided by the stamped metal, referring to patent no. 2153 issued to Moses LaFount on December 23, 1796, for a "Plate and hoop or band, to be used in the mounting of glass chandeliers, girandoles, or other lustres."[6] Matching wall lights in the Winterthur collection are similarly marked (NO. 304).

1. Chamber's *Cyclopaedia* of 1753, quoted in Hughes, *Table Glass*, p. 315.
2. Gerardus Duyckinck, *New York Mercury*, supplement, October 18, 1762.
3. Drop styles are illustrated in the 1812 trade catalogue of Thomas Osler and John Barton of Birmingham, manufacturers of glass chandelier furniture and "patentees of the improved icicle," reproduced in John P. Smith, *Osler's Crystal for Royalty and Rajahs* (London: Mallett, 1991), pp. 16–17.
4. Apsley Pellatt, *Curiosities of Glass Making* (1849; reprint, Newport, Eng.: Ceramic Book Co., 1968), pp. 122–23.
5. Parker's trade card is in J. Bernard Perret, "The Eighteenth-Century Chandeliers at Bath," *Connoisseur* 102, no. 446 (October 1938): 188, no. 11; Johnson's advertisement is cited in Geoffrey Wills, *Candlesticks and Lustres*, English and Irish Glass no. 6 (Guildford, Eng.: Guinness Superlatives, 1968), p. 14.
6. Bennet Woodcroft, *Alphabetical Index of Patentees of Inventions* (1854; reprint, London: Evelyn, Adams, and Mackay, 1969), p. 326. A similarly marked example is in Corning Museum, but the base of the glass is pressed; see Spillman, *Pressed Glass*, p. 24, no. 13.

300

301

CANDELABRA (ONE OF SIX)
LONDON, POSSIBLY WILLIAM
PARKER OR SUCCESSOR,
1790–1810

Colorless and blue lead glass; ormolu. Blown; drops are pressed and cut. Large urn cut with spiral gadrooning, fitted with a metal cover, and mounted on a pedestal foot of ormolu detailed with classical leaves, beading, and guilloche; square plinth of dark blue glass gilded on 2 sides with swagged paterae, and with trophy arrangement of urn and torches on one side, and a floral bouquet on the fourth side; plinth mounted on a square ormolu base on ball feet. Rising from the center of the urn and mounted in brass leaves is a cut pineapple supporting an urn-shape socket cut in a band of diamonds with panel cutting above and below; upturned rim cut with projecting tears, above a star-shape drip pan hung with tear and spangle drops. Flanking the pineapple are 2 panel-cut glass arms of S shape, each terminating in similar sockets and drip pans.
H: 22¾ in (57.9 cm)
History: found in Lisbon, Portugal
H. F. du Pont purchase, 1941: J. A. Lloyd Hyde, New York City
61.699.1 (mates are 61.699.2–.6)

Published: Smith and Hummel, "Winterthur Museum," p. 1282.

These elegant candelabras represent a stylistic departure from previous examples. The receiver for the branches is now a classical urn enriched with spiral cutting. The candle cups continue the urn form seen in the LaFount patent example, but here the exaggerated rims echo the pendant drops below. The arms are less dramatically curved and are paneled rather than notch cut or faceted as in the earlier styles of candelabras. The glass plinth has been given greater importance by being raised on a footed metal base and it is executed in deep cobalt blue glass that has been gilded in neoclassical motifs.

The festooned paterae seen here, as with the decoration of the related candlesticks in the collection (NO. 286), are reminiscent of the work of James Giles, a London decorator of porcelain and glass.[1] Giles went out of business in 1774, but the artisans of his atelier may have continued to enamel and gild on glass. Giles's ledger indicates that William Parker provided much of the glass he decorated. Parker was an important manufacturer of glass lighting devices, as evidenced by the chandeliers bearing his mark in the Assembly Rooms at Bath.[2]

These candelabras are said to have been purchased in 1798 by the Count of Porto Covo for his house in Lisbon, which later became the British embassy.[3] A set of wall sconces at Winterthur also came from that source (NO. 303). When Janet Schaw of Edinburgh traveled in Portugal in the mid 1770s she visited the home of Sir John Hort, British Consul General, and commented upon his "most brilliant cut crystal lusters."[4]

1. Delomosne and Son, *Gilding the Lily*, pp. 32–37.
2. Martin Mortimer, "Chandeliers at Bath," *Journal of the Glass Association* 2 (1987): 1–10; J. Bernard Perret, "The Eighteenth-Century Chandeliers at Bath," *Connoisseur* 102, no. 446 (October 1938): 187–92.
3. July 1, 1941, H. F. du Pont, Index to Purchase Records, p. 623, Registration Division, WM.
4. *Journal of a Lady of Quality; Being the Narrative of a Journey from Scotland to the West Indies, North Carolina, and Portugal in the Years 1774 to 1776*, ed. Evangeline Walker Andrews (New Haven: Yale University Press, 1922), p. 240.

302

CANDELABRA (ONE OF TWO) PROBABLY LONDON, POSSIBLY FALCON GLASSWORKS OF APSLEY PELLATT, 1815–30

Colorless lead glass; ormolu. Blown; drops are pressed and cut. Octagonal shaft cut with alternating ribs of pillar cutting and diamond diapering; stepped circular base with underside cut in alternating plain and diamond rays. Around shaft, above a metal fitting, is a shallow hemispherical drip pan, cut with 30 rays of alternating diamond diapering and pillar cuts, hung with double octagonal drops and icicle drops; extending from a mount are 2 ormolu S-curve arms with leafy base flanking a central stalk topped with a pineapple; the arms terminate in urn-shape glass sockets cut in diamonds with bobeches cut with alternating ribs of pillar cutting and diamond diapering, hung with octagonal and icicle drops.
H: 14⅜ in (36.5 cm)
H. F. du Pont purchase
59.507.1 (mate is 59.507.2)

This pair of lustres epitomizes the regency style in glass lighting devices. The cut decoration, which would have been described as "rich cut" in its day, features smaller, more deeply cut diamonds than those on eighteenth-century objects. Pillar cutting, a difficult technique that inspired mold-blown imitations (NO. 174), is also indicative of the 1815–30 period. The same

cutting can be seen on cameo-incrusted candlesticks and scent bottles made in London by Apsley Pellatt about 1820.[1] The drops of NO. 302 are very long icicles that glitter with the same effect as those of the large chandeliers (NO. 310).

1. Herbert W. L. Way, "Apsley Pellatt's Glass Cameos in the Collection of Mrs. Applewhaite-Abbott," *Connoisseur* 67, no. 265 (September 1923): 4, 6, 7.

Chapter 17
Wall Lights

303

WALL LIGHT (ONE OF SIX)
ENGLAND, 1790–1800

Colorless lead glass; ormolu. Blown; drops are pressed and cut. Hemispherical glass receiver cut in diamonds, fitted with metal cover and pendant below. Rising from the receiver is a solid, triangular, glass spire on paneled stem with bladed knop; at the top, a domed, cut canopy hung with double teardrops, surmounted by a diamond-cut pineapple on bladed-knop stem. From the receiver extend 3 panel-cut S-curve arms each terminating in an urn-shape socket with upturned rim shaped with vandyke cuts; star-shape drip pan below, each hung with single teardrops; the arms connected by a double chain of smaller drops with large pendant teardrops; circular metal wall mount.
H: 26 in (66.1 cm)
History: found in Lisbon, Portugal
H. F. du Pont purchase, 1948: J. A. Lloyd Hyde,
New York City
61.644.1 (mates are 61.644.2–.6)
Location: Du Pont Dining Room

Some eighteenth-century glass lustres or girandoles were placed on wood or gesso wall brackets. At the time of his death in Philadelphia in 1782, merchant Henry Keppel, Jr., owned "2 Cut Glass Lusters with gilt Prakits" that were valued at £10. This description is clarified in the inventory of his widow's estate taken at her death nine years later: "2 Glass Lustres £6, 2 Carved & gilt Brackets to ditto [£]2.5.0."[1]

The need for fixed illumination from a high position in a room was also met by mounting candelabras directly on the walls without using brackets. Known today as sconces, the term in eighteenth-century parlance apparently described candle arms mounted upon any vertical element hung on a wall. Glass sconces are listed in colonial household inventories as early as 1719. In 1727 appraisers recorded "a glass sconce in walnut frame with glass arms" in the parlor of Thomas Addison of Prince George's County, Maryland. Glass arms were attached to mirrors as well as quillwork and waxwork pictures (53.70). In Philadelphia William Vanderspiegel owned "a Glass Case of Wax work in Imagery with Glass Sconces," valued at £10.[2]

Like the set of six candelabras in NO. 301, these wall lights were supposedly acquired from the British Embassy in Lisbon, which had been the house of the Count of Porto Covo.

1. Henry Keppel, 1782-161, and Catherine Keppel, 1791-416, inventories, Philadelphia County Probate Records (microfilm, Downs, WL); C. Keppel reference courtesy of Doris Fanelli.
2. Capt. Isaac Leader inventory, 1719-169, Philadelphia County Probate Records (microfilm, Downs, WL); Probate Records, Prince George's County, liber 12, fol. 295, Maryland Hall of Records, Annapolis; William Vanderspiegel inventory, 1768-206, Philadelphia County Probate Records (microfilm, Downs, WL). For an eighteenth-century mirror with glass candle arms, see "Living with Antiques," *Antiques* 82, no. 6 (December 1962): 630.

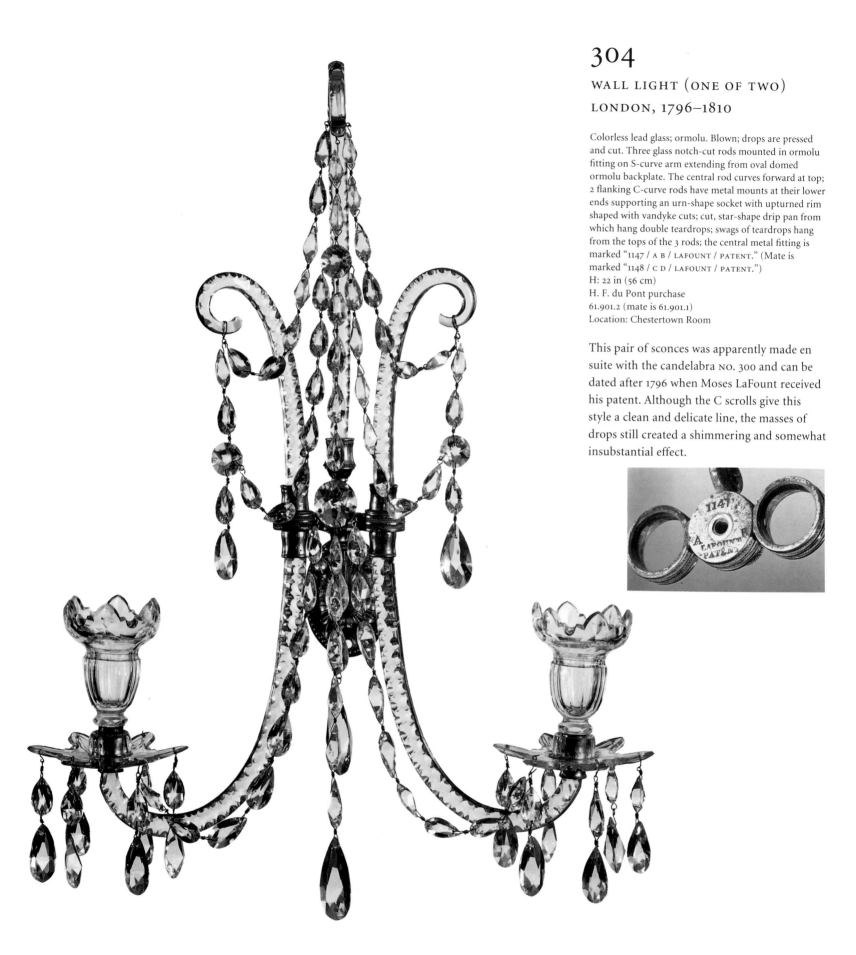

304

WALL LIGHT (ONE OF TWO)
LONDON, 1796–1810

Colorless lead glass; ormolu. Blown; drops are pressed and cut. Three glass notch-cut rods mounted in ormolu fitting on S-curve arm extending from oval domed ormolu backplate. The central rod curves forward at top; 2 flanking C-curve rods have metal mounts at their lower ends supporting an urn-shape socket with upturned rim shaped with vandyke cuts; cut, star-shape drip pan from which hang double teardrops; swags of teardrops hang from the tops of the 3 rods; the central metal fitting is marked "1147 / A B / LAFOUNT / PATENT." (Mate is marked "1148 / C D / LAFOUNT / PATENT.")
H: 22 in (56 cm)
H. F. du Pont purchase
61.901.2 (mate is 61.901.1)
Location: Chestertown Room

This pair of sconces was apparently made en suite with the candelabra NO. 300 and can be dated after 1796 when Moses LaFount received his patent. Although the C scrolls give this style a clean and delicate line, the masses of drops still created a shimmering and somewhat insubstantial effect.

305

WALL LIGHT (ONE OF TWO)
ENGLAND, 1800–1810

Colorless lead glass; ormolu. Blown; drops are pressed
and cut. An acorn-shape glass receiver, fitted with a metal
cover, is cut in diamonds, panels, and flutes with pendant-
cut pineapple in ormolu mounts. Rising from the receiver
is a tapered panel-cut glass tube enclosing a metal rod, the
glass with diamond-cut collars and a central ormolu foliate
fitting; at the top a triple cascade of metal bands from
which hang tear and rosette drops, surmounted with a
diamond-cut pineapple in metal mount. Extending from
the receiver are 3 S-curve panel-cut arms terminating in
fluted metal sockets above cut star-shape glass drip pans
from which hang double teardrops and a single large
spangle drop; from the shorter, central candle arm hangs a
rosette drop above a large spangle drop, the last connected
with the other 2 by swagged chains of teardrops. From each
socket rises a conical blown shade (possibly not original)
with engraved anthemia around the rim.
H: 32 in (81.5 cm)
H. F. du Pont purchase, possibly 1937: possibly R. W.
Lehne, New York City
58.817 (mate is 58.818)
Location: Lake Erie Hall

With its glass tubes, cut collars, and cascading
elements, NO. 305 is an unusual example of English lighting of the regency period. Certainly
the cascading drops would have had a remarkable effect when caught by candlelight below.

These may be the lighting devices R. W.
Lehne acquired from Kingston House in
Wiltshire.

306

WALL LIGHT (ONE OF FOUR)
ENGLAND, 1810–20

Colorless lead glass; ormolu. Blown; drops are pressed and cut. Two gadrooned and leaf-decorated ormolu rings, each with supporting metal inner rings and mounts, connected with chains of spangle drops; from the smaller, upper ring extend 3 feather-shape rods cut overall in diamonds and curved over at ends and connected with chains of spangle drops; from the outer rods hang spangle and icicle drops. Extending from the lower ring are 3 angular, panel-cut glass arms terminating in urn-shape sockets having a central diamond-cut band and upturned rims cut in serrated points and triangles of tiny cut diamonds; circular diamond-cut drip pans with serrated edges from which hang spangle and icicle drops; spangle and icicle drops hang directly from the metal ring; a pendant facet-cut glass ball at center bottom.
H: 28 in (71.5 cm)
H. F. du Pont purchase
61.1405.1 (mates are 61.1405.2–.4)
Location: Phyfe Room

This wall light and related chandeliers (NO. 310) illustrate the delicate proportions and rich detail of English lighting devices of the early nineteenth century. In contrast with the star-shapes and broad facets of eighteenth-century cut glass, the candle cups and drip pans are cut with small diamonds and serrations. The ornaments at the top evoke Prince of Wales feathers, a common motif of the regency period.

307

WALL LIGHT AND SMOKE GLASS
ENGLAND, 1820–40

Colorless lead glass; silver plate. Blown. Tall cylindrical
form tapered at base. Cut decoration: below rim a band
of diamond diapering with ribs of graduated lengths
above and below; around bottom, tall arches filled with
diamond diapering, and fans in between. Mounted at the
bottom in socket on scrolled arm of silver plate on
copper. Blown, domed smoke glass with downward-
folded edge (probably not original).
H: 17½ in (45.0 cm); Diam top of shade: 7⅝ in (19.5 cm)
H. F. du Pont purchase
61.802
Location: Readbourne Stair Hall

Glass wall lights were designed to protect a
flame from drafts in much the same way as
table-top India shades. An 1802 caricature of
Jamaican society depicts clusters of lights similar in shape to NO. 307. A Birmingham trade
catalogue of 1812 illustrates a "wall light for a
candle" that relates to Winterthur's, but the cut
decoration of NO. 307 indicates a later date of
manufacture.[1] Such cut patterns of diamonds
and fans ensured that the candlelight would
sparkle and provide a luxurious ambience. The
smoke glass was a practical necessity to protect
the wall and ceiling from smoke discoloration.

The thirty globe lamps in the stock of John
Long, a New York merchant in 1755, were earlier wall lights with round shades. The trade
card of William Parker shows a globular glass
shade mounted on an S-shape metal bracket
support (see p. 5, fig. 17). Another style is represented by a rare surviving example sold to
Nostell Priory in 1771 by Thomas Chippendale.
Its smoke glass was attached directly to the
globe by metal rods.[2]

1. The drawing by Ens. Abraham James (Barbados
Museum and Historical Society) is published in Jones
and Smith, *British Miliary*, p. 106. *A Book of Lamps,
Lanterns, &c. Manufactured at Birmingham* (1812), WL.
2. "Appraisements Made by Christopher Bancker and
Brandt Schuyler," p. 30, Downs, WL. Graham Hood,
"Refurnishing the Governor's Palace at Colonial
Williamsburg," *Antiques* 119, no. 1 (January 1981): 221.

Chapter 18
Chandeliers and
Hanging Lamps

308

CHANDELIER

ENGLAND, 1730–40

Colorless lead glass; iron. Blown. Hemispherical receiver cut overall in large diamonds. Iron shaft rising from the center carries a series of blown, cut-glass elements: a large and a smaller sphere separated by a tiered conical element; at the top, 2 angular knops of graduated sizes. Below receiver are hollow baluster elements cut with diamonds over panels; from the bottom of the shaft hangs a solid glass pendant formed of an angular knop with smaller pointed spire. From the receiver extend 12 S-curve round glass arms, each terminating in a flattened knop and cylindrical socket above a circular, ringed drip pan. Three drip pans are replacements.
H: approx. 50 in (127 cm)
History: Lord Henniker; Delomosne and Son
H. F. du Pont purchase, 1939: J. A. Lloyd Hyde and
Arvid O. Knudsen, New York City
64.1009
Location: Charleston Dining Room

Published: John D. Wood and Company, "Thornham Hall, Eye, Suffolk: Old English and French Furniture," (May 24–29, 1937), lot 115.
Fergus Graham, "Glass at the Antique Dealers' Fair—2," *Apollo* 26, no. 154 (October 1937): 216.
J. Bernard Perret, "The Evolution of the English Glass Chandelier," *Apollo* 30, no. 177 (September 1939): 101, fig. 1.
E. M. Elville, *English and Irish Cut Glass, 1750–1950* (London: Country Life, 1953), fig. 19.
Geoffrey Wills, *Chandeliers,* English and Irish Glass no. 7 (Guildford, Eng.: Guinness Superlatives, 1968), p. 3, fig. 1.

In the seventeenth century, chandeliers were fashioned of silver, brass, or carved wood and gesso. Some metal chandeliers were ornamented with beads of rock crystal; at the end of the seventeenth century French glassmakers began to substitute cut *pendeloques* of glass for the rock crystal. The concept of a chandelier primarily made of glass was developed in the very early eighteenth century, and by 1714 John Gumley was selling glass "schandelers" in London. Six years later Viscount Castlecomer's effects included a "large eight armed Glass-branch."[1]

From 1937 when NO. 308 was featured in the stand of Delomosne and Son at the London Antique Dealers' Fair, it has been recognized as one of the earliest English glass chandeliers in existence. Supporting the circa 1730 date is a similar chandelier that was installed at Emmanuel College Chapel, Cambridge, in 1732. Winterthur's chandelier originally hung in the grand hall on the ground floor of Thornham Hall, near Eye in Suffolk.[2]

With their bold spherical elements and curved candle arms that drop dramatically from the receiver, the early glass devices correspond to the brass chandeliers made throughout Europe in the first decades of the eighteenth century, but the cut glass sparkled more brilliantly than the most highly polished brass. On the first English glass chandeliers, only the elements on the central shaft are cut as a means of obscuring the metal supporting shaft; the arms and sockets are plain. Toward midcentury those elements also were cut with notches and diamonds to exploit to the fullest the refractive properties of lead-formula glass. The ringed ornamentation of the drip pans of NO. 308 repeats a treatment seen on the base of a four-light glass candelabra dating to circa 1725 and on other glass candlesticks of the period.[3]

There is no evidence that glass chandeliers were used in the American colonies in the early eighteenth century, but by the third quarter of the century a few may have hung in royal governors' mansions and a handful of public buildings. A pair of cut-glass chandeliers presented to the East India Marine Society in Salem, Massachusetts, in 1804 appear to have been made in the 1760–80 period, but it is not known if these rococo interpretations of the chandelier form were used in the colonies from that earlier date.[4] As in NO. 308, a large spherical element is a key feature of the Salem chandeliers; however, the arms are notch cut and of an exaggerated curve, dropping below the central pendant, and the top is a canopy form that later became a standard element (see NO. 309).

1. Ada Polak, *Glass: Its Makers and Its Public* (London: Weidenfeld and Nicolson, 1975), pp. 127, 143; *London Gazette,* April 6–10, 1714; *Post Boy,* June 21, 1720, quoted in R. W. Symonds, "Early English Hanging Light Fixtures," *Antiques* 22, no. 2 (August 1932): 52.
2. Martin Mortimer, "Chandeliers at Bath," *Journal of the Glass Association* 2 (1987): 2, pl. 2. William White, *History, Gazetteer, and Directory of Suffolk* (1844; reprint, Newton Abbot, Eng.: David and Charles, 1970), pp. 346–47. Thornham Hall was the home of the Major and Henniker families.
3. Mortimer, "Chandeliers," p. 1, pl. 1.
4. The chandeliers were presented by Capt. Benjamin Carpenter to East India Marine Society, whose building is part of Peabody Museum. One of the pair is in Jane C. Giffen, "Chandeliers in Federal New England," *Antiques* 101, no. 3 (March 1972): 533, fig. 12. For related chandeliers on the trade card of London glasscutters Maydwell and Windle, see Hughes, *Table Glass,* p. 60, pl. 28.

309

CHANDELIER

ENGLAND, 1790–1810

Colorless lead glass; iron; ormolu. Blown; drops are pressed and cut. Hemispherical receiver cut in overall diamond pattern. Rising above, on a central iron shaft, is a facet-cut cylindrical and knopped shaft; a large urn encircled by an ormolu mount, the glass cut in diamonds, panels, and swirl gadrooning; above, a facet-cut cylindrical and knopped shaft; at the top, an urn cut overall in diamonds above a domed, cut canopy hung with drops and chains of tear and spangle drops. Extending from the receiver are 16 tightly curved glass arms, panel-cut; the outer, lower 8 arms each terminate in an urn socket with upturned rim cut with projecting tears, above cut star-shape drip pan hung with tear drops; the upper, inner 8 arms support solid, cut spires rising above a small cut canopy hung with teardrops; chains of drops are swagged between the tops of the spires; the arms are also interconnected with festoons of drops and rosettes. Below the receiver a large, domed, cut canopy (possibly a replacement) hung with double teardrops and chains; a central cut pear-shape pendant.
H: approx. 62 in (157 cm)
History: found in Portugal
H. F. du Pont purchase, 1963: J. A. Lloyd Hyde and
Amos W. Shepherd, New York City
63.942
Location: Baltimore Drawing Room

Paul Bosc d'Antic wrote in 1780: "The English have a kind of glass for chandeliers which is perfectly beautiful. The chandeliers which they make from this, and which they polish in a most superior way and cut and arrange with the greatest art, reflect . . . all the colours of the rainbow."[1] Winterthur's stately example expresses to the fullest the neoclassical style of the form. The globular elements of baroque devices have given way to classical urns; the arms are panel cut, and the festoons of faceted drops convey an overall effect of delicacy and lightness.

Although a new type of chandelier was developed around 1800 that no longer emphasized a central axis (NO. 310), the central urn style of NO. 309 remained in demand into the 1820s. A larger chandelier of this kind but with more chains of drops still hangs in First Parish Church, Portland, Maine, having been purchased in New York in 1826. It is remarkably similar to one shown in the 1822 newspaper advertisement of New York glasscutter George Dummer, whose services included, "Chandeliers repaired, and orders executed to pattern." According to the *U.S. Directory* for 1822, Dummer was also an importer of glass whose shop was noted for its

"brilliant assortment of chandeliers," available in sizes ranging from four to forty-eight lights.[2]

Only in the federal period do glass chandeliers begin to appear with some frequency in American interiors. They were especially sought for churches, theaters, and other public rooms because they were the best way to light large spaces. In 1792 in one new theater in Philadelphia, "light [was] conveyed from cut glass chandeliers, suspended by gilt chains and brackets." The following year 3 glass chandeliers were acquired for the Assembly Rooms of Boston Theater, which was already lit by 4 large carved and gilded girandoles with 4 arms each, 10 single-arm girandoles—and 20 tin hanging candlesticks. Records indicate that one evening's illumination cost $31, with 23 pounds of spermaceti candles, 33 pounds of tallow candles, and 15 pounds of hog lard consumed.[3]

Several glass chandeliers similar to NO. 309 still survive in New England churches and meetinghouses, providing a touch of glittering luxury that seems at odds with the generally austere interiors. Of particular note is the chandelier presented by Hope Brown to First Baptist Church, Providence, in 1792, in memory of her father, Nicholas Brown. Because chandeliers were expensive they were often the gift of munificent patrons; the one given to Old South Church, Boston, in 1802, cost $800.[4]

There is less evidence of the use of glass chandeliers in private homes in the 1790s. One hung in the elegant drawing room at Mount Vernon. Thomas Roach, a New York wine merchant, owned a pair of glass chandeliers and a single one at the time of his death in 1798. A chandelier similar to NO. 309 still hangs in the Miles Brewton House in Charleston.[5]

Although cut-glass chandeliers like NO. 309 are traditionally attributed to Ireland and specifically to the Waterford glasshouse that opened in 1783, no documented example of a Waterford-made, or even an Irish-made, cut-glass chandelier has yet been traced.[6] Current scholarship tends to attribute most high-quality cut-glass chandeliers to London factories, several of which specialized in lighting devices.

Many of the chandeliers used in federal America were imported from England, but there is evidence that ones of Continental manufacture were used here as well. Two chandeliers presented to Independent Calvinistic Church of Newburyport, Massachusetts, are apparently of Continental origin, the gift of an English patroness of the founding minister. Acquired by du Pont, these were reassembled to form a single chandelier when installed at Winterthur (58.16). Glass chandeliers cut in the delicate style of English examples are shown in the trade catalogue of a Bohemian glass manufacturer. Perhaps the "German" cut-glass chandelier recorded in First Presbyterian Church of Pittsburgh was of this kind.[7]

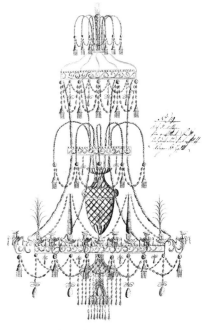

Most glass chandeliers were imported to a merchant's special order or formed part of his general stock, but some examples came to America by more circuitous routes. "Two fine glass branches and chains" given to Christ Church, Boston, by a Capt. Grushea and the owners of British privateer *Queen of Hungary* had been captured from a French vessel bound for Canada. Similarly, a glass chandelier hanging in Christ Church, Stratford, Connecticut, was originally destined for a Spanish convent, having been part of the cargo of a Spanish vessel taken by the British.[8]

The Dummer advertisement suggests that chandeliers of neoclassical style could have been made by American manufacturers. That American glasshouses were including some type of chandelier among their products by the 1810s is well documented; however, no surviving examples have been located. In 1817 a traveler reported: "At Messrs. Page & Bakewell's glass warehouse I saw chandeliers and numerous articles in cut glass of a very splendid description." In the Boston area New England Glass Company was prepared in 1819 to provide "*Chandeliers*—for churches and halls— made to any pattern or drawing." Likewise, the records of Boston and Sandwich Glass Company include references to chandelier balls, bowls, arms, drip pans, and smoke shades.[9]

1. Bosc d'Antic quoted in Ada Polak, *Glass: Its Makers and Its Public* (London: Weidenfeld and Nicolson, 1975), p. 147.
2. The Portland chandelier is shown in Jane C. Giffen, "Chandeliers in Federal New England," *Antiques* 101, no. 3 (March 1972): 530, fig. 5. Dummer advertisements in *New York Advertiser*, April 17, 1822, and *New York Commercial Advertiser*, January 3, 1825; Joshua Shaw, *U.S. Directory for the Use of Travelers and Merchants* (Philadelphia: J. Maxwell, 1822), p. 50.
3. *Massachusetts Magazine* 4, no. 9 (September 1792): 591; Joshua Taylor to Charles Bulfinch, cited in Giffen, "Chandeliers," p. 531.
4. Christopher Monkhouse kindly provided information on the Brown chandelier. Giffen, "Chandeliers," pp. 529–30.
5. R. W. G. Vail, ed., "A Dinner at Mount Vernon, from the Unpublished Journal of Joshua Brookes (1773–1859)," *New-York Historical Society Quarterly* 31, no. 2 (April 1947): 79; Thomas Roach inventory, New York City Inventories, Downs, WL. The Charleston fixture is in John Bivens and J. Thomas Savage, "The Miles Brewton House, Charleston, South Carolina," *Antiques* 143, no. 2 (February 1993): 304.
6. Warren, *Irish Glass*, pp. 217–18.
7. The benefactress was Lady Selina Huntington; the chandelier is shown in Giffen, "Chandeliers," p. 529, fig. 3; "The first Presbyterian meeting house has a very fine chandelier of German workmanship, lately presented to it by General O'Hara, of this place, but its magnificence glares in unbecoming contrast to the Quakerlike plainness of the house" (*The Pittsburgh Directory for 1819* [Pittsburgh: J. M. Riddle and M. M. Murray, 1819], p. 23).
8. Elise Lathrop, *Old New England Churches* (1938; reprint, Rutland, Vt.: C. E. Tuttle Co., 1963), pp. 25, 124.
9. Henry Bradshaw Fearon, *Sketches of America: A Narrative of a Journey* . . . (2d ed.; London: Longman, Hurst, et al., 1818), p. 204; "Chronicle: Domestic Glass Manufacturers," *Niles' Weekly Register* 17, no. 427 (November 13, 1819): 176. See for example, Sloar Book, August 11, 1827, in Leinicke, "Production," pp. 175–76, 300–302.

310

CHANDELIER

PROBABLY ENGLAND, 1810–35

Colorless lead glass; ormolu. Blown; drops are pressed and cut. A large circular metal ring supports 6 metal arms terminating in blown, cut-glass candle sockets of bulbous shape with scallop-cut upturned rims; below each socket is a hemispherical drip pan, cut in diamonds, from which hang spangle and icicle drops; strung from the large ring to a smaller upper ring are multiple chains of spangle drops; at the top, two tiers of icicle drops. Below the large ring hang four graduated tiers of icicle drops with a central, faceted, ball pendant.
H: approx. 56 in (142 cm)
H. F. du Pont purchase
61.1408
Location: Phyfe Room

The chains of facet-cut drops that had begun to obscure the vertical shafts of candelabras and chandeliers in the latter part of the eighteenth century eventually replaced them entirely. In this 1810–35 version there are no large blown and cut elements arranged on a central iron shaft; instead, long icicle and spangle drops form the substance of the device. Indeed, the arrangement of chains and tiers of drops becomes itself an enormous prismlike object, tapered from the top to a wide point then angled in to a point below.

Chandeliers like NO. 310 were made in Britain, France, and the United States and were fashionable through the second quarter of the nineteenth century.[1] Few are documented as to maker. The metal frame of an example similar to NO. 310 is stamped with the name Moss; because a William Moss appears as a cut-glass manufacturer in the Dublin directories for the 1823–26 period, he has been proposed as the source. However, chandeliers were not necessarily assembled by the firm that made the glass components. Thomas Osler of Birmingham, for example, became a "chandelier furniture maker," supplying glass drops and spangles to others.[2] As seen in NOS. 300 and 304, the name stamped on the metal parts was not that of the cut-glass manufacturer.

Records of the 1809 Sullivan Dorr house in Providence include specifications for a chandelier and prove that chandeliers like NO. 310 were hung in upper-class American homes of the early nineteenth century. A later version of the style can be seen in a painting of a fashionable New York parlor.[3]

The effect of the vertical chains of small drops stretched between two metal rings creates a graceful, shimmering cascade reminiscent of a waterfall. When lit in a mirrored room, such chandeliers become a thousand sparkling points and almost lose their sense of mass. This illusion could be quickly shattered, however, when a chandelier fell, as did the argand chandelier manufactured in 1840 by H. N. Hooper Co. of Boston for the House of Representatives in Washington a few months after installation. Weighing over 7,000 pounds and measuring 13 feet in diameter, the chandelier was ornamented with 2,650 cut prisms and 3,000 cut glass spangles and would have killed several distinguished politicians but for the time of day.[4]

1. An 1830s engraving after J. Gendall of Blades Upper Showroom, London (John P. Smith collection, exhibited at Dudley Art Gallery, Dudley, Eng., 1979), shows chandeliers of this style.
2. Warren, *Irish Glass*, p. 221, fig. 243; British Antique Dealers' Association advertisement, *Connoisseur* 180, no. 725 (July 1972): 38 (advertisement section); Peter Kaellgren, "Birmingham Cut Glass and the American Market: Examining an 1811 Account and its Context," *Glass Club Bulletin*, no. 158 (Spring 1989): 12.
3. Jane C. Giffen, "Chandeliers in Federal New England," *Antiques* 101, no. 3 (March 1972): 534, fig. 13; F. Heinrich, *Parlor of Mr. and Mrs. Ernest Fiedler* (1847; Museum of the City of New York), published in Edgar de N. Mayhew and Minor Myers, Jr., *A Documentary History of American Interiors* (New York: Charles Scribner's Sons, 1980), p. 106, fig. 48.
4. *Boston Transcript* as quoted in the *Maine Farmer* (Winthrop), January 2, 1841, reference courtesy of Earle G. Shettleworth, Jr.

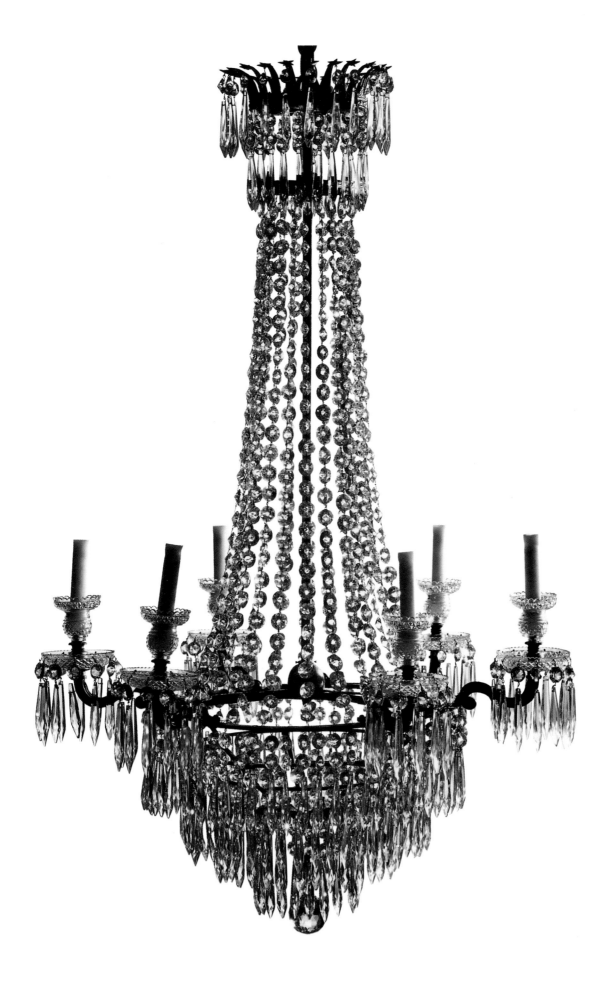

311

HALL LAMP AND SMOKE GLASS
ENGLAND, 1790–1820

Colorless glass; metal. Blown. Large globe of ogee shape
with outward-folded edge. Below rim a metal band with
serrated edge; metal fitting at bottom with pendant;
interior candle holder (not original). Chains connect
lamp to domed smoke glass with downward-folded edge.
H (globe only): 18 in (45.7 cm)
H. F. du Pont purchase: J. A. Lloyd Hyde, New York City
61.1455
Location: Montmorenci Stair Hall, floor 5

312

HALL LAMP AND SMOKE GLASS
ENGLAND, 1810–30

Colorless glass; brass. Blown. Globe of compressed
globular body curved in to cylindrical neck and everted
rim; exterior surface ground for frosted effect.
Polychrome enamel-painted decoration consisting of
leaves and flowers around the body, with stylized 3-leaf
motif around top of the neck; on the underside of the rim
a large diaper design. Around top edge a metal mount
with vertical leafy ornaments from which extend 3 chains
to upper domed smoke glass (not original); below, a
foliate brass mount and floral pendant.
H (excluding hanger): 7 in (17.8 cm)
H. F. du Pont purchase
64.783
Location: Portsmouth Room

In 1812 a Birmingham manufacturer sold
"hall lamps with glass shades" like NO. 311 in
sizes ranging from 8 to 11 inches, while another
trade catalogue of the 1830s shows similar
lamps 10 to 14 inches in size. NO. 311, one of
eleven hall lamps of this style at Winterthur, is
unusually large. Found by Lloyd Hyde in Canton, China, this must have hung in a palace
or institution.

A precursor of the style seen in NO. 311 is
on the 1760s trade card of William Parker (see
p. 5, fig. 17). More bell-like in shape, Parker's
candle lamp hung in one unit with its smoke
glass attached to the rim of the globe by
scrolled metal supports.

Glass hall lamps are recorded in American
documents from the 1770s. A "Large Globe
Lantern with an Iron chain," located in the
passage "upon the front stair case," was among
the furnishings destroyed in Gov. William
Tryon's house at Fort George in December
1773. There are numerous newspaper advertisements for glass hall lamps imported by American merchants in the federal period, but the

typical description, such as "a handsome assortment of Glass Lamps, for Entries and Halls,"
sheds no light on the details of shape and ornamentation.[1] A colorless glass example of the
style of NO. 311 still survives where it has hung
since 1817, the entry hall at Black Mansion,
Ellsworth, Maine. That the style was in considerable demand is indicated by the imitations
produced by rival Bohemian glassmakers who
sold to the American market and probably elsewhere.[2] The provenance of NO. 311 proves the
popularity of these English hall lamps throughout the world. In recognition of their use in Asia
they are often called Anglo-Indian lamps. They
remained in fashion in those markets for most
of the nineteenth century, making precise dating difficult.

Most lamps made in the style of NO. 311 were
colorless glass, yet the Winterthur collection
includes examples in green, amber, amethyst,
and blue. Several have prunted glass pendants
in lieu of metalwork. Although NO. 311 had a
device to hold four candles when Hyde found it,
period trade catalogues suggest that these lamps
were also fitted with oil-burning mechanisms.

The first American factory known to produce hanging glass lamps was Philadelphia
Glass Works, offering "lamps for halls, streets,
chambers, shops" in its February 22, 1775, newspaper advertisement. Nearly fifty years later
New England Glass Company was offering "cut,
painted, rough and plain Entry Lamps, newest
patterns." NO. 312 features painted floral decoration set off against a rough or wheel-ground
surface. This technique was used for candle
shades as well as hanging lamps.[3]

1. B. D. Bargar, ed., "Documents: Governor Tryon's House
in Fort George," *New York History* 35, no. 3 (July 1954): 302;
Harry Peters and Samuel Gedney advertisement, *Daily
Advertiser*, May 18, 1802, in Rita Susswein Gottesman, *The
Arts and Crafts in New York, 1800–1804: Advertisements and
News Items from New York City Newspapers*, Collections of
New-York Historical Society (New York, 1965), pp. 133–34,
no. 316.
2. See for example, no. 26, Gardiner's Island Glass
Catalogues, Downs, WL.
3. *Pennsylvania Packet*, February 22, 1775; *Boston Com-
mercial Gazette*, July 2, 1824, as quoted in Wilson, *New
England Glass*, p. 248; Brian Reade, "Architectural and
Domestic Metalwork: The Regency Period," in *The
Connoisseur's Complete Period Guides to the Houses,
Decoration, Furnishing, and Chattels of the Classic Periods*,
ed. Ralph Edwards and L. G. G. Ramsey (1958; reprint,
New York: Bonanza Books, 1968), p. 1187, pl. 67d.

Chapter 19
Oil Lamps

313

ARGAND LAMP (ONE OF TWO)
PROBABLY LONDON, 1800–1820

Colorless lead glass; brass, copper. Blown; drops are pressed and cut. Cylindrical glass shaft cut in diamonds on a brass foot and mounted at top with a bell-shape brass element; above, a hemispherical, cut-glass pan with spiky rim hung with octagonal and icicle drops; cylindrical brass fitting from which rises the spherical glass oil font, panel-cut above and below a band of diamonds; capped with spiral cut, flattened ball finial; 2 brass arms at either side supporting a burner mechanism with vertical foliate gallery holding a cylindrical glass shade with globular center section cut in diamonds.
H: 20⅞ in (53.0 cm)
H. F. du Pont purchase, before 1938
61.1070.1 (mate is 61.1070.2)

In 1784 Swiss physicist Ami Argand received an English patent for an oil lamp featuring a vertical draft tube surrounded by a circular wick to provide air to the center of the flame. A glass chimney kept the flame steady. Typically the font or reservoir for the oil was above and to the side of the burner. Argand lamps were commonly made entirely of metal except for the glass chimneys and shades. NO. 313 and its mate are unusual in that the base and font are also made of blown and cut glass.[1]

Argands were available in the United States soon after their invention, but they were expensive. The "patent lamps" sold by James I. Roosevelt in New York City in 1793 were probably argands. The household inventory of Thomas Learning of Philadelphia taken in 1796 included "2 Glass pattent lamps" in the front parlor downstairs valued at £2—almost as much as the glass chandelier that hung in his tea room. George Washington had five argands at Mount Vernon.[2]

Because of their shape argands were especially suitable for mantelpieces. For this purpose they were often marketed in pairs of single- or double-light fixtures; sometimes, two single-light lamps were designed to flank a central double-light fixture. In 1810 Robert Bach and Company in New York imported "ELEGANT LAMPS . . . from London, a few pairs of elegant one and two-light cut Glass Mantel Piece Lamps of the newest fashion."[3]

This revolutionary lighting device provided a light equivalent to about ten candles and was considered extremely bright. Count Rumford, who made a particular study of illumination and set out to improve certain failings of the argand lamp (see NO. 322), cautioned that "no decayed beauty ought ever to expose her face to the direct rays of an Argand lamp."[4]

1. Ronald Olmstead, "The Solar Lamps and Its Relatives," *Rushlight* 47, no. 2 (June 1981): 2369. A similar pair was sold in 1958; see Parke-Bernet Galleries, "Arts and Crafts of Pennsylvania, . . . Collection of the Late Arthur J. Sussel," pt. 1, sale no. 1847 (October 23–25, 1958), lot 566.
2. Roosevelt advertisement, *New-York Daily Advertiser*, June 15, 1793, quoted in Rita Susswein Gottesman, *The Arts and Crafts in New York, 1777–1799: Advertisements and News Items from New York City Newspapers,* Collections of New-York Historical Society 81 (New York, 1954), p. 102, no. 314. Learning inventory, 1796-435, Philadelphia County Probate Records (microfilm, Downs, WL), reference courtesy of Neil Larson. An argand that belonged to George Washington is in Jones and Smith, *British Military*, p. 105, fig. 126.
3. Bach and Co. advertisement, *New York Evening Post*, November 3, 1810, reference courtesy of Neil Larson.
4. An 1811 comment, quoted by Malcolm Watkins and cited in Jane Shadel Spillman, "Glass Lighting Devices," *Antiques* 98, no. 6 (December 1970): 917.

314, PL. 20

OIL LAMP

NEW JERSEY OR PENNSYLVANIA, 1810–40

Aqua glass. Blown. Spherical font with vertical lip; tall applied stem composed of hollow and solid knops of varying sizes on short cylindrical section at bottom; applied conical foot with downward-folded edge; ring-shape pontil mark.
H: 9¾ in (24.8 cm); Diam foot: 5¼ in (13.4 cm)
H. F. du Pont purchase, possibly 1925: possibly Renwick C. Hurry, New York City
68.717

Although using common window glass, the glassblower responsible for this oil lamp made a dramatic statement. By making it tall he increased the area that could be illumined. The blower created a stem in a time-honored way, with multiple knops, which in turn provided a firm handhold. Although the free-blown oil lamps associated with the Boston area have upturned saucer bases with folded edges (NOS. 315, 316), this lamp has a conical foot that harks back to the preceding century.

Many whale-oil glass lamps made before 1830 had their font openings fitted with agitable burners made of cork and holding one or two short metal wick tubes. Later, when more volatile burning fluids were introduced, metal screw-on burners holding diverging wick tubes were affixed to the fonts with plaster of paris.[1]

1. Jane Shadel Spillman, "Glass Lighting Devices," *Antiques* 98, no. 6 (December 1970): 920.

315, 316

OIL LAMPS

MASSACHUSETTS, 1813–30

NO. 315 (one of two). Blue and colorless lead glass. Blown. Colorless spherical font on solid cylindrical stem with central button knop; applied blue trumpet base with upturned rim and foot with downward-folded edge; pontil mark. Brass single-wick holder.
OH: 10 in (25.5 cm); Diam foot: 4⅜ in (11.2 cm)
H. F. du Pont purchase
64.1109 (mate is 64.1108)

NO. 316 (one of two). Colorless lead glass. Blown. Spherical font with collar below; cylindrical stem with button knops above and below ball knop; applied, tall trumpet base with upturned rim and downward-folded edge; pontil mark. Brass single-wick holder.
OH: 12¾ in (32.4 cm); Diam foot: 4⅝ in (11.8 cm)
H. F. du Pont purchase
64.1132.2 (mate is 64.1132.1)

Button-stem lamps similar to these were probably made by Thomas Cains at the glass factories he operated in South Boston from the time of the War of 1812. By 1826 the agent of New England Glass Company referred to lamps of "our old Button Stem patterns," and Boston and Sandwich Glass Company records contain references to "high" button-stem lamps, probably like NO. 316.[1] The button not only gave the lamps visual interest, it also provided a finger grip. The upturned, saucerlike feet were designed to catch any oil drips.

1. H. Whitney of New England Glass Company to W. E. Mayhew and Co., Baltimore, November 25, 1826, as quoted in Wilson, *New England Glass*, p. 240, see also p. 241; Bishop and Hassell, *Your Obdt. Servt.*, p. 89.

317

MINIATURE OIL LAMP
UNITED STATES, 1820–40

Colorless lead glass. Blown. Compressed globular font of irregular form curved in at top to circular opening; drawn stem and circular foot; blown in 3-part mold of geometric design (McKearin G III-4 variant): vertical ribbing around top; between horizontal rings are 3 repeat panels of sun-burst and diamond diapering, vertical ribbing below; rayed bottom (type III); pontil mark.
H: 2⅛ in (5.4 cm); Diam foot: 2⅛ in (5.4 cm)
H. F. du Pont purchase
59.3186

NO. 317 is one of a small group of lamps blown in three-part molds of geometric design. While the pattern here is similar to the G III-4 of the McKearin charts, it has single horizontal rings instead of triple rings above the band and double rings below. A distinctive mold defect that appears here as a vertical scratch through the sunburst panels is found on two other objects in the Winterthur collection, an inkwell (59.3179) and a salt (NO. 230), indicating they were blown in the identical mold.

Such diminutive lamps are often called sparking lamps, based on the notion that young lovers were permitted to be alone only as long as the lamp burned. It is more likely, however, that these functioned as night lights and not as timers for romantic encounters.

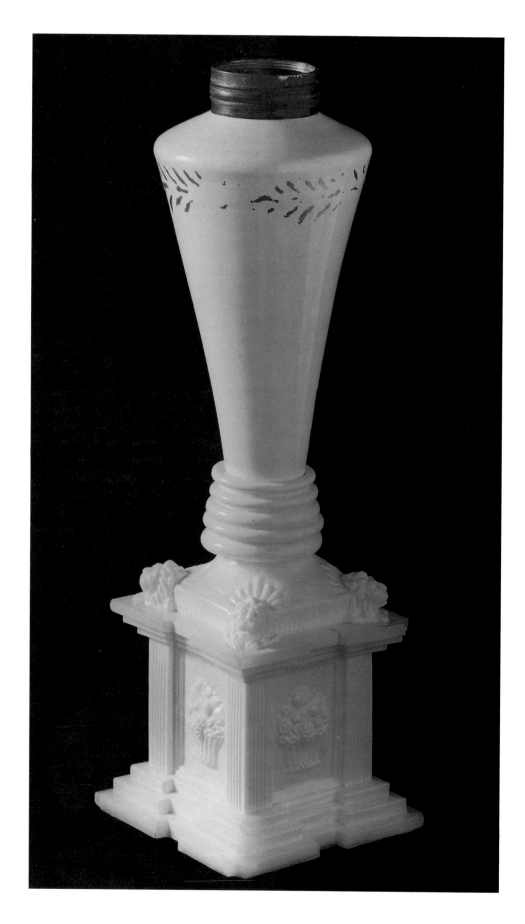

318

OIL LAMP
CAMBRIDGE, MASSACHUSETTS,
NEW ENGLAND GLASS COMPANY,
1827–40

Opaque white glass; brass. Blown; pressed. Blown conical
font angled in at top to circular opening mounted with
brass collar; around the widest point of the font are traces
of a gilded leafy band; annulated knop below. Pressed base
composed of 4-sided plinth on 3 steps; projecting fluted
pilasters at corners, each surmounted by a lion's head; on
each side in relief is a basket of flowers. Marked inside
base: "[N.E.G.C.O] / E.R:S.R."
H: 10¾ in (27.3 cm)
H. F. du Pont purchase
69.1031

After the technology of pressing glass became
widespread in the late 1820s, it was the moldmaker, not the glassworker, who was chiefly
responsible for the design and quality of the
finished product. Yet, as glass historian Kirk
Nelson has noted, "with the exception of the
lion head lamp, the work of these individuals
has not been identified." On Winterthur's
example the initials of New England Glass
Company are virtually obliterated, but the
moldmakers' initials are visible. It is believed
that these stand for Enoch Robinson and Spencer Richards. Robinson's 1826 patent for glass
doorknobs was one of the earliest patents relating to pressing technology; Richards took out a
patent for glass doorknobs in 1831.[1]

New England Glass Company originated
this architectural design for oil lamps, a sophisticated expression of the neoclassical style. The
basket motif, intimating the natural abundance
of the nation, relates to that of the rectangular
pressed salts also marked by the firm (NO. 236).
Boston and Sandwich Glass Company, founded
by a former agent of New England Glass Company, was quick to copy the design. Aside from
adding pad feet at the corners, the moldmakers
at Sandwich made only minor changes in internal dimensions and, of course, omitted the
initials. According to Nelson, an as-yet-
unidentified third factory may also have produced lion's head lamps. Examples are recorded
with spherical and conical fonts and in colorless
as well as opaque white glass.

In the summer of 1829, New England Glass Company had "commenced the manufacture of enamelled glass ware, which resembles the finest porcelain and pearl; and, surpassing what has been done in Europe, has extended it to the making of dishes, plates, nappies, cups, saucers, jelly, custard and egg cups, salts, knobs, etc." Although lamps are not mentioned in that commentary published by Hezekiah Niles, an advertisement in a Connecticut newspaper lists "enamelled glass lamps various patterns" among the wares of New England Glass Company. Gilding had been practiced at the factory from its inception. According to a report written in 1854, "other [glass]houses in the United States have attempted to gild their own work and have failed, this being the only establishment in which it is now carried on." A surviving recipe book for the factory includes a formula for gilding.[2]

1. Kirk Nelson, "Lion Head Lamps," *Maine Antique Digest* (October 1984): 4-a. Nelson identified "S. R." and has made a detailed study of the design of these lamps. For the complete mark, see Millard F. Rogers, Jr., "New England Glass Company Marks," *Antiques* 89, no. 5 (May 1966): 726, no. 8. Wilson, "American Contributions," pp. 199–200.
2. *Niles' Weekly Register* 36, no. 932 (July 25, 1829): 348; Kendall and Palmer advertisement, *Connecticut Courant*, October 6, 1829, as cited in Wilson, *New England Glass*, p. 289; 1854 report of Whitworth and Wallis for the British government as quoted in Watkins, *Cambridge Glass*, p. 49; Millard F. Rogers, Jr., "A Glass Recipe Book of the New England Glass Company," *Journal of Glass Studies* 7 (1965): 108–9.

319

OIL LAMP (ONE OF TWO)

PROBABLY NEW ENGLAND, 1830–45

Amethyst and colorless lead glass. Blown; pressed. Blown amethyst glass font of ogee form tapered in at top to small circular opening; colorless annulated knop below. Pressed base of colorless glass formed of a spreading section on a triple-step circular stem with interior ribbing; square foot with protruding rounded corners, ribbed on interior and exterior; pontil mark.
OH: 9⅜ in (23.9 cm); W base: 2¾ in (6.9 cm)
H. F. du Pont purchase, 1927: McKearins' Antiques, New York City
64.1128.1 (mate is 64.1128.2)

320

OIL LAMP (ONE OF TWO)

PROBABLY PITTSBURGH, 1835–50

Colorless lead glass. Blown; pressed. Blown font of
exaggerated pear shape, pattern-molded around base
with narrow flutes; annulated knop below. Pressed base
of 2 short rounded tiers with interior vertical ribbing, 2
higher tiers with exterior ribbing, each lower tier bears 4
protruding bullet-shape forms at the corners; 2 plain
steps below to a scallop-sided base with protruding
ribbed corners set on small pad feet.
H (glass only): 8⅝ in (22.0 cm); W base: 3¹⁄₁₆ in (7.8 cm)
H. F. du Pont purchase
59.1132 (mate is 59.1131)

321

OIL LAMP (ONE OF TWO)

PROBABLY NEW ENGLAND,
1835–50

Colorless lead glass. Blown; pressed. Blown font of pear
shape, engraved with stylized grapes and wheat sheaves,
with laurel band below; annulated knop below; hollow
blown shaft formed of a flattened knop above an acorn
knop engraved with angular Cs, annulated knop below;
pressed base composed of short cylindrical stem on 4-tier
square base, each tier shaped in scallops, bullet shapes on
top; pontil mark.
H (glass only): 10¹¹⁄₁₆ (27.3 cm); W base: 3⅝ in (9.22 cm)
H. F. du Pont purchase
59.1136

Many candlesticks and lamps were formed by combining blown and pressed elements. NO. 319 contains two colors of glass and has a font of neoclassical shape. Corning Museum has a lamp of the same elegant design but made of aqua glass.[1] NO. 320 features a bold font with pattern-molded detail, and NO. 321 proves that in spite of the inexpensive pressed base, the luxury techniques of cutting and engraving were sometimes applied to these kinds of lighting devices.

According to Boston and Sandwich Glass Company's Sloar Book, glassmakers made candlesticks and oil lamps of the same pattern at the same time.[2] That these elements can occur in various combinations should aid the attribution process, but as yet there are few thoroughly documented examples of either form. Candlesticks are known with the same pressed foot as NO. 321.[3] The knopped shaft of NO. 321 is unusual but relates loosely to that on a lamp attributed to Thomas Cains's Phoenix Glass Works, South Boston. A lamp with the same extraordinary base as NO. 320 but with a cut font of different shape has been attributed to western Pennsylvania. Lamps with the same panel-molded font of exaggerated shape have been assigned to both New England and Pittsburgh.[4]

The attribution of lamps like these to specific factories or even regions must await the discovery of well-documented examples or evidence from trade records. Pittsburgh glass was sold in eastern urban centers as well as in midwestern markets. By the same token, New England glass reached merchants in New Orleans and Kentucky. Makers closely copied one another's designs, and workmen frequently relocated.

1. Spillman, *Pressed Glass*, p. 213, no. 823; shown in color in Jane Shadel Spillman, *Glass Bottles, Lamps, and Other Objects*, Knopf Collectors' Guides to American Antiques (New York: Alfred A. Knopf, 1983), no. 316.
2. Leinicke, "Production," p. 274.
3. An example at Corning Museum is in Spillman, *Pressed Glass*, p. 206, no. 801. Another in Yale University Art Gallery is shown in Innes, *Pittsburgh Glass*, p. 239, fig. 238.
4. Spillman, *Pressed Glass*, p. 200, no. 783; Innes, *Pittsburgh Glass*, p. 238, fig. 236; p. 245, fig. 247. Spillman, *Pressed Glass*, p. 208, no. 809.

322

ASTRAL LAMP

CAMBRIDGE, MASSACHUSETTS,

NEW ENGLAND GLASS COMPANY,

1835–50

Black-amethyst and colorless glass; brass, steel. Columnar steel shaft with brass fitting at base and brass arms supporting ring-shape device for burning fluid; rectangular label on fitting marked "N. E. Glass Co. Boston."; dark

black-amethyst glass baluster stem with annulated knop at top and collar below; waisted section above circular, stepped foot; pontil mark. Blown colorless glass shade with facet-cut collar; the surface ground for frosted effect; cut rondels around top of neck; cut flower and leafy sprays around lower body.
OH: 17½ in (44.6 cm); Diam base: 5½ in (14.0 cm)
Museum purchase, 1952. Funds for purchase, gift of H. F. du Pont
52.165a, b

Published: Joseph T. Butler, *American Antiques, 1800–1900* (New York: Odyssey Press, 1965), p. 132.

The argand lamp (NO. 313) revolutionized lighting and sparked other inventors to develop further improvements. Among them was American Benjamin Thompson, better known as Count Rumford, a title bestowed upon him by the Elector of Bavaria. About 1806 the Count invented a balloon illuminator with a flat, circular reservoir attached with radiating arms to the base of the lamp. "By this contrivance," he wrote, "I got rid of the inconveniences that attend the use of inverted reservoirs; and I got rid of all shadows proceeding from the lamp." The resulting "Lampe Astrale" was patented in France by Bordier-Marcet in 1809 and 1810.[1]

As early as 1819, the year after it opened, New England Glass Company offered "Astral lamp shades—made to pattern."[2] For most astral lamps the shade was the only glass part, but in Winterthur's unusual example, the lower stem and foot are also fashioned of glass. The baluster style of the stem suggests a date no earlier than the late 1830s.

This shade was ground for a rough or frosted effect. A floral vine of cut and polished flowers offers contrast to the background, and the faceted collar is likewise left clear. Lamp shades were manufactured by numerous glasshouses and decoratively cut on the factory premises or by independent cutters. These were expensive, unlike the standard glass chimneys or tulip lamp glasses. In 1833 a Philadelphia merchant paid $1.25 each for astral shades made at Union Flint Glass Works. Those made at Baltimore Flint Glass Works cost $1.75 apiece.[3]

1. Ronald Olmstead, "The Solar Lamp and Its Relatives," *Rushlight* 47, no. 2 (June 1981): 2369–70.
2. *Niles' Weekly Register* 17, no. 427 (November 13, 1819): 176.
3. Record book of Thomas Barnes as quoted in Harrold E. Gillingham, "The Cost of Lamp Glassware," *Antiques* 28, no. 1 (July 1935): 23; Chapman-Baker Day Book, August 21, 1832, MdHS.

323

OIL LAMP (ONE OF TWO)

NEW ENGLAND, 1845–60

Amethyst glass. Pressed. Font in loop pattern with 6
protruding oval panels below a plain rounded top; knopped
stem; joining wafer below; octagonal baluster stem on
hollow square base.
H glass: 9¼ in (23.3 cm); W base: 3¼ in square (8.3 cm)
H. F. du Pont purchase
62.593.1 (mate is 62.593.2; same pattern in blue, 64.1110.1–.2)

324

OIL LAMP

PROBABLY NEW ENGLAND,

1845–60

Deep amethyst glass. Pressed. Ovoid font in loop pattern
with 6 protruding oval panels below a short rounded top;
joining wafer below; hexagonal stem with angular knops at
top and bottom; 2-tier hexagonal base.
H glass: 8¹³⁄₁₆ in (22.5 cm); W base: 4⅝ in (11.8 cm)
H. F. du Pont purchase
64.646

NOS. 323 and 324 illustrate lamp styles of the mid
nineteenth century. Their fonts echo the shapes
of earlier blown ones (NO. 319). The panel-
molded features of blown lamps like NO. 320
became more pronounced in the later pressed
loop patterns of NOS. 323 and 324.[1] The tall stems
show a move away from the elaborate and boxy
bases of the blown-pressed combinations and
toward the panel-cut stems of high-style tableware—a sleeker sense of design that is characteristic of pressed glass made in the middle years of
the nineteenth century.

1. A pair of lamps like NO. 324 was in the Elsholz collection,
Richard A. Bourne Co., "The Elsholz Collection of Early
American Glass," 3 vols. (December 9–10, 1986), 1: lot 556.

325

NIGHT LAMP

NEW YORK CITY, LEVERETT H. OLMSTED, CIRCA 1877

Blue glass; brass. Pressed. Spherical font on short vertical foot, pressed in 2-part mold; on one side the relief inscription "L. H. OLMSTED / NEW YORK." On the other, "LITTLE HARRY'S NIGHT LAMP"; flat bottom. Circular brass cap with wick holder.
OH: 2½ in (6.3 cm)
H. F. du Pont purchase
64.1493

This tiny lighting device, billed as "Little Harry's Odorless Safety Night Lamp," was advertised on the front page of the April 12, 1877, *Crockery and Glass Journal*.[1] Its chimney and shade, missing on the Winterthur example, were "combined in one" and made from "porcelain glass," and the font was made of flint glass. Although it weighed only two ounces the manufacturer assured the public that it would hold sufficient oil to burn twelve hours, at a cost of but a fraction of a penny per night. Perhaps the most significant feature claimed by the "patentee and sole manufacturer" was that it was "entirely free from odor while burning, and absolutely safe," a reference to the chief drawback of kerosene, which had been introduced as a replacement for whale oil in the 1850s.

Leverett H. Olmsted was a jack of many trades, according to the city directory listings for New York City. In 1869 he was listed as an engineer, the following year as a machinist, and in 1872/73 as a stationer who also dealt in hardware and bill files. "Sewing machine motors" and "machines" follow his name in the 1876 and 1876/77 directories. For 1878 and 1879/80, Olmsted's listing is "lamps," and he does not appear at all in the 1880/81 and later directories.

Made at a later date than most of the objects in the Winterthur collection, this lamp would have had special appeal for du Pont, who was known as Harry to his friends.

1. Advertisement reproduced in Innes, *Pittsburgh Glass*, p. 331, fig. 350.

326

WHALE-OIL LAMP FILLER WITH COVER

NEW ENGLAND, 1815–35

Colorless lead glass. Blown. Cylindrical body curved sharply at shoulder to narrow cylindrical neck with everted rim; applied rounded handle, curled back at lower terminal; applied hollow spout; low push-up in bottom; pontil mark. Conical cover with flattened ball finial and narrow tube extending through cork stopper.
OH: 5¼ in (13.4 cm); OL: 7 in (17.9 cm)
H. F. du Pont purchase, 1943: Winsor White, Mamaroneck, N.Y.
64.1134a, b

Although most commonly made of tin, several glass oil-lamp fillers are recorded, in bottle glass as well as refined colorless glass.[1] The requisites of the form were a strong handle and a curved spout with a tiny opening so the lamp fonts could be easily filled through the small burner opening.

1. McKearin and McKearin, *American Glass*, pl. 74, no. 10; pl. 61, no. 11; pl. 58, no. 9.

Bottles and Flasks

Without question, bottles were used in early America more than any other glass form. Virtually every household, no matter how modest, had a glass bottle or two. By the late seventeenth century, glass had replaced stoneware and earthenware bottles for the shipping and storage of many liquids and foodstuffs. Wines were typically matured in glass bottles. The demand for glass bottles was such that by 1700, some forty-two English glasshouses were producing annually 240,000 dozen of them.[1] Millions of English bottles were exported to the United States between 1650 and 1850, and millions of bottles were manufactured in American factories.

In spite of the vast importation of foreign bottles, and increasing domestic production, Charles Bagot, the British minister in Washington, reported in 1819, "It is a singular thing that there is no such thing as a pint bottle in the U. States. at least none are to be bought there." Thus, he urged his successor to bring his own pint bottles so he could bottle his Madeira.[2]

In Bagot's experience, Americans imported wines directly in large containers such as pipes or casks and bought empty bottles and did their own bottling. Others purchased wines and spirits from an importer who would then bottle the beverages for them, in their own bottles if they wished. Local brewers would likewise fill the bottles a customer supplied. Samuel Carpenter claimed that "those that send clean Bottles with good Corks, may have the best Beer."[3] Liquor merchants also purchased glass bottles for their trade and instituted the concept of returnable bottles at an early date. In 1767, Philadelphia merchant Elliot Duncan notified the public, "Four pence to be allowed on each Bottle of Wine or Ale, when the empty Bottle is returned," and brewer William Pusey advertised "The highest price given for empty Bottles." Snuff sellers were also anxious for bottles for their product: a Boston manufacturer declared that "Money or Snuff will be given for Bottles."[4]

As seen by the examples in the Winterthur collection, bottles came in a variety of shapes, sizes, and styles. Although manufacturers and retailers described bottles by size (pint, quart, etc.), measurements have proved that these were conceptual rather than actual designations and capacities varied widely.[5] Small bottles and vials were meant for such things as medicines and toiletries. Snuff bottles were square; some liquor bottles were also square so they could fit neatly into partitioned traveling cases. Pocket bottles were shaped so that a person could carry his refreshment conveniently in a pocket or travel bag.

Still, bottles were the most multipurpose glass form ever produced. In Virginia, archaeologists unearthed a wine bottle that had milk in it; another was filled with bird shot. The author of the first cookbook published in the United States recommended that damson plums be stored in snuff bottles. At Peale's Museum in Philadelphia, Henry Fearon saw "several quart bottles filled with ashes of the paper called 'Continental' money."[6]

1. John Houghton, *Husbandry and Trade Improv'd . . .*, cited in Ivor Noël Hume, "The Glass Wine Bottle in Colonial Virginia," *Journal of Glass Studies* 3 (1961): 93.
2. "Charles Bagot's Notes on Housekeeping and Entertaining at Washington, 1819," *Transactions, 1924–1926*, Publications of the Colonial Society of Massachusetts 26 (Boston, 1927): 442.
3. *Pennsylvania Gazette*, February 29–March 7, 1732.
4. Duncan broadside, HSP, Philadelphia. Pusey advertisement, *Pennsylvania Journal*, October 11, 1780. Peter Barbour advertisement, *Boston Gazette*, August 16, 1756, in George Francis Dow, *The Arts and Crafts in New England, 1704–1775* (Topsfield, Mass.: Wayside Press, 1927), pp. 280–81.
5. Jones and Smith, *British Military*, p. 14.
6. The corked bottle of milk is in Audrey Noël Hume, *Food*, Colonial Williamsburg Archaeological Series, no. 9 (Williamsburg, Va.: Colonial Williamsburg Foundation, 1978), p. 11, fig. 1. Noël Hume, *Glass*, p. 33. Amelia Simmons, *The First American Cookbook*, intro. Mary Tolford Wilson (facsimile ed.; New York: Dover Publications, 1984), p. 43 (originally published as *American Cookery*, 1796). Henry Bradshaw Fearon, *Sketches of America* (2d ed.; London: Longman, Hurst, Rees, Orme, and Brown, 1818), p. 154.

Chapter 20
Smelling, Snuff, and Medicine Bottles

327

SMELLING BOTTLE
ENGLAND, POSSIBLY NEWCASTLE
UPON TYNE, DECORATION
POSSIBLY BY WILLIAM BEILBY
WORKSHOP, 1775–90

Opaque white glass. Blown. Pear-shape with short cylindrical neck and solid oval foot; pontil mark. Enamel-painted decoration in puce: on one side, a rim border of graduated fronds and an exotic bird on a branch; on the other side, a scroll and leaf frame surrounding the black-enameled name, "E*Robson."
L: 3 in (7.6 cm)
Museum purchase, 1979: Maureen Thompson Antiques, London
79.3

Exhibited: Albert Amor gallery, "James Giles: China and Enamel Painter, 1718–1780," London, 1977.
Published: Sotheby Parke Bernet, "Catalogue of Fine English and Continental Glass and Glass Paperweights" (May 3, 1976), lot 20.
Albert Amor gallery, *James Giles: China and Enamel Painter, 1718–1780* (London, 1977), p. 45, no. 19.

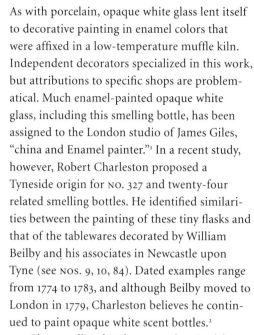

As with porcelain, opaque white glass lent itself to decorative painting in enamel colors that were affixed in a low-temperature muffle kiln. Independent decorators specialized in this work, but attributions to specific shops are problematical. Much enamel-painted opaque white glass, including this smelling bottle, has been assigned to the London studio of James Giles, "china and Enamel painter."[1] In a recent study, however, Robert Charleston proposed a Tyneside origin for NO. 327 and twenty-four related smelling bottles. He identified similarities between the painting of these tiny flasks and that of the tablewares decorated by William Beilby and his associates in Newcastle upon Tyne (see NOS. 9, 10, 84). Dated examples range from 1774 to 1783, and although Beilby moved to London in 1779, Charleston believes he continued to paint opaque white scent bottles.[2]

Glass smelling bottles were advertised frequently in American newspapers between 1760 and 1790. In 1768 Timothy Barret offered "enameled smelling bottles" just imported from London. The importance of this accessory to the eighteenth-century female was spelled out by Thomas Tisdale of Hartford who carried "Smelling Bottles of various shapes, so absolutely necessary for little Misses the approaching hot season and at the small price of 8*d.* each."[3]

1. *Enamel* was a term used in the eighteenth century to denote opaque white glass. For discussions of the Giles studio see R. J. Charleston, "James Giles as a Decorator of Glass," pts. 1, 2, *Connoisseur* 162, nos. 652, 653 (June, July 1966): 96–101, 176–81.
2. Robert Charleston, "A Group of Enamelled Opaque-White Glasses," *Burlington Magazine* 132, no. 1046 (May 1990): 328–35. Winterthur's smelling bottle is no. 25 on his checklist.
3. Barret advertisement, *Pennsylvania Chronicle*, February 22–29, 1768; Tisdale advertisement, *Connecticut Courant*, June 30, 1788.

328

SMELLING BOTTLE
PROBABLY NORWAY, POSSIBLY
UNITED STATES, 1780–1820

Colorless and blue lead glass. Blown. Irregular blue glass body of flattened spherical shape tapered to a cylindrical neck rising to a thick rounded collar; above, a wide, flaring neck; a colorless glass thread extends from the collar along the length of the body on either side and folds back on itself below the collar; applied solid foot of colorless glass; pontil mark.
L: 2¾ in (7.0 cm)
H. F. du Pont purchase
59.3013

Smelling bottles like NO. 328 were made in Norway in the late eighteenth century.[1] The glass industry there was established by Germans, but English workmen introduced lead-glass technology and English styles (NO. 224). Blue glass was especially popular around 1800 (NO. 146).

The early American glass industry was also characterized by an intermingling of Germanic and English traditions. At Manheim and Wistarburgh some German-style objects were blown of lead glass. Among them are the Wistarburgh tapersticks (NOS. 283, 284) that have the same irregular blue and thick, rounded collar as NO. 328.

The fashion for applied and pincered decoration on smelling bottles continued into the nineteenth century as proved by entries in the Boston and Sandwich production records in 1827 for pungents (smelling bottles) with three or four "pinches" or "pinchons."[2]

1. Ada Buch Polak, *Gammelt Norsk Glas* (Oslo: Gyldendal Norsk Forlag, 1953), pl. 77, no. 138.
2. The records are cited in McKearin and Wilson, *American Bottles*, pp. 380–81.

329

SMELLING BOTTLE (ONE OF
THREE)
ENGLAND OR UNITED STATES,
1780–1820

Amethyst lead glass. Blown. Flattened ovoid body with wide cylindrical neck; pattern-molded with 18 ribs swirled to the right; flat base with pontil mark. Others are blue and colorless. Another amethyst one is vertically ribbed.
L: 3⅛ in (8.0 cm)
H. F. du Pont purchase, 1928: McKearins' Antiques, New York City
59.3005 (mates are 70.392 [colorless], 70.393 [blue], and 70.394 [amethyst])

Published: Carlo Sellari, Dot Sellari, and the editors of Country Beautiful, *The Illustrated Price Guide of Antique Bottles* (Waukesha, Wis.: Country Beautiful, 1975), p. 377.

The rib-molded smelling bottle was a standard type blown in England and America during the eighteenth and nineteenth centuries. The ribs, ranging in number from eighteen to twenty-four, could be either straight or twisted. Examples are recorded in blue, green, amethyst, colorless, and opaque white glass. "Twisted" smelling bottles, some of opaque white glass, were among the products introduced at Manheim in 1769 by Stiegel's English glassblowers.

As the name implies, smelling bottles contained smelling salts (pungents), although some may have held fragrant scents.

> The snuff box and smelling bottle are pretty trinkets in a ladies pocket, and are frequently necessary to supply a pause in conversation, and on some other occasions; but whatever virtues they are possessed of they are lost by too constant and familiar use, and nothing can be more pernicious to the brain, or render one more ridiculous in company than to have either of them perpetually in one's hand.[2]

1. Palmer, "To the Good," pp. 218–19, fig. 12.
2. *Female Spectator*, 1750, as quoted in McKearin and Wilson, *American Bottles*, p. 378.

330

SNUFF BOTTLE

UNITED STATES, POSSIBLY
CONNECTICUT, 1797–1818

Olive green bubbly glass. Blown. Square body curved at shoulders to short narrow neck with everted lip; pontil mark. Pasted on one side: remains of a paper label printed in black with an Indian holding a pipe leaning on a cask inscribed "BEST VIRGINIA"; tobacco plant growing at right; below, the inscription "LOR[I]LLARD'S / MACCOBOY SNUFF, / SOLD at NO. 30 Chatham-Street, / [F]ive Doors F [torn] of the New-York/ [torn] [S]chool."
H: 5½ in (14.1 cm); W base: 2¾ in square (7.0 cm)
Museum purchase, 1962: John H. Martin, Woodstock, Vt.
62.158

331

SNUFF BOTTLE

UNITED STATES, 1858–70

Dark olive green nonlead glass. Blown. Square body with high shoulders curved in to wide circular opening with rounded lip; central smooth circular area on bottom with pontil mark. Pasted on one side: remains of a paper label printed in black with Indian holding smoking pipe and standing next to cask marked "BEST VIRGINIA." Below, "[SCO]TCH SNU[FF] / manufactured by / [SWE]ETSER BROTHER[S] / BOSTON, Mass., with parts of an additional notice below.
H: 4³⁄₁₆ in (10.7 cm); W base: 2⅜ in square (6.0 cm)
H. F. du Pont purchase
58.1976

Snuff was a preparation of tobacco intended for inhalation through the nostrils. The tobacco was treated with sauce composed of salt, aromatic substances such as oil of cinnamon, nutmeg, lavender, or rosewater, and was fermented over a period of time. It was taken for medicinal purposes but became fashionable—and addictive. Snuff boxes, filled from bottles like these, were the constant companions of men and women.

Scotch snuff was very popular in the colonies, but by the mid eighteenth century quality snuff was being made domestically. Among the American brands available before the Revolution were Weston's, which in 1773 was valued at 5s. 3d. a bottle, Hamilton and Leiper's at 3s. 6d., and Gilpin and Fisher's at 3s. 3d. Lorillard's

started in 1794 when Peter and George Lorillard erected mills in New York "for the purpose of manufacturing Scotch and Rappe Snuffs." The firm operated at the Chatham Street address until 1818.[1]

Snuff bottles were among the items advertised by most colonial glasshouses and continued to be manufactured by bottle factories throughout the nineteenth century. According to Boston city directories, Charles and George H. Sweetser operated their snuff and cigar business under the name Sweetser Brothers between 1858 and 1870. In spite of the years that separate them, the Lorillard and Sweetser bottles—and their labels—are remarkably similar.

1. For prices of snuff, see Margaret Coats inventory, 1773-264, Philadelphia County Probate Records (microfilm, Downs, WL). Notice in *The Diary; or, Evening Register*, August 29, 1794, quoted in Rita Susswein Gottesman, *The Arts and Crafts in New York, 1777–1799: Advertisements and News Items from New York City Newspapers*, Collections of New-York Historical Society 81 (New York, 1954), p. 188, no. 617.

332

PATENT MEDICINE VIAL

UNITED STATES, 1815–35

Pale aqua bubbly glass. Blown. Angular violin-shape body with short foot; wide cylindrical neck with applied, tooled lip; pontil mark. Blown in 2-part mold bearing inscriptions: on the obverse, "BY / THE / KINGS / ROYALL / PATENT / GRANT / ED TO"; on the reverse, "ROBT / TURLI / NGTON / FOR HIS / IN / VENTED / BALSOM / OF LIFE"; along one edge, "LONDON"; along the other, "JANY 26 1754."
H: 2¹¹⁄₁₆ in (6.8 cm); W: 1⅜ in (3.5 cm)
Museum purchase, 1975: Irvin and Dolores Boyd, Meetinghouse Antique Shop, Fort Washington, Pa. Funds for purchase, gift of the Claneil Foundation
75.224

Robert Turlington obtained a patent for his 27-ingredient panacea, The Balsam of Life, in 1744. It remained a popular—and costly —antidote on both sides of the Atlantic for nearly 100 years. One Philadelphia merchant had 2½ dozen Turlington's Balsam Bottles in stock at the time of his death in 1772; they were appraised for 1s. 6d. each. Francisco de Miranda provides an idea of the Balsam's healing powers. As his ship sailed out of Boston in 1784, "a great wave struck our pilot . . . leaving him with a contusion under the eye, which deprived him of his senses. (Fortunately he recovered the following day with a bit of Torlington which I had brought.)"[1]

After 1744 Turlington tried several different styles of bottles, then, spurred by unscrupulous people who bought empty bottles and "basely and wickedly put therein a vile spurious Counterfeit" formula, he settled on an angular style in 1754 that became the hallmark of his medicine. His action deterred no one, and the bottle was

pirated even into the twentieth century. Among glasshouses offering Turlington's bottles were South Boston, Dyottville, and Mount Vernon.[2]

Variations in the molds occur in the spelling of Balsam/Balsom, Royal/Royall, and in the date. NO. 332 probably dates from the second quarter of the nineteenth century.

1. Richard Parker inventory, 1772-133, Philadelphia County Probate Records (microfilm, Downs, WL); Francisco de Miranda, *The New Democracy in America: Travels of Francisco de Miranda in the United States, 1783–84*, trans. Judson P. Wood, ed. John S. Ezell (Norman: University of Oklahoma Press, 1963), p. 193.
2. For examples found in North American archaeological contexts, see Noël Hume, *Glass*, pp. 43–44, fig. 38–39; Jones and Smith, *British Military*, p. 96, fig. 115. For U.S. versions, see McKearin and Wilson, *American Bottles*, p. 292; C. Granger & Co., Mount Vernon Glass Works advertisement is reprinted in Harry Hall White, "New York State Glasshouses," pt. 2, *Antiques* 16, no. 3 (September 1929): 193, fig. 1.

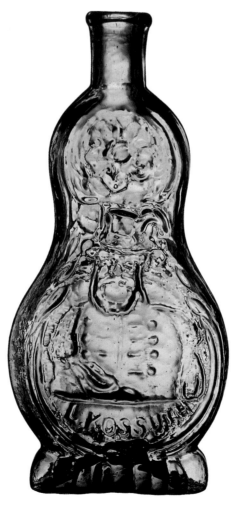

333

COLOGNE BOTTLE

UNITED STATES, CIRCA 1851–53

Aquamarine glass. Blown. Flattened violin-shape body with tall cylindrical neck tooled at lip, ribbed foot; pontil mark. Blown in 2-part mold with pictorial design: on the obverse, a bust portrait of Louis Kossuth, the inscription "L. KOSSUTH" curved below and a flower above his head; on the reverse, large oval panel with scroll ornament and stylized flower.
H: 5¹³⁄₁₆ in (14.8 cm); W: 2⅞ in (7.3 cm)
History: Philip Francis du Pont
Gift of Mrs. Harry W. Lunger, 1973
73.434

Decorative bottles of this size apparently held colognes and toilet waters of which there was a remarkable variety in the nineteenth century. Among them was Hungary water, which was perhaps the intended content of this particular bottle bearing the portrait of the Hungarian nationalist, Louis Kossuth. The major figure in the Hungarian uprising of 1848–50, Kossuth was released from imprisonment at the request of the United States government. He came to the U.S. in December, 1851, and for seven months toured the country in hopes of securing aid for his cause. Like other noted foreign visitors (see NOS. 276, 394), he was a target for immortalization in glass. Calabash-type liquor bottles (NO. 395) and rarer cologne bottles and sulphide paperweights were the principal commemoratives made for this visit.

Kossuth was not a celebrity universally admired. Many in Washington were disgusted by the "assumption and arrogance" displayed by the "great Behemoth of the Magyar race"— and were dismayed by the hotel bills that he and his entourage incurred at the expense of the United States government.[1]

1. Benjamin Perley Poore, *Perley's Reminiscences of Sixty Years in the National Metropolis*, 2 vols. (Philadelphia: Hubbard Brothers, 1886), 1:404–6.

Chapter 21
Wine and Other Round Bottles

334

WINE BOTTLE

ENGLAND, DATED 1726

Dark olive green nonlead glass. Blown. Squat globular body; tapered neck with applied, V-tooled string rim; conical push-up; pontil mark. Applied circular seal bearing inscription "John/DePeyster/1726."
H: 8 in (20.4 cm)
Museum purchase, 1960: The Old Print Shop, New York City
60.95

In England the wine bottle evolved from the globe-and-shaft form of the 1650s to the cylindrical bottle of the third quarter of the eighteenth century (NO. 336). The squat globular body of this bottle illustrates a stage in that process, here dated to 1726. Wine bottle was a generic term, for such bottles held porter, ale, beer, distilled liquors, fortified wines, and a variety of spirits.[1]

To personalize bottles a wafer or seal of glass was applied to the bottle and stamped in relief with a name, initials, or coat of arms and sometimes a date.[2] Dates on bottles were occasionally of commemorative significance rather than the date of manufacture, but because the shape of NO. 334 corresponds to other dated examples of the 1720s, the 1726 date probably does denote the year of manufacture.

Although seal bottles cost nearly one and one-half times unmarked bottles, many colonists owned them, as proved by archaeological as well as extant specimens.[3] Still, they represented but a fraction of the total number of such bottles shipped across the Atlantic.

Eighteenth-century American glasshouses made seal bottles in competition with the English imports. No mention of them is found in the extant records of the Wistarburgh factory in Salem County, New Jersey, but the bottle that bears the seal of proprietor Richard Wistar was undoubtedly blown there. In 1754 Thomas Lepper advertised on behalf of a New York City glassworks for "all Gentlemen that wants Bottles of any size with their Names on them," but no products of that factory have been identified.[4]

The original owner of NO. 334 was Johannes DePeyster (1694–1789), who married Anna Schuyler (1697–1750) and resided in Albany, where he served as mayor, city recorder, and commissioner of Indian affairs.[5]

1. Olive R. Jones, *Cylindrical English Wine and Beer Bottles, 1735–1850*, Studies in Archaeology, Architecture, and History (Ottawa: Environment Canada, National Historic Parks and Sites Branch, 1986), pp. 14–17.
2. The earliest datable English seal bottle (Corning Museum) was owned by Ralph Wormeley of Virginia who died in 1651; see Noël Hume, *Glass*, p. 34, fig. 23. Other dated seal bottles at Winterthur not included in this catalogue are as follows: 61.1332, dated 1719; 59.2969, dated 1750; 59.1978, dated 1774; 59.2970, dated 1789; 60.278, dated 1837; 65.2233, dated 1847.
3. In 1671 seal bottles cost 5s. per dozen while plain ones were 3s. 6d.; Sheelah Ruggles-Brise, *Sealed Bottles* (London: Country Life, 1949), p. 27. J. Paul Hudson, "Seventeenth-Century Glass Wine Bottles and Seals Excavated at Jamestown," *Journal of Glass Studies* 3 (1961): 78–89.
4. Palmer, "Glass Production," p. 86, fig. 6; the bottle is in the Corning Museum collection. Lepper advertisement, *New York Gazette*, November 18, 1754.
5. Waldron Phoenix Belknap, Jr., *The DePeyster Genealogy* (Boston: Privately printed, 1956), p. 33, pl. 5. An oil portrait of DePeyster (1718) is in the collection of New-York Historical Society.

335

WINE BOTTLE

ENGLAND, DATED 1739

Dark olive green nonlead glass. Blown. Octagonal body
with rounded shoulders; tall cylindrical neck with applied
V-tooled string rim; push-up; pontil mark. Applied
circular seal bearing a 6-point star above "-R-S-/1739."
H: 10⁹⁄₁₆ in (27.1 cm)
History: Alfred B. Maclay
H. F. du Pont purchase, 1945: Parke-Bernet Galleries, New
York City
59.1721

Published: Parke-Bernet Galleries, "Early American Bottles
and Flasks and Other Rare American Glass . . . Collected
by the Late Alfred B. Maclay," sale no. 644 (March 7–8,
1945), lot 463.

Blown in a mold of eight equal sides, this bottle
echoes the octagonal decanters that came into
vogue in England about 1730. As early as 1736

Christopher Pratt of Feversham was selling
quart-size, eight-square bottles from Newcastle
upon Tyne for 18s. per gross and pint-size versions at 16s. per gross. Two years later the stock
of Hoopers Glasshouse in Bristol included 46
dozen quart-size, eight-square bottles, valued
at 16d. per dozen, and 284 dozen pint-size
ones, valued at 14d. Dated examples and an
advertisement for Newcastle octagon bottles
prove that production continued into the
1770s. In Norway the form was manufactured
by the 1760s, but there is no evidence that
eight-square bottles were produced in the
American colonies.[1]

English green bottles were also shaped by
molds of eight unequal sides, creating a flatter,
more rectangular shape. Examples are known
with seals dated 1736, 1739, and 1745; others are
documented to the 1760s and 1770s. Merchant
John Greenhow, for example, owned bottles of
both eight-sided types, with seals dated 1769
and 1770.[2]

A bottle identical to NO. 335 is in the collection of Historic Deerfield; another was sold at
auction in 1990.[3]

1. Hughes, *Table Glass*, p. 278, pl. 210; Pratt advertise-
ment, *Kentish Post*, June 12, 1736, as quoted in Francis
Buckley, "Glasshouses on the Tyne in the Eighteenth
Century," *Journal of the Society of Glass Technology:
Transactions* 10 (1926):41; Hoopers inventory, collection
Bristol City Art Gallery; J. Stow's Bottle Warehouse
advertisement, *Ipswich Journal*, July 13, 1771, as quoted in
Buckley, *Old English Glass*, p. 51; Polak, "Illustrated
Price-List," p. 91.
2. Noël Hume, *Glass*, p. 36, figs. 27–28.
3. Christie, Manson and Woods, "English and
Continental Glass and Paperweights" (February 13,
1990), lot 30.

336

WINE BOTTLE

ENGLAND, DATED 1765

Olive green nonlead glass. Blown. Squat cylindrical body
with rounded shoulders, cylindrical neck with applied,
flattened string rim; push-up; pontil mark. Applied
circular seal bearing inscription "Sidney / Breese / 1765."
H: 11¼ in (28.7 cm)
H. F. du Pont purchase
65.2337

Exhibited: Minneapolis Institute of Arts, "The American
Craftsman and the European Tradition, 1620–1820," 1989.
Published: Palmer, "To the Good," p. 227, no. 84.

The cylindrical body and shorter neck are characteristic of midcentury production. The shape allows the binning of liquor bottles on their sides, which John Worlidge recommended in *Treatise of Cider* as early as 1676, "not only for preserving the Corks moist, but for that the Air that remains in the Bottle is on the side of the Bottle which it can neither expire, nor can new be admitted, the Liquor being against the Cork, which not so easily passeth through Cork as the Air."

Worlidge went on to write that "[s]ome [people] place their Bottles on a Frame with their noses downward for that end." Although this was probably an easier way to handle the globular-body bottles of that time, Worlidge did not find it a satisfactory method. There is little evidence, however, that bottles were commonly laid sideways until the mid eighteenth century when, by means of dip molds, they were blown in a cylindrical shape that would facilitate binning by this method. As explained by glass historian Olive Jones, the paraison is inserted through the top of the "mold, the bottle is blown and then withdrawn through the top of the mold. The mold may be in several parts but is not opened and shut during the blowing process. Dip molds form the body of the bottle and sometimes the base, but the shoulder neck, and finish and often the base were formed outside the mold."[1]

Sidney Breese (1709–67), the original owner, was a native of Wales who settled in New York City in 1730. He was a merchant who imported such English goods as looking glasses and fabrics.[2]

This is one of four bottles recorded bearing the Breese seal and date of 1765.[3] Although McKearin and Wilson have suggested that they were made in New York, no glasshouse was in operation there in 1765. Moreover, in color, thickness, empontilling, and finish the bottles are typical of English production. The only seal bottle documented to colonial American production, the RW bottle made at Wistarburgh, illustrates that with their wood-fired furnaces, colonial glasshouses could not make the thick-walled, dark green glass found in this and other bottles made in England's coal-fired furnaces. Moreover, the Wistar bottle has a

small pontil mark and a distinctive outward-folded lip that are not seen on NO. 336 or other English bottles.[4]

1. Worlidge quoted in Helen McKearin, "Notes on Stopping, Bottling and Binning," *Journal of Glass Studies* 13 (1971): 127; Olive Jones, "The Contribution of the Ricketts' Mold to the Manufacture of the English 'Wine' Bottle, 1820–1850," *Journal of Glass Studies* 25 (1983): 168–69.
2. *New-York Mercury*, June 1, 1761, as quoted in Rita Susswein Gottesman, *The Arts and Crafts in New York, 1726–1776: Advertisements and News Items from New York City Newspapers*, Collections of New-York Historical Society 69 (New York, 1938), pp. 133, 271. Sidney and Elizabeth Breese's great-grandson was Samuel Finley Breese Morse, artist and inventor.
3. Other examples are in Preservation Society of Newport County, Rhode Island; Los Angeles County Museum of Art; and Van Cortlandt Manor, New York. McKearin and Wilson, *American Bottles*, p. 204.
4. Palmer, "Glass Production," p. 86, figs. 6, 7.

337

WINE BOTTLE (ONE OF TWO)
BRISTOL, ENGLAND, HENRY
RICKETTS & CO., 1821–35

Dark olive green glass. Blown. Tall cylindrical body with rounded shoulders; tapering neck with down-tooled lip and string rim; push-up; basal ring bearing inscription "H. RICKETTS & CO. / GLASS WORKS BRISTOL"; blown in 3-part mold, the word "PATENT" around the shoulder. Applied circular seal bearing "W.M.C."
H: 10¹¹⁄₁₆ in (27.2 cm); Diam: 4¼ in (10.9 cm)
History: Philip Francis du Pont
Gift of Mrs. Harry W. Lunger, 1973
73.452.1 (mate is 73.452.2)

To achieve straight-sided bottles as well as those of square and octagonal shape, British glassmakers after 1730 used the dip mold technique. This process was revolutionized by Henry Ricketts of Bristol, who in 1821 took out a patent for an "improvement upon the construction of all moulds heretofore used in the manufacture of bottles," and an "entirely new method in the construction and operative movements and appendages of such moulds." Bottles blown with the aid of dip molds were by no means regular in shape or capacity; it was Ricketts's aim to form "nearly cylindrical" bottles, with "their height determined so as to contain given quantities or proportions of a wine or beer gallon measure, with a great degree of regularity or conformity to each other."[1]

The Ricketts patent involved a full-size, three-part mold consisting of a dip mold body part and two open-and-shut shoulder parts. The resulting mold seams ran horizontally around the shoulder and vertically up the neck. The patent also called for a mold to create a push-up in the bottom of the bottle and a removable letter plate for a basal manufacturer's mark.

Although the three-part mold was used in other branches of the glass industry, Ricketts apparently introduced the concept to bottle-making. He claimed his process would standardize capacities, but the interior measurements of the bottles could not be controlled, and capacities of Ricketts's bottles do, in fact, vary. Still, to this enterprising Bristol manufacturer must go the credit of changing the acceptable standards for the appearance of the wine bottle in England. His influence extended beyond British shores because at least nine American glassmakers in the 1840s came out with their own "patent" mold-blown bottles and marked them in a way similar to the Ricketts ones.[2]

1. Patent no. 4623, as quoted in Olive Jones, "The Contribution of the Ricketts' Mold to the Manufacture of the English 'Wine' Bottle, 1820–1850," *Journal of Glass Studies* 25 (1983): 167.
2. McKearin and Wilson, *American Bottles*, pp. 220–21.

338

BOTTLE

UNITED STATES OR EUROPE,
1830–50

Dark olive green nonlead glass. Blown. Body of barrel shape tapered at shoulder to cylindrical neck with down-tooled lip and string rim; patterned in 3-part mold of geometric design (McKearin G II-3): band of diamond diapering around shoulder; between plain horizontal bands are 4 panels of diamond diapering separated by plain vertical bands; diamond diapering below; plain bottom; pontil mark.
H: 5½ in (14.1 cm)
H. F. du Pont purchase, 1947: McKearins' Antiques, Hoosick Falls, N.Y.
59.3336

This rare mold-blown bottle features a geometric design similar to that seen in refined

tableware and decanters, but its finish is that of a wine or other utilitarian bottle. George McKearin attributed this bottle and another one like it to Keene Glass Works in New Hampshire.[1] That factory used three-part molds to make tablewares of unrefined glass, but NO. 338 is blown of an almost black-green glass, much darker than anything attributed to Keene. Moreover, the pattern itself is unrecorded except on these bottles. The lack of ribbing to outline the various panels and bands is aberrational in American three-mold patterns, so a foreign origin should not be dismissed.

1. The other is in McKearin and McKearin, *American Glass*, pl. 127, no. 3.

339

BOTTLE

PROBABLY NEW ENGLAND,
1780–1830

Olive green glass. Blown. Ovoid body tapered to tall cylindrical neck with applied lip; low push-up; pontil mark.
H: 5½ in (14.0 cm)
History: Philip Francis du Pont
Gift of Mrs. Harry W. Lunger, 1973
73.456.2

Bottles of the shape of NO. 339 were produced by numerous American glasshouses over a long period of time. New England glass factories of the federal period have been credited with most surviving examples. NO. 339 has a fairly small capacity, but the form occurs in very large sizes as well. These bottles were perhaps intended to hold such household liquids as vinegar and turpentine instead of serving as containers for alcoholic beverages.

340

BOTTLE

PROBABLY OHIO, 1815–45

Aqua glass. Blown. Spherical body with ridge around
shoulder formed by second gather; short cylindrical neck
with flaring, outward-folded lip; pattern-molded with 32
vertical ribs over 32 ribs swirled to right; applied disk foot;
pontil mark.
H: 4¾ in (12.1 cm); Diam: 3⁹⁄₁₆ in (9.1 cm)
History: Montague (?) collection
H. F. du Pont purchase, 1940: Neil C. Gest, Mechanicsburg, Ohio
59.3052

This is one of several similar bottles recorded,
although it is the only one without a handle.[1]
It is not known where these were made, but a
midwestern origin is likely because of the color
and pattern. The specific purpose of the bottle
is also unknown.

1. A handled example is at Corning Museum.

341–343, PL. 22

BOTTLES

OHIO OR WESTERN PENNSYLVANIA, 1820–50

NO. 341. Amber glass. Blown. Globular body; cylindrical neck with outward-folded lip; push-up; pontil mark.
H: 11¾ in (29.9 cm)
H. F. du Pont purchase, 1927: McKearins' Antiques, New York City
64.887

NO. 342. Aqua glass. Blown. Globular body; cylindrical neck with outward-folded lip; pattern-molded with 24 ribs swirled to right; push-up; pontil mark.
H: 7½ in (19.2 cm)
Gift of Charles van Ravenswaay, 1968
68.185

NO. 343. Amber-yellow glass. Blown. Globular body; tapering neck with outward-folded lip; pattern-molded with 24 ribs, dipped twice for a basket-weave effect; push-up; pontil mark.
H: 7⅝ in (19.5 cm)
Museum purchase, 1957: Neil C. Gest, Mechanicsburg, Ohio
57.132.2

Graceful globular bottles are characteristic of Ohio River valley production, although documented examples are unknown. Their brilliant colors and bold, pattern-molded designs relate to the tablewares associated with that region (for example, NOS. 118–20). Although plain bottles like NO. 341 were probably the most common, many pattern-molded bottles survive in collections today, especially ones with twenty-four ribs. Broken swirl or basket-weave examples are rare. The dating of these to the second quarter of the nineteenth century is confirmed by a remarkable aqua globular bottle with swirled ribs that has in its base the impression of an 1846 coin.[1]

1. John T. Gotjen, letter to the editor in "Notes," *Journal of Glass Studies* 24 (1982): 116.

Chapter 22
Case and Square Bottles

344

BOTTLE

CONTINENTAL EUROPE,
PROBABLY GERMANY, 1750–1800

Colorless nonlead glass; pewter. Blown. Rectangular body
with chamfered corners; rounded shoulders with ridge
formed by second gather; conical neck, the lip mounted
with pewter neck ring and screw top; low push-up; pontil
mark. Polychrome enamel-painted decoration: on one side
a heart above a standing bird; on the other, in script, "Herz
/ oben / vogel / unten."
OH: 6 in (15.4 cm); W: 2½ in (6.3 cm)
H. F. du Pont purchase
65.2276

This eight-sided form capped with pewter is
typical of central European glassmaking. Examples occur in colored glass, sometimes pattern molded in geometric designs. The form was
made from the seventeenth through the nineteenth centuries. The so-called half-post
method, whereby the second gather of glass is
clearly visible, is also typical of Continental production. It was a practice carried to American
factories by the many craftsmen who emigrated
from the Continent (NOS. 367, 368, 370, 372–79).

The exact purpose of these bottles is not
known, although the decoration and inscription
suggests NO. 344 had ornamental as well as functional value. Glasswares in this enamel-painted
style were long believed to have been made in
Manheim, Pennsylvania, but there is no documented example or written documentation to
support this idea (see NOS. 38–39).

345

CASE BOTTLE (ONE OF TWELVE)
EUROPE, 1775–1800

Dark olive green glass. Blown. Tall square bottle with four
flat sides tapered to base; rounded shoulders and short
cylindrical neck with applied V-tooled string rim;
push-up; pontil mark.
H (range): 9–9¾ in (23.0–24.8 cm); W base (range):
2½–2¾ in square (6.3–7.0 cm)
H. F. du Pont purchase
61.621.1 (mates are 61.621.2–.12)

Green case bottles, from pint to two-gallon capacities, were made square to fit in partitioned
wooden cases that held four to sixteen bottles.
Before about 1650 they were the only type of
wine bottle made in England, and excavations
of the earliest colonial settlements have yielded
numerous examples. Many seventeenth-century
ones were mounted with pewter or latten brass
screw caps.[1]

Inventory references to Danzig, Dutch, and
Holland cases of bottles imply that the Continent was the source of many case bottles used in
early America. Square case bottles made in the
Lowlands began to be imported into England in
quantity during the reign of James I.[2] This trade
may have continued after English manufacturers switched production at midcentury from
square bottles to the less difficult globular wine
bottle. That English glasshouses may have only
resumed the production of green case bottles in
the late 1760s, and did so at the instigation of
American merchants, is suggested by the correspondence between Ralph Carr, a merchant of
Newcastle upon Tyne, and his American customers. Carr wrote Philip Livingston of New
York in 1766:

> We have desir'd John Hodshon to send us
> one Bottle Case immediatly for as we have
> the best Glassmen in the world their can be
> no difficulty in their making the Bottles to
> fit the Cases & which will save the heavy
> duty upon foreign Glass.

In July Carr was able to report:

> We have also got the Square Bottles made
> which we hope will give Content, the mak-
> ers wanted to have Charged them at a good
> deal higher price for having never manufac-
> tured any before it took them much longer
> time, but as we buy Immense quantitys of
> their Goods we insisted upon having them
> at the price Mr. Hodshon says he pays by
> which you save the Enormous foreign duty

& there is no drawback. for the future you
can always order the Empty Cases to be
sent from Amsterdam.[3]

In the colonial era mold-blown case bottles
were made at Wistarburgh, Manheim, and
Germantown (now Braintree, Massachusetts),
all factories where German-trained craftsmen
were employed. A case-bottle mold was listed
in the 1752 inventory of Caspar Wistar's estate.

The popular association of green case
bottles with gin is supported to some extent by
period documentation. A Philadelphia estate
inventoried in 1764 included a case with 9
half-gallon bottles, 5 of them "full of Geneva
[gin]." Among the effects of another Philadelphia gentleman a few years later was "1 gin
case." The 1815 inventory of Pierre M.
LeBarbier DuPlessis included a "Gin Box with
12 Square Bottles," valued at $1.50. In the early
1800s John Innes Clark shipped 196 "empty
Gin cases" from Providence. Clark also sold
"Cordial Cases" empty as well as with 6 and 9
bottles, suggesting that cordials were also commonly stored in, and served from, case bottles.
At his death in 1757 Aaron Burr, president of
Princeton, owned a case with twelve bottles of
cordial water. The shipping records of Samuel
and William Vernon of Newport indicate that
cordials might include bordeaux brandy,
arrack, white Bengeracque, and "old
Margeaud."[4]

1. From one site in Martin's Hundred in Virginia, 108
bottles were found; see Ivor Noël Hume, *Martin's
Hundred* (New York: Alfred A. Knopf, 1982), p. 42. A case
bottle retaining its latten mount was excavated from a
seventeenth-century context at Flowerdew plantation;
Jane Towne to author, 1983. The 1674 inventory of Joseph
Pearce of Maryland included an "iron bound case wth 11
skrewed glass bottles" (Probate Records, Inventories and
Accounts, liber 1, fol. 364, Maryland Hall of Records,
Annapolis).
2. Eleanor S. Godfrey, *The Development of English
Glassmaking, 1560–1640* (Chapel Hill: University of North
Carolina Press, 1975), p. 228.
3. Carr to Livingston, March 3, July 10, 1766, Letterbook
of Ralph Carr, 1762–78, pp. 113, 115, Carr-Ellison Records,
Northumberland County Record Office, Newcastle upon
Tyne. Under the English excise tax regulations, exporters
received money back when they exported goods that had
been taxed.
4. Martin Ashburn inventory, 1764-59, William Wishart
inventory, 1768-171, and Pierre DuPlessis inventory,
1815-133, all Philadelphia County Probate Records
(microfilm, Downs, WL). Clark Invoice Book, p. 14, Burr
inventory, and Consignment of Samuel and William
Vernon for Bay of Honduras, September 23, 1766,
Downs, WL.

346

CASE BOTTLE SET (SEVENTEEN BOTTLES)

PROBABLY GERMANY OR BOHEMIA, 1780–1815

Colorless nonlead glass. Blown. Seventeen tall, straight-sided bottles of octagonal (1), hexagonal (4), triangular (8), and rectangular (4) cross-section; short cylindrical necks with ridge formed by second gather, everted lips; flat bases; ground pontil marks. Stoppers of solid glass, spherical form on tapered shaft. Each bottle has bands of shallow-cut ovals outlining shoulders and sides and large, abstract flowers; around the shoulders are gilded floral swags; gilded star on stopper.
OH (tallest): 12³⁄₁₆ in (31.0 cm); H (of bottle shown): 11½ in (29.2 cm)
H. F. du Pont purchase
57.841

NO. 346 demonstrates that colorless, glass case bottles were formed in a variety of shapes. Some cases were outfitted with drinking glasses, funnel and tray, in addition to bottles. Such sets could be found in homes but were mainly intended for the convenience of the traveler, as suggested by a New York merchant's advertisement for "Liquor cases with glasses and bottles for travelling." Indeed William Powell *was* traveling when his case bottle set was stolen in 1736: "On Monday, the 13th of February last was Stolen from on board a Cannoe lying at Stone's Bridge, a Holland's Case painted blue, about one Foot and a half square, there was in it 5 white Flint flowered case Bottles and one Canister with Sugar."[1]

Colorless case bottles were made in England, on the Continent, and in the United States. George Washington ordered an elegant English set in 1760.[2] Continental case bottles are typically blown of nonlead glass and have simple engraving or gilding. Often, as in NO. 346, they were made by the half-post method.

1. Harry Peters advertisement, *Daily Advertiser*, April 14, 1796, as quoted in Rita Susswein Gottesman, *The Arts and Crafts of New York, 1777–1799: Advertisements and News Items from New York City Newspapers*, Collections of New-York Historical Society 81 (New York, 1954), p. 101, no. 311; William Powell notice, *South Carolina Gazette*, March 13, 1735/6. This is a very early use of the term *flowered* to denote engraved decoration of floral design.
2. Washington's "Neat Mahogany Square Case with 16 Gall'n Bottles in ditto with ground Stoppers. Brass lifting handles & brass Casters" came from Philip Bell, London, and cost £17.17.0. It survives at Mount Vernon; see Christine Meadows, "The Furniture," *Antiques* 135, no. 2 (February 1989): 481–82.

347

CASE BOTTLE

FREDERICK COUNTY, MARYLAND,
ATTRIBUTED TO NEW BREMEN
GLASSMANUFACTORY OF JOHN
FREDERICK AMELUNG, DATED
1788

Colorless nonlead glass of gray tint. Blown. Square,
straight-sided body; rounded shoulders with ridge formed
by second gather; short cylindrical neck with everted lip;
flat base; pontil mark. Wheel-engraved decoration: on one
side, from a stylized ball and chain hangs a ring surrounding the inscription "B. Johnson / 1788"; 2 birds flank the
ball and stand upon a wreath that extends partly around
the ring.
H: 7⁵⁄₁₆ in (18.2 cm); W: 3⁹⁄₁₆ in (9.0 cm); D: 3⁷⁄₁₆ in (8.8 cm)
History: Col. Baker Johnson (1747–1811)
Museum purchase, 1973: James C. Brand, Morrilton, Ark.
73.357

Published: Lanmon and Palmer, "New Bremen," p. 57,
fig. 24b, c

This bottle is one of nine square or case bottles
that were made for Col. Baker Johnson of
Frederick, Maryland, who had a walnut case
fitted with partitions to hold the set.[1] Colorless
case bottles usually had glass stoppers (for example, NO. 346), but the Johnson ones were not
ground for stoppers and thus may have been
closed with corks.

The Johnson bottles are the only case
bottles that have been firmly associated with an
American glassworks of the eighteenth century.
Their attribution to the Amelung undertaking
is supported by the similarity of the engraving
to that on signed objects. The birds and date
numbers, for example, relate closely to those of
the Ghequiere tumbler (NO. 44); however, the
lettering is cruder and more angular than that
on other Amelung glasses.

Baker Johnson was the brother of Maryland's first governor, Thomas Johnson, to
whom the immigrant Amelung had brought a
letter of introduction. A prominent lawyer,
landowner, and promoter of American manufactures in western Maryland, Johnson had
interests in papermills, and ironworks—and
glasshouses that rivaled Amelung's establishment. Although the Johnsons doubtless hired
away some glassworkers from New Bremen,
their factories did not begin operation until
1792, so the New Bremen attribution for the
1788 set seems secure.

1. The case and eight bottles survive in various public and
private collections; see Lanmon and Palmer, "New
Bremen," pp. 56–57. James C. Brand to du Pont,
September 18, 1944, WM.

Chapter 23
Pocket Bottles

348–358, PLS. 5, 6, 15, 17

POCKET BOTTLES
MANHEIM, PENNSYLVANIA,
ATTRIBUTED TO GLASSWORKS OF
HENRY WILLIAM STIEGEL,
1769–74

NO. 348 (one of two). Light amethyst nonlead glass. Blown. Compressed spherical body with cylindrical neck; push-up; pontil mark.
H: 4⅝ in (11.8 cm); W: 3⅝ in (9.2 cm)
H. F. du Pont purchase, probably 1940: Neil C. Gest, Mechanicsburg, Ohio
59.3085 (mate is 59.3080)

NO. 349 (one of two). Amethyst nonlead glass. Blown. Compressed spherical body with tall cylindrical neck flared out at rim; pattern-molded with 20 vertical ribs to a circle on bottom; push-up; pontil mark.
H: 5⅜ in (13.7 cm); W: 3½ in (9.0 cm)
Museum purchase, 1951: Neil C. Gest, Mechanicsburg, Ohio. Funds for purchase, gift of H. F. du Pont
51.57 (mate is 59.3122)

NO. 350 (one of four). Amethyst nonlead glass. Blown. Compressed spherical body with cylindrical neck having an irregular rim; pattern-molded with rows of 12 "nipt" diamonds; push-up; pontil mark.
H: 5 in (12.7 cm); W: 3⅝ in (9.2 cm)
H. F. du Pont purchase
59.3155 (mates are 59.3090, 59.3123, 59.3134)

NO. 351. Blue nonlead glass. Blown. Compressed oval body with short cylindrical neck; pattern-molded with rows of 12 "nipt" diamonds; push-up; pontil mark. Pasted on one side is a paper label inscribed in ink "This bottle belonged to my maternal grandmother Rachel Ferm & contained Lavender water distilled by her. Darling Mother kept it during her life and her sister Rachel May was kind and gave it to me 5th mo 19 1878."
H: 5⅛ in (13.0 cm); W: 4 in (10.2 cm)
Museum purchase, 1979: Frank S. Schwarz and Son, Philadelphia. Funds for purchase partially supplied by Mrs. Harry W. Lunger in memory of Philip Francis du Pont
79.111

NO. 352 (one of two). Light amethyst nonlead glass. Blown. Compressed spherical body with cylindrical neck flared at rim; faintly pattern-molded with rows of 20 diamonds over probably 16 flutes; push-up; pontil mark.
H: 6 in (15.4 cm); W: 4⅛ in (10.5 cm)
H. F. du Pont purchase
59.3124 (mate is 59.3125)

NO. 353 (one of six). Deep purple nonlead glass. Blown. Compressed horseshoe-shape body with cylindrical neck; pattern-molded with rows of 28 ogival diamonds in honeycomb design above 28 ribs; push-up; pontil mark.
H: 5¼ in (13.4 cm); W: 3½ in (9.0 cm)
H. F. du Pont purchase
59.3081 (mates are 59.3082, 59.3084, 59.3099, 59.3129, 59.3138)

NO. 354 (one of thirteen). Amethyst nonlead glass. Blown. Compressed spherical body with cylindrical neck; pattern-molded with 2 rows of 5 large diamonds each containing 12-petal flower, above 30 ribs of varying heights; push-up; pontil mark.
H: 4¾ in (12.1 cm); W: 3½ in (9.0 cm)
H. F. du Pont purchase, possibly 1949: Neil C. Gest, Mechanicsburg, Ohio
59.3144 (mates are 59.3083, 59.3089, 59.3091, 59.3095, 59.3126, 59.3127, 59.3132, 59.3133, 59.3135, 59.3142, 59.3143, 59.3151)

NO. 355. Colorless nonlead glass. Blown. Compressed horseshoe-shape body, cylindrical neck; pattern-molded with 2 rows of 5 large diamonds each containing 12-petal flower, above 30 ribs of varying heights; push-up; pontil mark.
H: 4³⁄₁₆ in (10.7 cm); W: 3⅛ in (8.0 cm)
H. F. du Pont purchase, 1940: Edna M. Netter, Freehold, N.J.
59.3088

NO. 356. Light blue nonlead glass. Blown. Compressed spherical body with cylindrical neck; pattern-molded with 2 rows of 5 large diamonds each containing 12-petal flower, above 30 ribs of varying heights; push-up; pontil mark.
H: 5¼ in (13.4 cm); W: 3¾ in (9.5 cm)
History: found near McConnelville, Ohio
H. F. du Pont purchase, 1927: McKearins' Antiques, New York City
59.3131

Published: McKearin and Wilson, *American Bottles*, pl. 2.

NO. 357 (one of four). Light amethyst nonlead glass. Blown. Compressed oval body with cylindrical neck; pattern-molded with rows of 6 hexagons each containing 12-petal flower, above faint ribbing; push-up; pontil mark. Chipped below rim.
H: 6 in (15.4 cm); W: 4 in (10.2 cm)
History: found in Quakertown, Pa.
H. F. du Pont purchase, 1928: Neil C. Gest, Mechanicsburg, Ohio
59.3136 (mates are 59.3087, 59.3096, 59.3102)

Published: Neil C. Gest advertisement, *Antiquarian* 10, no. 6 (July 1928): 85.

NO. 358. Colorless nonlead glass. Blown. Compressed spherical body with cylindrical neck; pattern-molded with rows of 6 hexagons each containing 12-petal flower, above ribs of varying heights; push-up; pontil mark.
H: 5⅜ in (13.7 cm); W: 3⅞ in (9.8 cm)
History: Herbert Lawton
H. F. du Pont purchase, 1940: Neil C. Gest, Mechanicsburg, Ohio
59.3147

Published: Parke-Bernet Galleries, "Early American Furniture, Silver, and Paintings from the Collection of Herbert Lawton" (January 4, 1940), lot 33.

348

349

350

351

352

353

354

355

356

357

358

These pocket bottles represent the type of object that survives in largest number from the eighteenth-century American glass industry. The Winterthur collection alone includes thirty-seven; another sizeable cache is at Philadelphia Museum of Art.

The so-called diamond-daisy design (NOS. 354–56) is the most common, but plain flasks (NO. 348) and daisy-in-hexagon examples (NOS. 357, 358) are extremely rare. The majority are of amethyst glass; blue and colorless examples are rarely seen. NO. 356 is the only recorded diamond-daisy example in blue. Spectrographic analysis of the Winterthur and Philadelphia collections has revealed a remarkable homogeneity of composition.[1] Furthermore, close examination of the defects in the molded designs has shown that there was probably only one mold used for each pattern, which in turn suggests that a single manufacturer could have been responsible for the entire group of bottles. That manufacturer is believed to have been Henry William Stiegel. It is not known who supplied molds for his Manheim glassworks, but given Stiegel's other career as an ironmaster, the molds might have been made under his direct supervision.

The concept of decorative pocket bottles is rooted in Continental traditions. Floral molded patterns, not unlike the diamond-daisy and daisy-in-hexagon patterns, were made in South Germany and Bohemia in the eighteenth century.[2] The inspiration for those designs may have been cut floral motifs, common to case bottles, which were typically large scale and daisylike in detail (NO. 346). Many European bottles were blown by the half-post method, but, curiously, none of this group of American bottles exhibits this trait, even though immigrant German workmen probably made them. Continental flasks are generally flatter and wider than these, which are of fairly uniform size and have a distinctive puffy profile.

The attribution to the Stiegel factory is based on several factors. For the first five years of his business, Stiegel employed only German-trained workmen and produced primarily green

bottles and window glass. When nonimportation agreements in response to the Townshend duties of 1767 effectively removed English glass from the market, Stiegel revamped his factory to manufacture fine glass in the English style, and he hired English glassblowers and technicians. The exact nature of Stiegel's first American flint glass is uncertain: although some glass may have been blown entirely from remelted English lead-formula cullet, other refined and colored ware may have been made of nonlead formula glass. Only in 1771 was the factory able to produce lead glass from raw materials. In spite of the new English orientation of the Manheim works in its final years, 1769 to 1774, the German glassblowers continued to blow glass and doubtless drew on their native traditions for inspiration. It is in the cross-fertilization of English and German traditions that the unique character of Stiegel glass is apparent.[3] As essentially Continental forms made of refined nonlead glass, a result of the interest in English technology, these pocket bottles perhaps best illustrate the ongoing influence of the German workers. A list of products blown at Manheim between November 1769 and May 1770 includes 6,251 flint glass pocket bottles. That the list mentioned no common or green glass implies that the pocket bottles were blown of refined glass, and NOS. 348 to 358 may well represent that particular output of 1769–70.

Of the many pocket bottles that survive, only one has a history to the eighteenth century. Molded in the diamond-daisy design, the amethyst bottle bears diamond-point initials of its original owner, Elizabeth Shinn Armstrong (1748–1813) of Medford, New Jersey, who married John Tours Armstrong in 1764. The bottle descended in her family.[4]

The exact function of such bottles is problematical. The examples from the Armstrong and Ferm families were filled with camphor and lavender water in the nineteenth century, yet pocket bottles in eighteenth-century records are clearly linked with alcoholic beverages. The pocket or "half pint flat Dram Bottles" sold by merchant Thomas Tisdale were "suitable to carry the comfort of life into the field."[5]

1. For example the potassium/calcium ratios are consistent —roughly 2:1—and the bottles contain barium but no traces of either antimony or arsenic, the last typically occurring in German and Bohemian glass.
2. Palmer, "To the Good," pp. 230–31, no. 88. A flask molded in the diamond-daisy pattern is part of a collection of Venetian glass that has been at British Museum since 1860.
3. Palmer, "To the Good."
4. In the collection of Los Angeles County Museum of Art, see Leslie Greene Bowman, "An Engraved Stiegel Pocket Bottle," *Glass Club Bulletin*, no. 147 (Fall 1985): cover, pp. 3–5.
5. Tisdale advertisement, *Connecticut Courant*, June 21, 1790, quoted in Wilson, *New England Glass*, p. 28.

359

POCKET BOTTLE

PROBABLY CZECHOSLOVAKIA, 1915–30

Amethyst, bubbly nonlead glass. Blown. Flattened pear-shape body with cylindrical neck; pattern-molded with rows of 6 large diamonds each containing 12-petal flower, above 24 ribs of varying heights; push-up; pontil mark. Chipped neck.
H: 6 in (15.4 cm); W: 4 in (10.2 cm)
H. F. du Pont purchase, before 1939
59.3113

The dates at which du Pont acquired some rare mold-blown pocket bottles (for example, NOS. 356, 357) indicate the early passion of collectors for these wares. F. W. Hunter had featured the form in his 1914 book on Stiegel, and high prices soon followed: for the blue diamond-daisy (NO. 356) du Pont paid McKearin $2,250 in 1927. Such demand in the antiques marketplace encouraged the unscrupulous, and NO. 359 seems to be a fake intended to deceive.

When he inventoried the Winterthur collection in 1939, Neil Gest noted the "unique size and shape" of this bottle. It is pear-shape and flatter than the other flasks, lacking completely the characteristic puffy quality of the fifteen others in the pattern. The color has a decided pinkish caste, quite unlike the usual amethyst, and the glass is extremely bubbly. Although the diamond-daisy bottles at Winterthur and more than sixty others examined in other collections seem to have been blown from the same mold, exhibiting the same defects in the molded pattern, this bottle is of a completely different pattern, having six rather than five diamonds and twenty-four instead of thirty ribs below. When analyzed spectrographically, the bottle was shown to have an unusual composition.[1]

It is not known where NO. 359 was made. Czech glassmakers may have been responsible because they are known to have reproduced many types of glass that were popular collector's items in the early twentieth century. Curiously, however, no other examples from this mold have come to light. Other reproduction diamond-daisy flasks were blown in three-part molds with visible mold seams.

1. Its potassium level is roughly half of that found in authentic pocket bottles; Analytical Laboratory, Winterthur Conservation.

360, 361, PL. 5

POCKET BOTTLES

UNITED STATES, POSSIBLY NEW BREMEN GLASSMANUFACTORY OF JOHN FREDERICK AMELUNG, 1770–1800

NO. 360 (one of two). Pale amethyst nonlead glass. Blown. Large flattened oval body with short cylindrical neck; pattern-molded with rows of 8 large diamonds, each containing 4 ogival diamonds; push-up; pontil mark.
H: 6¾ in (17.3 cm); W: 5 in (12.8 cm)
H. F. du Pont purchase, 1948: Joe Kindig Antiques, York, Pa.
59.3008 (mate in darker amethyst is 59.3145)

Published: McKearin and McKearin, *Two Hundred Years,* pl. 1.
McKearin and Wilson, *American Bottles,* color pl. 2.

NO. 361. Blue nonlead glass. Blown. Compressed spherical body with cylindrical neck; pattern-molded with rows of 7 large diamonds, each containing 4 smaller ogival diamonds; push-up; pontil mark.
H: 5⅛ in (13.1 cm); W: 4¼ in (10.8 cm)
History: James Gabell
Museum purchase, 1952: Neil C. Gest, Mechanicsburg, Ohio. Funds for purchase, gift of H. F. du Pont
52.277

Published: McKearin and McKearin, *American Glass,* pl. 31, no. 6.

362

POCEKT BOTTLE

UNITED STATES OR

CONTINENTAL EUROPE, 1925–45

Colorless glass. Blown. Compressed spherical body with
short cylindrical neck; pattern-molded with rows of 7
large diamonds each containing 4 ogival diamonds;
push-up; pontil mark. Cracked.
H: 5 in (12.7 cm); W: 3⅞ in (9.8 cm)
History: from a Cincinnati collection
H. F. du Pont purchase, 1949: Neil C. Gest,
Mechanicsburg, Ohio
59.3130

Because fragments of this so-called checkered-
diamond pattern were excavated from the
site of Amelung's New Bremen glassworks,
NOS. 360, 361, and related salts (NO. 227) have
been attributed to that factory. The only presentation flask documented to New Bremen has a
narrow ovoid body with the puffiness of the
Stiegel-attributed pocket bottles (NOS. 348–58);
the flasks here are flatter and rounder. Unlike
the diamond-daisy and daisy-in-hexagon patterns associated with Manheim, the checkered-
diamond design is well known in European
production, and fragments of the pattern have
been found at Grünenplan, a German glassworks where Amelung had worked.[1]

Checkered-diamond flasks are recorded in
colorless and olive green as well as amethyst
and blue.[2] More than one glasshouse probably
made the pattern because as Winterthur's examples demonstrate, two different molds were
used, one with eight diamonds and one with
seven. (Salts were patterned in a seven-diamond
mold.)

The reproduction, NO. 362 blown of a very
clear glass, does not follow the shape of period
flasks. Its checkered-diamond pattern conveys
the effect of quatrefoils rather than diamonds.

1. Ivor Noël Hume, "Archaeological Excavations on the
Site of John Frederick Amelung's New Bremen Glassmanufactory, 1962–1963," *Journal of Glass Studies* 18 (1976):
185. The presentation flask, dated 1792, is shown in
Lanmon and Palmer, "New Bremen," pp. 72–73. An amber
example of South German origin is in Gustav E. Pazaurek,
"A German View of Early American Glass," pt. 1, *Antiques*
21, no. 4 (April 1932): 165, fig. 4. A ca. 1840 Norwegian
example is shown in Arnstein Berntsen, *En samling norsk
glass* (Oslo: Gyldendal Norsk Forlag, 1962), pl. 4, 336a.
2. A yellow-green one is shown in McKearin and
McKearin, *American Glass*, pl. 231, no. 4; another is in the
Billups collection, New Orleans Museum of Art, see
Corning Museum, *A Decade of Collecting* (Corning, N.Y.,
1962), p. 42, no. 66. A colorless one at Corning Museum
is pictured in Lanmon and Palmer, "New Bremen,"
pp. 118–19.

363

POCKET BOTTLE

UNITED STATES, 1800–1840

Colorless nonlead glass. Blown. Flattened oval body with tall cylindrical neck; pattern-molded with rows of 17 diamonds; push-up; pontil mark.
H: 5¹¹⁄₁₆ in (14.6 cm); W: 3¾ in (9.7 cm)
History: Philip Francis du Pont
Gift of Mrs. Harry W. Lunger, 1973
73.450.2

With its elongated body this flask represents a later version of the Stiegel type of pattern-molded bottle. The expanded diamond pattern offers no clue as to origin, but the shape and plain lip point to American rather than European manufacture.

364

POCKET BOTTLE

UNITED STATES, 1920–30

Pale amethyst lead glass. Blown. Flattened oval body with cylindrical neck having an irregular rim; pattern-molded with rows of 15 diamonds; push-up; pontil mark.
H: 6 in (15.4 cm); W: 4⅛ in (10.5 cm)
History: Prince Cantacuzene
H. F. du Pont purchase, probably 1949: McKearins' Antiques, Hoosick Falls, N.Y.
59.3086

Published: Parke-Bernet Galleries, "Early American Glass Bottles and Flasks, Collected by Prince Cantacuzene," sale no. 1001 (November 5, 1948), lot 136.

Pocket bottles molded with rows of fifteen diamonds were made in the nineteenth-century glasshouses of western Pennsylvania and Ohio, but this flask exhibits several characteristics that place it firmly in the twentieth century. Its pontil mark is a large and messy blob of glass inconsistent with the workmanship of the early period. The same excrescence is seen on other questionable glasswares, notably a related flask at Corning Museum and another ribbed flask formerly at Winterthur (see entry for NOS. 369–71). The difficulty the blower experienced in shearing the lip evenly is paralleled on some of the Mutzer group of spurious blown three-mold glass.[1] McKearin offered this flask to du Pont and claimed he had owned it nearly twenty years before (circa 1928), pushing the date of its manufacture into the 1920s. A similar flask sold at auction in 1942.[2]

1. Lanmon, Brill, and Reilly, "Suspicions," p. 166, fig. 31; p. 169, fig. 38.
2. McKearin to du Pont, December 13, 1949, WM; Parke-Bernet Galleries, "Early American Glass Collection of William W. Wood, 3d," sale no. 338 (January 22–23, 1942), lot 311.

365

POCKET BOTTLE

ENGLAND, POSSIBLY BRISTOL,

DATED 1806

Violet-blue lead glass. Blown. Flattened ovoid body with tall cylindrical neck; tooled lip; push-up; pontil mark. Gilded decoration: horizontal rings and leafy band around neck; on one side, in script, "Elizabeth / Morrys / 1806" above branches; on the other side, "Joseph / Morrys / 1806" above crossed branches.
H: 6⅛ in (15.6 cm); W: 3⅛ in (8.0 cm)
History: Philip Francis du Pont
Gift of Mrs. Harry W. Lunger, 1973
73.470

This presentation flask is typically English in its ovoid shape, tooled lip, rich blue color, and formal, gilded decoration. There was a strong tradition of gilded blue glass in Bristol. Isaac Jacobs, whose signature appears on numerous blue glasswares with gilding, opened Non-such Flint Glass Manufactory in Bristol in 1805.[1] Other glassmakers doubtless produced similar ware.

1. Witt, Weeden, and Schwind, *Bristol Glass*, p. 10.

366

POCKET BOTTLE

UNITED STATES OR ENGLAND,

1790–1825

Light green glass. Blown. Ovoid body with cylindrical neck flared at rim; pattern-molded with 12 vertical ribs; push-up; pontil mark.
H: 6½ in (16.5 cm); W: 2⅞ in (7.4 cm)
History: Philip Francis du Pont
Gift of Mrs. Harry W. Lunger, 1973
73.449.1

Narrow, pattern-molded bottles or vials, presumably of English manufacture, have been excavated from colonial American sites. They continued to be made into the nineteenth century by glasshouses on both sides of the Atlantic, but their exact function is unknown.[1]

1. Keith Vincent, *Nailsea Glass* (London: David and Charles, 1975), p. 51, fig. 44; Dr. Thomas Williams site, Historic Deerfield, Mass., has yielded such bottles. Collectors often describe them as nursing bottles.

365

366

367, 368

POCKET BOTTLES

NEW ENGLAND, 1800–1840

NO. 367. Olive green glass. Blown. Flattened spherical body; ridge around shoulder formed by second gather; cylindrical neck; pattern-molded with 32 fine ribs swirled to right in nearly horizontal design; push-up; pontil mark.
H: 6¾ in (17.2 cm); W: 5⅛ in (13.1 cm)
History: Philip Francis du Pont
Gift of Mrs. Harry W. Lunger, 1973
73.442.1

NO. 368. Yellow-green glass. Blown. Narrow horseshoe-shape body; ridge around shoulder formed by second gather; crooked cylindrical neck; pattern-molded with 36 vertical ribs over 36 ribs swirled to right; push-up; pontil mark.
H: 5⁵⁄₁₆ in (13.5 cm); W: 3⅜ in (8.5 cm)
History: Philip Francis du Pont
Gift of Mrs. Harry W. Lunger
73.440.4

Long known to collectors as Pitkins, pocket bottles with fine swirled ribbing were made throughout the United States; indeed, there is no proof that the Pitkin family manufactured them at their East Hartford, Connecticut, factory.[1] Examples with the shapes and colors of NOS. 367 and 368 are associated with New England factories, and bottles of broader body and other colors apparently originated in the Ohio River valley. Unlike eighteenth-century molded flasks and most nineteenth-century diamond-molded ones, Pitkins are usually fashioned by the half-post method, where a second layer of glass falls short of the full length of the first gather or post.

1. McKearin and Wilson, *American Bottles*, p. 328.

369–371

POCKET BOTTLES

OHIO OR WESTERN

PENNSYLVANIA, 1815–45

NO. 369. Yellow-amber glass. Blown. Compressed spherical body with cylindrical neck; pattern-molded with 24 ribs; pontil mark.
H: 4¾ in (12.1 cm); W: 3¾ in (9.6 cm)
History: Philip Francis du Pont
Gift of Mrs. Harry W. Lunger, 1973
73.448.1

NO. 370. Olive green nonlead glass. Blown. Flattened spherical body; ridge around shoulder formed by second gather; cylindrical neck; pattern-molded with 30 vertical ribs; push-up; pontil mark.
H: 6¼ in (15.9 cm); W: 5⅟₆ in (12.9 cm)
History: Philip Francis du Pont
Gift of Mrs. Harry W. Lunger, 1973
73.449.2

367

368

NO. 371. Pale green glass. Blown. Flattened oval body with cylindrical neck flared at rim; pattern-molded with 18 ribs swirled to right; push-up; pontil mark.
H: 6⅛ in (15.7 cm); W: 4¼ in (10.8 cm)
Gift of Charles van Ravenswaay, 1968
68.191

NOS. 369–71 represent a common style of flask made in midwestern glasshouses during the first half of the nineteenth century. The ribbed and swirl-rib patterns complement broad shapes typical of Ohio-area production. Historians have tried to associate the molds, identified by the number of ribs, with specific factories, but this is based largely on amateur excavations of Ohio glasshouse sites undertaken by Harry Hall White in the 1920s and 1930s.[1]

The ribbed example above is a spurious flask, relating most closely to these genuine midwestern examples but posing as a Stiegel-type when it came to Winterthur. Found in a small town in Virginia, the flask was the only teal green example Neil Gest had seen. Its brilliant color is one of the trouble signs because it was simply not made in the early glasshouses of America. H. F. du Pont's suspicions may have been aroused, but the rarity of the piece made

him want to believe in it: "It strikes me that the green flask is not quite as good a quality as we might expect from Stiegel, and I am afraid the color is a bluer green than the few pieces of glass I have." "Due to the uncertainty of this color harmonizing well in [his] cabinet," he did not want to pay top dollar. Still, he paid Gest $2,000 for it. Besides its unusual color (also seen in a spurious bowl), the flask differs markedly in its proportions from genuine flasks.[2] The lack of wear on the bottom is further indication of its lack of age.

1. See Francis J. Puig, "A Recent Accession: The Douglas Collection of Ohio Glass at the Minneapolis Institute of Arts," *Glass Club Bulletin*, no. 149 (Spring 1986): 12–16.
2. Du Pont to Gest, May 4, 1931; Gest to du Pont, May 5, 1931, WM. The flask is missing from Winterthur. The bowl is in McKearin and McKearin, *American Glass*, pl. 31, no. 7.

369

370

371

372–379

POCKET BOTTLES

PROBABLY OHIO OR WESTERN PENNSYLVANIA, 1815–45

NO. 372. Green bubbly glass. Blown. Elongated, horseshoe-shape body; ridge around shoulder formed by second gather; cylindrical neck; pattern-molded with 16 vertical ribs over 16 ribs swirled to left; push-up; pontil mark.
H: 7¼ in (18.5 cm); W: 4¼ in (10.9 cm)
History: Philip Francis du Pont
Gift of Mrs. Harry W. Lunger, 1973
73.439.2

NO. 373. Green nonlead glass. Blown. Flattened spherical body; ridge around shoulder formed by second gather; tall cylindrical neck; pattern-molded with 36 vertical ribs over 18 ribs swirled to left; push-up; pontil mark.
H: 6 in (15.2 cm); W: 5 in (12.8 cm)
History: Philip Francis du Pont
Gift of Mrs. Harry W. Lunger, 1973
73.444

NO. 374. Olive green, bubbly nonlead glass. Blown. Compressed oval body; ridge around shoulder formed by second gather; tall cylindrical neck; pattern-molded with 24 vertical ribs over 24 ribs swirled to right; push-up; pontil mark.
H: 6⅞ in (14.3 cm); W: 4½ in (9.5 cm)
History: Philip Francis du Pont
Gift of Mrs. Harry W. Lunger, 1973
73.446.1

NO. 375. Amber glass. Blown. Compressed spherical body; ridge around shoulder formed by second gather; cylindrical neck; pattern-molded with 30 vertical ribs over 30 ribs swirled to right; push-up; pontil mark.
H: 6⁹⁄₁₆ in (16.7 cm); W: 4¹³⁄₁₆ in (12.3 cm)
History: Philip Francis du Pont
Gift of Mrs. Harry W. Lunger, 1973
73.441.1

NO. 376. Pale aqua nonlead glass. Blown. Flattened pear-shape body; ridge around shoulder formed by second gather; short cylindrical neck; pattern-molded with 31 vertical ribs over 31 ribs swirled to right; push-up; pontil mark.
H: 6⅝ in (16.9 cm); W: 4¹⁵⁄₁₆ in (12.6 cm)
History: Philip Francis du Pont
Gift of Mrs. Harry W. Lunger, 1973
73.447.2

372

373

374

NO. 377. Aqua glass. Blown. Flattened spherical body; ridge below shoulder formed by second gather; tall cylindrical neck; pattern-molded with 32 vertical ribs over 32 ribs swirled to right; low push-up; pontil mark.
H: 7⅛ in (18.1 cm); W: 5 in (12.7 cm)
History: Philip Francis du Pont
Gift of Mrs. Harry W. Lunger, 1973
73.438.2

NO. 378. Amber-yellow, bubbly nonlead glass. Blown. Compressed spherical body; ridge around shoulder formed by second gather; wide short cylindrical neck; pattern-molded with 36 vertical ribs over 36 ribs swirled to right; push-up; ring-shape pontil mark.
H: 6³⁄₁₆ in (15.8 cm); W: 4⁹⁄₁₆ in (11.7 cm)
History: Philip Francis du Pont
Gift of Mrs. Harry W. Lunger, 1973
73.440.2

NO. 379. Olive green glass. Blown. Flattened spherical body; ridge below shoulder formed by second gather; cylindrical neck; pattern-molded with 38 vertical ribs over 38 ribs swirled to right; push-up; ring-shape pontil mark.
H: 6⅝ in (16.8 cm); W: 4⁵⁄₁₆ in (11.0 cm)
History: Philip Francis du Pont
Gift of Mrs. Harry W. Lunger, 1973
73.445

Using dip molds to achieve a basket-weave effect was an ancient technique. In the colonies, it was practiced at Wistarburgh, established by Caspar Wistar in southern New Jersey in 1739.[1] This broken-swirl decoration continued to be used by bottlemakers throughout the United States in the first half of the nineteenth century. As discussed in NOS. 367 and 368, certain differentiations in color and shape have been linked with eastern or western regions. Excavation of fragments of similar flasks in amber, aqua, and green from the site of an early New Jersey glassworks suggests that regional attributions should be made with considerable caution.[2]

375

376

377

NOS. 372 through 379, a selection from the collection formed by Philip Francis du Pont (1878–1928) and donated to Winterthur in 1973 by his daughter, Mrs. Harry W. Lunger, were chosen to illustrate the range of molds and colors. The collection includes several decorated in unusual molds, such as ones with thirty-one ribs (NO. 376) and thirty-eight ribs (NO. 379).

1. A green glass sugar bowl in the Newark Museum has the same basket-weave effect, see Palmer, "Glass Production," p. 91, fig. 16.
2. "Gloucester Glass Works, Clementon, New Jersey, circa 1800–1825," *Journal of Glass Studies* 10 (1968): 191–93.

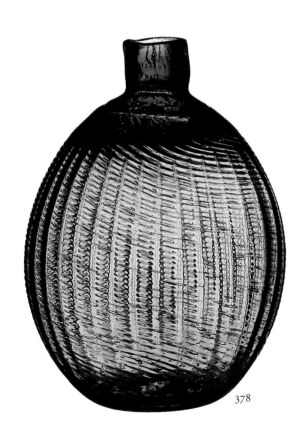

378

379

380

POCKET BOTTLE
PROBABLY SCANDINAVIA,
1810–40

Deep blue lead glass. Blown. Flattened spherical body with cylindrical neck; pattern-molded with 18 vertical ribs over 18 ribs swirled to right; pontil mark. Repaired rim chip.
H: 6⅛ in (15.7 cm); W: 5 in (12.8 cm)
History: Warner J. Steele collection, donated to Philadelphia Museum of Art in 1937 and deaccessioned in 1954
Museum purchase, 1970: Frank P. Ewing Antiques, Wilmington, Del.
70.438

NO. 380, rather wider and flatter than Ohio flasks, is probably the product of a Scandinavian glassworks. Its lack of proper footing is uncharacteristic of American bottles, and the herringbone effect of its patterning is associated with continental European style.[1] Although lead glass was blown in several Ohio factories, the midwestern pocket bottles are generally nonlead. Lead glass was made in Scandinavia in the nineteenth century.

1. Arnstein Berntsen, *En samling norsk glass* (Oslo: Gyldendal Norsk Forlag, 1962), pl. 24, no. 452.

381, 382

POCKET BOTTLES
UNITED STATES, 1820–45

NO. 381. Pale blue lead glass. Blown. Flattened oval body with tall tapering neck; patterned in 3-part mold of geometric design (McKearin G III-24): vertical ribbing around neck above horizontal ring and diagonal ribbing; a band of diamond diapering within horizontal rings; below are 9 large diamonds each containing a sunburst, with diagonal ribs in between; vertical ribbing around base below horizontal ring; rayed bottom (type IV); pontil mark.
H: 5¹³⁄₁₆ in (14.8 cm); W: 4 in (10.2 cm)
Museum purchase, 1958: James H. Rose and Earl Knittle
58.86

383

NO. 382. Colorless lead glass. Blown. Flattened spherical body with cylindrical neck; patterned in 3-part mold of geometric design (McKearin G III-23): diagonal ribbing around the shoulder within horizontal rings; wide band of diamond diapering; between horizontal rings are 9 large diamonds each containing a sunburst, with diagonal ribs in between; vertical ribbing around base; rayed bottom (type VI-A); push-up; pontil mark, iron oxide residue.
H: 5½ in (14.1 cm); W: 4⅛ in (10.6 cm)
H. F. du Pont purchase, before 1942: probably Charles Woolsey Lyon, New York City
59.3196

Examples of pocket bottles blown in three-part molds of geometric patterns are exceedingly rare, especially in blue. With their band of large diamonds containing large sunburst or stylized floral design, the G III-23 and -24 patterns are curiously reminiscent of the Stiegel-type diamond-daisy bottles (NOS. 354–56). Both NO. 381 and another blue one in the Garvan collection at Yale were found in Ohio, but New England is the more probable place of manufacture.

FIGURED FLASK
PORTUGAL, ATTRIBUTED TO
VISTA ALEGRE GLASSWORKS,
CIRCA 1829

Green, very bubbly nonlead glass. Blown. Ovoid body with wide cylindrical neck; blown in 2-part mold: on one side, a diamond pattern in oval panel surrounded by beads; on the other, 5 rows of 4-point stars in oval panel surrounded by grapevine motif; paneled edges; pontil mark.
H: 6½ in (16.5 cm); W: 3 in (7.6 cm)
History: Philip Francis du Pont
Gift of Mrs. Harry W. Lunger, 1973
73.433.1

This flask provides evidence of the foreign production of figured flasks because the design is shown in the 1829 illustrated trade catalogue of Vista Alegre Glassworks in Portugal.[1] The glass-

works had opened in 1824 and produced a wide range of utilitarian and table products.

This flask differs from American examples in the poor quality of the glass, in the narrow ovoid body, and in the style of the design. While this flask would not be mistaken for American production, Vista Alegre did make close imitations of a design attributed to Keene Glass Works (NO. 385). The factory also produced lead glass tablewares of the same mold-blown geometric designs that were made in New England (see NO. 99).

1. Vasco Valente, *O Vidro em Portugal* (Pôrto: Portucalense Editora, 1950), p. 83.

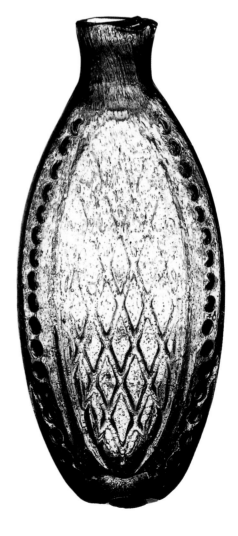

384

FIGURED FLASK

KEENE, NEW HAMPSHIRE, KEENE
GLASS WORKS, 1815–30

Olive green glass. Blown. Half-pint flask of rectangular
body with rounded shoulders and short, waisted neck
flared at rim; blown in 2-part mold (McKearin G VIII-10):
on each side, a sunburst with rays emanating from central
oval bearing inscription "KEEN"; horizontal ribbing down
edges; pontil mark.
H: 5⅞ in (15.0 cm); W: 3³⁄₁₆ in (6.1 cm)
History: Philip Francis du Pont
Gift of Mrs. Harry W. Lunger, 1973
73.423.4

385

FIGURED FLASK

NEW ENGLAND, POSSIBLY KEENE
GLASS WORKS, 1815–17

Green lead glass. Blown. Pint flask of angular body,
hollowed shoulders rising to thick cylindrical neck;
blown in 2-part mold (McKearin G VIII-3): an oval
sunburst on each side; horizontal ribbing down edges,
shoulders, and across neck; pontil mark.
H: 8¼ in (20.9 cm); W: 4½ in (11.4 cm)
History: Philip Francis du Pont
Gift of Mrs. Harry W. Lunger, 1973
73.423.7

386

FIGURED FLASK
WILLIAMSPORT, PENNSYLVANIA,
WILLIAMSPORT GLASS WORKS OF
WILLIAM IHMSEN, 1820–30

Light green nonlead glass. Blown. Pint flask of horseshoe-shape body with cylindrical neck; blown in 2-part mold (McKearin G II-10): on one side, "w. IHMSEN S" inscribed in a semicircle above an American eagle with wings raised, perched on oval panel inscribed "GLASS"; on the other, a sheaf of wheat above agricultural implements; vertical rib down edges; pontil mark.
H: 6¹⁵⁄₁₆ in (17.6 cm); W: 4⁷⁄₁₆ in (11.2 cm)
History: Philip Francis du Pont
Gift of Mrs. Harry W. Lunger, 1973
73.412.2

387

FIGURED FLASK
CAMBRIDGE, MASSACHUSETTS,
NEW ENGLAND GLASS COMPANY
OR NEW ENGLAND GLASS
BOTTLE COMPANY, 1818–30

Light green glass. Blown. Pint flask of rectangular body with rounded shoulders and tall cylindrical neck; blown in 2-part mold (McKearin G IV-27): on one side, Masonic archway and emblems; on the other, below a banner is an American eagle with wings partly raised, above an oval panel inscribed "NE/CO"; vertical rib down edges; pontil mark.
H: 7⅞ in (20.0 cm); W: 4¼ in (10.8 cm)
Museum purchase, 1982: W. M. Schwind, Jr., Antiques, Yarmouth, Maine. Funds for purchase, gift of Mrs. Harry W. Lunger
82.322

388

FIGURED FLASK
COVENTRY, CONNECTICUT,
COVENTRY GLASS WORKS,
CIRCA 1825

Olive green nonlead glass. Blown. Pint flask of
rectangular body with rounded shoulders and cylindrical
neck; blown in 2-part mold (McKearin G I-80): on one
side, a profile bust of DeWitt Clinton with "ᴅᴇ ᴡɪᴛᴛ
ᴄʟɪɴᴛᴏɴ" inscribed in arc above and "ᴄᴏᴠᴇɴᴛʀʏ" in
semicircle below around the letters "C-T"; on the other, a
profile bust of Lafayette with "ʟᴀꜰᴀʏᴇᴛᴛᴇ" in semicircle
above, horizontal bar and "T.S." below; horizontal
ribbing around shoulders and down edges; pontil mark.
H: 7⅝ in (19.4 cm); W: 4¼ in (10.8 cm)
History: Philip Francis du Pont
Gift of Mrs. Harry W. Lunger, 1973
73.405.2

389

FIGURED FLASK
PHILADELPHIA, KENSINGTON
GLASS WORKS OF THOMAS W.
DYOTT, CIRCA 1826

Pale aqua nonlead glass. Blown. Pint flask of horseshoe-
shape body with cylindrical neck; blown in 2-part mold
(McKearin G I-94): on one side, a large three-quarter
bust of Thomas W. Dyott inscribed in arc above, "T.W.
Dyott, M.D." surrounded by inscription, "ᴋᴇɴsɪɴɢᴛᴏɴ
ɢʟᴀss ᴡᴏʀᴋs ᴘʜɪʟᴀᴅᴇʟᴘʜɪᴀ"; on the other, three-
quarter bust of Benjamin Franklin surrounded by
inscription, "ᴡʜᴇʀᴇ ʟɪʙᴇʀᴛʏ ᴅᴡᴇʟʟs ᴛʜᴇʀᴇ ɪs ᴍʏ
ᴄᴏᴜɴᴛʀʏ"; vertical rib down edges; pontil mark.
H: 6¾ in (17.1 cm); W: 4⁹⁄₁₆ in (11.7 cm)
History: Philip Francis du Pont
Gift of Mrs. Harry W. Lunger, 1973
73.407.1

390

FIGURED FLASK

BALTIMORE, POSSIBLY
BALTIMORE FLINT GLASS WORKS,
1828–34

Light blue nonlead glass. Blown. Quart flask of
horseshoe-shape body with narrow cylindrical neck;
blown in 2-part mold (McKearin G I-21): on one side, a
profile bust of George Washington with "FELLS"
inscribed above and "POINT" below; on the other,
Baltimore's Washington Monument minus the statue;
vertical rib down edges; pontil mark.
H: 8¼ in (20.9 cm); W: 5⅝ in (14.3 cm)
History: Philip Francis du Pont
Gift of Mrs. Harry W. Lunger, 1973
73.400.1

391

FIGURED FLASK

ZANESVILLE, OHIO, SLIGO GLASS
WORKS OF THOMAS MURDOCK
AND JOSEPH CASSEL,
1832–CIRCA 1837

Blue-green, bubbly nonlead glass. Blown. Pint flask of
horseshoe-shape body with short cylindrical neck; blown in
2-part mold (McKearin G X-14): on one side, "ZANESVILLLE"
inscribed in semicircle above "OHIO" above bands of
diagonal and vertical ribbing; on the other, "MURDOCK" in
arc above "&/CASSEL," above diagonal and vertical ribbing;
vertical rib down edges; ring-shape pontil mark.
H: 6⅝ in (16.8 cm); W: 4⅛ in (10.4 cm)
History: Charles B. Gardner
Museum purchase, 1975: Robert W. Skinner Auctions,
Bolton, Mass. Funds for purchase, gift of Mrs. Harry W.
Lunger
75.192

392

FIGURED FLASK

BALTIMORE, BALTIMORE GLASS WORKS, 1840–50

Deep olive yellow nonlead glass. Blown. Pint flask of flattened oval body with tall cylindrical neck; blown in 2-part mold (McKearin G VI-3): on one side, Baltimore's Battle Monument with "BALTIMORE" in arc above; on the other, "LIBERTY / & / UNION" in straight lines; pontil mark. H: 6¾ in (17.1 cm); W: 4¾ in (11.9 cm)
History: Charles B. Gardner
Museum purchase, 1975: Robert W. Skinner Auctions, Bolton, Mass. Funds for purchase, gift of Mrs. Harry W. Lunger
75.193

393

FIGURED FLASK

BALTIMORE, BALTIMORE GLASS WORKS, 1847–48

Pale aqua nonlead glass. Blown. Pint flask of elongated horseshoe-shape body with tall cylindrical neck tooled at rim; blown in 2-part mold (McKearin G I-75): on one side, a profile bust of Zachary Taylor, inscribed above in arc "ZACHARY TAYLOR" and "ROUGH & READY" below; on the other, tall corn stalk with "CORN FOR THE WORLD" inscribed in arc above; pontil mark. H: 7⁷⁄₁₆ in (18.3 cm); W: 4⁷⁄₁₆ in (11.3 cm)
History: Philip Francis du Pont
Gift of Mrs. Harry W. Lunger, 1973
73.408.4

394

FIGURED BOTTLE

EVESHAM TOWNSHIP, BURLINGTON COUNTY, NEW JERSEY, MILFORD GLASS WORKS OF W. C. LIPPINCOTT & CO., 1850–53

Aqua nonlead glass. Blown. Quart bottle of calabash form; globular body with tall tapering neck and outward-folded, down-tooled lip; blown in 2-part mold (McKearin G I-101): on one side, a three-quarter bust of Jenny Lind within a wreath and inscribed "JENNY LIND" in arc above; on the other, glasshouse with smoking chimney, inscribed in arc above, "MILLFORA. G. WORK'S"; pontil mark.
H: 9⅞ in (25.1 cm); W: 5¹³⁄₁₆ in (14.8 cm)
History: Philip Francis du Pont
Gift of Mrs. Harry W. Lunger, 1973
73.428.1

395

FIGURED BOTTLE

PROBABLY PHILADELPHIA, KENSINGTON VIAL AND BOTTLE WORKS OF SHEETS AND DUFFY, CIRCA 1853

Amber-yellow glass. Blown. Quart bottle of calabash form; ovoid body with tall tapering neck and outward-folded, down-tooled lip; blown in 2-part mold (McKearin G I-112): on one side, a frigate with "S. HUFFSEY" inscribed on upper arc of paddle wheel and "U.S. STEAM FRIGATE / MISSISSIPPI / S. HUFFSEY" in

lines below; on the other, full bust of Louis Kossuth, inscribed "LOUIS KOSSUTH" in pointed arc above; broad flutes along edges; on the bottom, an oval with the legend, "PH. DOFLEIN / NTH. 5.TS.T 84" and "MOULD MAKER."; pontil mark with iron oxide residue.
H: 10½ in (26.7 cm); W: 5⅝ in (14.3 cm)
History: Philip Francis du Pont
Gift of Mrs. Harry W. Lunger, 1973
73.429.2

Published: Arlene Palmer Schwind, "The Glassmakers of Early America," in *The Craftsman in Early America*, ed. Ian M. G. Quimby (New York: W. W. Norton, 1984), pp. 187–88, figs. 11, 12.

396

FIGURED FLASK

LOUISVILLE, KENTUCKY,

LOUISVILLE GLASS WORKS,

1855–73

Aqua glass. Blown. Quart flask of flattened pear-shape body with cylindrical neck; blown in 2-part mold (McKearin G IX-6): on one side, 2 large 6-point stars above heart-shape scrolls framing the inscription "LOUISVILLE KY"; on the other, the same except inscribed "GLASS WORKS"; pontil mark.
H: 9 in (23.0 cm); W: 5½ in (14.0 cm)
Museum purchase, 1982: W. M. Schwind, Jr., Antiques, Yarmouth, Maine. Funds for purchase, gift of Mrs. Harry W. Lunger
82.321

397

FIGURED FLASK

PITTSBURGH, 1860–75

Aqua nonlead glass. Blown. Pint flask of rectangular body with rounded shoulders and cylindrical neck with string rim; blown in 2-part mold (McKearin G XI-9): on one side, a figure of a walking prospector, the inscription "FOR PIKE'S PEAK" above his head and "OLD RYE" below; on the other, an American eagle above an oval containing the inscription, "PITTSBURGH PA"; pontil mark.
H: 7⅝ in (19.5 cm); W: 4¼ in (10.8 cm)
Gift of Charles van Ravenswaay, 1968
68.199

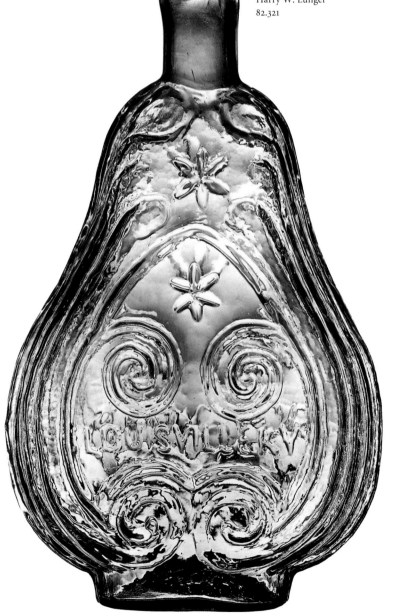

398

FIGURED FLASK

UNITED STATES, 1860–70

Green nonlead glass. Blown. Half-pint flask of rectangular body with rounded shoulders and tall cylindrical
neck; blown in 2-part mold (McKearin G XIV-9): on one
side, "TRAVELER'S" in semicircle above "COMPANION" in
straight line; on the other, "RAILROAD" in arc above
"GUIDE" in straight line; pontil mark.
H: 6¼ in (15.9 cm); W: 3⁵⁄₁₆ in (8.5 cm)
History: Philip Francis du Pont
Gift of Mrs. Harry W. Lunger, 1973
73.437.2

399

FIGURED FLASK

PITTSBURGH, FRANKSTOWN

GLASS WORKS OF WILLIAM

FRANK & SONS, 1866–74

Aqua nonlead glass. Blown. Pint flask of wide rectangular body with rounded shoulders and tall cylindrical
neck with string rim; blown in 2-part mold (McKearin
G XII-39): on one side, framed by leafy branches are
clasped hands upon a shield below a row of stars and
"UNION," and below, on an oval, the inscription
"W FRANK & SONS PITT."; on the other, a cannon next
to a flagpole with the United States flag; pontil mark.
H: 7⅞ in (20.1 cm); W: 4¼ in (10.8 cm)
Gift of Charles van Ravenswaay, 1968
68.198

400

FIGURED FLASK

BALTIMORE, BALTIMORE GLASS WORKS, CIRCA 1870

Amber-yellow nonlead glass. Blown. Pint flask of rectangular body with rounded shoulders, cylindrical neck and down-tooled lip with string rim; blown in 2-part mold (McKearin G XIII-54): on one side, a phoenix rising from flames above "RESURGAM"; on the other, "BALTIMORE" and "GLASSWORKS" in banners from top and bottom of an anchor; pontil mark.
H: 7⅞ in (20.1 cm); W: 3¹¹⁄₁₆ in (9.4 cm)
Gift of Mr. and Mrs. Donald Carpenter, 1974
74.14

Published: Arlene Palmer Schwind, "Some Notes on Baltimore Bottles," *Glass Club Bulletin,* no. 130 (Summer 1980): 7, fig. 2.

401

FIGURED FLASK

BALTIMORE, MARYLAND, MARYLAND GLASS WORKS OF JOHN L. CHAPMAN, 1850–62

Aqua, bubbly nonlead glass. Blown. Half-pint flask of rectangular body with rounded shoulders and tall cylindrical neck flared at lip; blown in 2-part mold (McKearin G XIII-9): on one side, figure of man dancing on board floor with "CHAPMAN." on panel below; on the other, a seated banjo player with "BALT. MD." on panel below; pontil mark.
H: 6⁵⁄₁₆ in (16.2 cm); W: 3⅜ in (8.6 cm)
History: Philip Francis du Pont
Gift of Mrs. Harry W. Lunger, 1973
73.432.3

NOS. 384 through 401 represent an important facet of bottle production in American glasshouses of the nineteenth century.[1] Known in the period as "figured flasks," these liquor bottles were blown in 2-part molds the designs of which provide an excellent index to popular taste of the time. A number of the earliest flasks carried simple geometric designs of classical inspiration that reflect broader currents in the arts (NOS. 384, 385). The importance of patriotic symbols is demonstrated by the proliferation of eagle flasks (NOS. 386, 397). NO. 387 clearly conveys the strong Masonic involvement of the American citizenry. Local pride is seen in bottles from the glasshouses of Baltimore that feature the famous Battle Monument and Washington Monument (NOS. 390, 392). The elegant "Resurgam" flasks of the Baltimore Glass Works celebrate one company's revitalization after a

disastrous fire (NO. 400).[2] Mold-blown flasks made after the Civil War feature designs relating to westward expansion (NOS. 397, 398). The usual genre scenes of the Chapman flask (NO. 401) apparently depict African-Americans and may have been derived from sheet music covers. For example, the song "Jim along Josey," published in 1840, shows a black boy dancing on a plank floor.

The portrait flasks produced in the United States are reminiscent of the head flasks of ancient Rome. Instead of mythological subjects, however, they honor both historical heroes and contemporary celebrities. Not surprisingly, George Washington's was the face most often rendered in glass; the philosophical ties the country felt with the ancient world are evident in his toga-clad likeness on NO. 390. Other heroes of the day who were toasted in glass included Mexican War heroes such as Gen. Zachary Taylor (NO. 393). Gov. DeWitt Clinton, famed for his vision in opening the Erie Canal, is paired in NO. 388 with Lafayette, the French hero of the American Revolution whose triumphant return in 1824–25 spawned a new era in souvenir goods. Other European celebrities who took the States by storm in the 1850s, Swedish singer Jenny Lind and Hungarian revolutionary Louis Kossuth, were also commemorated in liquor bottles (NOS. 394, 395). One glass manufacturer thought fit to immortalize his own likeness: Thomas W. Dyott, self-proclaimed doctor and entrepreneur, shares a flask with Benjamin Franklin (NO. 389).

Little is known about the moldmakers who were responsible for these designs or the process by which glassmakers chose designs for their flasks. NO. 395 is one of the few bottles that is documented to a particular moldmaker. Philip Doflein was a moldmaker in Philadelphia from 1842 to 1899. Recent research indicates that he was probably also responsible for the mold in which the Jenny Lind bottle (NO. 394) was blown.[3]

Many flasks are documented with a manufacturer's mark or place of manufacture, proving that glasshouses from New Hampshire to Kentucky were involved in the business. Unmarked flasks are often attributed to the same

factories responsible for marked examples of the pattern. It is just as possible, however, that other glasshouses, wanting to pirate a competitor's design, would produce unsigned versions. Fragments unearthed at factory sites have also offered a basis for attributions, but considering how cullet was recycled, such attributions must be made cautiously. Janice Carlson's study of the chemical compositions of Winterthur's pictorial flask collection suggests that spectrographic data can aid in determining a flask's manufacturer. Among other things, Carlson discovered only four bottles in the collection that had a high (30 to 40 percent) lead content.[4] This indicates that those factories had some connection with fine tableware production. NO. 385, previously attributed to Coventry Glass Works, where only bottles and utilitarian wares were made, should perhaps be reassigned to the glasshouse in Keene, where a bottle business succeeded a flint glass factory (see NOS. 52, 53). Wilson has attributed other lead glass flasks of related design to Keene.[5]

Figured flasks were produced in tremendous quantity; in one advertisement Dyott mentions he has 3,000 gross (432,000) flasks with his portrait.[6] Dyott prided himself on the fact that his was an alcohol-free company, even as he earned his living from the weakness of others. The temperance movement was gaining great strength throughout the nineteenth century, but as the number and variety of figured flasks suggest, America's thirst continued unabated.

1. For a complete discussion of American figured flasks, their production, use, design sources, etc., see McKearin and Wilson, *American Bottles*. A listing of other figured flasks at Winterthur is included in Appendix 2.
2. Arlene Palmer Schwind, "Some Notes on Baltimore Bottles," *Glass Club Bulletin*, no. 130 (Summer 1980): 6–8.
3. Edwin AtLee Barber, *American Glassware* (Philadelphia: David McKay Co., 1900), p. 79; Barber interviewed Doflein in 1896. See Miriam E. Mucha, "Solving the Mystery of Two Altered American Bottle Molds," *Journal of Glass Studies* 26 (1984): 111–19. Doflein probably added glass dealer Huffsey's name to his original Kossuth bottle mold about 1853 when the Milford Glassworks closed and Huffsey was able to acquire some of their molds.
4. Janice H. Carlson, "Compositional Characteristics of Some American Blown Glasswares" (November 1976), copy on deposit, WL.
5. Wilson, *New England Glass*, pp. 162–63.
6. Dyott advertisement, *United States Gazette*, March 3, 1825, as cited in Helen McKearin, *Bottles, Flasks and Dr. Dyott* (New York: Crown Publishers, 1970), p. 37.

Miscellaneous

402

SHEET OF CROWN GLASS
REDFORD, NEW YORK, REDFORD
GLASS COMPANY, 1831–51

Colorless glass of greenish tinge. Blown. Large circular disk tapering in thickness from about 4 inches in the center, where the pontil mark is located.
Diam: 46 in (117.0 cm)
H. F. du Pont purchase, after 1931: McKearins' Antiques, Hoosick Falls, N.Y.
56.520

In the eighteenth and nineteenth centuries, window glass was made either by the crown or by the cylinder method. Crown glass was the more desirable and more expensive type. In this process, about ten pounds of molten glass was gathered on the blowpipe and marvered and blown to form a flattened globe resembling a crown. The pontil rod was attached to the flat side opposite the blowpipe, then the glassblower cracked off the blowpipe, leaving a small opening. The glassmaker gradually enlarged the orifice through successive reheating and spinning until centrifugal force caused the crown to open into a disk. As explained in a period manual,

> the workman, taking great care to preserve, by a regular motion, the circular figure of the glass, proceeds to whirl it round with increasing velocity, until the aperture, now diminished to a ring of only a few inches diameter, suddenly flies open with a loud ruffling noise, like the rapid unfurling of a flag in a strong wind, and leaves the glass a circular plane or sheet, of from four to four and half feet diameter, of equal thickness throughout, except at the point called the bullion, or bull's eye, where it is attached to the iron rod.[1]

The 75¢ scrip issued by Redford Glass Company illustrates this phase of production. After annealing, the circular sheets, sometimes known as tables, could be cut into rectangular or square panes of desired sizes. The central pane with the bull's eye was popularly installed in transom windows over doors.

Before the Revolution, American glasshouses made window glass only by the cylinder technique, which was more familiar to the German craftsmen who dominated the industry. In that process, glass was blown and shaped to form a hollow cylinder. The cylinder was slit, put on an iron shovel, and placed in a special oven where the heat enabled the workman to flatten it.[2] Cylinder glass was more even in thickness than crown glass, but the metal shovels created an often unsightly rippling of the glass surface.

Crown glass from the factories of London and Bristol was imported for the windows of the finest colonial buildings. In 1781, while war was still raging, Robert Hewes built America's first crown glass factory in Temple, New Hampshire. It lasted only a short time, but Hewes immediately planned a new venture in Boston. Crown glass was apparently not made there, however, until 1796. Other crown glassworks came and went, and by 1831, when the Redford factory opened in New York, there was only one other glasshouse in the United States actively engaged in the manufacture of crown glass, viz. New England Crown Glass Factory near Boston. By contrast, twenty-three cylinder glass factories were in operation.[3]

Early in 1831 two Troy, New York, businessmen, Gershom Cook and Charles W. Corning, purchased land for a glassworks in Clinton County at a place on Saranac River known as Red Ford. From the record of the land transactions it is clear that Champlain Glass Works across Lake Champlain in Burlington, Vermont, was connected with the undertaking. Hezekiah Niles corroborated this when he noted that the Redford factory had "originated" in the one at Burlington.[4] John S. Foster, who had been superintendent of the Champlain works since it opened in 1827, came to Redford to oversee the construction and operations of the glasshouse. When it was incorporated as the Redford Glass Company in 1832, Foster was named as an owner along with Gershom Cook, Gurdon Corning, and Charles W. Corning. Production began in October 1831. During its first full year of operation, Redford Glass Company manufactured $78,000 worth of glass. Foster left in the spring

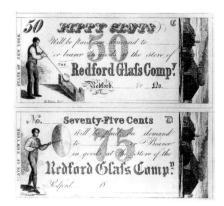

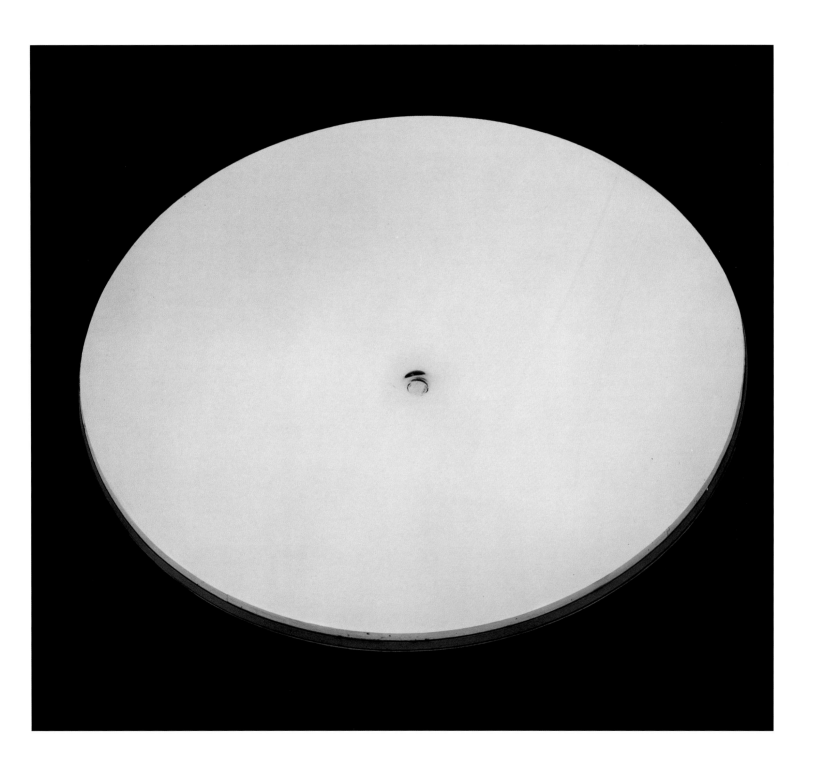

of 1833 and started a rival venture in Jefferson County that he named Redwood, perhaps out of spite. At Redford, glassmaking continued under the management of Noah H. Lund and several different proprietors. The glasshouse shut down in 1843, reopened in 1846, and closed permanently in 1851.[5]

According to Niles, the Redford products were "equal to those of the crown glass, of Boston." Judges of the manufacturing fairs of the American Institute in New York City awarded medals to Redford for the best crown glass exhibited in 1835 and subsequent years. Charles Goff, New York City agent for the factory between 1836 and 1844, described in an advertisement the two grades of crown glass then made at Redford:

> The Redford or first quality, is used throughout the United States and the Canadas, in all the first class of public and private buildings, also for Show Cases, Bow Windows, &c. It is called for in all Government contracts for Light Houses, Barracks, Rope Walks and Ship Houses; as its great thickness gives it an advantage over all thin Glass, so apt to crack by contraction in cold weather. Its surface not being polished after being blown, retains its enamel, lustre and hardness, and is not liable to the objection which applies to Plate Glass, of being easily and permanently bedimmed by dust. It being all of *extra thickness*, will, without injury, with-stand violent winds, hail storms, jars of cannon, &c., and its use in the end will prove most economical, independent of its adding so much to the beautiful appearance of all edifices. The Saranac, or second quality Redford, being stouter and stronger than any other Crown Glass in market, and 33⅓ per cent cheaper than the first quality, is in great request for Stores, Steam Boats, Canal Boats, Rail Road Cars and Green Houses. It is a most admirable article for Stores and Factories, where common thin Glass so soon gets broken.[6]

The company credited local white flint sand for the properties and qualities of their product. By 1850 the firm was offering three grades of extra-thick crown window glass measuring about ⅛ inch thick: a box of 100 panes of six-by-four-inch size cost $5.00 for grade A, $4.00 for grade B, and $3.00 for grade C. They also made a "new style" crown glass that was thinner, measuring a little over 1/16 inch thick, and ranging in price from $4.00 to $2.50.[7]

According to the advertisements, Redford's window glass adorned well-known buildings throughout North America. The first quality could be seen in New York at the Exchange on Wall Street, the Custom House, and the Astor House hotel. In Philadelphia first-quality Redford panes were installed in Girard College. According to the advertisement, North Carolina's capitol building as well as "all the Public Buildings at Washington" were fitted with the best Redford product. The Saranac quality could be seen in New York at Centre Market on Grand Street, Howard's Hotel on Broadway, and the Institution for the Blind. Among the numerous architects who attested to the quality of Redford glass were Robert Mills, Thomas U. Walters, and Ithiel Town. That Redford glass did enjoy the Canadian market as claimed is indicated by a notice in the *British American Journal*, placed by William Williams, Redford agent in St. Catherine's. In 1834 he notified the public that he had on hand, "all sizes of Crown Window Glass, of superior quality at the factory prices."[8]

Winterthur's remarkable uncut sheet, or table, of crown glass was once the gable window of the Benjamin Vaughan house, some fifteen miles from Redford on the highway between Plattsburgh and West Plattsburgh. Set into an

octagonal frame, the sheet was probably installed about 1840 when the house was enlarged. In 1931 Albert Banker, who then owned the house, sold the glass to "a New York antique dealer" for $500. When H. F. du Pont acquired it from George McKearin, he used it at Winterthur as a skylight on the eighth floor. In this he followed the suggestion of colonial glazier Obadiah Wells of New York, who in 1746 advertised "large Ball Eyes for Sky lights."[9] In addition to a smaller crown disk, the Winterthur collection also includes a sash window composed of small bull's-eye panes that supposedly came from the enclosed porch of the Redford Glass Company house, which was fitted with 182 such panes.

1. William Cooper, *The Crown Glass Cutter and Glazier's Manual* (Edinburgh: Oliver and Boyd, 1835), pp. 32–33. Crown glass sheets generally thicken gradually toward the central bull's eye.
2. For an illustration of the cylinder process, see Denis Diderot, "Manufacture des Glaces Souffleés," in *Recueil de Planches, sur les sciences, les arts libéraux, et les arts méchaniques, avec leur Explication* (Paris: Briasson, David, le Breton, 1765), 3: pls. 34–38.
3. *Address of the Friends of Domestic Industry, Assembled in Convention, at New-York, October 26, 1831, . . .* (Baltimore, 1831), pp. 125–26.
4. *Niles' Weekly Register* 42, no. 1072 (April 7, 1832): 90–91.
5. Information on the history of the Redford factory has been gleaned from the following sources: Warner McLaughlin, "A History of the Redford Crown Glass Works at Redford, Clinton County, N.Y.," in "New York State Antiques," ed. Janet R. MacFarlane, *New York History* 26, no. 3 (July 1945): 368–76. Harold A. Boire, "Redford—Rare American Glass," *Antiques* 68, no. 2 (August 1955): 135–39; "Redford Glass," *Antiques Journal* 11, no. 9 (September 1956): 10–13, 21. Clinton County Historical Museum, *Reflections: The Story of Redford Glass* (Plattsburgh, N.Y.: Clinton County Historical Association, 1979).
6. Charles Goff, "American Crown Window Glass," ca. 1843, Museum of American Glass at Wheaton Village, Millville, N.J.
7. M. Lane and Co., "Redford Glass Company's Prices Current of Crown Window Glass," Redford, N.Y., October 1850, Museum of American Glass at Wheaton Village.
8. Lane, Corning, and Suydam advertisement, *Globe* (Washington, D.C.), September 30, 1841; *British American Journal* (St. Catherine's, Ontario), June 17, 1834, reference courtesy of Janet Holmes.
9. "Dealer Pays $500 for One Pane of Glass," *Plattsburgh Daily Republican*, January 19, 1931; Allan S. Everest, *Pioneer Homes of Clinton County, 1790–1820* (Plattsburgh, N.Y.: Clinton County Historical Association, 1966); Wells advertisement, *New York Evening Post*, March 31, 1746.

403

WINDOWPANE

PITTSBURGH, BAKEWELL, PEARS, AND COMPANY, 1835–55

Colorless lead glass. Pressed. Rectangular slab; on one side, a relief design of wide Gothic window, with rosettes in the top, containing 3 double-arch sections with each arch topped with a rosette. Upper arches filled with rows of circles; a notched horizontal band below; lower arches filled with alternating rows of plain and stippled diamonds; above window are rosettes and scrolls with stippling in between; a row of beads outline the long sides of the pane. On the reverse smooth surface in the center is "BAKEWELL" in relief.
L: 6¹⁵⁄₁₆ in (17.6 cm); W: 4¹⁵⁄₁₆ in (12.6 cm)
Museum purchase, 1959: Patton's Antiques Shop, Duncansville, Pa.
59.23

This Gothic revival pane is one of several styles of pressed-glass windowpanes that bear the mark of Benjamin Bakewell's Pittsburgh firm. Other decorative panes were made and marked by Curling, Robertson, and Company in Pittsburgh and John and Craig Ritchie in Wheeling.[1]

In 1836 Bakewell advertised "pressed Panes for steam boats," but their intended location on those vessels is not clear. What pressed panes have survived from this period have emerged from furniture and door frames, found from Indiana to West Virginia. When he offered this pane to Winterthur, Gerald Patton informed Charles Montgomery that it was one of several he had found "mounted in pine frames." Two examples, one at Corning Museum and the other at Metropolitan Museum of Art, came out of a secretary desk from a home near Wheeling.[2]

The Gothic taste that was popular in the middle decades of the nineteenth century was expressed in cut, mold-blown, and pressed glass (for example, NO. 97).[3] Among the many other pressed-glass forms recorded in this style were salts, covered bowls, compotes, and lamps. The pointed arch was the characteristic emblem of the style in all media, but the idea of rendering an intricate Gothic window in miniature in a form that was itself part of a larger window was particularly ingenious. The clarity and precision of the design underscore the considerable skill of Bakewell's moldmakers.

1. Innes, *Pittsburgh Glass*, pp. 282–86.
2. Knittle, *Early American Glass*, p. 309; James H. Rose, "Lacy Glass Window Panes: Their Use, Process, and Origin," *Antiques* 51, no. 2 (February 1947): 120–21; Innes, *Pittsburgh Glass*, p. 284, fig. 303, no. 2, illustrates the Metropolitan Museum of Art example; Spillman, *Pressed Glass*, p. 72, no. 171.
3. Katherine S. Howe and David B. Warren, *The Gothic Revival Style in America, 1830–1870* (Houston: Museum of Fine Arts, 1976).

404

PESTLE OR LINEN SMOOTHER
PROBABLY ENGLAND, 1750–1800

Dark olive green, bubbly nonlead glass with amber striae. Tooled. Solid stem composed of 5 flattened ball knops, applied U-shape disk on top; applied disk base; smooth bottom.
H: 4⅞ in (12.4 cm); Diam base: 3¹³⁄₁₆ in (9.6 cm)
Museum purchase, 1956: Carl and Celia Jacobs, Southwick, Mass.
56.75.1

This curious glass object is often described as a linen smoother, and with its smooth, rounded base it could also have been used to spread out fine fabrics for darning. No period references to glass linen smoothers are known, but among the glasswares advertised by a Philadelphia merchant in 1776 were "sleek stones for silk stockings."[1]

Another possibility is that NO. 404 was designed as a pestle. An 1830 print, "The Apothecary," shows a similar object functioning in that way.[2] Whatever its purpose, its solid construction of sturdy bottle glass assured the object would survive hard use. Certainly the multiknopped stem afforded a good grip for the hand with the thumb resting comfortably in the top groove.

Examples like Winterthur's have been found in excavations of English glasshouses of the sixteenth and seventeenth centuries. One excavated from the Jamestown, Virginia, settlement is probably of English manufacture, but the form was made elsewhere in Europe.[3] In North America, glass mortars and pestles were manufactured as early as 1775.[4]

1. Joseph Stansbury advertisement, *Pennsylvania Evening Post*, April 30, 1776.
2. "The Apothecary"(Downs, WL) printed by E. Madeley and published by T. McLean, London.
3. R. J. Charleston, "The Vessel Glass from Rosedale and Hutton," in D. W. Crossley and F. A. Aberg, "Sixteenth-Century Glass-Making in Yorkshire: Excavations at Furnaces at Hutton and Rosedale," *Post-Medieval Archaeology* 6 (1972): 130, 144, 149. At least one linen smoother was recovered from the site of the seventeenth-century Denton glasshouse at Haughton Green, near Manchester; Ian Burgoyne, Pilkington's Glass Museum, to author, January 26, 1983. [Alice Winchester], "The Editor's Attic: An Obsolete Implement," *Antiques* 35, no. 6 (June 1939): 276. A Spanish example is in Harold Newman, *An Illustrated Dictionary of Glass* (London: Thames and Hudson, 1977), p. 185.
4. Kensington glassworks advertisement, *Pennsylvania Packet*, February 27, 1775.

405

FLOWER POT AND STAND
UNITED STATES, POSSIBLY NEW JERSEY, 1820–50

Opaque white glass of greenish translucency. Blown. Pot of tapered form with wide, outward-folded edge; high push-up in bottom with small hole in center; pontil mark. Circular stand with deep central well, curved rim with outward-folded edge; pontil mark.
OH: 4½ in (11.5 cm); Diam top of pot: 4⁹⁄₁₆ in (11.6 cm)
Museum purchase, 1957: McKearins' Antiques, Hoosick Falls, N.Y.
58.4.6a, b

Published: (possibly this one) McKearin and McKearin, *American Glass*, pl. 62, no. 6.

406, PL. 21

FLOWER POT
ENGLAND OR UNITED STATES, 1835–55

Deep green glass. Pressed. Heavy, tapered form with protruding rounded rim and 3 horizontal ribs beneath; the remaining body surface covered with fine horizontal ribbing; a laurel band and row of beads encircle the top; below, the body divided into 2 sections by 4 wide vertical ribs; in each section a pair of cornucopias flank a basket of flowers and fruit; a rope border below; recessed plain base; recessed foot; the bottom slightly concave around a central molded depression with small hole.
H: 3½ in (8.9 cm); Diam top: 4⅞ in (12.4 cm)
H. F. du Pont purchase
69.1344

Although the flower pot is a form more commonly associated with pottery, glass examples were made in different styles. As early as 1703 "3 glasse flowr potts" valued at 1s. 3d. were recorded in the appraisal of a Chester, Pennsylvania, estate, and "Glass Flower Potts" were advertised for sale in 1769 by a Charleston merchant.[1] At the Manheim, Pennsylvania, glassworks of Henry William Stiegel, glass flower pots were among the "extraordinary" items blown by Martin Greiner between 1764 and 1769.

The term *flower pot* may have denoted vases for cut flowers as well as containers in which plants were potted. The rich cut "Chimney Flower Pots and Ornaments" available in Petersburg, Virginia, in 1819 must have been expensive vases intended for mantel or hearth. A "Flower pot for Celery" was manufactured by Baltimore Flint Glass Works in 1834. In nineteenth-century ceramics trade catalogues, the term *garden pot and stand* describes objects like NOS. 405 and 406.[2]

Winterthur's glass flower pots clearly demonstrate that these containers could be quite ornamental in spite of their utilitarian function. Closely resembling porcelain, NO. 405 is blown of a dead white opaque glass that would effectively conceal the potting soil within. The deep green and fine horizontal ribbing of NO. 406 also served to detract the eye from earthy contents while the cornucopias and baskets express in crisp relief an appropriate theme of bounteous nature. No place of origin can be pinpointed for either pot. NO. 405 was in George McKearin's private collection, one of a pair he had found in South Jersey. Based on the area of discovery, McKearin had thought Millville a likely source. The design of the pressed flower pot recalls the salt dishes with baskets and cornucopia made in Massachusetts.[3]

1. James Cornish inventory, 1703-121, Philadelphia County Probate Records (microfilm, Downs, WL); James McCall advertisement, *South Carolina Gazette*, August 24, 1769.
2. T. Twitchell advertisement, *Petersburg Intelligencer*, January 8, 1819, reference courtesy of MESDA; "Invoice of Glass on Hand, 6 May 1834," Chapman-Baker Day Book, p. 11, MdHS; an example of a trade catalogue using this terminology is the Wedgwood catalogue for 1817, reproduced in Wolf Mankowitz, *Wedgwood* (London: B. T. Batsford, 1953), pl. 31.
3. L. W. and D. B. Neal, *Pressed Glass Salt Dishes of the Lacy Period, 1825–1850* (Philadelphia: Privately printed, 1962), pp. 17–18, 137–43, 213–17.

407

BELL-GLASS

UNITED STATES, 1815–40

Light green glass. Blown. Bell-shape form with slightly
flaring bottom edge; applied, molded handle of flattened
ball shape on short stem and wafer.
H: 15½ in (38.0 cm); Diam base: 16⁷⁄₁₆ in (43.0 cm)
H. F. du Pont purchase
54.545

Bell-glasses were designed to force delicate
plants and to protect them from cold and insects
during their growth. References to their use
occur in English sources from the 1650s, and the
name was derived from the shape. As explained
in a dictionary entry of 1728,

The *French* call them *Bells*, because they are
indeed made like a *Bell*, being about eighteen Inches broad at the Lower Part, and as
much in Height, with a great Button of the
same substance to take hold of them and
commodiously to place them.

Illustrations of seventeenth- and eighteenth-
century English garden implements show
bell-glasses that slope sharply from the top.
Winterthur's specimen has a more pronounced
shoulder and, in this, relates more closely to the
bell-glass pictured in Diderot.[1]

The popularity of glass gardening aids in the
American colonies has been documented in
Virginia, where archaeologists have unearthed
many fragments of bell-glasses of English manufacture. In the 1732 inventory of the estate of
Robert Carter of Corotoman there is mention of
"8 garden Virga Bell glasses" and "2 English
Ditto," a reference implying that bell-glasses
were made in Virginia as well as in England and
that the two kinds could be readily distinguished. There is no record, however, of a glasshouse operating in Virginia in the early part of
the eighteenth century.[2] The first clear reference
to American-made bell-glasses occurs in the

records of Stiegel's Manheim glassworks for April 1767, when his German-trained glass-blowers were credited with making garden bells. In the 1770s such bells were advertised by Philadelphia Glass Works.[3]

The nineteenth-century American origin of Winterthur's bell-glass is indicated by both its color and the details of its shaping. In English production, light green pharmaceutical glass was used only for small bell-glasses; ones of this large size were fashioned of dark green bottle glass. Eighteenth-century English examples excavated at Colonial Williamsburg have a wide, inward-folded edge, but Winterthur's has a plain edge. The earlier English ones have a handle formed by a trail of glass wound around a thick pontil scar while here the handle was molded and applied.

In 1816 a Boston glassworks advertised "Bell-glasses, tub'd and plain" and listed them with chemical and medical glasswares under the heading "APOTHECARIES' SHOP FURNI-TURE," which indicates the garden implements were probably blown of a light green or aqua glass. According to the factory price lists for 1818 and 1819, bell-glasses were sold by weight for 75¢ per pound.[4]

1. Robert Bradley quoted in Audrey Noël Hume, *Archaeology and the Colonial Gardener*, Colonial Williamsburg Archaeological Series, no. 7 (Williamsburg, Va.: Colonial Williamsburg Foundation, 1974), p. 62; Denis Diderot, "Agriculture et économie rustique, Jardin potager," *Recueil de Planches, sur les sciences, les arts libéraux, et les arts méchaniques, avec leur Explication* (Paris: Briasson, David, le Breton, Durand, 1762), 1: pl. 1, fig. 1.
2. See Noël Hume, *Archaeology and the Colonial Gardener*; "Carter Papers," *Virginia Magazine of History and Biography* 6, no. 3 (January 1899): 267, reference courtesy of Sumpter T. Priddy. There were two glass-making efforts in the Jamestown settlement, in 1608 and 1621, and archaeological evidence suggests that glass-making was attempted at Governor Berkeley's plantation at Green Spring in the 1660s. The next record of any interest in glassmaking in Virginia occurs in 1766: John Mercer of Marlborough plantation in Stafford County proposed unsuccessfully to fit up "a glass house for making bottles." See Ivor Noël Hume, *Here Lies Virginia* (New York: Alfred A. Knopf, Borzoi Books, 1968), pp. 144–45, 204–6.
3. Daybook, p. 122, Stiegel Records, HSP; *Pennsylvania Packet*, February 27, 1775.
4. Boston Glass Manufactory advertisement, *Columbian Centinel*, January 17, 1816, reproduced in Wilson, *New England Glass*, p. 202; Prices Current, South Boston, Edison Inst.

408, PL. 11

DISH COVER

POSSIBLY NEW YORK, POSSIBLY MOUNT VERNON GLASS WORKS, 1825–45

Green-blue nonlead glass. Blown. Circular domed form with applied solid mushroom-shape finial on wafer; pontil mark on top of knop; a rounded protrusion inside below finial. Blown in 3-part mold of geometric design (McKearin G I-30): diamond pattern at base of finial (probably type I) with double horizontal rings below; 21 broad vertical ribs encircle the body with 3 horizontal rings below; faint fluting around rim.
H: 4⅛ in (10.5 cm); Diam bottom: 6¹⁄₁₆ in (15.4 cm)
History: Crawford Wettlaufer; George S. McKearin Museum purchase, 1972: Richard H. and Virginia A. Wood Antiques, Baltimore. Funds for purchase, gift of Mrs. E. du Pont Irving
72.400

A somewhat smaller example of this rare form was published by the McKearins as a bell cover, presumably meaning bell-glass.[1] The size of NO. 408 and its patterned decoration indicate it was intended to function not in the garden but on the table as a dish cover. In 1817 Leeds Pottery in Yorkshire made conical covers for dishes 10 to 18 inches long. The pottery's ragout dishes, from 10 to 14 inches long, had domed covers similar to NO. 408.[2]

This cover was apparently blown from the same mold as a sugar bowl and cream jug in the Winterthur collection (NO. 174 and 58.4.4); all three share the same mold defects. Fragments found at the factory site and examples found in neighboring homes, have led to the attribution of this pattern to Mount Vernon Glass Works in New York.[3] The very similar G I-29 pattern, however, is attributed to Boston and Sandwich Glass Company (NO. 125).

Another mold-blown dish cover has been attributed to the glasshouse in Mantua, Ohio.[4]

1. McKearin and McKearin, *American Glass*, pl. 67, fig. 9, pp. 173, 270. The diameter of that example measures 5⅛ in.
2. The dish covers in the 1817 trade catalogue are reproduced in Donald Towner, *The Leeds Pottery* (New York: Taplinger Publishing Co., 1965), nos. 160–62, 213.
3. Harry Hall White, "New York State Glasshouses," pts. 2, 3, *Antiques* 16, nos. 3, 5 (September/November, 1929): 193–96, 394–96.
4. Pattern G II-33 in McKearin and McKearin, *American Glass*, pl. 118, no. 2.

409

PLATE

PITTSBURGH, STOURBRIDGE
FLINT GLASS WORKS OF THOMAS
AND JOHN ROBINSON, JR.,
1830–36

Colorless nonlead glass of gray tint. Pressed. Circular form with scalloped edge, circular well and wide curved rim; flat bottom with 8 knoblike protrusions around the edge. Smooth upper surface; relief pattern on underside: on base against a stippled ground are swags between palmettes, with oak leaves in between; this surrounds a ring with swagged background containing the inscription, "T & J. ROBINSON PITTSB.G"; in the center, 1 diamond and 4 ovals; around the rim a wreath of large oak leaves.
H: ⅞ in (2.2 cm); Diam: 5¾ in (14.6 cm)
Museum purchase, 1978: The Stradlings, New York City
78.42

This small plate, perhaps intended only as an advertising item, is distinguished by the mark, which identifies it as a product of Stourbridge Glass Works during the early 1830s partnership of Thomas and John Robinson, Jr., sons of the founder. T. & J. Robinson notified merchants in the fall of 1834 that they were manufacturing flint glasswares "in all its variety" and invited dealers to examine their assortment, adding that they were "disposed to sell low."[1] The Stourbridge line included fine cut and engraved glass as well as inexpensive pressed glass.

This pressed plate, made with a nonlead glass formula, has an unusual design quite unlike the John Robinson & Son boat salt of typical lacy style (NO. 235). The center bottom has a stippled background and a busy but crisp pattern of classical swags and leaves on which the factory mark is superimposed. In contrast is the decoration of the curved rim, where large and indistinct leaves are arranged on a plain ground.

Because it bears no relation to the usual lacy patterns associated with pre-1850 pressed glass, some historians have denounced the plate as a "decadent, cheap, late example of the decline of the true lacy."[2] The mark, however, clearly places the plate in the 1830s, the second decade of pressing technology and the supposed heyday of the lacy style. Perhaps the plate should instead be interpreted as an early experiment by the Robinsons to improve technology and eliminate the chill marks that made the stipple-ground lacy designs an almost essential camouflage for poor color and clarity. Like their father, John Robinson, Sr., who in 1826 secured a patent for pressing glass knobs in one action, the sons may have been actively involved in the technological advance of pressed glass. Because the lettering on this plate relates closely to that on mold-blown pocket bottles of Stourbridge manufacture, it is possible that the moldmaker Joshua Laird was responsible for both items.[3]

1. Robinson advertisement, *Pittsburgh Gazette*, October 6, 1834, as quoted in Knittle, *Early American Glass*, pp. 339–40.
2. Innes, *Pittsburgh Glass*, p. 262.
3. Helen McKearin, "The Case of the Pressed Glass Knobs," *Antiques* 60, no. 2 (August 1951): 118; McKearin and McKearin, *American Glass*, p. 347.

410, 411

BUTTER PRINTS
PROBABLY PITTSBURGH,
PROBABLY M'KEE AND
BROTHERS, 1862–72

NO. 410. Aqua, bubbly glass. Pressed. Solid disk with flat-based handle protruding from one side; the other with intaglio design of a bound wheat sheaf between 2 leafy fronds; around the rim are 2 serrated bands; "1862" in relief along edge of disk.
Diam: 4⅜ in (11.2 cm)
Gift of Mrs. Endsley P. Fairman, 1976
76.125

NO. 411. Aqua, bubbly glass. Pressed. Solid disk with knob handle protruding from one side; the other with intaglio design of a stylized, circular pineapple flanked by leafy fronds beneath; a serrated band around the rim; "1862" in relief along edge of disk.
Diam: 4⅜ in (11.2 cm)
H. F. du Pont purchase, 1928: Schuyler Jackson, Trenton, N.J.
59.2997

Exhibited: Corning Museum, "Pressed Glass, 1825–1925," 1983.

The designs of NOS. 410 and 411 are identical to those found on chip-carved wooden butter prints, which perhaps inspired the glass versions. Few are dated, but as collectible folk art items, many wooden prints have been attributed to the first quarter of the nineteenth century.[1] The pressing technology needed to make glass ones was developed in the later 1820s, but there is no documentation of glass butter prints being made much before the 1860s.

The Pittsburgh firm of M'Kee and Brothers included a glass butter print of a sheaf-of-wheat pattern in their trade catalogues for 1859/60, 1864, 1868, and 1871. The wholesale price ranged from $2.00 to $3.50 a dozen, with the highest price occurring in 1864 during the Civil War. A glass butter print that is very similar to the one shown by M'Kee was owned by Rhea Mansfield Knittle and published by her in 1929. Knittle also had a wooden one with a sheaf-of-wheat pattern that seems to be identical to Winterthur's glass version, which is sophisticated in its design and crisp in its execution.[2] The pineapple of NO. 411 is crude and stiff by comparison. Nonetheless, the date (presumably for a patent) and similar quality of glass suggest that the prints originated from the same factory.

These butter prints were patented one year after Alanson Slaughter introduced factory or creamery production of butter. Many farm women still continued their small-scale production, molding butter in one-pound cakes of cylindrical shape, about four inches in diameter.[3] Given their size, butter prints like NOS. 410 and 411 may have been used by those making butter to decorate and perhaps distinguish their cakes prior to packing for shipment to city grocers. Ordinary housewives may also have used butter prints to embellish slices of butter that were bound for the dinner table.

1. For a wooden example, see Beatrice B. Garvan, *The Pennsylvania German Collection*, Handbooks in American Art, no. 2 (Philadelphia: Philadelphia Museum of Art, 1982), pp. 70–72.
2. M'Kee Glass: (1859/60), p. 12; (1864), p. 55; (n.d.), pp. 96, 119; (1868), p. 145; (1871), p. 178; "Queries and Opinions," *Antiques* 16, no. 2 (August 1929): 138.
3. Susan Williams, *Savory Suppers and Fashionable Feasts: Dining in Victorian America* (New York: Pantheon Books, 1985), pp. 117–20.

412, 413, PL. 22

SPITTOONS

PROBABLY NEW YORK, POSSIBLY ELLENVILLE GLASS WORKS, 1850–80, POSSIBLY 1925–30 (NO. 413)

NO. 412. Amber and colorless bubbly glass. Blown. Squat globular body curved in at shoulder to narrow neck then flaring widely to rim with outward-folded edge; around body an applied band of colorless glass pulled up in irregular swagging; push-up; pontil mark.
H: 6⅛ in (15.7 cm); Diam top: 6⁹⁄₁₆ in (16.8 cm)
History: Olive Viber, Walden, N.Y.
H. F. du Pont purchase, 1931: McKearins' Antiques, New York City
59.3030

Published: McKearin and McKearin, *American Glass*, pl. 20, no. 1.

NO. 413. Amber glass. Blown. Compressed globular body curved in at shoulder to narrow neck flaring widely to rim with outward-folded edge; added gather of amber glass pulled up in swagging around body; push-up; pontil mark.
H: 6⅛ in (15.7 cm)
History: Olive Viber, Walden, N.Y.
H. F. du Pont purchase, 1931: McKearins' Antiques, New York City
59.3031

Although George McKearin suggested to H. F. du Pont that these containers "would be lovely for flowers," he did describe them for what they were, namely cuspidors. Ceramic cuspidors, or spittoons, were more common than glass ones. A rare record of glass spittoon production occurs in the 1859/60 M'Kee catalogue, where a glass spittoon of juglike form with handles is illustrated. NOS. 412 and 413 are quite different in shape, echoing ceramic spittoons of the eighteenth and early nineteenth centuries.[1] Typical ceramic spittoons from the 1850–1900 period were low and round with a top surface angled down to a central hole: they usually had a mottled amber-brown or Rockingham glaze. Whatever their shape or material, the need for spittoons throughout the United States was universally decried by nineteenth-century travel writers.

Determining the origin of heavily swagged glassware like NOS. 178, 412, and 413 is problematical. McKearin attributed the spittoons to Ellenville, but in 1923 one (possibly NO. 412) was thought to be from Millville, New Jersey.[2] McKearin claimed to have acquired both examples from Olive Viber of Walden, New York, a town near Ellenville, but because the swagging was achieved in two very different ways with different glass and the amount of wear varies greatly, they may not have been made at the same time. Indeed, NO. 413, with virtually no wear marks, may have been made in the later 1920s as a mate to that in the Temple sale, known to the maker only by photograph. However, another spittoon recently on the market was made in the same manner as NO. 413 and appeared to be of nineteenth-century manufacture.[3]

1. M'Kee Glass (1859/60), p. 20. The Leeds Pottery pattern book of 1812 illustrates ceramic "spitting pots" with and without handles; see Donald Towner, *The Leeds Pottery* (New York: Taplinger Publishing Co., 1965), nos. 123–24. Winterthur has a Worcester porcelain spittoon of this shape.
2. American Art Galleries, "Stiegel, Wistarberg, Sandwich, and Other Rare Early Glass Formed by Jacob Paxson Temple," (November 15–17, 1923), lot 492.
3. Skinner, "Early Glass, Bottles, and Flasks," sale no. 1279 (October 7, 1989), lot 708.

414

FURNITURE KNOBS

PITTSBURGH, BAKEWELL, PAGE,
AND BAKEWELL OR BAKEWELL
AND ANDERSON, 1825–35

Colorless lead glass. Pressed. Thick circular head on
threaded cylindrical stem with protruding disk at
bottom, from which extends a square shank bearing the
words "BAKEWELL'S PATENT" with a star on 2 corners.
The head has 8 round bosses against a diamond-stippled
ground with rope border; through the center, a narrow
screw hole.
L: 1⁹⁄₁₆ in (4.0 cm); Diam top: 2⅛ in (5.4 cm)
Gift of Richard Gould Antiques, 1970
70.403.1–.2

Glass was used to ornament American furniture at least as early as 1817, when a traveler
commented upon the beautiful effect of cut
glass on New York City cabinetwork. In 1824
Bakewell, Page, and Bakewell advertised "com-
mode and sideboard handles plain and cut,"
and "some excellent glass Knobs for Cabinet
Ware" were among the factory's products exhibited at the 1824 Franklin Institute Fair. An
advertisement for knobs available from Jersey
City Glass Company indicates the range of
styles available by 1830: "Plain, Fluted, Fine
Twisted, Coarse Twisted, Moulded and Sunflower, all of Superior Double Flint Glass. Also
the same as the above of the following colours,
viz. Deep Blue, Turquoise, Opal, Pearl, Agate
. . . Cut glass Knobs of any pattern . . . extra
rich Cut Glass Knobs."[1]

It was the manufacture of glass knobs that
apparently spurred the development of full
mechanical pressing in America. Nine of the
first fourteen patents relating to pressed glass,
issued between 1825 and 1833, concerned the
production of glass knobs for furniture and
doors. Conflicting claims of the various patentees led to complicated litigation.

These knobs, marked "BAKEWELL'S
PATENT," were made either under the Septem-
ber 9, 1825, patent issued to John P. Bakewell of
Bakewell, Page, and Bakewell or the May 14,
1828, patent issued to Thomas and John P.
Bakewell.[2]

1. Henry Bradshaw Fearon, *Sketches of America: A
Narrative of a Journey . . .* (2d ed.; London: Longman,
Hurst, et al., 1818), p. 24; *Western Reserve Chronicle*, March
19, 1824, reference courtesy of Mr. and Mrs. J. G.
Stradling; letter of commendation from the fair as quoted
in Innes, *Pittsburgh Glass*, p. 29; Jersey City Glass
Company advertisement, *Poulson's American Daily
Advertiser* (Philadelphia), March 4, 1830, as quoted in
N. Hudson Moore, *Old Glass, European and American*
(New York: Tudor, 1941), p. 274.
2. Wilson, "American Contributions," pp. 172, 174,
199–200; Helen McKearin, "The Case of the Pressed Glass
Knobs," *Antiques* 60, no. 2 (August 1951): 118–20; Kirk J.
Nelson, "The New England Glass Co. *vs* George W.
Robinson, Machinist," *Acorn* 1 (1990): 52, 63 n. 8. The role
of pressing in the Bakewell patents is not clear.

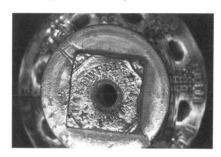

415

PLAQUE

PITTSBURGH, BAKEWELL, PAGE, AND BAKEWELL, CIRCA 1825

Colorless lead glass; white clay (sulphide). Pressed. Solid oval glass plaque containing sulphide profile portrait of George Washington facing left; on the underside, an elongated oval ground depression.
H: ¹¹⁄₁₆ in (1.7 cm); L: 3¼ in (8.3 cm)
H. F. du Pont purchase, possibly 1925: possibly Franklin Studio, Baltimore
59.1369

Published: Palmer, "American Heroes," p. 22, fig. 22.

In creating a sulphide portrait plaque, Benjamin Bakewell emulated a decorative form that English and French artisans had perfected about ten years earlier. The technique of cameo incrustation was probably initially inspired by portrait medallions of other materials that had chipped, faded, or become soiled: once a white clay profile was embedded in glass it was essentially indelible.

A Parisian master of the art, Barthélemy Despréz encased his clay images with such skill that they had an imposing, metallic appearance. He also heightened the effect by facet-cutting the edges of the plaque itself (NO. 417). Here, in a rare sulphide plaque identified as an American product, Washington is not as resplendent as his French-made counterparts because a trapped air bubble makes him appear to have a black eye. The glass was not faceted but merely cut to fit into a wooden or metal frame.

The identical Washington profile occurs in the bottom of two tumblers at Winterthur (NOS. 63, 65) and in tumblers in the collections of St. Louis Art Museum, Daughters of the American Revolution Museum, and Corning Museum. It is also the subject of the most ambitious of the Bakewell sulphide glasses, a cut-glass mantel ornament in Bergstrom Museum. A related but simpler ornament has been acquired by Western Reserve Historical Society.[1]

The source of this particular image of Washington is a medal for which Philadelphia die-sinker Christian Gobrecht may have been responsible because a plaster cast of this Washington medal is among the effects of his estate.[2]

1. See Palmer, "American Heroes," p. 23, fig. 23. Dean M. Zimmerman, "On the Cover," *Glass Club Bulletin*, no. 158 (Spring 1989): 2, 16.
2. James Ross Snowden, *A Description of the Medals of Washington . . . in the Museum of the Mint* (Philadelphia: Lippincott, 1861), pl. 6, no. 14. Artifacts from Gobrecht's estate are owned by Hanover Numismatic Society, Hanover, Pa., and are recorded in Decorative Arts Photographic Collection, WL.

416

DOORKNOB

PITTSBURGH, ATTRIBUTED TO BAKEWELL, PAGE, AND BAKEWELL OR BAKEWELL AND ANDERSON, 1826–35

Colorless lead glass; white clay (sulphide); metal. Pressed. Circular glass knob with rounded sides tapering to a short cylindrical shaft, attached to a brass cap with long metal pin; embedded in the glass is a sulphide profile portrait of Benjamin Franklin facing left; with the name "GOBRECHT" in relief on the shoulder.
Diam: 2¹⁄₁₆ in (5.2 cm)
H. F. du Pont purchase, 1969
69.1965

Published: Palmer, "American Heroes," p. 21, fig. 21.

This sulphide portrait of Benjamin Franklin was taken from the official medal of the Franklin Institute of Philadelphia. Christian Gobrecht, engraver and die-sinker, completed the die for the medal at the end of 1825, from the designs of Thomas Sully. The first medals were struck in 1826 and were presented to winning exhibitors at the institute's first annual industrial fair held in 1825. Benjamin Bakewell of Pittsburgh was awarded the silver medal for a pair of cut-glass decanters and was apparently inspired to use the medal as a model for his recently introduced cameo-incrusted glassware (see NOS. 63–65). In addition to doorknobs, there are examples of smaller furniture knobs, decanters, and a tumbler with this particular sulphide portrait of Franklin.[1]

Gobrecht may have supplied Bakewell directly with molds for the production of sulphide portraits, molds that were made from plaster casts of the original medals. Gobrecht's own plaster casts of the Franklin Institute medal and the Washington medal also used by Bakewell (NO. 415) descended in his family and are now in the collection of Hanover Numismatic Society in Pennsylvania.

1. A decanter is in Palmer, "American Heroes," pp. 18–19, figs. 17–18. Another example is in Jones Museum of Glass and Ceramics, Douglas Hill, Maine. The tumbler (Strauss collection, Corning Museum), differs from other Bakewell sulphide tumblers (NOS. 63–65) in having the sulphide on the side rather than in the bottom. A smaller knob for furniture is in Paul H. Dunlop, *The Jokelson Collection of Antique Cameo Incrustation* (Phoenix: Papier Presse, 1991), p. 50, no. 124.

417

PLAQUE (ONE OF TWO)

PARIS, BARTHÉLEMY DESPRÉZ, JR., 1815–25

Colorless lead glass; white clay (sulphide). Pressed. Thin glass oval with flat central section containing a sulphide profile portrait; the tapered edges cut with triangular facets. NO. 417 has a portrait of Benjamin Franklin facing left; impressed on the back of the sulphide: "DESPREZ, / Rue des Récolets / NO. 2 à Paris." The mate has a portrait of George Washington facing right.
L: 3¹⁄₁₆ in (7.8 cm); W: 2⅝ in (6.6 cm)
H. F. du Pont purchase
59.562 (mate is 59.561)

Published: Palmer, "American Heroes," p. 8, figs. 5, 6.

The sulphide portrait plaques by Despréz are superior examples of the art of cameo incrustation (see NOS. 63–65). No air bubbles detract from the striking silvery appearance of the images.

Barthélemy Despréz, Sr., was a modeler at the Sèvres porcelain factory between 1773 and 1783; later, he supervised the preparation of the clay bodies. By 1793 Despréz had established his own Paris factory for the production of porcelain medallions and cameos at No. 2, Rue des Récollets. His son and namesake had succeeded him by 1815 and in 1825 moved the business to a new location. The first mention of Barthélemy Despréz, Jr., in connection with sulphides occurs in 1819 when he received an award for cameos set in glass. Three years later *Le Bazar parisien* reported that Despréz "set cameos of different coloured clays in crystal glass and used them for decorating flasks, sweetmeat containers, vases, clocks, etc."[1]

The Despréz portrait of Franklin is after the Wedgwood medallion modeled by William Hackwood. Despréz also produced plaques with the same Franklin profile seen in the Bakewell tumblers.[2]

1. Régine de Plinval de Guillebon, *Porcelain of Paris, 1770–1850,* trans. Robin R. Charleston (New York: Walker, 1972), pp. 236–40.
2. Metropolitan Museum of Art, *Benjamin Franklin and His Circle* (New York: Metropolitan Museum of Art, 1936), no. 53; an example of Despréz's other Franklin sulphide (Historic Deerfield) is in Palmer, "American Heroes," p. 7, fig. 4.

418

BREAST PIPE

UNITED STATES, 1815–40

Colorless glass. Blown. Ovoid body with rounded bottom
and conical neck; from one side extends a long hollow
tube curved up at end; pontil mark.
H: 4¼ in (10.8 cm); L: 11½ in (29.2 cm)
Museum purchase, 1977: Wadsworth Atheneum,
Hartford
77.112

The production of apothecary and chemical
glasswares was an integral part of the glass
industry. For the storage, display, and dispens-
ing of medicinal powders, extracts, syrups, and
the like there were specie jars, salt mouths,
stopper rounds, and phials of all sizes. Glasshouses manufactured distillation apparatus
such as retorts and receivers. For medical treatment and personal hygiene they provided cup-
ping glasses, urinals, nipple shells, and breast
pipes, among other things.

Designed to draw milk from the breast by
suction, breast pipes were imported from England and Ireland during the eighteenth century. By the early 1770s they were blown in
Pennsylvania at the Manheim and Kensington
factories. In 1819 breast pipes made by South
Boston Flint Glass Works cost $3.50 a dozen.[1]

Relatively few examples of apothecary and
chemical glasswares have survived. Forms
probably changed little over time, and specific
factory attributions are difficult to make without supporting documentation.

1. Prices Current, South Boston, 1819, Edison Inst.

419

BIRD FOUNTAIN

ENGLAND, 1725–50

Colorless lead glass. Blown. Irregular conical body with
applied, pincered collar at top; above, an applied finial
blown in 2-part mold in form of human male head,
surmounted by an applied and tooled tricorn hat; short,
horizontal tube applied near base, opened on top to
form rectangular aperture with trailed rim; high push-up;
pontil mark.
H: 5⅞ in (14.7 cm)
History: T. Van C. Phillips, Jr.
Museum purchase, 1970: Pennypacker Auction Center
70.436

Published: Palmer, "Beer to Birdcages," p. 89, fig. 7.

420

BIRD FOUNTAIN

**PROBABLY MASSACHUSETTS,
1815–40**

Colorless lead glass. Blown. Pear-shape body with one
flattened side; blown in 3-part mold patterned with triple
vertical ribs (McKearin G I-12); applied collar; applied finial
of solid glass tooled into form of chicken; from flattened
side near the base extends a thick, mold-blown tube that
is hollow above a solid ramp of glass with an opening on the
upper surface; ground edge; push-up; ring-shape
pontil mark.
H: 5¾ in (14.6 cm)
H. F. du Pont purchase
59.3296

References to glass objects made for birds occur
in many written records of eighteenth- and early
nineteenth-century America, reflecting the fashion for keeping birds as pets. The forms include
fountains, boxes, glasses, cisterns, and pots.
Filled with water through the single opening in
the tube extension, fountains such as these operated on the principle of capillary attraction.
They were placed outside a birdcage with the
hopper extending through the bars so the bird
could drink.

Glass accoutrements for birdcages were made
by many factories in England and America. The
earliest English record of the form occurs in 1706
when T. Meyer, "at the Bird Cage in Long Acre,"

advertised his "so much approved and most convenient fashion Cristal Bird Glasses." In the American colonies, bird fountains were first advertised in 1732 by Rebecca Abbot of Boston. During the revolutionary war the Bristol glasshouse of Vigor and Stevens supplied bird pots and fountains to Frederick Rhinelander, a Loyalist merchant in New York City.[1]

Only one colonial glassworks, the Philadelphia Glass Works, is known to have produced birdcage glasses. In 1818 and 1819 the South Boston Flint Glass Works made bird boxes and founts, according to their price lists of those years.[2]

Fountains like NO. 419 with humorous anthropomorphic designs seem to have been popular from about 1720 through the end of the century. Several covered goblets dating between 1715 and 1730 have finials that are similar, mold-blown human heads wearing tricorn hats. Fragments of fountains matching Winterthur's have been excavated from Williamsburg sites of the 1770s. That they remained in fashion even later is suggested by a Thomas Rowlandson engraving of 1799 that clearly shows one of this type in use.[3]

The head of Winterthur's bird fountain is very simply rendered in contrast to other examples with more elaborate coiffures and higher, boldly shaped hats. The collar, a device used to conceal the junction of body and head, is flatter here and not as ruffled as that of other recorded fountains. Different faces, both male and female, are found on bird fountains, but none have been identified as portraits of particular individuals.

Winterthur's nineteenth-century fountain, NO. 420, has a tooled bird finial that reflects the function of the object. While this at first appears to be a whimsical addition, at least three other examples are recorded.[4] The body is still conical, but it was shaped in a three-part hinged mold. It may well represent the sort of fountains manufactured in South Boston and Sandwich.

1. Meyer advertisement, *Post Man* (London), February 12, 1706; Abbot advertisement, *New England Journal*, July 31, 1732, quoted in Wilson, *New England Glass*, p. 14; orders of March 21, 1778, and September 21, 1779, Letter and Order Book, 1774–84, Rhinelander Papers, NYHS.
2. *Pennsylvania Packet*, February 27, 1775. In 1818 boxes cost $2.00 a dozen and founts, $3.00; by 1819 these prices had been increased to $3.00 and $4.50 respectively; see Prices Current, South Boston, Edison Inst.
3. A goblet (Museum of the City of London) is in Buckley, *Old English Glass*, pl. 7. See Ivor Noël Hume, "Ornamental Glass Bird Fountains of the Eighteenth Century," *Antiques* 90, no. 2 (August 1966): 208–10.
4. Metropolitan Museum of Art; Sandwich Glass Museum; Richard A. Bourne Co., "The Elsholz Collection of Early American Glass," 3 vols. (December 9–10, 1986), 1: lot 561 (broken prior to sale).

421, PL. 20

ORNAMENT

UNITED STATES, 1825–50

Green-blue nonlead glass. Tooled. A bird with upright and pincered tail applied over a ball knop that is the top of a solid cylindrical stem with 3 ball knops and basal dome; applied disk foot; pontil mark.
H: 4⅞ in (12.4 cm); Diam base: 2⅜ in (6.0 cm)
H. F. du Pont purchase, 1946: McKearins' Antiques, Hoosick Falls, N.Y.
59.3033

422

ORNAMENT

UNITED STATES, 1830–65

Dark amber nonlead glass. Tooled. Wide-bodied turkey with pincered head and tail; applied short cylindrical stem and thick, irregular oval base with ridged, flat bottom.
H: 2⅞ in (7.3 cm); L: 3 in (7.7 cm)
History: possibly Rhea Mansfield Knittle
H. F. du Pont purchase
59.3338

Toys of unspecified types, whether for children or adults, were produced by many American glasshouses. NO. 422 is heavy enough to have had a functional use—a paperweight.

Glassmakers have long favored bird forms for tooled whimsical detail. The many examples of bird-embellished objects in the Winterthur glass collection indicate the range of possibility in this genre. The style was especially favored in Germany, and German immigrant craftsmen brought the taste for whimsy to colonial glasshouses.[1] The inspiration for NO. 421 may have come from English glassmaking, however, because a similar one of light green glass is at Sheffield City Museum. When du Pont acquired the aqua ornament in 1946 George McKearin believed it had been made at Redford Glass Company in New York, but other examples have been attributed to Pittsburgh, Sandwich, and New Jersey.[2]

The amber example may be the one published in 1928 as an example of midwestern glass.[3] At the time it was owned by the pioneer glass historian Rhea Mansfield Knittle of Ohio. The specific attribution of such whimsical wares is problematical, however, because dark amber glass was the common material used by bottle factories all across the country.

1. Franziskaner-Museums Villingen, *Schwarzwälder Glass und Glashütten* (Villingen-Schwenningen, Ger.: Schnurr Druck GmbH, n.d.), p. 94, figs. 44–47.
2. Mabel M. Swan, "Deming Jarves and His Glass-Factory Village," *Antiques* 33, no. 1 (January 1938): 27, fig. 7. This taller ornament (Sandwich Glass Museum) apparently descended in the family of Sandwich glassblower James D. Lloyd. For the Pittsburgh-attributed example (Henry Ford Museum, Edison Inst.), see Robert Bishop, *American Folk Sculpture* (New York: E. P. Dutton, 1974), p. 162, fig. 291.
3. Rhea Mansfield Knittle, "Rex Absolutus of the Monongahela," *Antiques* 13, no. 4 (April 1928): 291, fig. 3. For a similar example see Evelyn Campbell Cloak, *Glass Paperweights of the Bergstrom Art Center* (New York: Bonanza Books, 1966), pp. 130–31, pl. 45, no. 461.

423

JACOB'S LADDER ORNAMENT, PROBABLY NEW YORK OR NEW JERSEY, 1850–1900

Pale green glass. Tooled. Elongated and elastic obelisk form composed of a solid rod of glass folded at right angles and pulled upwards; at the bottom, a large spiral with rounded end.
H: approx. 27 in (68.6 cm)
H. F. du Pont purchase, 1930: Charles Woolsey Lyon, New York City
59.2634

Although some whimsical objects such as canes, hats, and crowns were made specifically for glassmakers' parades, others were intended to display the agility of the craftsman and the unique properties of glass, often for the entertainment of visitors to the glasshouse.[1] In fashioning this extraordinary Jacob's Ladder the glassmaker had to work quickly before the glass set up and became too hard to manipulate.[2] He pulled a long rod of glass and wrapped it around a tapered core or mandrel. The freestanding ladder also demonstrates the remarkable flexibility of tempered glass and sways at the slightest touch.

It is always difficult to attribute whimsies to individual factories or even regions; this one and a similar but smaller example at Bennington Museum were both found in New York. In November 1863, at the opening of Portland Glass Company in Portland, Maine, the workmen "politely turned out some small globes and specimens of Jacob's Ladder, which they presented to each [spectator] as mementoes of the interesting occasion." Jacob's Ladders are also recorded in English glassmaking.[3]

1. When Warren Gray visited the glasshouse at Suncook, N.H., in 1840, he watched the workers blow "several ladles, small globes, canes, and similar baubles for the Ladies & Gents who visited them in the course of the evening" (Gray as quoted in Wilson, *New England Glass*, p. 91).
2. While at Bethel, Jacob had a vision of a ladder reaching to heaven, Genesis 28:12.
3. *Eastern Argus* (Portland), November 12, 1863; Keith Vincent, *Nailsea Glass* (London: David and Charles, 1975), p. 79, fig. 85; Geoffrey Wills, *Novelties and Friggers*, English and Irish Glass series, no. 13 (Guildford, Eng.: Guinness Superlatives, 1968), p. 15.

Appendixes

Appendix 1: Blown Three-Mold Glass at Winterthur

CATALOGUE	MCKEARIN NO.	FORM	COLOR*	ACC. NO.	SOURCE
	G I-3 type 1	cruet	blue	73.462.1	Lunger gift 1973
242	G I-3 type 2	cruet	blue	70.382.1	Irving gift 1970
	G I-3 type 2	cruet	blue	70.3	
				82.2	Irving gift 1970
	G I-7 variant	cruet	amethyst	73.462.2	Lunger gift 1973
95	G I-8	wine decanter		56.36	Van Winkle gift 1956
420	G I-12	bird fountain		59.3296	
240	G I-24	caster set		83.10	Schwind 1983
	G I-24	condiment		70.380	Irving gift 1970
	G I-26	caster		70.379	Irving gift 1970
125	G I-29	cream jug	blue	73.463	Lunger gift 1973
174	G I-30	sugar bowl	aqua	59.3047	Gest 1945
	G I-30	cream jug	aqua	58.4.4	
408	G I-30	dish cover	aqua	72.400	museum purchase
	G II-1	small dish		59.3162	McKearin 1947
	G II-1	small dish		59.3163	McKearin 1947
	G II-1	small dish		59.3164	McKearin 1947
	G II-1	small dish		59.3165	McKearin 1947
	G II-1	small dish		59.3166	McKearin 1947
	G II-1	small dish		59.3167	McKearin 1947
338	G II-3	bottle	olive	59.3336	McKearin 1947
214	G II-6	bowl	green	54.36.2	
257	G II-6	vase	yellow	59.3003	Gest 1947
126	G II-6	pitcher	pink	59.3006	Gest 1947
274	G II-15	inkstand	gray/blue	59.3317	
	G II-15	inkstand	green	59.3321	
	G II-15	inkstand	amber	73.492	Lunger gift 1973
	G II-16	toy mug		59.3191	
	G II-16	toy wine		59.3230	one from Gest 1941
30	G II-16	toy wine		59.3231	
	G II-16	toy tumbler		59.3233	one from Gest 1941
	G II-16	toy tumbler		59.3234	
	G II-16	salt/toy bowl		59.3235	
	G II-16	hat salt		59.3298	
	G II-16	inkstand	olive/amber	70.387	Irving gift 1970
129	G II-17	cream jug	amethyst	59.3109	about 1940
	G II-18	salt (fake)	amethyst	59.3094	
206	G II-18	footed bowl		59.3183	?McKearin 1934
204	G II-18	footed bowl		59.3190	by 1939
246	G II-18	celery		59.3197	by 1939
98	G II-18	decanter		59.3206	

* Colorless unless otherwise noted.

CATALOGUE	MCKEARIN NO.	FORM	COLOR*	ACC. NO.	SOURCE
	G II-18	tumbler		59.3209	
	G II-18	tumbler		59.3211	
	G II-18	tumbler		59.3212	
	G II-18	tumbler		59.3214	
	G II-18	tumbler		59.3215	
193	G II-18	basket		59.3248	
	G II-18	tumbler		59.3254	
	G II-18	decanter		59.3257	
	G II-18	tumbler		59.3263	Parke-Bernet 1942
	G II-18	tumbler		59.3265	Parke-Bernet 1942
173	G II-18	sugar bowl		59.3271	Gest 1946
213	G II-18	butter tub		59.3275	Gest 1946
	G II-18	tumbler		59.3287	Sussel 1932
	G II-18	tumbler		59.3288	Sussel 1932
	G II-18	tumbler		59.3290	
	G II-18	tumbler		59.3292	by 1939
	G II-18	decanter		63.874	
	G II-18	tumbler		59.3335	
229	G II-18	salt		59.3331	by 1933
	G II-18	decanter		59.3328	
	G II-18	salt (fake)	amethyst	59.3097	
	G II-19	wineglass		59.3200	by 1941
	G II-19	wineglass		59.3201	by 1941
	G II-19	wineglass		59.3202	by 1941
27	G II-19	wineglass		59.3204	by 1941
	G II-19	wineglass		59.3239	by 1941
	G II-19	wineglass		59.3240	by 1941
28	G II-19	wineglass		59.3241	by 1941
	G II-19	wineglass		59.3242	by 1941
	G II-19	wineglass		59.3243	by 1941
	G II-19	wineglass		59.3244	by 1941
	G II-19	wineglass		59.3245	by 1941
	G II-19	wineglass		59.3246	by 1941
	G II-19	wineglass		59.3272	by 1941
	G II-19	wineglass		59.3273	by 1941
	G II-20 variant	tumbler		59.3208	
	G II-21	tumbler		59.3217	
	G II-21	tumbler		59.3256	
	G II-21	cream jug		59.3268	
147	G II-21	punch bowl		59.3274	by 1939
	G II-21	punch bowl		67.849	Parke-Bernet 1946
	G II-21	cream jug		59.3294	
246	G II-21	foot of celery		59.3197	by 1939
	G II-24	decanter		59.3199	
99	G II-27 variant	decanter	pale green	59.3320	Gest 1945
171	G II-32	sugar bowl	amethyst	59.3152	Gest 1931
172	G II-32	sugar bowl	amethyst	59.3153	Gest 1940

CATALOGUE	MCKEARIN NO.	FORM	COLOR*	ACC. NO.	SOURCE
	G II-34	tumbler		59.3293	by 1939
55	G II-34	tumbler		59.3330	Gest 1946
	G II-37	caster		59.3297	
131	G II-45 variant	cream jug	blue	72.117	Manheim gift 1972
	G III-2	decanter		59.3207	
96	G III-2	rum decanter		59.3303	by 1932
	G III-2	wine decanter		59.3304	by 1932
	G III-2	brandy decanter		59.3305	by 1932
	G III-2	gin decanter		59.3306	by 1932
	G III-4	inkstand		59.3179	Gest 1941
230	G III-4 variant	salt		59.3185	?Schubart 1926
317	G III-4 variant	miniature oil lamp		59.3186	
	G III-4	salt		59.3188	Parke-Bernet 1940
	G III-4	caster		59.3302	
215	G III-5	bowl		59.3160	Gest 1944 or 1946
	G III-5	bowl		59.3161	Gest 1944 or 1946
	G III-5	decanter		59.3171	
133	G III-5	pitcher (fake)		59.3180	Gest 1940
	G III-5	bowl (fake)		59.3187	Gest 1941
	G III-5	celery (fake)		59.3192	Gest 1940
	G III-5	decanter (fake)		59.3194	Gest 1944
	G III-5	decanter (fake)		59.3195	Gest 1944
	G III-5	decanter		59.3220	
132	G III-5	pitcher		59.3221	?Mason 1928
	G III-5	pitcher		59.3222	
205	G III-5	footed bowl		59.3232	Gest 1947
	G III-5	celery (fake)		59.3236	Sussel 1934
	G III-5	celery (fake)		59.3237	Sussel 1934
	G III-5	footed bowl		59.3247	Gest 1941
	G III-5	decanter (reproduction)		68.168	
	G III-6	tumbler		59.3181	
	G III-6	tumbler		59.3182	
100	G III-6	decanter/cruet		59.3249	McKearin 1947
54	G III-6	tumbler		59.3252	about 1940
	G III-6	tumbler		59.3253	about 1940
206	G III-6	foot of footed bowl		59.3183	?McKearin 1934
	G III-6	decanter		59.3307	McKearin 1947
	G III-6	cream jug		67.838	Gest 1941
	G III-6	bowl (fake)	blue	59.3284	Gest 1930
	G III-6	jug (fake)	blue handle	59.3277	Gest 1940
	G III-6	pocket bottle (fake)		59.3198	Gest 1945
	G III-6	tumbler (fake)		59.3193	Gest 1941
	G III-6	tumbler (fake)		59.3169	
216	G III-6	bowl (fake)	amethyst	59.3111	Gest 1931
	G III-6	pitcher (fake)	amethyst	59.3105	Gest 1929
	G III-6	salt (fake)	amethyst	59.3104	Gest 1947
	G III-6	salt (fake)	amethyst	59.3101	Gest 1931

CATALOGUE	MCKEARIN NO.	FORM	COLOR*	ACC. NO.	SOURCE
56	G III-10	tumbler		59.3170	Gest 1947
	G III-10	tumbler		59.3269	Gest 1940
	G III-10	tumbler		59.3270	Gest 1940
102	G III-12	toy decanter		56.38.36	Danby estate
	G III-12	toy decanter		59.3174	
	G III-12	toy decanter		59.3175	
	G III-12	toy tumbler		59.3205	
29	G III-12	toy wine		59.3228	Parke-Bernet 1940
	G III-12	toy wine		59.3229	Parke-Bernet 1940
	G III-12	toy jug		59.3309	Gest 1941
130	G III-12	toy jug		59.3310	Gest 1950
	G III-12	toy jug		59.3311	Gest 1950
231	G III-13	salt	blue	59.3278	Gest 1944
	G III-13	salt	blue	59.3279	Gest 1944
273	G III-13	inkstand	lavender	59.3323	Gest 1947
	G III-14	decanter		59.3308	
	G III-15	decanter		59.3332	
	G III-15	decanter		59.3333	Kindig 1948
121	G III-16	pitcher	blue	59.3280	Gest 1946
163	G III-16	sugar bowl	aqua	57.10.2	Gest 1956
	G III-16	decanter		59.3172	
	G III-16	decanter		59.3213	?McKearin 1947
53	G III-16	tumbler	blue	59.3282	McKearin 1946
256	G III-16	vase	aqua	59.3315	Gest 1947
	G III-16	decanter	green	59.3316	Gest 1947
	G III-16	pitcher	green	59.3318	Gest 1947
233	G III-18	hat salt		59.3267	
	G III-18	tumbler		59.3324	
	G III-18	tumbler		59.3325	
	G III-20	dish		59.3156	McKearin 1946
	G III-20	dish		59.3157	McKearin 1946
	G III-20	tumbler		59.3250	
	G III-20	tumbler		59.3251	
52	G III-20	mug		67.837	Parke-Bernet 1941
128	G III-21	cream jug	blue	57.10.3	Gest 1956
	G III-21	tumbler		59.3176	by 1939
	G III-21	cream jug		55.136.83	by 1939
	G III-21	tumbler		59.3177	by 1939
	G III-21	salt		59.3189	Parke-Bernet 1940
	G III-21	tumbler		59.3226	Sussel 1932
	G III-21	tumbler		59.3227	Sussel 1932
232	G III-21	salt		59.3238	Gest 1941
	G III-21	salt		59.3283	McKearin 1927
	G III-21	cream jug		59.3285	by 1933
	G III-22	tumbler		59.3314	
	G III-23	dish		59.3158	by 1932
	G III-23	dish		59.3159	?McKearin 1932

CATALOGUE	MCKEARIN NO.	FORM	COLOR*	ACC. NO.	SOURCE
127	G III-23	cream jug	blue	59.3276	by 1933
	G III-23	salt	blue	59.3281	by 1939
	G III-23	tumbler		59.3312	
	G III-23	tumbler		59.3326	
382	G III-23	pocket bottle		59.3196	?Lyon by 1942
381	G III-24	pocket bottle	pale blue	58.86	Rose and Knittle 1958
124	G III-24	pitcher	blue/colorless	59.3286	
123	G III-24	pitcher	yellow-green	59.3322	Gest 1947
	G III-24	tumbler		59.3313	
272	G III-25	inkstand	blue	59.3319	Gest 1947
	G III-26	cream jug	blue	73.297	
	G III-26	decanter		73.490	Lunger gift 1973
	G III-28	caster		59.3295	
	G III-28	caster		70.378	Irving gift 1970
	G III-29	inkstand	olive-amber	70.388	Irving gift 1970
247	G III-32	celery		59.3178	by 1946
	G III-32	celery		59.3223	?Gest 1946
	G III-32	celery		59.3224	
101	G III-33	decanter		73.489.1	Lunger gift 1973
	G III-33	decanter		73.489.2	Lunger gift 1973
249	G III-34	celery		59.3184	
248	G III-34	celery		59.3225	
58	G IV-2	tumbler		87.121	Kelly gift 1987
57	G IV-3	tumbler		83.2	Stradlings 1983
104	G IV-6	decanter		73.461	Lunger gift 1973
	G IV-7	decanter		59.3258	McKearin 1931
97	G IV-7	decanter		59.3260	McKearin 1931
122	G V-7	pitcher		76.32	Geesey gift 1976
103	G V-8	decanter		73.460.1	Lunger gift 1973
	G V-9	decanter		73.460.2	Lunger gift 1973
unrecorded pattern		hexagonal decanter		59.3255	Gest 1945
unrecorded pattern		footed bowl (fake)		63.53	
unrecorded pattern		basket	blue	77.45	museum purchase

Appendix 2:
Figured Flasks
at Winterthur

CATALOGUE	MCKEARIN NO.	COLOR*	ACC. NO.	SOURCE
	G I-11	aqua	73.403.1	Lunger gift 1973
	G I-14	aqua	73.403.2	Lunger gift 1973
	G I-17	pale green	73.400.3	Lunger gift 1973
390	G I-21	light blue	73.400.1	Lunger gift 1973
	G I-21	pale amethyst	73.400.2	Lunger gift 1973
	G I-24	aqua	73.401.2	Lunger gift 1973
	G I-24	deep olive	73.401.3	Lunger gift 1973
	G I-25	aqua	73.401.1	Lunger gift 1973
	G I-26	yellow-green	73.403.3	Lunger gift 1973
	G I-28	light blue	73.403.5	Lunger gift 1973
	G I-31	deep olive	73.403.6	Lunger gift 1973
	G I-34	deep olive	73.403.4	Lunger gift 1973
	G I-37	aqua	75.231	Porter gift 1975
	G I-38	green	73.402.2	Lunger gift 1973
	G I-39	aqua	68.206	van Ravenswaay gift 1968
	G I-41	blue	73.402.8	Lunger gift 1973
	G I-42	green	73.402.6	Lunger gift 1973
	G I-42	deep blue	73.402.7	Lunger gift 1973
	G I-43	yellow-green	73.402.9	Lunger gift 1973
	G I-50	pale aqua	73.402.3	Lunger gift 1973
	G I-55	pale olive	73.402.4	Lunger gift 1973
	G I-57	pale aqua	73.406.1	Lunger gift 1973
	G I-58	pale aqua	73.406.2	Lunger gift 1973
	G I-64	aqua	78.20	Lunger gift 1978
	G I-71	pale green	74.13	Carpenter gift 1974
	G I-73	colorless, green tint	73.408.1	Lunger gift 1973
	G I-73	pink-amethyst	73.408.2	Lunger gift 1973
	G I-73	yellow-green	73.408.3	Lunger gift 1973
393	G I-75	aqua	73.408.4	Lunger gift 1973
388	G I-80	olive	73.405.2	Lunger gift 1973
	G I-81a	olive	57.18.1	
	G I-86	olive	73.405.1	Lunger gift 1973
	G I-90	pale aqua	73.404	Lunger gift 1973
389	G I-94	aqua	73.407.1	Lunger gift 1973
	G I-96	aqua	73.407.2	Lunger gift 1973
	G I-99	deep green	73.428.3	Lunger gift 1973
	G I-100	aqua	73.429.1	Lunger gift 1973
394	G I-101	aqua	73.428.1	Lunger gift 1973
	G I-104	light blue	73.428.2	Lunger gift 1973
	G I-107	aqua	69.215	
	G I-111	aqua	73.409.1	Lunger gift 1973
395	G I-112	amber-yellow	73.429.2	Lunger gift 1973
	G I-113	olive-yellow	73.429.3	Lunger gift 1973
	G I-114	olive	73.409.2	Lunger gift 1973

* Colorless unless otherwise noted.

CATALOGUE	MCKEARIN NO.	COLOR*	ACC. NO.	SOURCE
	G I-117	aqua	73.410.1	Lunger gift 1973
	G I-121	aqua	73.410.2	Lunger gift 1973
	G II-6	pale blue-green	73.411.1	Lunger gift 1973
386	G II-10	light green	73.412.2	Lunger gift 1973
	G II-13/14 variant	aqua	73.415.1	Lunger gift 1973
	G II-17	aqua	68.203	van Ravenswaay gift 1968
	G II-17a	aqua	73.415.2	Lunger gift 1973
	G II-22	aqua	83.9	Schwind 1983, funds Lunger gift
	G II-26	aqua	73.412.4	Lunger gift 1973
	G II-31	pale aqua	73.414.1	Lunger gift 1973
	G II-31	deep green	73.414.2	Lunger gift 1973
	G II-36	aqua	68.201	van Ravenswaay gift 1968
	G II-38	aqua	73.412.3	Lunger gift 1973
	G II-42	pale green	73.417.2	Lunger gift 1973
	G II-44	pale green	73.417.1	Lunger gift 1973
	G II-49	pale yellow-green	73.416.2	Lunger gift 1973
	G II-52	aqua	73.413.1	Lunger gift 1973
	G II-54	pale aqua	73.413.2	Lunger gift 1973
	G II-56	aqua	73.416.1	Lunger gift 1973
	G II-61?		74.16	Carpenter gift 1974
	G II-63	deep olive	73.412.1	Lunger gift 1973
	G II-69	colorless	73.411.2	Lunger gift 1973
	G II-65?		73.222	
	G II-70	olive-amber	73.418.2	Lunger gift 1973
	G II-71	olive	73.418.1	Lunger gift 1973
	G II-72? variant	olive-amber	68.204	van Ravenswaay gift 1968
	G II-72	aqua	70.376	Irving gift 1970
	G II-86	olive-amber	70.374.1	Irving gift 1970
	G II-86	olive-amber	70.374.2	Irving gift 1970
	G II-92?	aqua	68.214	van Ravenswaay gift 1968
	G II-142	aqua	73.436.4	Lunger gift 1973
	G III-4	olive	70.373.1	Irving gift 1970
	G III-4	olive	70.373.2	Irving gift 1970
	G III-7	deep olive	68.205	van Ravenswaay gift 1968
	G III-14	green	73.419.1	Lunger gift 1973
	G III-15	aqua	73.419.2	Lunger gift 1973
	G IV-1	green	73.420.5	Lunger gift 1973
	G IV-3	colorless, amethyst striae	73.420.6	Lunger gift 1973
387	G IV-27	light green	82.322	Schwind 1982, funds Lunger gift
	G IV-28a?	green	73.420.2	Lunger gift 1973
	G IV-32	amber	73.420.1	Lunger gift 1973
	G IV-34	pale aqua	73.420.3	Lunger gift 1973
	G IV-37	pale green	73.420.4	Lunger gift 1973
	G IV-43	deep olive-amber	73.435	Lunger gift 1973
	G V-1	deep aqua	73.421.2	Lunger gift 1973
	G V-3?	olive-amber	68.207	van Ravenswaay gift 1968

CATALOGUE	MCKEARIN NO.	COLOR*	ACC. NO.	SOURCE
	G V-10	olive	73.421.1	Lunger gift 1973
392	G VI-3	deep olive yellow	75.193	Skinner 1975, funds Lunger gift
	G VI-4	amber	73.422.2	Lunger gift 1973
	G VI-4	emerald green	73.422.3	Lunger gift 1973
	G VI-7	pale aqua	73.422.1	Lunger gift 1973
	G VII-3	amber	73.424	Lunger gift 1973
385	G VIII-3	green	73.423.7	Lunger gift 1973
	G VIII-8	olive	73.423.5	Lunger gift 1973
384	G VIII-10	olive	73.423.4	Lunger gift 1973
	G VIII-16	green	73.423.6	Lunger gift 1973
	G VIII-20	aqua	73.423.2	Lunger gift 1973
	G VIII-25	amber	73.423.3	Lunger gift 1973
	G VIII-27	pale green	73.423.1	Lunger gift 1973
	G VIII-29	deep yellow-green	73.423.8	Lunger gift 1973
	G VIII-29	green	68.202	van Ravenswaay gift 1968
	G IX-2	aqua	68.208	van Ravenswaay gift 1968
396	G IX-6	aqua	82.321	Schwind 1982, funds Lunger gift
	G IX-12	olive-amber	73.425.2	Lunger gift 1973
	G IX-15	aqua	68.209	van Ravenswaay gift 1968
	G IX-25	green	73.425.1	Lunger gift 1973
	G IX-31	aqua	68.212	van Ravenswaay gift 1968
	G IX-32	aqua	68.211	van Ravenswaay gift 1968
	G IX-37	deep amber	73.425.3	Lunger gift 1973
	G IX-41	aqua	73.425.4	Lunger gift 1973
	G X-1	pale green	73.427.3	Lunger gift 1973
	G X-3	pale aqua	73.427.2	Lunger gift 1973
	G X-5	pale aqua	73.427.1	Lunger gift 1973
	G X-9	pale aqua	73.427.4	Lunger gift 1973
	G X-11	aqua	73.427.5	Lunger gift 1973
391	G X-14	blue-green	75.192	Skinner 1975, funds Lunger gift
	G X-16	pale blue-green	73.426.2	Lunger gift 1973
	G X-17	aqua	73.426.1	Lunger gift 1973
	G X-19	amber	73.426.3	Lunger gift 1973
397	G XI-9	aqua	68.199	van Ravenswaay gift 1968
	G XI-24	amber	73.437.3	Lunger gift 1973
	G XI-52	aqua	68.200	van Ravenswaay gift 1968
	G XII-6/8 variant	aqua	70.375.1	Irving gift 1970
	G XII-13	deep amber	73.436.1	Lunger gift 1973
	G XII-13	aqua	70.375.2	Irving gift 1970
	G XII-19	yellow	73.436.3	Lunger gift 1973
	G XII-34	aqua	68.197	van Ravenswaay gift 1968
	G XII-37	aqua	73.220	Carpenter gift 1973
399	G XII-39	aqua	68.198	van Ravenswaay gift 1968
	G XII-40	aqua	73.436.2	Lunger gift 1973
	G XIII-4	amber	73.430.2	Lunger gift 1973
	G XIII-6	aqua	73.430.1	Lunger gift 1973
401	G XIII-9	aqua	73.432.3	Lunger gift 1973

CATALOGUE	MCKEARIN NO.	COLOR*	ACC. NO.	SOURCE
	G XIII-12	olive	73.432.1	Lunger gift 1973
	G XIII-12?	pale gray-pink	73.432.2	Lunger gift 1973
	G XIII-18	pale aqua	73.437.4	Lunger gift 1973
	G XIII-35	deep amber	73.437.1	Lunger gift 1973
	G XIII-46	aqua	68.196	van Ravenswaay gift 1968
	G XIII-53	aqua	73.431.3	Lunger gift 1973
400	G XIII-54	amber-yellow	74.14	Carpenter gift 1974
	G XIII-56		73.431.4	Lunger gift 1973
	G XIII-58	lavender-blue	73.431.1	Lunger gift 1973
	G XIII-58	green-blue	73.431.2	Lunger gift 1973
398	G XIV-9	green	73.437.2	Lunger gift 1973

Reproductions of Figured Flasks

	G I-28	pale aqua	73.403.7	Lunger gift 1973
	G I-37	pink-amber	73.402.5	Lunger gift 1973
	G I-37	amber	71.234	Jester gift 1971
	G I-38	pink-amethyst	73.402.1	Lunger gift 1973
	G V-4	olive	73.421.3	Lunger gift 1973
	G V-5	pale green	63.12	

Appendix 3: Pressed Glass Cup Plates at Winterthur

CATALOGUE LEE-ROSE NO.	COLOR*	ACC. NO.	CATALOGUE LEE-ROSE NO.	COLOR*	ACC. NO.
13B		78.125.1	209		78.125.58
20		78.125.2	211		78.125.59
23 (two)		78.125.3, .4	212		78.125.60
28		78.125.5	215		78.125.61
41		78.125.6	216		78.125.62
95		78.125.7	216A		78.125.63
98 (three)		78.125.8–.10	217A		78.125.64
100A		78.125.11	231		78.125.65
104		78.125.12	235		78.125.66
120		78.125.13	242A		78.125.67
124B (two)		78.125.14, .15	246		78.125.68
126		78.125.16	255		78.125.69
129		78.125.17	256A		78.125.70
132		78.125.18	262 (three)		78.125.71–.73
134A		78.125.19	271A		78.125.74
136A		78.125.20	272 (six)		78.125.77–.82
145C (two)		78.125.21, .22	273 (two)		78.125.75, .76
147		78.125.23	284		78.125.83
147B		78.125.24	285		78.125.84
147C (three)		78.125.25–.27	292 (two)		78.125.85, .86
157B		78.125.28	315		78.125.87
158A (two)		78.125.29, .30	324		78.125.88
159		78.125.31	329		78.125.89
160A (two)		78.125.32, .33	332F		78.125.90
162A		78.125.34	373		78.125.91
162B		78.125.35	379 (three)		78.125.92–.94
164		78.125.36	388		78.125.95
166A		78.125.37	389		78.125.96
169A		78.125.38	390A		78.125.97
169B (two)		78.125.39, .40	395		78.125.98
170		78.125.41	397		78.125.99
172B (two)		78.125.42, .43	417		78.125.100
176		78.125.44	427		78.125.101
176A	blue-gray	78.125.45	429		78.125.102
176A		78.125.46	436A		78.125.103
180A (two)		78.125.47, .48	439		78.125.104
181A		78.125.49	440B (two)		78.125.105, .106
187 (two)		78.125.50, .51	441		78.125.107
191B		78.125.52	441A (two)		78.125.108, .109
192		78.125.53	445		78.125.110
196		78.125.54	447A		78.125.111
203		78.125.55	458A		78.125.112
204		78.125.56	459D	blue	78.125.113
208		78.125.57	465B		78.125.114

* Colorless unless otherwise noted.

CATALOGUE	LEE-ROSE NO.	COLOR*	ACC. NO.	CATALOGUE	LEE-ROSE NO.	COLOR*	ACC. NO.
	465O		78.125.115		667A		78.125.138
	476 (two)		78.125.116, .117		670		78.125.139
	515		78.125.118		670A		78.125.140
	517B		78.125.119		676B		78.125.141
	520A (two)		78.125.121, .122		676C		78.125.142
	522		78.125.120		677		78.125.143
	524		78.125.123	79	677A	violet blue	59.3076
	532		78.125.124		680		78.125.144
	535A		78.125.125		686		78.125.145
	547		78.125.126		691		78.125.146
	564 (two)		78.125.127, .128		692		78.125.147
	590		78.125.129		693		78.125.148
	593		78.125.130		694 (two)		78.125.149, .150
	595		78.125.131		699		78.125.151
	596		78.125.132	80	807	blue	59.3045
	610A		78.125.133		891 (two)		78.125.152, .153
	640		78.125.134		892		78.125.154
	643A (reproduction)		78.125.135		unclassified		78.125.155
78	651A	green	59.3073		unclassified		78.125.156
	661		78.125.136		unclassified	blue	78.125.157
	662		78.125.137		unclassified		78.125.158

Short-Title Bibliography

Baker, Gary Everett. "The Flint Glass Industry in Wheeling, West Virginia: 1829–1865." Master's thesis, University of Delaware, 1986.

Belden, Louise Conway. *The Festive Tradition: Table Decoration and Desserts in America, 1650–1900.* New York: W. W. Norton, 1983.

Bishop, Barbara, and Martha Hassell, eds. *Your Obdt. Servt., Deming Jarves: Correspondence of the Boston and Sandwich Glass Company's Founder, 1825–1829.* Sandwich, Mass.: Sandwich Historical Society, 1984.

Buckley, Francis. *History of Old English Glass.* London: Ernest Benn, 1925.

Charleston, R. J. *English Glass and the Glass Used in England, circa 400–1940.* London: George Allen and Unwin, 1984.

Delomosne and Son. *Gilding the Lily: Rare Forms of Decoration on English Glass of the Later Eighteenth Century.* London, 1978.

Jones, Olive R., and E. Ann Smith. *Glass of the British Military, 1755–1820.* Ottawa: Parks Canada, 1985.

Innes, Lowell. *Pittsburgh Glass, 1797–1891: A History and Guide for Collectors.* Boston: Houghton Mifflin, 1976.

Hughes, G. Bernard. *English, Scottish, and Irish Table Glass.* New York: Bramhall House, 1956.

Hunter, Frederick William. *Stiegel Glass.* 1914. Reprint. New York: Dover Press, 1950.

Knittle, Rhea Mansfield. *Early American Glass.* Garden City, N.Y.: Garden City Publishing Co., 1927.

Lanmon, Dwight P., Robert H. Brill, and George Reilly. "Some Blown 'Three-Mold' Suspicions Confirmed." *Journal of Glass Studies* 15 (1973): 143–73.

Lanmon, Dwight P., and Arlene M. Palmer. "The New Bremen Glassmanufactory of John Frederick Amelung." *Journal of Glass Studies* 18 (1976): 9–128.

Leinicke, Kris Gayman. "Production of the Boston and Sandwich Glass Company in the Year 1827." Master's thesis, State University of New York, 1986.

McKearin, George S., and Helen McKearin. *American Glass.* New York: Crown, [1941].

McKearin, Helen, and George S. McKearin. *Two Hundred Years of American Blown Glass.* New York: Bonanza, 1950.

McKearin, Helen, and Kenneth M. Wilson. *American Bottles and Flasks and Their Ancestry.* New York: Crown, 1978.

M'Kee and Brothers. *M'Kee Victorian Glass: Five Complete Glass Catalogs from 1859/60 to 1871.* Introduction and text by Lowell Innes and Jane Shadel Spillman. New York: Corning Museum of Glass in association with Dover Publications, 1981.

Noël Hume, Ivor. *Glass in Colonial Williamsburg's Archaeological Collections.* Colonial Williamsburg Archaeological Series, no. 1. Williamsburg, Va.: Colonial Williamsburg Foundation, 1969.

Palmer, Arlene. "From Beer to Birdcages: Glass in Colonial America." In *Delaware Antiques Show Catalogue,* pp. 81–89. Wilmington, 1974.

Palmer, Arlene. "Glass Production in Eighteenth-Century America: The Wistarburgh Enterprise." In *Winterthur Portfolio 11,* ed. Ian M. G. Quimby, pp. 75–101. Charlottesville: University Press of Virginia, 1976.

Palmer, Arlene. "American Heroes in Glass: The Bakewell Sulphide Portraits." *American Art Journal* 11 (January 1979): 4–26.

Palmer, Arlene. "'To the Good of the Province and Country': Henry William Stiegel and American Flint Glass." In *The American Craftsman and the European Tradition, 1620–1820,* ed. Francis J. Puig and Michael Conforti, pp. 202–39. Minneapolis: Minneapolis Institute of Arts, 1989.

Papert, Emma. *The Illustrated Guide to American Glass.* New York: Hawthorn Books, 1972.

Pepper, Adeline. *The Glass Gaffers of New Jersey.* New York: Charles Scribner, 1971.

Polak, Ada. "The 'Ip Olufsen Weyst' Illustrated Price-List of Eighteenth-Century Norwegian Glass." *Journal of Glass Studies* 11 (1969): 104.

Schwind, Arlene Palmer. "Pennsylvania German Glass." In *Arts of the Pennsylvania Germans,* ed. Catherine E. Hutchins, pp. 200–210. New York: W. W. Norton, 1983.

Smith, James Morton, and Charles F. Hummel. "The Henry Francis du Pont Winterthur Museum." *Antiques* 93, no. 6 (June 1978): 1282.

Spillman, Jane Shadel. *American and European Pressed Glass in the Corning Museum of Glass.* Corning, N.Y., 1981.

Thorpe, William Arnold. *A History of English and Irish Glass,* 2 vols. London: Medici Society, 1929.

Warren, Phelps. *Irish Glass: The Age of Exuberance.* New York: Charles Scribner's Sons, 1970.

Watkins, Lura Woodside. *Cambridge Glass, 1818 to 1888.* New York: Bramhall House, 1930.

Westropp, M. S. Dudley. *Irish Glass.* 1920. Revised edition. Dublin: Allen Figgis, 1978.

Wilson, Kenneth M. "American Contributions to the Development of Pressed Glass." In *Technological Innovation and the Decorative Arts,* ed. Ian M. G. Quimby and Polly Anne Earl, pp. 167–206. Charlottesville: University Press of Virginia, 1974.

Wilson, Kenneth M. *New England Glass and Glassmaking.* New York: Thomas Y. Crowell, [1972].

Witt, Cleo, Cyril Weeden, and Arlene Palmer Schwind. *Bristol Glass.* Bristol: Bristol and West Building Society in conjunction with City of Bristol Museums and Art Gallery, 1984.

MANUSCRIPTS

John Lee Chapman–William Baker Day Book. (Baltimore Flint Glass Works.) 1831–34. Maryland Historical Society, Baltimore.

J. S. Cunningham Account Book, Boston. 1826–27. Archives and Library, Edison Institute, Dearborn, Mich.

Vincent Gilpin and John F. Gilpin Invoice Book. 1828–38. Historical Society of Pennsylvania, Philadelphia.

"Prices Current of South Boston Flint Glass Ware." 1818–19. Archives and Library, Edison Institute, Dearborn, Mich.

Frederick Rhinelander Papers. New York Historical Society.

"Wheeling Flint Glass Works. Price Current of Glass Ware Manufactured by F. Plunket[t] and Co." (Original lost; photostat, Oglebay Institute–Mansion Museum, Wheeling, W. Va.)

Index

Botetourt, Gov., inventory of, 128, 248
Bottle, 343–85
Bovey, Christina Geeding, owner, 158
Bowl, 237–58; see also Sugar bowl and Footed bowl and Punch bowl
Boyd, Irvin and Dolores, dealers, 332
Boyington, Nancy, owner, 157
Bradley, Philip H. Company, dealer, 64, 236
Brand, James C., owner, 347
Breast pipe, 418
Breese, Sidney, owner, 336
Brevost, Antoinette, 107–8
Brianwood Antiques and Interiors, dealer, 49
Bristol, Eng., glass made in, 89, 337, 365, 350; glass exports from, 66, 68, 74, 129, 133, 150, 196, 247–48, 401
Brooklyn Flint Glass Works, N.Y., 92, 141, 164
Brooklyn, N.Y., glass in, 164
Brown, Hope, 326
Brown, Paul S., merchant, 80 n. 4
Bryant, Mrs. James, owner, 157
Bull's eye. See Crown glass
Burby, John, inventory of, 62 n. 2, 148 n. 1
Burford, Robert, glass engraver, 78
Burke, James, owner, 48, 111
Burkhardt, Robert, dealer, 142, 210, 217
Burne, W. G. T. Antiques, dealer, 212
Burner, for oil lamp, 333
Burr, Aaron, inventory of, 357
Burton, Charles, artist, 291
Busler, Ermina Morris, owner, 116
Busler, William Sherwood, owner, 116
Butland, James, glass manufacturer, 99, 153
Butler, Frances Anne. See Kemble, Fanny
Butter: cooler, 213, 247; print, 410, 411; tub, 213, 247
Byrd, William, diarist, 186

Cadwalader, Elizabeth, 228
Cadwalader, John, 69, 228
Cains, Thomas, glass manufacturer, 91, 114, 33, 80, 105, 149, 233, 239, 273, 334, 339
Calvert, Charles, inventory of, 221
Cambridge, Mass. See New England Glass Company
Cameo incrustation. See Sulphides
Can, 85, 93
Canada, glass in, 87, 260, 299; glass made in, 179; U.S. glass sold in, 388
Canby, Elizabeth Clifford Morris, owner, 188, 283
Canby, Samuel, owner, 300, 149
Candelabra, 297–302
Candle, 305
Candle shade, 294–96
Candlestick, 280–93

Cantacuzene, Prince, owner, 364
Cape, Brian, merchant, 129 n. 2
Capes, Richard, merchant, 246 n. 1
Carlen, Robert, dealer, 70, 207
Carlson, Janice, 385
Carpenter, Emmanuel, 69
Carpenter, Mr. and Mrs. Donald, donors, 400
Carpenter, Samuel, brewer, 343
Carpenter, Thomas, glass manufacturer, 191
Carr, Ralph, merchant, 357
Carre, Jean, glassmaker, 4
Carroll, Charles, of Carrollton, 266
Carter, Landon, 128
Carter, Robert, of Corotoman, inventory of, 392
Case bottle, 345–47
Cassel, Joseph, glass manufacturer, 391
Caster, 239, 240
Caster set. See Cruet set
Castlecomer, viscount, inventory of, 324
Celery glass, 243–50, 270
Centerpiece, table, 238, 240
Ceramics, relation to glass, 69, 119–21, 151, 155, 159, 182, 184, 191, 243–44, 276, 278–79, 300, 309, 393
Chain decoration: applied, 105, 114, 160; marvered, 149
Champagne glass, 79
Champlain Glass Works, 386
Chandelier, 308–10
Chapman, John L., glass manufacturer, 401; see also Baltimore Flint Glass Works
Charleston, Robert J., author, 261, 345
Charleston, S.C., glass in 66, 67, 74, 124, 129, 134, 221, 225, 226, 277, 326, 390
Checkered-diamond pattern, 227, 360–62
Cheetam, Anne, shop inventory of, 225, 260
Chemical glass, 400
Cherry, decanter for, 97
Childs, C. G., engravings by, 112
China Shop, dealer, 191
Chippendale, Thomas, 323
Churches, lighting fixtures in, 326–27
Cider glass, 57, 68
Cincinnati. See Order of the Cincinnati
Claret, decanter for, 84
Claret glass, 59
Clark, George R., donor, 66, 67, 34
Clark, John Innes, merchant, 357
Clark, Tracy, owner, 120
Clevenger Brothers, 218, 151, 171
Clevenger Brothers, N.J., glass manufacturer, 218, 151, 171
Clichy Glassworks, France, 275, 276, 278
Clinton, DeWitt, mold-blown portrait of, 388

Coats, Margaret, inventory of, 347 n. 1
Coats of arms: Pennsylvania, 33, 45; Schley, 16; U.S., 21–24
Coin glass, 105
Collamore, Horace, merchant, 136, 157
Cologne bottle, 333
Comet pattern, 138
Comfit glass, 185
Composition of glass, 1
Compote, 207–10, 237, 258; see also Footed bowl
Condiments, 266; containers, 224–42, 259
Connecticut, glass in, 51, 85, 150, 327; glass made in 112, 269, 291, 330, 388, 101, 179, 238, 248, 286, 345, 364
Cook, Gershom, glass manufacturer, 386
Cooper and Curtin, merchant, 66
Cooper, W. F., dealer, 298
Corning, Charles W., glass manufacturer, 386
Corning, Gurdon, glass manufacturer, 386
Cornish, James, inventory of, 390 n. 1
Costs of glassware (18th–19th century): general, 150–51, 156, 184, 221, 236, 239, 271, 275, 350, 393; of blown-over glass, 233; of cut glass, 106, 205, 239; of chandeliers, 326; of engraved glass, 108, 205, 310; of mold-blown glass, 106, 147, 156, 212, 236, 248, 251, 263, 268, 292; of paperweights, 296; of plain glass, 105, 156, 247, 310; of pressed glass, 212, 265, 309, 395; of toys, 81, 136, 145, 169; of window glass, 388
Coventry Glass Works, Ct., 388
Cowper, Ann Pierce Parker, owner, 197
Cowper, Thomas Frederick P. P., 197
Cowper, William, 232
Craig and O'Hara, glass manufacturer, 154
Cream jug, 105–11, 118, 123–25, 127–31, 134, 139, 143, 148; see also Jug and Pitcher
Crown glass, 402; process explained, 386
Cruet, 100, 241, 242; 134; set, 239, 240
Cullet, 1
Cummings, Alexander, author, 7
Cunningham, James S., merchant, 81 n. 1, 106 n. 1, 143, 169, 263
Cup plate, 78, 79, 80, app. 3
Curling, Robertson, and Co., glass manufacturer, 389
Cuspidor, 412, 413
Cut glass: development of, 302; fashion for, 5, 68, 226, 231; process 2 (ill.); see also Glasscutters
Cutting, as primary decoration, 26, 34–35, 63, 65, 70, 86, 92, 93, 148, 191, 195–97, 202, 239, 285, 287, 295–310, 313

Cylinder window-glass process, 386
Czechoslovakia, *359; see also*
  Bohemia

Dabney family, owner, *195, 196*
Daisy-in-diamond pattern. *See*
  Diamond-daisy pattern
Daisy-in-hexagon pattern, *357, 358*
Danby, J. K. estate, donor, *102,* 31
Daniels, Dorothy, author, 17
Dated glass, *44, 45, 47, 48, 62, 70, 113,
  334–36, 347, 365, 410, 411*
Davey, Elizabeth, inventory of, 121
Davey, John, 181
Davis, Charles K., donor, *42*
Davis, Jacob S., glass manufacturer,
  207
Davis, Pearce, author, 17
Decanter, *81–104,* 124; stoppers, 124,
  145
Delomosne and Son, dealer, *308*
Denmark, Mylenberg Glassworks,
  139
DePeyster, John, owner, *334*
Deshler, Mary Lefevre, owner, *149*
Design sources, for decorated glass,
  90, 111–12, 116, 279, 291
Desk accessories, *270–79*
Desprez, Barthelemy Jr., glassmaker,
  417, 398
Desprez, Barthelemy Sr., 399
Dessert glass, *179–201,* 218
DeVries, David Peterson, traveler, 59
  n. 1
Diamond patterns. *See* Pattern-
  molded designs *and* specific
  designs
Diamond-daisy pattern, *354–56, 359*
Diamond-point engraving *48, 71*
Dickinson, Mary, 121, 302 n. 1
Diderot, Denis, author, 1 (ills.), 2
  (ill.), 392
Dish, *195, 197–99, 201*
Dish cover, *408*
Dobbs, Arthur, inventory of, 247 n. 5
Dobson, John A., and Company, 114
Doflein, Philip, moldmaker, 395
Dog motifs, engraved, *60, 61, 64*
Dolphin design, *293*
Doorknob, *416*
Dowd, Eleanor M., owner, *111*
Downes, Marylyn Reeve, owner, *197*
Dram glass, *4*
Dramming, 62
Drawer pull. *See* Furniture knob
Drinker, Elizabeth, 88
Drinking glass, *1–80;* habits, 57–60,
  62, 74, 79, 85, 92, 118, 122, 127, 181,
  186, 343, 385
Drop pinching, process, 314
Drops, 314
du Pont, Eleuthère Irénée, 107
du Pont, Henry Francis: as glass
  collector, 19–29, 31–32, 36–38; as
  museum founder, vii; portrait of,
  19 (ill.)

du Pont, Philip Francis, owner, *89,
  101, 103, 104, 106–9, 118, 125, 241,
  264, 293, 333, 337, 339, 363, 365–70,
  372–79, 383–86, 388–90, 393–95, 398,
  401,* 33
Duffield, Joel, glassmaker, 173
Dulany, Daniel, inventory of, 88
Dummer, George, glasscutter, 326
Duncan, Elliot, merchant, 343
Dunmore, Gov., 125
DuPlessis, Pierre M. LeBarbier,
  inventory of, 357
Dupre, Augustin, medal by, 295
Durham, Lord, owner, *298*
Duyckinck, Gerardus, merchant, 314
  n. 2
Dyer, Walter A., 14–15
Dyott, Dr. Thomas W., glass
  manufacturer, portrait of, *389,* 153

Eagle design. *See* American eagle
  motifs
Eagles Mere, Pa., *116*
Eagles, Richard, inventory of, 94
Eating habits, 57–58, 218, 229, 237,
  246
Eberhardt, Martin. *See* Everhart,
  Martin
Edgerton, Mary, owner, *157*
Edmunds, James H., glass
  manufacturer, 249
Egg cup, 57
Ellenville Glass Works, N.Y., *412, 413*
Ellery, William, merchant, 85, 101
Elliott, John, glass manufacturer, 127;
  see also Philadelphia Glass Works
Elsholz, William J., owner, *292*
Emlen, Sarah Williams, owner, *45*
Enamel-painted glass, *9, 10, 15, 38–41,
  74–77, 84, 94, 145, 268, 282, 312, 327,
  344,* 2
Enameled glass, 66, 89; by New
  England Glass Co., 337
Encell, John, glassmaker, 153
England, glass exports from, 6–7, 68,
  74, 136, 218, 304, 332, 401; glass in,
  308, 3–4, 324, 328; glass industry in,
  4–5, 343; glass made in, *2–14, 20,
  26–28, 37, 48, 62, 73, 81–86, 89, 105–
  8, 113, 131, 144, 149, 154–56, 162, 180–
  92, 194–98, 202, 211–12, 224, 226,
  238, 239, 253, 280, 281, 285–87, 294–
  96, 298–313, 327, 329, 334–37, 365,
  366, 404, 406, 419; see also*
  individual cities
English glass, H. F. du Pont's
  collecting of, 24–25; collected by
  Winterthur Museum, 34
Engravers, glass, 2 (ill.), 10 (ill.),
  68–69, 75–76, 78, 108, 112, 127
Engraving, as primary decoration:
  diamond-point, *48, 70;* wheel, *8,
  12–14, 16–25, 33–35, 42–47, 49–51,
  60–62, 64, 66–68, 71, 83, 87, 88, 90,
  110–13, 115, 148, 158, 164, 321;* styles
  of, 66

Ensell, Edward, glassmaker, 154;
Ensell, Wendt and Company, glass
  manufacturer, 154
Eppes, John Wayles, 226
Eric, Mrs. Howard, owner, *3*
Europe, continental, glass exports
  from, 6–7, 92–93; glass made in, *1,
  15, 17–19, 21–24, 34, 35, 38–43, 49–51,
  61, 66–69, 74–77, 87, 88, 94, 131, 145,
  146, 148, 159, 160, 179, 251, 252, 268,
  270, 275–78, 282, 297, 328, 338, 344–
  46, 359, 362, 380, 383, 417; see also*
  individual countries
European glass, H. F. du Pont's
  collecting of, 24–25
European influence on American
  glass, 253, 280, 287, 296, 364
Everhart, Martin, glassmaker, 194
Ewing, Caleb, owner, *225*
Ewing, Frank P. Antiques, *380*
Exports of U.S. glass, 243

Faatz, Christopher, glass
  manufacturer, 207
Façon de venise glass, 4, 59
Fairman, Mrs. Endsley P., donor, *410*
Fakes/Reproductions, *109, 133, 170,
  216, 218, 359, 362, 364,* poss. *413;* 28,
  145, 263, 309, 370 (ill.)
Falcon Glassworks, London, *302*
Fearon, Henry, traveler, 343, 397 n. 1
Fenwick, Charles G., owner, *44*
Ferm, Rachel, owner, *351*
Figural decoration, *15, 40, 41, 63–65,
  71, 251–52, 268, 275–78, 286, 388–90,
  393–95, 397, 401, 415–17, 419; see also*
  Sulphides
Figured flask, *383–401,* app. 2; H. F.
  du Pont's collecting of, 24;
  collecting by Winterthur Museum,
  33
Filigree glass, *149;* 3 (ill.)
Finger bowl, *211*
Firing glass, *12, 19*
Fish, Mrs. Frederick S., owner, *152,
  176, 254, 257*
Flag, U.S., 25
Flayderman and Kaufman, dealer, 24
Flip glass, 85, 93
Flower pot, *405, 406*
Flower vases, *186–87, 251–69, 277*
Flute glass, *26,* 3
Foley, Daniel, glass manufacturer,
  157
Foltz, Conrad, glassmaker, 194
Footed bowl, *202–6, 238, 240, 245; see
  also* Compote
Ford, Henry, 27
Ford, John, glass manufacturer, 116
Fort Orange, Albany, N.Y., glass in,
  6, 59
Foster, John S., glass manufacturer,
  386
France, glass exports from, 109; glass
  made in, *34, 35, 61, 69, 148, 159, 275–
  78, 297, 417;* glassmaking in, 110, 114
Frank, William, and Sons, glass
  manufacturer, 399

Franklin, Benjamin, mold-blown portrait of, *389*; sulphide portraits of, *63, 64, 275, 416, 417,* 9, 68
Franklin Glass Works, Ohio, 160, 249
Franklin Institute, Philadelphia, 111, 136, 273, 397, 398 (ill.)
Franklin Studio dealer, *415*
Frankstown Glass Works, Pa., *399*
Freemason glass. *See* Masonic glass
Friese, John F., glass manufacturer, 78
Friese, Philip R. I., glass manufacturer, 78
Fruit bowl, 238, 240, 245; *see also* Footed bowl
Fruit: consumption of, 237; made of glass, *279*
Fry, Cornelius, 127
Fulford, John, inventory of, 94
Furniture knob, *414*
Furnival, Alexander, 78

Gabell, James R., owner, *157, 361*
Gadrooned glass, *105, 136, 176, 219, 243, 244, 255, 289, 290,* 271
Gaffield, Thomas, 114
Gallatin, Albert, glass manufacturer, 20, 194
Gallop, Mary, merchant, 67
Gardiner family, 100
Gardiner, John, 72
Gardiner's Island, N.Y., glass trade catalogues from, 72–73 (ill.), 75, 92–93 (ill.), 100, 132, 133 (ill.), 326 (ill.)
Gardner, Charles B., owner, *391, 392*
Garniture, 251, 252
Gaston, Frederick K., owner, *135*
Gayrard, Raymond, medal by, 116
Gedney, Samuel, merchant, 331 n. 1
Geeding, Christina, owner, *158,* 23
Geesey, Mrs. Titus, donor, *122,* 32
Geesey, Titus, owner, *122,* 268
Geeting, Catherine. *See* Geeding, Christina
Germany, glass exports from, 72, 92, 132; glass made in, *15, 21–24, 38–43, 74–77, 145, 251, 252, 282, 344, 346;* parallels to Amelung glass, 70
Gest, Neil C., dealer, *23, 24, 29, 30, 38, 46, 55, 56, 59, 99, 110, 119–21, 123, 126, 128, 130, 132, 133, 135, 152, 153, 157–60, 162, 163, 167, 168, 171–74, 176, 177, 178, 205, 213–16, 218, 226, 228, 231, 232, 238, 254, 257–59, 272, 273, 340, 343, 348, 349, 354, 357, 358, 361, 362,* 20–26, 28–29, 184, 210, 365, 370; inventory by, 19, 37 (ills.); portrait of, 28 (ill.)
Ghequiere, Charles, owner, *44,* 22–23
Gilded glass, *8–10, 49, 75, 89, 268, 286, 301, 318, 346, 365,* 2, 337 (by New England Glass Co.)
Giles, James, glass decorator, 303, 316, 345
Gilliland, James, merchant, 127, 226 n. 1, 277 n. 2

Gilliland, John Loftus, glass manufacturer, 136–37, 141
Gin, decanter for, 89
Ginsburg and Levy, dealer, 180, 189
Girandole, 314; *see also* Candelabra
Girard, Stephen, 112
Girl Scouts Loan Exhibition (1929), *176, 217,* 37, 203
Glassboro, N.J., glassmaking in, 191–92
Glasscutters, U.S., 70, 136–37
Glasse, Hannah, author, 221, 225
Glasshouse, image of, opp. 1 (ill.), *394*
Glassmaking: in Europe, 3–5; in U.S., 9–11
Glastenbury Glass Factory Company, 292
Glick, Philip, 210
Goblet, *3, 16, 35*
Gobrecht, Christian, engraver, *416,* 111, 398
Goddard, Abigail and William, 97
Goff, Charles, glasshouse agent, 388
Goodrich, Samuel Griswold, author, 62
Gothic style, *57, 58, 103–4, 143, 403*
Gould Antiques, Richard, donor, *414*
Gray, Samuel, merchant, 221 n. 2
Great Seal of the U.S., *21–24*
Greele, Mr., glass manufacturer, 207
Greene, John, merchant, 4, 6, 59–60
Greenhow, John, merchant, 350
Greenleafe, Catherine Wistar, 300
Greenwood, Edna, H., estate of, *184,* 224
Greiner, Adam, glassmaker, 207
Greiner, Martin, glassmaker, 151, 191, 260, 390
Greiner, Nicholas, glassmaker, 207
Gribbel, W. Griffin, owner, *152, 176, 257*
Grosz, Anthony, 97
Guest, George, 96
Guest, John, owner, *45*
Gumley, John, looking-glass manufacturer, 324

Hackwood, William, modeler, 399
Haedy, Christopher, glasscutter, 129, 298
Haines, Benjamin, glassmaker, 264
Half-post process, 356, 369
Hall lamp, *311, 312*
Hall, Margaret, (Mrs. Basil), traveler, 7, 297 n. 1
Hamersley, George, owner, *138*
Hamersley, Margaretta, owner, *138*
Hamilton, Ralph N., owner, *157*
Hamilton, Thomas, traveler, 58 n. 5
Hammer, Frederick, merchant, 6, 72
Hanging lamp, *311, 312*
Hannaford, Elizabeth, 181
Harper, Dolly Young, owner, *158*
Harrison, Thomas, glass manufacturer, 153
Harrison, William, author, 3

Hartshorne, Albert, author, 87
Harvey, Reuben, merchant, 238 n. 3
Haskell, Mrs. J. Amory, owner, *151*
Hat salt. *See* Salt, hat
Haynes, E. Barrington, author, 261
Henniker, Lord, owner, *308*
Henry VIII of England, inventory of, 3
Henry, William A., donor, *93*
Hertford, Countess of, quoted 279
Heston, Thomas, glass manufacturer, 191
Hewes, Robert, glass manufacturer, 386
Hewson, Connell and Company, glass manufacturer, 153
Higginson, Stephen, merchant, 101
Highmore, Joseph, painting by, 221
Hobbs, J. H., Brockunier and Company, glass manufacturer, 114
Hodges, Allan J., dealer, *198*
Hoffman, Bend and Company, auctioneer, 266
Holland. *See* Netherlands
Hollands decanter, 89
Honey pot, 214
Hooper, H. N. Company, lamp manufacturer, 328
Hoopers Glasshouse, Bristol, 350
Hort, John, diplomat, 317
Hostetter, Ira, owner, *47*
Howe, William T. H., owner, *29, 52, 121, 169, 178, 238,* 26
Huckle, Mr., glassmaker, 158
Huffsey, S., glass manufacturer, *395*
Hughes, G. Bernard, author, 298
Hunt, John, inventory of, 60 n. 2
Hunter, Frederick William, owner, *137, 255;* (author) 14, 19, 20–21, 25, 92, 150, 183, 284, 365
Hurdals Verk Glasshouse, Norway, *146*
Hurricane shade. *See* Candle shade
Hurry, Renwick C., dealer, *289, 290, 314,* 20
Hutchins, Thomas, 185
Hyde, J. A. Lloyd, dealer, *34, 35, 74, 77, 148, 169, 297, 301, 303, 308, 309, 311,* 23, 25

Iasello, Henry, owner, *292*
Ihmsen, Charles, glass engraver, 154
Ihmsen, William, glass manufacturer, *386*
Imported glass, 6–7, 72, 92, 133; colored, 134, 150; *see also* individual merchants or cities
India shade, 310; *see also* Candle shade
Ink bottle, 117
Inkstand, inkwell, 271–74
Innes, Lowell, author, 17
Ireland, glass exports from, 74, 157; glass made in, *12, 26–28, 86, 90, 113, 115* (signed), *131, 195, 196, 202, 295,* 228; glassmaking in, 228
Irving, Mrs. E. du Pont, donor, *60, 242, 271,* 33

Tryon, Gov. William, inventory of, 57 n. 4, 218, 330
Tumbler, *37, 38, 42, 44–48, 51, 53–71,* 85
Turlington, Robert, *332*
Twist stems. *See* Air-twist stem *and* Opaque-twist stem
Twitchell, T., merchant, 187 n. 6, 391 n. 2

Union Flint Glass Works, Pa., *78*; products of, 105, 106, 112, 138, 145, 153, 164, 251, 275, 340
United States Capitol, lighting in, 328
Urn. *See* Wine fountain

van Ravenswaay, Charles, donor, *342, 371, 397, 399,* 33
van Rensselaer, Stephen, author, 15
van Rensselaer, Jeremias, 57
Van Nostrand, L. G., author, 207
Van Winkle, William M., donor, *95,* 31, 184
Vanderspiegel, William, inventory of, 94, 101, 318
Vase, celery. *See* Celery glass
Vase, ornamental. *See* Ornamental vase
Vase, pyramid. *See* Pyramid vase
Vaughan, Benjamin, house of, 388 (ill.)
Venetian glass, influence of *1,* 3–4
Venice, *1*; glassmaking in, 3 (ills.), 4–5, 239
Vernon, Samuel, and William Vernon, merchants, 357
Verzelini, Giacomo, glassmaker, 4
Viber, Olive, owner, *412, 413*
Vigor and Stevens, Bristol, 66, 68 n. 2, 129, 196 n. 1, 248 n. 3, 401
Villiers, George, duke of Buckingham, 4
Virginia Company, 6,9
Virginia, glass in, *197;* 6, 125, 127–28, 164, 184, 187, 218, 221, 226, 332, 350, 391–92; for glass made in, *see* Jamestown
Vista Alegre Glassworks, Portugal, *99, 383*
Voltz, Conrad. *See* Foltz, Conrad

Wadsworth Atheneum, owner, *418*
Walbridge, William S., author, 15
Wales, Katherine, and Ethel Staniar, dealers, 27
Wall light, *303–7*
Wansey, Henry, traveler, 181
Washington, George: mold-blown portrait of, *390*; sulphide portrait of, *63, 65, 415, 417,* 84, 226, 326, 332, 358
Washington Monument, Baltimore, *390*
Water goblet, *35*
Waterloo Glass House Company, Ireland, *115*
Watkins, Helen DeLancey, owner, *26, 179, 188*
Watkins, Lura Woodside, author, 16–17
Watts, Hester, inventory of, 62 n. 2
Webster, owner, *258*
Wedgwood, Josiah, 111, 226 n. 2, 303
Weeks, Joseph D., author, 13, 17
Wells, Obadiah, merchant, 388
Wells, Thomas, glass manufacturer, 158
Wentzel family, glassmakers, 183
West Indies, glass in, 310
Westphalian glass imports, 72
Westropp, M. S. Dudley, author, 157
Wettlaufer, Crawford, owner, *408*
Wheeling, W.Va., glass made in, *79,* 138, 205, 270, 273
Whimsy, *423,* 36, 403
White, Harry Hall, author, 15, 107, 167, 174, 213, 370
White, Winsor, dealer, *282, 326*
Whitney, Henry, 123, 334 n. 1
Wikoff, Peter, glass manufacturer, 153
Williams, George Guest, owner, *45*
Williams, Lenore Wheeler, author, 15
Williams, William, merchant, 388
Williams, William P., dealer, *227*
Williamsport Glass Works, Pa., *386*
Willis, Katharine E., dealer, 27
Wilson, Kenneth M., author, 307, 351, 385
Window glass, *402, 403,* 11
Windowpane, *403*
Wine and water glass, 74
Wine bottle, *334–37*; fountain, *86*
Wineglass, *5–11, 13–15, 17, 25, 27, 28, 32,* 57–58; toy, *29–31*

Wines in colonies, 57, 127–28
Wing and Sumner. *See* Boston Glass Manufactory
Winterthur Museum: display of glass in, 36–39, 38 (ills.); glass collecting by, 31–35; Study Collection, 35
Winthrop, John, 60
Wishart, William, inventory of, 357 n. 4
Wisner, Elizabeth, owner, *116*
Wistar, Caspar, glass manufacturer, *36, 150, 225, 283, 284,* 9, 14, 15, 22, 175, 188; inventory of, 357; *see also* Wistarburgh Glassworks
Wistar family glass, 190
Wistar, Rebecca, owner, *283*
Wistar, Richard, glass manufacturer, *36, 150, 225, 283, 284,* 9, 22, 191–92; bottle with seal of, 9 (ill.), 349; *see also* Wistarburgh Glassworks
Wistarburgh glass: H. F. du Pont's collecting of, 19–20; collected by Winterthur Museum, 31; *see also* Wistarburgh Glassworks *and* Wistar, Caspar *and* Wistar, Richard
Wistarburgh Glassworks, *36, 150, 225, 283, 284,* 9 (ill.), 14, 191–92, 349; *see also* Wistarburgh glass *and* Wistar, Caspar *and* Wistar, Richard
Wood, Richard H., dealer, *47*
Wood, Richard H. and Virginia A., dealers, *8, 113, 201, 220, 269, 408,*
Wood, William W. III, owner, *120, 163, 167,* 20, 28
Woodward, Katharine, owner, *47*
Wrythen decoration, *2*
Wunsch Americana Foundation, donor, *115,* 34
Wythe, George, 218

Yates, Edward, cut-glass manufacturer, 137
Young, J. W., dealer, 27
Young, Naomi Elizabeth Beck, owner, 158

Zanesville Glass Manufacturing Co., 235
Zanesville Glass Works, 107
Zanesville, Ohio, *119, 120, 168, 169, 199, 200, 391,* 208

GLASS IN EARLY AMERICA
was designed and composed by
Katy Homans and Sayre Coombs,
and printed and bound by
Arnoldo Mondadori editore S. p. A.
The typeface is Adobe Minion,
the text paper is 90 lb. Gardamatte Brillante,
and the endleaves are Modigliani Perla.